EUROPEAN IMMIGRATION

European Immigration
A Sourcebook

ASHGATE

Published by
Ashgate Publishing Limited
Wey Court East
Union Street
Farnham
Surrey GU9 7PT
England

Ashgate Publishing Company
Suite 420
101 Cherry Street
Burlington, VT 05401-4405
USA

Ashgate website: http://www.ashgate.com

British Library Cataloguing in Publication Data
European immigration : a sourcebook
　　1. Migration, Internal – European Union countries
　　2. European Union countries – Emigration and immigration
　　3. European Union countries – Emigration and immigration –
　　Government policy
　　I. Triandafyllidou, Anna II. Gropas, Ruby
　　304.8'4

Library of Congress Cataloging-in-Publication Data
European immigration : a sourcebook / edited by Anna Triandafyllidou and Ruby Gropas.
　　　　p. cm.
　　Includes bibliographical references and index.
　　ISBN 978-0-7546-4894-9
　　1.　　European Union countries--Emigration and immigration. I. Triandafyllidou, Anna.
　　II. Gropas, Ruby.

　　JV7590.E946 2007
　　304.8'4--dc22

ISBN 978 07546 4894 9

Reprinted 2009

2006103131

Printed and bound in Great Britain by TJI Digital, Padstow, Cornwall.

Contents

List of Tables

List of Figures

Contributors

Rosana Albuquerque is Lecturer at the Department of Social and Political Sciences of Universidade Aberta (Portugal) and researcher at the Research Centre on Migration and Intercultural Relations. Presently, she is developing a PhD thesis on the social mobility of immigrant descendents of Portuguese-speaking African countries. Her main scientific interests are social mobility and stratification, political participation and citizenship.

Katia Amore (PhD) is an Associate Research Fellow at the Centre for Research in Ethnic Relation at Warwick University. Currently, she is conducting independent research on migration-related issues in Sicily working with local authorities and NGOs. She often posts on the blog migrationisland.org on issues related to migration and asylum.

Svetlozar A. Andreev is Junior Lecturer (returning scholar) at the Department of Political Science, Sofia University, Bulgaria and a Max Weber Fellow at the European University Institute in Florence, Italy. Previously, he was a postdoctoral fellow at the Centre for the Study of Democracy, University of Westminster, London, UK. During fall 2002 he held an OSI research grant at the Mirovni Institut in Ljubljana, Slovenia. His research interests include a wide range of topics, such as post-communist democratization, comparative regional integration and enlargement, European citizenship and legitimacy problems, and the future of EU borders.

Miguel Benito is director of the Immigrant Institute in Borås (Sweden). He is chief editor of the scientific journal *Aktuellt om migration* and managing editor of the *Journal of Intercultural Communication*, both online and issued by the Immigrant Institute. He is also Assistant Professor at the University of Borås and author of different books in library science. Born in Spain he has been working in Sweden since 1965. He also participates in governmental committees appointed to represent immigrant organizations.

Hassan Bousetta was awarded his PhD in Social Sciences from the Katholieke Universiteit Brussel (Belgium). He is currently an FNRS Research Fellow at the University of Liège (Belgium). His work focuses on the political participation of immigrant minorities and on local multicultural policies. He has also collaborated on several consultancy projects for cities (Paris, Antwerp, Bristol, Liège) and networks of cities (Eurocities, International Coalition of Cities against Racism).

Jan Černík is an Associate Research Fellow at the Institute of Ethnology of the Academy of Sciences Czech Republic. Presently, he is preparing a PhD thesis on the informal networks among Russian-speaking migrants. His research interests cover issues of the everyday economy, mutual solidarity and social isolation of migrants. He is also consultant of Caritas Czech for development projects in the Southern Caucasus.

Norbert Cyrus is research associate at the Interdisciplinary Centre for Education and Communication in Migratory Processes (IBKM) at the University of Oldenburg. Between 2004 and 2006 he was a researcher in the EU-funded research project POLITIS and since 2006 a coordinator of the EU-funded project WinAct. He has done research for ILO and public authorities in Germany on legal and illegal labour migration. His recent publications include *Trafficking for Labour and Sexual Exploitation in Germany: Study prepared for International Labour Organisation (ILO)* (Geneva, 2005) and *Handbuch Soziale Arbeit* (editor with A. Treichler, 2004).

Corina Demetriou is a researcher who writes reports and policy-papers on subjects relating to migration, discrimination, anti-nationalism and reconciliation. She has been involved in various campaigns, initiatives and NGOs on peace, reconciliation and equality. She studied international law and human rights and for years has been in private legal practice.

Boris Divinský studied Human Geography in Bratislava and worked in several universities abroad. He carried out the first survey of migration in Slovakia (IOM, 2003), followed by a larger and more comprehensive research on the impact of international migration on Slovak society published in 2005. As a freelancer, he focuses on the issues of immigration, asylum, integration of foreigners, acquiring citizenship, migration policy and management, institutional and legal aspects, xenophobia and social exclusion of foreigners, and other questions referring to international migration in Slovakia. He also co-chairs the Working Group for Justice and Home Affairs within the National Convent on the EU (consultative body for the Slovak Government).

Franck Düvell, PhD, is Senior Researcher at the Centre for Migration, Policy and Society (COMPAS), University of Oxford. From 2003–04, he was Jean Monnet Fellow at the Robert-Schuman Centre for Advanced Studies, European University Institute (Florence), and between 1998 and 2003 he was Research Fellow at the University of Exeter. He has been a lecturer in Sociology, political science and geography at the University of Bremen, Germany. His research focus is on irregular migration, European and international migration politics and on the ethics of migration control. He has published several books, chapters and articles, such as 'Internationale und europäische Migration' (Münster, 2006), 'Illegal Immigration in Europe' (Houndmills, 2005), 'Migration: Boundaries of equality and justice' (Cambridge, 2003, with Bill Jordan), 'Die Globalisierung des Migrationsregimes' (Berlin, 2003), and 'Irregular Migration: Dilemmas of transnational mobility' (Cheltenham, 2002, with Bill Jordan). Articles have been published in the *Journal for Ethnic and Migration Studies*, ACME, *Journal for Critical Social Policy*, Open Democracy, and IMIS-Beiträge. He is a member of the EU-funded Network of Excellence on 'International Migration, Integration and Social Cohesion' (IMISCOE).

Marco Goli (PhD Political Science, Copenhagen University, 2002) is involved in several comparative research programmes focusing primarily on the relationship between the market, the welfare state, civic society and ethnic minorities' strategies towards socioeconomic mobility in different discursive and institutional settings. Aspects of his research include: institutional and organizational deficiency, ethnic and social entrepreneurship, comparative national and local employment policies and strategies (SLIB), ethnic Business in Denmark (SLIB), substantial citizenship and democracy, comparative migration and integration policies. Currently, Dr Goli is leading two national comparative research programmes regarding employment policies in deprived urban areas of Denmark.

Carmen González Enríquez is Professor at the Spanish Universidad Nacional de Educación a Distancia (UNED), in Madrid. She has specialized on East European politics and international migration (irregular migration, public opinion, politics of fluxes' control and integration). She has published, among others, the books *The Politics of Memory* (Oxford University Press, 2001, with

A. Barahona y P. Aguilar) and *Spain and Immigration* (Fund. La Caixa, also on electronic version. 2001, with V. Pérez and B. Alvarez).

Ruby Gropas, PhD (Cantab), is a Research Fellow at the Hellenic Foundation for European and Foreign Policy (ELIAMEP) working on European integration, EU-Balkan relations and migration issues. She has done research work for UNHCR in Brussels and has worked for McKinsey & Company. Ruby Gropas is the Managing Editor of the *Journal of Southeast European and Black Sea Studies* (Taylor & Francis, London) and the author of *Human Rights and Foreign Policy* (Sakkoulas Editions, 2006).

Sonia Gsir is a research associate at the Centre for Ethnic and Migration Studies (CEDEM) at the Université de Liège. She is a PhD candidate in Political Science and her study focuses on multilevel governance of migration in the European Union. She has a BA in Romanic Philology and in 1995 she obtained an MA in International Relations and European Politics.

Krystyna Iglicka is Associate Professor at the L. K. Academy of Management. Her research areas include changes in fertility patterns during the demographic transition, strategies and mechanisms of emigration in the CEE region, labour mobility, East-West European migration, immigration and integration models, EU immigration policy, patterns of return migration, brain-drain and mobility of highly skilled labour. She was a Fulbright Fellow at the Department of Sociology (University of Pennsylvania) in 1999–2000 and a Fellow of the Polish Scientific Foundation, British Academy and, Foreign and Commonwealth Office Fellow at the University of London, 1996–1999. Works published by Krystyna Iglicka include 10 scientific books, nearly 40 articles in scientific journals published by American, British and Polish recognized publishers and around 20 policy-oriented expertises, reports and analysis.

Dirk Jacobs is Associate Professor in Sociology at the Université Libre de Bruxelles (Francophone university in Brussels) and the KUBrussel (Flemish university in Brussels). He obtained his degree in Sociology at Ghent University (1993) and his PhD in Social Sciences at Utrecht University in the Netherlands (1998). He has worked as a post-doctoral researcher at Leuven University.

Serge Kollwelter is a teacher. He is the chair of ASTI, a Luxembourgian NGO dealing with migration, asylum and integration (www.asti.lu). He is the coordinator of the Intercultural Documentation Center in Luxembourg (CDAIC). He carried out studies for MPG, EUMC, EUROFOUND on migration issues.

Ankica Kosic obtained her PhD in Social Psychology at the Faculty of Psychology, University of Rome 'La Sapienza' in 1999. In the period of 2001–2005 Dr Kosic was working as a Research Fellow at European University Institute, Italy, and currently she is a Marie Curie Post-doctoral Fellow at the University of Kingston, United Kingdom. Her research interest concerns the issues of immigrant integration, prejudice towards immigrants, and reconciliation between groups. She has published several chapters and articles.

András Kováts obtained degrees in Special Education and in Social Policy at ELTE University, Budapest. Currently living in Budapest, he has been conducting research on immigrant integration, immigration and asylum policy for the Minority Research Institute of the Hungarian Academy of Sciences. Since 1998 he has been in charge of coordinating the activities of Menedék – the Hungarian Association for Migrants, first as a programme co-ordinator, later as director. For the last few years he has also been involved in consultancy for various governmental bodies dealing with immigration and asylum related issues.

Albert Kraler is a researcher at the International Centre for Migration Policy Development (ICMPD, Vienna) and a lecturer at the Department of Political Science at the University of Vienna. Previously, he has held a Marie Curie Fellowship at the Centre for Migration Research at the University of Sussex (2003–04) and a research fellowship at the Department of Political Science, University of Vienna (2005–06). His research interests include migration policy, migration and statehood, the legal status of immigrants, and refugees.

Mikko Lagerspetz was born and educated in Turku, Finland. Since 1989 he has resided in Estonia, where he works as professor of Sociology and director of the Centre of Civil Society Studies and Development of the Estonian Institute of Humanities, Tallinn University. From August 2006 he is employed as professor of Sociology at the Åbo Akademi University, Turku, Finland. His research has focused on social problems, civil society, and identity.

Shahamak Rezaei has conducted the most comprehensive research project in Ethnic Entrepreneurship in Denmark, at the Danish Center for Small Business Research, University of Southern Denmark between 1998 and 2000. In 2001, he submitted his PhD dissertation entitled 'Business Dynamics amongst Immigrants: Self Employment and Network Relations – Blockage or Initiator of Socio-economic Mobility?' Shahamak Rezaei is affiliated as assistant Professor to the research group for 'Welfare State and Welfare Society' at Roskilde University. Shahamak Rezaei and Marco Goli are in co-operation with the Centre for Strategy & Evaluation Services ('CSES' – London), which has been retained by DG Employment and Social Affairs of the European Commission. They are in the process of carrying out the 'Non-discrimination mainstreaming impact assessment – Study of Community policies and legislation' assignment.

Silvain Sagne is licentiate in political sciences and constitutional law. He is a researcher at the University of Helsinki (CEREN) and has been in education for 20 years as a certified teacher (MAed) and pedagogical trainer for teachers. He has conducted different research studies based on education and participated on researcher-related dual citizenship; he is several times adviser in different Ministries in Finland as an expert in ethnic relations and has published and collaborated on a number of books. Silvain Sagne is finalizing his dissertation on 'Crossbred elite in Senegal'. His dissertation focuses on the process of transplantation of political ideologies, investigating the system of jurisdiction and the style of governance as a fruit of triple inheritance.

Sanna Saksela is a PhD candidate in Sociology at the University of Helsinki. Her PhD study focuses on how immigrant associations mobilize their members to participate in civil society and in what extent the policy-makers activate the associations to participate in the political decision-making process. Special attention is given to how institutional versus symbolic forms of power are used among policy makers and among members of non-national ethnic communities in Finnish society. Since 2001, Saksela has worked as a research assistant at the Centre for Research on Ethnic Relations and Nationalism – CEREN, University of Helsinki. She has also participated in national and international research projects dealing with immigration, civil society and local immigration policies.

Ulrike Schuerkens has doctorates in both sociology, and social anthropology and ethnology, from the École des Hautes Études en Sciences Sociales (Paris). She received the diploma 'Habilitation à diriger des recherches' from the University Paris V. Currently she is senior lecturer at the ÉHÉSS, Paris. Her main research topics are transnational migrations and social transformations.

Endre Sik, DSc, is Professor at ELTE University, Department of Minority Studies, Project Manager at TÁRKI, and Director of the National Focal Point of the European Union Centre for Monitoring Race and Xenophobia. For 10 years he was Chairman of Refuge – Association for Helping Migrants. He served as the president of the Hungarian Sociological Association.

Karin Sohler is currently completing a Masters degree (Migrations et relations interethniques) at the University of Paris and is a researcher in a comparative study on refugee participation and mobilization. Previously, she was an NGO legal adviser for migrants and refugees and a researcher at the European Centre for Social Welfare Policy and Research in Vienna. Her research topics include migrants' organizations and socio-political participation (co-author of *Migrantenorganisationen in der Großstadt*, Campus 2004), migrant transnational politics, discrimination of migrants in the labour market and related anti-discrimination policies.

Inese Šūpule is Senior Research Fellow at the Baltic Institute of Social Sciences. Since 2005 she has been a PhD student of Sociology in the Department of Social Sciences, at the University of Latvia. Her fields of specialization are transition to democracy, formation of civic society, political participation, migration, comparative values studies, ethnic studies, and society integration. Her recent publications include *Ethnopolitical Tension in Latvia: Looking for the Conflict Solution* (Riga, 2005), *Ethnic Tolerance and Integration of the Latvian Society* (Riga, 2004), and *Associational Voluntarism and Social Capital in the Baltic States* (Södertörns högskola, 2003).

Ana Teixeira, formerly a lecturer in sociology and a researcher at the Research Centre on Migration and Intercultural Relations at Universidade Aberta, is currently a PhD candidate in Sociology at the University of North Carolina at Chapel Hill. She is completing her doctoral dissertation in organizational legitimacy. Her main research interests include organizations, consumption, immigrants and ethnic minorities, and children.

Anna Triandafyllidou is Senior Research Fellow at ELIAMEP and at the Robert Schuman Centre of Advanced Studies, European University Institute in Florence. She is Professor at the College of Europe in Bruges. Her recent publications include: *Immigrants and National Identity in Europe* (Routledge, 2001) *Negotiating Nationhood in a Changing Europe* (Edwin Mellen Press, 2002) *Europeanisation, National Identities and Migration* (Routledge, 2003, co-editor), *Multiculturalism, Muslims and Citizenship: A European Approach* (Routledge, 2005,co-editor), *Transcultural Europe: Cultural Policy in the Changing Europe* (Palgrave Macmillan, 2006, co-editor), *Contemporary Polish Migration in Europe* (Edwin Mellen Press, 2006, editor), *What is Europe?* (Palgrave Macmillan, 2008).

Nicos Trimikliniotis is adjunct Assistant Professor of Law and Sociology at Intercollege; he directs the Cyprus National Focal Point for RAXEN. He has researched on migration, racism and discrimination, multiculturalism, ethnic conflict and resolution, constitutional and state theory. He is the Scientific Director for Cyprus for the EU-funded project, *The European Dilemma: Institutional Patterns and Politics of 'Racial' Discrimination* (2002–05) and 'Integration of Female Immigrants in Labour Market and Society (FEMIPOL)' (2006–07), Sixth Framework Program. He is a qualified barrister, holds an MA in Gender and Ethnic Studies and a PhD in Sociology.

Abel Ugba teaches Journalism at the University of East London. His educational and professional background relates to journalism and sociology. His research interests are in: production and uses of diasporic media, immigrant religious activities, identity, civic activism and trans-nationalism. Until 1998 when he returned to academia, Abel worked as a professional journalist in newspapers in Nigeria, Germany and Ireland. He was a co-publisher and the pioneering editor of *Metro Eireann*, Ireland's most popular multicultural newspaper.

Dita Vogel is Research Associate at the Interdisciplinary Centre for Education and Communication in Migration Processes (IBKM) at the University of Oldenburg, and international coordinator of the European research project POLITIS. She graduated in economics at the University of Cologne in 1989, obtained a doctorate on the fiscal impact of immigration at the University of Bremen in 1996, and was lecturer in Dutch Studies at the University of Oldenburg until 2004. She has carried out extensive comparative research on migration and migration policy, with grants from the German Marshall Fund of the United States, the European Union and the Deutsche Forschungsgemeinschaft, among others.

Jessika ter Wal is senior research fellow at the European Research Centre on Migration and Ethnic Relations (ERCOMER), Utrecht University. Her research is in the field of media and minorities (the representation of ethnic, religious and cultural diversity), and the measurement of migrants' experiences of discrimination. International publications on these topics include (with Maykel Verkuyten) *Comparative Perspectives on Racism* (Ashgate, 2000) and *Racism and Cultural Diversity in the Mass Media* (European Monitoring Centre on Racism and Xenophobia, 2002).

Niklas Wilhelmsson is a PhD candidate in Political Science at the University of Helsinki. Since 2001 he has been working as a research administrator and researcher at the Centre for Research on Ethnic Relations and Nationalism at the University of Helsinki. He has also served as assisting lecturer in political science at the Swedish School of Social Science at the University of Helsinki. He has participated in several national and international research projects dealing with immigration, political participation and local immigration policies. He has published several articles dealing with these issues.

Rita Zukauskiene, PhD, is Professor and Head of the Department of Psychology at Mykolas Romeris University in Lithuania. Her teaching and research mainly concentrates on developmental and personality psychology. Her main area of expertise is the systematic analysis of developmental trends of antisocial behaviour. She has published three books and over 30 papers in learned professional journals, with special emphasis on applying person-oriented approach in studying individuals.

Acknowledgements

This book is one of the first publications arising from our work in the Research Project: 'Building Europe with New Citizens? An Inquiry into the Civic Participation of Naturalised Citizens and Foreign Residents in 25 Countries' (abbreviated as POLITIS, contract no. CIT2-CT-2003-505987, and funded under the Sixth Framework Programme, Priority 7 Citizens and Governance in a Knowledge Based Society). This publication, and the realization of the POLITIS project in general, would not have been possible without the generous financial support of the European Commission and specifically the Directorate General for Research.

This is a truly collective piece of work. We would, therefore, like to express our special thanks to Carol Brown, Norbert Cyrus, Ankica Kosic, Alessia Passarelli, Doris Peschke and Dita Vogel for their direct and indirect contribution to this work, the interesting discussions we have had and their advice and support during the phase of writing and editing the manuscript. Thanks are also extended to all the POLITIS national experts who have contributed to this volume for their commitment and patience with our repeated intellectual and organizational requests. It has been a great experience to work closely with such a diverse and international group of people on a topic as exciting and as complex and multifaceted as contemporary immigration in the European Union.

A heartfelt thanks goes to Maria-Denise Gropas for her careful content and language editing of this work. The help of Karolina Tagaris has been most appreciated in formatting this work into a manuscript. We would also like to acknowledge the ever-generous institutional and personal support of ELIAMEP which has provided a warm institutional environment and a creative context for our work. Last, but as always not least, we would like to thank the three anonymous referees of Ashgate for their valuable feedback to the introductory and concluding chapters.

Anna Triandafyllidou and Ruby Gropas
Athens, 27 October 2006

Chapter 1

Introduction

Anna Triandafyllidou, Ruby Gropas and Dita Vogel

This chapter discusses the sociopolitical context of contemporary European migration. More specifically, we look at the impact that the end of the Cold War has had on migration in Europe, notably in terms of East to West population flows that involve not only the current EU25 member states but also countries of Eastern Europe and the Commonwealth of Independent States (CIS). We also discuss the emergence and diversification of migration forms including undocumented and shuttle migration, populations displaced for political reasons that are not, however, eligible for refugee status, as well as gendered migration. Through this, we aim at raising awareness of the universal usage of the terms 'immigrant' and 'immigration' that frequently suggests comparability where it does not, in fact, exist. Thus we point out major differences in the understanding of those terms in official statistics and current debates, while also discussing the divergence that may exist between official statistics and definitions of immigrant categories and the social reality on the ground. Last, we discuss the emergence of a common EU migration policy, and the challenges that lie ahead for European countries as regards the sustainable management of international migration.

General overview of migration patterns in Europe since the Second World War

The period immediately after the Second World War in Europe was characterized by large south-to-north flows originating from the northern Mediterranean countries (Greece, Italy, Portugal, and Spain). Western and Northern European countries such as Belgium, Britain, France, Germany and Sweden received migration from the south of Europe and the Mediterranean, but also experienced incoming flows from African, Caribbean and Asian countries. The post-war years were a period of reconstruction and industrial growth in a Europe that was short of labour after the disastrous Second World War. Thus, foreign workers came to meet domestic labour market needs and were often seen as temporary sojourners. The flows originating from outside Europe had largely to do with the colonial legacy of the receiving countries, especially Britain, France, Belgium and the Netherlands. Immigrants from former colonies were able to take advantage of an open policy towards labour migration and special rights (including in some cases full citizenship rights). These migrations were inscribed in the Fordist system of industrial production, and were often channelled through active recruitment policies of companies in the receiving societies and bilateral agreements between sending and receiving countries. While many of these immigrant workers indeed returned to their country of origin after some years, a considerable fraction eventually settled in the receiving societies and brought their families over, thereby raising important social and political challenges for integration that EU Member States continue to face today.

The migration dynamics in Europe changed in the early 1970s after the oil price shocks. Economic growth had been slowing down in Western Europe, structural change in labour markets was evident, and unemployment was growing, especially in the older industrial economies of

Britain and Belgium. As the European Communities pursued policies of economic integration, migration between Southern and Northern Europe gradually declined. By the time that Greece, Portugal and Spain joined the EEC, there were few migrants from these countries travelling for work to the northern Member States. At the same time, a certain level of industrial development accompanied by a wide expansion of the services sector in Southern Europe created employment opportunities, thereby restricting the 'push' factors to emigration. On the 'pull' side, Western and Northern European countries had put a stop to labour migration from the early 1970s onwards, aiming at 'zero immigration'. This equally reduced the flows from Asian and African countries to continental Europe and to Britain. Restrictive immigration policies were characteristic of many countries, including Britain and France, as a prerequisite for the successful integration of those already admitted. In other cases, such as Belgium, Denmark or Germany, admissions were restricted in line with domestic labour market needs, while integration remained a non-issue until the 1980s.

Population movements in Central and Eastern Europe (CEEC) were severely restricted during the post-war period and until 1989. Labour migration took place at a very limited scale and always through central planning and control. There was some exchange of workers between countries of the Warsaw Pact as well as small scale incoming migration (for labour or study purposes) from Communist countries in other continents (for example, the Socialist Republic of Vietnam or Cuba) to CEEC countries (for example East Germany or Poland). As regards outgoing migration from the CEEC to Western Europe or North America, for instance, this never stopped completely in spite of the heavy control measures implemented by communist states. Those who left CEEC for political reasons quickly found refuge in Western Europe. However, their numbers amount to several thousands over the entire period and cannot be compared in terms of magnitude with the large flows from Southern to Northern Europe or from countries in the developing world to Western and Northern Europe.

Since the 1980s, the situation has been changing yet again. The integration of the world economy through world trade and service agreements (GATT and GATS), the globalization of capital and labour and the rapid development of transport and communication networks have contributed to new types of population movements. At the same time, the geopolitical restructuring of Europe after 1989 has opened new opportunities for temporary or long-term migration within Europe as well as from third countries to CEEC and not just to Western Europe. The migration patterns of the last couple of decades are characterized by their fragmented nature: they include new forms of flexible labour, insecure legal status (often undocumented), variable duration, new gender roles and multiple destinations, all of which we explore in the sections below.

Migration in post-1989 Europe

The implosion of the communist regimes in Central and Eastern Europe (CEE) in 1989 has made the new context more volatile and dynamic. The closed borders between Eastern and Western European countries were suddenly opened and many CEE citizens, faced with the dismantling of the production system and welfare state in their countries of origin, started seeking better life chances and work opportunities in Western and Southern Europe. Similar to citizens from countries in the developing world, people from CEE were integrated into specific niches of domestic labour markets in the European Union. Moreover, the opening of the borders has led to diverse forms of population mobility that involve *Eastern, Central and Western/Southern* European countries in complex patterns (Wallace and Stola, 2001; Favell and Hansen, 2002).

These changes have subverted, if not openly at least tacitly, the proclaimed policy of zero migration in most European countries. Large numbers of migrants have arrived, worked and stayed – in various guises. They have entered either clandestinely or as asylum-seekers; but most commonly they have simply come via the pathways of globalization itself – with tourist or student visas which they then overstayed or abused, and at times even as business people (Jordan and Düvell, 2003). Both the more 'flexible', pro-globalization regimes of the UK and Ireland, and the more social protectionist regimes such as those in Germany and the Netherlands introduced new options for temporary legal migration, and built control facilities. These efforts contributed to shaping the country-specific forms of migration and the living conditions of migrants, with rather debatable effects on migration levels.

The line between economic migrants and persons moving for reasons ranging from political instability or oppression to ethnic strife in their countries of origin is increasingly blurred. Thus, people fleeing from political persecution sometimes opt for economic migration channels, both legal and undocumented, while some economically motivated migrants who leave their country in reaction to unemployment or poverty present their applications as asylum seekers (Wallace, 2002).

The governments of Southern Europe have been quite unprepared for the influx of migrants, and indeed when those migrants arrive in these states they usually come into societies that perceive themselves as largely monocultural and monoreligious. Important and unexpected challenges in Southern Europe have thus been raised. Southern European societies have slowly reacted to the presence of immigrants, firstly through repeated regularization programmes of undocumented workers and, secondly, with a view to integrating them both economically and culturally. Incidents of social unrest, highly visible cases of racism and ethnic prejudice have triggered a public debate on the cultural and political rights of immigrants. The former set of rights has been largely recognized even if institutionalized only to a limited extent, while the latter set still looms far behind, almost a taboo topic for Southern European societies.

The beginning of the new century has been characterized by further developments, either endogenous to the EU or exogenous and having to do with developments in the international arena.

Notably, both the European Commission and a number of the EU Member states announced a major shift in policy regarding the recruitment of skilled and unskilled workers from outside the Union. This came at a time when unemployment among EU citizens was still high – some 15.7 million (or 9.2 per cent of the labour force) in 2001 (Eurostat, 2001) – and social policies have focused on retraining and inclusion. This shift reflects growing concerns about bottlenecks and shortages, and the overall flexibility of the European social model (see Jordan and Düvell, 2003). Although the emphasis has been different among the various Member States, there is no doubt that an important change has been taking place regarding recruitment from outside the EU. For example, both Italy and Greece had unemployment rates of around 11 per cent in 1999, whereas Spain's unemployment rate exceeded 15 per cent in the same year. Nevertheless, Italy has admitted over 2.5 million, Spain about 2.5 million and Greece nearly 1.5 million immigrant workers in the last 15 to 20 years. This workforce is predominantly employed in agriculture, tourism, private care, catering and construction. In Italy, it also extends to small and medium-sized productive enterprises. Although initially admitted mainly through illegal channels, these workers have since been regularized through successive 'amnesty' programmes.

The second change followed the attack on the World Trade Centre and the Pentagon in the USA on 11 September 2001. As a direct result, security concerns closely related to migration became an urgent priority. The concern, or the perception, that irregular migration was becoming uncontrollable was already being voiced by politicians and the media; but the policy implications of the events of 9/11 complicated the migration debate further by bringing in additional dimensions. Simplified and even simplistic discourse signalled that migration, and even globalization itself, concealed a potential for terror attack and thus constituted a threat to security. As far as it is possible to ascertain, given the current information at hand, the perpetrators of these attacks were legal migrants and indeed their profiles – computer experts, technicians, diligent students – may be considered stereotypical of the skilled types of immigrant that the USA and the EU Member States are seeking (even competing) to attract. Further terrorist bombings in Madrid in March 2003 and in London in July 2005 have, however, indirectly confirmed the idea that migrants may constitute a 'threat' to western societies' well-being and cohesion, also leading to the interchangeable use of the words Muslims and immigrants as nearly synonymous. Needless to say, such a categorization ignores the rich variety of migrant groups and migration situations across the 25 European Member States.

New features of migration

While the chapters in this book mainly present the variety of migration experiences in EU countries, here we point to some specific features of contemporary migration flows – mainly those of the last 15 years – that tend to be referred to as new (King, 2002). While there is hardly any form of migration that has no historical precedent with some similar features (Bade, 2002), when we speak of new features of contemporary migration, we refer to the relevance, dominance and specific combinations of migration patterns that are largely shaped by economic conditions in a globalized world. Let us sketch some of these conditions that are related to labour supply and demand needs and that form a number of core workforce categories.

In the post-war era, the world was divided into a highly industrialized 'first' world with a growing services sector and a welfare state built up under the influence of organized labour. The 'second' world of communist states was characterized by state-driven industrialization and state-supplied services, complemented by a flexible barter economy that mitigated the harsh effects of failures in state planning. The so called 'third' world was characterized by a high dependence on the primary sector. This allowed for enormous wealth in the case of some oil-exporting countries and for disastrous poverty in the case of agrarian countries that tried to balance production for self-sufficiency with that for the world market, often failing in both. In some countries, some sectors and regions developed quickly to match the standards of the 'first' world, while others stagnated, leading to considerable tensions within the country.

High labour costs in 'first' world countries have promoted an unprecedented technological development that has spilled over to almost all other regions and countries of the world. Computers have become smaller, cheaper and more powerful, satellites are able to distribute TV programmes to the remotest regions of the world, public and private transport has multiplied with faster and relatively cheaper cars, trains and planes, as well as better airports and streets. These developments lead to ever closer connections of all those regions of the world with access to a reliable electricity supply and it has influenced the type of workforce required. In effect, production in these sectors is highly specialized, requiring a small elite of highly educated, highly organized and creative developers, engineers and managers (Type A), and a highly disciplined, well-educated production work force (Type B). This workforce is mainly situated in Western Europe, North America and Japan, but it is coming under increasing pressure from industrializing and democratizing regions, mainly in Asia and Eastern Europe. European and North American countries are increasingly seeking to attract highly skilled immigrants in an effort to stabilize locations and maintain work opportunities for their skilled labour force.

At a time when the movement of financial capital is largely liberalized, the wealth of a region depends largely on its capacity to supply a competitive combination of highly skilled Type A professionals with skilled and highly disciplined Type B workers in a stable, worldwide connected environment. These may form the core workforce of the internationally tradable services of global cities (Sassen, 1991), but also of prospering industrial regions in the old industrialized economies or newly industrializing states.

Such highly productive technology sectors are able to generate taxes for state services and welfare benefits. The state sector, with its spending on education, welfare and infrastructure is a necessary input for high-tech production insofar as it maintains a highly educated workforce, a stable political environment and a modern infrastructure. But it is also a cost factor for that production, as public employees, investments and welfare services have to be financed by taxes. Thus, the wage level in public employment and publicly organized employment is a crucial factor for the competitiveness of the high-tech sector. Employment with the state requires a certain degree of language capacities and country-specific knowledge and offers secure employment opportunities for native citizens of high- and low-skilled educational backgrounds (Type C and D respectively), but it is also often explicitly or implicitly reserved for citizens. This is most obvious in Luxembourg, where most citizens work for public authorities, but it is also present in all EU countries.

In addition, the sector providing services and other goods that are not internationally tradable is also an input and a cost factor for the high-tech sector. While some non-tradable goods and services also require high skills (Type E, for example, doctors, construction engineers), a considerable part of these activities can be performed with hardly any educational qualifications. Cleaning, gardening, looking after small children, caring for the physical needs of elderly and disabled persons, kitchen work in restaurants, delivering simple goods, hairdressing, simple renovating and construction work, can be done well by immigrants without qualifications and language capacity, but with the motivation to cope with low wages and endure unfavourable working conditions (Type F). The demand for Type F employment differs between states, and is most prominent in states where we find low levels of public services for children and the elderly and where highly qualified breadwinner couples have to resort to the private market to obtain labourers for these services (Sciortino, 2004). In this context, Type F workers are able to fill this need because of the low cost of their employment; that is, it is a cost item that can be relatively easily covered by the more qualified workforce.

At the same time, it is pertinent to note that the flexible and cheap labour provided by immigrants mainly from Central and Eastern Europe, Asia and Africa, has been contributing to growth in an increasingly deregulated economic environment of global cities. Recent studies (Reyneri et al., 1999) have shown that undocumented immigrant labour has had a positive economic impact, at least in the short term, on Southern European countries (Greece and Italy, in particular). Indeed, immigrants are likely to take Type F jobs for which the local unemployed do not compete. If they want to spend part of their earnings in their country of origin and consider their stay temporary, they find it easier to be content with lower wage levels than locals and endure more restricted housing arrangements. While native unemployed persons – among them many sons and daughters of post-war immigrants – would experience a declining standard of living by taking up a low-wage job in a prospering high-rent region, immigrants may perceive this change as a step forward when compared to their previous situation in their country of origin, or in any case a temporary 'sacrifice' that they are willing to accept in order to send a steady income back home. This is of course only the case if illegal arrangements do not lead them into a work relationship which involves dependency and deception.

In combination with low transport costs, these demand structures favour all sorts of temporary labour arrangements, whether legal or illegal. In addition, they contribute to a changed gender distribution of immigration. Many of these jobs are in private households and in fields that are traditionally associated with women. Women have become migration subjects in their own right, rather than being considered the accompanying 'luggage' of male 'breadwinners' who have migrated for work and have then brought over their spouse and children (Anderson, 2000; Anthias and Lazaridis, 2000; Kofman et al., 2000; Salih, 2001; Tastsoglou and Alipranti, 2003; Zontini, 2004).

There are also other forms of temporary migration, especially in Central and Eastern Europe and in areas of the Mediterranean. These may be categorized as new forms of mobility rather than migration proper, according to length of stay and/or repetition of travel for employment reasons (Peraldi, 2001, 2002; Wallace, 2002). They involve *shuttle migration* (repeated stays of a few months each, usually for informal work), *suitcase migration* (repeated trips of a few days or weeks each, mainly for trade and small business activities), and other petty trade and business activities related to the flourishing of 'bazaar economies' in Central and Eastern Europe and the wider Mediterranean basin. Such forms of migration have their origins in pre-existing state and economy structures such as the 'black market' during communist times, and the traditional open air markets in the Mediterranean. Moreover, they are further reinforced by the current economic and political transition processes in these regions that often lead people to invent new types of mobility and economic activity even if legal migration in the more 'traditional' sense of the term is impossible (because of migration policy restrictions) or undesirable (because of secondary jobs or welfare benefits in the home country).

This sketch of labour market trends in the global economy implies increasingly segmented labour markets. Polarized immigration in the lowest and the highest labour market segments is a general trend (see also, for example Jordan and Düvell, 2003). Immigration barriers for Type A professionals in tradable goods production are already low, and European states increasingly allow or consider allowing highly educated professionals in the production of non-tradables, for instance in the health services. However, absolute numbers are still low in the highly educated labour market segments. Professionals in state employment are still overwhelmingly recruited from the native population, while the middle class of production workers in high-tech fields is still very much protected from international labour competition by paperwork control and social control. At the other end of the spectrum, there exist numerous arrangements to allow, tolerate or accommodate immigration and temporary labour migration into the lowest strata of the labour market.

This constitutes a first overview of the different forms of migration that are present today, seen from a labour market perspective. This perspective alone is insufficient to understand the full range of migration push and pull factors; nor is it able to offer a complete understanding of who Europe's immigrants are today. Who comes as an immigrant – and under what employment conditions – is largely shaped by the migration histories and government policies of the individual EU Member States, or sometimes even of neighbouring Member States. Furthermore, there are many who arrive for reasons other than employment. This volume will, therefore, attempt to unfold the variety of paths and the diversity of migrant profiles that exist and to present the wide range of measures that have been taken by the EU Member States to deal with migration and its challenges.

Official definitions and social realities: who is an immigrant?

In order to proceed with this task, it is perhaps necessary to take a step back and tackle the obvious question of who is an immigrant according to official data and definitions. In doing this, we are confronted with the confusing reality that exists not only in terms of data and statistics, but also according to the gap that often exists between the formal status of an individual and his or her real situation in the host economy or society. Therefore, to address the question of who are Europe's immigrants, it is first necessary to turn to the richness of existing definitions in order to clarify the lack of common definitions and means of measurement.

Immigration is framed in quite different ways in each Member State, and statistical accounting follows national prerogatives rather than international standards. While standardized and well annotated tables – as presented by the Organization of Economic Cooperation and Development (OECD) – are of major use for the scientific community, they also suggest a comparability that does not in fact exist. This creates the temptation to interpret the available data without fully understanding the country's national background. Almost every Member State has different models of citizenship (and hence naturalization practices) and different 'national philosophies' of integration (Favell, 1998), which are reflected in migration statistics by default (Grieco, 2002). Indeed, each receiving country has its own system of national statistics as regards migration. Some countries monitor all the foreign-born, others monitor non-citizens; but as soon as migrants naturalize, they automatically disappear from migration statistics (for example, Germany or the UK) and still others keep more 'complete' records of native-born citizens, citizens of immigrant origin and non-citizens (for example, France or the Netherlands).

In the following sections, we briefly discuss how migrants are defined in different contexts ranging from official statistics, to political discussions and scholarly literature. It should be noted, however, that in an effort to achieve a comprehensive picture of migration in Europe today, we adopt an inclusive definition of immigrants. Basically, we define immigrants as foreign-born people and their immediate offspring, namely, first and second generation immigrants. Nonetheless, given various limitations of information, we would like to draw the reader's attention to the problems of this concept and discuss its overlaps with and differences from other concepts.

Foreign-born and natives

The distinction between 'foreign-born' and 'natives' is the most widely used differentiation in immigration. It defines immigrants as persons who have changed residence across borders. Indeed, personal migration experience is the decisive criterion.

In many sociological studies, the foreign-born are called 'first generation immigrants', while their offspring – born in the receiving country or immigrated with the parents at a young age – are called 'second generation immigrants.' The terms *allochthones* and *autochthones* are used by the Dutch state to define in a more precise manner the ethnic/national origin of a citizen or resident. This pair of concepts is a refinement of the country-of-birth criterion. It differentiates between *allochthones* as the foreign-born and their immediate offspring, taking the country of birth of the parents into account, and *autochthones* – native-born with two native-born parents. This criterion has been used in the Netherlands since the 1980s for official statistical purposes, allowing social scientists and migration experts to have a more inclusive approach to the Dutch population of immigrant origin, including the second generation (Centraal Bureau voor Statistiek, 2002).

Although 'foreign-born' seems to be an easy and straightforward concept, there are still some complications in the contemporary European situation. While people usually move across borders, in some areas of Europe borders have moved over people repeatedly during the last century. This has been the case in the aftermath of the Second World War and after 1989 in Central and Eastern Europe. Two examples are worth mentioning here to illustrate this complexity.

After the Second World War, Germany received some 12 million co-ethnic refugees of German origin, most of whom were expelled from regions that formerly belonged to Germany and became part of the independent Central and Eastern European countries. These people were born inside Germany's former borders but outside its subsequent borders. Given that Germany does not use the country-of-birth criterion in official statistics, it thereby renders this mass influx statistically invisible.[1] This is also true for contemporary ethnic German immigration from states that never had any affiliation with Germany.

Before 1989, the Baltic states were part of the Soviet Union. During this time, many Russians and citizens from other Republics of the Soviet Union (mainly Ukraine and Byelorussia) settled in Estonia, Latvia and Lithuania. These people moved to the Baltic states either of their own will or through forced migration as part of the dominant occupying majority. They were thus born inside the borders of the Soviet Union but at the same time outside the borders of the current Baltic states. However, after these countries gained independence in 1991, the Russian-speaking populations who chose to remain in these countries were assigned the peculiar status of *stateless permanent residents* of Latvia or Estonia. Although this category of persons did not undergo an international migration experience, but rather an internal domestic experience under particular circumstances, nonetheless, we have decided to include them in our definition of migrants.

Aliens and citizens under the influence of naturalization policies

Differentiating between foreign nationals and own nationals is still the most widespread criterion to measure foreign migration. It usually works well for new migration streams, but loses significance with increasing numbers of naturalizations and citizenship acquisition by birth. As policies regarding citizenship acquisition differ largely between EU Member States, the citizenship criterion measures completely different aspects with regard to migration.

People acquire their citizenship depending on their country of birth (*jus soli*) or by reference to their genealogical origin (jus sanguinis). Models of ethnic citizenship give preference to ancestry and, hence, to parents' and grandparents' nationality. Models of civic citizenship privilege the place-of-birth criterion, conferring citizenship to children born in their territory regardless of the nationality of their parents. In general, most citizenship regimes involve a combination of the two elements. Thus, in some cases, the *jus soli* principle is applied only if the parents of the child have lived for a certain time in the country, or, if the child herself/himself continues to live in that country. In other cases, a pure *jus sanguinis* regime is mitigated by a territorial element: children of foreign parents or foreigners born in a different country who are long-term legal residents are given the opportunity to naturalize if they wish to do so.

Generally speaking, the distinction between citizens and non-citizens (foreigners, be they temporary or long-term legal residents) is the main dividing line not only in the official statistics, but also in the public discourse in most countries. Data on the population by citizenship status are often used to frame migration-related issues. Let us, however, explore some concrete empirical examples with a view to highlighting the fuzzy edges of the distinction between citizens and aliens.

Most immigrants are foreign nationals at the time of migration. Exceptions include people of the same ethnic background who are granted citizenship upon arrival in the destination country through preferential channels. This is the case, for instance, of ethnic Germans from Central and Eastern European countries, from the Commonwealth of Independent States (CIS) (Münz and Ulrich, 1998), or of the Pontic Greeks from the former Soviet Republics of Georgia, Armenia, Kazakhstan and Russia (Triandafyllidou and Veikou, 2002). Similar, albeit not identical, is the case of residents from former colonies in a transition period, such as the Surinamese in the Netherlands, Commonwealth citizens in the U.K. or Algerians in France. Such cases are usually linked to particular historical circumstances.

---

1   They are included in the most recent microcensus which has yet not been analysed.

Different sets of exceptions are also made for the children or even grandchildren of former emigrants who may have inherited or re-acquired the citizenship of the country of origin. The case of Argentine citizens of Italian ancestry who are able to recover Italian citizenship if they prove that at least one of their grandparents had been an Italian citizen provides a good example (Pastore, 2001). The 'retornados' in Portugal are a similar case. These are former emigrants from Portugal and their offspring who settled in the Portuguese colonies in Africa, and who returned to Portugal after these countries gained their independence in the second half of the twentieth century.

Irrespective of some of the exceptions outlined above and to which we will return in the individual country chapters, it is standard practice that immigrants have the right to naturalize after a given period of time. This period tends to vary from one country to another and is usually between five and ten years of residence in the host country, and under specific conditions. In some countries these conditions refer mainly to the socio-economic realm, such as having a job and a stable residence and not having been convicted for certain crimes. In others, they also include cultural requisites such as language competence, familiarity with the customs and traditions of the country of settlement, and/or a feeling of belonging to that country. Applicants may or may not keep the citizenship of their country of origin. The conditions and procedures involved in the naturalization process influence the naturalization rate and, hence, the percentage of immigrants who become citizens.

Naturalization policies and practices blur the sociological distinction between immigrants and foreigners. While first-generation immigrants may naturalize, not all immigrants are considered foreigners. At the same time, while some non-citizens may have not experienced migration themselves, as they may have been born in their parents' country of settlement (that is, host country), they may still not be entitled to the citizenship of their country of birth. The obvious example of such a case was the German citizenship and migration policy until the year 2000. Today, more than one million out of its seven million foreign residents are native-born; that is, they are the offspring of immigrant parents or grandparents commonly referred to as second- or third-generation migrants.

In summary, naturalization policies greatly affect definitions and statistics about the immigrant population in a given country. In some countries, a considerable percentage of all first-generation immigrants are naturalized citizens, while the percentage in others is negligible. In some countries virtually all foreign nationals are foreign-born, while in others there is a considerable percentage of people born in the country who are foreign nationals. In yet other countries, naturalized citizens are considered migrants by the state and their (new) fellow nationals, while in other countries naturalized citizens become largely integrated in the host society and disappear from official statistics and, to a certain extent at least, from public opinion and media definitions of migrant populations.

Status and staying perspectives

When European states consider immigration policies, they often orientate themselves towards the classical immigration countries USA, Canada and Australia, with their sharp distinction between immigrants (with a permanent residence right) and non-immigrants (with a temporary residence right). The differentiation suggests that non-immigrants leave after a specified period of time, while immigrants come for permanent residence and stay permanently. Nonetheless, even in classical immigration countries, this categorization leads to problems, as it is built on rather simplistic assumptions about the immigration process. In the USA, there have been periods during which a large percentage of people who came with immigrant status left after some time. Today, many people who have (permanent) immigrant status in the USA were previously temporary migrants or even illegal entrants (Santel, 1998).

In most European states, there are few migrants who came with permanent residence status from the outset. Also, national policies vary not only in terms of citizenship acquisition rules but also with reference to migration status. Some countries, such as Ireland and Greece (Kassimis and Kassimi, 2004; Ruhs, 2004), have very recently developed a long-term immigrant category, as the need for such a category and for related policy provisions has emerged only during the last decade.

Most immigrants to Europe migrated with a temporary and/or uncertain staying perspective. They later decided to stay or were granted long-term residence status after several years of life and work in the receiving country. Here again the distinction between the different categories of seasonal, temporary and long-term migrants reflects the sociocultural norms and historical experiences of the receiving societies. Thus, the main 'hosts' of post-war Europe – Germany, France and the UK – had different expectations regarding the time perspective of their foreign workers. Germany saw immigration as a rotating guest worker scheme at the end of which migrants would return to their country of origin. This did not, however, eventually happen. Rather, a substantial portion of the migrants settled and brought their families in, considering Germany their new home. In France and the UK, expectations were more relaxed, not least because migrants came from former colonies and were thus perceived as sharing important cultural and historical links with the receiving society. However, indefinite stay permits were gradually restricted to those with French or British ancestry, respectively, and citizenship regimes became more restrictive. These changes emphasized the largely temporary perspective of international migration. Most receiving societies have difficulties in coming to terms with the idea that newcomers are there to stay permanently.

In reality, the distinction between temporary migrants and long-term or permanent immigrants is a criterion that differentiates migrants according to the host society's self-perception and policy objectives, and has little to do with actual migration processes. Migration policies often change, adapting to the migration trends and realities as well as to the perceived interests of the host society. Thus, people who came under rotation agreements were given indefinite stay rights and undocumented migrants received legal status. From this perspective, when we distinguish migrants according to their status, we do not imply a hypothesis about their future migration behaviour but, rather, relate to the legal ascription by the receiving state. In the analysis of issues such as integration and participation, researchers should not restrict their analysis to certain types of immigrants, since – from a historical and internationally comparative perspective – entry status is a very weak predictor of later settlement.

National majorities and ethnic minorities/diasporas

In certain cases, immigrants and their offspring from specific nationalities (these differ between Member States) are often seen as an ethnic minority in the receiving country. Ethnicity is not as objective a criterion as foreign-born or foreign national, but depends on self-perception and perception by others (Heckmann, 1992). In effect, ethnicity may be linked to culture, language or religion signalling the perceived belonging to a certain minority. This implies that boundaries of minority–majority perception may evolve and dissolve during migration processes. It is relevant to note here that, for immigrants from a certain country to be perceived as an ethnic minority within the receiving society, a substantial volume of immigration tends to be necessary.

Nonetheless, visibility is not only a matter of size of the population in question. Visibility may be higher if the minority is of a different phenotype (skin colour, face characteristics, overall complexion) making it easily distinguishable from the majority. Visibility may also depend on cultural factors such as dress codes and overall appearance of immigrant individuals that make them stand out from the majority 'crowd' (for example headscarf, Sikh turban and so on). Some groups are stigmatized by the political and public discourse as 'problematic', 'dangerous' or 'undesirable' aliens. Such negative stereotyping is often directed against Albanians in Greece, Algerians in France, Turks in Germany and Pakistanis in Britain.[2]

Although these populations are not part of our target group, it is worth considering whether countries with important historical minorities have a different way of dealing with immigration-related ethnic minorities. In addition, new migration may blend into traditional ethnic minorities. In Poland, for instance, recent Ukrainian economic migrants have settled in historical minority Ukrainian communities, a pattern echoed by recent Bangladeshi migrants in the UK. They thus both challenge and revitalize the minority institutions and may provide a test case as to whether institutional channels aimed at catering for the civic and political needs of historical minorities can be used by and for immigrant minorities.

Ethnicity perceptions in immigrant minorities do not necessarily overlap with country boundaries, nor do they necessarily coincide with migrants' self-perception. Kurds, for example, come from Turkey or Iraq and organize in Kurdish associations in the receiving countries. People from South America may see themselves and be perceived as *Latinos* in the receiving countries, while they would not have been aware of such a categorization before leaving their country of origin. Similarly, people from Sub-Saharan Africa are categorized generally as Africans, while they may internally differentiate not only in relation to their country of origin but also in relation to their ethnic or clan affiliation.

This brief overview of different dimensions that may be used to define who is an immigrant and what type of immigrant one is, shows on one hand the complexity of national realities in different Member States and, on the other, the divergence between countries and official definitions, public perceptions and sociological (research) understandings of migrants. The country chapters included in this book further highlight these differences and explain how they came about. In other words, they explore the historical processes and the policy developments behind these differences. In the concluding chapter, we take this issue further by comparing countries and seeking to identify not only mobility trends, but also 'migrant definition' trends across Europe.

European migration policy

The complex and dynamic picture of old and new migrations in Europe has also to be seen in the context of European integration. A unique feature of the European Union as a socio-political entity is the expansion of its boundaries. The entry of 10 new member states in May 2004 has made its dynamic character ever more salient while also changing the legal definition of who is an international migrant in EU territory. However, public perceptions of who is an '*extracomunitario*' (non-EU citizen) take more time to change. In the meantime, the EU continues to expand, welcoming Bulgaria and Romania in 2007 and with the expectation to include the Balkans and Turkey in the next decade or so.

---

2   In this book we are concerned with immigrant minorities only, not historical ones. Historical minorities are native populations of a different ethnicity or nationality that were nevertheless part of the country from its very moment of state formation or pre-modern migration movements. Well known cases of national minorities are the Basques in Spain and France, the Irish in the UK, Hungarians in Romania and Slovakia. However, most – if not all – European countries have one or several historical ethnic/national minorities living in their territory.

The inclusive nature of the Union, however, raises a number of identity questions which relate to both the notion of 'European-ness' or a European identity, and to the national identities of Member States or of minorities within them. The process of constituting the European Union opens up a tri-polar identity space in which existing forms of collective identification have to be re-negotiated and re-defined. This space is characterized by the simultaneous existence of three levels of identity and governance: the transnational or European level, the national or Member State sphere, and the local-regional context, which includes minorities and immigrant communities. Within this context, the dominance of the nation-state as a political agent and of national identity as the primary form of collective identification are put into question (Zapata-Barrero, 2001).

The process of Europeanization affects immigrant communities and minorities living in Europe both directly and through the channels of national states. First and foremost, the Amsterdam Treaty (AT) has incorporated migration policies into the Treaty of the European Communities as Title IV on 'Visas, Asylum, Immigration and Other Policies related to the Free Movement of Persons' (Hailbronner, 1998). Following the AT, the Treaty for a European Union (TEU) states (Article 2) that it is the EU's objective

> to maintain and develop the Union as an area of freedom, security and justice, in which the free movement of persons is assured in conjunction with appropriate measures with respect to external border controls, asylum [and] immigration.

Thus, what was previously characterized as an area of common interest among Member States, has become a policy objective of the EU. Nonetheless, the AT has guaranteed a balance between national control and supranational governance by introducing a limit to the jurisdiction of the European Court of Justice (ECJ) on migration policies, a limit that does not exist in other areas (Article 68 TEC; also Stetter, 2000, p. 95). Discussing the legal and institutional details of the AT provisions concerning migration goes beyond the scope of this volume. It is, however, worth noting that the AT shifted the focus from inter-governmental cooperation to protect a common interest to supranational governance.

The Directorate General for Freedom, Security and Justice (DG FSJ) has been actively engaged in preparing the ground for the development of a common EU immigration policy, issuing a series of relevant Communications and Council Directive proposals in recent years (http://europa.eu.int/pol/justice/index_en.htm). Negotiations among the Member States have been intense. Among recent developments, we note the Council Directives on family reunification and on the status of long term resident,[3] on common asylum procedures[4] and on the common efforts to combat illegal migration.[5] After lengthy negotiations and failure to reach an agreement, the proposal for

---

3   25/11/2003, Council Directive, 2003/109/EC of 25 November 2003 concerning the status of third-country nationals who are long-term residents. Official Journal L 016, 23/01/2004, p. 0044–0053, and 22/09/2003. Council Directive 2003/86/EC of 22 September 2003 on the right to family reunification, Official Journal L.251 , 03/10/2003 p. 0012–0018.

4   25/02/03. Council Regulation (EC) No 343/2003 of 18 February 2003 establishing the criteria and mechanisms for determining the Member State responsible for examining an asylum application lodged in one of the Member States by a third-country national.

Official Journal L 050, 06/02/03 p. 0001–0010. And 06/02/03. Council Directive of 27 January 2003 laying down minimum standards for the reception of asylum seekers

Official Journal L 031, 06/02/03 p. 0018–0025.

5   11/02/2002, COM 2002 071 final.52002PC0071. Proposal for a Council Directive on the short-term residence permit issued to victims of action to facilitate illegal immigration or trafficking in human beings who cooperate with the competent authorities. Decision follow-up; 10/07/2001. Council Directive 2001/51/EC of 28 June 2001 supplementing the provisions of Article 26 of the Convention implementing the

a common policy on managing labour migration (both for employed persons and for independent professionals) is again open for discussion.[6] In sum, there has been progress in the building of a common EU migration policy, but such progress is slow and is characterized by the lowest common denominator approach. Directive proposals are systematically watered down through the negotiations between Member States who seek to protect their national interests and national immigration policies. Defining who is an immigrant, why, how and for how long they come and stay in a member state, remains largely tied to national government decision-making and national migration policy traditions.

Informal discussions with DG FSJ officials (notes from seminar at the College of Europe, Bruges, 15 March 2005) confirm that border control is the most successful sector of migration policy at the EU level. Co-operation and transfer of knowledge in this area has been intense in the past few years during the pre-accession negotiations of the 10 new Member States. Such co-operation systematically continues with both the remaining accession countries and in the context of the EU neighbourhood policy in the Mediterranean and Eurasian region. However, border control is only one area of migration policy which is indispensable, although it cannot obscure the pressing problems and challenges of the overall management of economic migration and immigrant integration that European societies face.

The contents of this book

The concurrence of these migration categories and migration patterns outlined above has led to the present situation of a profoundly diverse immigrant population in the EU 25 host countries. Thus, each EU Member State is looked at in detail in the 25 subsequent country chapters.

Each country chapter follows a similar structure. In the first instance, each chapter clarifies the categories of persons who are considered as migrants in the member state and includes an explanation of the national statistical data provided. This is followed by an overview of the recent migration history (that is the last 10 to 15 years) and the individual migration policies of each EU country, along with an analysis of how these have influenced the categories of migrants that exist across the 25 states.

The common traits and comparative dimensions are brought out in the concluding chapter. The final chapter not only brings forward the various categories of immigrants in the EU today, it also provides a schematic grouping of the EU Member States based on their characteristics. Without over-simplifying the distinctive features particular to each country, the 25 Member States are grouped in five subsets based on their experiences of migration: a) old host countries; b) recent host countries, c) countries in transition, d) small island countries and e) non-immigration countries.

Schengen Agreement of 14 June 1985. OJ L 187 of 10/07/01, p. 45 (carriers liability); 02/06/01. 301L0040. Council Directive 2001/40/EC of 28 May 2001 on the mutual recognition of decisions on the expulsion of third country nationals. Official Journal L 149, 02/06/01 p. 0034–0036; 25/11/03. COM (2003) 727 final. Proposal for a Council Decision Establishing a secure web-based Information and Coordination Network for Member States' Migration Management Services (ICONET) of 25/11/03. And 29/01/02. COM 2001 567 final. 52001PC0567. Proposal for a Council decision adopting an action programme for administrative co-operation in the fields of external borders, visas, asylum and immigration (ARGO), Official Journal C 025 E, 29/01/02 p. 0526–0530.

6   11/01/2005, Com/2004/0811 Final, Green Paper on an EU Approach to Managing Economic Migration 11/07/2001, Com (2001), **386**. Proposal for a Council directive on the conditions of entry and residence of third-country nationals for the purpose of paid employment and self-employed economic activities. Official Journal C 332 E, 27/11/01 p. 0248–0256. Decision follow-up.

The first group refers to Northern and Western EU Member States, or what we can also refer to as the traditional host migration countries. Their migration history is very different and the migrant population much more varied. France, Germany, Belgium, the Netherlands and the UK have a long migration history principally because of their colonial history, and this is similarly in Denmark and Sweden, which have a longer experience with immigrants. These countries are generally faced with the challenge of combating the social exclusion and marginalization of second- or third-generation immigrants. Associated with this is the fact that economic crises and social frustration are exacerbating xenophobic reactions of the majority populations, while the religious factor is becoming increasingly visible and present within the immigrant population. Nevertheless, these countries have the most far-reaching multi-cultural policies and, in many cases, immigrant populations have been granted the right to vote in local elections, thereby enhancing their political participation in the host country. In these countries the focus of attention has shifted from issues of regularization to issues of participation and integration.

The second subset includes the Southern European countries (that is, Italy, Greece, Spain and Portugal) that in the course of less than two decades have become host countries. Their emigration patterns of the past have been reversed in spite of high rates of unemployment among native workers. This shift in European migration patterns partly reflects a gradual improvement in the economic situation and the living conditions in Europe's southern countries, but in part it is also an unintended side effect of the restrictive measures taken by the UK, France, Germany, and Switzerland. The immigration experience in these countries has been characterized by the absence of a consistent migration policy with a long-term approach on issues of regularization and integration. This has led to an increase of illegal immigration and of migrants remaining in these countries unofficially, with their papers not always in order. This irregular or illegal status has implications not only for their employment security, but also for the extent of their integration into the host society. The large inflow of undocumented immigrants that has been common to these Member States has led to repeated regularization programmes. For example, the country chapters look into the five such programmes that have taken place in Italy since 1986, involving more than two million immigrants; the two such programmes in Greece, with the third currently under way; the four regularization initiatives in Portugal since 1992; and the three such programmes undertaken by Spain, with its third and most far-reaching regularization scheme in 2005. These regularization programmes confirm that such strategies do not solve in the long term the challenge of dealing with undocumented migration, if they are not part of a wider scheme of immigration management and integration policies.

The third subset is made up of the Central and Eastern European countries (CEE). Along with the political, social and economic transition which occurred in this region after the 'Autumn of Nations' in 1989, the mechanisms and patterns of migration have changed with regard to these countries as well. Central European countries appear to be in the preliminary stage of an immigrant flow not only from the former Soviet Union countries, or from neighbouring nations with which there was a formal relation (for example Czechoslovakia and former Yugoslavia) but also from the Far East and from the West. During more recent years, CEE countries have become an attractive destination for entrepreneurs from Western Europe and the USA. They mostly carry out economic activities in the tertiary and quaternary sectors as highly-skilled managers, experts, consultants, scientists and so on. Immigrants from Asian countries mostly use CEE countries for temporary stay in transit towards Western Europe. The most visible group among these have been the Vietnamese in the Czech Republic, Poland and Slovakia, and the Chinese in Hungary and Slovenia. There have existed so-called 'international co-operation schemes' in educational and employment sectors between some of these countries, but since 1989 other forms of inflow have developed, from illegal entry, to temporary stay and arranged marriages through to the setting-up of business and permanent settlement through formal means.

Cyprus and Malta form a different category combining a small population, a growing influx of immigration over the past decade and continued emigration. Being at the geographic periphery of the EU they are also called to manage increasing numbers of illegal immigrants and asylum seekers.

The Baltic states, Slovenia and Slovakia are identified as non-immigration countries, given that the former steady migration flows from the former Soviet Union or Yugoslavia have, overall, ceased since the 1990s and 2000s. At the same time, the emigration flows that were characteristic of the first years after their independence also appear to be levelling out. The issue of stateless persons is of particular interest in this set of EU Member States and is looked at particularly in the Latvian and Estonian chapters.

Moreover, the concluding chapter puts forward a typology of the main migration pathways that can be traced within the European Union. Eight old and new migration pathways are thus identified: the pathway of co-ethnics and returnees, the colonial and post-colonial pathway, the pre-1989 internal migration pathway, the labour migration pathway, the asylum-seeking pathway, the pathway of temporary and seasonal migration, the 'gold-collar' pathway, and the pathway of irregular migration.

To conclude, the final chapter offers a comparative overview of immigrant integration practices regarding naturalization regimes, the granting of local voting rights and the extent of immigrant participation in the civic and political life of the host countries.

Thus, this book is a synthesis of existing data and provides a concise overview of recent migration history throughout the European Union. It is based on secondary sources in English and in the national language of each Member State, as well as on international and European migration statistics. It aims to serve as a useful and comprehensive reference volume for students, practitioners and scholars working on migration in Europe.

References

Anderson, B. (2000), *Doing the Dirty Work? The Global Politics of Domestic Labour*. London: Zed Books.

Anthias, F. and Lazaridis, G. (eds) (2000), *Gender and Migration in Southern Europe: Women on the Move*. Oxford: Berg.

Bade, K.J. (2002), *Europa in Bewegung: Migration vom späten 18. Jahrhundert bis zur Gegenwart*, München: Beck.

Centraal Bureau voor Statistiek (2002), *Allochtonen in Nederland 2001*. Heerlen/ Voorberg: CBS.

Eurostat (2001), *The Social Situation in the European Union*. Luxembourg: Office for the Official Publications of the European Communities.

Favell, A. (1998), *Philosophies of Integration: Immigration and the Idea of Citizenship in France and Britain*. London: Macmillan.

Favell, A. and Hansen, R. (eds) (2002), 'EU Enlargement and East-West Migration', *Journal of Ethnic and Migration Studies*, Special Issue, **28**(4), October.

Hailbronner, K. (1998), 'European Immigration and Asylum Law under the Amsterdam Treaty', *Common Market Law Review*, **35**(5), 1047–1067. [DOI: 10.1023/A%3A1018659109304]

Heckmann, F. (1992), *Ethnische Minderheiten, Volk und Nation: Soziologie Inter-ethnischer Beziehungen*. Stuttgart: Enke.

Jordan, B. and Düvell, F. (2003), *Irregular Migration: The Dilemmas of Transnational Mobility*. Cheltenham, UK & Northampton, USA: Edward Elgar.

Jordan, B., Stråth, Bo and Triandafyllidou, A. (eds) (2003), 'From Guardians to Managers: Immigration Policy Implementation in Europe', *Journal of Ethnicity and Migration Studies*, **29**(2).

King, R. (2002), 'Towards a New Map of European Migration', *International Journal of Population Geography*, **8**, 89–106.

Kofman, E., Phizaklea, A., Raghuram, P. and Sales, R. (2000), *Gender and International Migration in Europe; Employment, Welfare and Policies*. London: Routledge.

Münz, R. and Ulrich, R. (1998), 'Germany and its Immigrants: a Socio-Demographic Analysis', *Journal of Ethnic and Migration Studies*, **24**, 25–56.

Pastore, F. (2001), 'Nationality Law and International Migration: the Italian Case', in Hansen, R. and Weil, P. (eds) *Towards a European Nationality*, 95–118. New York: Palgrave.

Peraldi, M. (ed.) (2001), *Cabas et Containers. Activités marchandes informelles et réseaux migrants transfrontaliers*. Paris: Maisonneuve & Larose.

Peraldi, M. (ed.) (2002), *La Fin des Norias?* Paris: Maisonneuve & Larose.

Reyneri, E., Baganha, M., Dal Lago, A., Laacher, S., Palidda, S., Papantoniou, A., Papantoniou, M., Solé, C. and Wilpert, C. (1999), *Migrants' Insertion in the Informal Economy: Deviant Behaviour and the Impact on Receiving Societies (MIGRINF)*. Comparative Reports, Brussels: TSER Programme (Contract No. SOE2-CT95-3005), unpublished project report.

Salih, R. (2001), 'Moroccan Migrant Women: Transnationalism, Nation States and Gender', *Journal of Ethnic and Migration Studies*, **27**(4), 655–71. [DOI: 10.1080/13691830120090430]

Santel, B. (1998), 'Auf dem Weg zur Konvergenz? Einwanderungspolitik in Deutschland und den Vereinigten Staaten im Vergleich', *Zeitschrift für Ausländerrecht und Ausländerpolitik*, **1**, 14–20.

Sassen, S. (1991), *The Global City: New York, London, Tokyo*. New Jersey: Princeton University Press.

Sciortino, G. (2004), 'When Domestic Labour Is Not Native Labour: the Interaction of Immigration Policy and the Welfare Regime in Italy', in Gorny, A. and Ruspini, P. (eds) *Migration in the New Europe: East-West Revisited*, 168–88. London: Palgrave.

Stetter, S. (2000), 'Regulating Migration: Authority Delegation in Justice and Home Affairs', *Journal of European Public Policy*, **7**(1), 81–103. [DOI: 10.1080/135017600343287]

Tastsoglou, E. and Maratou Alipranti, L. (eds) (2003), 'Gender and International Migration: Focus on Greece', *The Greek Review of Social Research*, Special Issue 110 A.

Triandafyllidou, A. and Veikou, M. (2002), 'The Hierarchy of Greekness: Ethnic and National Identity Considerations in Greek Immigration Policy', *Ethnicities*, **2**(2), 189–208.

Wallace, C. (2002), 'Opening and Closing Borders: Migration and Mobility in East Central Europe', *Journal of Ethnic and Migration Studies*, **28**(4), 603–625. [DOI: 10.1080/136918302 1000032227]

Wallace, C. and Stola, D. (eds) (2001), *Patterns of Migration in Central Europe*. London: Palgrave.

Zapata Barrero, R. (2001), 'The Limits of a Multinational Europe: Democracy and Immigration in the European Union' in Requejo, F. (ed.) *Democracy and National Pluralism*. London: Routledge.

Zontini, E. (2004), 'Immigrant Women in Barcelona: Coping with the Consequences of Transnational Lives', *Journal of Ethnic and Migration Studies*, **30**(6), 1113–1144. [DOI: 10.1080/13691830 42000286278]

Internet-based references

Grieco, E. (2002), 'Defining 'Foreign Born' and 'Foreigner' in International Migration Statistics', *Data Insight, Migration Information Source*, 1 July 2002 (available at www.migrationinformation.org, accessed 22 August 2006).

Kassimis, C. and Kassimi, C. (2004), 'Greece: A History of Migration', *Migration Information Source*, June 2004 (available at http://www.migrationinformation.org/Profiles/display.cfm?ID=228, accessed 22 August 2006).

Ruhs, M. (2004), 'Ireland. A Crash Course in Immigration Policy', *Migration Information Source*, October 2004 (available at http://www.migrationinformation.org/Profiles/display.cfm?ID=260, accessed on 25 August 2006).

Chapter 2

Austria

Albert Kraler and Karin Sohler

Throughout the twentieth century, Austria was a country of both immigration and emigration. However, its migration history in the twentieth century is characterized by several major breaks, all of which led to important reconfigurations of the patterns of migration and the emergence of completely new migratory phenomena. In the post-war period, migration is largely associated with 'guest worker migration', which started in the early 1960s. Originally, 'guest worker' migration – as the very name suggests – was designed as a temporary, rotating migration, but the system developed into a mixed form of circular and permanent migration. Because of labour recruitment, immigrants from Turkey and former Yugoslavia – the major countries of origin of labour migrants – still form the majority of immigrants. Indeed, in 2005 they comprised 54 per cent of a total foreign population of approximately 788,000 persons. Yet, as a result of the 'new immigration' from other, mostly Eastern European, countries and from Africa and South-East and Central Asia, the immigrant population is increasingly diversifying.

During the Cold War period, Austria was also an important country of transit and asylum for refugees from communist-ruled Eastern Europe. During the 1980s, however, the importance of 'cold war refugees' declined and the share of asylum seekers from other countries of origin progressively increased. The inflow of immigrants from Eastern Europe following the end of exit controls in 1989, and the influx of refugees from former Yugoslavia after 1991, resulted in the almost doubling of the population with foreign citizenship between 1988 and 1993. After 1993, the foreign resident population continued to grow, but at a much lower rate. Since 2001, because of a rise in immigration from EU countries (notably Germany), high levels of family reunification involving naturalized migrants and high levels of asylum applications, net immigration has again markedly risen. The total foreign population has risen to 788,609 or 9.6 per cent of the total population in 2005,[1] while an estimated 15 per cent of the total population are foreign born.

Major developments in Austria's immigration policy

Until the early 1990s, Austria designed its migration policy exclusively on the basis of economic considerations. Indeed, the government left the determination of migration levels largely to the 'social partners' comprised by organized labour and employers. However, major transformations in the political system – notably the erosion of the dominance of the traditional ruling parties,[2] and the emergence of opposition parties who used migration to sharpen their profile and to mobilize voters[3]

---

1   Statistics Austria, POPREG, <http://www.emn.at/module-Documents-view-cid-1-did-7.phtml>, accessed 24 March 2006.

2   Social Democratic Party, SPÖ; the Austrian People's Party, ÖVP.

3   The Populist Freedom Party and the Green Party.

– made migration a central theme of political debates and undermined the power of social partners to decide on migration policy in a technocratic manner and behind closed doors.

By the late 1980s, following a marked rise in the number of asylum applications, asylum had also become an increasingly contentious political issue. In particular, the massive inflow of Romanian asylum seekers in 1990 created the impression of an impending asylum crisis and gave rise to intense public debate in which asylum and immigration issues became increasingly intertwined. Moreover, migration was reframed as a security issue. In this context, the Ministry of the Interior became the leading actor in designing migration policy. After the fall of the Iron Curtain, rising inflows of new labour migrants from Eastern Europe and refugees from former Yugoslavia increased the pressure on policy-makers to undertake a comprehensive reform of immigration legislation. Another reason for reform widely acknowledged at the political level stemmed from the growing recognition that the existing legal framework governing migration, still relying on the 'rotation model', had become inadequate to deal with the long-term presence of immigrants.

In an initial step, asylum was reformed in 1991. Fast-track procedures and the concepts of 'safe third country' and 'safe country of origin', both of which were subsequently applied to several Eastern European countries (Hungary, Slovakia, Romania), were introduced (Kraler and Stacher, 2002). After lengthy discussions, the first major reform of immigration legislation was adopted in 1992. Contrary to the initial progressive impetus of the reform, notably the idea to guarantee residence security for long-term immigrants and their descendants, the emphasis of the legislation was on restricting immigration. The most important novelty introduced by the 1992 Residence Act was annually fixed quotas determining the maximum number of first permits issued to different categories of migrants according to demographic, labour market and social considerations ('capacities of reception'). Long-term immigrants were, in many respects, worse off than before the reform. The restrictive quota system and the provisions on the issuing and renewal of residence permits had the effect of increasing both residence insecurity and the numbers of (long-term settled) immigrants and their family members who were withdrawn or denied regular status either because of the exhaustion of quotas or for procedural reasons. In addition, the new legal provisions left considerable scope for administrative discretion. This, in turn, also involved administrative decisions being frequently overturned by the country's higher courts (Jahwari, 2000).

Reforms for the tightening of border control, policing measures and freedom of movement provisions for EEA citizens had already been anticipated in view of Austria's accession to the European Economic Area in 1993, as well as the European Union and the Schengen Group in 1995. Even before accession, Austria had become strongly involved in European policy harmonization on external border control and asylum policies, in many ways acting as a precursor in introducing the respective policies.

After several abortive attempts to reform immigration legislation, a new Immigration Act was finally adopted in 1997. One of its major objectives was to address the obvious shortcomings of the 1992 act, and, in particular, the precarious legal situation for settled migrants and their descendants (Bauböck and Perchinig, 2006). Under the slogan 'integration before new immigration', its declared intention was to promote the integration of settled immigrants while endorsing the restrictive position on immigration. The most important novelty introduced by the reform was the principle of 'consolidation of residence'. This principle enhanced the protection from expulsion as well as the duration of residence, and established an absolute right to remain for foreign children born or raised in Austria.

In 2000, the long-time coalition of the Social Democratic Party (SPÖ) and the Austrian People's Party (ÖVP) was succeeded by a centre-right government coalition, led by the ÖVP with the populist Freedom Party (FPÖ) as the junior party in government.

Between 2000 and 2006, the ÖVP-FPÖ[4] coalition undertook three major revisions of immigration and asylum legislation. The first reform, in 2002, introduced new regulations on four important aspects.

First, labour immigration of low skilled workers was formally ended by abolishing the quota for workers and replacing it with a quota for 'key personnel', that is, highly skilled migrants. In order to qualify as 'key personnel', prospective migrants had to meet a minimum wage initially set at €2,016 per month (which has since increased to €2,250).[5]

Second, as compensation, the employment of (unskilled) temporary labour was greatly facilitated by allowing seasonal workers in employment sectors other than those which had traditionally employed seasonal migrants, as well as by extending the employment period to up to one year.

Third, all new immigrants from third countries and third country nationals who had immigrated to Austria after 1998 were obliged to sign the so-called 'integration agreement' and to attend mandatory language classes. Because of various exemptions from the requirement, as well as the option to prove language proficiency in other ways, only a few migrants covered by the regulation actually attended these courses.

Finally, the 2002 reform also harmonized immigration legislation with employment regulations by introducing a 'residence certificate', which migrants can obtain after five years of residence and which provides unlimited access to employment. (The residence certificate was replaced by the Settlement Permit (EC) in the 2005 reform implementing the directive on third-country nationals who are long-term residents of a Member State).

From the late 1990s, Austria had become one of the main receiving countries of asylum seekers in Europe, because of her geographical position and her role as a Schengen-border country. In response, asylum policies increasingly focused on restricting access both to the territory and to asylum procedures. The centre-right government continued this line of policy-making. The 2003 reform severely cut back procedural guarantees,[6] although several of these provisions were subsequently annulled by the Constitutional Court (ECRE, 2005).

In mid-2005, immigration legislation was again completely revised, this time including residence regulations, asylum, and police enforcement measures (BGbl. 100/2006). To a large degree, the immigration reform was made necessary by EU legislation which had to be transposed, but a range of other provisions were also reformed. In particular, the conditions to fulfil under the 'integration agreement'[7] were enhanced and its scope extended to further categories of migrants which were formerly exempted.

Moreover, in a move to clamp down on 'fake marriages', the application for residence permits of spouses of an Austrian or EEA citizen have been made more difficult. At the same time, state

---

4   In April 2005, Jörg Haider relaunched the FPÖ under the name of 'League for the Future of Austria' (BZÖ), thus effectively splitting the party into two. Although all but two FPÖ MPs support the League, the splitter FPÖ has much more support among the electorate, evident in the 2005 provincial elections in Vienna.

5   The minimum wage requirement created considerable difficulties in the health sectors. As a consequence, the threshold for nurses and carers was lowered to €1,500 (König and Perchinig, 2005).

6   For example, limiting the rights of appeal by excluding new evidence during appeal procedures, or by excluding residence rights (protection from expulsion) for appeals against certain negative decisions (concerning inadmissible applications according to the Dublin regulations, or safe third country) or for subsequent applications.

7   Most importantly, the level of language proficiency a migrant has to meet was enhanced, as was the number of course hours an immigrant has to attend (300 instead of 100).

powers increasingly and systematically investigate suspected cases of marriages of convenience.[8] In conjunction with a transfer of responsibilities for issuing short-term residence permits to provincial authorities, this has created considerable hardship for many bi-national couples involving (former) asylum seekers.

In summary, the 2005 reform massively increases the powers of state organs to clamp down on migrants in an irregular situation (for example by extending the maximum duration of detention pending deportation from 6 to 12 months), while maintaining the restrictive position towards new immigration and elevating the integration requirements demanded of new migrants.

In contrast to immigration policy, citizenship policies had largely remained at the margins of political debates. A modest reform of nationality law in 1998 introduced 'integration' as a guiding principle in respect of naturalization, but upheld most other provisions of nationality legislation[9] (Waldrauch and Çinar, 2003).

However, in 2005 and closely tied to the reform of immigration legislation, a major reform of the Nationality Act took place which, for the first time, dealt with citizenship as an intrinsic element of the overall migration regime. Its main objectives were to:

- bring citizenship legislation in line with immigration legislation, notably by making eligibility for citizenship dependent on the possession of a long-term residence permit for the last five years before application;
- reduce the number of different waiting periods and increase the minimum time after which nationality can be obtained;
- tighten conditions for the acquisition of nationality, such as the sufficient financial means clause and the condition to show a clean criminal record;
- make acquisition dependent on a relatively high level of German language proficiency and the successful completion of a citizenship test, in which the applicants' knowledge of Austrian history, geography and political system will be tested.

As a result of the higher costs involved in assessing applications for nationality, fees for naturalization have been considerably increased as well.[10] Even more than the 1998 reform, the 2005 reform defined citizenship as a reward which only the most deserving foreigners should be granted (Valchars, 2006).

The immigrant population in Austria: main demographic and social features

Despite the restrictions on labour migration, immigration levels continue to be pronounced. In fact, net migration to Austria has risen sharply during the last five years in particular, as shown in Table 2.1.

---

8   The permits now have to be applied for from abroad, whereas previously they could be obtained in Austria irrespective of the former (irregular) status of the spouse. In a similar vein, civil registrars have now to report marriages involving a third-country national to the Aliens Police.

9   Notably the *ius sanguinis* principle in regard to the transmission of nationality to children, different waiting periods for different categories of migrants wishing to naturalize, absolute entitlement to naturalization after 30 years, and regular discretionary naturalization after 10 years.

10   See *Der Standard*, 'Staatsbürgerschaft: Gebührenerhöhung für Küberl, ungeheuerlich (03 March 2006). Federal fees have been increased from EUR 725 to EUR 900 for regular naturalizations. The fees for the extension of naturalization to spouses have been increased from EUR 174 to EUR 700, while for the co-naturalization of children EUR 200 (previously no fee) has to be paid. In addition, provincial authorities administering naturalizations usually demand additional provincial fees.

Table 2.1   Net migration* by citizenship category (1996–2004)

	Net migration Total	Net migration of Austrian Nationals	Net migration of Non-Nationals			
			Total	Former-Yugoslavia	Turkey	Others
1996	3,880	-4,306	8,186	-1,367	1,068	8,485
1997	1,537	-5,603	7,140	-2,010	1,777	7,373
1998	8,451	-5,913	14,364	2,719	1,959	9,686
1999	19,787	-5,313	25,100	6,650	3,499	14,951
2000	17,272	-4,315	21,587	2,798	3,394	15,395
2001	32,964	-12,408	45,372	9,223	7,769	28,380
2002	33,507	-20,283	53,790	9,597	7,876	36,317
2003	36,297	-14,802	51,099	9,391	7,091	34,617
2004	50,582	-10,039	60,621	n.a	n.a	n.a
1996–2004	204,277	-82,982	287,259	37,001**	34,433**	155,204**

*Net migration or migration balance is defined as the difference between the number of emigrants and the number of immigrants to a country.
**1996–2003.
Source: Statistics Austria; Figures for 2004: http://www.statistik.gv.at/fachbereich_03/Wanderungen.pdf.

Between 1991 and 2005, the foreign resident population increased from 517,690 (6.6 per cent of the total population) to 788,609 (9.6 per cent of the total population).[11] To some extent, the growth of the foreign resident population (in particular during the 1990s) is a consequence of the *jus sanguinis* principle, as a result of which children born to parents of foreign citizenship in Austria automatically obtain the nationality (or nationalities) of their parents. In 2001, 116,015 (or 16.3 per cent) of the overall foreign resident population were born in Austria.

At the time of the latest census (2001), the total foreign-born population stood at just over one million, or 12.5 per cent of the total population. Table 2.2 gives a breakdown of the population by country of birth and citizenship category. In conjunction with continuing high levels of immigration and naturalizations (some 195,000 foreigners were naturalized between 2001 and 2005),[12] the total foreign-born population can be estimated at about 1.2 million, or close to 15 per cent of the resident population in 2005.[13]

---

11   Statistics Austria, POPREG, <http://www.emn.at/module-Documents-view-cid-1-did-7.phtml>, accessed 24 March 2006.
12   For (2001–04): Statistics Austria, <http://www.emn.at/module-Documents-view-cid-1-did-43.phtml> accessed 24 March 2006; For 2005: Press Release Statistics Austria Nr. 8.523-32/06 'Wieder weniger Neo-Österreicher', 23 February 2006, <http://www.statistik.gv.at/cgi-bin/pressetext.pl?INDEX=2006008972>, accessed 24 March 2006.
13   Own estimate. The estimate is based on the difference between the total number of foreign-born and the foreign-born population with foreign citizenship at the time of the census, to which the estimated foreign-born population with a foreign citizenship on 01/01/05 and the number of naturalizations between

Table 2.2   Population by country of birth and citizenship category (2001)

Country of Birth \ Citizenship	Total	Austrian nationals	Foreign nationals
Total	**8,032,926**	**7,322,000**	**710,926**
Austria	7,029,527	6,913,512	116,015
Abroad – All Countries	**1,003,399**	**408,488**	**594,911**
BiH	134,402	18,342	116,060
Bulgaria	7,039	2,875	4,164
China	6,799	2,712	4,087
Croatia	38,808	14,449	2,439
Czech Republic	54,627	46,100	8,527
Egypt	9,168	4,818	4,350
France	5,903	2,325	3,578
FYROM	13,948	2,154	11,794
Germany	140,099	79,397	60,702
Greece	3,060	1,501	1,559
Hungary	30,953	18,203	12,750
India	8,163	3,680	4,483
Iran	11,459	5,348	6,111
Iraq	3,101	1,601	1,500
Italy	28,099	17,638	8,461
Netherlands	5,248	1,921	3,327
Nigeria	2,913	799	2,114
Philippines	8,881	5,673	3,208
Poland	41,671	20,531	21,140
Russian Federation	6,644	2,643	4,001
Serbia and Montenegro	143,077	35,422	107,655
Slovakia	15,981	8,417	7,564
Slovenia	21,021	14,694	6,327
Sweden	3,214	995	2,219
Switzerland	11,713	7,124	4,589
Turkey	125,026	31,898	93,128
U.S.A.	7,371	2,464	4,907
Ukraine	3,272	1,439	1,833
United Kingdom	6,786	2,382	4,404

Source: Statistik Austria (2002): Volkszählung 2001. Hauptergebnisse I – Österreich. Vienna: Statistics Austria, available at http://www.statistik.gv.at/gz/publikationen.shtml.

In 2005, 74 per cent of the foreign resident population came from outside the EU25 and 80 per cent from outside the EU-15. While the share of the successor countries of the former Yugoslavia

2001 and 2004 were added. To estimate the foreign-born population with foreign citizenship, the ratio between foreign- and Austrian-born foreigners at the time of the census was used.

and Turkey has decreased considerably since the 2001 census, a majority of foreign nationals still originate from traditional countries of labour recruitment. With regard to the latter, the majority are from Serbia-Montenegro (17.5 per cent of the total foreign population), Turkey (14.8 per cent) and Bosnia Herzegovina (11.5 per cent). Owing to relatively high (and increasing) numbers of German nationals, EU15 nationals have become a relatively large share of the foreign resident population (19.6 per cent).

Nationals from new EU Member States account for 6.8 per cent, of which Slovaks, Hungarians and Poles make up the overwhelming majority. Most of these immigrants can be assumed to stem from the post-1989 wave of immigration. This can mainly be deduced from the fact that most of the earlier refugees from Czechoslovakia, Hungary and Poland have since been naturalized. In addition, there is a growing immigrant population from 'non-traditional' countries such as Iran, India, the Philippines and Egypt, thereby reflecting the diversification of the countries of origin of immigrants.

The gender composition of the immigrant population still reflects the history of an initially male dominated labour migration shaped by the 'guest worker model' However, the gender imbalance has significantly decreased over the past 10–20 years, especially with regard to the more settled immigrant communities. By contrast, a stark gender imbalance still characterizes some more recent immigrant communities with very specific immigration histories, notably Egyptians and Nigerians – where males dominate – and Filipinos, of whom the majority are females. Similarly, the immigrant population is significantly younger than the non-migrant population. The differences become most pronounced when the age structure of the foreign nationals is compared to that of Austrian nationals. Thus, 43 per cent of the foreign population is below 30 years of age, whereas the corresponding figure for Austrians is 33 per cent. By contrast, only 8 per cent of the foreign population belongs to the age group 60 and above, as compared to almost 22 per cent of Austrian nationals.[14]

As a legacy of selective labour recruitment and the placement of first generation immigrants in unskilled or low-skilled jobs, the majority of immigrants remain employed in low-paid, blue-collar jobs with a high risk of unemployment. The persistent ethnic segmentation of the labour market and the relatively low levels of socio-professional mobility, however, also reflect the prevailing restrictive legal conditions for foreigners during much of the 1990s. Equally important, foreign workers were (and continue to be) employed mainly in small and medium-sized enterprises with inherently limited career possibilities. By contrast, larger enterprises were almost entirely controlled by the state, and, reflecting the strength of trade unions, consciously did not employ foreign workers (Demel et al., 2001). In 2000, more than three-quarters of non-nationals worked in blue-collar jobs (Raxen Focal Point for Austria 2003: 16). The share of non-nationals is particularly pronounced in agriculture (34.6 per cent in 2005), the food industry (17.7 per cent), textiles and clothing (23.4 per cent), construction (19.7 per cent) and restaurants and bars (31.7 per cent) (Biffl, 2005, p. 26). The unemployment rate is, on average, one to two per cent higher than that of nationals. Reflecting the inferior position of non-nationals in the labour market, average monthly income of non-nationals was EUR 343 below that of nationals in 2000 (the average monthly income of foreigners stood at €1,637) with income differentials being highest between Austrian and foreign males (€503 or 22 per cent less) (Raxen Focal Point for Austria 2003: 17, 50). The generally low social position of immigrants is also reflected by the fact that more than 25 per cent of immigrants are at risk of falling into poverty (BMSGK, 2004, p. 21). Stark inequalities between migrants and natives also characterize the educational system. For example, while 93 per cent of 17-year-old Austrians

---

14   Source: see footnote 1.

attend secondary school, only 60 per cent of Turkish and former Yugoslavian students do (see NCP, 2004, p. 48f).

Immigrant rights and participation in public life – issues of immigrant integration

For various reasons such as the restrictive regime governing the acquisition of citizenship, the fact that migrants who entered Austria between the late 1980s and the early 1990s have become eligible for citizenship only fairly recently, and policies of states of origin in regard to renunciation of citizenship, the share of Austrian citizens with a migrant background has increased significantly only since the 1990s. Thus, the political opportunity structure for the majority of immigrants is still largely shaped by the specific discriminatory legal framework for foreigners. Overall, political opportunity structures in Austria have to be regarded as rather closed and it is only fairly recently that Austria has offered a pathway to legal integration for long-term immigrants. The barriers to full civic, social and political participation, however, remain high. With the transposition of the Directive on Long-Term Residents (2003/109/EC) in the most recent immigration reform, long-term immigrants enjoy the same range of social and civic rights as nationals and EU citizens. As a result, however, the fault line is now between those immigrants who have access to 'denizenship' and those who do not.

In the Austrian context, the civic and political participation of (non-EU) immigrants has been limited in particular with regard to two dimensions:

- voting rights
- interest representation in the employment sphere and workplace democracy.

With the exception of EU citizens who vote at the local level, voting rights have remained exclusively tied to Austrian nationality. In December 2002, the Vienna City Council introduced the local vote for district council elections for long-term third-country nationals with a minimum residence of five years (Waldrauch, 2003). However, the electoral law was successfully challenged before the constitutional court. As a result, the majority of immigrants remain excluded from political participation and representation at the local level.

Until recently, immigrants' rights to representation in the employment sphere (both representation in works councils at the shop floor level and in the statutory representative bodies at national and provincial level, as well as in the Chamber of Labour and the Chamber of Commerce) were restricted. Although allowed to vote, non-nationals were barred from standing for office. The denial of the right to stand for office in interest representation was unique in Europe, as representation in works councils was elsewhere considered as an employment, rather than a political, right (Pühretmayer, 1999; Gächter, 2000). Only after a judgement by the European Court of Justice in September 2004[15] were the relevant provisions finally amended in December 2005.

The denial of the right to stand for election has arguably had a tremendous effect on the patterns of immigrants' political socialization. While works councils are formally independent from trade unions, holding office as a shop steward has traditionally been a major entry gate into the trade union hierarchy. In addition, both trade union activists and delegates of the statutory chambers have been a traditional source of recruitment for political parties. Surveys, on the other hand, have shown that migrants are keen for political representation, particularly in the workplace. Also, migrants declare comparably high trust in these institutions (Jenny, 2003).

---

15   European Court of Justice, 'Judgement in Case C-465/01 of 16 September 2004'.

A recent study on immigrant politicians (Grasl, 2003) shows that participation in migrants' community organizations was also important in promoting political participation and integration in political parties, predominantly in left-wing political parties. At the same time, political parties are increasingly becoming aware of naturalized immigrants as potential voters (most evident in the 2001 and 2005 elections for the Vienna City Council). Virtually all parties (including the FPÖ) are now recruiting candidates of immigrant background. Nevertheless, they are rarely placed in favourable positions on candidate lists and thus have only very limited chances of obtaining a mandate.

However, there are also other important venues for immigrant participation, notably through associations. As several recent studies have shown, the number and activity spectrum of migrant associations have greatly increased. And they became increasingly important with regard to the mobilization and collective representation of immigrants' interests during the 1990s (Bratić, 2003; Kroissenbrunner, 2003; Waldrauch and Sohler, 2004). While associations continue to be primarily orientated towards sports, cultural, and religious activities, certain segments became more professionalised and orientated towards integration services during the 1990s. Partly as a result, they have also become more politicised in terms of demanding immigrant rights and confronting racism and xenophobia (Waldrauch and Sohler, 2004). These developments are the result of various factors, including the political and legal context during the 1990s and the increasing importance of the second generation as activists in associations (Bauböck and Perchinig, 2006). To some degree, however, they are also the result of the emergence of integration policies on a municipal level, as part of which several municipalities have funded immigrant associations, have promoted umbrella organizations or have established advisory bodies. Perhaps the most important example is Vienna. A special body – the Viennese Integration Fund[16] – has not only provided funding for immigrant associations but has also provided new channels of participation, notably in the form of the 'integration conference'. This is an umbrella organization for immigrant organizations whose purpose is to provide a networking and service structure for immigrant associations and advocacy groups dealing with immigrant issues, as well as being a structure that could serve as an arena for voicing immigrant concerns. Similar participatory bodies also exist in other municipalities.

On the national level, the elaborate legal framework concerning the recognition of faith communities has clearly had a positive impact on the integration of religious minorities. In particular, the institutionalization of Islam in Austria (Islam is represented by the Islamic Faith Community in Austria) has helped to forge an amenable relationship between the Muslim community and the state, and between the Muslim Community and other faith communities. This has greatly assisted in responding swiftly to public debates and specific problems.

A separate legal framework exists for autochthonous ethnic minorities (the so-called 'Volksgruppen'). It gives the six recognised autochthonous minorities[17] a series of specific cultural and representative rights such as bilingual education, provided the proportion of ethnic minority members in a given education district exceeds certain thresholds, representation of ethnic associations in the national minority advisory council, state support for linguistic and cultural activities and so on. In contrast to the territorially defined recognized ethnic minorities, the new minorities resulting from immigration do not have any entitlements to cultural or other minority rights, although there is a certain overlap between immigrant and autochthonous ethnic communities (notably among Czechs, Slovaks and Hungarians).

---

16   In 2004, the Integration Fund was incorporated into the city administration, following an official shift in integration policies from a minority to a diversity management approach.

17   These are Carinthian and Styrian Slovenes, the Croatian minority in Burgenland, the Hungarian minority in Vienna and Burgenland, the Czech and Slovak minorities in Vienna, and Roma and Sinti (all Austrian provinces).

Public and media discourses on migration

In stark contrast with the 1970s and 1980s, when immigration hardly featured in public debates, immigration has become a high profile issue since the 1990s. In general, public discourse on migration is characterized by anti-immigrant attitudes and outright xenophobia, and highlights the negative implications of migration.

A major shift in public discourse occurred after the fall of the Iron Curtain, with Romanian asylum applicants being at the centre of public debate. In contrast to the traditional sympathetic portrayal of refugees from Eastern Europe as genuine victims of communist rule, public discourse on Romanians emphasised their 'otherness' – their poverty, ill health, the general backwardness of the country and the endemic violence characterizing Romania (see Matouschek, Wodak and Januschek, 1995, p. 59). In a second phase, Romanians were increasingly seen as economic migrants rather than as refugees, and were associated with all sorts of petty crime, not least since many of them entered the country illegally after the imposition of a visa requirement. Public discourses on Romanians and, subsequently, on asylum seekers in general were significant in that they increasingly shifted the terms of the overall debate on migration to security issues ('illegal migration', 'bogus asylum seekers', trafficking and smuggling of migrants, organised crime, and so on) and in that they reframed migration policy as a matter of policing. The shift of responsibility within the government from the Ministry of Social Affairs to the Ministry of Interior as lead agency for immigration policy in the late 1980s may have helped to reinforce the changes in perception of, and in policies towards, immigrants (Sohler, 2000).

Mobilization against immigration by the FPÖ, reached its height in 1992/93, when the FPÖ organised a petition under the slogan 'Austria first', calling for a restriction of immigration and tighter border and internal controls. In response, a wide range of NGOs, public figures, church organizations and others organised a mass demonstration for tolerance and against xenophobia, the so-called 'Sea of Candles' (Lichtermeer), in which some 300,000 people participated, making it the largest demonstration of the post-war period.

Two key events in 1999 were particularly significant for a revival of massive political mobilization against racism and xenophobia. In early May 1999, Marcus Omofuma, a Nigerian failed asylum seeker died from suffocation as a result of gagging while being deported from Vienna to Sofia. The incident provoked massive outrage over inhuman deportation practices as well as police practices towards Africans in general, which were denounced as 'institutional racism' by various activists. Numerous demonstrations were held in response to the tragic death of Omofuma calling for political consequences.[18] A month later, a large police raid was carried out against an alleged Nigerian 'drug cartel' ('Operation Spring'), which led to the arrest of over 100 persons, including a renowned Nigerian writer, activist and long-term resident of Austria. The timing of the raid was closely related to anti-racist campaigning and, from the perspective of the police, anti-racist campaigning by Africans was perceived as 'undermining police and the rule of law' (see Kravagna, 2004, p. 70). The raid not only delegitimized and criminalized the entire African community, but also effectively aimed at undermining anti-racist mobilization, with the support of Austria's largest tabloid, Die Krone. In addition, both the Omofuma incident and the alleged large-scale involvement of African asylum seekers in drug trafficking were one of the main campaigning issues during the election campaign preceding the October 1999 general elections.

---

18   The most important consequence was the establishment of a human rights commission (Menschenrechtsbeirat) charged with monitoring detention and expulsion practices (see Waldrauch and Sohler, 2004, p. 379); <http://menschenrechtsbeirat.at>, accessed 28 March 2006.

The EU's eastern enlargement has led to an intense, albeit short-lived, public debate on the levels of immigration to be expected from the new Member States and about 'restricting' access to the labour market. Consequently, Austria was – along with Germany – one of the main proponents of long transition periods, only after which would unrestricted access to national labour markets be granted. Fears of mass migration are (along with religion) also the main issues discussed in relation to Turkey's candidate status for accession to the EU, which is rejected by the overwhelming majority of the population and most political parties. Interestingly, the most recent public controversy on the negative effects of labour migration in the context of massive structural unemployment was triggered by rising numbers of (seasonal) migrants from Germany (notably Eastern Germany) which, ironically, was initiated by a joint programme of Austrian and German labour market authorities (König and Perchinig, 2005).

During the 1990s, 'integration' had become an increasingly important issue in public discourse. However, so far, the debate is almost exclusively concerned with perceived integration deficiencies of immigrants and has a strong assimilationist undertone. In general, it rests on the assumption that migrants are reluctant to integrate and, therefore, have to be coaxed to do so, by force if necessary (König and Perchinig, 2005).

The country's Muslim community has only recently become an issue in debates on integration, with a focus on alleged integration deficits as well as gender inequalities and gender roles within the Muslim community. In contrast to other European countries, however, issues such as the wearing of headscarves, the alleged development of 'parallel societies', or radical Islam, have remained marginal in public discourse and on the whole rather non-controversial (König and Perchinig, 2005). However, in the run-up to the 2006 general elections, the alleged unwillingness of Muslims to integrate has become a major issue of public debates, fuelled both by the far right and the ÖVP Minister of the Interior.

The low score achieved by Austria in the 2003 Pisa-Study[19] (it moved down several ranks in comparison with the previous study) has led to a sharp controversy over the negative impact of immigrant children and the performance of the education system in general. Rather than addressing possible root causes (notably the stratified nature of the education system, which reproduces and exacerbates social inequality, the little support for children for whom German is a second language), the immediate reaction of government politicians was to call for mandatory supplemental language courses for immigrant children along the lines of the integration agreement. Moreover, it was perceived that immigrant children burden the education system.[20]

Clearly, the focus of the wider public debates on migration is rather limited. In most debates, the focus of the debate is centred on the negative aspects allegedly associated with migration. These range from crime to, abuse of benefits by 'undeserving foreigners', high unemployment, residential and other localised conflicts and, increasingly, the threat to social cohesion and cultural homogeneity supposedly posed by migrants.

Concluding remarks

Despite evidence to the contrary, the official line continues to be that Austria is not a country of immigration. In a similar vein, the increasing diversity of Austrian society as a result of migration is

---

19   The PISA programme (Programme for International Student Assessment), conducted every three years, is a standardized survey-cum-assessment programme. See www.pisa.oecd.org, accessed 19 July 2006.

20   See for example *Der Standard*, Langjähriges ideologisches Zerwürfnis' – Migrationsforscherin im Interview, 1 December 2004.

rarely acknowledged, let alone welcomed, in public. On the contrary, the integration and citizenship tests introduced in 2002 and 2005 also send a clear symbolic assimilationist message both to immigrants and the wider public. While the government has repeatedly expressed its commitment to integration, integration is largely understood as an obligation of migrants (especially of those defined as 'culturally different'), rather than as a process engaging Austrian society as a whole.

However, with a foreign-born population of about 15 per cent and high levels of new immigration, Austria has turned into one of the major countries of immigration in Europe. Yet, the visibility of immigrants in the public realm remains low and migrants continue to be represented as a social group which is marginal to Austrian society at large. Arguably, however, the public representation and perception of immigrants is gradually changing as a result of several sociological, economic and political developments. Among them are an increasing proportion of naturalized citizens, the emergence of a broad spectrum of migrant associations, including interest organizations defending the rights of immigrants, and the increasing importance of immigrant-led businesses and so on. As a result of these developments, immigrants are increasingly being recognized as voters, clients, and consumers.

Austria's accession to the EU in 1995 and, more recently, the accession of the 10 new Member States in May 2004, has meant that an increasing number of migrants are – by and large – no longer subject to the strict migration controls in place to control the movement and residence of third-country nationals. In addition, mostly because of family ties to Austrian citizens, the overwhelming majority of third-country nationals entering Austria as new immigrants are not subject to the annual quota of around 8,000 – a measure which has thus largely lost its relevance as an instrument of migration control. As a result of these developments, immigration policy has increasingly lost its capacity to influence, let alone determine, levels of migration. However, as recent reforms in Austria show it is enormously effective in creating barriers which deprive immigrants of equal rights.

References

Bauböck, R. and Perchinig, B. (2006), 'Migrations- und Integrationspolitik' in Dachs, H. et al. (eds) *Politik in Österreich: Das Handbuch*. Vienna: Manz.

Bratić, L. (2003), 'Sozio-politische Netzwerke der Migrantinnen aus der ehemaligen Sozialistischen Föderativen Republik Jugoslawien (SFRJ) in Österreich', in Fassmann, H. and Stacher, I. (eds) *Österreichischer Migrations- und Integrationsbericht*, 395–411. Klagenfurt/Celovec: Drava Verlag.

Gächter, A. (2000), 'Austria: Protecting Indigenous Workers from Immigrants', in Penninx, R. and Roosblad, J. (eds) *Trade Unions, Immigration and Immigrants in Europe (1960–93): A Comparative Study of the Attitudes and Actions of Trade Unions in Seven West European Countries*, 65–89. New York and Oxford: Berghahn Books.

Grasl, A. (2003), 'Sichtbar werden', in *Wiener Hefte zu Migration und Integration in Theorie und Praxis*, 1/2003, Special Issue Defizitäre Demokratie – MigrantInnen in der Politik, 141–51.

Jawhari, R. (2000), *Wegen Überfremdung abgelehnt*. Vienna: Braumüller.

Jenny, M. (2003), 'Politikinteresse und Bereitschaft zur politischen Partizipation bei Migrantinnen in Wien', in *Wiener Hefte zu Migration und Integration in Theorie und Praxis*, 1/2003, Special Issue Defizitäre Demokratie – MigrantInnen in der Politik, 127–40.

König, K. and Perchinig, B. (2005), 'Austria' in Niessen, J., Schibel, Y. and Thompson, C. (eds) *Current Immigration Debates in Europe: A Publication of the European Migration Dialogue*,

Brussels: Migration Policy Group (available at http://www.migpolgroup.com/infopages/3000. html).

Kraler, A. and Stacher, I. (2002), 'Austria: Migration and Asylum Patterns in the 19th and the 20th century', in *Historische Sozialkunde. Geschichte – Fachdidaktik – Politische Bildung*, Special Issue 2002 – International Migration, 50–65.

Kravagna, S. (2004), 'Making Crime: Die staatliche Konstruktion der nigerianischen Drogenmafia in Österreich', *Stichproben Wiener Zeitschrift für Kritische Afrikastudien*, 6(2004), 61–88.

Kroissenbrunner, S. (2003), 'Islam, Migration und Integration: sozio-politische Netzwerke und Muslim-Leadership', in Fassmann, H. and Stacher, I. (eds) *Österreichischer Migrations- und Integrationsbericht*, 375–94. Klagenfurt/Celovec: Drava Verlag.

Matouschek, B., Wodak, R. and Januschek, F. (1995), *Notwendige Maßnahmen Gegen Fremde? Genese und Formen von rassistischen Diskursen der Differenz*. Vienna: Passagen Verlag.

Pühretmayer, H. (1999), *Das Passive Wahlrecht für Migranten und Migrantinnen zum Betriebsrat in der Bundesrepublik Deutschland und in Österreich. Ein Vergleich*. Wien: Projekt-Endbericht.

Sohler, K. (2000), 'Vom "Illegalen" zum "inneren Feind"', *Kurswechsel*, 1(2000), 53–64.

Valchars, G. (2006), *Defizitäre Demokratie: Staatsbürgerschaft und Wahlrecht im Einwanderungsland Österreich*. Vienna: Braumüller.

Waldrauch, H. and Çinar, D. (2003), 'Staatsbürgerschaftspolitik und Einbürgerungspraxis in Österreich', in Fassmann, H. and Stacher, I. (eds) *Österreichischer Migrations- und Integrationsbericht*, 261–83. Klagenfurt/Celovec: Drava Verlag.

Waldrauch, H. and Sohler, K. (2004), 'Migrantenorganisationen in der Großstadt', in *Entstehung, Strukturen und Aktivitäten am Beispiel Wien*. Frankfurt/Main: Campus Verlag.

Internet-based references

Biffl, G. (2005), *Zur Niederlassung von Ausländerinnen und Ausländern in Österreich*, Vienna: WIFI (available at http://www.bmi.gv.at/downloadarea/asyl_fremdenwesen/NLV_2006endg_0509.pdf).

BMSGK, [Bundesministerium für Soziale Sicherheit, Generationen und Konsumentenschutz] (2004), *Bericht über die Soziale Lage 2003-2004*, Vienna: BMSGK (available at http://www.bmsg.gv.at/cms/site/attachments/9/2/3/CH0338/CMS1064227005975/beriht_ueber_die_soziale_lage_2003_-_2004.pdf).

Demel, K. et al. (2001), 'Die soziale Mobilität der AusländerInnen' in Ein, B. (ed.) *Zur Arbeitsmarkt – und Sozialstrukturanalyse der Großstadt*, Vienna: Universität Wien (available at http://www.oefm.org/documents/KFMob.pdf).

ECRE [European Council on Refugees and Exiles] (2005), *Country Report (2004) – Austria*, London: ECRE (available at http://www.ecre.org/country04/Austria%20FINAL.pdf).

Raxen Focal Point for Austria (2003), *Migrants, Minorities and Employment in Austria*, Vienna: Raxen Focal Point for Austria (available at http://eumc.eu.int/eumc/material/pub/RAXEN/3/emp/AT.pdf).

Waldrauch, H. (2003), *Immigration and Integration of Foreign Nationals: Flows, Stocks and Policies in Austria. Fieri Country Profile*, Turin: Fieri (available at http://194.116.10.213/fieri/ktml2/files/uploads/servizi/schede%20paese/austria%20engl.pdf).

Chapter 3

Belgium

Hassan Bousetta, Sonia Gsir and Dirk Jacobs

Belgium has a peculiar form of federalism. The federal state has both territorial and group-based federated entities, respectively known as 'regions' and 'communities'. As a result, public policy making is often a matter of multi-levelled governance (Favell and Martiniello, 1998). Migrant policy is no exception. It is fragmented across the various levels of the federal state (national level, community level and regional level) and, therefore, in the Belgian context it is advisable to speak about 'migrant policies' in the plural rather than 'migrant policy' in the singular. The migrant integration policy, however, has become a policy competence of the 'subnational' federated entities. As a result, a wide variety of – sometimes even contradictory – migrant-related policies and practices have come to coexist in Belgium. Equally, there has been an influence of Europeanization. The process of European integration has substantially marked the Belgian approach towards immigrants, increasingly distinguishing EU-citizens from third-country nationals (Martiniello and Rea, 2003, pp. 1–2). It should be noted, however, that immigrant admission policy has always remained an exclusively national prerogative.

Before looking into some of these migrant policies, let us first briefly discuss the recent history of Belgian migration patterns. After the Second World War, Belgium concluded bilateral agreements with Mediterranean countries in order to revitalize the exploitation of its coal mines and to rebuild the country. Italians were the first to be recruited to work in the mines through the Protocol signed between Belgium and Italy in June 1946 (Martens, 1976, pp. 67–70). In 1956, however, two major, fatal mining accidents prompted Italy to demand better conditions for its workers. Given the reluctance to accommodate the safety-related demands of the Italian Government and the competition with neighbouring countries for foreign labourers, Belgium was forced to further expand its area of recruitment. Unlike other former colonial states, however, Belgium never opted to recruit labourers from its colony, the Congo, or from protectorates Rwanda and Burundi. It had enough trouble trying to guarantee sufficient labour for colonial exploitation in Central Africa itself and, thus, did not consider Central African immigration a sensible option. As a result, from 1956 onwards, other groups of guest workers were being attracted from countries like Spain, Greece, Morocco, Turkey, Algeria, Tunisia and Yugoslavia. The largest group of new immigrant low-skilled labourers to settle in the 1960s undoubtedly came from Morocco. A large majority of them settled in the major cities and especially in Brussels. Large-scale recruitment of foreign labourers, combined with the arrival of their families and the relatively high birth rate of immigrants on Belgian soil, soon led to a substantial increase in the proportion of foreigners. In the 1960s and early 1970s, a considerable number of the new immigrants were non-active dependants of guest workers. Immigration of dependants through family reunion had been actively stimulated in the 1960s, resulting from the wish of Walloon politicians to use immigration for demographic purposes (Sauvy, 1962; Martens, 1973, pp. 235–236). Family reunification was equally seen to be an asset in the competition with neighbouring countries to attract foreign labourers (Martens, 1973, p. 107).

Owing to economic recession, in 1974 the Belgian Government decided to stop all new immigration and active recruitment of non-EC guest workers. Nevertheless, for certain categories of specialized workers (for instance Polish mechanics) occasional exceptions were still granted. Parallel to these new restrictions, the government regularized undocumented migrants, mostly Moroccans and Turks. Moreover, family reunion of non-EC-immigrants was still allowed, partly because of the demographic deficit in Wallonia. At the same time, ongoing EC-immigration, especially from neighbouring countries, gained momentum.

As far as non-EU-citizens are concerned, at the end of the 1980s, a 'new' category of immigrants came to the fore, consisting of asylum seekers mainly originating from Eastern Europe, Africa and Asia. The arrival of asylum seekers in Belgium was by no means a new phenomenon, but clearly one which gained importance in the overall migration flows at the end of the 1980s and throughout the 1990s. The new patterns of migration and the growing variety of nationalities triggered quite some political debate. In public discourse, distinctions between clandestine undocumented migrants, refugees, asylum seekers and other newcomers were blurred. Parallel to this development, there was an overall trend of criminalizing migrants (Brion et al., 2001).

Major developments in Belgium's immigration policy

Belgium has recently adjusted its admission policy within the framework of the Schengen co-operation and as a result of the process of European integration. It also modified its legislation in response to a number of domestic developments with regard to migration. In this context we can mention peaks in asylum seeker application numbers (in 1993, 1999 and 2000), problems linked to the detention and expulsion of foreigners, mobilization of undocumented migrants, the use of Belgium as a transit country to the UK, xenophobic sentiments within public opinion and pro-immigrant countermobilization.

Since becoming a signatory party of the Schengen Agreements, Belgium has modified its legislation accordingly. The internal border control was suppressed and a zone of free movement (for EU-citizens) was created. Because of Belgium's geographical position and of socioeconomic factors, the number of EU-citizens – especially Dutch and French – has been rising constantly over the last 15 years.

Visa policy has been progressively aligned to European practices. As far as long-term visas are concerned, two particular categories of migrants are of special interest. Firstly, foreign students are granted temporary residence permits each year. Such permits are restricted to higher education purposes only. Belgium receives quite a significant number of foreign students (around 10 per cent of the student population). More than half of the foreign students come from EU countries, while the rest originate largely from Africa. Secondly, family reunification remains an important admission channel. It is regulated by the Aliens Law of 15 December 1980 (law regulating access to the territory, the sojourn, the settlement and removal of foreigners) and by the bilateral agreements concluded after 1945. According to Belgian law, certain family members (namely spouse and children) of a non-EU citizen with a residence permit longer than 3 months are eligible for family reunification. The spouse must be at least 18 years old, whereas the children must be under 18. There are also provisions to avoid chain migration. The family member joining a foreigner in Belgium is granted a one year residence permit and only later might an unlimited residence permit be granted (Gsir, Martiniello and Wets, 2003, p. 65). Recent legislative modifications suggest a trend to attempt to limit family reunification. Thus, in 2006, the government decided to penalize sham marriages or even the attempt to conclude such marriages (Gsir et al., 2005, p. 45).

Regarding admission for work purposes, even if the suggestion of allowing quotas of immigrants was at one point raised by the Ministry of Home Affairs in 2003, quotas have never officially been introduced in the post-1974 period (Gsir et al., 2005, p. 43). Figures are, however, interestingly stable. Around 100,000 labour permits were issued between 1974 and 1984, with about one-third of them being issued to newcomers. From 1985 to 1993, once again some 100,000 labour permits were issued (with around 27,000 to newcomers). All this was done within the framework of a longstanding legislation. The original 1936 law on foreign workers regulation was replaced by a new law in 1999, amended in 2003 (Ouali, 2004, p. 29). Some provisions were taken to facilitate the employment of specific categories of foreigners. On the one hand, highly skilled workers were allowed more flexibility in renewing their labour permit for another four years and even longer. On the other hand, under certain conditions, the category of foreigners who do not need labour permits was enlarged. It now includes foreigners with unlimited residence permits, sportspersons, providers of services and postdoctoral researchers. Furthermore, supplementary to the existing labour permits (Permit A: unlimited in time and jobs and Permit B: limited in time – up to one year – and restricted to one job), the new legislation created Permit C (limited to one year but valid for several jobs). This new permit targeted asylum seekers, foreign students, victims of smuggling and regularized foreigners in particular.

Since the end of the 1980s, Belgium has modified its asylum system several times in order to make the procedure simpler, more rapid, and more efficient from an administrative point of view. Reducing the number of asylum applications is undoubtedly the main objective of the asylum policy. A constant decrease in the rate of acknowledgement of refugee status (now about 10 per cent) can be observed over the last 15 years. The peak inflows of asylum seekers in 1993 and 2000 led Belgium to open several 'reception centres' in order to be able to respond. As a signatory of the Dublin Convention, Belgium applies the principle of only considering case files which have not been considered in other countries. In 2001, there was a major change in the asylum system. Since that time, instead of financial help, asylum seekers have only been provided with help in kind and must remain in 'reception centres' to receive it. The government also decided to apply the LIFO principle (Last In, First Out) to give priority to the handling of the more recent asylum applications and, if they do not meet the criteria, to repatriate them swiftly.

Furthermore, the Belgian Government has taken various measures to limit irregular migration such as immigration law enforcement, carriers' sanctions or penal measures towards citizens, smugglers or traffickers. Detention of irregular migrants developed in the 1990s as an instrument to facilitate the removal of undocumented migrants from the territory. This harsh policy is also meant to deter new potential migrants. In 1995, a law regulated the creation of detention centres for rejected asylum seekers and irregular migrants. In a nutshell, most recent developments in asylum regulations attest to tougher policy schemes and are meant to have a deterrent effect.

The end of the 1990s was marked by several migration related events, such as the death of a young Nigerian migrant during the attempt to expel her and, consequently, the mobilization of undocumented migrants (Ouali, 2004). A coalition change led to a number of new compensatory decisions in this area. An important one was the regularization campaign, agreed upon in December 1999 and launched in January 2000. Four criteria were taken into account: having a pending asylum petition for an abnormally long time (at least four years for individuals and three for families); suffering serious illness; impossibility of returning to the country of origin, and strong and sustainable ties in Belgium (at least 6 years in Belgium without receiving an order to leave the territory). All the undocumented migrants present in Belgium before 1 October 1999 could qualify for regularization providing that they fulfilled one of the four criteria. Around 60,000 migrants took part in the regularization campaign and at least 42,000 of them (from 2000 onwards) received legal status. While in total 140 nationalities were represented, applicants mainly originated from the former Belgian colonies (especially the Congo), North Africa and Turkey. There is still campaign pressure for a new mass regularization, but public authorities routinely stress the 2000 regularization campaign had an exceptional character.

The immigrant population in Belgium: main demographic and social features

In January 2005, Belgium had 10,445,852 inhabitants, of whom 870,862 were foreigners (residents not holding Belgian citizenship). This amounts to approximately nine per cent of the whole population, spread in different proportions over the three Belgian regions (Table 3.1). In proportional terms, of the three regions, Brussels-capital is host to the largest number of foreign residents (close to 30 per cent). In 1999, European and non-European citizens accounted for more or less similar shares (15 per cent of the population), but the high rate of naturalization among non-Europeans and EU enlargement mean that the balance now stands at 16 and 10 per cent respectively.

Table 3.1   Foreign population in Belgium on 1 January (1999–2005) by region

	1999	2000	2001	2002	2003	2004	2005
Belgium (total country)	891,980	897,110	861,685	846,734	850,077	860,287	870,862
Brussels	272,146	273,613	262,771	260,040	260,269	263,451	265,511
Flanders	289,065	293,650	280,962	275,223	280,743	288,375	297,289
Wallonia	330,769	329,847	317,952	311,471	309,065	308,461	308,362

Source: Institut National de la Statistique (INS).

Among the foreign population, 12 nationalities are dominant. Table 3.2 shows clearly that the largest foreign groups are EU nationals from Italy (because of the aforementioned earlier labour recruitment from Italy) and from neighbouring countries.

In terms of geographical distribution, the various foreign groups are differently located in the three regions. For example, Italians and French are mainly located in Wallonia, whereas the Turkish group is mostly located in Flanders. Remarkably, 50 per cent of the non-EU citizens residing in Brussels are Moroccans.

The figures on the foreign population are, however, misleading if taken at face value. It is not known how many children of foreign residents acquired Belgian nationality with the 1985 introduction of *jus soli*, the acquisition of nationality on the basis of the place of birth, its extension in 1991 and consequent changes in nationality legislation. We can only make educated guesses. Let us consider the example of Brussels. In the 1991 Census, 53,983 Belgians did not have Belgian nationality at the time of birth and, hence, made use of the naturalization procedure. As a result, at least 34.1 per cent of Brussels' inhabitants were of foreign origin in 1991. Owing to the evolution of the nationality legislation and demographic developments, in 2005 probably around 10 per cent of Brussels' population were Belgians of foreign descent who acquired citizenship through *jus soli*, naturalization, or the other systems for acquiring Belgian nationality. One can thus estimate that today approximately 40 per cent of Brussels' inhabitants are of immigrant origin.

Table 3.2   Immigrants according to country of origin in January 2002 (top 12 countries)

Country	Number (1/01/2002)
Italy	190,792
France	111,146
Netherlands	92,561
Morocco	90,657
Turkey	47,044
Spain	44,962
Germany	34,667
United-Kingdom	26,365
Portugal	25,755
Greece	17,579
Congo (RDC)	13,670
United-States	11,814

Source: N. Perrin, Gédap-UCL, http://www.dofi.fgov.be/fr/statistieken/belgian%20migration/cijfergegevens.htm.

As was stressed earlier, many recent newcomers have entered Belgium hoping to acquire refugee status. On the eve of the 1990s, the annual number of new asylum seekers stood at 12,945 and it kept growing until 1993, when it reached its peak of 26,717. Following this, the number of asylum seekers amounted to approximately 11,500/year and increased again until 2000 to reach the maximum number recorded in Belgium up till now, a total of 42,691. The various wars in the Balkans can explain these figures. From 2001 onwards, the number has been constantly decreasing, undoubtedly because of harsher policy. Although asylum seekers came from over 100 different countries, the majority originated from the following countries: former Yugoslavia, former USSR, Romania, the Congo, Pakistan, Nigeria, Bulgaria, Turkey and Ghana. Over the years, the number of asylum seekers from Eastern European countries has also become increasingly important. In 1996, 54.8 per cent of asylum seekers originated from Europe, 28 per cent from Africa, and 11 per cent originated from Asia. The same distribution per continent can also be observed for subsequent years. Nonetheless, the nationalities vary slightly. Thus, in 2004, 47 per cent of asylum seekers originated from Europe (Russia including Chechnya, Serbia and Montenegro including Kosovo, and Slovakia), 34 per cent originated from Africa (mainly the Republic of the Congo, Angola and Cameroon) and 19 per cent originated from Asia (mainly Iran and Armenia).

The only figures at hand are those – in accordance with the 1951 Geneva Convention – of refugees applying for asylum. Not surprisingly, there is no clear view on numbers of undocumented refugees (or other undocumented immigrants). Moreover, it is extremely difficult – if not impossible – to know precisely how many applicants whose asylum demand was rejected actually left or were expelled from the country or even remained in the country with an irregular or semi-irregular status. Different estimating techniques have been used but all of these figures have to be considered with caution. One of the methods, such as regularization data for instance, indicates 71,500 migrants without legal residence at the beginning of 2000 (Belgian Contact Point, 2005, pp. 26–27). Regarding the countries of origin of irregular migrants, police data show that from 1998 until 2004 the intercepted migrants were mainly from Yugoslavia, Romania, Poland, Morocco, Algeria, Afghanistan, Albania and Russia.

Immigrant social and political rights and participation in public life

General policy framework

The overall framework for any policy regarding immigrants in Belgium was devised in 1989 by the Royal Commissariat for Migrant Policies. This was an official government body set up to develop and monitor integration policy.[1] The Flemish and Francophone policies towards immigrants have all taken pieces from the integration framework of the Royal Commissariat as guidelines for their own policy efforts.[2] Nevertheless, the linguistic cleavage (French/Flemish) has triggered divergent types of attitudes and policy frameworks with regard to the settlement and integration of immigrants in the different parts of the country (Bousetta, 2000b).

Mirroring Dutch policy, the Flemish government has had a clear preference for supporting migrant organizations which are willing to cooperate in federations and are coordinated by quangos.[3] In addition, the Flemish government has financially supported local initiatives aimed at urban renewal and the integration of deprived groups in disadvantaged neighbourhoods. In 1998, the Flemish government adopted a new overarching policy framework clearly based on the recognition of ethnic-cultural groups and including both (settled legal) migrants and refugees and groups with nomadic lifestyles ('gypsies') as its target groups. Parallel to this 'multicultural policy', the Flemish government also developed policy measures that are said to be aimed at the 'assimilation' of newcomers (Jacobs, 2004). Since the end of the 1990s, the Flemish have been preparing and experimenting on the so-called citizenship trajectories (*inburgeringstrajecten*), in which lessons in the Dutch language and lessons of introduction to Flemish/Belgian society are to be taken by certain categories of immigrant newcomers. The aim is to actively promote a certain degree of language and cultural assimilation. This scheme, once again borrowed from the Netherlands, has become compulsory for (most) non-EU newcomers in Flanders from April 2004 onwards, and is optional in Brussels.

The Francophone and Walloon governments have not been willing to recognize the participation of immigrants in society as specific ethnocultural groups. Although in practice often primarily directed towards ethnic groups, the dominant category used in policy is 'people of foreign origin'. Other policy initiatives may also target immigrants but may not be labelled as immigrant policies. The same can be said of several measures taken by the Brussels-Capital region. The large numbers of foreign residents and the de facto residential concentration of ethnic minorities have, nevertheless, forced officials in Brussels towards a multicultural stance. In contrast to the Flemish situation, special programmes for newcomers on the Francophone side are quite limited and mainly focused on learning the French language.

---

1   In 1993, it was replaced by the Centre for Equal Opportunities and Fight against Racism.

2   Following the Royal Commissariat, integration is the insertion of migrants into Belgian society according to three guiding principles: 'a) assimilation where the 'public order' demands this; b) consequent promotion of the best possible 'fit' in accordance with the orientating social principles which support the culture of the host country and which are related to 'modernity', 'emancipation' and 'true pluralism' – as understood by a modern western state; c) unambiguous respect for cultural diversity-as-mutual-enrichment in all areas' (KCM, 1989, pp. 38–39).

3   Quangos are quasi non-governmental organizations. They are formally independent of government but to a great extent subsidized by government and function according to government guidelines.

Competing Flemish-francophone approaches towards immigrants' civic participation

Owing to the complex institutional framework of the Belgian federal political system, both the Flemish and Francophone communities have jurisdiction with regard to policies concerning immigrants or ethnic minority groups in the Brussels-Capital Region. As a result, two contradicting policy approaches coexist within the same territory. This being said, it should be pointed out that the difference between the Flemish and Francophone approach for dealing with multi-ethnic issues is very much interconnected with, and instrumental to, strategies used by the political establishment of both linguistic groups as contenders in the political field of Brussels (Jacobs, 2000). Their divergent positions on integration policy allow them to protect and reinforce their respective positions in the multinational political arena. In addition to opening its education system in Brussels to all potential pupils (and thus now hosting about one-third of all children), and stimulating multilingual cultural events, the Flemish community has for example made substantial efforts to woo immigrant associations in Brussels. These activities are, at least partially, strategic attempts on behalf of the Flemish government in Brussels to incorporate immigrant (often Francophone) self-managed organizations into its policy networks, hoping thereby to strengthen the Flemish community's sphere of influence within the Brussels-Capital Region. Immigrant associations, of course, welcome Flemish efforts as interesting new possibilities for funding and lobbying. They can now go 'shopping' for funding and influence in either the Flemish or the Francophone community and can strategically opt for different forms of collective mobilization – stressing either ethnic identity or neutral forms of social insertion (Jacobs and Rummens, 2003). As a result of the Francophone approach, many immigrants are active within the structures of existing social organizations (such as trade unions) and anti-racist organizations. The fact that migrant associations are treated as legitimate partners for discussion and policy initiatives by the Flemish authorities has, however, also enhanced the creation of self-managed organizations and processes of ethnic mobilization.

Enfranchisement

Until recently only Belgian citizens were allowed to participate in elections. Belgian politicians have been remarkably reluctant in enfranchising foreign residents. This was, as has been extensively discussed elsewhere (Jacobs, 1998, 1999, 2001), mainly due to the polarization and the electoral struggle over the anti-immigrant vote in the 1980s and early 1990s. It has also been the result of the disruptive effect of the Flemish-Francophone cleavage in the second half of the 1990s. It took till early 1999 before Belgium finally enfranchised EU citizens in compliance with the Maastricht Treaty and the derived European directives. Foreign residents from EU-countries were therefore able to participate in the most recent local elections which took place in October 2000. To be able to participate, they had to register in advance as voters. It should be noted that voting is compulsory for Belgians. Non-EU citizens, however, were not allowed to vote in local elections. A special clause in the constitution stipulated that the electoral laws could only be modified to enfranchise third-country nationals after the year 2001. The electoral law was modified in 2004, following a heated political debate which brought the government very close to a crisis. Third-country nationals participated for the first time in local elections in October 2006, albeit only as voters and not as candidates.

Nationality law

Nationality is an essential instrument for any discussion on participation, especially political participation, since the vast majority of political rights are associated with nationality. The intergenerational transmission of citizenship (*jus sanguinis*) constitutes the basic principle of access to Belgian nationality. Children born to Belgian nationals are automatically attributed Belgian nationality at birth. However, *jus soli* has gradually been introduced into Belgian nationality law. Although the 1999 reform was supposed to allow a larger participation of former foreign residents in the 2000 local elections, it only had limited effect on the increase of Belgian voters for the October elections, because of slow implementation. The 1984 and 1991 reforms are hence to be considered most relevant for the political participation of Belgians of immigrant origin in the 2000 local elections.

In 1991, the importance of *jus soli* in Belgium's nationality law was significantly enhanced. While in 1984, double *jus soli* was still linked to the voluntary choice of the parent(s), it was implemented (quasi-) automatically from 1 January 1992 onwards. The new procedure was introduced for the so-called 'third-generation immigrants'. Every child born on Belgian soil of a parent also born in the territory automatically acquires Belgian nationality. There is, however, a 'residence' condition for the parent(s) (they must have been living in Belgium for at least five years of the ten years preceding the birth of the child). Furthermore, a new option-procedure was introduced for the 'second-generation immigrant' born on Belgian soil. Belgian nationality can be acquired for a child born on Belgian soil by declaration made by the parent(s) on behalf of the child under several conditions. If the parents have not made or could not make use of the opportunity to opt for Belgian nationality for their child born on Belgian soil, the person involved can him- or herself still opt for Belgian nationality between the ages of 18 and 22 (option procedure of 1984). Additionally, a new procedure was introduced allowing persons born in Belgium and who have, since birth, resided in Belgium, to acquire Belgian nationality between the ages of 18 and 30. Belgian nationality is automatically granted unless the 'district attorney' disagrees. In 2000, the conditions for the option procedure were simplified. Adults born in Belgium or having lived in Belgium for seven years with permanent residence status can opt for Belgian nationality, except in the event of a refusal from the 'district attorney'.

In Belgium, naturalization is discretionary. When it is refused, there is no right of appeal. Discretionary naturalization is, in essence, not a right but a favour which one can be granted. This is symbolically made clear in the Belgian system in which naturalization is still 'politically' decided upon by Parliament. Renunciation of the previous nationality is, in principle, not a condition of acquiring Belgian nationality, although simultaneous possession of Belgian nationality and that of most other European countries is ruled out by the Treaty of Strasbourg (6 May 1963). From 1996, all adults who had been resident in the country for five years (three years for refugees) could apply for naturalization. The applicant had to prove his/her integration into Belgian society. Furthermore, some Belgian people were asked to be guarantors, in other words, to vouch for a particular applicant. The application was sent to the Chamber (one of the two bodies of Parliament), which decided whether the applicant would be granted Belgian nationality. Since 2000, the residence requirement has been reduced. Henceforth, all adults who have been residing in Belgium for three years (two years for refugees) can apply for naturalization. Moreover, the test of integration has been dropped altogether. Paradoxically, there is no clear-cut language requirement for naturalization since Flemish and Francophone politicians could not agree on precise modalities.

Public and media discourses on migration

One of the consequences of 9/11 is without any doubt that the issue of multiculturalism and the position of Islam within Belgian society have been put centre-stage in political and public debates. Any observer who would undertake a quick scan of the focus of contemporary Belgian media attention would have to conclude that the issue of cultural diversity – and in particular the position of immigrant Muslim minority groups – is currently seen to be standing at the heart of public life. The preoccupation of managing ethnic, cultural and religious diversity in the public space did not suddenly appear with the tragic events in New York and Washington. Indeed, it has been a recurring issue for – albeit fragmented – debate in Belgium since the mid-seventies (Jacobs and Swyngedouw, 2002).

What is new in the content of the debate, however, is the peremptory negative character of the arguments produced. The most radical opponents of multiculturalism have shaped a dialogue space in which the claim for identity difference and recognition of minority groups is deeply questioned. Authoritative arguments vis-à-vis ethnic and religious minorities have heavily challenged the discourse and ideal of a society where difference is mutually enriching. In many such debates, the incorporation of Islam and of Muslims is central, both implicitly as well as explicitly (Bousetta and Jacobs, 2006, pp. 23–36).

In the Belgian context, the question of dealing with ethnic diversity – at least when being considered independently of the linguistic divide in the country – was initially conceived as an issue limited to handling the consequences of recruitment of a temporary foreign labour force in an ad hoc manner. In the course of the 1970s and 1980s, the issue of multiculturalism gradually came to be seen independently of issues of migration and mobility. If the management of cultural diversity in the public space can no longer be thought of in the framework of earlier migration waves alone, nor can it be conceived as a matter to be dealt with merely in the private sphere.

Fundamentally, the issue at stake is how to conceive a public space able to welcome and organize a peaceful coexistence of culturally and religiously different minority and majority groups. Such a challenge raises the question of the principles along which we need to reorganize public space in an accommodating way for all groups involved. Just as the nineteenth century struggles of the working class were articulated in terms of social justice, the contemporary claims of minority groups manifesting themselves in multicultural societies need to be read as a quest for what political philosophers have called a principle of ethnocultural justice (Kymlicka, 2001).

One would wish for a serene climate in which to pursue the debate on multiculturalism, but this is far from being a readily available option. These debates are, on the contrary, developing in a nervous atmosphere. In Belgium, the context is marked by the fact that the question has reached a high level of political centrality, especially in Flanders (the Dutch speaking part of Belgium) where the extreme-right wing party Vlaams Belang (former Vlaams Blok) obtained no less than 25 per cent of the popular vote in the June 2004 regional and general elections. Pushed in the back by a strong xenophobic far-right movement, the government and political parties are ceaselessly led to comment and make political statements about the perceived failures of multicultural coexistence. As a consequence, public deliberations on the issue of dealing with ethnic diversity take place against a backdrop of political manoeuvres seeking to woo either ethnic minority voters – especially in Brussels (Jacobs, Martiniello and Rea, 2002) – or, more often, the anti-multiculturalism and/ or xenophobic voters (Jacobs and Rummens, 2003). Not surprisingly, the tensions generated by international developments also shape the debate. In 2004, the war in Iraq, the Israeli-Palestinian conflict, and the unstable situation in Afghanistan all contributed to a mutual lack of confidence between 'the West' and 'the Arab-Muslim world'. The consequences are not merely diplomatic, but also affect domestic politics, in Belgium as in other European countries. The relationship between Arab and Muslim minorities on the one hand and the majority groups of the European societies where these minorities live and reside on the other, feels the repercussions of these tensions. The worries raised in mainstream public opinion by acts of political violence in the world in the name of Islam raise questions about the nature of European Islam and the degree of loyalty of European Muslims. This was only exacerbated in Belgium in November 2004, following the murder in

Amsterdam of the controversial Dutch film-maker and publicist Theo Van Gogh by a young Dutch Muslim extremist of Moroccan origin.

Interestingly, the focus on Islam and the pressure on multicultural discourse in Belgium have, however, not directly led to an overall change in actual policy. As has been the case in the past, policy is still often pragmatic in nature and a wide variety of (sometimes contradictory) policies and practices coexist in Belgium. In some instances, a crude assimilationist line is being taken, while in other instances ethnic diversity is being encouraged. Ethnic difference can both be neglected and denied or accommodated, depending on the issue we are dealing with and the actors involved. On the ground, policy may be of a de facto multicultural nature, while all involved will heavily deny it has anything to do with the idea of multiculturalism. A strict assimilationist policy scheme may be announced but, in the end, it may not be so strictly implemented.

Concluding remarks

Belgium has for a long time been an immigration country. The post-Second World War period was marked by the arrival of immigrants from several Mediterranean countries. Italians, Greeks, Spaniards, Moroccans, Turks, Algerians, Tunisians, and Yugoslavians were actively recruited by the Belgian Government and rapidly invited to be joined by their families. Most of them have settled in Belgium. After 1974, inflows of immigrants (EU−citizens, highly skilled workers, family members, foreign students and irregular migrants) did not stop in Belgium. They even remained particularly important during the 1990s and then mainly consisted of asylum seekers. Instead of developing proactive migration policies, Belgium has been dealing with the changes in its migration and post-migration context by adopting generally ad hoc measures and several times modifying the Aliens Law of 15 December 1980.

Around 10 per cent of the population is foreign in Belgium. This immigrant population is unevenly spread across the regions and cities. Brussels is a particular case in point, where almost one in three inhabitants is a foreigner. Nationality figures, however, do not give a clear picture of the number of people of immigrant origin. Owing to ongoing liberalization of the Belgian nationality law, a large number of foreigners have acquired citizenship. At the start of the new millennium, Belgium had one of the most open nationality legislations in the world.

Immigrants and their offspring have, for long, been perceived as workers and not so much as civic and political actors. Despite that, they have always developed forms of political activity either at the margins or outside the Belgian political institutions in order to improve their living conditions or, more generally, to improve their position in society. The forms of participation of immigrants largely depend on the political opportunity structure available at certain times, namely the conditions for access to political and civil rights, the degree of openness of political parties and civil society associations, the electoral system, and so on. As an increasing body of research literature has shown, institutional factors can indeed explain a large part of the conditions under which immigrants may participate in society (Bousetta, 2000a, 2001; Jacobs and Swyngedouw, 2002). The evolution of nationality legislation, for instance, has allowed a very effective opening of Belgian political institutions to the multicultural reality of the country. This is also true for the citizenship of the European Union which has allowed EU citizens to participate actively in local and European elections without any nationality requirement. Immigrants and foreigners are now active in all fields of Belgian society. Over the last 15 years, they have become increasingly visible in public life by actively engaging in public debates about issues of direct concern to them.

There has been fragmented debate about the management of diversity stemming from migration in Belgium since the mid-1970s. Fear of a white backlash and anti-immigrant populism has been a constant in public discourse. Rhetoric about immigrants has tended to be quite negative. After the events of 9/11, public discourses focused heavily on multiculturalism and the place of Islam in Belgium. Ever since, debate on ethnocultural diversity has continued to linger in a fairly tense atmosphere. At the same time, however, the myth of zero immigration is increasingly being challenged. Furthermore, several policy developments attest to the progressive acknowledgement by political elites that Belgium is, de facto, a country of immigration and that it is rapidly becoming a multicultural society. Last but not least, immigrant origin citizens have gained increasing public visibility and have – with varying success – at repeated times raised their voice in the political arena. Most politicians creatively try to juggle both positively framed integration and antidiscrimination policies on the one hand, and harsh asylum policy and populist anti-immigrant discourse on the other. As a consequence, it is not always possible to provide a clear-cut image of Belgian migration and integration policies and discourses.

References

Bousetta, H. (2000a), 'Institutional Theories of Immigrant Ethnic Mobilisation: Relevance and Limitations', *Journal of Ethnic and Migration Studies*, **26**(2), 229–45. [DOI: 10.1080/136918 30050022785]

Bousetta, H. (2000b), 'L'impact des divisions communautaires sur l'intégration des étrangers: le cas de la Belgique', in McAndrew, M. and Pagé, M. (2000) *L'éducation dans les sociétés divisées*, 59–81. Montréal: L'Harmattan.

Bousetta, H. (2001), *Immigration, Post-Immigration Politics and the Political Mobilisation of Ethnic Minorities: A Comparative Case-Study of Moroccans in four European Cities*, unpublished PhD thesis, Katholieke Universiteit Brussel.

Bousetta, H. and Jacobs, D. (2006), 'Multiculturalism, Citizenship and Islam in Problematic Encounters in Belgium', in Modood, T., Triandafyllidou, A. and Zapata-Barrero, R. (eds) *Multiculturalism, Muslims and Citizenship: A European Approach*, 23–36. London: Routledge.

Brion, F., Rea, A., Schaut, C. and Tixhon, A. (eds) (2001), *Mon délit? Mon origine. Criminalité et Criminalisation de l'Immigration*. Brussels: De Boeck Université.

Favell, A. and Martiniello, M. (1998), *Multinational, Multicultural and Multilevelled Post-National Politics in Brussels, Capital of Europe*, paper presented at the ECPR Joint Sessions, Warwick University, March.

Gsir, S., Martiniello, M. and Wets, J. (2003), 'Belgium Report', in Niessen, J. and Schibel, Y. (eds) *EU and US approaches to the Management of Immigration: Comparative Perspectives*, 47–76. Brussels: MPG.

Gsir, S., Martiniello, M., Meireman, K. and Wets, J. (2005), 'Belgium', in Niessen, J., Schibel, Y. and Thompson, C. (eds) *Current Immigration Debates in Europe: Publication of the European Migration Dialogue*, 41–46. Brussels: MPG.

Jacobs, D. (1998), *Nieuwkomers in de politiek* [Newcomers in Politics]. Ghent: Academia Press.

Jacobs, D. (1999), 'The Debate over Enfranchisement of Foreign Residents in Belgium', *Journal of Ethnic and Migration Studies*, **25**(4), 649–64.

Jacobs, D. (2000), 'Multinational and Polyethnic Politics Entwined: Minority Representation in the Region of Brussels-Capital', *Journal of Ethnic and Migration Studies*, **26**(2), 289–304. [DOI: 10.1080/13691830050022811]

Jacobs, D. (2001), 'Immigrants in a Multinational Political Sphere: the Case of Brussels', in Rogers, A. and Tillie, J. (eds) *Multicultural Policies and Modes of Citizenship in European Cities*, 107–122. Aldershot: Ashgate.

Jacobs, D. (2004), 'Alive and Kicking? Multiculturalism in Flanders', *International Journal on Multicultural Societies*, 6(2), 189–208.

Jacobs, D. and Rummens, S. (2003), 'Wij zeggen wat ù denkt: Extreem-rechts in Vlaanderen en nieuw radicaal-rechts in Europe', *Krisis, tijdschrift voor empirische filosofie*, 4(2), 41–59. (We say what you think: The extreme right in Flanders and the new radical right in Europe).

Jacobs, D. and Swyngedouw, M. (2002), 'The Extreme Right and Enfranchisement of Immigrants: Main Issues in the Public Debate on Integration in Belgium', *Journal of International Migration and Integration / Revue de l'intégration et de la migration internationale*, 3(3–4), 329–44.

Jacobs, D. and Swyngedouw, M. (2003), 'Politieke participatie en zelforganisatie van allochtonen in de Brusselse gemeenten: Een verkenning', in Witte, E., Alen, A., Dumont, H., Vandernoot, P. and De Groof, R. (eds) *De Brusselse negentien gemeenten En Het Brussels Model − Les dix-neuf communes bruxelloises et le modèle bruxellois*, 261−90. Brussels: Larcier. (Political participation and self-organization of allochthones in the Brussels municipalities).

Jacobs, D., Phalet, K. and Swyngedouw, M. (2002), *Social Capital and Political Participation among Ethnic Minority Groups in Brussels, A Test of the Civic Community Argument of Fennema and Tillie*, paper presented at the Workshop Political Participation for Immigrants and their Descendants in Post-War Western Europe at the ECPR Joint Workshop Sessions, March; Turin.

KCM (Koninklijk Commissariaat voor het Migrantenbeleid) (1993), *Tekenen voor gelijkwaardigheid* [Signing for equality]. Brussels: KCM.

Kymlicka, W. (2001), *Politics in the Vernacular*. Oxford: Oxford University Press.

Martens, A. (1973), *25 Jaar Wegwerparbeiders, Het Belgische Immigratiebeleid na 1945*. Leuven: KULeuven. (25 Years of disposable workers. The Belgian immigration policy after 1945).

Martens, A. (1976), *Les Immigrés, Flux et Reflux d'une Main-d'oeuvre d'appoint: La Politique belge de l'immigration de 1945 à 1970*. Louvain: Presses Universitaires de Louvain.

Ouali, N. (2004), 'Analyse des données démographiques et des demandes d'asile', in Desmarez, P., Van der Hallen, P., Ouali, N., Degraef, V. and Tratsaert, K. (eds) *Minorités ethniques en Belgique: Migration et marché du travail*, 9−34. Ghent: Academia Press.

Sauvy, A. (1962), *Rapport sur le problème de l'économie et de la population en Wallonie*. Liège: Editions du Conseil Economique Wallon.

Internet-based references

Belgian Contact Point (2005), *Illegally Resident Third Country Nationals in Belgium: state approaches towards them and their profile and social situation*. Brussels: European Migration Network (available at http://www.dofi.fgov.be/fr/1024/frame.htm).

Martiniello, M. and Rea, A. (2003), *Belgium's Immigration Policy Brings Renewal and Challenges*, Migration Information Source (available at http://www.migrationinformation.org/Profiles/display.cfm?ID=164).

Chapter 4

Cyprus

Nicos Trimikliniotis and Corina Demetriou

This chapter discusses the context that has transformed Cyprus from an emigration to an immigration country. It examines public discourse, the legal status and the social position of migrants and asylum-seekers. This is set against the historical and political backdrop of Cyprus, dominated by the 'national' problem, which keeps the island divided.

Cyprus abandoned the restrictive immigration policy followed until 1990 in an effort to meet low-skill labour shortages generated by an economic development model based on mass tourism and services. Today, the total number of non-Cypriot residents is estimated to be between 80,000 and 100,000. This represents approximately 10 per cent of the total population which resides in the south of the island, including an estimated 10,000–30,000 undocumented migrant workers, consisting mainly of 'overstayers'. Most immigrants are employed in domestic work, the service industry (tourism, trade), the manufacturing industry, agriculture and construction, in low-paid and low-status jobs.

The change of policy resulted from a shortage of labour for low-skilled labour intensive jobs (Matsis and Charalambous, 1993). Moreover, the slowing down in economic growth in the 1990s, together with the rise of inflation, formed the basis for abandoning restrictive labour policies. In addition, Cyprus' path toward accession to the EU and other developments in the international arena influenced the government's opening up of the labour market (Trimikliniotis, 1999). With the change of policy in 1990, the criteria for granting permits were extended and a procedure was outlined for employers to recruit staff from abroad.

The policy assumption was that the employment of migrant workers would be short-term, temporary and restricted to specific sectors and specific employers. In the end, however, this policy proved to be ill-founded. The institutional framework has failed to properly accommodate and encourage the civic participation of migrants. As a result, these groups of people have not been provided with the space to develop a sense of belonging to Cypriot society. It is only very recently that debates on the rights of migrant workers and multicultural society have emerged. Nonetheless, these are largely still focused on regularization rather than on tolerance and integration. Migrants and asylum seekers face a rather hostile environment in society, including hostile media and an unsympathetic immigration regime based on 'control.' That said, some encouraging signs are beginning to emerge.

Major developments in Cyprus' immigration policy

To appreciate the context of migration to Cyprus one has to locate migration within the politically turbulent historical setting of the island, in which ethnic conflict has prevailed over other issues. Since independence in 1960, the political stage and public debates have been dominated by inter-ethnic relations, the violent clashes between the two constitutionally 'recognized communities',[1] namely Greek-Cypriots (82 per cent) and Turkish-Cypriots (18 per cent), and by the 1974 foreign military interventions which still keep the island divided today.[2] This chapter will concentrate on the territories controlled by the Republic of Cyprus, which are located in the southern part of the island.

Cyprus had historically been a country of emigration toward richer countries. As is usually the case in former British colonies, many Cypriots migrated to the UK, as well as to other destinations such as Australia, the United States and South Africa. In fact, the number of Cypriots living abroad is equivalent to nearly half the island's population. The military invasions of Greece and Turkey in 1974 left the country divided and society and the economy devastated. There was an 18 per cent fall in GNP between 1973 and 1975, a 30 per cent rise in unemployment, mass poverty and a loss of 37 per cent of the country's territory.

The 1974 events, by default, created the preconditions for rapid modernization, in spite of the severe drop in the GNP and the sharp rise in unemployment and poverty. Cheap labour was initially provided by the Greek Cypriot displaced persons who fled from the north and settled in the south. But concerted effort by the Government, political parties and trade unions created the conditions for the economic development subsequently experienced and for the labour shortages which resulted.

To meet these shortages, the government begun to issue individual visas to migrant workers for employment, which were short-term and restricted to specific sectors. Although the actual developments of the past decade reversed the dominant presumption that immigration would be temporary, a number of institutional devices which had been designed with that presumption in mind have resulted in an institutional framework with the following characteristics. First, work permits are granted on the condition that each migrant worker is attached to a specific employer without the freedom to change jobs unless the original employer consents to such a change. Second, work permits are granted annually and with a maximum period of initially six and then four years. The policy is reviewed on an irregular basis. At the end of March 2005 it was reduced to four years, and six additional months could be granted on exceptional humanitarian grounds. Pending the accession of Romania and Bulgaria to the EU, no maximum stay was provided for Romanians and Bulgarians, although there have been several instances of deportations of such nationals. Structurally, this produces and reproduces a framework of precariousness and exclusion. Third, evidence of non-compliance by employers with labour laws is abundantly recorded by Parliamentary reports in 1997, as well as Reports by the European Commission against Racism and Intolerance (see ECRI, 2001, 2005; Trimikliniotis and Pantelides, 2003; Harakis et al., 2005). It is worth noting that few initiatives have taken place to unionize or otherwise organize migrant workers.

The change of immigration policy in 1990 which opened up the island's doors to migrants was the result of the following factors. On the one hand, economic developments such as the world-wide growth in tourism resulted in economic growth which increased the demand for labour in Cyprus. On the other hand, political developments such as the collapse of the Soviet Union resulted in the migration of labour from ex-Soviet countries. This was coupled with the migration of a large number of Pontic Greeks from the Caucasus region who received Greek nationality and

---

1   Only the Greek-Cypriots and the Turkish-Cypriots are recognized by the Cyprus Constitution as 'communities', endowed with specific power-sharing rights; three other ethnic groups (Armenians, Latins, Maronites) are treated as 'religious groups' and have certain 'minority rights' (see Trimikliniotis, 2006).

2   First there was a military coup which was instigated by an army intervention by Greece with the assistance of local extremists. It was followed by an invasion and occupation by Turkey.

were, thus, able to migrate to Cyprus with the minimum of formalities. In addition, the Gulf War, successive crises in The Gulf Region and unrest in Israel and Palestine contributed to the inflow of both economic and political refugees from the affected regions.

Before its accession to the EU, Cyprus was the only country to allow Russian nationals to enter without visas. This was an initiative taken in an effort to attract businesses, holidaymakers and much-sought-after capital. This policy has resulted in several thousands of Russians migrating to Cyprus and establishing offshore businesses, Russian schools and Russian churches. Following its EU accession, Cyprus was forced to adopt a more restrictive policy in granting entry rights to Russian nationals. However, many of those who came to Cyprus in the 1990s have settled on a temporary residence visa which is renewed annually.

The policies and practices governing migrant workers from the moment of entry, their working conditions and their legal and social rights, are set out in the agreement between the Cyprus government, the employers' organizations (OEV and KEVE)[3] and trade unions (PEO, SEK, DEOK and some sectional unions).[4] This is known as the 'tripartite system'. The criteria, originally compiled in 1991[5] and reaffirmed in 2004, stipulate that migrant workers are granted the same employment terms and all other rights enjoyed by Cypriot workers, derived from existing collective agreements and social security schemes. A study carried out by the State Planning Bureau, however, refers to the need to 'take into account the element of *temporality* as well as other factors' (Planning Bureau, 1989, p. 3). This allows for flexibility in the interpretation of the policy. Furthermore, the same study recognizes that there are 'no efficient mechanisms to monitor this' (Planning Bureau, 1989, p. 4). This problem is also recognized in the 1997 Reports of the Parliamentary Commissions on Employment and Social Insurance and on Human Rights.

By and large, as a result of EU accession, and a more active role by NGOs and some trade unions, there has been an on-going debate about the employment of migrant workers in Cyprus, with a focus on their labour rights. At the same time, there have also been strong anti-immigrant sentiments expressed in various debates and media discourses (see ECRI, 2001, 2005).

In a paper submitted to the tripartite committee on labour issues in August 2005, the Ministry of Labour outlined the basis for a general strategy whose primary goal is to 'curb' the 'uncontrollable influx of foreign workers' (that is, third-country nationals employed in Cyprus). This strategy is proposed so that a number of 'principles and aims' are met:

- to 'ensure the security and protection of the state and its citizens and the promotion of the common/public interest';
- to safeguard human rights;
- to cover extraordinary and/or specialized (authentic) needs of the labour market, providing that the preference regime for Cypriot and Community persons is maintained;
- to cover the strategic developmental goals of the Strategic Development Plan;
- to ensure the standard policy for the full utilization of the local human resources, particularly the utilization of the inactive female population, the prevention and combating of youth unemployment, the encouragement of the extension of working life and the integration of vulnerable groups in the labour market.

---

3   OEV is the acronym for Organization of Employers and Manufacturers. KEVE is the acronym for Chamber of Commerce and Manufacture.

4   PEO is the left-wing union and stands for Pan-Cyprian Federation of Labour. Together with the right-wing SEK (Confederation of Cypriot Labour) they are the largest trade union. DEOK is a small Democratic Labour Federation of Cyprus.

5   Circular of the Dept. of Labour of the Ministry of Labour and Social Insurance ref. T.E. 48/83 dated 02/12/1991.

Essentially, the paper proposes a quota system for each sector and for the country as a whole, but the policy paper is rather vague and general. For instance, it sets a compulsory 30 per cent maximum quota for third-country foreign labourers for all businesses and also per sector without, however, clearly specifying the various sectors. The main features of the Government paper include a quota on the employment of 'foreigners' both at the national level and on a sector basis. It allows 'foreign workers' the right to change employer after the first year but within the same job and sector. Moreover, there is a six-week maximum period for such a request to be considered. There is a priority-based system in which the first priority in employment, after Cypriots and EU nationals, is given to nationals from EU accession countries, followed by third-country nationals who can be employed in specified economic sectors and under strict criteria. Furthermore, applications must be made from outside Cyprus. Work permits are granted, as a matter of third priority, to asylum seekers and foreign university students who have been studying in Cyprus for three year courses and may work only upon completion of their first year of study. Media reports refer to the policy as a 'break' with the employment of foreign migrant labour. Moreover, the system is prone to fail for the simple reason that quotas do not work; rigidity and bureaucracy are likely to grow even further.

Another development is the introduction of the 2004–2006 Cyprus National Action Plan for Social Inclusion. This Action Plan views 'immigrants' as 'groups at risk', and recognizes that it is a group whose members are 'at risk of exclusion'. This follows the second ECRI Report which referred to migrants as 'a vulnerable group'.

EU accession has also created 'Europeanized' arguments regarding migration. Accession to the EU has allegedly made Cyprus an attractive destination for migrants and asylum-seekers and the response of policy-makers has been to keenly transform themselves to 'border-guards of Europe'.[6] Cyprus is a prime instance of a southern European country which functions as the 'entrance hall' to the EU and often serves as a 'waiting room' for many migrants who have Northern European countries as their final destination (Anthias and Lazarides, 1999, p. 3).

The Cyprus government failed to transpose Directive 203/109/EC[7] before the deadline of 23 January 2006. Moreover, the surge of deportations of immigrants who had been in the country for several years before the set deadline attracted criticism from the media, the Ombudsman (the national Equality Body under law transposing Directive 2000/43/EC) and NGOs. A number of Supreme Court decisions[8] were issued during 2005 and in early 2006 cancelling some of the many deportation orders issued by the Migration Office. In his reasoning for one of these decisions, the judge stated that although non-transposed directives cannot be applied directly, the implementation of the aims and effects of such directives is encouraged, and that national laws must be interpreted in a manner consistent with the directives even if not yet transposed.[9]

Meanwhile, a bill was submitted and discussed in Parliament to amend the antiquated law on Aliens and Migration. The law eventually passed purports to transpose Directive 2003/106/EC on long-term migrants. The government's intention to include a requirement for proficiency in the Greek language and Cypriot history met with strong resistance from trade unions and was eventually dropped. The Chief Immigration Officer is currently facing disciplinary proceedings for

---

6   During the EU Thessalonica summit, the President of Cyprus offered to share 'expertise' in dealing with migrants and asylum-seekers with the European Union.

7   The Directive requires Member States to introduce laws granting migrants who have been lawfully in the country for 5 years and over the right to 'long-term residence status'.

8   *Mahmoud Adil v the Republic of Cyprus* (13/01/06); *Maher Ahmet Baskouj v the Republic of Cyprus* (17/01/06); *Nebojsa Micovic v the Republic of Cyprus* (Case No. 1012/2005, dated 18/11/05).

9   *Nebojsa Micovic v the Republic of Cyprus.*

failure to implement the law and for continuing to deport persons entitled to long-term residence status.[10]

Matters relating to the control of the borders fall within the ambit of the powers of the executive, who are under a duty to apply the rights derived from domestic and international law. They are subject, of course, to judicial supervision. The general rubric of judicial control of the executive on matters relating to immigration and nationality falls under the category of proper exercise of discretion. This is under the principle of *legitimacy*, justification of administrative acts, the principles of equality, and natural justice. The interpretation of the law by the Courts and its implementation by immigration officers has shown a tendency to considerably enlarge the scope of state discretion which often leads to discriminatory behaviour. Indeed, immigration officers in Cyprus have already been criticized by the Second ECRI Report for discriminatory behaviour.[11]

The process of 'Europeanization' has enabled a gradual change in attitude and has resulted in the harmonization of Cypriot laws.[12] However, the immigration model itself, which is primarily based on the employment of migrant workers on a short-term, temporary and restricted-to-specific-sectors basis, is likely to remain essentially in place. This is mostly because the changes brought about by the transposition of the *acquis* involve only the opening up of the doors to European citizens; the restrictive approach towards third-country nationals remains (Trimikliniotis and Demetriou, 2005). Discrimination occurs in the labour market, education, housing and other services, as well as in the way migrants are depicted by the media. We could safely assume that the structural and institutional aspects of the status of most immigrants are likely to remain those of 'third-country nationals' (Trimikliniotis and Pantelides (2003).

The immigrant population of Cyprus: main demographic and social features

Within sixteen years there has been a large increase in the total number of legally employed and undocumented migrant workers. As the Tables (below) indicate, there is a discrepancy in the figures for migrant workers provided by various Government Departments and the Statistical Service. The Cypriot authorities have supplied an annex to the Third ECRI Report on Cyprus in which they refer to the rise in the number of non-Cypriots from 20,000 in 2000 to 75,000 in 2005. This number does not include: illegal immigrants, mostly overstayers, who are estimated to be around 40,000; asylum seekers; Europeans and non-Europeans of various categories. Nor does it include 'a considerable number of visitors', such as retired persons, students and those on permanent residence permits. According to the Asylum Service of the Ministry of Interior there are a total of 22,963 asylum seekers.[13]

---

10   Interior Ministry official Giorgos Giorgallis was quoted in *The Cyprus Mail*, 24 July 2005.
11   The second ECRI report reads: 'Concern is also expressed at reports of discriminatory checks on the part of immigration officers of non-whites coming to Cyprus.'
12   Directives 43/2000 and 78/2000 were transposed via new legislation which came into force on 1 May 2004, upon accession into the EU.
13   Information provided by the Ministry of Interior on 10 January 2006.

Table 4.1   Economic indicators and migration

	1996	1997	1998	1999	2000	2001	2002	2003	2004
Economically active population	306,000	307,600	311,100	318,200	324,900	329,9	326,133	341,203	354,686
Gainfully employed population	28,5900	28,6100	28,8800	29,4700	30,1800	30,7800	32,1900	32,5300	33,3100
% of unemployment	3.1	3.4	3.3	3.6	3.4	2.9	3.9	4.1	4.7
[Legal] Immigrants	16,723	19,310	20,713	24,059	26,398	30,196	57,504	62,705	71,434
% of immigrants with active population	5.5	6.28	6.66	7.6	8.12	9.16	17.86	19.27	21.44
Net migration	5,300	4,800	4,200	4,200	3,960	4,650	6,885	12.342	15.724

Sources: Labour Force Survey 2003 and 2004, Cyprus Statistical Service; Labour Statistics 1999 and 2003, Cyprus Statistical Service; Demographic Report 2004, Cyprus Statistical Service; Industrial Statistics 2004, Cyprus Statistical Service; Estimations of future needs on migrants employment between 2004–2007, Human Resources Authority, March Edition 2004; 2003 Annual Report, Ministry of Labour and Social Insurance.

Table 4.1 provides a breakdown of the total number of migrants into different categories. Each one of the categories listed is independent of the other, in the sense that there is no overlap. It is noteworthy that the category of migrant workers with work permits does not include Greek nationals, offshore company personnel, or Pontic Greeks who, once granted Greek nationality, are entitled to enter and work in Cyprus with few formalities. It is thus not entirely clear who is actually included in the category 'EU nationals' which appears below.

Table 4.2   Categories of migrant workers in Cyprus

	2003	2004	2005
Migrant workers with work permits	38,000	40,000	52,000
Pontic Greeks (non passport holders)	10,000	10,000	10,00
Greek Citizens (including Pontic Greek passport holders)	10,000	10,000	21,294
Migrant workers in offshore companies	5,000		
Asylum Applications (cases)	4,032	8,284	7,291
Undocumented Migrant Workers	5,000–15,000	10,000–30,000	10,000–30,000
Total			80,000–100,000

It is important to clarify that no accurate record exists, and that Table 4.2 is compiled by the author of this chapter based on information from the Cyprus Statistical Service, the Population Archive and various informal estimates that have been averaged out. In addition, regarding the distinction between Greek nationals and Pontic Greeks, Pontic organizations claim that the total number of Pontic Greeks is between 20,000 and 30,000, of whom only half have Greek passports. As it is not possible to verify these figures, we have taken as given what seems to be a 'consensus' amongst most persons with 'specialized knowledge' (ministry officials, organizations, researchers and so on). The Population Archive does not keep separate figures for Pontic Greeks.

Table 4.3   **Distribution of migrant workers in sectors of the economy**

Sector	1997	1998	1999	2000	2001	2002	2003	2004	2005
Agriculture	1647	1681	1862	2018	2456	2933	3414	3823	3578
Manufacturing	2011	2058	2108	2052	2550	2854	3524	3883	3959
Fishing								46	42
Mining								55	60
Waters supply/ electricity and gas								9	8
Construction	1445	1463	1552	1398	1884	2592	3553	4614	4495
Tourism	3044	3804	4682	3761	5851	7288	7672	3351	2958
Wholesale / Retail/repairs	1269	1420	1429	1554	1951	2810	3487	4193	4692
Education								564	582
Restaurants								4838	4984
Health and Social activities								765	823
Other Trade Activities	1255	1425	1558	1629	2189	2441		1288	1446
Transport							1388	750	802
Intermediary Financing Organisations Services								215	263
Domestic Labour	5467	6100	6925	7597	9515	10677	12248	14648	15863
Entertainment	1420	1425	1436	1440	1200	1200	1333	1118	1200
Other	2041	2185	2169	2578	2860	3346	3810	4	5
Total	18344	20136	22263	22398	28267	33700	39041	45182	46880

Source: Own compilation.

Table 4.3 was given to the social partners by the Department of Labour in July 2005. There is some variance with the figures provided by the Statistical Service. Moreover, they do not include EU nationals, the Pontic Greeks, students, asylum-seekers or refugees. Nor does the Table provide an estimate of the undocumented workers in Cyprus.

There are two categories of Greek passport holders: migrant workers from mainland Greece and Pontic Greeks who have immigrated to Cyprus from the Black Sea via Greece. Through a bilateral agreement with the Greek Government, Greek citizens (including Greek passport holders of Pontic origin) enjoy permanent residence rights as well as the right to work in Cyprus. In the offshore business sector, most non-Cypriot employees originate from Central and Eastern Europe, mainly Russia and the former Yugoslav Republics.

Most domestic workers originate from South-East Asia and especially the Philippines, Sri Lanka and India. The main sectors in which migrant workers are employed are: agriculture, manufacturing, construction, hotels, restaurants and trade. In the latter three sectors, the majority of migrant workers originate from Central and Eastern Europe and particularly the Balkans. In the former three sectors, which are low skill, low-status and hard working environments, a significant number of Asian workers are employed.

According to the Cyprus Statistical Service Demographic Report, in 2003 there were 10,353 'short-term immigrants'[14] and 16,779 'long-term immigrants'.[15] Overall, long-term immigrants work and reside under a more favourable regime. Their salaries tend to be higher and many have their families with them. Depending on the length of their stay, long-term migrants have a better chance of getting acquainted with rules and procedures and of joining trade unions.

In the early to mid-1980s many affluent Lebanese, Kuwaitis, Palestinians and people from other Arab countries arrived in Cyprus following the collapse of Beirut and the general unrest in the Middle East. These were not migrant workers, but business and other affluent people. More people from the Gulf area arrived in Cyprus during the Gulf War, most of whom left Cyprus and returned to their countries of origin as soon as stability in those countries was restored.

In the early 1990s, many Eastern Europeans, both business people and temporary workers, started migrating to Cyprus following the collapse of the Soviet Union. These were mostly from Russia, former Yugoslavia (primarily Serbs), Bulgaria and Romania. Serbs and Russians were, to a large extent, welcomed by the Greek-Cypriots because of their common religion (Christian Orthodox). The 1999 war in Yugoslavia brought an additional number of Yugoslavians (Serbs) to Cyprus. A small number of the Eastern Europeans in Cyprus are affluent businessmen or highly educated persons occupying managerial positions in the offshore industry, residing under a temporary residence permit. This type of permit is easily renewable so long as they operate or hold a position in a business enterprise in Cyprus.

Naturalization

By 31 December 2003, 2,295 persons had acquired citizenship in Cyprus by naturalization and 9,018 by marriage. In general, the Cyprus government is cautious over granting citizenship to non-Cypriots allegedly because this is an issue that touches upon demographics. Demographics is one of the several dimensions of the Cyprus problem and is at the centre of heated debates (Trimikliniotis, 2006).

Law 141 (I) 2002 stipulates that a non-Cypriot who resides lawfully in the country may acquire citizenship via naturalization under certain conditions. The Interior Minister may grant citizenship to an adult and 'fully able' 'alien' applicant, if the Minister is satisfied that the applicant meets a number of criteria. Such criteria include lawful stay in the country for the preceding 12 months preceded by an additional uninterrupted stay of seven years, 'good character' and 'intention to reside in the Republic'. However, satisfying the Interior Minister is not sufficient. The law vests the Council of Ministers, the highest body in the executive hierarchy, with the discretion of granting, or not, citizenship. In practice, this discretion tends to be exercised by declining citizenship applications.

Immigrant rights and participation in public life – issues of immigrant integration

The current institutional framework hardly provides the space for the civic participation of immigrants. It is, therefore, hard to differentiate between restrictive and encouraging legal

---

14   The definition provided by the Statistical Service for this term is 'persons entering Cyprus with the intention of remaining less than one year'.

15   Long-term migrants are defined by the Statistical Service as 'persons entering Cyprus with the intention to settle, or to stay for one year or more'.

conditions. There are obviously 'restrictive conditions' that prohibit political participation in elections (restrictions on voting and on standing for office), unless full citizenship is granted, but there are no formal prohibitions of membership in parties and organizations, rights for self-organization, public rallies, and so on, although there have been cases where the contract of employment of migrants in certain sectors prohibited involvement in political activity.

Overall, the situation in Cyprus can be described as rather disappointing on the issue of the civic participation of migrants, but there are some encouraging signs. The rights guaranteed under the Constitution and the ECHR are generally respected, with some exceptions. Nevertheless, migrants face a tough regime because, on the whole, issues relating to their stay are considered as falling outside of these legal provisions. The recently enacted anti-discrimination legislation transposing Directives 43/2000 and 78/2000 has had some impact on the situation of migrants in Cyprus. Nevertheless, the areas affected by these new laws are mostly employment-related and only indirectly affect migrants' level of civic participation.

The main focus of the migrant support and solidarity NGOs in Cyprus is to protect the basic rights of migrants in terms of regularization and labour disputes. Lack of funding and understaffing, however, restrict the activities of many NGOs. It is worth noting that the promotion of encouraging conditions for civic participation such as foreigners/immigrant committees, quotas and subsidies to ethnic organizations have not been at the top of their agendas. Over recent years, some migrant support initiatives have developed, but the sector remains small and the media do not always give it the space and attention it requires.

Some public awareness campaigns and discussions have taken place, aimed at disseminating information about the harmonization process and the changes made in the field of non-discrimination. These, however, have not gone beyond the anti-racism discourse and into the sphere of promoting civic participation (see Trimikliniotis and Demetriou, 2005).

The institutional framework

The right to freedom of association and membership in trade unions is guaranteed by the Constitution and the laws on trade unions. Although the insistence of trade unions that upon entry to Cyprus, migrant workers ought to enjoy the same rights as Cypriot workers is reflected in the 'Criteria', in practice there are violations of the rights of migrant workers, particularly in sectors that are not unionized. Complaints of non-compliance by employers are regularly filed with the Ombudsman's office (see Trimikliniotis, 1999; ECRI Reports, 2001, 2005; Trimikliniotis and Pantelides, 2003).

While in certain unions the percentage of migrant workers is very high,[16] there are no third-country nationals elected to the leadership of any trade union. This presumably reflects the discouragement they feel because of the short-term nature of their stay in Cyprus.

A highly controversial clause has found its way into the specimen agreement which some migrant workers applying for a work permit in Cyprus are requested to sign. This clause expressly prohibits the political participation of migrant workers and is often used by employers to prevent migrant employees from becoming members of a trade union, thus arbitrarily classifying trade unionism as a 'political activity'. The Cypriot Constitution grants the right of political participation and the right to be a member of a trade union to all, citizens and non-citizens alike, rendering the said contractual provision unconstitutional. However, this is hardly ever brought to the attention of

---

16   More than half of the members of SEGDAMELIN-PEO (agricultural and port workers) are migrants; more than one-third of the construction workers of PEO are also migrants; and the same is true for about one-third of SYKSKA-PEO (tourism trade union); one in six of SEMMIK-PEO (metal and wood workers union); one in six in SEVETTYK (clothing, commerce and trade workers and nurses).

the migrant applying for a work permit and if and when a migrant discovers the unconstitutional dimension of this provision, the cost of pursuing such a case through the courts is probably higher than the benefit it will bring. The Ombudsman issued a recommendation, pursuant to a complaint, criticizing the aforementioned contractual condition. This recommendation, however, has yet to be complied with by the authorities.

Another important dimension of Cyprus' accession to the EU is the anti-discrimination laws purporting to transpose Directives 2000/43/EC and 2000/78/EC.[17] However, in order for the new rights and procedures to have any impact on the situation of migrants, a certain degree of awareness, literacy and knowledge of Greek are necessary, which are lacking at the moment. In the case of recourse to the courts, money and time are also needed. Besides, as foreseen in the Directives, these laws have no application in issues relating to entry visas and work permits of third-country nationals in Cyprus, where discriminatory treatment continues to be widely practised.

Public and media discourses on migration

There is a regular pattern, largely media generated, highlighting the 'negative' social consequences of the presence of migrants in Cyprus, the dangers from 'excessive numbers', the 'floods', 'hordes' or 'waves' of migrants who are allegedly just waiting for the opportunity to 'move in' and exploit the opportunities that are available to them (work, social welfare, education and so on). Studies show that such patterns have repeatedly emerged since 1990 (Trimikliniotis, 1999, 2001, 2005b; Harakis et al., 2005). In recent years, the ghettoization and generally poor accommodation of migrants has attracted a lot of public comments. Some have been critical of the authorities and others have had racist connotations. For instance, whilst in 2004 the Mayor of Limassol highlighted the problem of the impoverished ghettoes of migrants and called on the state to recognize the contribution of migrants to Cypriot society and the economy, in 2005 the Mayor of Nicosia told the press that the accommodation conditions of migrants 'downgrade' the city. This statement attracted criticisms from the national Equality Body and the Commission on Journalistic Ethics, who issued reports on the matter.

Public discourse on migration is frequently connected with unemployment, 'welfare chauvinism' and talk of 'job stealing'. This was particularly the case after 1990, with the change of migration policy. At the time, a xenophobic attitude was adopted mainly by trade unions and individual politicians (see Trimikliniotis, 2005b) connecting the inflow of migrant workers to the 'rise' in unemployment among Cypriots. In addition, the government's social welfare department (Ergatiko Vima 8 September 1993) has experienced 'concern' about the 'social problems resulting from the presence of foreign workers', such as marriages of convenience in order to secure the right to stay in Cyprus, the 'suffering of underage children as a result', as well as 'affairs mainly between Cypriot men and female workers' many of which lead to 'the break-up of marriages'.[18]

Connections are also made in some press articles between migrants and disease or crisis. Headlines have appeared with phrases such as 'Foreign workers are a real cancer' or referring to undocumented workers as a 'gangrene', a 'plague' or a 'headache'.

Extensive references are also made to the country's size and its capacity to integrate migrants. 'Cyprus is too small to absorb the current number of foreign workers' is a phrase often heard in

---

17   The Equal Treatment (Racial or Ethnic Origin) Law (2004) No. 59 1) / 2004 (31/01/03); the Combating of Racial and some other Forms of Discrimination (Commissioner) Law No. 42 1) / 2004 (19/03/04) (See Trimikliniotis, 2005a).

18   In reply to questions by journalists, the government's Social Welfare Department 'expressed concern' about such cases (Ergatiko Vima 08/09/93).

public discourse. The social paradigm on which this statement rests is derived from the 'host-immigrant' model theory, according to which migrant workers are considered a 'threat' to the fabric of society.

Moreover, immigration is frequently associated with the Cyprus problem. The argument often invoked to justify the restrictive immigration policies is that Cyprus is semi-occupied by the Turkish army, its 'national survival' is under threat and the settlement of foreigners must be restricted so that its demographic character is not altered. This is intended to be juxtaposed to Turkey's policy of encouraging the settlement of Turkish nationals in the occupied north of Cyprus, the number of whom by now far exceeds that of the local population, thereby rendering the resolution of the 40-year-old conflict even more complicated than it was at first.

Closely connected with this is the perceived tension between national culture and heritage on the one hand, and 'alien cultures and religions' on the other. The concern with migrants as 'carriers of different attitudes, principles and values', who have the potential to 'influence social institutions', is a widespread notion. This is marked by a failure to contextualize the issue within the current social reality of globalization and multiculturalism.

The 'connection' between immigration and criminality is equally one of the media's favourite themes, also used by populist, right-wing or ethnonationalist politicians and the police. This practice has been repeatedly criticized by the national Equality Body. The media often record such statements made by politicians or the police without criticizing their underlying message and usually accompany the text with photos of dark-skinned persons in handcuffs, thereby reinforcing the connection.

Undocumented workers or illegal immigrants are frequently the subject of media reports which, though in some cases sympathetic, generally tend to portray them as a menace. This is in line with the view often expressed by the trade unions and the authorities. A conclusion that may safely be drawn is that the media tend to be sympathetic when covering heart-breaking stories of individual migrants and less sympathetic or even at times xenophobic when they refer to migrants as a group or a section.

Finally, a small number of media reports started appearing, mostly following Cyprus' accession to the EU, in which the ill-treatment of migrants by their employers and by the police was highlighted. These reports are often merely recording statements to that effect made by the National Equality Body, NGOs and international bodies such as ECRI and UNHCR.

It may generally be argued that left-wing and liberal journalists and politicians take a more sympathetic view of migrants and migration, although it is impossible to generalize. The discourse of the right-wing trade union SEK has generally been more xenophobic than that of the left wing trade union PEO, whose reservations were more focused on the alleged negative employment and welfare impact. Nonetheless, before 1995 PEO also used phrases such as 'the danger of alien cultures' and blamed immigration for the rise in unemployment among locals. Over the years, and particularly following Cyprus' accession to the EU, discourses have become a little milder and less xenophobic, as social partners began to accept that immigration is an inevitable and, in some respects, necessary reality. Left-wing trade union PEO, the employers' union OEV and in some contexts right-wing trade union SEK now acknowledge that there is no connection between immigration and unemployment amongst Cypriots. The view publicly expressed by the Ministry of Labour and the other social partners continues to connect immigration with unemployment, often invoking studies which are not made publicly available. However, references to 'alien cultures' have been toned down.

Concluding remarks

Since 1989, Cyprus, a country divided by ethnic conflict, has moved from being a country of emigration to one of immigration. It remains a largely racist and xenophobic society and at a structural, institutional and political level, vital changes are required to address this problem. Third-country migrants are routinely dehumanized and are reduced to mere economic instruments performing menial tasks that Cypriots will not perform. Also, migrants from acceding countries and EU countries are now very much part of the labour force in society at large. The educational system has not been able to properly integrate and meet the needs of an increasingly multicultural society, as it is by design an ethnocentric system (Trimikliniotis, 2004).

To discuss the integration and civic participation of migrants requires a serious change in the whole way in which migrants are perceived and structurally located in Cypriot society. In particular, it requires a radical reform of the current system: the immigration model for migrants ought to shift from the short-term temporary model to a policy of granting long-term status to migrants who have a vested interest in adapting and producing in Cypriot society. At policy level, the whole approach to immigration policy must break away from the ideology of 'control' and, in particular, border control and move towards a more proactive and positive approach towards immigrants and immigration. The basis of the model of reception of migrant workers ought to be based on a multi-cultural model that promotes dialogue, equality, belonging and respect for difference.

Of course, Cypriot society is undergoing an economic, social and political transformation. Following EU accession, it is rapidly becoming increasingly 'Europeanized'. In addition, the opening-up in 2003 of the sealed checkpoints dividing north and south has brought Cypriot society into contact with the other ethnic community which lived so close and yet so far apart for over 40 years. Racism and exclusion in Cyprus requires comprehensive measures for institutional reform, as well as a re-working of the political and ideological discourses that define the 'nation', citizenship and 'belonging'. Moreover, accession to the EU should be seen as a challenge to improve, modernize and question policies, institutions and practices which are in need of reform. Rather than viewing the harmonization with the EU merely as a technocratic process, it should be approached as a challenge in order to be able to move forward, particularly when it comes to matters that affect the lives of vulnerable groups in society. In this sense, harmonization must be seen in the broader context of tackling intolerance, bringing about social equality, participation, solidarity and understanding to enhance the best resources of Cypriot society and its people, including its migrants.

References

Anthias, F. and Lazarides, G. (1999), 'Introduction', in Anthias, F. and Lazarides, G. (eds) *Into the Margins: Exclusion and Migration in Southern Europe*. Avebury: Aldershot.

ECRI (2001) (European Commission against Racism and Intolerance), *Second Report on Cyprus*. Strasbourg: Council of Europe.

ECRI (2005) (European Commission against Racism and Intolerance), *Third Report on Cyprus*. Strasbourg: Council of Europe.

Harakis, K. et al. (2005), *Αντικοινωνική Συμπεριφορά των Νέων στην Κύπρο: Ρατσιστικές Τάσεις* [Anti-social Behaviour of Youth in Cyprus and Racist Trends]. Athens: Sakkoulas.

Matsis, S. and Charalambous, A. (1993), 'The Demand and Supply Dimensions of the Labour Market: The Issue of Foreign Labour' in Demetriades, E.I., Khoury, N.F. and Matsis, S. (eds)

Labour Utilization and Income Distribution in Cyprus, 23–54. Department of Statistics and Research, Nicosia: Ministry of Finance, Cyprus.

Planning Bureau (1989), *Study on Labour Shortage: A Note on Importing Labour from Abroad*, September 1989, Nicosia.

Trimikliniotis, N. (1999), 'Racism and New Migration to Cyprus: The Racialisation of Migrant Workers', in Anthias, F. and Lazarides, G. (eds) *Into the Margins: Exclusion and Migration in Southern Europe*. Avebury: Aldershot.

Trimikliniotis, N. (2001), 'Europeanisation and Modernisation: Locating Cyprus in the Southern European Context', *The Cyprus Review*, **13**(2), Autumn 2001, 47–74.

Trimikliniotis, N. (2004), 'Mapping Discriminatory Landscapes: Ethnic Discrimination in a Divided Education System', *The Cyprus Review*, **16**(1), Spring 2004, 53–86.

Trimikliniotis, N. and Pantelides, P. (2003), 'Mapping Discriminatory Landscapes in the Labour Market', *The Cyprus Review*, **15**(1), Spring 2003.

Trimikliniotis, N. (2005b), 'Socio-political Developments and Impacts – Cyprus Report', Workpackage 5, *The European Dilemma: Institutional Patterns and the Politics of 'Racial' Discrimination*, Research Project Xenophob, EU Fifth Framework Programme 2002–2005.

Trimikliniotis, N. (2006), 'Nationality and Citizenship in Cyprus Since 1945: Communal Citizenship, Gendered Nationality and the Adventures of A Post-Colonial Subject in a Divided Country', in Bauböck, R., Perching, B. and Sievers, W. (eds), *Citizenship Policies in the New Europe*, IMISCOE Series. Amsterdam: Amsterdam University Press.

Internet-based references

Trimikliniotis, N. (2005a), Report on Measures to Combat Discrimination in the EU.

Trimikliniotis, N. and Demetriou, C. (2005), 'Active Civic Participation of Immigrants, Cyprus' in POLITIS (ed.) *An Inquiry into the Civic Participation of Naturalised Citizens and Foreign Residents in 25 Countries* (available at http://www.uni-oldenburg.de/politis-europe/download/Cyprus.pdf).

Chapter 5

Czech Republic

Jan Černík

Until the last decade of the twentieth century, the Czech Republic was a country of emigration. Nearly three million Germans were expelled from Czechoslovakia after the Second World War. And during socialism, the country lost approximately 500,000 citizens, even though emigration was illegal. The two main waves of emigration, in 1948 and 1968, were politically and economically motivated as people fled the country's totalitarian regime. Approximately 220,000 Czechs and Slovaks returned to Czechoslovakia after the Second World War. During the late 1940s and 1950s, about 7,000 Bulgarians and 12,000 Greeks settled in the depopulated frontier areas.[1] During the socialist/communist era, immigration mainly took place within the framework of intergovernmental agreements. Indeed, foreign labourers from other socialist countries (Angola, Cuba, Korea, Mongolia and Vietnam) were sent to Czechoslovakia in the 1970s and 1980s.

In the early 1990s, the Czech Republic, along with other countries of Central and Eastern Europe, became part of a buffer zone of international migration from east to west. Democratization and liberalization of political and economic relations brought about a relatively free movement of people. Over a fairly short period, especially in the mid-1990s when migration legislation was liberal and economic relations favoured immigration, many foreigners came to the Czech Republic to work. From the Czech side, the preference was for the short-term, temporary migration of workers into specific segments of the economy. Ethnically selected migration of Czech compatriots from the former Soviet Union in the post-1989 period was welcomed by public opinion and political elites.

While significant emigration was expected, it did not actually take place and, in fact, over the last decade, the Czech Republic has increasingly become a destination country for immigrants and, to a lesser extent, asylum seekers. Finally, Czech migration policy has developed in the context of its EU accession and the need to address current migration challenges.

Major developments in the Czech Republic's immigration policy

The first immigration inflow after 1989 was the return of descendants of Czech emigrants and their family members from neighbouring Ukraine and Belarus. This took place between 1991 and 1993, followed by a second wave of repatriation between 1993 and 2001 from Kazakhstan. An inflow of foreigners from third countries to the Czech Republic increased after the Velvet Revolution when entry into the country was liberalized. The division of the Czechoslovak Federal Republic in 1993 brought about a change in migration. The majority of Slovaks who had permanently settled in the Czech Republic (close to half a million individuals) were granted Czech citizenship. An agreement on free movement between the Czech and Slovak Republics stimulated a new wave of immigration

---

1   Czechoslovakia admitted leftist partisans and their families from northern Greece after the Greek Civil War (1945–1949).

from the Slovak Republic, and these immigrants became the biggest group of permanently settled immigrants in the Czech Republic (Drbohlav, 2004).

Permanent immigration into the Czech Republic gradually gained importance principally because of the country's economic transformation, changing geo-political factors and for cultural reasons.

First, the Czech economy's demand for both skilled and unskilled labour, mainly in the manufacturing and construction sectors, steadily grew. Moreover, given that the Czech Republic had one of the highest per capita incomes in the region of the CEEC, this constituted a significant 'pull' factor for immigrants. In addition, the Czech Republic and the GDR constitute the most western parts of the former Soviet empire. The border with Austria and Germany has attracted transit migrants while the prospect of EU integration played an important role in influencing the patterns of permanent immigration. Moreover, the country's links with other 'post-colonial' countries of the Soviet empire, and its access to Western Europe, determined the patterns of migration trends in Central Europe. Immigrants from the former Soviet Union and Yugoslavia found a similar heritage of socialism in the Czech Republic to the ones which they are familiar with from their countries of origin. The language barrier for immigrants from the aforementioned countries was insignificant, as Russian remained highly useful and the different Slavic languages share many features which make them mutually understandable or, at least, easy to learn. These and other similar cultural features work particularly in favour of Slovak and Polish immigration.

At the same time, the emigration of Czechs to countries of the European Union, and particularly Germany and the United Kingdom, steadily grew in the early 1990s. In 1992 and 1993, between 0.4 per cent and 0.8 per cent of the domestic labour force – 27,000 and 49,000 people respectively – occupied seasonal or commuting jobs in Germany (OECD, 2004). However, the data collected in host countries soon after the year 2000 reveal a rather low number of Czech citizens residing abroad. Based on OECD Statistics, Czech emigration into EU countries appears to be one of the lowest among the ten countries of Central and Eastern Europe (OECD, 2004).

Czech migration policy

Czech migration policy and practice were more improvisational than planned during the 1990s. 'At least until 1999, the policy had been concerned with measures within a more or less static model. Unambiguously, passive attitudes prevailed over the active ones' (Drbohlav, 2004, p. 75). The Czech Republic was going through the complicated process of disintegration and economic and political transformation. The process of accession to the European Union gradually influenced and prioritized the objectives of Czech migration policy. These included combating illegal migration, defining a comprehensive asylum policy and harmonizing migration policies with the EU's common standards. The institutional and legal harmonization of the Czech Republic with the EU was a formative element of Czech migration policy. In January 2000, a key Act came into force, Act No. 326/1999 Coll. on the Residence of Aliens in the Territory of the Czech Republic. The new Act on the Residence of Aliens changed the migration environment, as it established administrative control of the residence of foreigners, control of the administration of migration itself, and the harmonization of Czech migration law with the legal conventions of European countries. A result of this new Act was both tougher control and administrative restrictions for both first-time migrants and foreigners residing in the territory of the republic. As a result of the new Act, a significant group of immigrants was rendered illegal, and the administrative process for both migrants and the police became increasingly overloaded. This was complemented by the regulation of visa policy according to the standard regime in the EU countries (visa regimes towards the Ukraine, Russia and other countries of the former USSR) and specific laws regulating the employment and entrepreneurial activities of foreigners. In 2004, the amendment of Act No. 325/1999 Coll. on Asylum restricted the employment of asylum seekers during the first year of the procedure.

The political framework for the integration of foreigners in the Czech Republic was established by the *Concept on the Integration of Foreigners* (hereinafter Concept), a document that the Czech Government endorsed on 11 December 2000.[2] The Minister of the Interior was, until 2003, entrusted with co-ordinating and supervising activities aimed at achieving these aims. Moreover, an advisory body called the 'Committee of the Ministry of Interior for the preparation and implementation of the policy of the government of the Czech Republic in the area of integration of foreigners and the inter-community development' (henceforth Committee) was established. Representatives of the Czech Government, the civil sector, the academic community and the territorial administration took part in the Committee. In accordance with the government's decision No. 126 of 11 February 2004, the co-ordination of the implementation of the Concept was transferred to the Ministry of Labour and Social Affairs (MoLSA) and a MoLSA Committee was formed. The Ministries that took part in the Committee were responsible for developing integration policies for the period 2004–2006 and for drafting the *Situation Analysis and the Status of Foreigners*. The Updated Concept on immigrant integration (approved in 2006) emphasizes an individual – rather than group – approach to the integration of foreigners. The main priorities are economic self-sufficiency, knowledge of the Czech language, relationship with the majority population, and the orientation of foreigners in the host society.

Even before 1 May 2004 (date of accession to the European Union), the Czech Republic had already accepted a number of harmonizing legislative changes affecting both foreigners' residency conditions within its territory and the institutional framework for their integration. A pilot project entitled *Active Selection of Qualified Foreign Workers* was also developed as part of the Czech Republic's immigration policy. It is a recruitment instrument similar to the so-called Quebec System that supports foreign experts immigrating to the Czech Republic along with their families. It also gives them the opportunity to obtain a permanent residence permit within a considerably shorter period than that usually required (only two-and-a-half years). The applicant has to either be a citizen of Belarus, Bulgaria, Canada, Croatia, Kazakhstan, Moldova, Serbia and Montenegro or Ukraine, or a graduate from a university or tertiary education institution in the Czech Republic irrespective of nationality. It also provides a valid visa for over 90 days for the purpose of employment or a long-term residence permit for the purpose of employment and a work permit in the Czech Republic.

The Ministry of the Interior also regulates projects directed at a group of potential migrants from Ukraine, Moldova, Georgia and Armenia. The aim of these projects is to prevent illegal migration by improving human capital and life conditions of target groups or migratory counselling services.[3]

The first half of the 1990s is characterized by a period of *laissez-faire* migration policy. The inflow of migrants occurred through a visa-free regime with former USSR and Balkan countries. During that period, an institutional framework was established for distinctive groups of migrants such as asylum seekers and ethnic Czechs from Eastern Europe and Asia. The entry of the Czech Republic into the European Union structures, and the need to regulate migration inflow, brought about the emergence of a migration policy. This was marked by increasing state control over

---

2   Some elements of the integration policy were established in the late nineties, but it was rather more technical or organizational issues regarding the settlement of compatriots and recognized refugees. The political framework of the integration of foreigners was outlined in the 'Principles of the Concept of Integration of Foreigners' in 1999.

3   These projects are part of the Czech Government's programme of international development cooperation.

migration, and resulted in the introduction of a restrictive alien and asylum law in 2000. Currently, citizens of third countries are required to apply for a 90-day-and-over visa at the Czech embassy in their home country for purposes of family unification, employment and entrepreneurship. This visa type is valid for one year. During their stay in the Czech Republic, migrants might request a permit of long-term residence at their place of residence. This legal status is more flexible. It allows a change of purpose of stay and it is possible to obtain the permit for a duration of two years. Permanent residence also translates into the enjoyment of similar rights to Czech citizens. Its validity is for five years.[4]

The current state of the migration policy is still influenced by the application of the legal norms of the European Union. Indeed, particular concepts of national migration policy are formulated into governmental declarations such as integration policy, or into a programme of active immigration policy.

Naturalization

The naturalization of foreigners is regulated by the Act on Acquiring and Losing Czech Citizenship (No. 40/1993). It does not allow for double citizenship apart from in exceptional cases (for instance Slovakia). In the Czech Republic, the right of children to acquire citizenship is governed by the principle of *jus sanguinis*. Additionally, knowledge of the Czech language is required.

There is no right to receive citizenship through the process of naturalization.[5] A foreigner can apply for Czech citizenship after five years of permanent residence in the Czech Republic. According to the recent Alien law, the permit for granting permanent residence status to a foreigner can be obtained after ten years of residence under a long-term visa have been completed. This results in a 15-year period preceding the application for citizenship. This length of time required was criticized by NGOs and experts. Nowadays, the Council Directive 2003/109/EC on long-term residents sets the period for granting permanent residence status in the Czech Republic at five years. This implies a ten-year waiting period for the right to request Czech citizenship.

Between 2001 and 2005 Czech citizenship was granted to 15,870 people, of whom 9,691 had Slovak citizenship. Former citizens of Czechoslovakia and their descendants have privileged access to Czech citizenship. They receive citizenship (after a five-year waiting period) by merely declaring that they wish to become Czech citizens, rather than having to go through the lengthy administrative process that non-former Czechoslovakia citizens must go through to obtain Czech citizenship.

The immigrant population in the Czech Republic: main demographic and social features

The period of 'transition' in the Czech Republic was characterized by transit migration from Eastern Europe and Asia to the EU countries. The Czech Republic has gradually become the most exposed country in terms of immigration rates in the region of the CEEC (Wallace and Stola, 2001; Drbohlav, 2004; OECD, 2004).[6] As Table 5.1 shows, the total number of foreigners legally residing

---

4   Paradoxically, permanent residents in the Czech Republic from third countries have easier access to labour markets than they would in member countries of the EU who still have restricted employment for citizens of the new Member States [especially Germany, Austria, and others].

5   But former citizens of Czechoslovakia received Czech citizenship by simply declaring their nationality/citizenship to the appropriate authorities.

6   The Czech Republic has the highest immigration growth rate in a sample of selected countries of the OECD. Immigrant population increased by 18 per cent between 1990 and 2002 (OECD, 2005, p. 43).

in the Czech Republic on 30 June 2006 is 295,955 – or approximately 2.5 per cent of the total population. One third of these are foreigners living in the Czech Republic on the basis of family reunification, and two-thirds are economic migrants. Estimates of figures of illegal migrants vary between 100,000 and 200,000 individuals.

Table 5.1   Foreigners in the Czech Republic on 30 June 2006

Citizenship	Total	Permanent residence
Total	295,955	125,849
Ukraine	93,466	20,201
Slovakia	54,201	21,520
Vietnam	38,566	28,248
Poland	18,386	11,341
Russian Federation	16,910	7,148
Germany	8,116	4,099
Moldova	5,352	973
Bulgaria	4,610	2,553
United States	3,928	2,134
China	3,790	1,771

Source: Directorate of Alien and Border Police, Ministry of the Interior

The Czech Republic has gradually become a new country of immigration, especially for people from the former socialist world. For migrants from countries of the Far East, the USA and South Asia, the Czech Republic remains a country of transit or of temporary stay.

The most favoured migratory destination is the capital city, Prague (up to 4 per cent of the total population), and its surrounding regions. Important migratory destinations are regional capitals (Karlovy Vary, Brno, Plzeň and Ostrava).

Ukrainians

The circular migration of workers from Ukraine proved to be the most dynamic and visible pattern of migration into the Czech Republic in the early 1990s. The number of Ukrainian citizens residing in the Czech Republic dramatically increased. In 1996, when visa applications were accepted for business reasons rather than just for labour, a new trend began. From 1996, entry to the Czech labour market became noticeably easier for migrants as shareholders of formal entrepreneurial entities such as cooperatives or trading companies. The rising trend of Ukrainians arriving in the Czech Republic continued between 1997 and 1999 with an increase from 43,402 to 65,883 persons. Ukrainians work mainly in the construction industry, but a significantly growing percentage of Ukrainian women have started to work in manufacturing and agriculture. These workers periodically return to Ukraine, and they usually use their income from the Czech Republic to increase their standard of living at home (Uherek et al., 2006). The pattern of circular migration of Ukrainians also involves illegal or quasi-legal regimes of migration, provided by an informal network (Černík, 2006). In any case, only 17 per cent of Ukrainian citizens hold permits of permanent residence in the Czech Republic.

Vietnamese

Vietnamese 'socialist guest workers' and students (approximately 23,000 in the mid-1980s) have remained in the Czech Republic despite the directive for temporary immigration of Vietnamese and the expensive return programme provided by the Czechoslovak Government in the early 1990s. Vietnamese from the former GDR, Vietnam and CIS countries have found a profitable economic niche in the Czech Republic (Brouček, 2004; Kocourek, 2004). They were pulled by market opportunities unleashed in the first half of the 1990s by the hunger for consumer goods felt by the post-socialist society and by the cross-border petty-trade of cigarettes and alcohol with Germany and Austria. The number of Vietnamese has been increasing because of the high birth rate among the immigrant community, as well as their continuous immigration into the Czech Republic (the total figure was 23,924 in 2001 and 34,179 in 2004). Indeed, Vietnamese children constitute an important second generation of immigrants in the Czech Republic. Recently, the Vietnamese have been undergoing a radical cultural change, such as the rapid loss of their native language amongst the second generation, and the fragmentation of the closed community.

Russians

Citizens of Russia represent rather different type of foreign entrepreneurs in the Czech Republic. The number of Russian citizens has been constantly increasing, except in the year 2000, when a visa regime between Russia and the Czech Republic was put in place. The Russians who come to the Czech Republic are mostly economic elites or groups from the higher middle strata of Russian society. They are pulled by the political stability and an environment which favours investment. The Russian population is concentrated in Prague and Karlovy Vary, a spa city in the western part of the Czech Republic, where they invest in hotel facilities and services. What is remarkable is the low rate of employment amongst Russians residing in the Czech Republic. Only 2,689 of the 15,032 citizens of the Russian Federation were employed or held a trade licence in the Czech Republic in 2004. This means that just 18 per cent of Russians actually work in the Czech Republic. The rest are family members or stakeholders. It should also be noted that an important group of Russian citizens in the Czech Republic are Chechen refugees or asylum seekers.

Balkans

Migration from the former Yugoslavia started relatively early with people escaping the civil war and the consequent economic struggle characterizing the region in the first half of the 1990s. Many young and skilled people left Serbia because of their dissatisfaction with limited social mobility caused by the Mafia-style regime of Slobodan Milošević and economic sanctions imposed by the United Nations. A significant immigration group is from Bulgaria.

Chinese

They began arriving in Czechoslovakia via Hungary in 1992 and 1993 (Moore-Mezlíková, 2003; Obuchová, 2003). The Czech Republic represented *terra incognita* for them. For many of the settled Chinese, the Czech Republic became the first transition country in their plans for economic expansion towards the rest of Europe. Many of the Chinese residing in the Czech Republic were already entrepreneurs engaged in international trade between China, Hungary and Russia. One third of them held permanent resident permits. The number of Chinese citizens who settled in the Czech Republic was relatively stable and has been decreasing. The figures of illegal and asylum migration for the Chinese have been constantly on the rise because Central Europe has become an important transit zone on the Russian route to Western Europe.

Asylum seekers

The number of asylum seekers remained stable until 1997. Up until then approximately 2,000 applicants requested asylum each year. From 1997, the figure increased rapidly and reached its peak in 2001 with more than 18,000 applicants. By 2001, the Czech Republic had become the ninth most popular destination in Europe for asylum seekers, and the eleventh in the world.

Since February 2002, when the amendment of the Act on Asylum entered into force, the number of applications has fallen by approximately 50 per cent. In December 2004, 1,623 persons held asylum status in the Czech Republic. They are groups of people originating from the former Soviet Union and Eastern Europe.

Illegal migrants

Estimates of illegal migrants in the Czech Republic vary between 100,000 and 200,000. According to an analysis by Drbohlav, it is estimated that approximately 165,000 irregular migrants are active in the Czech labour market and, in addition to these, another 30,000 dependants are estimated to be living in the Czech Republic (Drbohlav, 2004).

Immigrant rights and participation in public life: issues of immigrant integration

The civic participation of migrants is a relatively new issue for Czech society. On the one hand, there is the integration strategy implemented in 2000 and regulated by the *Concept of integration of foreigners in the territory of the Czech Republic*, which encourages foreigners' civic participation. On the other hand, the real practices are quite different and effective solutions of the problems of civic and political participation of migrants are still lacking. Czech integration policy has been implemented since 2000, but the relatively short period of its implementation, among other factors, accounts for the wide gap still existing between policy and practice. Concept, as a key document, gives attention to the political participation of foreigners. In essence, the public administration has prepared political instruments fashioned on the model of the recommendations drawn up by the Council of Europe or other international institutions.

Nonetheless, the process of implementing policy into practice has been repeatedly paralysed by old-fashioned and restrictive legislative norms, as well as by the conservative character of state institutions. The lack of political motivation is (de)forming the institutional nature of civic participation of immigrants in the Czech Republic. For most of the decision-makers, integration issues are still administrative tasks which are implicitly covered by the European Union. This perception is also reflected in the restrictive policy of naturalization in the Czech Republic. Furthermore, citizenship is used as a restrictive measure, framing the key legal norms for civic and political participation for so called 'third-country' nationals. The lack of political motivation is also reflected in rather weak financial support for integration programmes.

The central issue is the response of immigrants to specific structural opportunities for their participation in public life put in place by state institutions and other administrative entities. This includes 'gatekeepers' of the political system, such as trade unions, the NGO sector, political parties, ethnic and religious organizations and various forms of affirmative action. The main characteristics of the institutional setting and civic participation of immigrants in the Czech

Republic are centralization, the NGO sector, a limited number of ethnic associations for activities in cultural affairs, and a disproportion between the participation of naturalized immigrants and that of foreigners.

The lack of systemic linkage of Czech integration policy between central institutions and regional or local gatekeepers of immigrants' participation undermines the possibility of large-scale participation. A limited attempt was made by establishing the District Advisory Councils for the Integration of Foreigners in 2001. These Councils would have on their board foreigners, local NGO networks and district officials. The administrative level of district was rejected, however, during a reform of state administration in 2002. The necessity of the systemic linkage between levels of public administration within the framework of Czech integration policy is included in the Updated Concept of immigrant integration.[7]

Currently, the formal direct participation of immigrants in the democratic process takes place at the level of central state institutions, where some foreigners and their supporting institutions are lobbying for their concerns. The Committee for the Rights of Foreigners was established under the Czech Government's Council for Human Rights. Several immigrants' representatives participate in the initiatives of this committee as representatives of the NGO sector. The importance of the Council lies in its official mandate to comment on new or changed legislation. The Committee is a useful platform for communication between NGOs and state bodies. The Council also has the authority to push for legal improvements. For instance, the Committee has been negotiating to push through legal measures which would grant immigrants the right to vote in municipal elections. The Committee formulates evaluations and recommendations which are directed to the competent state bodies and discusses concrete causes for the violation of the rights of foreigners. Representatives of the Ministries are obliged to explain and justify the steps taken by state institutions.

The second significant forum is the Council for the Integration of Foreigners, at the Ministry · of Labour and Social Affairs [MoLSA]. This is a recently established policy-making board at governmental level. The Council for Integration is also a body for cooperation and implementation of the Czech integration policy across all levels of public administration. Here, several organizations more or less voice migrants' concerns. Nevertheless, the NGO sector remains more influential in voicing the concerns of immigrants.

The Committee at the Council for Human Rights is influential in its direct functional feedback to legislative and administrative practice, but is unable to influence municipal and regional administrative practice, since it is focused at government level.

Functional limitations (in the broad sense of civic participation) are given by their focus on an actual public administration at the highest level (national legislation and administrative practice of governmental bodies). The Council at MoLSA has an indirect influence on further improving the situation of immigrants. Members participate in the development of the political documents of the government of the Czech Republic. The co-ordination role of the Council at MoLSA represents two important aspects: first, policy-making at the level of state executive institutions and, second, interconnection with European structures. Both the 'gateways' mentioned could be very important for the promotion of migrants' civic participation. Nevertheless, in practice, their impact is rather weak, indirect and selective, as only very few selected foreigners are engaged in the policy-making process.

The Department for Migration and Integration of Foreigners at MoLSA has been communicating with NGOs and religious societies, which play a substantial role in defending the rights and interests of foreigners at the local level. As mentioned above, the implementation of foreigners'

---

7   The Updated Concept formalizes existing informal links as further modes of co-operation between levels of governance in the Czech Republic.

integration is not a mandatory task for public administration at the regional and local levels. The model of implementation of the Czech integration policy which is outlined has been spreading at the regional and local levels in recent years. NGOs are the main implementers here.

Currently, the measures taken by the state result in a high degree of centralism and paternalism on behalf of 'the gatekeepers'. A similar situation could be detected in Germany in the 1970s, where immigrants were objectified. A similarity with the German example can be observed in the efforts to create an umbrella organization of foreigners. The establishment of an umbrella organization of immigrants is under way now, and its particular effects suggest ways of uniting the voices of immigrants through journals, conferences, round tables and so on.

There is no visible sign of the inclusion of immigrants in the political mainstream of the Czech Republic. In brief, the two most important points are that foreigners from non-EU countries do not have the right to vote at any level and, with a few exceptions, foreigners have no access to elected or appointed functions. The right to vote for third-country nationals is blocked by two Acts regulating the Election to Municipalities and the Municipal Administration. According to Uhl (2003) there is an undifferentiated approach to foreigner's political and other public participation in the Czech Republic. Uhl points out that the 'mere fact of the possibility to command or not to command political rights does not depend on any type of residence permit' (Uhl, 2003, p. 85).

The civic participation of immigrants through trade unions is undermined by a restrictive labour law against foreigners. These obstacles force migrants to practise forms of quasi-legal opportunities to work. Despite their powerful status, trade unions mostly limit their activities for migrants to several small-scale projects focused on the publication and dissemination of information leaflets.

The Ministry of Culture has a specific programme of subsidies for ethnic minorities, financed in part from the state budget. As a result, cultural affairs are the focus of immigration associations. Conditions of the migration programme differentiate two types of subsidized activities. The first includes, among others, multicultural and multiethnic events, film and music festivals. The second involves cultural issues of a particular community, journals, dance classes and others. The most active associations are Armenian, Vietnamese, Ukrainian, Bulgarian and Russian.

The limited number of sources of finance determines the character of activities supported. Thus, for example, important issues such as education, social assistance and legal counselling do not match the aims of most subsidy programmes.[8] The city mayors have adopted the same approach and support similar activities within the framework of the subsidy programmes for national minorities.[9]

Foreigners do not have rights as ethnic and national minorities in the Czech Republic. The Czech minority law operates with the term national minority, which is defined as a 'community of citizens of the Czech Republic who are distinguished from other citizens usually by common ethnic origin, culture and traditions. They are a numerical minority of the population and they

---

8   The subsidy programmes for the integration of foreigners exist within the framework of the state budget (this is separate from the subsidies for national minorities).

9   The legal act on the rights of members of national minorities obliges the state to provide subsidies in order to sustain the culture, traditions and languages of the national minorities. The subsidies are granted to radio and television broadcasting in the respective languages of the minorities. The minority law also obliges local municipalities (with up to ten per cent minority inhabitants) and regional governments (with up to five per cent minority inhabitants) to create councils for national minorities. The councils have to consist of a minimum of half of the representatives of the national minorities. The municipal council is an initiating and control organ and its function is consultative. The regional council will have a co-coordinating role. At the governmental level there is a council for national minorities, which consists of representatives of recently recognized national minorities (Slovaks, Germans, Poles, Roma, Bulgarians, Croats, Hungarians, Ruthenians, Russians, Greeks and Ukrainians).

declare their will to be recognized as a national minority' (Legal Act No. 273/2001 Col.). Civic and political rights are granted to the state-recognized national minorities. Thus, the structure for the pursuit of political and civic participation of national minorities is useful for the pursuit of the political and civic participation of foreigners. Several ethnic organizations cover non-citizen members of communities (despite the narrow definition of national minorities). Some Ukrainian, Bulgarian, and Russian organizations try to represent both citizens and foreigners in the fields assigned by the minorities' law.

In many regards, Czech minority policy and law have set preconditions for the creation of structural opportunities for the civic participation of immigrants although contemporary practice has reproduced the gap between naturalized members of minorities and immigrants from third countries. The forming of minorities by immigrants from third countries is examined in the following two parts.

The resulting situation is the practice of a double standard approach to ethnic communities. One aspect is the 'ethnic multiculturalism' of the Czech minority policy towards institutionalized national minorities. The second is the exclusion of immigrant groups from civic rights. Czech minority policy hangs between two contradictions: the declared concepts of multiculturalism and certain segregating effects of citizenship in the Czech legal framework. The cultural rights of some groups have doubled, namely in cases of concurrent members of institutionalized national minorities and citizens of EU countries.[10] On the other hand, the cultural rights of certain groups of immigrants who are neither EU citizens nor members of recognized national minorities are restricted. Lastly, the groups which consist of both citizens of the Czech Republic and immigrants from third countries are split by internal conflicts. The minorities' policy de facto segregates distinctive groups of one ethnic background, namely the naturalized cultural elite, from vital strata of immigrants.[11]

Public and media discourses on migration

Recent public discussions on issues related to migration can be divided into four distinct categories. First, the refugees. Second, the demographic decline of the autochthonous population of the Czech Republic and the economic needs of the labour market. Third, the illegal aspects of migration and, fourth, the integration of foreigners. In the Czech media, commentaries and reports on international events relating to migration, such as the crisis in Darfur, the escalating of ethnic/religion tensions in the Netherlands, or troubles in French suburbs, have been emerging. The process of the construction of a European asylum and immigration policy is also closely observed by several Czech journalists. The xenophobic element appears in the propaganda of several extreme right-wing parties and it is mostly directed towards Roma people. 'Islamophobia' is also surfacing in the Czech media. Several misguided articles describe the presence of a small and unproblematic Muslim population, or tourists from Arab countries, in the Czech Republic in the context of global terrorism.

The issues faced by asylum seekers have dominated migration in the media since the beginning of the 2000s. Now, the issue of asylum has become more distinguished from other migration themes in the Czech media. Many journalists commented on the influx of Chechen refugees in

---

10   The Act on National Minorities guarantees the same rights for EU citizens as the new School Act.

11   The example of an intra-ethnic segregating effect of the double-faced policy could be illustrated with the civic participation of Ukrainians in the Czech Republic. It seems to demonstrate a kind of gap – of cultural misunderstanding – between naturalized minorities and the immigrant community: representatives of national minorities are mainly naturalized intellectuals or sometimes elderly people, who are often not successful in finding a visible response to their activities from their migratory compatriots.

the spring of 2003. It represented the last mass flow of refugees into the Czech Republic, and it was preceded by an inflow of Georgian and Armenian asylum seekers. The war in Chechnya and its aftermath have become focal themes of several journalists. Relatively large-scale protests were organized in support of the Chechen refugees and against the war in Chechnya. The introduction of asylum seekers into camps and local communities is constantly presented in the media as a 'typical' migration issue. Since accession to the EU, the issue of asylum has been withering away in the media. Currently, the central issue is the health care system for asylum seekers in the Czech Republic.

The Czech population is sensitive to issues of criminality or illegality which are associated with international migration. For instance, cases of detection of bands of smugglers or gangs specializing in the trafficking of humans have been publicized. As a result, police activities connected to these cases and presented in the media have been projected by the audience onto all illegal foreign workers. They have greatly contributed to producing ethnic stereotypes of certain groups of immigrants. For instance, Albanians are depicted as drug smugglers, Russians as the Mafia, Ukrainians as illegal workers, and Vietnamese as petty-traders (Karhanová and Kaderka, 2003). The latter group is the target of more detailed reporting, as journalists are concerned with the transformation of the Vietnamese community and its growing second generation.

Both of the themes described above are closely connected with issues of integration. For instance, the Czech President has recently started discussions on the question of 'the rights of immigrants' (Klaus, 2003). Among the concrete issues of integration, the conditions of temporary workers from Ukraine in the Czech Republic have increasingly attracted the attention of the media over the past two years. Journalists write about the discriminatory behaviour of Czech officials, especially that of alien and border police. All of these articles have been written as appeals for the improvement of living and legal conditions of temporary workers in the Czech Republic.

Concluding remarks

The Czech Republic is one of the so-called 'new Member States of the EU.' Following the collapse of the communist regime, Czechoslovakia/the Czech Republic was affected by the turbulent development of migration. That abrupt situation created the need for regulative and control mechanisms which did not exist institutionally. The aim of these mechanisms was to manage migration flows in the Czech Republic as a buffer zone of migration until accession to the EU. European institutions and their legal framework became a useful instrument for the establishment of Czech migration policy. The migration policy was partly a product of ad hoc solutions to particular events or situations. Up until then, the legal framework and institutional practice of migration did not respect the economic concerns of migrants. Because of solid economic growth, the Czech economy faces increasing labour shortages. The gap between labour supply and demand is insignificant in percentage terms and is filled with migrant workers from the Ukraine and other former Soviet Republics. Usually paid much less than Czech workers, Ukrainians or Moldovans help maintain the Czech economy's growth. Despite the economic benefit, these people have only limited opportunities to work legally in the Czech Republic because of administrative measures or rigid bureaucratization and legal barriers. Most labour migrants depend on the services of the informal infrastructure, thereby limiting their civic participation.

The current situation of the country can be compared to the history of the so-called new immigration countries. Third-country migrants have been coming to the Czech Republic with a view to long-term residence or circular labour migration. Despite the considerable development in creating superstructural elements (legislation, administrative practice, government initiatives) at the central level for the integration of foreigners, the implementation of the declared policy has been characterized by considerable shortcomings. Czech migration policy is more coherent regarding asylum or development co-operation with resource countries, but it is more or less incoherent for short-term labour migration or permanent immigration. The Czech population is not explicitly xenophobic, but the incorporation of migrants into public space is blocked by a glass wall of social distance.

References

Brouček, S. (2004), *Integrace Vietnamského etnika v ČR*. Prague: Institute of Ethnology of the ASCR.

Černík, J. (2006), 'Of Clients and Chereps: The Organisational Structures of Ukrainian Labour Migration', in Szczepaniková, A., Čaněk, M. and Grill, J. (eds) *Migration Processes in Central and Eastern Europe: Unpacking the Diversity*. Prague: Multicultural Centre.

Concept of Integration of Foreigners on the Territory of the Czech Republic (2006), Resolution of the Government of the Czech Republic No. 126 (Prague).

Drbohlav, D. (2004), *Migration Trends in Selected EU Applicant Countries*. Vienna: International Organisation for Migration.

Klaus, V. (2003), *Co s přistěhovalci?* Prague: Lidové noviny, 18 January 2003.

Kocourek, J. (2004) 'Vietnamci', in Ezzedine-Lukšíková, P. and Drbohlav, D. (eds) *Integrace cizinců v ČR – Studie arménské, in vietnamské a ukrajinské komunity v Praze a Středočeském kraji*. Prague: IOM.

Uherek, Z. et al. (2006), *Migrace do České republiky, sociální integrace a lokální společnosti v zemích původu*. Prague: Institute of Ethnology of the ASCR.

Wallace, C. and Stola, D. (2001), *Patterns of Migration in Central Europe*. New York: Palgrave.

Internet-based references

Moore-Mezlíková, M. (2003), *Číňané v České republice, 1992–2002: Zrod a formování symbolické komunity*, Prague: Research report for Ministry of Interior (available at http://www.cizinci.cz/publikace-a-vyzkum.shtml?x=496).

Obuchová (2003), *Čínská komunita v České republice 2001*, Prague: Research report for Ministry of Interior (available at http://www.cizinci.cz/publikace-a-vyzkum.shtml?x=115).

OECD (2004), *Trends in International Migration 2003*, Paris: Sopemi.

Moore-Mezlíková, M. (2003), *Číňané v České republice, 1992–2002*.

Karhanová and Kaderka (2003) *Obraz cizinců v médiích*, Prague: Research Report for Ministry of Interior (Prague: Institute of Czech Language), of the ASCR (available at http://www.cizinci.cz/files/clanky/121/Obraz_cizincu_v_mediich.pdf).

Uhl, P. (2003), 'Politická participace cizinců a sdružování v odborových svazech', in *Komparativní studie programu Mig Race, Poradna Pro občanství, občanská a lidská práva*. Prague: Open Society Fund (available at http://www.migraceonline.cz/studie_f.shtml?x=133842).

Chapter 6

Denmark

Marco Goli and Shahamak Rezaei

Issues related to the integration of immigrants have been widely discussed in Denmark since the beginning of the 1970s. But the new millennium brought with it tensions for the Danish public and for Danish politics regarding what is seen by many as 'the failure of integration policy'.

After coming into government in 2001, the new Liberal–Conservative coalition introduced a fundamentally different policy for migration and integration. This new policy created many institutional and administrative changes and affected migration considerably. For instance, not only was there a remarkable reduction in the number of immigrants entering the country, but there was also a decline in the support given to immigrant populations' participation in civic areas. It seems that the scope, content and intensity of the debate, as well as the overall discursive structure and institutional setting, have been undergoing important changes.

Based on empirical evidence and theoretical articulation, this chapter posits a rather cautious hypothesis. Our argument follows that growing religious identification among immigrants and attachment to religious organizations and associations, as well as development of the so called 'Parallel Society'[1] (Rezaei and Goli, 2006) seems to reduce immigrants' overall participation in democratic processes. The empirical challenge would be to determine whether the new Danish policy on migration and integration, together with the dominant discourse in Danish media and public debate, provides the religious and ethnic identification and participation with an attractive mode of civic and political participation among immigrants; whether these are newcomers or 'old' immigrants.

There exists a rather substantial variation in the extent to which immigrant groups are represented in public debate. It appears that the most politically active immigrants at the local and national levels and in the media are individuals who focus on issues related to Islam, or are considered to have Islamic affiliations. Danish policy of contradiction (that is formal openness and substantial closure), especially with regard to substantial inclusion in the concept of 'the Danes', leaves the ground open for non-democratic forces. Below, we will introduce the major developments in Danish immigration policy, the main characteristics of its immigrant population, immigrant participation in different spheres of life and, finally, the public and media discourse with regard to immigration. The structure and content of the following presentation attempt to bring empirical evidence to bear in support of our aforementioned argument.

---

1   In the Danish context the term 'Parallel Society', originally established as an academic empirical term of reference as an 'Ideal Type model' by Rezaei and Goli (2002) refers to 'setting up, following and monitoring alternative standards of behaviour, goals, principles and norms by minorities, specifically ethnic minorities'.

Major developments in immigration policy in Denmark from 1990 onwards

The history of the new immigrants in Denmark began in the late 1960s and early 1970s. Several thousand people mainly from Turkey, Yugoslavia and Pakistan, seeking vacancies at the bottom of the labour market, chasing their dreams of fortune, found their way to 'the country up north'. International and national industry were growing rapidly, the Danish welfare state and the public sector were expanding, the educational system was flourishing, and the willingness of the national labour force to be employed in manual labour jobs was low. Many other structural changes were taking place (Goli, 2002). Immigrant workers could help by filling in the gaps, at least for a while, until the economy could be restructured and adjusted to new circumstances. This conception was a matter of consensus between many actors such as the Danish Government, trade unions, the public and the media in Denmark (Sørensen, 1988).

During the first years of the 1970s, the overall expectation of Danish society, the Danish Government, trade unions, employee organizations and the immigrant population themselves, was that they would eventually return to their countries of origin. They would either do so when new circumstances in the labour market no longer presented a need for them, or when they had saved enough money to improve their life conditions back home (Sørensen, 1988; Goli, 2002). In the meantime, their participation in civic life was extremely poor and limited. They were the unknowns, the strangers.

Shortly after, in the following years of economic recession, immigrants became 'Last hired – first fired'. In the meantime, they had already brought their relatives to Denmark in search of a new life.

Realizing the situation and the sudden unemployment levels among immigrant workers, the Danish Government introduced the first 'immigration-stop' at the beginning of the 1970s. The stop was officially announced as being a temporary measure, yet in practice became a permanent one, although it was not effective in practice (Hjarnø, 1996). Because of their lawful right to family reunification, the number of immigrants kept on increasing. Years after, developments in the international arena and growing unrest in many countries resulted in a further influx of immigrants.

The 1980s became the decade of political mobilization among immigrants, supported by public funds and by left-wing parties and trade unions (Goli, 2002).

By the mid-1990s the immigrant population (refugees included) demanded to be considered as 'ethnic minorities' (Goli, 2002). Nowadays in the Danish public debate the term 'ethnic minorities' refers exclusively to immigrants and descendants whose country of origin is either 'non-western' (that is, not in the industrial world) or non-EU. Ethnicity became a major issue and 'culture' a battlefield in the public debate (Schierup, 1994).

The new millennium began with an intensified, from time to time ideological, polarization and hectic political and public debate on migration and integration. In the 2001 election, the majority of the Danish electorate distanced themselves from the Social democrats' and Social liberals' policies on migration and integration. The winning coalition, Liberals and Conservatives, were then helped in office by the right-wing party's (DF) parliamentary support. The far right party had become the third biggest party in the country. A new, in many respects fundamentally different, approach to immigrants (presented below) supported by the public, was then introduced.

The immigrant population in Denmark – main demographic and social features

By 1 January 2004, the immigrant population (including refugees) in Denmark amounted to 442,036, or 8.2 per cent of the total Danish population. The immigrant population includes people of both 'western' (29.2 per cent) and 'non-western' / third- country (70.8 per cent) origins.

By 1 January 2003, the rate of employment among immigrants from third countries was only 47 per cent. In comparison, the equivalent rate for Danes was 77 per cent.[2] Immigrants from Somalia, Lebanon, Afghanistan and Iraq have the lowest employment rates.

Major immigrant groups

Turks, Pakistanis and Yugoslavs, that have traditionally been the main immigrant population groups in Denmark, remain the largest immigrant groups. Recently, however, refugees from Iraq, Iran, Somalia and Bosnia have also been growing in numbers. The table below shows the main immigrant groups found in Denmark in 2007.

Table 6.1   Major immigrant groups by country of origin (1 January 2007)

Country of origin	Immigrants	Descendants	Total	Percentage (%) of total immigrant population
Turkey	30,887	23,370	54,257	12.3
Former Yugoslavia	30,416	8,305	38,721	8.8
Iraq	20,701	4,970	25,671	5.8
Lebanon	12,101	9,689	21,790	4.9
Pakistan	10,689	8,561	19,250	4.4
Somalia	11,774	5,589	17,363	3.9
Iran	11,730	2,483	14,213	3.2
Vietnam	8,643	3,812	12,455	2.8
Sri Lanka	6,815	3,509	10,324	2.3
Afghanistan	8,986	1,247	10,233	2.3
Morocco	4,948	3,851	8,799	2.0
Other countries	180,112	28,848	208,960	47.3
All countries	337,802	104,234	442,036	100.0

Note: The term 'immigrants' includes both foreigners and naturalized citizens. The term 'descendants' means children born in Denmark – children born in other countries are classified as immigrants themselves. Source: Integration Miinistry.

---

2   The unemployment rate refers to the official definition made by Statistics Denmark. Unemployed are those who participate in the labour market (are available for jobs but don't have any).

In 2004, 40.4 per cent or 178,491 of the total immigrant population (including descendants) in Denmark were Danish citizens of a different ethnic/national background. Up to 2003, a growing number of immigrants and descendants applied successfully for Danish citizenship. In 2006/2007, 3,952 immigrants and descendants became Danish nationals, as compared to 9,316 in 2001/2002. This dramatic reduction was due to the fact that the requirements for becoming a Danish national became more demanding in 2002. These new requirements include documentation of a certain level of fluency in the Danish language, familiarity with Danish society and its basic values, Danish culture and history. Moreover, the applicant must prove a minimum continuing residence of nine years in the country. This latter requirement is also dependent on, among other things, the applicant's national background or the status of their residence. Thus, in the period 2002–2003, there was a rather dramatic 77.2 per cent reduction in issued citizenship. In 2003/04, 4,885 individuals became Danish nationals. The tendency towards adopting Danish citizenship seems to be much more widespread among descendants, where 64.5 per cent – almost twice the rate among immigrants, – are Danish citizens

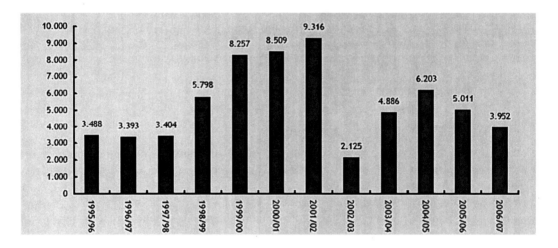

Source: Tal & Fakta, Integrationsministeriet, 2007

Figure 6.1   Number of citizenships issued

Table 6.2 shows the number of foreign nationals according to their national background.

Table 6.2   Foreign citizens as of 1 January 1980, 1993, 1997, 2000, 2001 and 2002 (in nominal terms)

	1980	1993	1997	2000	2001	2002
Foreign citizens total	99,796	180,103	237,695	259,357	258,629	266,729
Scandinavia, the EU and North America	54,667	59,531	72,298	78,764	79,668	80,911
Immigrant countries total	41,940	79,020	92,927	99,615	99,424	101,063
Asylum seekers	3,189	41,552	72,470	80,978	79,537	84,755
Largest immigrant population groups (country of origin):	29,555	54,280	59,758	59,394	57,126	55,285
- Turkey	14,086	33,653	36,835	36,569	35,232	33,383
- Former Yugoslavia	7,126	11,154	12,804	12,137	11,530	11,474
- Pakistan	6,400	6,259	6,736	7,115	7,071	7,160
- Morocco	1,943	3,214	3,383	3,573	3,293	3,268
Refugee countries total	3,189	41,552	72,470	80,978	79,537	84,755
- Afghanistan	26	667	1,637	2,878	4,200	7,061
- Ethiopia	74	436	517	558	521	520
- Iraq	102	4,385	8,066	12,687	13,821	16,541
- Iran	215	8,248	7,029	5,702	5,013	4,906
- Former Yugoslavian states	0	152	19,380	22,925	23,424	23,880
- Lebanon	156	4,203	4,368	3,418	2,538	2,349
- Romania	49	997	1,117	1,099	1,106	1,176
- Somalia	102	2,089	9,683	14,265	14,447	14,585
- Sri Lanka	181	5,672	5,415	4,851	4,293	4,112
- No citizenship	965	10,185	10,166	7,588	5,532	5,020
- Vietnam	1,319	4,518	5,092	5,007	4,642	4,605

The following table shows the number of naturalizations among certain national categories of immigrant and descendants in Denmark.

Table 6.3   Naturalizations by national background (1995, 1999, 2000, 2001 and 2002)

	1995	1999	2000	2001	2002
Europe (A)	2,083	5,072	5,900	5,342	7,340
- Yugoslavia (former)	413	709	1,523	1,137	3,413
- Turkey	797	3,154	2,787	3,130	2,418
Africa (B)	311	903	2,371	1,751	3,396
- Morocco	122	322	485	213	313
- Somalia	12	215	1,189	1,074	2,263
North America (C)	46	58	53	65	74
- USA	36	51	38	38	60
South and Latin America (D)	94	149	255	251	334
Asia (E)	2,202	4,765	7,844	3,631	5,137
- Afghanistan	24	98	276	215	301
- Iraq	177	918	2,210	871	1,161
- Iran	531	914	1,105	437	519
- Lebanon	216	601	1,099	309	376
- Pakistan	145	463	545	297	573
- Sri Lanka	635	523	819	365	594
- Thailand	56	137	214	124	172
- Vietnam	137	439	647	318	508
Oceania (F)	8	19	16	13	13
Stateless/others (G)	516	1,450	2,372	849	1,006
All (A+B+C+D+E+F+G)	5,260	12,416	18,811	11,902	17,300

Residence

The growth in immigrant population in recent decades from 3.0 per cent of the total population in 1980 to 8.2 per cent in 2004 is mostly due to the growth in three categories:

- people who have attained temporary and/or permanent residence in the country on the basis of their status as political or de facto refugees
- people who have residence in the country in accordance with their right to family reunification and/or marriage
- people who were born in the country (descendants).

Statistically, since 1995, refugees and people who came through the family reunification pathway before 1 January 2004 account for 75.7 per cent of all third-country nationals residing in Denmark.

The following table specifies the basis for residence for selected immigrant groups.

Table 6.4   Residence permits issued, by reason (2001–2006)

Category	2001	2002	2003	2004	2005	2006
Business & study	10,001	13,310	16,778	19,887	24,988	28,448
EU	5,950	6,041	6,475	7,904	9,916	12,802
Family reunification etc.	14,140	9,943	5,733	4,718	4,341	4,198
Asylum	6,263	4,069	2,447	1,592	1,147	1,095

Source: Based on statistics from Ministry of Integration, Tal & Fakta, 2006.

Going back to the new Danish migration and integration policy and its electoral promises on reduction of newcomers, the Ministry for Integration reports that residence permits based on asylum, family reunification or marriage have been reduced in recent years. According to the Ministry the number of residence permits granted on the grounds of family reunification in 2004 is 3,013. In 2003 there were 4,791 and in 2002 there were 8,151.

Illegal immigrants

There is no systematic and reliable estimate of the number of illegal immigrants in Denmark. But it is officially acknowledged that illegal immigrant workers, especially from Eastern Europe, or new EU Member States, are occasionally employed on a temporary basis under inferior working conditions in specific branches such as construction, small enterprises, domestic work and agriculture. Another group of people without a legal residence permit are asylum seekers whose applications for asylum have been turned down but who have not left the country and, instead, make a living illegally in enterprises owned by immigrants of either their own ethnic background or other immigrants (Rezaei, 2004). Regarding the issue of illegal immigrants, the Danish political and public debate during the last decades has almost exclusively focused on illegal economic activities among immigrants from non-western countries. More recently, however, illegal and informal economic activities among immigrants from western countries or their exploitation by Danish employers have also been included in the agenda.

Immigrant rights and participation in public life – issues of immigrant integration

From the very beginning, the core of the Danish Government policy debate has somehow been centred on the rights and duties of the immigrant population toward the Danish state and society (Sørensen, 1988; Goli, 2002). With the new Liberal–Conservative Government that came to power in 2001 some researchers argue that a new era of migration and integration policy has begun (Torfing, 2003). They refer to a process of discursive change that is regenerated and reproduced through daily practice. Torfing (ibid.) refers to the situation at hand as a shift from a welfare paradigm to a workfare paradigm, a shift from the attitude of 'What can we do for you?' to the attitude of 'What can you do for us and for yourself?', a shift from qualifying immigrants to meet the demands of the labour market through a long process of education and cultural adjustments, to a policy of making 'productive individuals out of immigrants'.

Discursive shift or not, this might explain the dramatic change of integration policy that has been introduced and institutionalized by the Liberal–Conservative Government and which, from time to time, has brought Danish policy on integration and migration onto the front page of the media around Europe and the world. The fact is that, in spite of much resistance from the opposition coalition in Danish politics, there has not yet been either an alternative put forward to challenge the new policy or any convincing efforts to move the average Danish voter's preferences and perspectives with regard to migration and integration.

New immigrants from non-western countries with a perspective to stay – a description which refers to the type of permit they have – receive a 'Citizen in Denmark' booklet published by the Ministry of Integration in several immigrant languages. The booklet presents Denmark as the land of opportunities and emphasizes that immigrants can practise their religion as they wish, start an association or join one to fulfil their individual or collective goals, and there are lots of political, cultural, societal or religious activities they can participate in. The newcomers are encouraged to take part in the political and societal life of their municipality.

Among other information provided to newcomers in this booklet are references to the freedom of religion, freedom of media, freedom of speech and freedom of association, while relevant parts of the Danish constitution are highlighted. According to the booklet, there are 150 large and small religious communities in Denmark, 90 religious societies, and the right to conduct religious ceremonies is granted to priests, imams, rabbis and other religious representatives along with the right to build temples of worship, run schools and publish their ideas freely. Such encouragements follow the principle of participation in democratic processes which is highlighted in the publication (ibid., p. 61).

Since 1981, immigrants have the right to participate, both as voter and candidate, for seats in local elections after three years of residence. After nine years of residence they can apply for Danish citizenship, implying the right to vote in general elections and run for parliament. The applications are granted, depending on appropriate behaviour and the fulfilment of certain other requirements such as being over the age of 18, not having a criminal record, not owing money to welfare institutions and so on.

Following the law of integration of 1999, municipalities with a certain size of immigrant population have been able to establish Local Integration Councils (Integrationsråd). By 2001, there were 48 such councils established around the country. The task of the councils is to give advice on local integration policies. They can also be an arena for political participation of immigrants on integration issues. Records of the participation in Integration Councils (2006) in the municipality of Copenhagen showed a very unsatisfactory level.

All citizens have the right to start an organization or association. The only requirement is to hold a meeting, a general assembly, to decide the objectives of the association. Danes are famous for their tendencies to facilitate and participate in associations and according to the publication, 73 per cent of the Danish population are members of more than one association. Newcomers are encouraged to participate in associations, as these are considered the key to Danish society. According to this welcome-publication there are about 200 associations whose activities are specifically ethnic-related, including cultural, political and friendship associations.

The objectives of many of these associations are typically to strengthen the ties between immigrants and Danes. Also, participation in media debate is underlined, and there are radio and television broadcasting on a local level for different immigrant populations, highlighting and dealing with their specific problems. Immigrants are known statistically and publicly for what is considered culturally founded talent and potential for establishing themselves as entrepreneurs, creators of small businesses. The government has introduced several institutional measures to develop that talent.

Before the shift in policies in 2001, immigrants' participation in society was not only encouraged by a fast track to legal equality and equal welfare rights, but also by substantive subsidies to immigrant associations. These measures to encourage participation have been reconsidered and mostly stopped.

The change of integration policy includes, among other things, a differentiation among people with regard to social rights. The Introduction Benefit (*introduktionsydelse*) amounts to about 52–77 per cent of the average benefit for people on welfare. In other words newcomers get a lower welfare benefit than people who have lived in Denmark longer. This reduction has been explained by the government as an attempt to provide a greater economic incentive to get a job as quickly as possible. Togeby (2003) characterizes the actual outcomes of the policy as a weakening of those resources that must be in place before immigrants can actually use their formal and equal rights to participation. A second part of the new policy is related to a new set of conditions that have to be met before family reunification and marriage. The new requirements are that both parties should be over 24 years old, that they should fulfil some other economic requirements, and that they should prove that the sum of their common ties/attachments to Denmark and Danish society is greater than their attachments to the country of the spouse.[3] This policy too has been repeatedly criticized on the same grounds (among many others by UN human rights organizations, and European Human Rights commissioner Alvaro Gil-Gobles (Danish National TV – Nyheder, 14 July). It is considered as a reduction of immigrants' civil rights.

According to the new policy the spouse (the possible newcomer) cannot receive any benefits from the welfare state, and all her/his living expenses must be covered by the husband or the wife during the first 7 years of residence. Hence, the economic incentives are also strengthened by the principle that indicates that people with stronger ties to the labour market can get unlimited residence faster than others.

Dealing with the shift in integration policy, Togeby (2003) concludes that in spite of the formally declared goals of the government for furthering cultural diversity and participation, following the change of policy in 2002 cultural openness has been under considerable pressure: 'The absence of polyethnic rights makes it difficult for ethnic minority members to actually unfold their cultural diversity'. More specifically, polyethnic rights include having substantial government subsidized facilities to learn mother tongues, run private schools, run self-managed organizations and so on. Protecting these types of rights has obviously not been the new policy. On the contrary, many of these rights have been abolished or restricted in practice. At the same time, as a part of the new policy, immigrant associations and organizations have lost public financial support.

The ongoing discussion about the Muslim population's right to have and to run a cemetery in accordance with their own religion seems to be a good example. According to the law, the minorities have the right to exercise religious priorities, including running their own churchyards. But at the same time the institutional setting indicates involvement from the public administration to initiate and realize such projects. This involvement has proved to be very complicated. After a long period of negotiations, a licence has been issued to facilitate Muslim graveyards in areas belonging to the Copenhagen municipality. Evidence shows that the municipality of Copenhagen had demanded extortionate prices for this, and the case came before the court. The focus of political and public debate on Islam and Muslims has generated new and more religion-grounded mobilization among Muslims. Prior to the last election, a Danish-Muslim organization announced its active participation in the next election in favour of the opposition and against the Liberal–Conservative Government. They have sued Danish national public service television for propaganda against

---

3   Integrationsministeriet, Notat, J.nr:2006/4199-639. Among many other aspects the information needed for the evaluation of the attachment includes job, residence permit, citizenship: http://www.nyidanmark.dk/NR/rdonlyres/152A9DA0-5C2E-4E35-B44A-5E726A486206/0/fae1_ansoegningspakke_aegtefaelle_eng_application_spouses_endelig_240107.pdf.

Islam by repeatedly showing the assassinated Dutch director van Gogh's documentary and on 6 January 2005 they demanded a publicly administered mosque tax similar to the church tax paid by members of the Danish national church. Reflecting on the lack of substantial opportunities for practice of cultural priorities and engagement on different premises, Manu Sareen, an integration consultant in Copenhagen municipality, and author of a publicly debated book on arranged and forced marriage among immigrants, argues: 'The young immigrants and descendants feel that they are being pushed out of Danish society and they increasingly withdraw themselves. That movement makes integration a rather impossible project. Politicians must go the opposite way; they should let young immigrants and descendants enter society on their own cultural and religious premises' (*Jyllands-Posten*, 29/12/03).

If we were to divide the areas of immigrant participation into political, economic, social, cultural and religious areas, it is clear that immigrant participation in the economic sphere is the area that receives prime attention. This follows the idea that economic self-sufficiency is at the core of civic participation. With regard to immigrant participation in the political sphere, it seems that quantitative surveys on the participation of immigrants in politics at the national and local level have received some attention, especially during the last three to five years. But immigrants' participation in politics cannot be considered as a high priority area. Owing to a consensus established and reproduced from the very beginning of the new history of migration in the 1970s, the question of immigrant participation in the economic sphere has traditionally been closely tied to two concerns. Firstly, the concerns about the Danish welfare state, its efficiency, its future, its possible reforms and so on. Secondly, economic participation is usually studied as a parameter closely connected with the structure of the Danish labour market. The areas of focus very often include aspects such as incentives, motivation to work and discrimination. Recently, the opportunity structure has come to be seen as a product of interconnection and interplay between three factors: the Danish welfare state, the structure of the Danish labour market, and the possibilities that are products of development of the 'immigrant society' it self. The last is recently referred to as 'The Parallel Society'.

Political participation

About 1.5 per cent of the total electorate have an immigrant background. Participation of immigrants in local elections is much lower than the average. Slightly more than one per cent or 49 of the total seats of municipality committees around the country have an immigrant background, while 1.1 per cent of the total number of seats in the national parliament are occupied by individuals of immigrant descent. In the 2001 national election there were 14 immigrants and descendants of immigrants running for a seat in parliament. The equivalent figure in the 2005 election was 21, from the following national backgrounds: Pakistan 5, Turkey 5, Morocco 3, Syria 2, India 2, Taiwan 1, Lebanon 1, Uruguay 1 and Somalia 1. Until the latest election there were two MP's with a (non-western) immigrant background in the national parliament, but the latest national election (February 2005) brought in one more representative with a (non-western) immigrant background.[4] Descendants and second- generation immigrants seem to have fairly average participation levels in political parties, unions and grass roots associations (Togeby, 2003).

In the publication 'Impression Management and Political Entrepreneurship in Denmark' Necef (2002) presents a comparative study of immigrant elite strategies to influence the policy and public debate. Necef takes a closer look at the institutional and discursive structure of the channels of political influence for immigrant political entrepreneurs. Outlining the political opportunity

---

4   All three Members of Parliament are Muslim.

structure, the dominant discursive environments, and the election system in Denmark, Necef discusses the conditions and circumstances that ambitious immigrant political entrepreneurs must deal with in order to become successful (Necef, 2002, p. 30).

Other studies show that immigrants' engagement in their own organizations is carried by the elite, and many immigrants feel that their concern and political preferences are not represented in a satisfactory manner by Danish political institutions. That is considered as the main reason why immigrants establish their own organizations (Mikkelsen, 2002, p. 100).

Migrant and ethnic minority volunteering

According to Mikkelsen (2005, p. 117) the participation of immigrants in civic associations and other associations is very poor: 7.1 per cent participate in Parent committees in schools, 3.4 per cent in associations in housing sectors, and 8.5 per cent in free-time association such as clubs, 11.7 per cent in multiethnic associations and 1.2 per cent in political associations. But there are major variations in the levels of participation among different categories of immigrants. The highest level is represented by immigrants of Iranian descent (0.61) the lowest among immigrants of Pakistani descent (0.21). Immigrants from Iranian and Pakistani descent who represent the opposite ends of engagement in associations are, on the other hand, very close to each other when it comes to spare-time activities. Both represent a very high level of engagement in clubs (such as sport clubs, and so on) while immigrants of Turkish descent seems to prefer participation in more ethnic orientated forums. Mikkelsen concludes: 21 per cent of immigrants are engaged in spare-time activities that involve people of Danish descent, while 45 per cent prefer activities that one way or another exclude people of Danish descent and 34 per cent are active in spare-time activities that are mixed (Danes and immigrants).

Labour market related and other aspects of civic participation

Thirty-seven per cent of immigrants are members of a labour market organization (2003). Participation in labour market organizations is dependent on many factors, including length of residence and the very character/structure/organization of the Danish labour market, to mention just a few (Rezaei, 2004). Mikkelsen (ibid.) shows that, as far as immigrant participation in labour market organizations is concerned, representation of immigrants from Iran, Pakistan, Turkey and former Yugoslavia in trade unions is above average, while that of immigrants of Somali, Iraqi and Palestinian origin is below average. Taking the institutional structure of the Danish labour market into account, Mikkelsen (ibid.) emphasizes that immigrants' membership of a labour market organization cannot be taken as an indicator of active participation.

Another aspect of immigrant participation that seems to receive growing attention from decision makers and community actors is connected with participation in housing areas (Iversen et al., 2001). Studies (see Mikkelsen, 2002) show that participation of immigrants in matters connected to their housing is rather poor. The study shows that in some urban areas where the immigrant population accounts for about 50 per cent of residents, only about 18 per cent of the members of residents' committees were individuals of immigrant background. Other studies indicate that immigrants only make up 1–2 per cent of the total number of residential committee members nationally (Togeby, 2003).

Mikkelsen (2007) has emphasized the impact of religious organizations and associations, specifically the Islamic ones, as creators of identity among immigrants. During recent years, probably because of the international and national politicized public debate on Islam, Islam seems to have become a major unifying factor among Muslim immigrants. Dealing with immigrants' activities in the religious sphere of life, Mikkelsen shows that 10 per cent of immigrants go to a religious association, while 25 per cent (mostly Somalis, Pakistani, Turkish and Palestinian immigrants) often go to a mosque (Iranians and Yugoslavs are very rare visitors to a religious association). Rezaei (2003) has found that immigrants with stronger ties to religious associations and mosques are typically characterized by a distance from the Danish population and by difficulties with the Danish language; the question of integration does not seem to occupy their minds very much. Many of them wish to get back home, in spite of very long residence (more than 20 years) in Denmark or even at times despite having being born in the country. Rezaei (2004) has shown that the same segment usually invest their money in the country of origin.

Public and media discourses on migration

Few studies have investigated the Danish media discourse on immigration and immigrant-related issues. Based on an empirical investigation of the daily news flow on ethnic affairs in the dominant news media, Hussain et al. (1997) and Hussain (2000) argue that the Danish media have played an important role in the (re)production of a prejudiced discourse on ethnic minorities. In this discursive process, Muslim minorities have been the primary victims, argues Hussain (ibid.): 'In the absence of social interaction between the majority population and minority groups, the cognitive frame of reference through which members of the ethnic majority premise their arguments is largely based on mental models of ethnic events that are constituted by media-mediated themes and topics on minority issues in the daily news flow of the national media.' After the 9/11 events and their aftermath, the Danish media focus on Islam has intensified. Most issues discussed in relation to the immigrant population are in one way or another related to the question of Islam. Among issues that are specifically highlighted in the media, Hussain underlines:

- the question of cultural integration of immigrants and descendants into Danish values
- the role of Muslim religious leaders (Imams) in the integration process
- the question of gender-relations among Muslim immigrants
- arranged and/or forced marriages
- divergence and convergence between immigrants' and Danes' values
- dilemmas related to collective and individual freedoms, freedom of expression, speech and association.

The limits of tolerance

A brief look at the newspapers and electronic media during recent years – even with the very recent Mohammad cartoon excluded – supports the findings of Hussain (op. cit.). A review of 800 articles of Danish media coverage in summer 2001 shows that 95 per cent of them were about Islam, and in particular of a rather negative image of Islam and Muslims. In recent years, other issues, not specifically related to Muslim immigrants, that have received particular mention include the question of ghettos and their impact on immigrants' cultural and societal integration; the shadow economy, untaxed activities and other illegal transactions through immigrant ethnic networks; youth criminality and urban gangs among immigrant descendants; the future of the Danish welfare state and the role of immigrants; institutional problems and challenges related to immigrants' participation in the Danish labour market; and the disconcerting gap between immigrants' and descendants' educational preferences and behaviour, and the actual and future needs of the Danish labour market.

Other practical and institutional issues such as the question of discrimination, the possible and actual impacts of the states' and municipalities' policy toward integration have also been repeatedly highlighted in the media.

In conclusion, the four major topics dominating the media debate during recent years are:

- Islam, Danish values and integration values
- ghettos and concentration
- the shadow economy and its relation to immigrants' possibilities for socio-economic mobility.
- labour market and immigrant children's education.

The Liberal–Conservative Government that came to power in 2001 had made explicit promises to its voters that it would reduce the number of asylum seekers, stop arranged and forced marriages among immigrants and change the premises and objectives of the integration and migration policy. Since then, indeed, a series of major institutional changes have been introduced, and it seems that the implementation of the new policy has been successful in the sense that the practice of integration and migration policy has followed the desired political changes. Facilitating active participation of immigrants and descendants was put at the top of the political agenda from the beginning of the Liberal–Conservative coalition government.

In sum, the goals of the new integration policy are to encourage and create participating and taxpaying citizens who are equal to other citizens in every manner. They should be guaranteed equal rights and formal and substantial opportunities for participation in society's political, economic, social, religious and cultural affairs. The political desire is that the individual immigrant should develop an understanding of the basic Danish values and norms. And the goal of public servants is to ensure that the individual immigrant becomes economically self-sufficient as soon as possible (the law on integration, 2001).

Concluding remarks

By 1 January 2004, the immigrant population (including refugees) in Denmark amounted to 442,036, or 8.2 per cent of the total Danish population. The immigrant population includes people of both 'western' (29.2 per cent.) and 'non-western'/third-country (70.8 per cent.) origins. The terms 'immigrants' (indvandrere) and 'ethnic minorities' refer both in the political vocabulary and in the public debate to immigrants of 'non-western' descent. Turks, Pakistanis and Yugoslavs, traditionally the main immigrant population groups in Denmark, remain the largest immigrant groups. Recently, however, refugees from Iraq, Iran, Somalia and Bosnia have also been growing in numbers.

By 1 January 2003, the rate of employment among immigrants from third countries was only 47 per cent. In comparison, the equivalent rate for Danes was 77 per cent.[5] Immigrants from Somalia, Lebanon, Afghanistan and Iraq have the lowest employment rates. The core of the new discourse on both immigration and integration policy, introduced by the Liberal–Conservative Government, and widely supported both by voters and opposition, is the change of the institutional focus from 'welfare' to 'workfare', cutting down the number of new immigrants and the attachment to the labour market almost exclusively as the channel to integration into Danish society.

---

5   The unemployment rate refers to the official definition made by Statistics Denmark. Unemployed are those who participate in the labour market (are available for jobs but don't have any).

As far as the policy of 'integration' and challenges of immigrant participation in state institutions, civic society and media are concerned, Danish discourse, not yet contested or substantially challenged by the media, the public or the opposition, must be considered a primordial discourse (as the opposite of the instrumental or rational discourse) on ethnicity (Hutchinson and Smith, 1996). Such a discourse puts the collective differences in focus. All other things being equal, this discourse and policy minimize the chances of an 'ethnic person' (that is, an individual who by others and mainstream institutions is considered to think and act according to their ethnic affiliation and not by rational considerations) participating in the mainstream labour market or in other spheres of mainstream social and political life in Denmark. The empirical study (Goli, 2002) shows that being labelled by presumed ethnic affiliation in the Danish context is a disqualifying factor, indicating limited knowledge of Danish culture and society, lack of knowledge about how to behave as well as how to handle a situation 'the Danish way', both explicitly and implicitly emphasized as 'the rational way'. Danish public servants know that *Ethnic means trouble!* (Goli, 2002).

Developments in recent years have added a new issue to the Danish public and academic debate on immigrant participation. It is widely acknowledged that many immigrants spend most of their lives in the so called 'parallel society'. Compensating for its marginal position in the labour market and other societal spheres, the immigrant population seems to have found alternative ways of participation. It goes through the informal economy, where welfare benefits are combined with illegal incomes. 'The parallel society' means that the immigrant population, seeking acknowledgement and support, turns to its own community, informal institutions and associations and network in order to improve its life situation. These typically mono-ethnic and closed networks and associations operate on the basis of different standards of exclusive mutual trust as responses to the situation, which is almost permanently politicized through political and public debate in the media.

The overall and alarming conclusion of the studies referred to in this chapter is that the consequence of the Danish integration discourse is that the immigrant population has been pushed towards its own networks and towards social and economic exclusion from Danish society. That is a disconcerting consequence.

References

Goli, M. (2002), En verden til forskel – Diskursiv inkonsistens og institutionel ineffektivitet, Case: Institutionalisering af etnisk ligestilling på det statslige arbejdsmarked i Danmark. Denmark: Institut for Statskundskab, Københavns Universitet.

Hussain, M. (2000), 'Islam, Media and Minorities in Denmark', *Current Sociology*, **48**(4), 95–116.

Hussain, M., et al. (1997), *Medierne, Minoriteterne og majoriteten Denmark*. Nævnet for etnisk ligestilling.

Hutchinson, J. and Smith, A.D. (eds) (1996), *Ethnicity*, Oxford University Press.

Integrationsministeriet (2002), *Medborger i Danmark – en håndbog for nye borgere*. Denmark: Integrationsministeriet.

Integrationsministeriet (2003), *Regeringens integrations- og udlændingepolitik*.

Iversen, R.B. et al. (2001), *Borgerinddragelsens flertydighed- En antropologisk undersøgelseaf viden og magt på integrationsområdet i Indre Nørrebro Bydel*. Denmark: Institut for Antropologi, Københavns Universitet.

Mikkelsen, F. (2002), *Indvandrerforskning i Danmark*. Denmark: Amid 19/2002.

Mikkelsen, F. (2007), *Indvandrerorgansiationer I Danmark*. Forthcoming.

Necef, M.Ü. (2002), *Impression Management and Political Entrepreneurship in Denmark*. Odense: Universitets Forlag.

Rezaei, S. (2003 and 2004), *Indvandrernes netværksrelationer – blokering eller afsæt for socioøkonomisk mobilitet?* Denmark: Det Samfundsvidenskabelige Fakultet, Syddansk Universitet, Syddansk Universitetsforlag.

Rezaei, S. and Goli, M. (2006), *Indvandrernes tætte netværk – Katalysator eller hæmsko*. Roskilde: Universitets Center.

Schierup, C.U. (1994), *På kulturens slagmark*. Denmark: Syddansk Universitetsforlag.

Sørensen, W. (1988), *Der kom fremmede*. Denmark: Center for kulturforsknig v/Århus.

Togeby, L. (2003), *Fra fremmedarbejdere til etniske minoriteter*. Denmark: Magtudredningen.

Torfing, J. (2003), 'Den stille revolution i velfærdsstaten – fra forsørgelse og hierarki til aktivering og netværksstyring', in Madsen, P.K. et al. (eds) *Drivkræfter bag arbejdsmarkeds-politikken Denmark*. SFI.

Internet-based References

Integrationsministeriet. *Tal & Fakta*, 2007 (available at http://www.nyidanmark.dk/NR/rdonlyres/87B88864-2494-4029-91B5-F33A1CB80A17/0/tal_og_fakta_juni_2007_2.pdf).

http://www.nyidanmark.dk/NR/rdonlyres/01D113D6-EA0D-4DB6-B2F9-DA47A6706EFF/0/tal_og_fakta_2006.pdf.

Chapter 7

Estonia

Mikko Lagerspetz

Major developments in Estonian immigration policy

The fall of real socialism and the dissolution of the Soviet Union brought several newly independent countries to the map of Europe. Whereas there were thirty-three nations competing in football's European Nations' Cup in 1992, the number of contestants in 1996 was 48 (Pierson, 1996, p. 13). Estonia was one of the 'new' countries, but Estonian independence has a longer history. Its tradition of independent statehood dates from the years 1918–1940 (see Raun, 1987). The country, which was previously successively ruled by Germans, Danes and Swedes, became a Russian province in 1721 and remained as such until it was declared an independent republic on 24 February 1918. Between 1939 and 1940, the Estonian Government found it impossible to refuse to give its consent to the Soviet Union's demand to locate several military bases in the country. These concessions were soon followed by outright occupation and the country's incorporation into the Soviet Union as a new Soviet Socialist Republic. Estonia shared this fate with its southern neighbours Latvia and Lithuania, the two other Baltic republics. Like many other countries of Central and Eastern Europe, in the late 1980s they became the scene of mass movements for democratization and national liberation. Estonia was able to free itself from the collapsing Soviet central government on 20 August 1991, shortly before the final dissolution of the Union itself in December 1991 (see, for example, Lieven, 1993/94).

The period of Soviet rule brought about a massive change in the ethnic composition of the country's population of slightly over one million people (see Table 7.1). In the 1930s, 'non-titular' nationalities in Estonia[1] made up 12 per cent of the total population. During the period of large-scale industrialization, which took place especially during the 1960s and 1970s, significant numbers of Russians and other ethnic groups from different parts of the Soviet Union settled in Estonia. In 1989, the percentage of ethnic Estonians in Estonia had dropped to 61 per cent. The proportion of immigrant workers became largest in the North-Eastern region, where large industrial plants were situated. Also in the capital, the proportion of 'non-ethnic' Estonians approached one-half of the population. In addition to industrial workers, they included military and administrative personnel. The minorities continue to be concentrated in these geographic areas.

After the restoration of Estonia's independence in 1991, the citizenship status of its inhabitants was defined according to whether they or their parents or grandparents had been citizens of the independent Estonia (1918–1940). In this way, those settled during the Soviet time and their descendants were defined as non-citizens – as immigrants. According to the latest census of 2000, the number of foreign citizens and persons without citizenship residing in Estonia was around

---

1   In Estonian official discourse, they are mostly referred to as 'Non-Estonians' (*mitte-eestlased*). Confusingly, this term is applied irrespective of whether the persons referred to are Estonian citizens or not. In statistics, 'ethnicity/nationality' (*rahvus*) refers to self-reported ethnic belonging and is independent of both citizenship and mother tongue.

270,000, which equates to 20 per cent of the country's total population of 1.37 million. During the 1990s and 2000s, no significant immigration into Estonia took place. In 2000, the total number of resident foreign citizens from outside the former Soviet Union was fewer than 2,000 people.

Since the beginning of the 1990s, there has been a downward trend of both the total population and the proportion of minorities. This is related, firstly, to the age structure and a fall in the birth rate and, secondly, to large-scale emigration. From 1990 to 1993, almost 80,000 people left Estonia, mostly for Russia and other countries of the Commonwealth of Independent States (CIS) (Lagerspetz and Vogt, 1998, p. 73). Since then, the general population decline due to emigration, low birth rate and unfavourable age structure has not changed the proportions of the various ethnic groups.

Table 7.1   Ethnic breakdown of Estonia's population (1934, 1989, 2000)*

	1934		1989		2000	
	'000s	%	'000s	%	'000s	%
Estonians	993	88	963	61	930	68
Russians	93	8	475	30	351	26
Germans	16	2	3	0.2	2	0.1
Swedes	8	0.7	0.3	0.02	–	–
Jews	4	0.4	5	0.3	2	0.1
Finns	–	–	17	1	12	1
Ukrainians	–	–	48	3	29	2
Belarusans	–	–	28	2	17	1
Others	13	1	30	2	27	2
Total	1,126	100	1,566	100	1,370	100

*All numbers are from population censuses.
Sources: Lauristin & al. 1997; Statistical Office.

Immigration became a hotly debated issue in the course of the revolutionary events of the late 1980s. At that time, immigration was equivalent to the inflow of labour and retired military officers from other parts of the USSR, which had already led to a major change in the population's ethnic composition (see Table 7.1 above). Along with a growing linguistic Russification of public life, the independence activists interpreted immigration as a threat to the future existence of the Estonian nation. Between 1988 and 1990, the public debate on both issues became central in the political life and media, which were gradually being freed from censorship (see Lagerspetz, 1996, pp. 57–60; 80–101).

The country's citizenry became defined by the 1992 *Citizenship Act* as consisting of the pre-1940 citizens and their descendants only, thereby granting no automatic citizenship to Soviet citizens who had arrived in Estonia during Soviet rule, or even to those who were born of such parents. Instead, they were expected to undergo a naturalization process. It is worth noting, however, that children born of stateless parents in Estonia were exempted from this process from 1998 onwards. The relevant policy measures introduced since 1992 have involved the definition of legal statuses and rights of different groups of people considered as immigrants. Second, they have addressed what has in broad terms been called integration issues.

When analysing the development of immigration and minority policies, scholars tend to distinguish between three different, consecutive phases during the period of Estonia's new independence (for example Vetik, 1999; Pettai, 2000; Heidmets and Lauristin, 2002; Jurado, 2003; Kõuts and Tammpuu, 2002; Lauristin and Heidmets, 2002; Ruutsoo, 2002). The development can be presented as a gradual shift from initial rejection and non-recognition of the Russian-speaking immigrants by the majority population, towards acknowledging them as fellow members of Estonian society. No doubt, the first phase was a continuation of the debate initiated by Estonian pro-independence activists in 1988. During the second half of the 1990s, the government became growingly conscious of a need to adopt more active and less exclusionist policies. An official State Programme was launched in 2000 (see below) with the aim of integrating the immigrants/ minorities into the new society now dominated by the Estonian language and ethnic Estonians. These events denote another turning point in both policy and discourse alike. The change in discourse is very recent, as it is only since 2004 that both the media and administrators have taken up the issue of Estonia's policy towards new immigration. This change is related to the country's altered international position as a member of the European Union (EU).

The discursive and policy changes have been attributed to different causes. For instance, the role of international organizations such as the Organization for Security and Cooperation in Europe (OSCE), the EU and the Council of Europe (COE) have been frequently mentioned (for a thorough analysis, see Jurado, 2003). Estonian scholars tend to stress the importance of internal developments for policy change, such as the consolidation of the overall political framework, the lack of clear-cut differences of economic status between ethnic Estonians and Russian-speakers, processes of cultural modernization and westernization, and socio-psychological factors (Heidmets and Lauristin, 2002, pp. 322–330; Lauristin and Heidmets, 2002).

The immigrant population in Estonia: main demographic and social features

According to the 2000 population census, there are 1.37 million people living in Estonia, 80 per cent of whom are citizens of Estonia, 6.3 per cent citizens of Russia and 0.7 per cent citizens of other countries. Among the latter, approximately 4,000 people (0.3 per cent of the population) are citizens of other EU countries, mainly Latvians, Lithuanians and Finns. The citizenship of 0.6 per cent of the population is unknown, and 12.4 per cent of the population are without citizenship. Whereas the share of ethnic Estonians among the total population is 67.9 per cent, their share among the citizens is higher (84.2 per cent). Correspondingly, a large number of people with an ethnicity other than Estonian are either citizens of foreign countries or, more frequently, stateless.

Of the 252,266 persons born outside Estonia, 96,079 were Estonian citizens either by naturalization or by birth. Some of the remainder were stateless (80,642), Russian citizens (67,780) or citizens of other countries. It should be noted that a majority of the currently stateless persons (88,847), and a large portion of the resident Russian citizens (17,761) were, in fact, born in Estonia.

The system of different legal statuses for people of different national or ethnic origins has been summarized in Table 7.2 below. Estimates of the number of legal residents in each category are based on the 2000 census. By 2005, the number of citizens had grown to 1,154,000, while the number of holders of permanent residence permits had diminished to around 203,000 (*Postimees*, 31 May 2005).

Table 7.2   Population of Estonia by legal status (2000)

Legal residents 1,370,000					Illegal residents 5–10,000?
Citizens of Estonia		Non-citizens			
• by birth and naturalized 1,096,000		• foreign citizens 95,000 • stateless persons 170,000 • persons with unknown citizenship 9,000			
Estonians 922,000	Members of national minorities 174,000	Holders of permanent residence permits ~230,000	Holders of temporary residence permits ~40,000	Asylum seekers < 10	

Note: The estimate of the number of illegal residents was presented in 2002 by the Office of the Minister Without Portfolio responsible for population issues.

The annual number of new residents is limited by an immigration quota of 0.05 per cent of the present population. This quota does not apply to immigrants from the EU, the European Economic Space, Switzerland, the USA, Japan, ethnic Estonians, or family members of present legal residents. Residence permits are either temporary (up to 5 years) or permanent (from July 2006, long-term – see below), and the rights granted to holders of the two different kinds of permits differ mainly in two respects. First, the holder of a temporary residence permit is not allowed to work without a work permit. Second, only the holders of permanent (or long-term) residence permits have voting rights in local elections. As to other rights, the two categories of persons are treated equally. Holders of temporary residence permits are usually those who entered the country after the end of the Soviet rule. In 2005, the total number of holders of residence permits was 244,254. Among them, 41,067 held a temporary residence permit and the remaining 203,187 persons had been granted permanent residence permits (*Postimees*, 31 May 2005: 6).

A permanent residence permit can be achieved after the expiration of the temporal residence permit. According to an amendment in 1997 (Riigi Teataja, 1997) of the 1993 Aliens' Act, persons who had applied for the temporary permit before 12 July 1995 were automatically entitled to a permanent residence permit at application. At the same time, however, the amendment introduced a regulation according to which temporal residence for the purpose of work or studies does not entitle one to apply for a permanent residence permit (§ 12(3) of the Aliens' Act). This created a curious situation that lasted until July 2006, since immigrants who arrived after 1995 were not on equal terms with the previous settlers regarding their possibility of gaining permanent residence permits and, eventually, Estonian citizenship. This particular problem was recently solved by a law amendment which, however, seems to have created a new anomaly. On 19 April 2006, the Parliament made a number of changes to the Act. The term 'permanent residence permit' has now been substituted by 'long-term residence permit'. The new regulations also entitle temporal residents with a view to work, to apply for the long-term permit. As a new requirement for persons between 15 and 65 years of age, the amendment introduces the passing of an examination of basic skills in the Estonian language (information from the Estonian Parliament's website *http://web. riigikogu.ee*, accessed 25 May 2006). Again, present holders of permanent residence permits are automatically entitled to the long-term permit, while new applicants will have to fulfil the language requirement. According to a remark by the Legal Chancellor, the particular paragraph introducing this new requirement was not to be implemented before 1 June 2007 (*Eesti Päevaleht*, 20 April 2006).

The Refugees Act (1997) specifies the procedures and conditions under which one may apply for asylum in Estonia. If the person is granted asylum, they will receive a temporary residence permit. Since the adoption of the Act, the yearly number of applicants has remained very small; twelve at its peak, and usually fewer than ten people applying. As of June 2005, only four people had been granted refugee status (*Postimees*, 16 June 2005: 6). According to information given by authorities to the European Commission against Racism and Intolerance (ECRI, 2006), the processing of an asylum claim took an average time of one-and-a-half months in 2004. The time was significantly shorter than it had been in 2002 when the Commission's previous report was being prepared.

The last category of third-country nationals residing in Estonia involves illegal residents. According to a 2002 estimate of the Estonian Ministry of Population, their number ranges between 5,000 and 10,000. As a rule, they had lived in Estonia before independence, and were ineligible for Estonian citizenship. Moreover, they have not applied for residence and work permits for different reasons, and are unknown to any population register. Most of them are severely marginalized socially. Their residence permit applications are treated as parts of the overall yearly immigration quota (0.05 per cent of the population).

In legal terms, the people who came to live in Estonia from other parts of the USSR during the Soviet rule are considered immigrants. However, many of them have lived in the country for a long time, they form a large part of the population and are active in all spheres of society. A large part of the non-citizen residents were born in Estonia and are, thus, second-generation immigrants. Although the Soviet-era immigrants belong to several ethnic groups, Russian is the first language for most of them.

There are two groups that may be defined as return migrants. Among the Soviet settlers who arrived after the Second World War there were some people with Estonian ancestry whose forefathers had migrated from Estonia to Russia during the nineteenth century. As they are not descendants of the citizens of the 1918–1940 Estonian Republic, they have had to apply for naturalization in order to become citizens of independent Estonia. Another group of return migrants are the Estonians who escaped from the country during the Second World War and who lived in exile in the West for several decades. They are entitled to Estonian citizenship by birth and hold the same rights as citizens born in Estonia. Although the *Citizenship Act* contains a prohibition on double nationality, revocation of Estonian citizenship is possible only on the person's own application. In the 2000 census, 186 resident Estonian citizens were reported to be in possession of a second citizenship.

Finally, during the 1990s and 2000s there has been an immigrant influx from countries outside the former Soviet Union. In the 2000 census, the largest group of foreign citizens from outside the former Soviet Union were 926 Finnish citizens. The other groups were much smaller, German, U.S. and Swedish citizens being the largest groups with 147, 145 and 137 persons respectively. The total of all immigrants, excluding citizens from the former Soviet Union republics, included 131 persons from Asia, 12 from African countries, 186 from the Americas, six from Australia and one from New Zealand.

Regarding the integration of immigrants into the labour market, there is no legal discrimination on the grounds of the job seekers' origins. However, parts of the Estonian labour market have, in practice, become segregated along ethnic lines. The share of employees belonging to ethnic minorities is lower than their share of the population within agriculture, commerce, education and public governance. Their share is considerably larger among industrial and transportation workers. This pattern was already visible during the Soviet regime. A hierarchic division also emerged during the 1990s. On one hand, the share of ethnic Estonians in managerial positions has grown. On the other, so has the share of minorities among unskilled workers and the unemployed (Asari, 2002, p. 223). The wages of employees belonging to the majority population are significantly higher, even when the effects of gender, education, position and branch of economy are eliminated from the analysis (Krusell, 2002, p. 205).

Lastly, according to the Constitution (Article 30), state agencies and local governments must employ Estonian citizens. However, the Constitution allows for exceptions in accordance with other legislation. The Language Act (1995) defines the minimum levels of fluency in Estonian that are required from holders of different jobs within the public sector. These language requirements are one reason for the less than proportional representation of other than ethnic Estonians in public offices, even when compared to their share of Estonian citizenry.

Immigrant rights and participation in public life – issues of immigrant integration

The most important legal acts that define rights and entitlements for immigrants and minorities are the *Citizenship Act, the Aliens' Act, the National Minorities' Cultural Autonomy Act, the Language Act, the Refugees Act*, and the other general Acts regulating political and administrative procedures, education, health and social services and so on.

The Constitution forbids discrimination on the basis of nationality and states, and provides that 'rights, freedoms and duties of each and every person, as set out in the Constitution, shall be equal for Estonian citizens and for citizens of foreign states and stateless persons in Estonia' (Article 9). Among these rights, as stipulated in subsequent articles of the Constitution, are the right to political opinion, freedom of speech, the right to address and receive answers from state agencies, local governments, and their officials, the right to assembly and the right to form and be a member of non-profit organizations and unions. Only Estonian citizens, however, may belong to political parties.

For Estonian citizens, there is universal suffrage from the age of eighteen. Foreign citizens and stateless persons are entitled to vote in elections for local government councils, if they hold permanent resident permits and have legally resided in the territory of the relevant municipality for at least five years by 1 January of the election year. The right to run as a candidate in elections is granted to Estonian citizens only.[2] In November 2001, an amendment to the Riigikogu Election Act and the Local Government Council Election Act was passed, which abolished the previous requirement that candidates must be proficient in the Estonian language and, thus, improved the access of naturalized and minority citizens to the political process.

There has been a long-standing controversy over the future of secondary school tuition in Russian, and several previous decisions to change over to Estonian-language schools have been postponed. The amendment of 2000 to the *Basic Schools and Upper Secondary Schools Act* states that Estonian is the language of instruction in the upper secondary school (to be implemented from the academic year 2007/2008). However, the same amendment defines 'the language of instruction' as the language in which at least 60 per cent of the teaching of the curriculum is given. This would allow schools to continue teaching some subjects in Russian. Whether the decision will be implemented within the given time frame, or will be postponed again, remains to be seen. Some politicians have publicly doubted the practical possibilities of achieving the task within the planned period. The then Prime Minister, Juhan Parts, announced his stance in September 2004, namely that Russian-language secondary education should remain available after all (*Eesti Päevaleht*, 16 September 2004).

A possible mechanism for maintaining schools and other cultural institutions functioning in minority languages was designed by the *National Minorities Cultural Autonomy Act* enacted in

---

2   With the exception of elections to the EU Parliament, in which all resident EU citizens have both the right to vote and the right to stand as candidates.

1993. Following the example of a similar act of 1925, the law allows every minority of at least 3,000 members to create a representative body with the task of organizing the minority's cultural and educational life. The same right is extended to the historical minorities (Germans, Jews, Swedes), which numbered 3,000 members before the war. To use this right, citizens willing to participate in the establishment of a cultural autonomy will have to register themselves, and a representative council has to be elected by at least 50 per cent of the registered members of the minority. It is stipulated that only Estonian citizens can be registered as members. The necessary act of implementation was not adopted before 2003 (*Riigi Teataja* 2003, 40, 25) and so the institutions designed by the Act became established for the first time by Ingrian Finns in May 2004 (Roov␣li, 2004) and, following them, by the Estonian Swedes in February 2007 (*Kulturrådet*, 2007). Obviously, the procedure requires a particularly large amount of organizational work and dedicated resources, while the law gives no guarantees of financial support from the public authorities.

In order to address the issue of ethnic diversity, several governmental institutions and action programmes have been initiated. In May 1997, the Estonian Government assigned responsibilities on population and integration issues to a *Minister without Portfolio*. The Minister reports directly to the Prime Minister and coordinates such policy areas as population policy, implementation of integration policies, naturalization and citizenship issues, issues related to the national census (in collaboration with the population census and statistics committees) and refugee issues. Within the Ministry of Internal Affairs is the *Department of Foreigners*, which is a small office with a broad scope of responsibilities, from visa regulations to planning policy in the areas of citizenship, aliens' problems, refugees and illegal immigration. Within the *Ministry of Culture* there has been no separate department for minority issues since 1997, but it has, nevertheless, regularly allocated finances in support of the cultural activities of minority organizations. From 1999, the *Legal Chancellor* has been empowered to fulfil certain functions of an ombudsman. In an attempt to increase the visibility and accessibility of the institution, the Office of the Legal Chancellor opened a regional office in Ida-Virumaa (North-Eastern Estonia) in June 2001.

The *President of the Republic's Roundtable on National Minorities* was established in 1993 as a standing conference of politicians and representatives of ethnic minorities and people without citizenship. It intended to provide a forum for dialogue and thus defuse the potential for open ethnic conflict. However, it lacks a mandate to treat the problems it identifies and has not played any visible role in the public debate so far. The Roundtable has a part-time presidential plenipotentiary, a part-time assistant and a small budget.

State policies towards non-citizens and ethnic minorities have, since 2000, been formulated in a general action plan called *Integration in Estonian Society (2000–07)*. The programme is coordinated by the *Non-Estonians' Integration Foundation*, a quasi-governmental non-profit entity created in March 1998 to coordinate the use of integration resources, including foreign funding. In 2003, the Estonian Government allocated, through the Integration Foundation, 7.9 million crowns (EUR 508,000) for integration-related activities, while the foundation's total budget – including foreign funding – amounted to 53.4 million crowns (EUR 3.4 million) (*Integration Yearbook, 2003*, 2004: 78). The programme discusses integration in Estonian society as being shaped by two processes: firstly, *the social harmonization of society* around 'a strong common national core' based on knowledge of the Estonian language and Estonian citizenship; and secondly, *the opportunity to maintain ethnic differences* based on the recognition of the cultural rights of ethnic minorities. When the programme has been assessed, the very fact of its development and implementation has been regarded as a significant achievement in itself. However, certain shortcomings have been pointed out (*Minority Protection*, 2002). Firstly, the implementation has concentrated on the education and language sectors, which have received three-quarters of the total financing of the programme (approximately EUR 14.4 million for the period 2000–2003), leaving the fields of legal-political and socio-economic integration dependent on their inclusion in other government programmes. Although the programme stresses the objective of combining integration with the maintenance of strong minority identities and the minority citizens' competence in their ethnic cultures, its implementation has been accused of being rather assimilationist in practice. It seems that, at present, a definition of 'integration' which would be shared by the government, the general public, and the representatives of minority organizations does not exist.

Different studies on political participation (for example Rose, 2000; Rikmann and Lagerspetz, 2003; Raudsaar and Kasemets, 2004) suggest that both non-citizens and Russian speaking citizens have less trust in political institutions than citizens belonging to the majority population. They are also less satisfied with the flow of information available to them regarding the activities of public institutions. Non-citizens seem to be less likely than Estonian citizens to protest against the authorities for actions that they consider unjust. Moreover, 30 per cent of non-citizens maintained that their right to participate in public life had not been sufficiently guaranteed (as compared to 17 per cent of the Estonian citizens) (Rikmann et al., 2002). A measure of civic participation calculated by Raudsaar and Kasemets (2004, p. 167) gave similar results. At the same time, it has been suggested that, in comparison with economically weak groups within the majority population (such as rural people and those with basic education), the passivity of the Russian speakers is more due to the lack of information and participation channels, rather than to frustration or disappointment (Rikmann and Lagerspetz, 2003, p. 18). In comparison with their percentage of both the total population and that of the electorate, members of minority nationalities are under-represented at both central and local government levels.

Some political parties have claimed to represent the Russian-speaking minorities. At present (2006), there are 20 political parties registered in Estonia, four of which have profiled themselves as representatives of Russian-speaking minorities (The Estonian United People's Party; The Baltic Russian Party in Estonia; The Russian Party in Estonia; The Party of Russian Unity). Parties and electoral unions of ethnic minorities have (since the parliamentary elections of 2003) influence at the local level only, mainly in the capital Tallinn and in the towns of the North-Eastern industrial region. It seems that even the minority population prefers to vote for candidates belonging to the Estonian-speaking mainstream parties. The Centre Party (*Keskerakond*) has many Russian-speaking members and is the strongest party both in Tallinn and in the North-Eastern region. The share of non-citizens voting in the local elections has dropped from 53 per cent in 1993 (with a peak of 85 per cent in 1996) to 43 per cent in 1999. A similar, but less steep, drop also characterizes the voting activity of the majority population (*Minority Protection*, 2002, 233).

With regard to the participation of immigrants and minorities in non-governmental organizations (NGOs), it is worth noting that the NGO sector in general has rapidly expanded during the last ten years. However, the number of Russian speakers' organizations has definitely remained lower (Lagerspetz, Rikmann and Ruutsoo, 2002). Population surveys regularly conclude that non-citizen and Russian speakers are less likely to be members of NGOs. Here, however, trade unions are an exception. The Central Organization of Estonian Trade Unions came into being as a wholly voluntary organization in 1990 to replace the Estonian branch of the official Soviet Labour Confederation. However, the share of organized labour of all employees has continuously diminished, being at present a mere 11.8 per cent (*Eesti Päevaleht*, 21 November 2005). Trade union membership is still usual among workers of large-sized industrial plants, among whom many are Russian speakers, especially in the North-Eastern region. Trade unions are rather invisible in the service sector and in small enterprises. As a result, the share of organized labour among ethnic Estonians is smaller than that among minority citizens and non-citizens.

Few non-governmental organizations deal directly with human rights and issues connected with minority rights. Instead, several organizations represent the (above all, cultural) interests of their ethnic groups in Estonia (see Lagerspetz and Joons, 2004, p. 76f.). Many of them are members of the *Estonian Union of National Minorities*. For Russians, *The Union of Slavic Educational and Charitable Societies in Estonia* is the dominant cultural organization, uniting more than 20 organizations under its umbrella, and conducting a regular series of cultural events and activities.

Financial support has been given to the activities of NGOs through local government, the Ministry of Culture and government-funded foundations. Usually, funding is given on the basis of applications and descriptions of projects. However, representatives of the minority organizations have repeatedly challenged the effectiveness of funding on that basis. Sometimes the funding actually received remains invisible in statistics or financial reports. This is the case, for instance, when a local government lends rooms without rent for courses or other events run by an organization of an ethnic minority.

Public and media discourses on migration

The discourse on immigrants and migration has so far been intertwined with the debate on issues such as the integration of minorities, citizenship policies and language policies. The development of public and media discourses can also be divided into three subsequent periods.

At the beginning of Estonian independence, the relationship between the government – now representing a former Soviet minority suddenly turned majority – and the Russian-speaking population was far from friendly. It should also be noted that Russian troops were still present in Estonia until August 1994. This created suspicion between the government and the Russian-speakers, who were sometimes seen as a 'fifth column' (Jurado, 2003). Thus, for a number of years, government policy was centred on changing the ethnic balance by encouraging the emigration of Russian-speakers (*Minority Protection* 2002: 195).

The second period covers the mid-1990s and was characterized by a softening of the original controversy between ethnic Estonians and Russian-speakers, and an emerging dialogue between the Estonian Government and Max van der Stoel, the High Commissioner on National Minorities (HCNM) of the OSCE. According to Jurado (2003), around 1997 a change in the domestic political discourse occurred and the parliamentary debate on minority issues became related to security concerns, and the need to avoid conflict both with Russia as well as internally with the country's own minority population.

This was reflected not only in relevant research that aimed to propose new policy initiatives and domestic legitimacy (Pettai, 2000) but also in the adoption of an official resolution on the principles of minority policy by the Parliament in June 1998. In line with the parliamentary resolution, the government adopted an interim Action Plan, and the next cabinet launched a more detailed *State Integration Programme* in 2000 (see above). Since then, the parliamentary debate seems to include more references to the moral desirability of different policy options and follows the Council of Europe discourse (Jurado, 2003). This might be a sign of two important changes in the political climate surrounding minority issues. First, minorities are no longer perceived as a threat to national security; and second, the European ideas of multiculturalism have received growing attention and have gradually replaced the ethnocentric ideas that were characteristic of the initial years of the Estonian nation-building process.

Estonia's EU accession has added some new migration-related issues to the current debate. On one hand, the increased mobility of labour has given Estonian citizens a chance to emigrate to other EU countries. This involves both unskilled workers and some highly skilled professionals, such as doctors and nurses. The fairly large emigration of people from the latter category has been seen as a problem. On the other hand, Estonian migration policy is now discussed in the context of a co-ordinated EU approach to migration. The EU in general, including Estonia, has an ageing population. In 1998, the fertility rate dropped to 1.21 and has now only crept back to 1.38 (2002) (Vetik, 2003, p. 78). In the public sphere, immigration is frequently referred to as a possible means of supporting the sustainability of the pensions system, as well as a way of keeping labour costs low. In general, there is no lively debate over migration-related issues, and popular attitudes towards immigration and immigrants seem to be either uninterested or negative.

At the same time, some issues related to the immigrant/minority population remain unresolved and continue to be debated. The most crucial issue is the future of the Russian language in secondary education. Here, the opinions of the authorities, of minority organizations and of the teachers of Russian schools still seem to lie in opposition to each other.

Concluding remarks

Estonia's immigrant population is almost entirely a result of Estonia's occupation by the Soviet Union during the Second World War. Having been defined as immigrants ex post facto, the Soviet-era settlers in Estonia can be described as belonging to a 'post-colonial' or an 'new imperial' minority (Sicakkan, 2004, pp. 50–51) – a rare phenomenon in today's Europe. Most rights guaranteed for Estonian citizens are guaranteed for other permanent legal residents as well. This especially covers welfare rights, economic rights and basic legal rights. For most purposes, the same also applies to holders of temporary residence permits. However, the legislation still seems to need developing. This is apparent from the recent changes to the present Aliens' Act. The most visible differences between people of different citizenship status are, however, concerned with political rights.

Estonia's policies and public debate on immigrants and national minorities have until very recently dealt only with the old minorities and/or the Soviet-era settlers. The new immigrants to the independent Estonia have remained rather invisible for debate, research and policy development. The first initiatives to deal with the children of new immigrants within the system of education have been taken only recently, and research on them is almost non-existent. Although new immigrant groups are small, they are, nevertheless, growing, and there is a pressing need to develop a conscious immigration policy reflecting Estonia's position as an EU member state.

References

Asari, E-M. (2002), 'Eesti keele oskuse ja kodakondsuse mõju mitte-eestlaste tööturuvõimalustele' [The impact on non-Estonians' labour market position of their knowledge of Estonian language and citizenship status], in Saar, E. (ed.) *Trepist alla ja üles: edukad ja ebaedukad postsotsialistlikus Eestis* [Up and Down the Stairs: The Successful and the Unsuccessful in Post-Socialist Estonia], 210–35. Tallinn: Teaduste Akadeemia Kirjastus.

Eesti Päevaleht, 16 September 2004; 21 November 2005; 20 April, 2006.

Heidmets, M. and Lauristin, M. (2002), 'Learning from the Estonian Case', in Lauristin, M. and Heidmets, M. (eds) *The Challenge of the Russian Minority: Emerging Multicultural Democracy in Estonia*, 319–32. Tartu: Tartu University Press.

Integration Yearbook 2003 (2004), *Integration Yearbook/Integratsiooni Aastaraamat 2003*. Tallinn: Integration Foundation/Integratsiooni Sihtasutus.

Jurado, E. (2003), 'Complying with European Standards of Minority Education: Estonia's Relations with the European Union, OSCE and Council of Europe', *Journal of Baltic Studies*, **XXXIV**(4), 399–431.

Kõuts, R. and Tammpuu, P. (2002), 'Changing media discourse on minority issues: From ignorance towards recognition', in Lauristin, M. and Heidmets, M. (eds) *The Challenge of the Russian Minority: Emerging Multicultural Democracy in Estonia*, 305–16. Tartu: Tartu University Press.

Krusell, S. (2002), 'Eestlaste ja mitte-eestlaste palkade erinevus' [Differences between wage levels of Estonians and non-Estonians], in Saar, E. (ed.) *Trepist alla ja üles: edukad ja ebaedukad postsotsialistlikus Eestis* [Up and Down the Stairs: The successful and the unsuccessful in Post-Socialist Estonia], 191–209. Tallinn: Teaduste Akadeemia Kirjastus.

Kulturrådet (2007), 'Kulturrådet' (available at www.estlandssvensk.ee, accessed 29 June 2007).

Lagerspetz, M. (1996), *Constructing Post-Communism. A study in the Estonian social problems discourse*. Turku: Annales Universitatis Turkuensis.

Lagerspetz, M. and Joons, S. (2004), *Migrants, Minorities, Belonging and Citizenship: The Case of Estonia*. Bergen: BRIC/University of Bergen.

Lagerspetz, M., Rikmann, E. and Ruutsoo, R. (2002), 'The structure and resources of NGOs in Estonia', *Voluntas*, 13(1), 73–87.

Lagerspetz, M. and Vogt, H. (1998), 'Estonia', in Berglund, S., Hellén, T. and Aarebrot, F. H. (eds), *The Handbook of Political Change in Eastern Europe*, 55–88. Cheltenham, UK and Northampton, MA, USA: Edward Elgar.

Lauristin, M. and Heidmets, M. (eds) (2002), *The Challenge of the Russian Minority: Emerging Multicultural Democracy in Estonia*. Tartu: Tartu University Press.

Lauristin, M. and Vihalemm, P. with Rosengren, K. E. and Weibull, L. (eds) (1997), *Return to the Western World: Cultural and Political Perspectives on the Estonian Post-Communist Transition*. Tartu: Tartu University Press.

Lieven, A. (1993/1994), *The Baltic Revolution. Estonia, Latvia, Lithuania and the path to independence*. New Haven and London: Yale University Press.

Minority Protection... (2002), *Monitoring the EU Accession Process: Minority Protection, Volume I. An Assessment of Selected Policies in Candidate States*. Budapest & New York: Open Society Institute.

Pettai, V. (2000), 'Competing conceptions of multiethnic democracy: Debating minority integration in Estonia', paper presented at the European Consortium for Political Research, Joint Sessions Workshop on 'Competing Conceptions of democracy in the Practice of Politics', April 14–19, 2000, Copenhagen Denmark (available at http://www.ut.ee/SOPL/cv/pettai/Competin.pdf, accessed 12 November 2004).

Pierson, C. (1996), *The Modern State*. London and New York: Routledge.

Postimees, 31 May 2005; 16 June 2005.

Raudsaar, M. and Kasemets, A. (2004), 'Eesti osalusdemokraatia proovikivi: poliitiline aktiivsus ja usaldus' [The touchstone of Estonian participatory democracy: Political activity and trust], in Kalmus, V., Lauristin, M. and Pruulmann-Vengerfeldt, P. (eds) *Eesti elavik 21. sajandi algul: ülevaade uurimuse Mina. Maailm. Meedia tulemustest* [Life-World in Estonia at the Beginning of the 21st Century: An overview of results from the study 'Me. The World. The Media'], 165–82. Tartu: Studia Societatis et Communicationis I.

Raun, T. U. (1987), *Estonia and the Estonians*, Stanford: Hoover Institution Press.

Riigi Teataja [the official gazette publishing legislative acts] (available at www.riigiteataja.ee, accessed 30 May 2006).

Rikmann, E., Lagerspetz, M., Pernik, P. and Tuisk, T. (2002), *Poliitilise osaluse dilemmad Eesti poliitilises kultuuris: kuuluvus ja kodanikuidentiteet* [The dilemmas of political participation in Estonian political culture: Belonging and civic identity] (Research report commissioned by the Chancellery of the Estonian Parliament) (available at www.riigikogu.ee/osakonnad/msi, accessed 30 May 2006).

Rikmann, E. and Lagerspetz, M. (2003), 'Kodanikuidentiteet ja poliitiline osalus' [Civic identity and political participation], in Vetik, R. (ed.) *Eesti inimarengu aruanne 2003. Inimarengu trendid ja ühiskondliku kokkuleppe vajadus* [Estonian Human Development Report 2003. Human development trends and the need for social agreement], 15–19. Tallinn: TPÜ RASI.

Roováli, K. (2004), '2,800 Eesti ingerlast valib mais kultuuriomavalitsuse' [2,800 Estonian Ingrians will elect Cultural Autonomy Board in May]. *Postimees*, 29 March 2004, 3.

Rose, R. (2000), *New Baltic Barometer IV: A survey study*. Glasgow: University of Strathclyde/ Studies in Public Policy No. 338.

Ruutsoo, R. (2002), 'Discursive conflict and Estonian post-communist nation-building', in Lauristin, M. and Heidmets, M. (eds) (2002) *The Challenge of the Russian Minority: Emerging Multicultural Democracy in Estonia*, 31–54. Tartu: Tartu University Press.

Saar, E. (ed.) (2002), *Trepist alla ja üles: edukad* ja *ebaedukad postsotsialistlikus Eestis* [Up and Down the Stairs: The Successful and the Unsuccessful in Post-Socialist Estonia]. Tallinn: Teaduste Akadeemia Kirjastus.

Sicakkan, H. G. (2004), *Belonging and the Quality of Citizenships: A comparative study of new public spaces in six European countries*. Bergen: BRIC/University of Bergen.

Third Report... (2006), *Third Report on Estonia. Adopted on 24 June 2005*. Strasbourg: European Commmission against Racism and Intolerance/Council of Europe CRI(2006)1.

Vetik, R. (1999), *Inter-Ethnic Relations in Estonia 1988–1998*. Tampere: Acta Universitatis Tamperensis.

Vetik, R. (ed.) (2003), *Eesti inimarengu aruanne 2003. Inimarengu trendid ja ühiskondliku kokkuleppe vajadus* [Estonian Human Development Report 2003. Human development trends and the need for social agreement]. Tallinn: TPÜ RASI.

Chapter 8

Finland

Silvain Sagne, Sanna Saksela and Niklas Wilhelmsson

Until recently, Finland was a country of emigration rather than of immigration. After the Second World War nearly 700,000 Finns migrated to Sweden, North America, Australia and other countries, mainly because of rapid structural changes in Finnish society (Forsander, 2002; Sandlund, 2004). Historically, migration to Finland has been very limited. During the first three decades of the twentieth century, Finland received refugees from both Russia and the Central European countries. At that time Finland did not have a migration policy, and attitudes towards refugees where generally reserved. During the Second World War, many Ingrian Finns moved to Finland from the Soviet Union but in the peace treaty Finland bound itself to send them back. This still has an impact on immigration to Finland today, since Ingrian Finns are presently regarded as return migrants with special status to return to Finland (Similä, 2003, p. 99).

In the decades after the Second World War the Finnish borders were tightly controlled and migration was very limited. During the 1970s and 1980s small groups of Chilean and Vietnamese refugees moved to Finland, while immigration in general remained modest (Valtonen, 1997). After the breakdown of the Soviet Union, Finland quickly converted into a receiving country for immigrants. The main immigration flows that have targeted Finland came from the former Soviet Union areas. The war in Somalia and former Yugoslavia and other restless areas in Africa and Asia are other big sources of immigration (mainly refugees and through family reunification) (www. mol.fi).

Finnish migration is closely related to its history and its peripheral location. There has never been great pressure for migration and neither has there been a labour shortage. Finnish migration policy has also traditionally been rather restrictive because of the country's geopolitical location.[1] (Forsander, 2002, p. 23; Similä, 2003, p. 99). The main reasons for increased immigration to Finland are to be found in allowing return migration, in having larger refugee quotas and in increased labour migration especially from neighbouring countries. We can assume that two of the drivers for increased immigration are the dissolution of the Soviet Union and Finland's joining the EU in 1995.

The rapid increase in migration at the beginning of the 1990s occurred simultaneously with the economic depression, which led to an increase in racism and xenophobic behaviour (Similä, 2003; Jaakkola, 2005).

Major developments in Finnish immigration policy

Even though immigration to Finland increased during the 1990s, the immigrant population is still small and amounts to only circa 2–3 per cent of the population of 5.2 million. The major inflows

---

1   Immigrants and refugees have been viewed as a threat to national security and immigration has been considered a politically delicate issue in relation to the neighbouring Soviet Union.

of foreign population towards Finland have included (Jasinskaja-Lahti, Liebkind and Vesala, 2002, p. 17):

- return migration of people of Finnish descent from Sweden and the former Soviet Union (Finnish Swedes and Ingrian Finns)
- refugees and family reunification (UN quota refugees and other refugees)
- marriage
- labour migration.

The first legislation regarding immigrants and immigration was the Aliens Decree that entered into force in 1919. It was broad and manifested the role of the state in controlling immigration through passports, visa and residence permits. During the 1930s the legislation became more detailed and the rights to asylum were defined. During the first three decades of the twentieth century, immigration to Finland was very limited and consisted mainly of Russian refugees. It reached its peak in 1922 when 33,500 Russian refugees moved to Finland. During the 1930s mainly Jewish refugees from Central Europe arrived in Finland. The Finnish Government took a cautious position towards Central European refugees, in view of its good relationship with the Nazi regime (Similä, 2003, p. 99). This was reflected in the Foreigners Decree of 1938, which tightened the stance against foreigners and authorized the foreign police to monitor foreigners. Even though the Aliens Decree of 1942 redefined the grounds for asylum, there were very limited attempts during the inter-war years in developing Finnish asylum policy. This reflected the difficult foreign political situation Finland was in at the time[2] (Lepola, 2000, pp. 39–44). During the Second World War, 63,000 Ingrian Finns moved to Finland from the Soviet Union. In the peace treaty Finland bound itself to send the Ingrian Finns back. About 8,000 of the Ingrian Finns stayed in Finland while 55,000 were later sent back to the Soviet Union (Similä, 2003, p. 99). After the Second World War the number of foreigners living in Finland was very low. It has been estimated that only about 7,500 foreigners were living in Finland in 1955 (Forsander, 2002, p. 25).

Until 1983 immigration and the rights of foreigners was governed through Decrees. The first Finnish Aliens Act entered into force as late as 1983. It was a necessary step to take, due to discrepancies between the Finnish legislation and international human rights agreements. The 1983 Aliens Act strengthened the legal protection of foreigners and granted foreigners permission to appeal before the courts.

The breakdown of the Soviet Union and the influence of international agreements opened up Finnish society at the beginning of the 1990s. Economic growth and a growing labour shortage opened the discussion about recruiting foreign labour. The increasing number of foreigners living in Finland and the critique of Finnish legislation led to the adoption of a new Aliens Act which entered into force in 1991. The 1991 Aliens Act received a lot of criticism. The Act was both unclear and in conflict with other Finnish legislation and with international agreements – concerning family reunification, among other issues – which made it difficult to maintain a coherent immigration policy. While drawing up the new legislation, the Committee on Immigration suggested that, because of its ageing population, Finland should be aiming for a more active immigration policy. The Amsterdam Treaty also started a process towards harmonizing immigration and asylum policies

---

2   Finland has been characterized as a country between East and West. Between the World Wars the relationship between Finland and the Western European countries developed while, at the same time, the country remained influenced by developments in the Soviet Union. In 1939, the Winter War broke out between the Soviet Union and Finland which continued – except for some shorter periods of peace – until the end of the Second World War.

amongst the EU-countries, which also poses new challenges for the Finnish legislation (Forsander, 2002, pp. 26–27). The reform of the Aliens Act led to the adoption of a new Aliens Act in 2004.

The Aliens Act defines the rules for long-term residence of foreigners in Finland. Foreigners are usually first issued a temporary residence permit that is valid for a limited period. A permanent residence permit can be issued to a person who has resided in Finland on a temporary residence permit for two consecutive years. Any permanent residence permit may be refused on specific grounds such as being guilty of a crime or some other reprehensible conduct. The application for a residence permit is made to the local police authorities. If the local police consider that the application has to be rejected, the final decision is taken by the Directorate of Immigration. In the event of a negative decision the applicant may appeal to the County Administrative Court. The highest instance for appeal is the Supreme Administrative Court. The residence permit is important, since it gives access to Finnish social security. Social benefits and social services are based on residency and not citizenship. A person migrating to Finland can be considered to be residing in Finland and have access to social security immediately after entering the country if the purpose is permanent residence and the person is holding a residence permit that is valid for at least one year.

Even though Finnish legislation has eased up, Finnish migration policy can still be judged as restrictive. Also, the Finnish refugee quota is small and very few refugees are given a Convention status. There has also been a reduction in asylum applications, especially from the Eastern European countries after the introduction of accelerated asylum procedures with the possibility of rapid expulsions in 2001. The introduction of the rapid expulsions came as a reaction to the increasing number of Roma asylum seekers from Romania, Slovakia and the Czech Republic (Similä, 2003, p. 4). This procedure has been highly criticized.

The Directorate of Immigration and the Ministry of Labour select the refugees who are admitted to Finland within the annual refugee quota. The refugee quota is verified in the State budget each year. In co-operation with the Ministry for Foreign Affairs and the Ministry of the Interior, the Ministry of Labour annually presents a proposal to the government concerning the regional allocation of the refugee quota. The selections are usually based on interviews conducted in refugee camps, during which the grounds for granting a residence permit are examined. A representative of the Security Police also participates in the interviews.

Finnish immigration policy has traditionally been built on a homogenous national population, and immigration to Finland has, thus, generally required biological or family ties to Finland (Forsander, 2002, p. 23). Ingrian Finns were granted the special right of return migration, on the grounds of their Finnish descent, by a decision made by President Mauno Koivisto in 1990 (Söderling, 2004, p. 47). The decision led to a huge increase in the immigration of people from the former Soviet Union. Since then, the authorities have introduced stronger regulations concerning the necessary documentation and language skill that a person of Ingrian descent should have before s/he can enter the country. In September 2004 there were still 22,000 Ingrians lining up for entry interviews in Russia and Estonia (www.uvi.fi).

Traditionally, it has been difficult to receive a work permit in Finland but, as a reaction to the increasing labour shortage and because of increasing international co-operation, the number of foreign workers in Finland has increased and the granting of work permits has become more flexible. In 2000, 15,000 work permits were issued (Sorainen, 2003, pp. 14–15).

Naturalization

The principal rules for Finnish citizenship are based on the principle of descent; in other words, being born to a Finnish parent. Even if a child is born abroad, but at least one of the parents is

Finnish, the child will automatically receive Finnish citizenship. A child born in Finland whose parents are not Finnish citizens will not receive Finnish citizenship automatically unless he or she is in danger of being stateless (Lepola, 2004, p. 4).

The Finnish Nationality Act also makes it possible for foreigners to acquire Finnish citizenship, provided they fill certain criteria. Foreigners are expected to have satisfactory oral and written Finnish or Swedish skills. A foreigner must have lived in Finland for six years and have adequate means of subsistence before he or she can apply for citizenship. For refugees and stateless persons, special rules are applied and the period for obtaining Finnish citizenship may be shorter. Persons with Finnish spouses can receive Finnish citizenship after five years of residence in Finland. Spouses need to prove they have lived together and have done so for the past three years. The Nationality Act also guarantees the acquisition of Finnish citizenship for a former Finnish citizen and Nordic citizens after two years of uninterrupted stay in Finland. Even though Ingrian Finns are given special rights to move to Finland because of their Finnish descent, they have not been granted privileged status regarding citizenship (see Lepola, 2004, p. 4; Nationality Act 359/2003).

The rules for applying Finnish citizenship are not definite. Even if a foreigner meets the criteria for Finnish citizenship, the application may be rejected by the authorities. Only children who have been adopted by Finnish parents, former Finnish citizens, citizens of other Nordic countries, and young people (age 18–23) who have lived in Finland for at least 10 years have an absolute right to claim Finnish citizenship. Since 2003 it has been possible to hold dual citizenship, which means that foreigners do not have to give up their former citizenship when they are granted Finnish citizenship (Lepola, 2004, pp. 4–5).

In total, 28,709 foreign citizens received Finnish citizenship between 1999 and 2003. Of these, 13,588 are from Europe, 6,592 from Asia, 4,612 from Africa, 856 from America and 45 from Oceania. The largest groups of European immigrants who received Finnish citizenship between 1991 and 2003 came from Russia, Estonia and Sweden. The largest African groups receiving Finnish citizenship during the same period were Somalis, Moroccans and Ethiopians, while the largest Asian groups receiving Finnish citizenship were Vietnamese, Iraqi and Chinese. Immigration from North and South America and Oceania has generally been smaller and less permanent, which is also indicated by the number of people who have received Finnish citizenship (Sagne, Saksela and Wilhelmsson 2005, p. 12).

Integration policies

The integration policies and policies concerning foreigners living in Finland have changed since the beginning of the 1990s because of increased migration to Finland, membership of the European Council and EU membership. The Finnish integration law is extensive and in a comparative perspective a fairly developed structure (Lepola, 2000, pp. 416–417; Salmenhaara, 2002, p. 61). The Finnish Integration Act came into force on 1 May 1999 and aims to provide immigrants with a knowledge of Finnish, information about Finnish society and culture, and possibilities of education and work. The main emphasis of the immigration and refugee policy programmes is on the rapid and flexible integration of immigrants. Integration refers to participation in the economy, politics and social life of the society on an equal basis, and rights and obligations equal to those of the native population. Immigrants should, at the same time, have the right to maintain and develop their own culture and religion (Integration Act 493/1999, §1). The objective is to support the integration of immigrants, including refugees, into the Finnish labour market and society by designing individual integration plans for persons who have moved to Finland and have a home municipality in Finland (Integration Act 493/1999, §3). The law requires all municipalities to have an integration programme, on the basis of which individual integration paths for all immigrants are built, and whose aim is full membership in society and employment. A three-year individual integration plan is drawn up for every immigrant. All unemployed immigrants or immigrants living on social welfare are required, within a year after coming to Finland, to draw up an individual integration plan together with the authorities, and to participate in the education and other measures stated in the plan. In addition to education and language education the plan might also include work training and support (Salmenhaara, 2002, p. 61).

The Finnish anti-discrimination laws are fairly extensive. The main anti-discrimination provisions have been laid down in the Constitution, the Equality Act and the Penal Code. In addition, there are many individual acts dealing with labour life and prohibiting discrimination in their particular sphere of application. Discrimination based on sex is specifically dealt with in the Act on Equality between women and men. Most anti-discrimination provisions explicitly prohibit discrimination on a wide variety of grounds and contain a clause according to which discrimination based on other personal characteristics is prohibited as well. Section 6 of the Finnish Constitution provides for equality and non-discrimination on a wide variety of grounds such as health, disability, sex, ethnic origin, language, religion and belief. The constitution aims to guarantee formal equality – that is, that people are to be treated similarly in similar circumstances – but it also aims to enhance the achievement of full substantive equality in practice. The constitutional prohibition can be the subject of direct court action.

The purpose of the Equality Act, which came into force in February 2004, is to foster equality and enhance the protection of those who have experienced discrimination. The Equality Act prohibits discrimination based on age, ethnic origin, disability, sexual orientation or other personal characteristics. The term ethnic origin refers to both immigrants and old ethnic minorities and the aim of the law is, thus, to protect all people living in the country from discrimination. In addition to national legislation, the international human rights law provides added protection from discrimination. Even though the Finnish integration and anti-discrimination legislation is extensive, the administrative policies and practice have been criticized due to their un-adaptive and bureaucratic nature. Researcher Perttu Salmenhaara, for example, has stated that the normalizing and controlling aspects of the Finnish welfare state are emphasized at the cost of efficient and humane integration and migration management. The bureaucratic practice and the policies carried out by civil servants should be more adaptive and efficient and the focus should be put on long-term results (Salmenhaara, 2002, p. 63).

The immigrant population in Finland: main demographic and social features

Migration to Finland can roughly be divided into five categories: refugees, including UN quota refugees and so called de facto refugees; family reunifications; remigration; labour migration and migration for other reasons. The most common reasons for migrating to Finland are marriage and family purposes, return migration and asylum seeking (Jasinskaja-Lahti, Liebkind and Vesala, 2002, p. 17). The special feature of the Finnish case is that the number of immigrants, compared to other Western European countries, is still very low. Most immigrants have lived in the country for a very short time and Finland has traditionally not been a country of destination for refugees. The proportion of labour migration is very small, there is a special composition of immigrants with regard to countries of origin and a high proportion of marriages between Finns and immigrants (Similä, 2003, pp. 101–102).

Since the beginning of the 1990s, the foreign-born population in Finland has increased rapidly. The number of foreigners legally living in Finland without citizenship quadrupled between 1990 and 2005, from 26,300 to 113,850. During the same period the number of foreign-born Finnish citizens and residents doubled from 77,000 to 176,000, constituting three per cent of the total Finnish population. The number of residents whose first language is not Finnish or Swedish has increased from 43,000 in 1992, to 144,000 in 2005 (Statistics Finland, 2005). The census figures can be judged to give a reliable picture of immigrants in Finland, because the number of illegal or un-registered immigrants is estimated to be low. Most illegal immigrants enter the country legally, but are judged as illegal immigrants since their residence permit, visa or visa-exempt period has expired. It has been estimated that there could be around 10,000 illegal immigrants in Finland who have entered on tourist visas and are working temporarily in Finland. There are only a very limited number of people who have entered the country illegally, or who are illegally staying permanently in the country (Similä, 2003, p. 107).

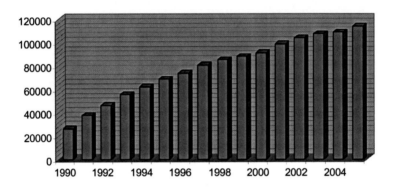

Source: Statistics Finland.

Figure 8.1   Foreign citizens in Finland (1990–2005)

In total, by the end of 2005, the Finnish population amounted to 5,255,580 of whom 176,612 were born abroad. Among the permanent population in Finland, 5,141,728 have Finnish citizenship, while 113,852 people are of another nationality. Finland is a bilingual country with Finnish and Swedish as the official languages. People in Lapland have the right to use Sami in schools and handle their affairs with authorities in their own language. Of the Finnish population, 4,819,819 people had Finnish as their mother tongue, 289,675 had Swedish as their mother tongue and 1,752 had Sami as their mother tongue. In total, there were 144,334 persons who had a foreign language as their mother tongue. Russian is, by far, the most common foreign mother tongue in Finland. There are also considerable groups with Estonian, English, Somali, Arabic, Albanian, Kurdish and Vietnamese as their mother tongue (Statistics Finland, 2005).

Table 8.1   Population according to nationality, mother tongue and state of birth (2005)

Population   5,255,580

Nationality		Mother tongue		State of birth	
Finnish	5,141,728	Finnish	4,819,819	Finland	5,078,968
Foreigners in total	113,852	Swedish	289,675	*Born abroad in total*	176,612
Biggest groups:		Sami	1,752	*Biggest groups:*	
Russian	24,621	*Foreign languages in total*	144,334	Former Soviet Union	40,196
Estonian	15,459	*Biggest groups:*		Sweden	29,527
Swedish	8,196	Russian	39,653	Estonia	12,597
Somalian	4,704	Estonian	15,336	Somalia	5,060
Serbian and Montenegrin	3,321	English	8,928	Former Yugoslavia	5,030
Iraqi	3,267	Somali	8,593	Russia	4,748
Chinese	2,992	Arabic	7,117	Germany	4,555
German	2,792	Kurdish	5,123	Iraq	4,352
British	2,762	Albanian	5,076	China	4,123
Turkish	2,621	Chinese	4,613	Thailand	3,551
Thai	2,605	Vietnamese	4,202	Great Britain	3,497

Source: Statistics Finland.

Russian immigrants form the largest immigrant group, amounting to approximately 25,000 persons (Russian citizens). Of all immigrants coming to Finland from the former Soviet Union area, 60–70 per cent are Ingrian return migrants. Ingrians are people of Finnish decent who moved from Finland to Ingria in the 16th and 17th centuries.[3] A majority of the Ingrian immigrants have never visited Finland before and do not speak Finnish. Russian immigrants have also moved to Finland for marriage and employment purposes (Jasinskaja-Lahti, Liebkind and Vesala, 2002, p. 18).

Estonians form the second largest immigrant group in Finland, and total approximately 15,000 persons. Almost half of the Estonian immigrants are Ingrian Finns. After Estonia gained independence from the former Soviet Union and was confronted with economic problems and unemployment, some Estonians moved to Finland for better job opportunities and higher salaries (Sorainen, 2003, pp. 14–15).

Somalis form the largest refugee group in Finland, with about 5,000 people. Most of the Somali refugees came to Finland through the Soviet Union at the beginning of the 1990s when civil war broke out in Somalia (Alitolppa-Niitamo, 2004; Sandlund, 2004, p. 5). Other large refugee groups in Finland are people from the former Yugoslavia, Iraq and Iran. Other significant immigrant groups are mainly labour immigrants from other EU countries and the USA (Statistics Finland, 2005).

Labour migration has been growing in recent years, mainly because of increased labour migration from neighbouring countries, but is still comparatively low. Recruitment of skilled labour from abroad is still extremely low compared to the other EU countries. Most immigrants arriving in Finland don't have a job waiting for them. The threshold is high for entering the labour market in the Nordic welfare societies, where there is a high rate of unemployment among immigrants (Forsander, 2002, p. 28). Almost one-third of all foreign nationals living in Finland are unemployed. Among some nationalities unemployment has been considerably higher. Refugees and asylum seekers especially have had difficulties in finding a job in Finland and many are working in sectors where income is low and the employment situation is unstable (Salmenhaara, 2002, p. 51). Immigrants are mostly employed in industry and in the service sector, and are overrepresented in sectors such as cleaning and public transportation. In 1997, 36 per cent of immigrants were employed, 28 per cent were unemployed, 11 per cent were students, 1 per cent were retired and 24 per cent were something else. Fifteen per cent of the employed immigrants were working in the metal industry, electronics industry and the forestry industry, 15 per cent were working in the restaurant sector, 9 per cent were working in cleaning, 8 per cent were working in health care, 6 per cent were working in the construction sector and 6 per cent in teaching. Although unemployment is high among immigrants in Finland, the danger of an ethnification of poverty is small because of social welfare services (Forsander, 2002, pp. 127–282).

Immigrant rights and participation in public life – issues of immigrant integration

According to the European Commission against Racism and Intolerance (ECRI) Finland has, in the last few years, taken a number of significant measures to include immigrants and minority groups in the policy development process (ECRI, 2002, p. 5).

The right of foreigners to participate in associations and political parties has increased during recent decades. According to the association law of 1919 (Association Act 1/1919) foreigners were not allowed to participate in political organizations or organizations with political purposes. With the revision of the association law in 1989, foreigners were granted the same rights as Finnish citizens to participate in organizations (Association Act 503/1989).[4] This also made it possible for

---

3   Ingria is an area around St Petersburg.
4   Parties in Finland are governed through the Association Act and the Party Act.

immigrants to join, or establish their own, associations with political goals, such as youth parties and labour unions. Immigrants nowadays also have similar rights to Finnish workers to join labour unions.

The political rights of foreigners have also been extended. Since 1976, the right to vote and the right to be a candidate in municipal elections were granted to the nationals of other Nordic countries after three years of residence. Since 1995, EU citizens and citizens of Iceland and Norway who are 18 years of age are entitled to vote in municipal elections if they have been living in the municipality for more than 51 days before the elections. Other nationals are entitled to vote in the local elections after two years of residence.[5] The right to stand as a candidate and to participate in parliamentary elections requires Finnish citizenship. The same applies for voting in presidential elections. In European Parliamentary elections, citizens of other EU Member States have the right to vote if they have lived in Finland for two years.

The Finnish state has recently taken some legislative measures in order to lower the threshold for participation and to incorporate immigrants in the decision-making process both at the national and the local level. The Integration Act requires the municipalities to give societal education and guidance in order to make societal participation easier (Saksela, 2005).

In general, foreigners and immigrants have not been very visible in Finnish politics. Some immigrants and foreigners have used their right to establish associations, publish newspapers and organize demonstrations, but their activities have mainly targeted their own nationality or language group (Lepola, 2004, p. 8). In Finnish politics in general, immigration issues have become more prominent only in recent years. Some political parties have established immigrant working groups and the number of political candidates with an immigrant background has increased significantly during the recent elections. In the municipal elections of 2004, 75 immigrant candidates were nominated in the capital region, of whom only three were elected (Wilhelmsson, 2004). The electoral participation among immigrants having voting rights has remained low. In the 1996 municipal elections only 17 per cent of immigrants in the capital region voted and in 2000 only 14 per cent, thereby probably reflecting a lack of integration into Finnish society (Hellsten and Martikainen, 2001, pp. 52–53).

Advisory boards both at the national and at the local level have been established in order to get the voices of immigrants heard and in order to give immigrants a better chance to express their political opinions. However, there are still problems in the sharing and dissemination of information between authorities and immigrants and in the division of work between different authorities (Saksela, 2005). The first national advisory board for migrants, the Migration Commission (SAN) was appointed by the Council of State in 1970. The board later merged with the Advisory board for Refugee Affairs (Refugee Commission) to form the Advisory Board for Refugee and Migration Affairs (PAKSI). The Ministry of Labour was in charge of PAKSI together with the Ministry of Health and Social Affairs. The increased number of immigrants and refugees at the beginning of the 1990s required new kinds of institutional arrangements. In 1998, at the request of the Ministry of Labour, the Council of State appointed the Advisory Board for Ethnic Relations (ETNO), a broad-based consultative expert organ, which gives statements on matters relating to refugees and migration and on racism and ethnic relations. A variety of linguistic and cultural minorities are broadly represented on the Advisory Board (www.mol.fi).

Local multicultural advisory boards have been established in the largest communities. The Multicultural Advisory Councils of Espoo and Vantaa and the Advisory Council for Foreigners in Helsinki were established after the Integration Act came into force. The main function of these councils is to coordinate and advise different delegations for immigration affairs, and to follow

---

5   Chapter 4, section 26 (1) Municipality Act, on 2 December 1995.

the outcomes of the integration programmes as well as the work done by the delegation for ethnic discrimination and racism. Members of immigrant associations do participate in the working groups of the Multicultural Advisory Council in Espoo and Vantaa. They are not involved in the decision-making, but do contribute to the planning of integrative issues. The Advisory Council for Foreigners in Helsinki is also planning to involve members of immigrant associations and representatives of immigrant groups (Saksela, 2005).

Public and media discourses on migration

Media policy

The new Constitution of Finland (731/1999) that entered in force in 2000 underlines the freedom of expression for all. The immigration policy programme also underlines the importance of supporting the media activities of immigrant communities and their associations. The role of the media has also been noticed in the Government Action Plan to Combat Ethnic Discrimination and Racism. It was acknowledged that immigrants and immigrant associations need funding for their publicity activities and the Ministry of Education has started to support the media activities of immigrants as well as of national ethnic minorities. Currently, the number of journals, radio and television programmes among immigrants and national ethnic minorities is growing. Print media is, however, still the most dominant form of ethnic media.[6] There are also radio programmes that are produced together with immigrants and old national minorities, such as Radio Sputnik by the Russians and 'Lähiradio' (a local community radio programme in Helsinki). The action plan also stressed that the majority culture media should give opportunities to representatives of ethnic minorities to participate in the production of media. During recent years especially the national television and Radio broadcast company YLE has acknowledged the interest among immigrant and other ethnic groups in expressing their opinions.

The media discourse

There are a few issues concerning immigration and immigrants that have regularly been discussed in the Finnish press. A study of the Finnish press showed that about 20 per cent of the newspaper articles dealing with ethnic minorities and immigration focused on the relationship between ethnic minorities, 16 per cent dealt with aspects related to legislation and authority actions and crimes committed by members of ethnic minorities, and 9 per cent focused on labour market issues. Among the legal and authority issues, the new Aliens Act and the procedure of rapid expulsions have received a lot of attention in the media. During 2004 a comparatively large number of Roma people from Slovakia came to Finland seeking asylum because of the circumstances in their country of origin. This received a lot of media attention and was linked to the debate on the new Aliens Act and rapid expulsions.

Other significant themes that have been discussed are the effect of the transition period law on the structure of the labour market, the effect of founding a discrimination board, and the effect of the Equality Act.[7]

---

6   There are several periodicals published among the old minorities in Finland: Jews, the Roma, the Tatars and the so-called old Russians.

7   The percentages are based on a research project conducted by the Department of Journalism at the University of Tampere. The results are based on media monitoring of seven major newspapers: *Helsingin*

There has been a long-standing debate on how to deal with immigration in general and on the need of labour migration to Finland (Sorainen, 2003, pp. 6–19). The debate has focused on the unfavourable age structure of the country and its possible consequences and policy orientation, including debates on immigration policy and the need for increased labour migration. Opinion has been divided between those favouring increased labour migration and those against it. Connected to this, there have been discussions on the EU-enlargement process and the issue of the illegal labour market. One of the recent, most visible, and highly debated issues has been the immigration of Estonian workers to Finland after Estonia joined the EU, and its impact on the Finnish labour market. There is also a recurring debate in the media on how to deal with the integration of immigrants, and on how well integration policies work.

Recent global phenomena such as tensions between Muslims and non-Muslims have been mentioned much more frequently in the media since 9/11 and the wars in Afghanistan and Iraq.[8] The reporting has not been entirely negative towards Islam; on the contrary, there seems to be an increased awareness and consciousness on the part of journalists when dealing with issues concerning ethnic minorities and immigrants (Sandlund, 2000, 2002; Raittila, 2002; Haavisto, 2004, p. 18).

Concluding remarks

Finland has traditionally been a country of emigration. During the 1960s and 1970s many people migrated from the country because of structural changes in Finnish society. Traditionally, Finnish migration policies have been restrictive and the number of immigrants has been low. Immigrants now amount to approximately three per cent of the population. Finland has been faced with increased immigration since the beginning of the 1990s and this development will probably continue in the future. Finnish migration is closely related to its history and to its peripheral location. There has never been great pressure for immigration and neither has there been a labour shortage. Finnish migration policy has also traditionally been rather restrictive because of the country's geopolitical location.

The main reasons for increased immigration to Finland are to be found in allowing return migration, in having larger refugee quotas, and in increased labour migration especially from neighbouring countries. The major inflows of foreign population towards Finland have included: the re-immigration of people of Finnish descent from Sweden and the former Soviet Union (Finnish Swedes and Ingrian Finns), refugees and family reunification (UN quota refugees and other refugees), marriage and labour migration. We can assume that two of the drivers for increased immigration are the dissolution of the Soviet Union and Finland's joining the EU in 1995. The rapid increase in migration at the beginning of the 1990s occurred simultaneously with the economic depression, which led to an increase in racism and xenophobia.

Like many other West-European countries, Finland will suffer from an ageing population and will consequently need more foreign labour. The ageing population and low birth rates have influenced and shaped attitudes towards foreigners. The present government perspective states that Finland needs labour migration in order to meet the needs of the labour market. The Finnish Government has already taken action to manage the immigration issue by softening the immigration laws.

Sanomat, Ilta Sanomat, Iltalehti, Aamulehti, Turun Sanomat, Kymen Sanomat and *Kaleva.*

8   Results are based on a media monitoring project carried out by the Centre for Research on Ethnic Relations and Nationalism (CEREN) at the Swedish School of Social Science at the University of Helsinki, and include the monitoring of several major Swedish language newspapers and the major Finnish language newspaper.

The Finnish Government has also made significant efforts to improve the position of immigrants in Finland. The Finnish integration law is extensive and, comparatively speaking, a fairly developed structure. The law requires all the municipalities to have an integration programme, on the basis of which individual integration paths for all immigrants are built, the aim of which is full membership of society and employment.

The right for foreigners to participate in associations and political parties has been extended during recent decades. In general, foreigners and immigrants have not been very visible in Finnish politics. Some immigrants and foreigners have used their rights to establish associations, publish newspapers, and organize demonstrations, but their activities have mainly targeted their own nationality or language group. In Finnish politics in general, the immigration issue has become more prominent in recent years. Some political parties have established immigrant working groups and the number of political candidates with an immigrant background has increased significantly during the recent elections. Electoral participation has remained very low among immigrants. In recent years, immigrant advisory boards have been established both at the state and at the municipal level, in order to improve both the formal and informal participation of immigrants in the policy-making processes.

Immigrant groups in Finland are generally small and heterogeneous, which makes it hard for them to get organized. In the future, more emphasis should be put on the collaboration between immigrants and mainstream society. Although immigrant associations participate in integrative projects and on advisory boards, there is a need to pay attention to the way interaction takes place. Namely, instead of organizing projects for immigrants these should be done together with them.

References

Alitolppa-Niitamo, A. (2004), *The Icebreakers. Somali-speaking Youth in Metropolitan Helsinki* . *with a Focus on the Context of Formal Education.* Finland: Hakapaino.

ECRI (European Commission against Racism and Intolerance) (2002), Second Country Report on Finland. Strasbourg.

Forsander, A. (2002), *Luottamuksen ehdot. Maahanmuuttajat 1990-luvun suomalaisilla työmarkkinoilla.* Finland: Vammalan kirjapaino.

Haavisto, C. (2004), 'Etniska minoriteter och etnicitetsfrågor i Hufvudstadsbladet och Vasabladet', *CEREN Occasional Papers*, **4**, 2004.

Hellsten, V. and Martikainen, T. (2001), 'Nuoret ja uusi politiikka. Tutkimus pääkaupunkiseudun nuorten poliittisista suuntauksista', *City of Helsinki Urban Facts Research Series*, 2001:2. Helsinki.

Jaakkola, M. (2005), *Suomalaisten suhtautuminen maahanmuutajiin vuosina 1997–2003. Työpoliittinen tutkimus 2005.* Helsinki: Hakapaino.

Jasinskaja-Lahti, I., Liebkind, K. and Vesala, T. (2002), *Rasismi ja syrjintä Suomessa. Maahanmuuttajien kokemuksia.* Helsinki: Gaudeamus.

Lepola, O. (2000), *Ulkomaalaisesta suomenmaalaiseksi. Monikulttuurisuus, kansalaisuus ja suomalaisuus 1990-luvun maahanmuuttopoliittisessa keskustelussa, Suomalaisen kirjallisuuden seuran toimituksia 787.* Helsinki.

Lepola, O. (2004), 'Does Immigration Challenge the Finnish Nation?', in Castrén, A-M., Lonkila, M. and Peltonen, M. (eds) *Between Sociology and History*, Suomalaisen kirjallisuuden seura, 268–88. Helsinki.

Raittila, P. (ed.) (2002), *Etnisyys ja rasismi journalismissa.* Suomen journalistiliitto, mediakriittinen julkaisusarja 6. Vammala: Vammalan kirjapaino OY.

Sagne, S., S. Saksela and Wilhelmsson, N. (2005), Active Civic Participation of Immigrants in Finland. Country Report Prepared for the European research project POLITIS. Oldenburg.

Saksela, S. (2005), 'Maahanmuuttajayhdistysten ja viranomaisten välinen yhteistyö' in T. Joronen (toim.) *Maahanmuuttajien elinolot pääkaupunkiseudulla. Helsingin kaupungin tietokeskus*, 89–115. Helsinki: Yliopistopaino.

Salmenhaara, P. (2002), *Maahanmuuttajat, etniset vähemmistöt ja työmarkkinat. Tutkimusraportti.* Ihmisoikeusliitto 2002.

Sandlund, T. (2004), 'Introduction', in Sandlund, T. (ed.) *GLOCALMIG: Minorities, Migrants Belonging and Citizenship, Glocalization and Participation Dilemmas in the EU and Small States*. Bergen: BRIC Publishers.

Sandlund, T. (ed.) (2000), *Rasism och etnicitet i den finlandssvenska tidningspressen*. SSKH Meddelanden 57. Helsingfors: Universitetstryckeriet.

Sandlund, T. (ed.) (2002), *Etnicitetsbilden i finlandssvenska medier*. SSKH Meddelanden 62. Helsingfors: Universitetstryckeriet.

Similä, M. (2003), 'Immigrants and Minorities in Finland: Problems and Challenges', in Turton, D. and Gonzalez, J. (eds) *Immigration in Europe: Issues, Policies and Case Studies*, 97–112. Spain: Artes Graficas Rotegiu.

Söderling, I. (2004), 'Finland and Sweden Footsteps, Differences and Similarities in Immigration and Integration Policies', in Kärki, K. (ed.) *Power and Control: Perspectives on Integration and Multiculturalism in Europe*. (The Family Federation of Finland, The Population Research Institute D), 43/2004. Turku.

Sorainen, O. (2003), *OECD Sopemi – Trend in International Migration*. Finland: Sopemi.

Valtonen, K. (1997), *The Societal Participation of Refugees and Immigrants* (Canada and Trinidad: Case Studies in Finland). Vammala: Vammalan Kirjapaino.

Wilhelmsson, N. (2004) (unpublished paper) *Political Participation of Immigrants in Finland. An analysis of the voting behaviour of four immigrant groups in the Capital region.*

Internet-based references

Ministry of Labour (available at http://www.mol.fi, accessed 20 November 2004).

Statistics Finland (available at http://www.tilastokeskus.fi, accessed 10 November 2004, 15 December 2005, 5 May 2006).

Directorate of immigration (available at http://www.uvi.fi, accessed 1 November 2004).

Legal Sources

Integration Act (L 493/1999)
The Aliens Act from 1991
Association Act (L 1/1919)
Association Act (L 503/1989)
Constitution of Finland (731/1999)
Nationality Act (L 359/2003)

Chapter 9

France

Ulrike Schuerkens

While the percentage of immigrants in France has remained the same since 1975, immigration has changed a lot: family reunification has become the main reason for entry, female immigration has increased and immigrants have begun to come from more faraway countries (Tribalat, 1996). Frequently, immigrants work as unskilled or low- skill labourers (52 per cent of men and 23 per cent of women; 42 per cent of these immigrants occupy jobs as unqualified workers). Their over-representation in industry and construction has diminished over recent years. People born in France with two immigrant parents represent five per cent of those under the age of 66. Children of immigrants often have difficulties in school, but no more than children with the same socioeconomic characteristics. In 1999, immigrants represented 7.4 per cent of the population living in the French metropolitan territory (INSEE, 2001). Immigrants born in Algeria, Tunisia and Morocco represent 30 per cent of all immigrants. More and more immigrants are arriving from Sub-Saharan Africa, Turkey and Asia. Thirty-five per cent of immigrants live in the Paris metropolitan area. In 2002, 53 per cent of immigrants aged 15 or more had a job or were looking for a job, while 16.4 per cent were unemployed. The latter is twice as high as unemployment among 'native' French people. According to their country of origin, they have more (Arab and African countries, Turkey) or less (Spain, Italy, Portugal) chance of being unemployed (Miller, 1981). Among the former, one out of five aged between 25 and 59 is unemployed. Another tendency has been the increase in ethnic shops and businesses, which has contributed to a new cycle of integration of these groups in French society (Tavan, 2005).

As Guiraudon notes (2006), the premise of French official policy has long been a form of assimilationist republicanism. Throughout the country's immigration history (ranging from the post-colonial migrants), foreign migrant Belgian, Italian and Polish blue collar workers have been expected to become French through their equal access to the neutral institutions of the Republic (for example the schools), their inclusion in the labour market and related social institutions. However, economic restructuring led to a deterioration of immigrants' working conditions. Economic stagnation also led to a rise in ethnocentric sentiment and a shift towards anti-immigration discourse and support for extreme-right political parties. This was also reflected in urbanization trends, with a large portion of the middle-class moving out of mixed neighbourhoods and schools, thereby leading to the creation of immigrant ghettos characterized by socioeconomic exclusion and inequalities, with demands for political inclusion and cultural recognition remaining largely unmet.

This chapter discusses immigration policy developments in France during the last 15 years, outlines the demographic and social composition of the immigrant population currently resident in the Republic and reviews the participation of immigrants in the public life of the country. The French media debate on migration is also commented upon while, in the concluding section, the future challenges of immigration and immigrant integration for France are considered.

Major developments in France's immigration policy

In 1984, the French Government admitted that immigrants stayed longer in the country than they were supposed to. After three years of legal stay, they could then receive a permit, which allowed them to stay for ten years. Immigration became a political factor.[1] Non-EU immigrants began to play a role as groups who triggered political sympathies or antipathies (Fassin et al., 1997). The right-wing National Front with Le Pen obtained votes among popular voters with anti-immigrant politics. In 1993, the conservative government introduced new difficulties in obtaining the resident permit. For instance, immigrant spouses of French citizens had to wait two years after their wedding before they could obtain residence.

Applying for asylum became easier than obtaining a legal immigrant status. But an asylum seeker could not work while her/his application was being processed. In 1998, a law facilitating the reunification of families and obtaining a resident permit was voted (Chevènement law, 11 May 1998). Students, researchers, and artists have received special permits, as have retired people who travel from their country of origin to France. The law regulating refugees has been widened in its scope (1998) so that people persecuted as freedom fighters in their home countries have also been able to obtain this. Since 1993, young immigrants born in France can obtain French nationality without a formal procedure upon the age of majority (Brubaker, 1997; Cesarani and Fulbrook, 1996). Access to French nationality has been opened to everybody who has spent five years in the country.

Since the early 1990s, immigration has been met with increasing reluctance by public opinion and policy-makers alike. It has been related to security issues, both in relation to international terrorism and with regard to its posing an economic 'threat' to French jobs and to the social security system. There has been an increase of xenophobic attitudes among groups who, some years earlier, had voted for left-wing parties (Noriel, 1996).

The French law on foreigners (1998) regulates immigrants' right of residence on French territory (see Blion et al., 2003, pp. 13–14). Many immigrant groups (EU nationals, Algerians) depend on special agreements with their countries of origin. Since 1974, the application of the Decree of the 2 November 1945 concerning the conditions of entry and residence of immigrants in France has made access to employment dependent upon a residence permit. Currently, it is nearly impossible to migrate to France for the purpose of employment. The only legal way to enter and work in France is family reunification. Special cards exist for several privileged groups, such as students, scientists and artists. There is no work permit as such, except for traders and artisans. Foreigners who have the right to work in France without authorization are: EU members, citizens of Andorra and Monaco, those with a residence permit (a ten-year certificate for Algerians) or a temporary residence permit with the mention 'private and family life' (Blion et al., 2003, p. 12), and some other categories such as media correspondents, sailors and so on. A European Union national has the right to work without a permit. Except for the categories mentioned above, all foreigners who wish to stay in the country for more than three months need to hold a residence permit in order to obtain a certificate allowing them to work. Obtaining a residence permit is dependent upon the reason for entry into French territory.

Two types of residence permits exist. 'Residence permits (Cartes de résidence) are valid for ten years and grant an automatic right to work. Temporary permits (Cartes temporaires) are valid for one year and give limited access to employment to certain categories of applicants (Blion et al., 2003, p. 14). These latter permits are delivered 'to those able to prove family ties ('private and family life' category), scientists, artists, students and visitors' (Blion, op. cit., 15). With the

---

1   This first part of the chapter is based on information given in Blanc-Chaléard (2001).

exception of students, who must apply for authorization, holders of this permit are automatically eligible to work in France. 'Algerian nationals holding a temporary permit (one year) have the right to obtain a ten-year residence permit provided they give proof of regular, effective and uninterrupted residence in France for the last 3 years' (Blion, ibid.). They must have a stable and sufficient income during their stay. Furthermore, they are not required to hold a professional card in order to be self-employed.

Non-Europeans do not have free access to work. While they may ask for the right to work in France, 'their 'applications are almost systematically rejected as European preference is systematically invoked' (Blion, ibid.). Indeed, the situation of the labour market is often invoked as a reason for rejecting an application. Applications in special categories, such as scientists, can be submitted with a letter from the employer. 'If authorization is granted, it gives the right to a one-year work permit, and has to be renewed every year' (Blion, ibid.). A new amendment signed on 1 July 2001, 'allowed citizens of Algeria and Tunisia to be included in the general regulations of the 2nd November 1945 Decree, which applies to nationals of other countries' (Blion, op. cit., 16). Tunisians can benefit from all new mentions regarding temporary permits created by the law (1998) ('private and family life', 'visitors'). To obtain a long-term residence permit, foreigners must have sickness insurance. After 3 years, third-country nationals can ask for a ten-year residence permit. After five years, a residence permit may be automatically obtained upon application (for more see Blion et al., 2003, pp. 13–16).

An important recent movement is that of the *sans-papiers*, who are African illegal migrants (Freedman and Tarr, 2000 and Freedman, 2004). These migrants 'without papers' attracted widespread media attention for having staged a hunger strike and for the police breaking down the doors of a church in Paris with a view to expelling them (1996). This expulsion mobilized the French population who supported the movement with demonstrations and public petitions. The larger movement of the mid-1900s followed a series of legalizations introduced by right-wing governments, which had, in the first instance, pushed many immigrants into a situation of illegality.

This movement began in March 1996 when 300 Africans, mainly from Mali and Senegal, occupied a church in Paris. The aim was to put pressure on the government to regularize their situation in France. The expulsion four days later put an end to this adventure. But at the end of June 1996, another church was occupied. Meanwhile, mediators composed of scientists, lawyers, and other personalities had met the government, but their propositions were rejected. In other French towns, hunger strikes and occupations followed. At the end of August 1996, over a thousand policemen expelled the *sans-papiers* from the Parisian church. Blacks were arrested and white people, the supporters, were allowed to go free. The violence of the police intervention provoked a wave of public support and demonstrations in favour of the group (Simeant, 1998).

At the end of the year, the same right-wing government introduced new bills relating to illegal residence and work in France which found little opposition from left-wing members of Parliament. Associations defending immigrants' rights and the extra-parliamentary left organized a campaign against these bills. The bill was then re-worded. The left-wing government elected in 1997 organized a regularization of half of the 160,000 *sans-papiers*. They received legal residence permits for one year which, in reality, did not do very much other than perpetuate their state of uncertainty.

The right-wing government, elected in 2002, tried to resolve the issue by clarifying procedures for prefectures dealing with claims for residency papers and by deciding to expel those without papers. But the resistance of the *sans-papiers* and the mobilization of their supporters continued. The question of the *sans-papiers* has occupied an important place in the debate over immigration in France during recent years, highlighting the boundaries between citizens of the EU and those from outside Europe. As Freedman underlines, the debate has not only tackled immigration rules, but the nature of citizenship, inclusion and exclusion (Freedman, 2004, p. 81). Foreigners living in France without legal residence papers have become politically active and have engaged with French authorities. Balibar suggests (1999) that this mobilization has contributed to a new 'active citizenship'.

The urban riots during three weeks in autumn 2005 were the most important in France since 1968 (Roy, 2005; Le Goaziou and Mucchinielli, 2006). The impression that the police looked down on and punished youths of immigrant origin was one of the main motifs. The media discourse presented this violence as the result of permanent discrimination in housing and labour. Urban districts such as the French *cités* were built in the 1950s and 1960s, as estates of large buildings, of a sort which do not exist in other countries, designed expressly to house poor families (Wikipédia, 2006). The construction of these buildings was influenced by the socialist housing politics of the USSR.

In 2005, French President Jacques Chirac characterized the social situation as a crisis of meaning and identity which questioned the French policy of integration. In a television announcement, he focused on the diversity of French society and the necessity to underline principles such as equality and solidarity. According to reports of the DCRG (Direction Centrale des Renseignements Généraux), the urban riots took place in common urban districts and were not organized by centralized groups. Young French citizens of the second generation of immigrants were organized around a common feeling of exclusion and not according to their ethnic or geographic origins. Those who destroyed buildings or cars were largely thought to have no employment prospects.

The immigrant population in France: main demographic and social features

According to the last census from 1999, there were 4,306,094 immigrants in France (Lebon, 2000). Forty-five per cent of them possess European citizenship, 39.3 per cent African citizenship (including Algerians, Tunisians, and Moroccans), 12.7 per cent Asian citizenship, and 3 per cent American and Oceanic nationalities (see Table 9.1).[2]

Immigrants represent 7.4 per cent of the total population of France. In 1999, 63.9 per cent of immigrants had foreign citizenship and 36.1 per cent had obtained French nationality. This translates approximately into 1.56 million people (see Table 9.2). Spaniards and Italians obtained French nationality; so did immigrants from South-East Asia who often came for political reasons. A quarter of Algerian and Moroccan immigrants chose French nationality. Turkish and Portuguese have, more often than not, maintained their original nationality.

---

2   This part of the chapter is based on information given in INSEE (2005).

Table 9.1   Immigrants by country of origin in 1999

Nationalities	Total	Percentage
Total	**4,306,094**	**100.0**
European nationalities	**1,934,144**	**45.0**
Spanish	316,232	7.4
Italian	378,649	8.8
Polish	98,571	2.3
Portuguese	571,874	13.3
Other	568,818	13.2
African nationalities	**1,691,562**	**39.3**
Algerians	574,208	13.4
Moroccans	522,504	12.1
Tunisians	201,561	4.7
Others	393,289	9.1
American and Oceanic nationalities	**130,394**	**3.0**
Asian nationalities	**549,994**	**12.7**
Turkish	174,160	4.0
Cambodia, Laos, Vietnam	159,750	3.7
Other Asian countries	216,084	5.0

Source: INSEE 2005, 49.

Table 9.2   Population of France by nationality and place of birth (1999)

Nationality	Place of birth		Total
	In France	**In a third country**	
Total	52,650,000	5,870,000	58,520,000
'Native' French	51,340,000	1,560,000	52,900,000
Naturalized French	800,000	1,560,000	2,360,000
Foreigners	510,000	2,750,000	3,260,000

Note: Foreigners, according to INSEE, are persons who do not possess the French nationality; immigrants are persons who were born in a foreign country and who may or may not posess French nationality. Thus, the total immigrant population in France amounts to 4,310,000 (i.e. 2,750,00 foreigners born outside France and 1,560,000 naturalized French).
Source: INSEE 2005, 35.

In 1999, the number of female migrants was higher in the oldest age groups (65 and over) and in the 19–45 age group. After 1990, most of the immigrants were women and half of them were aged between 22 and 34 upon their arrival in France. Approximately 47 per cent of the female immigrants lived in a couple before migration, as opposed to 30 per cent of men. For women, reuniting with their husbands is one of the reasons for migration, while men often prefer to have settled before starting a family. Female immigrants do not participate in large numbers in the labour force: two-thirds of male immigrants are active in the workforce, as opposed to less than half of the female immigrant population. Twenty-five per cent of women are unemployed, as opposed to

19 per cent of men. The age structure of immigrants is different from that of French nationals. Two thirds are aged 25–64, while only half of French nationals are in this age group. Thirteen per cent of immigrants are less than 25 years old. The older age groups can be found in those groups with an earlier immigration history, namely Italians, Spaniards and Poles. Turks, South-East Asians, and Africans have the highest percentage of young people under the age of 25.

According to *Le Monde*, in 2003, there were 52,204 asylum seekers (2, 23 October 2004). The same year, OFPRA (Office Français de Protection des Réfugiés et Apatrides) recognized 9,790 refugees (INSEE, 2005, p. 74): 1,058 originated from Russia, 4,314 from Africa (1,141 from the Democratic Republic of the Congo), 2,669 from Asia (857 from Turkey and 645 from Sri Lanka) and 366 from the Americas (296 from Haiti).

The educational level of immigrants has risen during recent decades. In 1999, 41 per cent of immigrants had no diploma or only a primary school education. Twenty-seven per cent had an intermediate level, 11 per cent had a secondary level (baccalauréat) and 21 per cent held a university degree. There are, nevertheless, huge differences according to the countries of origin (the level of the European countries is higher than that of Turkey).

Immigrant rights and participation in public life – issues of immigrant integration

The legal framework

Third country nationals who wish to become French nationals can do so more easily, compared to other countries of the European Union such as Germany. Foreigners do not have political rights, such as voting, before their naturalization. They have the right to participate in trade unions, but they should remain politically neutral. There are, for example, certain restrictions on the functions of a labour union delegate who is a third-country national.

There has always been a hiatus in France between the right of foreigners to work and the right to be represented and to participate in public life (Delemotte and Chevallier, 1996). In France, a few local migrant councils were introduced in the 1990s. However, they had only a consultative role and their competencies were limited to municipal interests. Nevertheless, these councils have the advantage of associating migrants with political decision processes in the country of immigration and familiarizing the national population with the idea of the participation of foreigners in political life (Favell, 1998).

Economic migrants from non-EU countries often experienced rather reduced political rights in their countries of origin. Given that they often risked being expelled for political reasons, many immigrants perceived politics as a taboo, and a topic of distrust (See Blanc-Chaléard, 2001, pp. 83–89). Nonetheless, there were forms of expression open to immigrants in France: consultative local rights, participation in associations and strikes, to name but a few. Certain conflicts had an influence on political decisions by their duration and extension[3] that, in principle, transgressed the strict political neutrality that the French state required from immigrants.

Immigrants thus used political resources unknown to the public powers (Wihtol de Wenden, 1988, p. 216). In enterprises, immigrants were sometimes mobilized on an ad hoc basis depending on the issue that was being fought over by the labour unions. These included their professional and geographic mobility and their representation in trade unions, for example.

In the 1980s and 1990s, the life of immigrants continued to be a focus of politicization (Quiminal, 1991). The cleaners of the Paris underground went on strike, clandestine immigrants

---

3   For instance, the Sonacotra conflict described by Quiminal (1991).

and youth in the suburbs demonstrated. These conflicts were handled at the local participant level and, wherever possible, the help of mediators was sought. With these actions, immigrants entered the French political sphere, where they tried to exercise influence. The defence and expression of their interests thus left the political periphery and turned to the French political centre.

Immigrants had, by the mid-1980s, been settled for a long time and were interested in the local context where they lived. Political leaders began to tackle the problem of immigration. But its use was always an indicator of the balance of power between the different parties. In certain towns, extra-municipal commissions were installed with the aim of giving a voice to immigrants (Créteil, Guayancourt). But the political challenge was minimal (Delemotte and Chevallier, 1996). A consultative participation in the local activities was progressively accepted, but a local vote was, as revealed by national polls, more or less rejected (Wihtol de Wenden, 1988, p. 261).[4]

The election of President Mitterrand in 1981 brought a change in politics regarding immigrants. Even if the targets remained unchanged (putting an end to incoming flows and integrating those already in the country), some references were changed. The expulsion of young immigrants ceased and the right of family reunification was underlined. Moreover, immigrants received the right to associate under the same terms as French nationals, as expressed in the 1901 law. Lawyers received the right to monitor governmental expulsion decisions. Efforts were made to favour the expression and representation of immigrants in a multicultural France.

In 1984, a work permit, including the right to stay in France for ten years, was created. Spouses or children of French nationals, parents of French children, refugees or residents in France for more than 15 years could acquire this permit. From that moment, legitimacy based on labour was abandoned. The National Council of Immigrant Populations (CNPI) was established in 1984, had to counsel the government, and was composed of immigrants, leaders of enterprises and labour unions, civil servants, and personalities from the associations. In 1983, a law proposal designed to create consultative councils of foreign communities was suggested. But these forms of consultation were met by a lack of motivation and means of the municipalities and their difficulties to find interlocutors. The greatest problem was the National Front, which tried to politically and legally counteract the mayors who installed commissions for immigrants.

Different laws that went in the direction of greater equality between foreigners and French nationals were voted in. Temporary residents could marry without the authorization of the Minister of the Interior; employers of clandestine immigrants risked the confiscation of their materiel and their products, and irregular immigrant workers received social security benefits, holidays and the ability to be defended by a labour union; the situation of irregular foreigners with a stable job could be regularized. Second-generation immigrants could, henceforth, remain in France if they had lived there for a long period. Expulsions had become exceptional measures.

Obtaining the right to vote for immigrants is blocked in France by ideological reasoning which links it to citizenship, nationality and territory. Because immigrants do not have the right to vote in local elections (except, recently, EU nationals), and do not constitute a political influential group, immigration has been used as a challenge in local political discourse. This topic has an ideological meaning for the extreme right-wing party, the National Front, which has tackled topics such as insecurity, the level of tolerance, foreigners and 'the myth of the number of foreigners'.

Immigrants who have been excluded from the local and national scene have begun to play an important role, even if they have been less an actor and more a subject of political discourses. At the national level, immigration has become a subject that has to be tackled by those who look for legitimacy. At the local level, immigration has played the role of destabilizing electors, who were worried by a multiethnic society, clandestine immigrants and huge numbers of immigrants. So

---

4   For examples of these commissions, see pp. 262–64.

these electors have tried to reorganize the right/left cleavage. At an international level, immigration has formed a challenge to negotiations between France and countries of departure (for example Algeria). The status of immigrants has thus become the result of these different elements.

The visibility of a generation with an immigrant background and possessing French nationality or dual citizenship status poses the question of social, cultural and political legitimacy in the French political order. Immigrants in France total about four million people, including the flows of clandestine people and those acquiring French nationality.

Political rights of immigrants

The associative movement gave immigrants the possibility to exercise the political right to associate (Le Huu Khoa, 1995). Often, immigrants from non-EU countries had other, more pressing, problems to resolve than the right to vote (Geisser 1997). As early as 1982, Algerians and Moroccans originating from countries maintaining strong political and economic ties with France underlined that they favoured equal social and trade union rights. The right to vote, according to them, did not equate to the equality of rights (see Wihtol de Wenden, 1988, p. 308). They preferred to demand the right to express themselves (see Andrieu, 2001).

The political class in France is more or less hostile to the political rights of immigrants. Some of the most common arguments still discussed (see Wihtol de Wenden, 1988, p. 312; Blanc-Chaléard, 2001, pp. 90–93) are:

- The right to vote is granted in the form of 'a compensation' following successful socialization in the receiving state in order to permit the immigrant to assimilate (such as the right to vote after naturalization or after a long stay).
- Immigrants are, according to some political leaders, 'not educated enough' to exercise this right; they have to be prepared, for example, with a local consultative participation that permits acculturation.
- Perhaps the right to vote is not the best-adapted solution to the political attitudes of immigrants, who prefer forms of collective expression (associative life, strikes, and so on). Political parties have, thus, directed the debate towards these collective rights during recent years.

But French law does not exclude every possibility for foreigners to exercise certain public activities, such as participation in the constitution of a public elective organism. They are voters and can be elected by parent associations in schools and to social security schemes, and they can be electors for the constitution of certain courts, such as the tribunals of rural leases, and they can be members of industrial tribunals, but they cannot be elected. Moreover, foreign students have the right to vote in universities (see Wihtol de Wenden, 1988, p. 313).

What, then, are the obstacles? In order to extend the right to vote and to be elected by foreigners, a revision of the Constitution is necessary. The fact that the electors of the municipal councillors are in an indirect way also the electors of the senators is problematic.[5] The electors are considered in the French constitution to form the *peuple* that is constituted by French citizens and not foreign citizens. The French position regarding political rights remains tied to the idea of national citizenship. The right to vote is linked to naturalizations that can usually be obtained after a lengthy procedure of two or three years.

---

5   The 1958 constitution states: 'Sont électeurs, dans les conditions déterminées par la loi, tous les nationaux Français majeurs des deux sexes, jouissant de leurs droits civils et politiques.'

Even if there has been some discussion on this topic during recent decades, public opinion has always been hostile to giving foreigners the right to vote in their local areas. As a result, politicians have never decided to change the position. A complicating event was the Maastricht Treaty and the European vote. EU citizens were given the right to vote in local elections in the country in which they were resident, even without having the nationality. At the 2001 municipal elections, the right-wing party was firmly against granting voting rights to non-nationals from outside the EU. The left-wing party was more divided. The Green Party suggested a constitutional bill, but the then Prime Minister, Jospin, argued that the conditions at the time were not favourable for the adoption of such a measure. Freedman reports: 'In December 2002, several associations organized a "referendum" on the right to vote for foreigners. This "citizens' vote" was organized in 70 towns and cities across France and permitted those who supported the idea of extending the right to vote for immigrants to go and vote for this idea in associational headquarters, in markets or in The Town Hall' (Freedman, 2004, p. 94).

Nevertheless, the situation of French nationals of immigrant origin was somewhat better in local and municipal politics. As Oriol (2001) found for the 2001 municipal elections, 7.6 per cent of the candidates were of 'foreign origin', and 4.6 per cent of these were of Maghreb origin. All parties, even the extreme right party, presented candidates of immigrant origin. However, not all parties managed to elect them. The majority of the elected representatives were from left wing parties and were from the Maghreb. They were integrated in the political system because their presence was related to the 'difficult' suburbs (Oriol, 2001, p. 96). These candidates are, in fact, closer to 'civil society' and to French cultural diversity. Even if they are French nationals, their small number displays their marginalization and a level of exclusion.

Another important topic is the headscarf issue. The question is whether Muslim girls should or should not be allowed to wear their *foulards* in the secular French school system (Delmas, 2006). In fact, the French idea of assimilation demands some kind of cultural uniformity. Fear of the spread of Islamic fundamentalism has created tensions within French society. The 'affaire des foulards' has been an ongoing political debate since it first appeared in the headlines in France in October 1989, when a headmaster in a suburb of Paris refused to allow three Maghrebi girls to come to school wearing their head-scarves, arguing that this would be against the French principle of secularism in schools. 'The majority of the newspaper reports focused on the affair as a challenge to secularism in the French education system' (Freedman, 2004, p. 132). Political parties were divided: the National Front considered the wearing of a headscarf as a sign of an Islamic 'invasion' in France. An opinion poll at the time showed that 75 per cent of those questioned were hostile to girls wearing headscarves in schools (*Le Monde*, 20 November 1989). Numerous later polls confirmed this tendency. The Socialist Party was divided on the topic, as was the moderate right. Finally, the Socialist Minister for Education, L. Jospin, turned to the *Conseil d'État* which considered that wearing a religious sign was not sufficient reason for excluding girls from school.

In 1994, the topic re-emerged when F. Bayrou, the right-wing Minister for Education, argued that 'ostentatious' religious symbols should not be allowed in schools. SOS-Racisme, who had previously supported the girls, changed to supporting the government's idea. The leaders of this association declared that the growth of Islamic fundamentalism was a real danger in many suburbs with huge immigrant populations. In 1994, the Ministry of the Interior estimated that less than 5 per cent of all Muslim girls were wearing headscarves to school. The *Conseil d'État* ruled the following year that it was up to each head-teacher to consider the case before excluding a girl. Most recently, the right-wing government solved the problem by making the wearing of headscarves in schools illegal from September 2004. The right-wing parties argued in support of the law and although the Socialist Party was more moderate, they argued that they were fighting for secularism. A survey carried out for *Le Figaro* showed that 55 per cent of respondents were favourable to the law (8 November 2003). It seems that this law has brought to an end to years of dispute over the topic, arguing with success for the secularism of the French education system with 639 girls wearing headscarves at the beginning of the school year and with only 47 girls excluded from schools up to February 2005 (*Metro*, 15 February 2005).

The associative movement

Associations have gradually developed into mass movements. In the 1980s, there were 850 Arab movements (women, youth and intercultural associations), 350 Turkish movements (divided by their religious and political currents), 250 South-East-Asian refugee associations, about 1,000 self-help associations, and a very feeble movement of refugees from Latin America (see Wihtol de Wenden, 1988, p. 364). Many of these associations have received financial assistance from the *Fonds d'Action Sociale* (FAS).[6] To give some figures, in the 1990s, the FAS distributed 1.3 billion French Francs (about 20 million euros) to immigrant associations (Wihtol de Wenden and Leveau, 2001, pp. 110–111).

In fact, Freedman argues that '[f]or some advocates of post[-]National citizenship, the lack of formal voting rights and the right to be elected is not an important barrier to citizenship, since political citizenship might be provided in the form of participation through associational movements or other alternative forms of participation' (Freedman, 2004, p. 89). But it can be argued that the lack of representation of ethnic minorities in France's National Assembly is illustrative of a sort of exclusion. Indeed, the last National Assembly had one Muslim member of Parliament from Mayotte, and two women of Maghreb origin who are senators in the *Palais de Luxembourg* (the French Senate) (Hajji and Marteau, 2005, p. 123). At the 2001 municipal elections, 5.6 per cent of the local councillors were of immigrant origin and 3.5 per cent of Maghreb origin (Freedman, 2004, p. 96). Freedman continues that '[t]he participation of immigrants in associations is not perceived by the French state as a transition towards full political participation, but as a substitute for full political citizenship ... It is argued that participation in such associations provides a real participation in local affairs ...' (Freedman, 2004, p. 98).

Immigrants are often engaged in cultural associations in France. Some group members of Arab and Asian origin are also engaged in religious associations (see Le Huu Khoa, 1995). Those of Arab origin who are naturalized French citizens are rather active in political parties that consider these people as a guarantee against problems caused by Muslim fundamentalists in France. Political elites of African and Asian origin are rather rare in France (see Douma, 2003). African groups are particularly active in France, but their civic activities are directed towards their country of origin (Daum, 1998). Some ten years ago, Arabs were rather active, too. These associative activities have experienced a decline due to a recent focus on social promotion at the individual level in this group. Yet the headscarf issue has provided a new impetus to their civic activities. Asian groups were rather active in the 1970s and 1980s, but with their integration in French society, most active militants left the associations and turned to family activities. It seems that parent associations continue to be a major focus for all groups.

---

6   *Fonds d'action sociale* – Social Action Fund set up in 1959, now called FASILD (*Fonds d'action sociale pour l'intégration et la lutte contre les discriminations* – Social Action Fund for Integration and Anti-Discrimination). This organization has financed many studies on immigration topics by university researchers or independent researchers, associated with universities and has continued to play an important role as an institution financing associations and research on immigrant topics.

The active civic participation of first-generation immigrants in France is rather low compared to the majority of the population. Radical Muslim groups, even if their influence is rather small in France, also play a role in the civic movement (Hajji and Marteau, 2005, pp. 62–75).

The relation between engagement in ethnic or migrant organizations and political activities is rather strong for Arabs with French nationality, as their engagement has permitted them to begin political careers in national political parties at the local, regional, national and even supra-national (EU) levels. Asians and Africans are more concerned with activities related to the promotion of their own community. Asians are often rather well integrated in French society, even if they try to focus more on communal ties than on mainstream society organizations. Africans' civic activities are more directed towards their own countries. Overlaps can be found for some men in trade union membership and for both men and women in parental associations. Yet most often, overlaps and transitions concern immigrants who have been naturalized, such as the *beurs*[7] who are engaged in French political parties.

Public and media discourses on migration

In France, the current public discussion on migration is related to a plethora of issues. At the end of 2004, media attention was concentrated on the female headscarf, which had been forbidden in state schools since the beginning of the new school year (2004–2005). The veil, as well as other religious signs such as the cross, is excluded from public life in so far as the state is secular and religion is reserved to the private sphere. Obviously, this topic has attracted a great deal of public interest with schoolgirls refusing to abandon the veil and discussions with the school administration. A few girls (47) have been excluded from certain schools after months of public discussion because they were not ready, as most other Muslim girls are, to abandon their veil.

Another topic which has attracted media interest is the free circulation of migrants originating from Eastern European countries which became part of the European Union in May 2004. The media have underlined that poor people from the East had already entered with a tourist visa before the admission of their countries to the EU. Those who wish to enter through legal means are, according to the media discourse, often students.

Another interesting point is the suggestion that immigrants are a remedy against an ageing French population. There are two topics linked to this in the media discourse; on the one hand, the fear of being confronted by a lack of labour and, on the other, the hope of providing a balance with an ageing French population. The media, *Le Monde* above all, underline that it is no longer the poorest people who migrate as was the case in the past, but that, rather, it is the middle classes and students who are the most mobile. The Minister of the Interior – and now President of France – N. Sarkozy is in favour of the quota system defended by other European countries, permitting only so-called 'useful' migrants. Intellectuals underline that the economic necessities of the countries of origin and the interests of the migrants should also be taken into account (Schuerkens, 2005, 2006).

A recent book by Hajji and Marteau (2005) provides some interesting insights into the portrayal of Islam in the media. The authors find that fear of Muslims has entered the media. After the high number of votes in favour of Le Pen at the 2002 presidential elections, the press no longer wanted to be perceived as a medium which avoided touching upon ethnic topics. Yet French television journalists seem to be biased by information obtained from the police who are faced with a particular type of social reality unknown to those journalists who cover these topics in the media.

---

7   The notion *beur* expresses a bi-cultural identity – both Arab and French and belonging to both cultures.

Moreover, in films, Arabs and blacks continue to play the roles of delinquents. Journalists from visible minorities have tried to change this situation by asking media managers to respect ethnic diversity and by insisting on giving French people of foreign origin roles other than those of the 'fanatic terrorist'. One early result has been the summer replacement (2006) of the news journalist of TF1 at 8 p.m. by a black French journalist.

Hajji and Marteau (op. cit.) present the opinion of the Rector of the Paris mosque, Dalil Boubakeur, who believes that the media create antagonistic situations and insist on particular signs in order to convince the public. According to him, the media portray a 'typical' Muslim with a beard or a woman with a headscarf and not, for instance, a scientist. This situation means that large groups feel misrepresented by the media (see Geisser, 2003). An ethnic press, ethnic radio and ethnic television have therefore developed during recent years (for example, Beur FM and Beur TV).

The French media extensively covered the political unrest in the French suburbs of October and November 2005. French commentators have described this societal crisis as the attack of a post-colonial proletariat and of the 'enemies of our world'. They have pointed to the failure of the French model of multiculturalism, the crisis of urban areas, even the development of a parallel society placed outside the laws of the Republic. Of course, the social and political interests of the observers have inspired the coverage of the riots. The right-wing government has placed the emphasis on internal competition between poor groups ('those who have success' against 'those who do not want to get out of a difficult situation', 'the victims' against the 'perpetrators, 'French people' against 'polygamous families'). In fact, this treatment of the problem has permitted the breaking-down of uncoordinated resistance to an order characterized by social inequality. Even the left-wing parties did not offer a way out of the crisis. An organization around common political options of actors of different professional, confessional and geographic origin may permit an improvement in the situation of these young immigrants who protested after the death of two youngsters in the Parisian suburb of Clichy-sous-Bois. The verbal attacks of Sarkozy, who announced the 'nettoyage au Kärcher' (cleaning by using a Kärcher pressure washer) of the 'racaille' (rabble, mob) first ignited the unrest.[8]

Concluding remarks

This chapter has tackled the main features of immigration policy in France since the early 1990s. It has presented the demographic and socioeconomic characteristics of the immigrant population. The chapter has also given a short outline of the media discourse on migration during the last two decades. As was shown by the recent Parisian suburban unrest, immigrant integration policy needs to be reconsidered in order to address long-term challenges of immigration in France and not to react to problems by short-term and uncoordinated policy measures. Until recently, policy design has managed migration on an ad hoc basis and according to each government's priorities, combined with policy initiatives at the EU level.

---

8   The papers published in November and December at riotsinfrance.org are relevant for reference.

References

Andrieu, C. et al. (eds) (2001), *Associations et champ politique: La loi de 1901 à l'épreuve du siècle*. Paris: Publications de la Sorbonne.

Balibar, E. (1999), 'Le droit de cité ou l'apartheid?', in Balibar et al. (eds) *Sans-papiers: l'archaïsme fatal*. Paris: La Découverte.

Blanc-Chaléard, M. (2001), *Histoire de l'immigration*. Paris: La Découverte.

Blion, R. et al. (2003), *EU and United States Approaches to the Management of Migration: France* (published online), Niessen, J. et al. (eds). Brussels: Migration Policy Group. www.migpolgroup. org.

Brubaker, R. (1997), *Citoyenneté et nationalité en France et en Allemagne*. Paris: Belin.

Cesarani, D. and Fulbrook, M. (eds) (1996), *Citizenship, Nationality and Migration in Europe*. London and New York: Routledge.

Daum, C. (1998), *Les associations de Maliens en France. Migrations, développement et citoyenneté*. Paris: Karthala.

Delemotte, B. and Chevallier, J. (eds) (1996), *Étranger et citoyen. Les immigrés et la démocratie locale*. Paris: L'Harmattan.

Delmas, C. (2006), *Das Kopftuchverbot in Frankreich. Ein Streit um die Definition von Laizität, Republik und Frauenemanzipation*. Frankfurt a.M, et al., P. Lang.

Douma, J. (2003), *L'immigration congolaise en France. Entre crises et recherche d'identité*. Paris: L'Harmattan.

Fassin, D. et al. (1997), *Les lois de l'inhospitalité: Les politiques de l'immigration à l'épreuve des sans-papiers*. Paris: La Découverte.

Favell, A. (1998), *Philosophies of Integration: Immigration and the Idea of Citizenship in France and Britain*. Basingstoke: Macmillan.

Freedman, J. (2004), *Immigration and Insecurity in France*. Aldershot: Ashgate.

Freedman, J. and Tarr, C. (eds) (2000), *Women, Immigration and Identities in France*. Oxford: Berg.

Geisser, V. (1997), *Ethnicité républicaine: Les élites d'origine maghrébine dans le système politique français*. Paris: Presses de la Fondation Nationale des Sciences Politiques.

—— (2003), *La Nouvelle islamophobie*. Paris: La Découverte.

Guiraudon, V. (2006), 'Different Nation, Same Nationhood: The Challenge of Immigrant Policy', in Culpepper, P. D., Hall, P. A. and Palier, B. (eds) *France: the Politics that Markets Make*, pp. 129–50. Basingstoke: Palgrave-Macmillan.

Hajji, S. and Marteau, S. (2005), *Voyage dans la France musulmane*. Paris: Plon.

INSEE (2001), 'La Population étrangère en France', in *Recensement de la Population de 1999*. Paris.

—— (2005), *Les immigrés en France, Édition 2005*. Paris.

Le Goaziou, V. and Mucchinielli, L. (eds) (2006), *Quand les banlieues brûlent ... Retour sur les émeutes de novembre 2005*. Paris: La Découverte.

Le Huu Khoa (1995), *Asiatiques en France: Les expériences d'intégration locale*. Paris: L'Harmattan.

Lebon, A. (2000), *Immigration et présence étrangère en France en 1999*. Paris: La Documentation Française.

Miller, M. (1981), *Foreign Workers in Western Europe. An Emerging Political Force*. New York: Praeger.

Noiriel, G. (1996), *The French Melting Pot: Immigration, Citizenship, and National Identity*, translated by Geoffroy de Laforcade. Minneapolis/Saint-Paul: University of Minnesota Press.

Oriol, P. (2001), 'Les Français d'origine étrangère aux élections municipales de 2001', *Migrations société*, **77**(13), 41–54.

Quiminal, C. (1991), *Gens d'ici, gens d'ailleurs*. Paris: Chr. Bourgois.

Schuerkens, U. (2005), 'Social Transformations and Transnational Migrations: A Theoretical Approach', Special Monographic Issue of *Current Sociology*, 'Social Transformations and Transnational Migrations', **53**(4, 2) 535–54.

—— (2006), 'Migration and Development', in Leonard, T.M. (ed.) *Encyclopedia of the Developing World*, **2**, 1039–46. New York: Routledge.

Simeant, J. (1998), *La Cause des Sans-papiers*. Paris: Presses de la Fondation nationale des Sciences politiques.

Tavan, C. (2005), 'Les immigrés en France: une situation qui évolue', in *Insee Premiere, n° 1042*.

Tribalat, M. (1996), *Faire France: Une enquête sur les immigrés et leurs enfants*. Paris: La Découverte.

Wihtol de Wenden, C. (1988), *Les immigrés et la politique*. Paris: Presses de la Fondation Nationale des Sciences Politiques.

Wihtol de Wenden, C. and Leveau, R. (2001), *La Bourgeoisie: Les trois âges de la vie associative issue de l'immigration*. Paris: CNRS Editions.

Internet-based references

Roy, O. (2005), *The Nature of French Riots* (available at https://riotsfrance.ssrc.org/roy, 18 November 2005).

Wikipédia (2006), 'Emeutes de 2005 dans les banlieues françaises' (available at http://fr.wikipedia.org/wiki/Émeutes_de_2005_dans_les_banlieues_françaises, accessed 22 April 2006).

Chapter 10

Germany

Norbert Cyrus and Dita Vogel

Who is an immigrant in Germany? Indeed, political debates for a long time refuted the notion that there are any 'immigrants' in Germany. The ongoing immigration was, for a long time, not officially acknowledged as immigration but, rather, it was labelled as the return of ethnic Germans, the temporary recruitment of workers, or the temporary reception of asylum seekers and civil war refugees (Cyrus and Vogel, 2005). But de facto immigration numbers in this 'no-immigration-country' regime were substantial. Experts estimate that about 30 per cent of the population residing in Germany was born abroad or has ancestors which immigrated to Germany after 1945 (Bade and Münz, 2002, p. 11). Only with the passing of the new Immigration Act in 2005 did the official position acknowledge that immigration takes place and should be properly managed and statistically counted in the future. Moreover, the integration of newcomers with the perspective to stay should be promoted along with more secure residence rights and integration courses (Bade, Bommes and Münz, 2004).

In the current situation of hardly any net immigration (BAMF, 2005a), public debates focus more and more on integration issues. In recent years, many integration-related issues have dominated the headlines in public discourses for weeks. These included poor records of immigrant children in schools, violence in neighbourhoods with a high share of immigrant population in big cities, high unemployment among foreign nationals, Muslim teachers' claims to wear headscarves in class, the situation of women in Turkish immigrant families. These debates contributed to and reinforced the image that immigration is a problem, that immigration control should be more strictly enforced, and that integration policies failed in the face of immigrant communities who are largely refusing integration. Politicians have repeatedly and successfully made use of these opinions to win elections (Meier-Braun, 2002).

Public debates fail to recognize that a large part of the current problems are due to non-integration policies as a means of enforcing immigration control. A large proportion of those who have secure residence rights or even German citizenship today were, initially and for many years, subject to policies of disintegration: short-term residence permits, exclusion from the labour market or from certain professions, exclusion from political rights and from certain social rights. Even today, there is a considerable minority within the foreign population with insecure residence rights and the constant threat of deportation, even after long-term residence of more than ten years.

In this paper, we sketch the development towards this situation, focusing on the last two decades. In the final remarks, we will ask what this could mean for determining who is an immigrant in the future.

Major developments in Germany's immigration policy

From the beginning of industrialization in the second half of the nineteenth century, German territories turned from an area of emigration to one of immigration (Herbert, 1986; Bade, 2003).

The long and changeable history of migrant workers' attraction include the recruitment of seasonal workers for German agriculture during the empire until 1918 and the unscrupulous organization of forced labour by the Nazi regime (1939–45).

After the Second World War, millions of German refugees from former territories settled in the two German states, but the migratory situation soon began to develop differently. The German Democratic Republic (GDR) closed its borders, but because of an increasing lack of labour, in the early 1980s it began 'importing' migrant workers, mainly from other socialist states such as Poland, Cuba, Mozambique and Vietnam in particular. On the other side of the wall, the Federal Republic of Germany (FRG) accepted the influx of GDR citizens who escaped for political, social and economic reasons. After 1955, the FRG signed the so-called guest-worker recruitment programmes in order to organize the temporary employment of migrant workers from ten states, mainly from the Mediterranean basin. An estimated total of fourteen million migrant workers had come to West Germany and most had left when the recruitment programmes were terminated in 1973. Workers with a job were allowed to remain, which had the unintended effect of stabilizing the settlement of many of these 2.7 million recruited foreign workers since they had, by law, no chance of returning to Germany once they had left.

The subsequent period 1973–1990 was characterized by the immigration of family members of these recruited workers and the beginning of immigration of refugees and asylum seekers from politically unstable countries in Latin America, Africa, Asia and Europe (in particular Turkey and, later, civil war refugees from former Yugoslavia). The few citizens from socialist countries who managed to come to Germany were generally accepted as political refugees.

Since the mid-1970s, the immigration of ethnic Germans from Poland and later Romania and the late successor states of the USSR started and reached a peak in the early 1990s.

In 1990, a major revision of the Foreigner's Law was enacted after a long and heated debate. The migration policy became characterized by the officially declared targets to prevent the further entry of immigrants from non-EU countries, to foster the return of foreign nationals and to promote the integration of the legally residing immigrants, and in particular the recruited workers and their families. All in all, the 1990 Foreigner's Law had introduced more and better legal claims instead of far-reaching discretion of authorities at the local level, leading to more secure rights for settled immigrants.

But the 1990 Foreigner's Law had been prepared before Germany faced major immigration challenges from the collapse of the communist regimes in Eastern Europe. It was not sufficient to cope with the extraordinary situation after the fall of the Berlin wall in November 1989, which was an important event in German history, including its migration history. The following years were characterized by a pragmatic 'muddling through' in reaction to new developments and concerns. In the first half of 1990, Western Germany faced a massive influx of immigrants with the right to housing and basic income: East-Germans, ethnic Germans from Eastern Europe, and asylum seekers from all over the world, but mainly from Europe. This development put immense pressure on the local communities in Germany which were responsible for providing shelter and subsistence for these immigrants. Immigration from Eastern to Western Germany reduced quickly in the course of the unification of Germany in 1990. At the same time, ethnic German immigration was restricted by a de facto quota, while the first legislative restrictions came into force only in 1993. Asylum seeker numbers multiplied until 1992. In 1993, the constitutional right to asylum was severely restricted, and a number of legislative and administrative measures made access to the asylum procedure much more difficult and curtailed social and juridical rights during the procedure.

In the same period, border control was completely reorganized. At the EU borders in the west and south, border control changed from inspection units sitting at ports of entry to mobile units looking for illegal immigrants. Access from the east had formerly been neatly sealed by the nearly impermeable walls erected by the German Democratic Republic. After unification, a completely new border control regime was built up at the border with Poland and the Czech republic.

While the conservative German Government tried to cope with the increasing immigration from Central and Eastern Europe, mainly by restricting immigration opportunities and increasing border control, it expanded inter-governmental agreements for the temporary employment of workers from Central and Eastern Europe. It also introduced regulations, in the form of a quota, for admitting Jewish refugees from Russia.

Towards the end of the 1990s, net immigration was reduced to a trickle. When a coalition of the Social Democratic Party and the ecologically and more pro-migration orientated Green Party formed a so-called 'Red-Green government' in 1998, it was faced with expectations to introduce paradigmatic changes in the field of migration and integration and to take care of a 'normalization' of migration policies (Bommes, 2001). Indeed, the Red-Green government launched some immigration legislation projects immediately, and after its re-election in 2002. This was nonetheless done cautiously and with a continuous tendency to more restrictive regulations in response to harsh critique from the opposing parties and media (Hell, 2005).

Naturalization reform

The first of the most important initiatives was the naturalization reform: the new 'Red-Green government' launched a new naturalization act with a provision for a limited *jus soli* and double citizenship. After fierce protest initiated by the Christian Democratic Party on the eve of a state election, the opportunity for double citizenship was reduced to a temporary status for the second generation with the obligation to decide on the retention of one citizenship later on. The law stipulates – provided that the parents possess a secure residence status – that children of foreign nationals born in Germany will receive German citizenship on a preliminary basis, regardless of whether they possess another citizenship. However, the legal requirements foresee that naturalized persons with dual citizenship have to opt for one citizenship only by the age of 23. Thus, German citizenship will be automatically withdrawn if a naturalized adult with double citizenship does not renounce the other citizenship. It will be up to the courts to decide on the constitutionality of this provision.

After the enactment of the law, naturalization issues stirred little public attention until 2005. The full consequences of the law reform appeared only after the coming into force of the provisions. It turned out that this regulation collided with a well- known practice of Turkish citizens who return their Turkish citizenship in order to acquire German citizenship, and regain it afterwards as a second citizenship.[1] As a consequence, some 10,000 'double citizens' were faced with the legal fact that they were no longer German. The German authorities offered citizens who had re-acquired another citizenship after naturalization to repeat the naturalization procedure under the condition that the German citizenship will become exclusive.

A labour market initiative

Only when an initiative to introduce a work permit scheme for computer experts in 2000 was implemented at the demand of IT enterprises and gained wide public acceptance, did the Red-Green government feel encouraged to take up an initiative for a complete reform of the Foreigners' Law. The Federal Minister of the Interior appointed an Independent Commission on Immigration. Following the argumentation of the Independent Commission (Kommission Zuwanderung, 2001),

---

1   See www.migration-info.de/migration_und_bevoelkerung/archiv/ausgaben/ausgabe0502.htm.

political and societal elites in all fields recognized that immigration is an inevitable aspect of globalization and that, rather than being prevented, it should be managed properly. Shortly after the publication of the Commission report in the summer of 2001, the Ministry of the Interior launched an immigration bill that made some use of the Commission's results but was in many details more restrictive.

Increased security concerns

The incident of 11 September 2001 coincided with the debate on the more open proposals of the Commission and the bill of the Ministry of the Interior. After 9/11, security issues were emphasized in the debate on immigration and the aspect of policing immigration gained increasing relevance. In this situation, the Christian Democratic Party returned to an even more restrictive stance in order to win votes (Meier-Braun, 2002). After a contradictory vote in the second chamber of Parliament, the new law was firstly enacted, came partly into force in July 2002, and was finally stopped by the Constitutional Court for procedural reasons in December 2002 after a legal action taken by the Christian Democratic Party.

New immigration law

In 2002, the Red-Green coalition government was re-elected in a close vote, but for major reforms like the immigration law, it still needed the consent of the opposition because of the Christian Democrat majority in the second chamber. After lengthy negotiations with limited information given out to the public, they finally agreed on a new immigration law and voted accordingly in parliament. The 'Law for Managing and Containing Immigration and for the Regulation of the Residence and Integration of EU Citizens and Foreigners' came into force in January 2005. As in the original version, the terminology and the legal framework changed – although not as much as originally planned – but actual policy instruments remained the same in many policy fields (Vogel and Wüst, 2003).

An important aspect of the new law is the introduction of obligatory integration courses for new entrants. Integration courses have a main focus of language acquisition (600 hours) and some limited introduction to the German civic order (30 hours). They are publicly financed with a contribution by the immigrants themselves. This is waived in cases of low income. Earlier immigrants with secure residence status do not enjoy an individual right to participate in such courses. They may participate when ongoing courses are not filled with newly arrived immigrants, but in cases of unemployment or of perceived integration deficiencies, the authorities may even oblige long-term residing immigrants to participate (Beauftragte der Bundesregierung für Migration und Integration, 2005).

In November 2005, after early elections, the Christian Democratic Party and the Social Democratic Party formed a 'great coalition' government. This new government emphasizes the difficulties rather than the opportunities related to migration. The new government continues with the legislation projects of its predecessor but stresses restrictive instruments and authoritative measures in order to control migration, return unwanted immigrants and demand more integration efforts from immigrants. Again and again, politicians mainly but not only from the Christian Democrats launch new restrictive proposals – such as the duty to speak only German in schoolyards, or the deportation of immigrants who refuse integration or harder punishment of forced marriages in the criminal law – with limited chances of succeeding in the legislative process and even lower chances of leading to substantial changes in the social reality in case of enactment. In addition, the legislator discusses a number of adjustments to the immigration law in order to implement

EU directives. As a rule, the new coalition government opts for the most restrictive admissible regulations (for a more detailed account of recent immigration policies, see also Cyrus and Vogel, 2005).

In this situation, welfare organizations and immigrant lobbyists are consistently lobbying to get the issue of tolerated immigrants on the agenda. 'Tolerance' is a formal acknowledgement of the impossibility of removing a person, and it gives access to some social rights, but only limited labour market access. Among the more than 200,000 so-called 'tolerated' persons in Germany there are people with residence of more than ten years. In Germany, there have been no regularization programmes for undocumented immigrants, but a number of status adjustment programmes for long-term tolerated immigrants in the 1990s (Cyrus and Vogel, 2005), and a new programme is being considered. Recently, lobby campaigns countered the emotional campaigns of restrictionists, trying to draw attention to the issue by focusing on well educated, well integrated young people who have spent most or all of their life in Germany and are now faced with exclusion from the labour market or even deportation, because of their parents' status.

The immigrant population in Germany: main demographic and social features

Owing to inconsistent legal treatment of immigration, there is no clear picture available of the stock of immigrants, that is the foreign-born population, in Germany. German migration statistics are based on residence registers, which count all regular German and foreign residents, including short-term residents such as seasonal workers. Official statistics do not differentiate between foreign-born and natives, but only between foreign nationals and Germans. Hence, there is no secure information on the number of foreign-born or naturalized German citizens. The foreign-born and their offspring can only be identified in the most recent microcensus survey that published initial data after this chapter was finalized. According to this survey, 15.3 million residents (20 per cent of the population) are either foreign-born or children of foreign-born in 2005.[2] The population with immigration backgrounds can be traced back to a variety of immigration patterns (Sachverständigenrat für Migrationsbericht, 2004; Sachverständigenrat für Zuwanderung und Integration, 2004). Most important were the following:

Between 1945 and 1949, about twelve million German nationals fled to the Federal Republic of Germany, mainly from the former German territories and some other areas of Eastern Europe, and settled in Germany (Münz, 2001).

Between 1955 and 1973, an estimated fourteen million workers from countries of the Mediterranean basin entered Germany on the basis of bilateral recruitment agreements in order to take up temporary employment. The majority of these recruited workers had returned by 1973, when a recruitment stop was declared. In that year about 2.7 million workers were in Germany, many of whom decided to stay.

The subsequent immigration of relatives of foreign nationals living in Germany became an important channel for permanent settlement. In 2003, the German visa-authorities issued 76,077 visas for family-related permanent immigration.

Since the 1950s, more than four million persons benefited from organized programmes for the reception of ethnic Germans, initially from Poland and Romania and, later, from the former Soviet Union. The immigration of ethnic Germans peaked after 1989. Indeed, between 1990 and 2003, 2.4 million ethnic Germans arrived.

---

2   Press release Beauftragte der Bundesregierung für Integration. Berlin, 06/06/06, http://www. integrationsbeauftragte.de/gra/presse/presse_1342.php.

Between 1990 and 2003 the German authorities admitted altogether 179,934 persons as Jewish quota refugees who came exclusively from the area of the former Soviet Union. Currently, about 15,000 persons immigrate annually.

Between 1990 and 2003 asylum authorities decided more than 2.69 million asylum applications and rejected most of them. Although being obliged to leave the country, many rejected applicants managed to remain in Germany.

During the 1990s civil war in former Yugoslavia, about 350,000 refugees were accepted as civil war refugees on a temporary basis. Of these, only 20,000 victims of civil war atrocities remained in Germany, while the rest returned.

Another immigration pattern that contributes to the officially registered foreign population concerns temporarily admitted migrant workers and students. Altogether 271,000 seasonal workers and on average 43,000 foreign contract-for-services workers were employed in 2003. About 180,000 foreign students (with a foreign school certificate, not foreign nationals who study after completing a German school) were registered in 2003.

Since the information on immigration is so inconsistent, this section focuses on the information of foreign nationals only. In 1991, there were about 5.9 million foreign nationals in the Federal Republic of Germany. This quickly rose to 7.3 million in 1996. The stock figure stabilized around this number until 2003, but decreased to 6.7 million foreign nationals in 2004. This reduction of 600,000 persons is mainly the effect of an adjustment of statistical categories. As a matter of fact, the available figures show that, currently, Germany does not receive much new immigration. The migration statistics since 1998 show a balanced or rather modest positive net migration balance.

One important factor why the foreign population does not increase is naturalization. Between 1994 and 2003 more than 1.2 million foreign nationals received German citizenship, of whom more than 0.5 million were Turkish citizens. Of foreign nationals, 5.3 million are also foreign-born, while 1.4 million were born in Germany (see www.destatis.de). Among foreign nationals not older than 17 years, 69 per cent were born in Germany. This situation will definitely change because of the new nationality law that came into force 2000 (as explained in Section 2 of this chapter).

The figures (Table 10.1) indicate that at the end of 2005, approximately 32 per cent (2.1 million) of the foreign population came from an EU Member State and a further 48 per cent (3.2 million) from other European countries. The remaining foreign residents came from Asia (12 per cent), Africa (4 per cent), America (3 per cent), and some were stateless or of a nationality not determined (1 per cent).[3] The largest in number were Turkish (26 per cent), Italian (8 per cent), Polish (5 per cent), Greek (5 per cent) and Serbian-Montenegrin (4 per cent).

The average duration of residence for foreign nationals was 16.8 years at the end of 2005.[4] The foreign population is, however, divided with respect to the length of stay and residential rights. More than one-third of the foreign population has lived in Germany for more than 20 years, and about two-thirds (4.6 million persons) for at least 8 years, thereby fulfilling one of the basic requirements for naturalization. About 21 per cent of all resident foreign nationals were born in Germany. Among the resident Turkish nationals, 34 per cent were born in Germany, among Italian nationals 30 per cent, and among Dutch nationals 28 per cent. The share of women is 48 per cent, their average age is 35.6 years, and their average stay is 16 years. The average age of foreign men is 36.4 years and their average stay 17.6 years.

---

3   http://www.destatis.de/presse/deutsch/pm2006/p1340025.htm, accessed 02/05/06.
4   http://www.destatis.de/presse/deutsch/pm2006/p1340025.htm, accessed 02/05/06.

Table 10.1   Basic figures for the foreign population in Germany (2005)

Category	Arrivals	Departures	Resident foreign population at 31 December 2005
Total of European nationals	**281,591**	**213,223**	**5,375,180**
of whom:			
Total of European Union	166,767	124,919	2,144,648
of whom:			
Italy	12,269	18,245	540,810
Poland	75,273	40,139	326,596
Greece	5,734	10,413	309,794
Total of other European countries	114,824	88,304	3,230,532
of whom:			
Turkey	31,375	23,142	1,764,041
Serbia and Montenegro	12,340	8,152	297,004
Total Asian countries	**68,369**	**42,744**	**826,432**
Total African countries	**21,057**	**13,636**	**274,929**
Total America	**26,556**	**17,640**	**208,200**
Total Australia und Oceania	**1,726**	**1,270**	**10,157**
Stateless or unknown	**2,194**	**1,662**	**60,913**
Total foreign population	**401,493**	**290,175**	**6,755,811**

Source: Ausländerzentralregister.

According to the latest available data, about two million foreign nationals reside in Germany with a temporary or an insecure residence status, and 180,000 foreign nationals with only a tolerated status. In general, about 1.1 million foreign refugees lived in Germany in 2003. Of these, 115,000 were acknowledged asylum seekers, 75,000 were quota refugees, 188,000 were Jewish quota refugees from CIS countries, 416,000 were de facto refugees and 166,500 were persons belonging to another category (Sachverständigenrat für Zuwanderung und Integration, 2004, p. 60).

In some districts of big cities with a large share of immigrants, children with immigrant backgrounds account for the majority in the schools. According to all available studies among the international Pisa studies, the school system does not deal with this concentration in an appropriate manner.

The economic integration balance is problematic (OECD, 2005). In summer 2004 the unemployment rate among foreign nationals was 20.1 per cent while the overall unemployment rate was 11.7 per cent. At 8.4 per cent, the rate of social assistance recipients is higher among foreign nationals than among German nationals with a rate of 2.9 per cent. Among the foreign social assistance recipients, 10 per cent are EU-citizens, 9 per cent are recognized asylum seekers, 1 per cent is civil war refugees and 80 per cent are other categories of foreign residents including Turkish nationals and tolerated persons (Franz, 2004). However, the economic integration problems are somewhat overemphasized by statistical distortion, since those foreign nationals that are better off and more successful 'disappear' with naturalization from the statistics of foreign nationals and leave the less successful behind.

Undocumented immigrants are not included in all quoted figures. Estimates indicate that as many as one million persons who live in Germany are without proper documents (Alt, 2003; Cyrus, 2005a). This means that, on the one hand, the figures of foreign nationals lead to an underestimation of the real amount of *immigration* caused by ignorance of the omitted categories (ethnic Germans, naturalized citizens and undocumented immigrants), and on the other hand, that there is an over-estimation due to the inclusion of foreign nationals born in Germany (Migrationsbericht, 2004, p. 129). As a matter of fact, experts agree that the quality of data sources in the field of immigration and integration is badly insufficient (Sachverständigenrat, 2004, p. 396ff; BAMF, 2005b, p. 3).

Immigrant rights and participation in public life – issues of immigrant integration

The current legal framework for immigrants' civic participation in Germany is laid down by the basic law and a number of specific laws and regulations. As a rule, newly arriving ethnic German immigrants enjoy full political rights from the beginning. But, according to the basic law, *foreign nationals* cannot possess full civic rights. The missing German citizenship excludes foreign residents from political rights, namely active and passive voting rights. But apart from political decision-making, non-citizens enjoy far reaching entitlements. With reference to the human rights norms codified in the international human rights conventions, the basic law includes the principles of non-discrimination and the rule of law. Immigrants are hence entitled to the services of a number of legal and social institutions, although in some domains this occurs with particular restrictions (Davy, 2001).

Basic and citizens' rights   Foreign non-citizen residents enjoy freedom of speech, of press and of information (Article 5 Basic Law).

Voting rights   According to a 1990 Federal Constitutional Court ruling, an extension of the right to vote and run for office at local level to non-nationals is currently not constitutionally possible in Germany (Shaw 2002, p. 30). This principle encompasses elections at Federal, state and local level. Only EU-citizens enjoy voting rights in local level elections as well as for the European parliament, but not at Federal and state level.

Participation in political parties   Although non-citizens do not possess the right of membership of political parties, they are not excluded by law from becoming a member. They are, nonetheless, definitely excluded from internal party procedures to appoint candidates for political office as they do not possess the voting right.

Representation in local decision-making   Since the early 1970s, several types of 'foreigners' advisory councils' have been instituted and gradually framed by legal regulations of the federal states (Länder). In some states they consist only of non-citizens while in other states representatives from local councils and administrations also are involved. The non-citizen members are sometimes appointed by local authorities, and in some federal states elected in ballots by the locally registered non-citizen population. As a rule, the main and common characteristic of all foreigners' advisory council is their political insignificance. In some municipalities they have the right to put a resolution on the record of the local council but, as a rule, they are only allowed to make non-committal statements.

Membership of German associations   German law does not offer special restrictions regarding foreign nationals' membership of German associations. As with political parties, the decision to accept non-citizens rests with the associations and clubs.

Representation on workers councils   With a reform of the industrial constitutional law in 1972, every non-citizen regardless of residence status enjoys active and passive voting rights for the workers councils, namely the central institution for industrial co-determination.

Right to assemble and establish associations   The constitutional law warrants the freedom to assemble in public (Art. 8 Basic Law) and the right to establish associations (Article 9 Basic Law) to German citizens only. However, non-citizens are free to set up an association and enjoy the opportunities to launch political activities and to establish self-organizations. But these foreigners' associations are subject to special clauses of the German association law, with restrictions applying, for example, for security reasons or when peaceful cohabitation is threatened. The legislator tightened the special regulations in 2002 in response to the terrorist attacks of 9/11, and lowered the threshold which allows the government to forbid foreigners' associations.

The evaluation of rights depends on the focus. Those scholars who focus on the level of classical *political rights* emphasize exclusion, while those who rather concentrate on *social rights* underline the far-reaching equal status. It is noteworthy that the anti-discrimination law was only introduced in 2006. The German legislator was reluctant to implement the European norms (Treichler, 2004).

While immigrant associations traditionally met with distrust in the German public debate (Herbert, 1986; Bade, 2003), several political and societal developments led public authorities to begin to launch institutional measures for the promotion of immigrant participation. Since the late 1970s, more and more recruited workers lost the 'illusion of return' and began to direct the focus of their interests and concerns to life in Germany. According to their social and cultural background and to their specific situational demands, immigrants began to set up associations which serve their religious, social or cultural needs and in the course of time started to demand recognition and support from German authorities.

Today, immigrant associations receive assistance from several different programmes and government levels which aim to promote the integration of immigrants. On the federal level, public authorities spent €574 million in 2003 and €496 million in 2004 for the infrastructure of integration measures for immigrants (including ethnic Germans) and for language training. A few immigrant associations indirectly benefited from the funds when they acted as supplier of projects such as language or professional training courses. However, the German welfare associations were the main recipients. Also, on the local level, additional programmes for the promotion of integration and participation of immigrants were launched, and indeed, many municipalities established special programmes (Sachverständigenrat für Zuwanderung und Integration, 2004, p. 248). With respect to this development, an observer stated that the societal framework for immigrant associations has improved in recent years. Owing to a change of paradigm, the work that immigrant associations have been doing for decades is now recognized and new options are being opened up so that immigrant associations may apply for public funding (Jungk, 2002, p. 2). The beginning of scientific considerations of immigrants' civic participation in Germany can be traced back to the late 1970s. Several scholars conducted mostly smaller research projects on integration and participation of settled foreign workers. Today, a large number of scientific studies that examine aspects of the civic participation of immigrants are available. But these studies rather deal with more general forms of participation, membership patterns, and immigrant associations. Recently, the Federal Ministry for the Family commissioned a literature review with particular reference to voluntary engagement of foreign nationals. The report indicated 32 research projects and 49 publications on immigrant integration and participation (Huth, 2002). Our own enquiry (Cyrus, 2005b) with a broader interest yielded many more scientific publications dealing with different national groups and aspects of civic participation of immigrants. The research encompasses several nationalities, but the focus is on citizens of those countries that Germany once had recruitment agreements with, namely Italy, Spain, Yugoslavia and, above all, Turkey.

Initially, recruited foreign workers either established cultural clubs or founded religious associations. Political divisions in some countries of origin (that is, mainly, Turkey and Yugoslavia) instigated a fragmentation of immigrant associations between ethnic groups or political factions from the same country, while Spanish immigrants tended to join in parents' associations (Weiss and Thränhardt, 2005). With the ongoing settlement process, immigrants established sport clubs, parents' associations and immigrants' interest groups with the general objective of improving the situation in the host country. The focus of orientation shifted increasingly from homeland-related issues to matters related to the immigrant situation in the host country. Today, second- and third-generation foreign nationals are mainly members of German sport clubs and they are – because of their socio-economic position – overrepresented in trade unions when compared to German nationals of the same age. The most important group of active civic participants are immigrants from Turkey who are overrepresented in the local foreigners' advisory boards.

Public and media discourses on migration

The debate of the early 1990s was characterized by efforts to cope with the massive influx of immigrants and soon focused on the admission of refugees and asylum seekers and the regulation of temporary recruitment of CEE-workers (Cyrus, 1994; Meier-Braun, 2002), while the existence of a stable resident foreign population became more and more accepted. But immigration remains a contested issue. It was only for a rather short period, around the turn of the millennium, that the debate showed a tendency in favour of more liberal immigration management. All relevant political actors seemed to agree that at least properly managed immigration is necessary and beneficial for Germany. The main arguments in favour of a more liberal immigration regime were the economic demand for highly qualified workers and the efforts to reduce the demographic gap (Kommission Zuwanderung, 2001). However, the attack against The Pentagon in Washington and the World Trade Center in New York on the 11 September 2001, and the economic decline of the IT industry around the same time, changed the situation and fuelled the renaissance of non-immigration opinions.

Recent recommendations for more liberal immigration management in favour of a modest labour market quota cautiously formulated by an official expert council (Sachverständigenrat für Zuwanderung und Integration, 2004) met with firm refusal and caused the subsequent abolition of this expert council. Such a reflex-like and harsh rejection of proposals in favour of more proactive immigration management indicates that the political culture of the self-declared non-immigration country remains salient. Immigration in Germany is still predominantly framed as being detrimental for the state and society.

Islam and the potential threat by Islamist organizations have repeatedly made the headlines in Germany. External incidents like the 9/11 terrorist attack and the recent killing of a Dutch film director have been discussed, but internal affairs such as the legal ban on headscarves for teachers in office or the discussion about forced marriages have also contributed to the perception of an Islamic danger. Surveys reveal an increasingly negative public attitude towards Islam and immigrants with an Islamic background (Statistisches Bundesamt, 2005, p. 589f). The comparative Pisa study – an international ranking of the efficiency of school systems – positioned Germany in the lower ranks. This caused debates about the deficiencies of the highly segregated German school system. Looking at the causes of Germany's poor achievement, it turned out that children with a blue collar or migrant background were particularly involved. In order to explain the overall miserable balance of the integration of immigrants, the politically framed term 'parallel society' is frequently used in the public debate. This term suggests that immigrants actively and deliberately segregate, refuse to acquire basic cultural techniques (language, education) and thus provoke high rates of unemployment and social assistance receipt. The use of the term 'parallel society' obscures the fact that the long lasting and still salient non-immigration policy has contributed to the current situation.

Several studies show that the media coverage in Germany delivers a rather negative picture of immigration, thereby reinforcing the negative attitude of the population towards immigration and foreigners. Afternoon television talk shows, popular among the less educated youth and young adults, transmit as an unspoken message the concept of distinct cultures and national traits (Thomas, 2003). The media coverage in television, film and print-media portrays immigrants rather as objects that cause problems for the receiving country (for an overview see Merten et al., 1986; Schatz et al., 2000; Hess-Lüttich, 2003).

The negative discourse in media and politics is not without effects. Surveys show that the rejection of immigration is increasing among the German population. The results of the continuous survey (ALLBUS) indicate that the public attitude towards immigration became more liberal between 1980 and 1994, but then turned into a more hostile and negative opinion. According to continuous surveys, 61 per cent of respondents in 1991 and then 72 per cent in 2002 were in favour of restricting the influx of migrant workers, refugees and ethnic Germans (Sachverständigenrat für Zuwanderung und Integration, 2004, p. 381). The expectation that immigrants should adopt a German life-style was supported by 65 per cent in 1980 and dropped to 50 per cent in 1996. In 2000, however, this increased to 72 per cent (Sachverständigenrat für Zuwanderung und Integration, 2004, p. 381f; Statistisches Bundesamt, 2005, p. 586).

From personal observations, we would like to add that local media often cover a wider selection of immigration-related topics than the national discourse. Here, we also find coverage of the efforts of school classes and soccer clubs to oppose the deportation of their fellow students or players. We find that the positive aspects, such as the achievements of immigrant entrepreneurs or the events of local cultural initiatives of immigrant background, are also given coverage.

Concluding remarks

Who are Germany's immigrants? This contribution has sketched the development of the current migration situation, which is characterized by a highly fragmented immigrant population. The rising number of naturalized immigrants – largely of ethnic German or Turkish background – with full rights is still largely invisible in official statistics. The foreign national population is diverse in several respects. With regard to citizenship, Europeans both from EU and non-EU countries still dominate, with an increasing proportion of non-European residents. With regard to immigration, it has to be noted that official statistics include foreign nationals born in Germany, immigrants with a secure status, temporary residents such as seasonal workers and exchange students, as well as asylum seekers and tolerated refugees. Status does not necessarily correspond with length of stay, as there are people who have lived in Germany for more than a decade, yet who still have no secure status. Net immigration is currently negligible and, hence, current debates focus more and more on integration issues, failing to recognize that a large part of the perceived problems are due to non-integration policies as a means of enforcing immigration control.

Who will be Germany's future immigrants? The new Residence Act of 2005 foresees that Germany will receive immigrants with a long-term staying perspective for family and labour market reasons (Cyrus and Vogel, 2005). Their integration will be promoted by obligatory and state-supported language courses that are framed as 'integration courses'. Public discussion acknowledges that there will be a need to attract highly qualified immigrants in the future and foresees a gate for them. This gate, however, is currently nearly closed as a result of restrictive implementation in the face of high unemployment figures. It can be assumed that, for example, foreign students in Germany who find a job after their studies will profit from this gate in the future.

At the same time, the immigration law is control-minded and restrictive with respect to unwanted immigrants from poorer countries who try to gain asylum or protection. If German immigration policy fails to develop a more coherent approach and proceeds with increasingly restrictive procedures, two developments will probably occur. First, the group of migrants that is neither removed nor granted the prospect of a secure stay will continue to be a distinctive feature of the German immigrant population. Faced with a harsh exclusionary disintegration policy, this group will not only have problems in Germany, but will also become increasingly problematic for German society. Second, with negligible asylum acceptance rates and hardly any other options to gain regular status for political or humanitarian reasons, the number of persons without any status will start to rise again.

While past immigration was highly segmented with regard to status, future immigration will be largely split into three groups: immigrants with the prospect of a secure stay, integration promotion and equal rights; temporary and tolerated immigrants with a legal stay but faced with an extremely exclusionary disintegration policy; and temporary and permanent illegal migrants faced with the difficulties of survival in a highly organized society.

These tendencies may be cushioned, compensated for, and finally reversed by other developments in German society. These may include the support of immigrants by the church, labour unions and welfare organizations at the national level, pragmatic coalitions of immigrant activists and administrations at the local level in individual cases, and increasing activities of Germans with an immigrant background. It remains, moreover, an open question whether Germany's negative attitude towards immigration will continue to influence future common European immigration policy or whether a more coherent and liberal approach developed on the European level will shape Germany's future immigration policy.

References

Alt, J. (2003), *Leben in der Schattenwelt: Problemkomplex illegale Migration*. Karlsruhe: von Loeper Literaturverlag.

Bade, K.J. (2003), *Migration in European History*. Oxford: Blackwell.

Bade, K.J. and Münz, R. (2002), 'Einführung: Migration und Migrationspolitik – säkulare Entscheidungen für Deutschland', in Bade, K.J. and Münz, R. (eds) *Migrationsreport 2002; Fakten, Analysen, Perspektiven*, 11–30. Frankfurt am Main and New York: Campus.

Bade, K.J., Bommes, M. and Münz, R. (eds) (2004), *Migrationsreport 2004: Fakten – Analysen – Perspektiven*. Frankfurt am Main: Campus.

BAMF (Bundesamt für Migration und Flüchtlinge) (2005a), *Migration, Integration und Asyl in Zahlen*. Nuremberg: Selbstverlag.

BAMF (Bundesamt für Migration und Flüchtlinge) (2005b), *Die Datenlage im Bereich der Migrations- und Integrationsforschung: Ein Überblick über wesentliche Migrations- und*

Integrationsindikatoren und die Datenquellen, BAMF-working papers 1/2005. Nuremberg: Selbstverlag.

Beauftragte der Bundesregierung für Migration, Flüchtlinge und Integration (2005), *Bericht der Beauftragten der Bundesregierung für Migration, Flüchtlinge und Integration über die Lage der Ausländerinnen und Ausländer in Deutschland*. Berlin: Selbstverlag.

Bommes, M. (2001), 'Bundesrepublik Deutschland: Normalisierung der Migrationserfahrung', in Bade, K. (ed.) *Einwanderungskontinent Europa: Migration und Integration am Beginn des 21. Jahrhunderts*, 49–60. Osnabrück: Rasch.

Cyrus, N. (1994), 'Flexible Work for Fragmented Labour Markets: The Significance of the New Labour Migration Regime in the Federal Republic of Germany', *Migration – A European Journal of International Migration and Ethnic Relations*, **26**, 97–124.

Cyrus, N. (2005a), *Trafficking for Sexual and Labour Exploitation in Germany*. Geneva: International Labour Organization.

Cyrus, N. and Vogel, D. (2005), 'Germany', in Niessen, J., Schibel, Y. and Thompson, C. (eds) *Current Immigration Debates in Europe: A Publication of the European Migration Dialogue*. Brussels: Migration Policy Group.

Davy, U. (ed.) (2001), *Die Integration von Einwanderern: Rechtliche Regelungen im europäischen Vergleich*. Frankfurt am Main and New York, Campus.

Franz, V. (2004), 'Arbeitslosigkeit und Sozialhilfebezug: Inwieweit Sind Migranten von Hartz IV betroffen?' *Aid – Ausländer in Deutschland*, **20**(3).

Hell, M. (2005), *Einwanderungsland Deutschland? Die Zuwanderungsdiskussion 1998–2002*. Wiesbaden: VS-Verlag.

Herbert, U. (1986), *Geschichte der Ausländerbeschäftigung in Deutschland, 1880 Bis., 1980; Saisonarbeiter, Zwangsarbeiter and Gastarbeiter*. Bonn: Dietz.

Hess-Lüttich, E.W.B. (2003), 'Interkulturelle Medienwissenschaft und Kulturkonflikt', *Linguistik online*, 14, 2/3: 89–106.

Huth, S. (2002), *Ergebnisse der Literaturrecherche. Recherche zum freiwilligen Engagement von Migrantinnen und Migranten – Konzepte, Recherche und Ausarbeitung der Dokumentation*. Bonn: Broschürenstelle des BMFSFJ.

Jungk, S. (2002), *Politische und soziale Partizipation von Migrantinnen und Migranten und ihren Selbstorganisationen – Möglichkeiten der Mitwirkung, Inanspruchnahme und Chancen in Deutschland* (Vortrag zur Tagung 'Politische und soziale Partizipation von MigrantInnen mit Schwerpunkt KurdInnen', veranstaltet von NAVEND e. V, 18 January 2002). Düsseldorf, Solingen: Landeszentrum für Zuwanderung NRW.

Meier-Braun, K.-H. (2002), *Deutschland, Einwanderungsland*. Frankfurt am Main: Suhrkamp.

Merten, K. et al. (1986), *Das Bild der Ausländer in der deutschen Presse: Ergebnisse Einer systematischen Inhaltsanalyse*. Frankfurt am Main: Dagyeli.

Migrationsbericht (2004), *Migrationsbericht 2004: Bericht des Sachverständigenrates für Zuwanderung und Integration im Auftrag der Bundesregierung in Zusammenarbeit mit dem Europäischen Forum für Migrationsstudien (efms) an der Universität Bamberg*. Nuremberg: BAFL.

Münz, R. (2001), 'Deutschland wird Einwanderungsland – Rückblick und Ausblick', *Zuwanderung und Asyl* (Band 8 der Schriftenreihe des Bundesamtes für die Anerkennung ausländischer Flüchtlinge, Bundesamt für die Anerkennung ausländischer Flüchtlinge), 173–214. Nuremberg: Selbstverlag.

OECD (2005), *Labour Market Integration of Immigrants in Germany*. Paris: OECD.

Sachverständigenrat für Zuwanderung und Integration (2004), *Migration und Integration – Erfahrungen nutzen, Neues wagen. Jahresgutachten 2004 des Sachverständigenrates für Zuwanderung und Integration.* Nuremberg: BAFL.

Statistisches Bundesamt (2005), *Datenreport 2004: Zahlen und Fakten über die Bundesrepublik Deutschland. Zusammenarbeit mit dem Wissenschaftszentrum Berlin für Sozialforschung (WZB) und dem Zentrum für Umfragen, Methoden und Analysen, Mannheim (ZUMA).* (Zweite, aktualisierte Auflage). Wiesbaden: Statistisches Bundesamt.

Schatz, H. et al. (eds) (2000), Migranten und Medien. *Neue Herausforderungen an die Integrationsfunktion von Presse und Rundfunk.* Wiesbaden: Westdeutscher Verlag.

Thomas, T. (2003), *Deutsch-Stunde: Zur Konstruktion nationaler Idenität im Fernsehtalk.* Frankfurt am Main: Campus.

Treichler, Andreas (2004), 'Wi(e)der Fremdenfeindlichkeit und Rassismus. Europäische. Grundlagen und menschenrechtliche Perspektiven der Antidiskriminierungsarbeit', in Treichler, A. and Cyrus, N. (eds) *Handbuch Soziale Arbeit in der Einwanderungsgesellschaft*, 71–98. Frankfurt (Main): Brandes und Apsel.

Unabhängige Kommission Zuwanderung (2001), *Zuwanderung Gestalten – Integration fördern*: *Bericht der Unabhängigen Kommission Zuwanderung.* Berlin: Bundesministerium des Innern.

Vogel, D. and Wüst, A. (2003), 'Paradigmenwechsel ohne Instrumentenwechsel? – Kontinuität und Wandel im Politikfeld Migration', in Seeleib-Kaiser, M., Gohr, A. and Wiesbaden, W. (eds) *Sozial- und Wirtschaftspolitik unter Rot-Grün*, 265–86. Opladen: Westdeutscher Verlag.

Weiss, K. and Thränhardt, D. (eds) (2005), *Selbsthilfe: Wie Migranten Netzwerke knüpfen und soziales Kapital schaffen.* Freiburg im Breisgau: Lambertus Verlag.

Internet-based references

Cyrus, N. (2005b), 'Active Civic Participation of Immigrants in Germany', Country Report prepared for the European Research Project POLITIS. Oldenburg: IBKM (available at http://www.uni-oldenburg.de/politis-europe/download/Germany.pdf).

Chapter 11

Greece

Ruby Gropas and Anna Triandafyllidou

Until recently, Greece was a migration sender rather than host country. A brief historical overview of immigration trends into Greece since the twentieth century is limited mainly to inflows from the Balkans due to the Balkan Wars, to refugees from Asia Minor (approximately 1.4 million in the 1920s and again around 350,000 in the 1950s from Istanbul) and from Egypt. These refugees were principally of Greek origin; they were integrated into the host society very quickly, primarily for foreign policy reasons, and their impact on the Greek economy and commerce was positive. Nevertheless, the economic underdevelopment of the country did not encourage immigration into Greece. On the contrary, Greeks emigrated in significant numbers mainly to Northern Europe (Germany, Belgium), the USA and Australia. Emigration, however, nearly came to a halt in the mid to late 1970s after the tightening up of migration regimes in Northern Europe.

After the geopolitical changes of 1989, the country was quickly converted into a host of mainly undocumented immigrants from Central and Eastern Europe, the former Soviet Union and the Third World. The dramatic and sudden increase of immigrant influx was an unexpected phenomenon for both the government and the population. The new situation has been characterized by administrative and political confusion with regard to migration policy, and an over-representation of irregular/illegal immigrants working in conditions of informality across the Greek economy. An increase in xenophobic behaviour and racism has been registered from the mid-1990s.

Major developments in Greece's immigration policy

It is commonly stressed that Greece, traditionally an immigrant-exporting country, has increasingly confirmed its status as a destination country. In particular, major population inflows towards Greece during the last 20 years have included:

- co-ethnic returnees, notably the Pontic Greeks, arriving from the former Soviet Republics (Georgia, Kazakhstan, Russia and Armenia);
- immigrants of Greek descent, notably ethnic Greek Albanian citizens (Vorioepirotes);
- economic immigrants from non-EU countries (other than the categories mentioned previously, for example Ukrainians, Russians, Filipinos, Bangladeshis);
- a smaller number of returning Greek migrants from Northern Europe, the USA, Canada and Australia.

On the eve of the 1990s, Greece lacked a legislative framework for the control and management of immigration. The first law that tackled the influx of foreigners into the country was Law 1975 of 1991 with the eloquent title 'Entry, exit, sojourn, employment, removal of aliens, procedure for the recognition of refugees and other measures'. The aim was mainly to curb migration, to facilitate removals of undocumented migrants apprehended near the borders and, if possible, to remove illegal aliens sojourning in Greece. The law made nearly impracticable the entry and stay of economic migrants seeking jobs.

In the years that followed, hundreds of thousands of immigrants came to Greece without documents or permits. They either crossed the northern mountainous borders between Albania or Bulgaria and Greece on foot at night, or landed with small dinghies on the Greek islands of the Aegean or Crete (usually with the 'help' of human smuggling networks). Some arrived at Greek airports with tourist visas which they overstayed and others crossed the northern Greek borders by bus, pretending that they were travelling for leisure. It became increasingly evident that immigrants were here to stay and that the new phenomenon could not merely be managed through stricter border control and massive removal operations.

The presidential decrees 358/1997 and 359/1997 inaugurated the first immigrant regularization programme, which took place in spring 1998. In total, 371,641 immigrants applied for the white card (limited duration permit) which was the first step in applying for the temporary stay permit or green card (of one-, two- or five-year duration). Only 212,860 undocumented foreigners managed to submit an application for a green card. The main reason for this was that while this first regularization programme was ambitious in its conception and rather open in its conditions, it met with insurmountable organizational and practical difficulties. For one, the state services responsible for managing the programme were hardly prepared to receive and process the hundreds of thousands of applications. In addition, proof of legal employment for a minimum number of days was an important prerequisite; the reluctance of many employers to pay social insurance contributions made it very difficult for many applicants to meet this requirement. As a result, a significant number of applications were unsuccessful in passing to the second but necessary phase of the green card application phase and, despite the repeated extensions of the deadlines, presumably fell back into undocumented status.

Nonetheless, this programme lay the first foundations in Greece for an institutional framework able to deal with immigration. In addition, the data collected through the regularization procedure offered some first insights into the socioeconomic and demographic features of the immigrant population.

According to data collected by the Employment Institute (OAED), 44.3 per cent of all foreigners who applied for the regularization of their working and residence status in the months of January to May 1998 were concentrated in the wider metropolitan area of Athens. Of these applicants, 52.7 per cent were Albanians, 6.1 per cent Pakistanis, 4.8 per cent Bulgarians, 4.5 per cent Romanians and another 4.5 per cent Poles. In addition, there were more female applicants among the following population groups: Bulgarian, Polish, Ukrainian and Filipino.

In 2001, and before the first regularization programme had come to a close, the government issued a new law (Law 2910/2001) entitled 'Entry and sojourn of foreigners in the Greek territory. Naturalization and other measures'. This law had a twofold aim. First, it included a second regularization programme that aimed at attracting all the applicants who had not been able to benefit from the 1998 'amnesty', as well as the thousands of new immigrants who had, in the meantime, arrived in Greece. Second, the new law created the necessary policy framework to deal with immigration in the medium to long term. Thus, it provided for issues relating to border control as well as for channels of legal entry to Greece for employment, family reunion, return to their country of origin (for ethnic Greeks abroad), and studies or asylum seeking. It also laid down the conditions for the naturalization of aliens residing in the country.

Another 370,000 immigrants applied to acquire legal status within the framework of the new programme. Even though the implementation phase had been more carefully planned, organizational issues arose quickly. In the Athens metropolitan area in particular, the four special immigration offices set up by the regional government to receive and process the applications were unable to deal with the huge workload they were faced with. Following repeated recommendations on behalf of trade unions, NGOs and the Greek Ombudsman, the law was revised and the relevant deadlines extended. Nonetheless, resources were still insufficient as work and stay permits continued to be issued for one-year periods only. Hence, by the time one immigrant was done with the issuing of her/his papers, s/he had to start all over again to renew them. In addition to the cumbersome nature of the procedure, the costs (in money but also in time spent queuing) associated with this renewal process incurred by the migrants constituted a further hindrance. Only in January 2004 (Act 3202/2003) did the government decide to issue permits of a two-year duration, thereby facilitating the task of both the administration and the immigrant applicants.

In 2001, the government issued a three-year programme: *the Action Plan for the Social Integration of Immigrants* (for the period 2002–2005). This Plan includes measures for their inclusion in the labour market, their access to health services and, overall, a series of measures promoting cultural dialogue and combating xenophobia and racism within Greek society. Unfortunately, many of the provisions of this programme have remained on paper only.

In August 2005, the Greek Parliament adopted a new immigration bill on 'Entry, stay and integration of third-country nationals in Greece' to come into force on 1 January 2006. The objective of this new legislation is to rationalize the coordination of Greece's immigration policy, simplify procedures and cut red tape, and adapt Greek legislation to the new EU directives regarding family reunification and long-term resident status. The core innovative features include unifying residence and work permits into one document, clarifying family reunification conditions, addressing the status of victims of human trafficking and strengthening regional migration commissions. However, this bill has been criticized by non-governmental organizations, immigrant associations, academics and opposition parties for continuing to ignore the majority of the country's illegal migrant population, for not effectively transposing the European Commission directives on family reunification and long-term resident status into national legislation, for introducing ill-designed integration tests in relation to the adoption of long-term resident status, and for imposing unreasonably high fees for stay/work permit applications. The Greek Minister of Interior has reacted to criticisms by noting that the necessary changes will be made if gaps or problems surface during the law's implementation.

The immigrant population in Greece: main demographic and social features

At the 1991 census, Greece had 10,260,000 residents of whom 167,000 were foreigners. Following the most recent census of March 2001, there are 10,964,020 inhabitants in Greece, of whom 797,091 are foreigners. These figures are shown in Table 11.1. The 2001 census gives the most complete picture of the immigrant population in Greece, as it has attempted to cover both legal and undocumented aliens. Among these foreigners there are only 47,000 citizens from the EU15 Member States (that is, before the enlargement which was concluded on 1 May 2004). Comparing the data of the two censuses it becomes clear that the demographic growth of Greece in the last decade is almost entirely due to the arrival of non-EU workers and their families.

Table 11.1   Total population and immigrant stock in Greece (1991 and 2001)

Population – official data	1991	2001
Total population of Greece	10,260,000	10,964,020
Of whom foreigners	167,000	797,091
In %	2	7

Source: National Statistics Service of Greece, www.statistics.gr.

With regard to the 762,000 immigrants for whom we have detailed demographic data, the percentage of men is slightly higher than that of women (54.5 per cent and 45.5 per cent respectively). Most immigrant men and women declare employment as their main reason for coming to Greece (54 per cent in total). The second most important reason for settling in the country is family reunion (about 100,000 people in total, that is 13 per cent), while approximately 50,000 persons have identified return to their country of origin as the third most important reason for migration to Greece. The census included another category (apart from work, family, return, studies and seeking asylum), which was ticked by 164,180 individuals (roughly equally divided between men and women). In spite of the large number of people registering under this category (over 20 per cent of all foreigners), there is no available information as to what these 'other reasons' may consist of.

The largest group of immigrants are from the Balkan countries. More than half of all foreigners registered in the census and for whom we have detailed demographic data, are Albanian citizens (that is 438,000 or 57 per cent). The majority of these (240,000, that is 54 per cent) stated that they came to Greece to find employment, while 70,000 (15 per cent) came for family reunion, and about 10,000 (or 2.3 per cent) as co-ethnic returnees. About one-third of Albanians work in the construction sector and another 20 per cent in agriculture.

The second largest national group (with a very large difference from the first though) are Bulgarian citizens with 35,000 individuals registered at the census, and two-thirds (more than 27,000) have identified work as the principal reason for their immigration to Greece. Roughly one-third of Bulgarians work in agriculture and another third in private care and house cleaning services.

Alongside the non-EU citizens, we should consider in substance even if not in form, the co-ethnic returnees from the former Soviet Republics, generally referred to as Pontic Greeks, who arrived in Greece in the late 1980s and early 1990s as economic migrants. According to the special census administered by the General Secretariat for Greeks Abroad (GSGA) in the year 2000, 152,204 Pontic Greeks had settled in the country. More than half of them (about 80,000) came from Georgia, 31,000 came from Kazakhstan, 23,000 from Russia and about 9,000 from Armenia.

It is unclear how many ethnic Greek Albanians (*Vorioepirotes*) (not included in the GSGA data) had already been naturalized and, hence, appeared as Greek citizens in the 2001 census. It is estimated that about 100,000 Albanian citizens who live in Greece have been issued with the Special Identity Card for ethnic Greeks from Albania.

Furthermore, nearly one-half of the migrants have secondary education (including technical schools) while approximately one-tenth have higher education. A qualitative analysis of the educational levels of the various nationalities shows that, in comparative terms, Albanians have the lowest level of education and former Soviet citizens the highest. In terms of higher education, females have the larger share of the total, while males appear to predominate in all other educational categories (Kassimis and Kassimi, 2004).

In sum, we estimate (see Table 11.2) at about 1.25 million the total number of immigrants (including co-ethnics) living in Greece in 2005. This amounts to just under 12 per cent of the total population. It is unclear how many among them have a legal stay and work status. Among the legal immigrants, a large majority regularized their status through the two 'amnesty' programmes mentioned above, while a smaller number either came legally or took advantage of the special provisions for co-ethnics.

Table 11.2   Foreign and foreign-born population in Greece (2005)

Total number of foreigners – Data from census of 2001 *Main nationalities in descending order*	797,091
Albanians	438,000
Nationals from EU15	47,000
Bulgarians	35,000
Georgians	20,000
Romanians	20,000
Russians	17,500
Cypriots	17,000
Poles	13,000
Pakistanis	10,000
Ukrainians	10,000
Indians	10,000
Other categories of foreigners or foreign-born	
Pontic Greeks*	152,204
Undocumented immigrants**	300,000
Total Immigrant and Ethnic Returnee Population (rounded to the nearest thousand)	1,250,000

General Secretariat for Greeks Abroad; Special Census of 2000.
**Authors' rough estimate of the undocumented immigrant population currently present in Greece. This estimate is based on the authors' own perception and on discussions with other social and policy actors including immigrant organisations and NGOs.*

To obtain an understanding of immigrant insertion in the Greek labour market, it is useful to look more closely at the case of Albanians, who account for more than half of the total foreign population. Lambrianidis and Lyberaki (2001) have shown how Albanian workers in Thessaloniki (the second largest city in Greece) have moved from unskilled farm work into construction, small-firm employment, semi-skilled work and transport services. The authors have highlighted the upward socioeconomic mobility of Albanian immigrants who, through increased language skills and a better understanding of employment possibilities in Greek society, have managed to improve their employment situation and income. It is also worth noting that in the period covered by the research, the first regularization programme took place, thus enabling immigrant workers to obtain legal status and hence to enjoy insurance benefits. Among the sample studied by Lambrianidis and Lymperaki, 82 per cent declared that they held steady employment and 57 per cent paid social insurance. About one-third of men interviewed worked in construction and one-third of women in house cleaning. Among women another third were housewives while, among men, 24 per cent worked in small industries. These findings are confirmed by Hatziprokopiou (2003), who shows that

Albanian immigrants in Thessaloniki, apart from construction and domestic services, are employed in small enterprises (commerce, transportation, hotels and restaurants) and in small- and medium-scale manufacturing. Contrary also to earlier studies (Iosifides and King, 1998), Hatziprokopiou notes that at the time of his interviews, most interviewees had legal status and social insurance.

The insertion of Albanian and other foreign workers into the Greek labour market at a time of relatively high structural unemployment reveals the structural imbalances of the Greek economy. Indeed, the Greek economy is characterized by insufficient labour supply and an over-regulated and rigid job market. At the same time, low productivity sectors are over-represented in the economy. Under these circumstances, the plentiful, cheap, flexible and often informal work provided by immigrant workers has fulfilled the needs of the Greek job market, counteracting some of these imbalances.

Naturalization

A special comment about naturalization in Greece is in order here. Law 2130/1993 states that immigrants who wish to become Greek citizens have to be resident in Greece for more than ten years in the last twelve (previously the requirement was for eight years in the last twelve). This is one of the longest residence requirements for naturalization – together with Swiss legislation – in Europe. Law 2910/2001 (Articles 58–64) made the conditions and procedure even more cumbersome: a high fee is to be paid by the applicant (over 1,300 euros) and the decision is discretionary. Furthermore, authorities are not required to reply within a specified time and need not justify a negative decision to the applicant. If an applicant is rejected, s/he may apply again after one year.

These articles (58–64) have been subject to criticism by NGOs, the liberal press and international organizations (ECRI, 2004) for being discriminatory and unfair. ECRI in particular has raised concerns regarding the preferential path to citizenship available to individuals of Greek origin, noting that there are subjective elements in the assessment of such origin, making the applicants liable to discrimination. Also, ECRI (2004, paragraph 64) notes that such distinctions between presumed co-ethnics and others create uncertainty among the latter and false expectations among the former with regard to the kind of rights and/or treatment that they are entitled to.

Immigrant rights and participation in public life – issues of immigrant integration

In Greece, immigrant participation in public life has been hampered by the long-standing undocumented or insecure status of most immigrants. Moreover, the flawed organization of both regularization programmes made immigrants particularly suspicious about the intent of such programmes and, paradoxically, encouraged them to remain in the shadow of Greek society and economy. Besides, most immigrants were too busy making ends meet and not being caught by the police to find the time (and energy) to organize in associations.

Taking into account that foreigners – including those of Greek ethnic origin – constitute about 12 per cent of the total Greek population and nearly 15 per cent of the Greek labour force, their record of civic activism is truly limited. It is fair to say that the institutional and legal framework of migration in Greece has up to now provided them with very limited opportunities to participate in public life.

Section II of the Greek Constitution (2001), referring to Individual and Social Rights, sets out 18 sets of rights applicable to all individuals living in Greece. Of these, there are eight articles in which the exercise of a right is reserved to Greek citizens only. Thus, immigrants who are legal residents do not have the right to rally (Article 11) nor to enter into associations (Article 12). Moreover, Law 2910/2001 and Circular 32089/10641/26.5.1993 of the Ministry of the Interior discriminate against immigrants with regard to the processing of and response to naturalization applications. Such provisions do not impede civic participation as such, but generally create a climate of mistrust between the state and the immigrant aspiring to become a national and to be fully integrated into the host society. Furthermore, Law 2910/2001 states that immigrants are required to report any change of address, job or employer to the authorities, though restrictions on mobility within Greek territory do not apply.

Perhaps the most important issue that is particular to the Greek case is the fact that the Greek state has distinguished between immigrants of Greek ethnic origin and others (Triandafyllidou, 1996; Triandafyllidou and Veikou, 2002). The former have been granted special status. Co-ethnics from the former Soviet Republics were treated as returnees and a preferential path to naturalization was made available to them, and though ethnic Greek Albanian citizens were discouraged from naturalizing, they were issued special identity cards. These cards carried with them eligibility for specific welfare benefits, even if their holders were not granted Greek citizenship. This policy of preferential treatment has raised numerous legal problems and created unease among the population (ECRI, 2004). Overall, this distinction may have encouraged the civic participation and integration of Pontic Greeks and ethnic Greek Albanians (*Vorioepirotes*) while discouraging the more active inclusion of 'other' immigrants.

With regard to formal participation in the country's political life, voting and standing for elections at the national level is still restricted to Greek citizens. EU citizens residing in Greece can participate in European elections and in local elections though, until the previous elections in 2002, participation has been at rather low levels. Immigrant naturalization and full political participation overall remains a sensitive issue. There are no special consulting or other bodies at the state or local level encouraging immigrant participation even without the right to vote. Given that non-Greeks do not have political rights, it follows that they cannot become official party members. The exception is with regard to Cypriots who are able to be party members. In the context of our research, this raised the question of the extent to which immigrants can exercise their right to association in the political sphere. Interviews that we conducted with representatives of the main political parties, however, shed some light on the informal inclusion of immigrants in the political sphere. In recent years, there have been a number of parliamentarians who include immigrants in their team, and some political parties refer to immigrants who are informally closely associated with the party or who participate (generally as observers) in party conventions as 'friends of the party.' This informal network and affiliation facilitates a flow of information between the immigrant communities and the political elites.

Although to some extent many aspects of the picture painted here are rather bleak, there are a handful of positive highlights regarding immigrant integration. During the last years, Greek NGOs and state organizations have participated more actively in the European Social Fund and European Commission programmes combating discrimination and exclusion. They have thus contributed to public awareness campaigns in favour of immigrant inclusion in Greek society. However, such campaigns are far from gaining prime time visibility of the kind that perceived immigrant criminality has been receiving for several years now.

Intellectuals, NGOs and particularly the Greek Ombudsman (http://www.synigoros.gr/allodapoi/) have been increasingly active in promoting and protecting immigrants' human and more general sociopolitical rights. Trade unions have tried, to a certain extent, to encourage immigrant workers' membership. Trade unions in specific trades, for example the builders' union, have formally been pro-immigrant as a means to secure their native members' rights and to avoid illegitimate competition from immigrants accepting work for lower pay and without welfare benefits. However, on the whole, trade unions have not been at the forefront of pro-immigrant civic or political activism.

There are also a few examples of naturalized immigrants (generally having obtained Greek nationality through marriage) who have become increasingly civically and politically active – particularly as regards their participation in political parties. These, however, remain exceptions.

Public and media discourses on migration

An early study prepared for the Council of Europe (Spinellis et al., 1996) identified the following themes as the main focus of the press coverage on migration:

- immigrants increase unemployment among natives;
- immigrants are responsible for an increase in criminality (these mostly involve property-related offences, but also drug trafficking and rape);
- the main 'solutions' to the 'immigration problem' include stricter laws and harsher enforcement, especially concerning border control;
- ethnic origin and/or nationality tend to be highlighted, particularly in the case of Albanians.

Looking at the media coverage and political discourse nowadays, a decade after this study was undertaken, improvement is unfortunately rather limited. Since the late 1990s, the coverage of cultural and ethnic diversity has been marked by an improvement, resulting in more balanced accounts of immigration and minority issues, albeit sidestepping the issue of minority and immigrants' rights.

In a recent study by Triandafyllidou and Veikou (2002) focusing on media reporting on minority and immigration issues in the mid to late 1990s, the author distinguishes between two main categories of newspapers and television channels and their respective attitude towards minority issues. A large part of the daily press and private television stations adopt a nationalist, xenophobic and even racist standpoint, promoting a view of Greece as culturally and ethnically 'pure' and homogeneous. The right-wing press and private television channels in particular show little sensitivity towards cultural difference and tend to stigmatize and discriminate against immigrants and minorities.[1] A few dissenting voices, including state television channels, mainstream and left-wing newspapers, adopt a more careful and sensitive approach when reporting on ethnic issues and towards minority and immigration matters, and are characterized by a relative openness to cultural and ethnic diversity with only a mildly nationalist viewpoint. Nonetheless, they fail to react and criticize verbal harassment, the racist attitudes and behaviour exhibited by the majority of the political elite. At the risk of generalizing, the media which are characterized by an extremely nationalist-xenophobic discourse mostly have a right-wing orientation, while the mildly nationalist, more-sensitive media belong to the centre and left wing of Greek politics. Granted, there are exceptions to this rule; for example, the nationalist camp also includes left-wing newspapers, while traditional right-wing newspapers are also found in the moderate side.

---

1   Greece's historical minorities include the following national, ethno-linguistic and religious groups (percentages refer to the total resident population): Roma 3.3 per cent; Arvanites 2 per cent; members of the Macedonian minority 2 per cent; Vlachs 2 per cent; Turks 1 per cent and Pomaks 0.3 per cent. Religious minorities, which include Catholics, Protestants and new religious movements, make up nearly 1 per cent of the population. Among these minorities, the Greek State only recognizes the existence of Turkish Muslims, the Roma population and Greek Catholics and Protestants (Minority Rights Group (MRG), 1994; Triandafyllidou, 2002).

To a significant extent, reporting on minorities and immigrants is couched in conspiracy theories rhetoric and an overall perception of national threat. In these cases, the Greek nation's cultural, ethnic or even religious 'purity' and well-being is perceived to be threatened by internal or external 'enemies'. The common feature of the various 'enemies' singled out at different times and with regard to different issues or events is predominantly their non-Greek origin and culture; they may either be historical enemies (for example Turks) or national traitors (for example members of the Macedonian minority). In other words, reporting concentrates more on the presumed threat to the country and the people than on practical issues of minority and immigrant integration. This becomes a distorting lens for reading and interpreting the actions and words, often taken out of context, not only of the presumed 'enemies' but also of any third parties intervening in a given matter. Such third parties include fellow EU Member States, European or other international bodies, the US Government, and even Greek non-governmental organizations defending minority rights.

'Political correctness' or minority sensitivity is far from being common practice, especially in the language used by tabloids and newspapers adopting extreme nationalist views. Accusations of racism are denied and any anti-racist argument is turned on its head; authors are not racist, they simply point to the danger or damage inflicted on the country and its people by foreigners. Karydis (1996) and Pavlou (2001) point to the invented reality of news bulletins. Pavlou argues that the press discourse reproduces police bulletins and systematically 'recycles' criminal news, so that they appear to be more frequent than they actually are. Overall, the media rarely define concepts such as 'racism', 'anti-racism', or 'cultural diversity'. Diversity is represented as 'a deleterious thing', 'hybridization', a loss of 'purity' or cultural and political autonomy, while homogeneity and nationalism are praised as 'a desirable thing'. It is worth noting that the more moderate media adopt a more open and sensitive stance. They report the arguments of the different parties involved in minority or immigrant matters, and avoid the use of offensive terms such as 'barbaric', or 'inhuman.' Their accounts, to the extent that this is possible, constitute a more even-handed approach to the issues or events reported. Nonetheless, criticism towards other newspapers or television programmes for using racist language and/or inciting ethnic hatred is exceptional. By failing to clearly stand up for minority rights and individual civil rights, the moderate, 'impartial' media do little to thwart intolerance and racism. There are few studies analysing directly and in detail the language used in news or commentaries on migration (Petronoti, 2000; Triandafyllidou, 2000, 2001; Pavlou, 2001) and no studies as yet that examine the ways in which news-making practices and routines affect the content and form of migration reporting.

A few words on the current issues that tend to attract most of the media attention may be indicative of the issues relating to migration that are perceived as being important by the host country's population, and of the general public's sensitivities with regard to the immigrant population's living conditions. References to immigrants may be grouped under the following four general themes.

Immigrant criminality

Both petty crimes against one's property and more serious crimes (for example armed robbery, murder, drug or women and children trafficking) are often related to immigrants in television bulletins and newspaper reports. The media tend to reproduce ethnic prejudice by reporting and commenting on national categorizations of crimes (for example Albanians are involved in all sorts of trafficking, extensive presence of the Albanian Mafia, Russian and Ukrainian women are generally employed in the sex industry, Romanian criminals, Bulgarian children are sold to families wishing to adopt). Suspects or convicted perpetrators are referred to by their nationality or ethnic origin.

Illegal immigrants attempting to enter Greece

Stories of boats captured or shipwrecked off the shores of various Greek islands with scores of illegal immigrants hidden below deck are very common in the printed and audio-visual press. Reporters emphasize in particular that a) in their attempt to seek a better life, hundreds and thousands of people (principally from Asia) are prepared to risk their life, and b) these people are exploited by 'inhuman' traffickers who charge exorbitant amounts to bring them illegally to Europe with no consideration for their safety and life.

Trafficking of women

Stories of women from Eastern Europe, Russia, Ukraine and Moldavia especially, who are brought to Greece under false work pretences and are then forced into prostitution are very frequent. Reports (undercover and news documentaries) tell the stories of young girls and women who are either brought into Greece illegally and, therefore, have no papers or whose passport and papers are 'confiscated' by bar-owners and human traffickers, and who therefore have no possibility of resorting to the authorities to be protected and are sexually exploited in Athens and in rural areas. Such stories frequently allude to the involvement, or at the very least the acquiescence, of the local police authorities.

Immigrant children in state schools

There are many reports and articles on the growing number of children in state schools. On the one hand, particular emphasis is on schools where children of immigrant origin have become the majority and how this influences schooling. It is often argued that because of Greek-language difficulties that some children of immigrant origin may have, teaching is slowed down, leading many Greek parents to prefer private education or relocating to neighbourhoods with smaller immigrant populations in order to offer their children a 'better' education. On the other hand, there is an almost yearly recurrent theme of immigrant children coming top of their class.

In parallel to the above sombre description of the media landscape, there are growing trends of increased sensitivity towards minority and immigrant problems, of increasing acceptance of diversity within Greece, and a tendency to give voice to minorities themselves as well as to NGOs active in the field. These trends mainly characterize the moderate and progressive segment of the press and television channels. Critical accounts of the poor social and economic conditions of specific minorities (mainly Roma and Muslim Turks) and immigrant labourers (Albanians in particular) are given, and related state policy is criticized. Also, success stories of young immigrant pupils, foreign musicians, actors or writers and intellectuals, mainly of Albanian nationality, are reported in magazines and newspapers, and more rarely in television programmes. Nonetheless, minority or immigrant rights are never on the media agenda as collective political rights. The coverage concerns mainly the improvement of their living or working conditions, their access to education or work, but not their politicization as non-Greek cultural or ethnic groups that comprise a part of Greece.

It is interesting to note that over the last couple of years, popular television programmes, serials and reality shows have been including immigrants in their casting. More importantly, though, small television stations such as Kanali 10 provide news updates in Russian and Albanian and certain radio stations in the Attica prefecture cater to the immigrant communities (such as national broadcasting ERA, or Radio 98.4, and so on).

The modest positive change in the media coverage of minority and immigration issues may be related to cultural initiatives undertaken by known artists and media people promoting understanding and receptiveness towards diversity. In addition, there has been a mobilization of NGO activists and a small number of intellectuals to whom the more moderate newspapers occasionally give access. Last but not least, the more balanced accounts of immigration issues in particular are related to the positive role that immigrants are perceived to be playing in the national economy. This includes taking care of the elderly or of younger children, or catering to labour shortages in low-status and low-paying jobs in agriculture and the service sectors; overall, this has made the Greek people and media more open to them.

Concluding remarks

At the dawn of the twenty-first century, Greek society finds itself transformed when compared to the 1980s. Modern Greece is now fully integrated in the European Union and the Eurozone, albeit still with a very large informal economy that is very difficult to combat. The country is facing the economic and cultural tensions of globalization and at the same time has become host to nearly a million immigrants in little more than a decade. The native population is rapidly ageing, causing a preoccupation, among other things, with the state welfare system. The relatively high internal unemployment is paradoxically coupled with severe labour shortages in some sectors.

With regard to the major 'national issues', Greece has aligned itself with its major EU partners in most international questions and with regard to Turkey's entry to the EU. Moreover, during the last decade, steps have been taken for a more open policy towards the country's historical minorities – in particular towards the largest one, the Muslim minority of western Thrace. Greek authorities have made hesitant steps towards immigrant incorporation in Greek society – for example the inclusion of immigrant families in state housing for the first time in October 2004. Nonetheless, most Greek citizens still hold xenophobic and racist attitudes with regard to immigrants (Eurobarometre, 1997, 2000), Albanians in particular. Immigrant participation in public life is very limited. Ethnic associations are few and relatively small. Foreigners' participation in mainstream organizations such as political parties or trade unions is formally welcome but in effect marginalized.

In this chapter we have analytically reviewed the main features of immigration policy in Greece since the early 1990s. We have also presented the demographic and socio-economic profile of the immigrant population and have critically discussed their limited participation in Greek public life. The chapter also presents a short overview of media discourses on migration during the past 10 to 15 years, highlighting the selective representations and references of migrants that persist, both in terms of use of language and choice of news items.

The contours of the immigration situation in Greece are rather disappointing. After nearly 15 years of massive migration, the country still strives to accept its role as a host society. Migration policy planning lacks a mid- to long-term perspective and policy measures up to now have been reactive, short-term and fragmented. Immigrant integration policy needs to be reconsidered to address the social and economic challenges of migration. At the same time a proactive migration planning and a realistic migration control policy is necessary to manage migration through legal channels, avoid the proliferation of undocumented migrants and combat human trafficking in the region of Southeast Europe. Until recently, policy design has adapted to policy initiatives at the EU level but has failed to take a more future-orientated, pro-active perspective.

As regards the context of heightened security awareness following 9/11 and the Madrid and London bombings, Greek governments have paid less attention to international terrorism threats (even if security was a top issue on the Olympic Games 2004 agenda) while giving more emphasis to regional security threats related to political instability in neighbouring Balkan countries (Albania, Kosovo, FYROM) and overall the question of Turkey's European future. Thus, although security is an issue on the Greek migration policy agenda, it has not radically affected the options and views of Greek governments on the issue.

References

ECRI (2004) (European Commission against Racism and Intolerance) *Third report on Greece,* adopted on 5 December 2003, published 8 June 2004. Strasbourg: Council of Europe, CRI (2004) 24.

Eurobarometre (2000) *Special Report: Racism and Xenophobia in Europe,* October 2000, No. 138.

Hatziprokopiou, P. (2003) 'Albanian Immigrants in Thessaloniki, Greece: Processes of Economic and Social Incorporation', *Journal of Ethnic and Migration Studies,* 29(6), 1033–1057. [DOI: 10.1080/1369183032000171357]

Iosifides, Th. and King, R. (1998) 'Socio-spatial Dynamics and Exclusion of Three Immigrant Groups in the Athens Conurbation', *South European Society and Politics,* 3(3), 205–229.

Karydis, B. (1996) *Immigrant Criminality in Greece: Theoretical and Criminal Policy Issues* (in Greek). Athens: Papazisis.

Lambrianidis, L. and Lyberaki, A. (2001) *Albanian Immigrants in Thessaloniki, Greece* (in Greek). Athens: Paratiritis.

Minority Rights Group (1994) *The Slavomacedonian Minority in Greece: A Case-study in Balkan Nationalism.* MRG International, The Southern Balkans, 1994/4.

Pavlou, M. (2001) 'Racist Discourse and Immigrants in the Press of a Candidate 'metropolis': The Contraband Merchants of Fear', in Marvakis, A., Parsanoglou, D. and Pavlou, M. (eds) *Immigrants in Greece* (in Greek). Athens: Ellinika Grammata.

Petronoti, M. (2000) *Migration and Migrants.* Official and Unofficial Discourse, paper presented at a conference on Immigration into Greece: Social Exclusion, Xenophobia and Policies of Incorporation/Integration in the Labour Market and Society, 26 September 2000. Athens, Greece.

Spinellis, C., Dermati, S., Koulouris, N., Tavoulari, M. and Vidali, S. (1996), 'Recent Immigration and Protection of Migrants: Human Rights in Greece', *Chroniques,* 9, 67–96.

Triandafyllidou, A. (1996) 'Greek Migration Policy: A Critical Note', *Synthesis: Review of Modern Greek Studies,* 1(1), 15–22.

Triandafyllidou, A. (2000) 'The Political Discourse on Immigration in Southern Europe: A Critical Analysis', *Journal of Community and Applied Social Psychology,* 10(5), 373–89. [DOI: 10.1002/1099-1298%28200009%2F10%2910%3A5%3C373%3A%3AAID-CASP595%3E3.0.CO%3B2-R]

Triandafyllidou, A. (2001) *Immigrants and National Identity in Europe.* London: Routledge.

Triandafyllidou, A. (2002) 'Greece', in ter Wal, J. (ed.) *Racism and Cultural Diversity in the Mass Media: An Overview of Research and Examples of Good Practice in the EU Member States, 1995-2000,* 149–72. Vienna: EUMC.

Triandafyllidou, A. and Veikou, M. (2002) 'The Hierarchy of Greekness: Ethnic and National Identity Considerations in Greek Immigration Policy', *Ethnicities,* 2(2), 189–208.

Internet-based references

Eurobarometre (1997) *Special Report, Racism and Xenophobia. Human rights and Immigration in the European Union*, Eb 47.1, December 1997, No. 113 (available at http://europa.eu.int/comm/public_opinion/archives/eb_special_en.htm).

Kassimis, C. and Kassimi, C. (2004) 'Greece: A History of Migration', *Migration Information Source Journal*, June 2004 (available at http://www.migrationinformation.org/Profiles/display.cfm?ID=228, accessed 24 August 2006).

Chapter 12

Hungary

András Kováts and Endre Sik

Immigration in contemporary Hungary is not a new phenomenon, but the democratic transition after 1989 brought with it a fundamental shift. At present, there is only 1.5–2 per cent of the population who are immigrants, the overwhelming majority of whom are ethnic Hungarians from neighbouring countries (mostly Romania) who aim to work, study or permanently settle in Hungary. Non-Europeans comprise only one-tenth of the immigrant population. The present legal and institutional frameworks of the country's immigration policy have been laid down and formulated in the past 16 years, and are highly influenced by a peculiar characteristic of the immigrant population and migratory movements. Indeed, the dominant discourse in Hungary regarding foreigners is very much focused on issues related to the diaspora which are closely related to the Hungarian community on the other side of the border. Consequently, it is not surprising that the institutional and legal setting of immigrants' participation overlaps with diaspora-related issues. Migration-related discourses in contemporary Hungary are mostly in the context of a shrinking Hungarian population, and of border control and security. Another aspect of migration policy debates is the issue of labour migration and its effect on the domestic labour market. The apparent contradiction between facilitated immigration and the government's explicit aim to preserve ethnic Hungarian communities outside the country's borders often shapes the outcome of these debates. The issue of immigrants' civic participation is not a relevant issue in contemporary Hungary, and its direct legal regulation practically does not exist. Finally, there are three main types of immigrant community organizations identified in this paper: non-European human rights and advocacy organizations, Chinese cultural and commercial lobby groups, and ethnic Hungarian agencies.

This chapter offers an overview of Hungarian immigration policy and the size and trends of immigrant stocks in Hungary; it discusses briefly the question of the Hungarian diasporas in neighbouring countries as well as the participation of immigrants in Hungarian public life. Last but not least, the chapter reviews the media coverage of immigration issues and concludes on future migration challenges for Hungary.

Major developments in Hungary's immigration policy

Definition of immigrants

There is no established definition for immigrants in Hungary and the use of the term 'immigrant' is rather ambiguous in legal, political and social discourses. The narrowest definition most often used by legal and policy documents is rather technical, as it states that all foreign citizens who stay in the country with any purpose apart from tourism are considered immigrants.

This definition is based on citizenship but some clarification is needed. On the one hand, it covers all foreigners who stay in the country for over a year regardless of purpose (excluding tourism). On the other hand, returnees who are not foreign citizens and have spent more than a year abroad are excluded. This group is especially important in the Hungarian case since political emigrants of the previous decades and their descendants return to Hungary with Hungarian passports, and in increasing numbers, to set up business or enjoy their pension in their homeland.

On the other hand, labour migrants who stay for a shorter period are also considered immigrants. Labour migration in the Central and Eastern European region, including Hungary, has been characterized as a short-term and commuting migration. Work permits are often issued for a period shorter than a year. Work permits may also cover daily (and short-term) commuters. These latter have an important effect on local and sub-regional labour markets.

Until the late 1990s, there was a significant influx of asylum seekers and refugees from Romania and Yugoslavia and later on from Afghanistan and Iraq. However, the number of those seeking asylum in Hungary has dropped dramatically in the last five years. Moreover, people who are granted refugee status or humanitarian protection also tend to leave the country after staying for a few years.

While it is impossible to estimate both their number and their effect on the labour market, non-registered (illegal, clandestine) labour migrants can also be found in Hungary. Their presence in agriculture, construction and the service industry of certain regions is well known and important.

For the purposes of comparative analysis, the term foreign-born population in contemporary Hungary would be misleading (Juhász, 2003). In Hungary – as well as in other countries in Central Europe – there have been such boundary fluctuations that a birthplace which at the time of birth was Hungarian will often later belong to another country. Consequently a large proportion of the currently foreign-born population consists of elderly people who, because of numerous shifts of the national borders over the past 85 years, are today considered foreign-born.[1]

A brief historical overview of immigration into Hungary

At the turn of the nineteenth century Hungary was an emigration country, sending millions of poor young males (mostly from the fringes of the Monarchy) to the USA (Zolberg, 1989; Tilly, 1990). As a result of the peace treaties concluding the First World War, Hungary lost a substantial part of its territory and, as a consequence, an ethnically highly homogeneous population was created which was very receptive towards patriotic, even chauvinist or irredentist ideologies. Ethnic Hungarians moved in large numbers from the territories cut off from Hungary by the new state borders after 1920. The Second World War was also followed by large-scale resettlement movements along ethnic lines (ethnic Germans were expelled to Germany and their homes filled with ethnic Hungarians who were in turn expelled from Czechoslovakia). For the following four decades, communism transformed Hungary into a virtually closed country, with very limited and state-controlled inward and outward migration.

The claim that Hungary was a closed country during communism is based upon the fact that between 1949 and 1989 there was practically no immigration into Hungary. The only exceptions were the politically motivated migrations of Greek and Chilean communists, who were granted asylum in the early 1950s and 1970s. In contrast, mass emigration occurred only once (after the failed revolution in 1956 when about 200,000 people left the country). Despite the seemingly

---

1   Such historical events were the changes of borders following the Versailles peace treaty closing the First World War, the border revisions made during the Second World War, the annexations, withdrawals, and subsequent changes of population. Other historical events, such as the Second World War and the 1956 revolution, also influence the limited value of the concept of foreign-born population. About 6,000 of those living in Hungary with permanent residence permits were actually born in present-day Hungary. They left Hungary, acquired citizenship elsewhere, and have recently returned.

sealed borders, there was a continuous flow of emigration from Hungary between 1956 and 1989. Indeed, it is estimated that at least another 200,000 people left the country in this period.

Between 1988 and 1989, with the ever-growing number of people arriving from the neighbouring countries, a *quasi* refugee regime emerged in Hungary. The term 'quasi' refers to the fact that Hungary signed the 1951 Geneva Convention in late 1989 and, consequently, though the Constitution contained the concept of asylum, no asylum seeker could formally get refugee status. However, both the media and politicians referred to migrants as 'refugees'. This can be explained by the political context in which the overwhelming majority of these 'quasi-refugees' were mainly ethnic Hungarians fleeing from communist Romania. The total population of Hungary during the period was about ten million, and the annual number of immigrants between 1988 and 1991 ranged between 23,000 and 37,000. Of these, it is estimated that about 80 per cent were ethnic Hungarians from Romania, Ukraine and Yugoslavia.

The sudden large inflow of migrants (mostly from Romania), was followed by a considerable outflow due to their return home or departure for a third country. A second large inflow caused by the Yugoslavian conflict was also followed by a significant outflow in the mid-1990s. In the last decade, migration has stabilized to an estimated 14–15,000 immigrants per annum (Juhász, 2003).

Hungary's accession to the European Union has not brought dramatic changes in the migration trends of the country. Although the number of labour immigrants has been increasing for the past few years, it is still very low compared to the total available workforce. Despite expectations and often fears, the number of those who seek asylum in Hungary has not grown, but rather, has kept decreasing since EU accession.

The general legal framework of immigration

Following the democratic transition, Hungary acceded to universal and regional conventions (1951 Geneva Convention, 1967 New York Protocol, ECHR, CE Prevention of Torture, UN Torture, UN Covenants) of international humanitarian law. These have been embodied into the Hungarian legal system.[2]

Numerous provisions can be found in bilateral agreements that Hungary signed with European states referring to substance of the international legal instruments or to autonomous rules relating to migratory movements. These are agreements with neighbours on border regime, readmission of nationals and third-country nationals who have passed the border illegally, on visa-free travel, on cultural exchange, as well as on employment, vocational training or the retraining of workers in some European states. These contracts provide the framework for lawful entry, residence and certain activities of nationals on a mutual basis.

The right of repatriation and free movement (travel out of Hungary) are regulated in the Constitution as basic rights of nationals and lawfully residing foreigners in Hungary. The Act on Entry, Residence and Immigration to Hungary (No. 39 of 2001, hereinafter: Alien Act) and its executive decrees[3] regulate the general policing rules on foreigners. These provisions cover requirements of lawful entry and residence in Hungary, issuing the visa and identity documents of various groups of foreigners. The Act on Hungarian Citizenship (No. 55 of 1993) and its executive decree issued by the Cabinet (No. 125/1993) is considered a major pillar of immigration policy. Although there are some benefits for ethnic Hungarians, recognized refugees and family members

---

2   In particular into Chapter XII of the Constitution.

3   Issued by the Cabinet (No. 170/2001), Minister of the Interior (No. 23/2001), Minister of Justice (No. 27 and 40/2,001) and Minister of Foreign Affairs (No. 23/2001).

in naturalization proceedings, the acquisition of citizenship is based on individual and considerable efforts of the applicant for social, linguistic and economic integration regardless of roots, qualification, age and occupation. Multiple nationality is permitted and citizenship is provided for stateless or abandoned children born in Hungary. However, neither first- nor second-generation immigrants can automatically obtain citizenship, as 12–13 years in Hungary are required.

Diaspora politics

The overwhelming majority of immigrants are from neighbouring countries and mostly have an ethnic Hungarian background. The dominant discourse in Hungary regarding foreigners is focused very much on issues related to the diaspora on the other side of the border. Consequently, it is not surprising that the institutional and legal setting of immigrants' participation overlaps with diaspora-related issues.

The status of ethnic Hungarians living in countries adjacent to Hungary has always been part of the discussion on immigration legislation. Hungarian governments have always aimed to encourage ethnic Hungarians to remain in their place of birth. Unlike the German approach, Hungary's policy toward co-ethnics abroad has thus developed as a policy of shaping national identity and not as an immigration policy (Tóth, 2000; Melegh, 2002). The Hungarian immigration and naturalization system has often been criticized for being indifferent towards ethnic Hungarians who 'return to their motherland', despite certain benefits for ethnic Hungarians and persons of Hungarian ancestry in the immigration and naturalization process. The so-called Status Law, ostensibly intended to be a set of legal instruments to support ethnic Hungarians in neighbouring countries, stirred domestic political debates in 2001 and 2002, resulting among other things in a set of proposed measures regulating seasonal employment in Hungary. In reality, because of the limited scope of benefits provided both in the 'Status Law' and in the treaty, both failed to have any impact on migration. The number of work permits issued under their provisions is insignificant compared to the total number of work permits per year. According to both experts and the media, this is because the procedure to obtain such a permit is extremely slow and bureaucratic.

The public and political debate on the status of ethnic Hungarians living across the state borders emerged again in late 2004. This time the issue of granting Hungarian citizenship to those who request it and are able to prove their Hungarian origin was raised by the World Federation of Hungarians, a political lobby group active both in Hungary and in the diaspora. The campaign, eventually endorsed by the right-wing opposition parties and opposed by the Government, ended in a public referendum in December when the majority of the voters rejected the idea of even discussing the possibility of granting extraterritorial citizenship rights to non-immigrant, non-resident fellow Hungarians.[4]

The relevance of diaspora politics in contemporary Hungary is well illustrated by the existence of two special bodies: the Office for Hungarians Living Across the Border and the Standing Hungarian Conference.

The Office for Hungarians Living Across the Border was established in 1992 with the aim of carrying out Government policy. The Office was first located within the Prime Minister's Office, and was then integrated into the Ministry of Foreign Affairs in 1998.

As an institution of dialogue among the representatives of the government, the parties in the Parliament and Hungarian communities of the diaspora, the Standing Hungarian Conference was set up in 1999. The body comprising numerous sub-committees plays a vague political role: the

---

4   The debate is well documented by the Institute of National and Ethnic Minority Research of the Hungarian Academy of Sciences at the following website: http://www.kettosallampolgarsag.mtaki.hu/.

Parliament only 'welcomes its establishment' and calls upon the government 'to give a yearly report on its operation and execution of the political proposals of the Conference concerning Hungarians across the border'. Thus, the government has wide room to manoeuvre, to exchange views, to reconcile divergent opinions, to find political consensus or to maintain the veneer officially. According to the government's interpretation, the main national task is to develop the connection between Hungarians living beyond the borders and those living within, and it is centred on the fields of education, culture, economy, healthcare, welfare, local government and regional relations. This is done in order to 'remain resident in the homeland, yet to preserve national identity'.

The Conference issues proposals, but their relevance, the decision-making procedure, and publicity have not been defined. As such, the Conference may be considered a shadow or a substitute body of genuine negotiation, discourse or compromise-making. However, it is sufficient to legitimize the diaspora policy in its present state.

The immigrant population in Hungary: main demographic and social features

The number of immigrants is established as the sum total of foreigners legally residing in the country according to various administrative registers (Hárs and Kováts, 2005). For migration statistics, the main and most common data sources are the 2001 National Census Database, the Register of Foreigners based on the data of the Office of Immigration and Nationality of the Ministry of the Interior (OIN) and published by the Hungarian Central Statistical Office (HCSO). This statistical database includes foreigners who stay in Hungary for longer than a year. Beyond these, the OIN publishes statistical data (mostly on migration flows and administrative actions concerning immigrants) on its homepage.[5]

The number of foreigners who stay in the country over a year is stable, around 1.2–1.5 per cent of the native population. This number has been slowly but steadily growing in the past decade. According to the most recent figures, there was a nine per cent increase in the past year, amounting to 155,000 immigrants in the country in January 2006 (Statisztikai Hivatal, 2006). In Hungary, the overwhelming majority of immigrants are of European origin. Half of them are Romanian citizens (mostly ethnic Hungarians), about a tenth are from Yugoslavia or Ukraine (most of them are ethnic Hungarians as well) and nearly a quarter from EU Member States (see Table 12.1).

---

5   http://www.bmbah.hu/statisztikak.php.

Table 12.1   Immigrants in Hungary by sending country and region (1 January 2004)

	Male	Female	Total	Share of immigrants by sending region	Share of immigrants by sending countries in the region
	Number			%	
Europe (EU 15) of whom:	52,146	58,769	110,915	85.2	100
European Union	10,729	14,255	24,984		22.5
Romania	27,071	28,605	55,676		50.2
Yugoslavia	6,640	5,727	12,367		11.1
Ukraine	6,033	7,063	13,096		11.8
Asia of whom:	8,207	6,508	14,715	11.3	100
China	3,713	3,077	6,790		46.1
Others	2,764	1,715	4,479	3.4	
Total	63,117	66,992	130,109	100	

Source: Központi Statisztikai Hivatal, 2005.

According to the available statistics of the foreign register and the 2001 census data on resident immigrants, resident foreigners (immigrants) constitute about 1.3 per cent of the total population. The census data categorized both third-country nationals and dual (Hungarian and any foreign) citizens (the majority of them returnees) as immigrants. Furthermore, immigrants in Hungary appear to be better educated and to have higher labour market status than the native population (Gödri and Tóth, 2005). In terms of gender distribution, there are slightly more men than there are women. This gender gap used to be much more pronounced in the early 1990s, particularly because of the war in neighbouring Yugoslavia. Table 12.2 sets out some of these figures.

Table 12.2   Gender distribution of native population and resident immigrants (per cent)

	Men	Women	Total
Natives	47.6	52.4	100
Immigrants of whom:	49.2	50.8	100
Foreign citizens	48.7	51.3	100
Dual citizens	51.6	48.4	100

Source: Census 2001.

The share of immigrants in the older age-groups is relatively low compared to that among the locals. In middle age groups (30–59) and young adults (20–29) the share of immigrants is rather high. The proportion of elderly people in the group of dual citizens is more similar to that of the Hungarians, but there is a significantly higher share of youngsters (below 19) among them (Table 12.3).

Table 12.3   Age distribution of native population and resident immigrants (per cent)

	Younger than 19	20–29 years old	30–59 years old	Older than 60	Total
Natives	23.2	15.6	40.7	20.5	100
Immigrants of whom:	21.2	24	43	11.8	100
Foreign citizens	20	26	43.6	10.4	100
Dual citizens	27.6	13.1	39.9	19.4	100

Source: Census 2001.

It is worth noting that immigrants' level of education is considerably higher than that of the locals. The proportion of those with secondary and higher education among migrants is significantly higher than that among Hungarians over 18. This may be explained by the different age-structure of immigrants (the proportion of younger and thus better educated generations is much higher among them). In each category, those with dual citizenship have the highest education level among all groups, as Table 12.4 shows.

Table 12.4   Level of education of native population and resident immigrants (per cent)

	Share of the population having concluded:		
	primary education (8 years) in the population over 15	secondary education in the population over 18	higher education in the population over 25
Natives	88.8	38.0	12.5
Immigrants of whom:	92.1	57.3	25.3
Foreign citizens	91.7	56.0	24.2
Dual citizens	94.5	65.1	31.4

Source: Census 2001.

According to the census data, 36 per cent of the total Hungarian population are employed, as opposed to 42 per cent of immigrants. Altogether, the labour market position of resident foreigners is much better than that of locals (Table 12.5). This is partly due to the different age structure but can also be contributed to their better education, as well as to the selective effect of the immigration system, which requires regular legal employment (or at least regular income) in Hungary in order to obtain long-term residence permits.

Table 12.5   Labour market position of native population and resident immigrants (per cent)

Labour market position	Employed	Unemployed	Inactive	Dependent	Total
Natives	36.1	4.1	32.5	27.2	100
Immigrants	42.2	3.6	20.2	34	100
of whom:					
Foreign citizens	43.4	3.8	18.9	33.9	100
Dual citizens	35.7	2.6	26.9	34.8	100

Source: Census 2001.

Resident immigrants who are employed (42 per cent of the total immigrant population) have quite good status in the labour market. A greater proportion of them – as compared to Hungarians – work as professionals. Again, the share of professionals is especially high among dual citizens (38 per cent). The share of immigrants is above the natives' among service workers; while in other activities (less qualified non-menial jobs and industrial or construction menial jobs) their share is below that of locals.

This seemingly better socio-economic situation of immigrants may seem peculiar compared with other European countries. The explanation lies in the immigration system itself, which is largely selective toward favouring long-term residents with a relatively stable economic background. Immigration itself is still at a very early phase – it is still the first-generation labour immigrants who dominate the statistics – family unification and asylum play a minor role in the general picture, and usually these two are associated with social and integration problems. Another issue is the relatively fast track towards naturalization: especially for those with an ethnic Hungarian background, who disappear from the immigration record within a few years. Foreigners doing low-skilled or menial jobs in agriculture or the construction industry are often commuters or stay on a short-term visa, and are therefore not recorded in the immigration stock – further biasing the figures.

Refugees and asylum seekers are not that common in Hungary. From 2001 onwards, the number of those seeking asylum in the country started to decrease rapidly (See Table 12.6.) and even a great proportion of those who registered as asylum seekers had left the country before the official decision was taken. The recognition rate of refugees is very low (between 100 and 200 people annually) and the number of foreigners who live in Hungary as refugees is approximately 500 (Balogi, Kováts and Simon, 2005).

Table 12.6   The number of asylum seekers and their distribution by origin (2002–2005)

Year	Number of asylum seekers	European	Non-European	Total
		%		
2002	6,412	6.88	93.12	100
2003	2,401	24.45	75.55	100
2004	1,600	31.44	68.56	100
2005	1,609	36.29	63.71	100

Source: OIN statistics.

As for illegal migration, various sources suggest that most undocumented immigrants are weekly or monthly commuters from the neighbouring countries. These are mostly migrants who work in the seasonal sectors (agriculture, construction) of the informal economy (Sik, 1999, 2002), or as tourist traders working at the open-air markets (Czakó and Sik, 1999). There are no reliable data available on the size and scope of illegal immigration. However, most analysts believe that illegally employed foreign workers greatly outnumber those with work permits. It is estimated that in the high season, the number of illegal foreign workers may be the double those with permits (Juhász, 2003).

In sum, immigration in contemporary Hungary can be characterized by the following:

- The number and proportion of immigrants is low (1.5–2.0 per cent of the population).
- Immigrants mostly come from the neighbouring European countries, and most of them are of Hungarian ethnicity.
- The proportion of asylum seekers among immigrants is very low and has been steadily decreasing since the late 1990s.
- Immigration is mainly a demand-driven, sub-regional labour migration, often based on seasonal or temporary employment; movement of family members and family unification is less significant.
- Immigrants have a better social and economic position than the native population. This is largely due to their different age structure (higher proportion of population of an active age among them), and their higher level of education. Their advantage is reflected by their better labour market position in comparison with the local population.
- Irregular (illegal) immigration mostly involves either transiting through the country or engaging in seasonal or temporary employment. Permanent settlement is not typical for undocumented migrants in Hungary.

Immigrant rights and participation in public life – issues of immigrant integration

The issue of immigrants' civic participation is not a relevant one in contemporary Hungary, as its direct legal regulation practically does not exist. This means that neither restricting nor encouraging conditions can be identified. The general framework is the legal structure of NGO activity which is fully EU-compatible (Tóth, 2003, 2004). A good example of this relaxed but not exactly encouraging attitude is that though Hungary did not sign the European Council's Convention on the role of foreigners in local politics, this is not explicitly forbidden. Indeed, there was one case in the 2002 local elections where an immigrant won the election on the strength of the votes of settled migrants in the area.

Another aspect of the institutional setting of migrants' public (but not civic) activity is their role in politics and in state organizations. Owing to the ethnic characteristic of Hungarian immigration, there are 'dissidents' of the communist period who have returned, as well as people who settled in Hungary from the ethnic Hungarian communities in neighbouring countries and who are now active in politics.

However, the former 'dissidents' either never lost their Hungarian citizenship[6] or could be re-naturalized after the fall of communism. Consequently during the first years of post-communism there were several cases of ethnic Hungarians living in various EU countries who played a significant role in shaping domestic politics.

---

6   According to the Hungarian constitution those who were born Hungarian cannot give up their citizenship and cannot be excluded except under special conditions.

Ethnic Hungarians from neighbouring countries migrated to Hungary during communism mostly through fake marriage or through applying for Hungarian citizenship. Many used to be active in the underground civil movements or as intellectuals, and later some also became active politicians.

Finally, in relation to Hungarian diaspora politics, ethnic Hungarians living in neighbouring countries also play an important role in Hungarian political and civic life. There is the already mentioned Hungarian Standing Conference which covers all Hungarian Parliamentary parties as well as representatives of Hungarian parties in the parliaments in all neighbouring countries. This institution has a major role in defining Hungarian diaspora politics. Moreover, some representatives of these organizations are also very active in Hungarian politics and civic activities.

As for the civic integration of immigrants, three major types of community organizations can be identified. The first group consists of asylum seekers and refugees as well as temporary residents mainly from African countries and from Afghanistan, organizing and volunteering for self-established human rights organizations (Marton, 2001; Olomoofe, 2001). These organizations usually maintain the double aim of providing legal support and other types of assistance for their clients on the one hand, and of improving intercultural understanding and fighting racism and discrimination on the other.

The second major group is the Chinese population, which forms the largest immigrant population from outside Europe. This community has been present in Hungary since the late 1980s, and its pattern of integration is characterized by strong self-organization and mobilization both in cultural and commercial activities. Indeed, the two are often interlinked. However, their impact upon the host society is minimal; that is, activities are more or less restricted to issues related to their own community.

The third group or community consists of ethnic Hungarian immigrants from across the borders, who are often referred to as quasi-diaspora migrants. The members of this community partly focus on the process of establishing their own organizations and provide self-help in settling in Hungary. This is the result of their desire to preserve their social capital and culture rooted in their communities across the borders.

Preserving culture and maintaining cultural or national identity forms the core of civic activities. Indeed, it is listed among the major goals of almost every civic organization or movement representing the aforementioned three immigrant communities. Religious associations (churches, congregations) can also be found in the major immigrant groups such as Transylvanian Hungarians, Chinese or Africans in Budapest. Other kinds of activities were pursued only by certain immigrant communities, depending on the particular needs and capacities of the relevant groups: powerful political activism in the form of lobby groups is typical of the Chinese community; economic associations for mutual aid or interest representation appear among Transylvanian Hungarians and the Chinese; human rights associations are established or maintained mainly by African immigrants.

The relation between migrant and majority organizations is relevant only in the field of refugee integration. A few but visible refugee self-help groups play a role in the integration of the small number of refugees in Hungary. However, this role is mostly restricted to some cultural activities such as football games between refugees and Hungarians, attending Refugee Day celebrations, and community events organized by Menedék – the Hungarian Association for Migrants (the dominant NGO providing integration-related services to migrants).

Public and media discourses on migration

Current migration debates are determined by the fact that contemporary Hungarian society is a relatively ethnically homogeneous society, and that the small group of immigrants mainly consists of ethnic Hungarians from the neighbouring countries.

Migration-related discourses in contemporary Hungary mostly occur in the context of the shrinking of the Hungarian population, and of border control and security. Moreover, there exists an apparent contradiction between facilitated immigration and the constitutional responsibility that attributes responsibility to the Republic for ethnic Hungarians outside the country's borders.

The demographic issue received political and public attention with hysterical overtones in 2000 with a report containing an analysis and policy recommendations on migration prepared by a research team of the Demography Research Institute of the Central Statistical Office (Hablicsek and Tóth, 2000). It came in the wake of the United Nations' study of 'replacement migration' in Europe, which suggested that Europe would have to absorb 159 million immigrants if it was to maintain sustainable demographic trends. The release of the report and the Prime Minister's subsequent comment that Hungary should be able to draw on a pool of hundreds of thousands or even 1.5 million potential ethnic Hungarian workers from neighbouring countries[7] was the first instance in which migration aroused significant public debate. Following the report, the government established a Population Committee to study ways to confirm what it saw as negative population trends. The committee, which had a subcommittee on migration, received a mandate to develop a strategy to introduce a national population programme. The strategy was published in December 2003 as a policy document (see Kormánybizottság, 2003), devoting a full chapter to the issue of immigration. However, to date, no concrete measures have been introduced to implement the programme itself. The document is just another example of the controversial and ambiguous approach towards the present immigration situation in Hungary. Besides recognizing the importance of facilitating the long-term settlement and integration of qualified labour immigrants, it omits the fact that the majority of this group is from the Hungarian communities outside the borders. Furthermore, it explicitly states that members of these communities should not be encouraged to emigrate to Hungary and that the government should give cultural and economic support in order to make them remain (ibid., pp. 33–36).

The issue of illegal foreign labour was used by the then-opposition Socialist Party as a dangerous threat in its 2002 election campaign. It was the time when the Status Law was debated in the Parliament and the government held bilateral discussions with its neighbouring countries. According to press reports, socialist leaders maintained that the government wanted to 'unleash millions of Romanian workers' – which for many ordinary Hungarians translates into Gypsies – on the Hungarian job market. To allay critics' fears, the government made the work permit procedure more bureaucratic and, as a result, the number of permits issued under this provision has remained insignificant.

Another initiative to tackle the problem of lacking a comprehensive migration policy was the establishment of the Inter-Ministry Committee on Migration by the Prime Minister's Office in April 2004. The Committee, which consists of political secretaries of state from several Ministries[8] as well as from the Office of Hungarians Across the Border (the relevant Government office dealing with the affairs of the Hungarian Diaspora), and the political Secretary of State responsible for

---

7   This statement was interpreted by the Hungarian press as an encouragement to immigration, but the Prime Minister later clarified that he had in mind Hungarians abroad as an economic resource for the 'mother country' (Melegh, 2002).

8   These include: Ministry of Interior; Health, Social and Family Affairs; Employment and Labour; Economy and Transport; Justice; Foreign Affairs; Education; Finance.

national security, was set up with the explicit aim of harmonizing and coordinating activities that are closely linked with the country's EU membership.[9] According to its mandate, the main task of the Committee is to lay down the foundations of the national migration strategy by gathering and analysing relevant data and formulating a proposal for a long-term migration policy.

By late August 2004, the Committee had come forward with a draft proposal for the Migration Strategy of the Republic of Hungary. After some inter-ministry consultations, the draft was amended in November 2004 and sent out for consultation to the relevant Ministries. In spring 2005, the document was sent back to the Committee for a thorough revision, as it was found inappropriate. After a thorough revision, the proposal was approved in November 2005 by the Ministries involved, but in spring 2006 it had still not been made official. There were no wider consultations or communications on the matter, and neither the academic nor the NGO communities have been involved in the process. Finally, the general public has not been involved either.

The main policy debate in 2004 and 2005 was centred on the issue of labour market liberalization in the context of immigrant labour. According to the National Action Plan for Employment (NAP), the Government's position is that labour immigration is not an alternative to the low labour supply and mismatches; the primary aim should be mobilization within the domestic labour market, and this should be reflected by the NAP, not encouraging labour immigration. Another aspect behind the lack of policy responses is the surprisingly rigid position on other Member States' restrictions on free movement of labour from new Member States. Hungary applies equal measures on the basis of reciprocity, but beyond this there is an argument saying that non-EU citizens should not enjoy a better position in the labour market than those who come from another Member State. Thus, any policy promoting the employability of third country nationals should not offer a better position than that of those EU nationals whose participation in the labour market is restricted due to reciprocity. A third aspect which is reflected by the NAP is the controversial approach to the overwhelmingly ethnic characteristic of labour immigration into Hungary. Immigration policy should reflect the preferential treatment of ethnic Hungarians, but expressing or even implying a resettlement (facilitated immigration) approach in the national diaspora policy should be avoided.

From time to time the social causes of xenophobia, and its relation to anti-Semitism, and anti-Gypsy attitudes, as well as the political aspects of the spread of such values are debated both in the media and in Parliament.

The year of Hungary's accession to the EU, 39 per cent of Hungarians claimed that the free movement of Hungarians to the other EU countries was disadvantageous. Forty-seven per cent of them considered the increasing possibility of EU citizens settling down in Hungary as a disadvantage. Moreover, 82 per cent of the Hungarian population would have forbidden foreigners from buying Hungarian land.

The currently most discussed issue related to the diasporic nature of the Hungarian migration processes is the aforementioned referendum on 5 December 2004 on the granting of Hungarian citizenship (that is, dual citizenship) to all ethnic Hungarians[10] living outside the borders of Hungary. The debate around this topic covers (in an extremely over-politicized and distorted way) all relevant aspects of the contemporary migration trends in the country such as the extent to which:

---

9   The Committee was set up by a Government Decision (No. 2104/2004).

10   A Hungarian is a person who claims the so-called 'document of Hungarianness' (or, as it is officially called, 'Hungarian National Identity Card') and identifies oneself with the Hungarian nation (in a cultural sense).

- granting dual citizenship of ethnic Hungarians living across the borders would contribute to their migration into Hungary;
- the present labour immigration structure would change due to the better prospects of finding employment elsewhere in the EU with a Hungarian passport;
- diaspora politics would be affected by dual citizenship, and how this might influence the migration regime in Hungary and its neighbours.

The referendum on double citizenship failed, as less than 25 per cent of the eligible voters turned up to vote. Consequently, Parliament was not obliged to pass a new law granting Hungarian citizenship to all members of the quasi-diaspora. However, the issue remains at the top of the agenda for both national and diaspora politics, and greatly influences migration policy.

Concluding remarks

Although the issue of immigration has not played a significant role in contemporary Hungarian political debates, there are certain issues which should no longer be deferred. Although the legal and institutional framework of the country's immigration policy has been put in place in the past two decades, the conceptual foundations of a comprehensive migration policy are still missing. There is a set of societal issues that are yet to be discussed and debated publicly in order to reach a social and political consensus in setting the aims of the national migration policy. One such issue is that the migration of ethnic Hungarians from neighbouring countries should be considered as a social fact and that diaspora politics should be shaped acknowledging this fact. Another issue is the very restrictive approach toward labour immigration which is not endorsed by the actual situation of the labour market. Whereas immigrant labour can and in fact does contribute to the economic development of the country, there is no evidence of its impact on legal employment of nationals.

According to expert opinions, the present characteristic of immigration into Hungary is not likely to change in the short term. Hence, there is no reason to apply restrictive measures against those who choose Hungary as their temporary or permanent residence. Encouraging the relatively low social and political participation of immigrants will inevitably contribute to the formulation of a comprehensive and effective migration policy in Hungary.

References

In English

Czakó, Á. and Sik, E. (1999) 'Characteristics and Origins of the Comecon Open-Air Market in Hungary', *International Journal of Urban and Regional Research*, **23**(4), 715–37.

Hárs, Á. and Kováts, A. (2005) 'Hungary' in Niessen, J. and Schibel, Y. (eds) *Immigration as a Labour Market Strategy – European and North American Perspectives*, 89–110. Brussels: Migration Policy Group.

Marton, K. (2001) 'In what Ways Are the Afghans Different?' in Nyíri, P., Tóth, J. and Fullerton, M. (eds) *Diasporas and Politics*, 27–41. Budapest: MTA PTI (Centre for Migration and Refugee Studies).

Melegh, A. (2002) *Globalisation, Nationalism and Petite Imperialism*, Manuscript.

Olomoofe, L. (2001) 'Africans in Budapest: An Emerging Subculture?' in Nyíri, P., Tóth, J. and Fullerton, M. (eds), 62–69.

Sik, E. (1999) 'The Spatial Distribution of Informal Marketplaces and Informal Foreign Traders in Contemporary Hungary', in Feige, E.L. and Ott, K. (eds) *Underground Economies in Transition*, 275–306. Aldershot: Ashgate.

Sik, E. (2002) 'Informal Labour Market-Place on the Moscow Square', in Neef, R. and Stanculescu, M. (eds) *The Social Impact of Informal Economies in Eastern Europe*, 231–47. Aldershot: Ashgate.

Tilly, C. (1990) 'Transplanted Networks', in Yans-McLaughlin, V. (ed.) *Immigration Reconsidered*, 79–95. Oxford: Oxford University Press.

Tóth, J. (2000) 'Diaspora Politics: Programs and Prospects', in Kiss, I. and McGovern, C. (eds) *New Diasporas in Hungary, Russia and Ukraine*, 96–141. Budapest: Open Society / COLPI.

Tóth, J. (2004) 'NGO Sector and its Participants in Legislation Process in Hungary', *Public Law and Institutions in the 21st Century* (Pécs), 131–40.

Zolberg, A. (1989) 'The Next Waves: Migration Theory for a Changing World', *International Migration Review*, Fall, XXIII, 403–430.

In Hungarian

Balogi, A., Kováts, A. and Simon, D. (2005) *Zárótanulmány az, Empirikus kutatás* a *menekültek társadalmi integrációjáról c. kutatás eredményeiről*. Budapest: ICCR, manuscript.

Gödri, I. and Tóth, P.P. (2005) *Bevándorlás és beilleszkedés, A szomszédos országokból Mayarországra irányuló bevándorlás az ezredfordulón*. Budapest: Központi Statisztikai Hivatal Népességtudományi Kutatóintézetének jelentései, 80.

Hablicsek, L. and Tóth, P.P. (2000) 'A nemzetközi vándorlás szerepe a magyarországi népesség számának megőrzésében, 1999–2050' in *Demográfia*, **2000**(1), 11–46.

Központi Statisztikai Hivatal (2005) *Magyar statisztikai zsebkönyv, 2004*. Budapest: KSH.

Központi Statisztikai Hivatal (2006) *Népmozgalom 2005 január-december*. Budapest: KSH.

Tóth, J. (2003) 'Non-profit szervezetek a nemzetközi jogi színtéren', Acta Juridica et Politica, Tomus LXIII Fasc. 20.

Internet-based references

Juhász, J. (2003) *Hungary: Transit Country between East and West*, Migration Information Source, European Country Profiles, Migration Policy Institute (available at http://www. migrationinformation.org/Profiles/display.cfm?ID=181).

Kormánybizottság, N. (2003) *A Népesedéspolitikai Kormányprogram koncepciója 2003* (available at http://misc.meh.hu/binary/5507_nepesedesiprogram_koncepcio.pdf).

Chapter 13

Ireland

Abel Ugba

Ireland has transformed from a country of emigrations to one of 'in-migrations' within 10 years. However, despite decades of intermittent and sometimes massive emigrations, there were immigrants and minority ethnic groups in the country long before the recent dramatic increases in 'in-migrations' (for a fuller analysis, see Keogh, 1998; MacEinri, 2000; Lentin, 2001; Goldstone, 2002). According to the 2002 census, approximately 6 per cent of Ireland's 3.9 million population were not Irish and another 1.3 per cent were only part-Irish (CSO, 2002). The majority of non-Irish residents are British and nationals of other countries in the West. These countries dominated migrations to Ireland in the decades before the 1990s. The greater and more diversified in-flows of migrants that began in the mid-1990s have, however, resulted in dramatic changes on Ireland's sociocultural and demographic landscapes.

This analysis challenges monocausal interpretations that identify Ireland's recent economic boom as the only reason for the increased presence of immigrants in twenty-first century Ireland. While acknowledging the role played by the Celtic Tiger (or Ireland's recent economic boom) in attracting migrant workers, it identifies the other factors that have brought Ireland to the attention of immigrants, such as her links to regional and international organizations, and burgeoning influence and status in international politics and the multiplicity of armed and civil conflicts in many parts of the world. The rest of this analysis examines the reactions of the Irish state and the public to the increased presence of immigrants. It also identifies the major immigrant groups in Ireland and examines the patterns of immigrant participation in public life.

Major developments in Ireland's immigration policy

Ireland did not participate in a significant way in earlier post-Second World War overseas recruitment of labour by some countries in the West or in the influx of former colonial subjects into mother-countries (Faist 2000; Marren 2001; Martin 2001). However, Irish immigration policies resemble those that had been enacted by countries such as Germany and the United Kingdom which were intended to dissuade the long-term presence of immigrant and minority ethnic groups (Rasmussen, 1996; Bade, 2003). This is the result both of the increased harmonization of immigration and asylum policies among EU member-countries and of Ireland's historical aversion to the 'other' as demonstrated by her contentious relationship with the Travellers (an indigenous cultural minority) or her racially-motivated reaction to the in-flows of Jews before and during the Second World War (Keogh, 1998; Goldstone, 2002; O'Connell, 2002; McVeigh 1992, 2002). Recent developments in immigration policies can be discussed under these three themes:

- asylum policies
- immigration and residency
- citizenship.

Asylum policies

Since the 1990s there have been swift increases in asylum applications although the numbers have fallen in recent years. There were a total of 424 applications in 1995, up from 39 in 1992. This rose dramatically to 1,179 in 1996 and to 7,762 in 1999. In 2000, the number of applicants (including re-applications) stood at 10,938. It fell slightly to 10,325 in 2001 and rose again to 11,634 in 2002. The total number of applications in 2003 dropped to 7,900. It slipped further to 4,766 in 2004, to 4,323 in 2005 and to 4,314 in 2006, the lowest number since 1998. Nigerians accounted for the highest number of applicants in 2005 and, for every year since 2000, they have accounted for between 30 per cent and 40 per cent of total applications (ORAC, 2007).

In Ireland, refugees can be broadly divided into Geneva Convention applicants and programme refugees. Programme refugees are a pre-specified number of asylum seekers who have arrived for a specified period as a result of a government decision to waive the requirements of a formal application under the 1951 Geneva Convention. Although they are granted the entitlements of a 'recognized' asylum seeker from the moment they arrive in Ireland, they are still confronted with problems of social isolation and racism. In the 1990s programme refugees came to Ireland from Bosnia, Croatia and Kosovo. Before that there had been programme refugees from Vietnam and Chile.

Generally, asylum applications in Ireland are made under the terms of the 1951 United Nations Geneva Convention and the 1967 New York Protocol. Both the Convention (which Ireland signed in November 1956) and the Protocol (Ireland signed in November 1968) have been incorporated into Irish refugee law by means of the 1996 Refugee Act. The Refugee Act has been amended by Section 11(1) of the 1999 Immigration Act, Section 9 of the 2000 Illegal Immigrant Trafficking Act, and Section 7 of the 2003 Immigrant Act. The Refugee Act, which came into effect in November 2000, establishes the Office of the Refugee Application Commissioner (ORAC), which determines asylum applications in the first instance and the Refugee Appeals Tribunal (RAT), which hears appeals against the decisions of the ORAC.

Those whose applications receive a positive response from the ORAC are granted refugee status following approval from the Minister of Justice, Equality and Law Reform (hereafter referred to as the Minister of Justice). Unsuccessful applicants can appeal to the RAT. They can also appeal to the Minister of Justice for permission to remain in Ireland on humanitarian grounds if the RAT rejects their appeal (Refugee Act, 1996). Those whose applications for leave to remain are rejected are issued with deportation orders and their cases are transferred to the Garda National Immigration Bureau (GNIB), the body that enforces immigration laws.

Asylum laws and policies in Ireland have also been influenced by multilateral agreements among Member States of the European Union. The Dublin Agreement, which attained a convention status in 1996, allows Member States to deny an application for asylum if the applicant passed through a 'third safe country' to the country where the application is being made. This Agreement was incorporated into Irish laws in August 1997, and it came into effect the following month (Cullen, 1998). The list of 'safe' countries includes Romania, Bulgaria and the ten countries that have joined the EU since May 2004 (Refugee Act, 1996). The Illegal Immigrant Trafficking Act implemented in November 2000 and the 2002 Carriers' Liability Bill are modelled on provisions of the Inter-Governmental Council (IGC) joint position paper. The Act introduced the fingerprinting of asylum applicants aged 14 and above while the Bill requires transporters to ensure that passengers brought into Ireland by them are in possession of valid travel documents.

In Ireland, asylum seekers do not have the right to gainful employment and access to third-level education is problematic. On 26 July 1999, the government implemented a 'one-off' decision to allow asylum seekers who had been in the country for up to one year to work. It refused to extend or repeat the gesture despite pleas from asylum seekers' groups, community and church leaders and employers (Tróicare and ICJP, 2002). Until 2000, the majority of asylum seekers were housed in and around the Greater Dublin Area. In December 1999, the government announced a new policy of 'dispersal', which meant that asylum seekers would be assigned to designated accommodation centres all over Ireland. It also announced that social welfare cash payments would be replaced by direct provision of meals and other necessities to asylum seekers. Under the new arrangements, adult asylum seekers would receive €19.10 weekly while children get €9.50. In contrast, homeless people and others on full-board accommodation receive an additional €60 weekly. Under welfare laws, anyone who has insufficient means to meet his or her needs is entitled to €128.80 per week from the state. The new policy did not affect asylum seekers' entitlements to medical cards, child benefit and free legal services.

Until May 2003, community welfare officers could in exceptional circumstances allow asylum seekers to move out of direct provision and to receive mainstream welfare benefits, including rent supplement for private rental accommodation. In a move described by the Irish Refugee Council as 'a serious retrograde step' (Haughey, 2003c), the government changed the policy in 2003, making it obligatory for all new arrivals to live in accommodation centres (Tróicare and ICJP, 2000, p. 26; Haughey, 2003b, Butler, 2003). Government officials said the changes were aimed at cutting costs and at making Ireland less attractive to asylum seekers. A report by the Free Legal Advice Centres (FLAC) described 'direct provision' as 'inhumane and discriminatory' and said the policy was 'gravely detrimental to the human rights of a group of people lawfully present in the country' (FLAC, 2003).

In mid-2003, about 4,500 asylum seekers were accommodated in 53 direct provision centres in Ireland (Haughey, 2003b; FLAC, 2003). At the beginning of 2005 there were 6,127 asylum seekers in 63 accommodation centres. The largest centre in Mosney housed 761 people while the one in Athlone had 359 residents. The number fell to 3,874 in January 2006, reflecting both the dramatic reduction in the number of asylum applicants in Ireland and the relocation to private accommodation of immigrant parents of Irish children, who have successfully applied for a residence permit (Sanctuary, 2005; Sanctuary, 2006).

Immigration and residency

The major developments in immigration and residency policies in Ireland since the beginning of the 1990s have been aimed at ensuring measured but discriminatory inflows of migrant workers while limiting the entry of asylum seekers. This section analyses specific policies on migrant workers and general ones relating to long-term settlement of immigrants in Ireland.

Permits for non-Irish and non-EU (including EEA[1]) nationals to work in Ireland operate on two tiers: the work permit and the work visa/work authorization. Workers who come into the country on a work permit are 'tied' to a particular employer. In fact the application for the permit is made by the employer on behalf of the employee and it is issued to the employer. This means that the worker is not allowed to seek a different employer even when he/she is displeased with the situation. Indeed, cases of gross abuse and exploitation of workers have been documented in media reports (Crosby, 2001; Haughey, 2002). Work permits are issued for a short duration, usually for six months or one year but they can be renewed.

Even in the days when it desperately sought workers overseas, the government never officially removed the provision that requires employers to offer vacant positions first to Irish and EEA citizens and then to non-Irish/EEA nationals if these had not been filled. However, in the heydays

---

1   The EEA consists of EU countries, Iceland, Liechtenstein, and Norway.

of the Celtic Tiger and debilitating workers' shortages, government officials turned a blind eye to this requirement. At the beginning of 2002, however, as the sudden downturn in the economy resulted in increased job losses, it reaffirmed this restrictive requirement. It would no longer consider applications for new work permits unless they were accompanied by a letter from Foras Áiseanna Saothair (FÁS) confirming that 'all reasonable efforts have been made by the employer to find an Irish or other EEA national to fill the vacancy on offer' (Lucey, 2001; DTEE, 2006). In 2003, the government further restricted the hiring of foreign workers to certain types of job and also announced that all sorts of overseas recruitment would be drastically reduced from May 2004 in expectation of workers from the ten new EU countries (Haughey, 2003a). Under the new policies, employers are required to register vacant positions with FÁS for a period of four weeks. FÁS is required to send notices of the vacancies to its local offices nationwide and to other European Economic Area (EEA) public employment services.

The working visa/work authorization scheme was introduced in 2000. Applicants process their application at the Irish embassies in their countries of permanent residence or directly by post to the visa office in Dublin. Working visas are issued to non-EU and non-EEA immigrants who require entry visas to Ireland while work authorizations are issued to those who do not require entry visas. Working visas and work authorizations are usually valid for two years, or three months in the case of Candidate Nurses. Workers in these categories are allowed to change their employers within the same skills category after arrival in Ireland as long as they have valid permits to work and reside in the country (www.entemp.ie). Working visa immigrants can apply for family reunification after three months in the country. Those on work authorization can come to Ireland with their family since they do not require entry visa.

Until 2004, spouses of work permit holders or of working visa/work authorization immigrants were not permitted to take up gainful employment (Donnellan, 2003). Following pressure from immigrant workers, employers and NGOs, the government changed this policy in 2004 (Holland, 2004). The spouse of a work permit holder can take up a job so long as there is an employer willing to apply for a work permit on his or her behalf. These spouses can take up any kind of job, the application is exempt from work permit fees and the potential employer is not obliged to advertise the job or position with FÁS. However, a spouse whose husband or wife is working in a different field to that for which the work permit or working visa or authorization was originally granted may be disqualified from taking a job.

Not unexpectedly, there have been greater inflows (but not the flood predicted by sections of the Irish mass media) of migrant workers from the ten countries that joined the European Union in May 2004. In the absence of official statistics, the applications for Personal Public Service (PPS) numbers have been used to determine the number of migrants from these countries. The PPS number is required for tax and employment purposes and for most transactions with government departments. From May to December 2004, a total of 53,582 applications were made by migrants from the ten new states. This increased to 109,951 in 2005. In 2004, immigrants from Poland accounted for nearly 50 per cent of total applications, followed by immigrants from Lithuania.

This trend was accelerated in 2005 with applicants from Poland accounting for 63,523 (more than half) of the total applications. Lithuania came a distant second with a total of 18,488 applications. In both years, the least numbers of applicants came from Slovenia and Cyprus, according to statistics obtained from the Department of Social and Family Affairs. In anticipation of greater migrant inflows from these countries and perhaps to stem the 'tide' that never happened, the government had disqualified migrants from these countries from claiming supplementary welfare allowance, rent allowance and other social welfare related payments. These measures were repealed in 2006 after a ruling by the EU Commission that they amounted to discrimination (Sanctuary, 2006).

The next section examines some of the most profound changes in residency policies in the past 15 years.

Foreign students   Statistics for this category of immigrants are haphazard and unreliable. Whereas the bulk of students in the past mostly came from North America and Europe, according to the Higher Education Authority (www.hea.ie), more students are now coming from Asia and Africa. However, the HEA statistics do not cover many private colleges and language schools. The number of language schools has increased dramatically in the last decade but there are also no reliable statistics on the actual numbers of students. Immigrant students, including those in language schools, are entitled to work for a maximum of 20 hours a week. It is common knowledge that many work full-time with the active connivance of their employers, many of whom often exploit these workers. Introduced at the beginning of this decade as part of the measures to wrest a slice of the English language market from the United Kingdom, the policy has attracted many immigrant groups to Ireland.

Family reunification migrants   Fewer immigrants have come into Ireland via the family reunification route. This is largely due to the lengthy and strict application procedures. The criteria are non-standardized and the decision processes are not transparent. Though applications are made to the Minister for Justice, the ORAC is charged with processing them and with making recommendations to the Minister. The Minister exercises discretionary power in granting or rejecting applications based on ORAC's recommendations. Between 2001 and the end of 2003, a total of 544 persons were given approval to join their relatives in Ireland. At 227, the number approved in 2002 was the highest, followed by 192 in 2003 (information received from the Department of Justice press office, 2004). A total of 317 new applications were made in 2004. Of the 556 new applications received in 2005, 384 were processed and forwarded to the Minister for approval. In 2005, the highest numbers of applications were made by Somalis (12 per cent), followed by Nigerians (10 per cent) and the Democratic Republic of the Congo (9 per cent) (Sanctuary, 2005; Sanctuary, 2006).

Illegal migration   There are relatively few avenues to enter into Ireland illegally because the country, unlike most countries in continental Europe, has no land borders with any country. In addition, the sea- and airports have been rigorously policed in recent years. However, anecdotal evidence suggests that there are illegal immigrants in the country. Most of them are asylum seekers whose applications have failed or other 'legal' immigrants whose residence permits/visas have expired but who have chosen to remain either by obtaining false documents or by simply inhabiting the underworld of undocumented immigrants. Although there are no official statistics for these categories of 'immigrants', it is generally believed that they constitute a small minority. Since 2003, the Garda Immigration Bureau has carried out sporadic but massive searches of private homes aimed at identifying, arresting and deporting illegal immigrants.

Residence permit   Up until early 2003, immigrants, including asylum seekers, who become parents of a child or children born in Ireland, and therefore an Irish citizen, could also apply for a residence permit solely on that basis. Section 2.1 of the Irish Constitution, including Article 2 adopted as part of the 1998 Belfast Agreement, grants the right to naturalization to every child born in the island of Ireland (Dooley, 2003; *The Irish Times* 2002). In a famous judgement in what is now known as the 'Fajujonu case', the Irish Supreme Court ruled in 1989 that the children of non-citizens had a constitutional right to the 'company, care and parentage' of their parents within a family unit. That ruling effectively compelled the state to grant residence permit to such parents (*The Irish Times* 2002; Dooley, 2003). The numbers of immigrants relying on this avenue to establish the right of residency grew sharply from the beginning of the twenty-first century after Ireland's stricter immigration and asylum policies made it difficult for immigrants, especially asylum seekers, to establish a presence in the country. Between 1996 and the end of 2001, a total of 4,859 people were granted rights to remain in Ireland on this basis, while the number of births in 2001 to non-Irish nationals in the Dublin-based Rotunda hospital was reported by the Irish Times to be one in five (*The Irish Times* 2002).

The government's decision to abandon this policy followed another Supreme Court decision on 23 January 2003 in a case involving a family from Nigeria and another from the Czech Republic (*The Irish Times* 2002; Haughey, 2000c, 2003d). The court ruled that immigrant parents of Irish citizen children and their non-Irish siblings could no longer apply for a residence permit solely on that basis. The ruling was applied retroactively to include all parents whose children were born before the court ruling (but not those who had been granted a residence permit), including those whose applications were pending. As of 19 February 2003 when the Minister for Justice issued orders to stop granting residence permits to immigrant parents of Irish citizens, there were 11,493 outstanding applications (Department of Justice, 2004). Of these, 9,631 applicants had been or were still in the asylum system and 1, 862 were non-asylum related.

The Coalition Against the Deportation of Irish Children (CADIC) spear-headed a campaign to persuade the Minister for Justice to have a change of heart over the outstanding applications. Having run, and won (with the support of 78.9 per cent of the population), a referendum in June 2004 to change Ireland's citizenship entitlement and allow only children born in Ireland whose parent or parents is/are a citizen to achieve Irish citizenship, the government announced at the end of 2004 a new policy that would allow immigrant parents to reapply for a residence permit (see Lentin and McVeigh 2006 for a nuanced analysis). The new policy effectively removed the threats of deportation that had dangled over the heads of these immigrants since February 2003. Under the new policy that came into effect in January 2005, applicants would have to prove, among other things, that they are of good character and that they have the possibility to become self-sufficient in two years from the time they are granted residency rights. They are also required to give an undertaking not to invite other members of their family outside of Ireland to live with them. Out of the 17,877 applications received by the Department as of mid-December 2005, 17,660 had been processed. A total of 16,704 persons were granted residency rights and 956 were refused (Sanctuary, 2006). The state officially ended the receipt and processing of applications in January 2006.

Deportations, which had always been an element of Irish immigration policies, acquired new salience during this time and up till the end of 2005. The majority of the over 550 deportations in 2003 were to countries in Eastern Europe. In 2003, the Garda National Immigration Bureau embarked on the joint chartering of aircraft with immigration authorities in the United Kingdom and the Netherlands to facilitate deportations to Nigeria, China, Romania and other countries in Eastern Europe. Whereas 2,866 deportation orders were signed by the Minister for Justice in 2004, only 599 deportations were carried out. The majority of deportations were to Romania (250), Nigeria (77), Moldova (57) and China (18). In 2005, 396 deportations out of the 1,838 orders signed by the Minister were effected. The highest number of deportations were to Nigeria (135), followed by Romania (122) and China (18). A total of 335 people were repatriated 'voluntarily'. Between 1999 and 2005, a total of 12,660 deportation orders were issued and 2,664 deportations were carried out, while 2,855 people were repatriated 'voluntarily' (Sanctuary (2005); Sanctuary (2006).

Citizenship policies

The most profound change in Irish citizenship law took effect in January 2005. In June 2004 Irish citizens had voted overwhelmingly to repeal Article 9 of the Irish Constitution, which grants the right to naturalization to every child born in the island of Ireland. Since January 2005 immigrants born in Ireland whose parent or parents are not citizens can apply for citizenship if their parent 'has, during the period of four years immediately preceding the person's birth, been resident in the island of Ireland for a period of not less than three years' (Irish Nationality and Citizenship Act, 2004). In addition, spouses of Irish citizens and asylum applicants who have attained refugee status can apply for naturalization after three years. Also, immigrants (excluding asylum seekers and students) who have legally resided in the country for five years are entitled to apply for naturalization. There is also a provision for applying for leave to remain in the country indefinitely if an immigrant has lived in Ireland for eight years.

The immigrant population in Ireland: main demographic and social features

Whereas large numbers of in-migrants in the 1990s consisted of returned Irish migrants, citizens of the UK and of the other EU countries, there were also inflows from North and South America, Asia and Africa (see Figure 13.2 and Table 13.2). As the analyses in the previous sections demonstrate, the vast majority of non-EU immigrants are migrant workers. Emigrations have, since the mid-1990s, consistently outstripped immigrations, as Figure 13.1 and Table 13.1 illustrate.

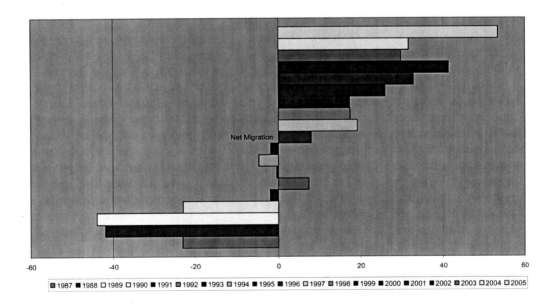

Figure 13.1   Estimated net migration (1987–2005) ('000s)

Table 13.1   Estimated net migration (1987–2005) ('000s)

	1987	1988	1989	1990	1991	1992	1993	1994	1995	1996	1997	1998	1999	2000	2001	2002	2003	2004	2005
Net Migration	-23.0	-41.9	-43.9	-22.9	-2.0	7.4	-0.4	-4.7	-1.9	8.0	19.2	17.4	17.3	26.0	32.8	41.3	29.8	31.6	53.4

The results of the 2002 Census (CSO, 2002) also showed that 5.8 per cent of Ireland's 3.9 million residents were non-Irish citizens. The largest number of these came from England and Wales (182,624), Northern Ireland (49,928), the USA (21,541) and Scotland (15,963). The other large groups include Nigeria (9,225), Germany (8,770) and France (6,794).

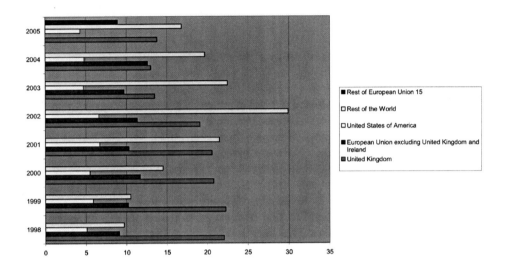

Source: Central Statistics Office.

Figure 13.2   Estimated migration inflows (1998–2005) ('000s)

Table 13.2   Estimated migration inflows (1998–2005) ('000s)

		1998	1999	2000	2001	2002	2003	2004	2005
All Persons Inward Migration	United Kingdom	22.1	22.3	20.8	20.6	19.1	13.5	13.0	13.8
	European Union excluding United Kingdom and Ireland	9.1	10.2	11.7	10.3	11.3	9.7	12.6	..
	United States of America	5.1	5.9	5.5	6.7	6.6	4.7	4.8	4.3
	Rest of the World	9.7	10.5	14.5	21.5	29.9	22.5	19.7	16.8
	Rest of European Union 15	..	..	..	..	..	..	..	8.9

However, the demographic landscape has changed considerably since 2002 with increased inflows from non-EU and non-western countries – see Figure 13.2 and Table 13.2 above. The increased inflows from China, the Philippines and Poland have resulted in a greater presence of these nationals.

A recent report in *The Observer* put the 'official' number of Poles working in the construction industry in Ireland at 100,000 and the 'unofficial' at more than 200,000 (Media Guardian, 2006).

In the midst of the dramatic increases in 'in-migrations', emigrations have been sustained, albeit at a much reduced rate. The majority of recent emigrants are young and they tend to return after a few years. The April 2004 Population Estimates revealed that 18,500 persons emigrated from Ireland in the previous 12 months, the lowest since 1987. More than half of them (54 per cent) were between the ages of 15 and 24.

Immigrant rights and participation in public life – issues of immigrant integration

The active participation of immigrants in public life is, to a large extent, influenced by the status and conditions of their residency. Anecdotal and experiential knowledge suggests that immigrants with long-term or permanent residence status and those who have Irish citizenship have taken a more confident and committed approach to participation in public life. The picture is a lot more complex than the one painted here. There are immigrants who have been active in public life despite having uncertain or precarious residence status. For others, their civic activism is informed by their pre-immigration education and experience, while others are compelled to tread the path of active civic participation because of the peculiar difficulties they face in Ireland (see Ugba, 2005, for a fuller analysis). In relation to politics and electoral participation, there are specific regulations under Irish laws and those will be analysed later in this section. The next section will elucidate the relationship between general immigration policies and immigrant participation in public life.

As documented above, there are different regimes in Ireland for receiving and integrating asylum seekers, foreign workers, students and family reunification migrants. Whereas students, migrant workers and their relatives/dependants have access to all levels of education, asylum seekers have access only to primary and secondary education. In addition, they do not have the right to gainful employment (with the exception of a small number of asylum seekers allowed to work in 2001 – see Troiciare and ICJP, 2002), secure and private accommodation or to travel out · of the country. While these restrictions have barred asylum seekers from participating in some civic activities, many have been engaged in activities mostly aimed at changing these and other restrictive immigration policies and at combating racism. Examples of immigrant-led groups in this respect include the Association of Refugees and Asylum Seekers in Ireland (ARASI), the African Refugee Network (ARN), the Nigerian Support Group (NSG) and the Asylum Seekers Group Ireland (ASGI).

There are no similar restrictions on the participation of immigrant workers in public life. However, there are financial difficulties as well as specific institutional requirements that discourage participation. A recent report by Integrating Ireland identified discriminatory fees, language problems, problems with the recognition of earlier educational achievements and 'various social welfare traps and barriers' as some of the obstacles to immigrant participation in education (Integrating Ireland, 2005). The report recommended a review of the existing admissions systems to facilitate access to higher education for immigrants who have not gone through the Irish secondary school system.

The civic activities of many foreign workers have been focused mainly on changing discriminatory employment, healthcare and social welfare policies. The paths of many immigrant workers to such activism are usually the trade unions and other kinds of pressure groups. There are no constitutional and institutional barriers to membership of trade unions for foreign workers but immigrant membership of many unions have, until recently, been low because some immigrants were not clear on what their rights in this respect are. Others who were not envisaging a long or permanent presence in the Irish labour market did not feel compelled to join the unions (Ugba, 2005).

Religious activism is one area where immigrant participation appears to be most intense and voluntary, less problematic and apparently unhindered by precarious residence status or length of time in Ireland. The most innovative and dramatic change in Ireland's religious and cultural landscape is not the participation of immigrants in 'mainline' Irish churches but the birth and spread of immigrant-led religious groups – from a variety of Christian churches to several mosques in Dublin and elsewhere (Ugba, 2003, 2005, 2006a, 2006b, 2007). It has been relatively easy for immigrant groups to set up places of worship and to publicly demonstrate their beliefs, partly because the institutional requirements are not stringent. For individual immigrants, religion appears to be a convenient and adaptable baggage, which they are able to fold up, transport and unfold, in new circumstances with minimal difficulties.

Immigrants have also been active in media production, particularly in the 'ethnic' media sector (Ugba, 2002). The launch of *Metro Eireann* on 17 April 2000 marked a turning point in this respect, as it stimulated greater intellectual and public debates on the role of ethnic minority media in Ireland. It also opened the floodgates to the birth of many other publications and provided additional opportunities for immigrant civic participation. The use of new Information and Communication Technologies (ICTs) to enhance participation in public life is becoming widespread. Most immigrant groups have set up websites for publicising their activities and facilitating information interchange.

Political and electoral participation involves specific rules and conditions (see Fanning, Mutwarasibo and Chedamoyo, 2003, 2004 for details). Whereas only Irish citizens can take part in referenda and vote in some kinds of elections, citizens of EU countries can vote only in European and local elections while 'every person who is a citizen of Ireland or ordinarily resident in the State and has reached the age of 18 years' can vote and be voted for in local elections (www.environ.ie). Up until the 2004 elections, immigrant participation in the political and electoral processes was low-key. However, about 20 immigrants contested the June 2004 local elections. The two who got elected were Nigerians.

Public and media discourses on migration

In the late 1990s and early 2000s, when Ireland recorded its highest numbers of asylum seekers, anti-immigration groups and some sections of the media capitalized on the prevailing sense of bewilderment to stir up anti-immigrant sentiments. Groups like the Immigration Control Platform launched campaigns aimed at getting the government to adopt more restrictive and exclusionary policies. While the government professed a commitment to its obligations under the Geneva Convention, some government Ministers made unsubstantiated distinctions between 'genuine' refugees and those they termed as 'bogus', 'economic migrants' or 'welfare scroungers' (Cullen, 2000; Guerin, 2002).

Racism and racial attacks directed at immigrants rose in almost equal proportion to anti-refugee tirades from official and unofficial quarters (Brennock and Haughey, 2003; Haughey, 2000a, 2000b; McCarthy and Rafferty, 2002). A development parallel to the rise in racism and racially-biased media discourse (Haughey, 2001) is the development of an anti-racism sector that spans governmental and non-governmental initiatives and groups. The National Consultative Committee on Racism and Interculturalism (NCCRI) was established in 1998 to facilitate dialogue between government agencies and non-government organizations (www.nccri.ie) while the Equality Authority, a government-funded body charged with initiating anti-discrimination laws, was established in 1999 (www.equality.ie). The 1998 Employment Equality Act and the 2000 Equal Status Act outlaw discrimination on nine grounds, including gender, race, religion and membership of the Traveller community. The Equality Status Act also established the Equality Tribunal, an independent and quasi-judicial forum that hears or mediates complaints of alleged discrimination under the equality legislation. Its decisions and mediated settlements are legally binding (www. equalitytribunal.ie).

However, Lentin and McVeigh (2006) have argued that 'the cooption of anti-racism by state(s) and the reformulation of anti-racism as 'integration', 'diversity' and 'interculturalism' mark the end of anti-racism as anti-state racism political action'. According to them, 'anti-racism based on a 'partnership' model – and including anti-racist organizations fully funded by the Department of Justice – is dominated by white Irish people, often informed by a sense of the colonial past and of anti-Irish racism, all convincing themselves that they are working in partnership with people of colour'. Perhaps in acknowledgement of these views, the anti-racism movement has witnessed some transformations in recent years as immigrant groups and members of Ireland's only indigenous ethnic/cultural minority – the Travellers – have struggled to assert their voice and place.

Concluding remarks

In a space of ten years, Ireland's sociocultural and demographic landscape has experienced dramatic changes. This analysis has attempted to contextualize the most profound of these changes and identify their causes, trajectories and implications. As in most countries in the West, the most recent developments have seen dramatic decreases in asylum applications (www.unhcr.org), without corresponding decreases in the numbers of immigrant workers. These latest developments are, perhaps, an indication of future trends. However, it is safe to conclude that the developments of the last ten years have inscribed multi-ethnicities and other forms of cultural diversities on the Emerald Isle on a scale far greater than it had ever known.

References

Bade, K.J. (2003), *Migration in European History*. Malden, Mass. and Oxford: Blackwell Publishing.

Brennock, M. and Haughey, N. (2003), 'Judges Apologise to Non-Nationals for Remarks about Immigrants'. Dublin: *The Irish Times*, 21 February.

Butler, P. (2003), 'FLAC Criticises Direct Provision'. Dublin: *The Irish Times*, 17 July.

CSO (Central Statistics Office) (2002), *Census Results*. Dublin: CSO.

—— (2003), *Population and Migration Estimates*, April. Dublin: CSO.

Crosby, J. (2001), '108 Cases under Scrutiny for Breaches of Labour Laws'. Dublin: *The Irish Times*, 8 June.

Cullen, P. (1997), 'EU Refugee Treaty Takes Effect, but Ireland Still Has no Law on Asylum'. Dublin: *The Irish Times*, 29 August.

—— (2000), *Refugees and Asylum Seekers in Ireland*. Cork: University Publishing.

Donnellan, P. (2003), 'Driving our Nurses Away'. Dublin: *The Irish Times*, 12 July.

Dooley, R. (2003), 'State is Obliged to Protect Irish-Born Children'. Dublin: *The Irish Times*, 21 November.

DTEE (2006), *Work Permits Statistics by Nationality*, www.entemp.ie.

Faist, T. (2000), *The Volume and Dynamics of International Migration and Transnational Social Spaces*. Oxford: Oxford University Press.

Fanning, B., Mutwarasibo, F. and Chedamoyo, N. (2003), *Positive Politics: Participation of Immigrants and Ethnic Minorities in the Electoral Process*. Dublin: Africa Solidarity Centre, www.africacentre.ie.

—— (2004), *Negative Politics, Positive Vision: Participation of Immigrants and Ethnic Minorities in the 2004 Local Elections*. Dublin: African Solidarity Centre, www.africacentre.ie.

FLAC (2003), *Direct Discrimination? An Analysis of the Scheme of Direct Provision in Ireland*. Dublin: Free Legal Advice Centres.

Goldstone, K. (2002), 'Christianity, Conversion and the Tricky Business of Names: Images of Jews and Blacks in the Nationalist Irish Catholic Discourse', in Lentin, R. and McVeigh, R. (eds) *Racism and Anti-Racism in Ireland*. Belfast: BTP Publications.

Guerin, P. (2002), 'Racism and the Media in Ireland: Setting the Anti-Immigration Agenda', in Lentin, R. and McVeigh, R. (eds) *Racism and Anti-Racism in Ireland*. Belfast: BTP Publications.

Haughey, N. (2000a), 'Ignorance and Poverty Add to Racial Tensions in Dublin'. Dublin: *The Irish Times*, 6 May.

—— (2000b), 'Refugee Group Chairman Urges Action after Assault'. Dublin: *The Irish Times*, 4 December.

—— (2000c), 'State Contesting Right of Non-EU Parents of Irish Children to Stay'. Dublin: *The Irish Times*, 9 January.

—— (2001), 'The Media and Racism', in Farrell and Watt (eds) *Responding to Racism in Ireland*. Dublin: Veritas Publications.

—— (2002), 'Foreign Worker Scheme Suspended to Stem Abuse'. Dublin: *The Irish Times*, 30 October.

—— (2003a), 'Employers Told Number of Work Permits to be Cut from Next Year'. Dublin: *The Irish Times*, 13 September.

—— (2003b), 'FLAC Censures Asylum-Seeker Housing Scheme'. Dublin: *The Irish Times*, 11 July.

—— (2003c), 'State Housing for New Asylum-Seekers'. Dublin: *The Irish Times*: June 12.

—— (2003d), 'Residents of Limbo'. Dublin: *The Irish Times*, 7 June.

Holland, K. (2004), 'Rule Change for Spouses of Non-EU Nurses Welcomed'. Dublin: *The Irish Times*, 7 January.

'Integrating Ireland' (2005), *International Students and Professionals in Ireland: An Analysis of Access to Higher Education and Recognition of Professional Qualifications*. Dublin: Integrating Ireland.

Irish Nationality and Citizenship Act (2004), Dublin: Government Printing Press.

Keogh, D. (1998), *Jews in twentieth-century Ireland: Refugees, Anti-Semitism and the Holocaust*. Cork: Cork University Press.

Lentin, R. (2001), 'Responding to the Racialisation of Irishness: Disavowed Multiculturalism and its Discontents', *Sociological Research Online* (available at http://www.socresonline.org.uk/5/4/lentin.html).

Lentin, R. and McVeigh, R. (2006), *After Optimism? (Ireland: Racism and Globalisation)*. Dublin: Metro Eireann Publications.

Lucey, A. (2001), 'Employers Angered at New Rules over Work Permits'. Dublin: *The Irish Times*, 31 December.

MacEinri, P. (2000), *Immigration into Ireland: Trends, Policy Responses, Outlook*. Cork: ICMS (www.migration.ucc.ie/irelandfirstreport.htm).

—— (2001), 'Immigration Policy in Ireland', in Farrell and Watt (eds) *Responding to Racism in Ireland*. Dublin: Veritas Publications.

Marren, P. (2001), 'Causes of International Migration', in Whelan, T.R. (ed.) *The Stranger in our Midst: Refugees in Ireland – Causes, Experiences, Responses*. Dublin: Kimmage Mission Institute of Theology and Cultures.

Martin, F.S. (2001), 'Global Migration Trends and Asylum', *Journal of Humanitarian Assistance* (available at http://www.jha.ac/articles/u041.htm).

McCarthy, P. and Rafferty, M. (2002), 'Ethnicity, Class and Culture in Dublin' in *Studies*, **94**, 338–64.

McVeigh, R. (1992), 'The Specificity of Irish Racism'. *Race and Class*, 33:4.

—— (2002), 'Is there an Irish Anti-Racism? Building an Anti-Racist Ireland', in Lentin, R. and McVeigh, R. (eds) *Racism and Anti-Racism in Ireland*. Belfast: BTP Publications.

Media Guardian (2006), 'Dublin Heralds a New Era in Publishing for Immigrants', 12 March.

O'Connell, J. (2002), 'Travellers in Ireland: An Examination of Discrimination and Racism' in Lentin, R. and McVeigh, R. (eds) *Racism and Anti-Racism in Ireland*. Belfast: BTP Publications.

ORAC (2007), 'Monthly Asylum Statistics Published by the Office of the Refugees Application Commissioner' (available at www.orac.ie/Pages/Statistics.htm).

Pollak, A. (1999), 'Welcome to Dublin, Unless You're Black'. Dublin: *The Irish Times*, 24 April.

Rasmussen, H.K. (1996), *No Entry: Immigration Policy in Europe*. Copenhagen: Copenhagen Business School Press.

Refugee Act (1996). Dublin: Government Printing Press.

Sanctuary (2005), *A bi-monthly newsletter on asylum, refugee and migrant matters from a religious perspective*, published by Refugee & Migrant Project of Irish Bishops' Conference. January, No. 33. Maynooth, Ireland.

—— (2006), January, No 36.

Staunton, D. (2003), 'Concern over EU 'safe' Countries List'. Dublin: *The Irish Times*, 10 October.

—— (2002), Irish-Born Deportees Editorial, *The Irish Times*, 10 April.

'Tróicare and the Irish Commission for Justice and Peace (ICJP)' (2002), *Refugees and Asylum Seekers: A challenge to solidarity*. Dublin: Tróicare/ICJP.

Ugba, A. (2002), 'Mapping Minorities and their Media: Ireland' (availabe at www.lse.ac.uk/collections/EMTEL/Minorities/papers/minoritymedia_ireland.doc).

—— (2003), 'African Churches in Ireland', *Asyland*, Autumn. Dublin: Irish Refugee Council.

—— (2005), 'Active Civic Participation of Immigrants in Ireland: A Contribution to a Project on Immigration Civic Participation in the 25 EU Countries' (available at www.uni-oldenburg.de/politis-europe/download/Ireland.pdf).

—— (2006), 'African Pentecostals in 21st Century Ireland', *Studies*, **95**(378), 163–73.

—— (2006a), 'African Pentecostals in 21st Century Ireland', *Studies*, **95**(378), 163–73.

—— (2006b), 'Between God and Ethnicity: Pentecostal African Immigrants in 21st Century Ireland', *Irish Journal of Anthropology*, 9(3), 56–63

—— (2007), 'African Pentecostals in twenty-first century Ireland: Identity and integration' in Fanning, B. (ed.) *Immigration and Social Change in Ireland*. Manchester and New York: Manchester University Press.

Internet-based references

www.cso.ie: official website of Central Statistics Office (February 2007).

www.equalitytribunal.ie: official website of the Equality Tribunal (October 2004).

www.equality.ie: official website of the Equality Authority (October 2004).

www.entemp.ie: official website of the Department of Enterprise, Trade and Employment (October 2004).

http://www.environ.ie: official website of the Department of Environment, Heritage and Local Government (October 2004).

www.hea.ie: website of the Higher Education Authority.

www.integratingireland.ie: website of Integrating Ireland, network of community and voluntary groups (October 2004).

www.justice.ie: official website of the Department of Justice, Equality and Law Reform.

www.metroeireann.com: official website of Metro Eireann (October 2004).

www.nccri.ie: official website of the Consultative Committee on Racism and Interculturalism (October 2004).

www.orac.ie: official website of the Office of the Refugees Application Commissioner (ORAC) (February 2007).

Chapter 14

Italy

Ankica Kosic and Anna Triandafyllidou

Like other countries in Southern Europe, Italy has, in the course of less than two decades, rapidly and unexpectedly changed from a country of emigration to one of immigration. The immigrant population is approximately three million people out of a total of 58 million inhabitants.[1] While the immigrant population amounts to just under 5 per cent, among them, asylum seekers (successful and rejected ones) are only a tiny fraction.

Immigrants come to Italy mainly in search of employment and of a better life. They come from many different countries and continents of origin,[2] profess different religions, and carry with them a mosaic of cultures and habits.

Italy has developed a piecemeal approach to immigration, lacking until recently a comprehensive and consistent policy framework. Because of its geographical position, this country is highly exposed to penetration by illegal immigrants from the south and from the east. Moreover, like other southern EU countries, Italy has a widespread informal economy, thereby providing fertile ground for illegal migration to operate in. Combating undocumented immigration and the trafficking of human beings is a priority for both security and foreign policy. It is also an issue to which public opinion is extremely sensitive.

Despite several regularization programmes enacted since the late 1980s,[3] allowing the legalization of more than two million immigrants, immigrant integration is still at an early stage in Italy. Significant steps toward integration were taken in the period 1998–2001, when a centre-left government was in power. The Berlusconi government on the other hand put more emphasis on tight management of flows, limited the scope of integration to legal migrants only, and made the procedures involved in obtaining or renewing legal status even more bureaucratic and cumbersome. Nonetheless, in 2002, this centre-right government enacted the largest regularization programme ever, involving 700,000 immigrants. At the same time, public opinion remains concerned about immigrants 'invading' their national territory, as well as endangering their national welfare and identity.

Major developments in Italy's immigration policy

Although the history of immigration into Italy is a relatively recent phenomenon, it can be divided into different phases or periods in relation to the numbers and socioeconomic features of the

---

1   This includes an estimate of undocumented migrants present in Italian territory.
2   The main three groups, Romanians, Moroccans and Albanians, account for only 30 per cent of the immigrant population, while the first ten nationalities account for just over 50 per cent of the total immigrant population.
3   1986, 1990, 1996, 1998 and 2002.

immigrants, their absorption into the labour market and the immigration policies adopted by the Italian state.

In contrast to other EU countries, immigration to Italy did not begin in a period of reconstruction and economic development. Rather, it took off during a period of economic recession characterized, among other things, by an increase in the rate of unemployment.

The first flow of immigrants into Italy started in the mid-1970s and included relatively limited numbers of students and refugees from different countries. The significant increase in the number of immigrants in Italy was witnessed after 1984, in the period when Britain, Germany and France closed their borders to immigrants, and when flows were, therefore, partially diverted towards Southern Europe. The first comprehensive immigration law was introduced into Italian legislation in 1986 (Law 943/1986). It regulated the entry of immigrants seeking employment and provided amnesty for undocumented immigrants who could prove such employment. Since the idea behind that law was that the immigration phenomenon was limited and transitory, it contained no rules aimed at encouraging integration (Campani and De Bonis, 2003).

The period between 1990 and 1996 was characterized by migratory flows mainly from the Balkan region and Eastern Europe. This was a period of transition for the Italian political system (D'Alimonte and Bartolini, 1997), political crisis and corruption scandals,[4] and the emergence of new parties being hostile towards immigration (for example *Lega Nord*). Italian immigration policy also had to adjust to emerging European migration policy (Butt, 1994; Stetter, 2000) and the attention paid by northern EU member states to the weak borders of the southern European countries. Through Law 39/1990, most commonly known as the 'Martelli Law,[5] immigration began to be considered as a long-term phenomenon in Italy. This law defined special provisions regarding immigration, including the annual planning of migratory flows, and certain norms regarding the rights and obligations of foreigners in Italy. These involved their stay and work conditions as well as other matters concerning family reunification and social integration.

The second half of the 1990s saw a major settlement of immigrants in Italy and a higher number of requests for family reunification. The centre-left government in power between 1997 and 2001 tried to implement a new immigration policy (Law 40/1998). This was the so-called *Turco-Napolitano* law or the Single Text – *Testo Unico* – which set annual quotas for immigration flows and established a set of measures and consultative bodies aimed at immigrant integration. Annual flows were to be based on triennial plans to be prepared by the government. Workers could enter and stay in Italy under the following conditions: a) for seasonal employment (within the annually defined quotas); b) if they had an offer of employment in Italy (again within the annual quotas predefined by the government; stay permits for work purposes were initially issued for one year); and c) if they were 'sponsored' by an Italian or a foreign citizen legally residing in Italy. Law 40/1998 stated that integration policies should ensure parity of access to public services (see also Zincone and Ponzo, 2006).

The immigration policy landscape has changed again since 2002, when the centre-right government coalition at the time adopted a new, more restrictive law 189/2002 (known as the *Bossi-Fini* law). This law specifies that all 'social integration measures' are limited to legal immigrants, and introduces a more repressive policy toward undocumented immigrants through the use of compulsory repatriation. Conditions for issuing or renewing a permit vary in line with the reasons for entering Italy (for example dependent employment, self-employment, family reunification,

---

4   The *Mani pulite* ('Clean hands') investigation that started as a local scandal in Milan soon took on huge dimensions as it revealed widespread corruption among the political and economic elites. Two-thirds of the members of Parliament ended up under investigation by the Public Prosecutor.

5   Claudio Martelli was the deputy prime minister who promoted this legislation.

study and so on). The residence permit cannot last more than the work contract and a maximum period of nine months has been defined for seasonal workers, one year for temporary workers, and no more than two years for other workers (that is for work on a self-employed basis, work as an employee for an indefinite period and family reunification). Non-EU workers can enter Italy on a 'residence contract' (*contratto di soggiorno* only). This is a contract of dependent employment signed by the employee and the employer. Upon expiration of the contract, the immigrant worker is allowed to stay in Italy for another six months in search of employment. It also establishes a needs-test for foreign workers, similar to the one existing in other EU countries such as Germany or Greece. The employer is obliged to advertise the job opening for at least 20 days. If s/he finds no Italian citizen or legal resident able to take up the offer, the prefecture authorizes the entry of a new non-EU worker.

The centre–left coalition that has been in government since April 2006 has prepared a new immigration bill that is currently (spring 2007) under discussion in Parliament and will become effective in January 2008. This bill includes an important innovation, notably the introduction of a points-based entry system whose aim is to manage more efficiently incoming flows of economic migrants. The new government is also processing proposals regarding the concession of the right to vote in local elections to non-EU citizens who reside in Italy, and changes in the citizenship law that would ease naturalization requirements for non-EU citizens.

Annual quotas for immigration

The management of foreign labour flows in Italy essentially centres on the quota system. There is a three-year programme which spells out the quotas for each period. Nonetheless, on 30 November of each year, the Ministry of Labour publishes the positions (*flussi di ingresso*) available for the following year. These quotas are decided on the basis of the estimated need for foreign labour as provided by local and regional labour offices of the Ministry, and employers' associations in each region or province. The quotas have always fallen short of national estimates of demand for foreign labour (as estimated by the Excelsior Unioncamere, 2004) and applications to provincial labour offices almost always exceed the available quotas (Zanfrini, 2003). The national quotas are divided in relation to four parameters (Chaloff, 2003):

- Regional, with the overall quota divided into sub-quotas for the 20 regions, which then allocate the quotas to the country's 104 provinces.
- Type of labour, with the usual divisions being seasonal, dependent work and self-employment. In 2006, seasonal work permits were issued only to citizens of Serbia-Montenegro, Croatia, Bosnia and Herzegovina, Macedonia, Bulgaria and Romania, to the citizens of those countries with which seasonal labour agreements have been signed (Tunisia, Albania, Morocco, Moldavia and Egypt), and to those individuals who had seasonal work permits issued in the previous three years (thus allowing past workers to return, regardless of nationality). The remaining 170,000 permits had to be distributed between dependent work and self-employment.
- Job category. In 2006, 45,000 permits were reserved for housekeepers and private carers and 4,000 for highly skilled professionals (some special categories are exempted from the quota).
- Nationality, with some sub-quotas reserved for citizens of specific nationalities. One part of the preferential quotas is reserved to workers of Italian origin (whose parents were Italian in ascendant line within the third degree) who wish to enrol in the list. In 2006, the

decree established a quota of 500 immigrants of Italian origin from Argentina, Uruguay and Venezuela, for seasonal, dependent or self-employed work.

Legal entry for work was set at 58,000 persons in 1998, increasing to 83,000 in 2000 and to 170,000 in 2006. Of these, 50,000 permits were assigned to seasonal work and 78,500 to dependent non-seasonal work. Students and other foreigners with non-work permits have the option of converting to work permits within the limits of the quota (3,500 in 2006 of whom 2,000 in dependent work and 1,500 in self-employment). It is worth noting that family reunification in Italy is exempt from the quotas, and that those with a family permit are allowed, but not required, to work.

Although annual quotas are to be used for immigrants entering Italy through the legal procedure for employment purposes, they have often been used by undocumented immigrants who already reside and work in Italy in order to legalize their status. Indeed, the initial legal provision was adapted to reflect reality by allowing undocumented immigrant workers to apply for a residence permit from within Italy, provided their employer is willing to undertake the procedure of regularization (Triandafyllidou and Veikou, 2001).

The gap between the planned legal quotas, the demand for foreign labour and the immigration pressure from non-EU countries continuously produce large numbers of undocumented immigrants. Italy's geographical location in the centre of the Mediterranean and its extensive coastline make it a relatively accessible country to illegal immigrants. It is also common practice for immigrants to enter Italy on a tourist visa and overstay and/or abuse their visa. Furthermore, the existence of a considerable informal economy, the rapid growth of the domestic and personal services sector and the predominance of small businesses where unregistered labour can be hidden with greater ease, provide work for undocumented migrants.

The systematic inflow of undocumented immigrants has led to periodic regularization programmes. Five such programmes have taken place in the last 20 years: 1986, 1990, 1995, 1998 and 2002, involving more than two million immigrants. These programmes provide an indication of the number of undocumented immigrants residing in Italy in each period. It should be noted, however, that some were repeat regularizations of immigrants who had fallen back into an irregular status after failing to meet the criteria for a permit renewal.

The latest regularization, in September 2002 (approved by Law 189/2002), aimed to regularize two types of irregular immigrant workers: maids and private carers, on one hand, and workers in factories and industry (mainly in the north of Italy) on the other. Previously, documented immigrants whose residence permits had expired were also eligible to apply, provided they had been hired before 10 June 2002, and had never received an expulsion order. There were 704,113 such applications – indeed, a record number compared to all other regularization programmes in Southern Europe (Caritas, 2004). The impact of this regularization was to increase the legally resident population of foreigners by about 50 per cent in some areas of northern Italy.

The Italian immigrant population: main demographic and social features

As can be seen in Table 14.1, between 1986 and 2005, the legally resident foreign population in Italy rose from under 300,000 to an estimated 3.0 million (including EU Member State nationals, and minors), thereby accounting for 5.2 per cent of the total resident population (Caritas, 2005, p. 97). The legally resident foreign population rose by 4 per cent from 1991 (see Table 14.2), also because of workers regularized under the 2002 Law. Among immigrants with legal stay status, short-term employment contracts predominate (70.6 per cent), whereas long-term employment contracts are rather rare. Fewer women than men have a work contract for an indefinite period.

Table 14.1   Foreign residents in Italy holding a residence permit (1986–2005)

Year	Total with residence permits	Of whom non-EU
1986	289,068	151,714
1990	550,457	422,489
1995	677,791	563,158
1996	729,159	606,974
1997	986,020	857,897
1998	1,022,896	887,689
1999	1,090,820	948,692
2000	1,340,655	1,194,792
2001	1,379,749	1,233,584
2002	1,448,392	1,308,335
2003	1,503,286	1,352,420
2004	2,193,999	2,040,530
2005	3,035,000	

Note: The table refers to the total number of foreign citizens (excluding minors) residing legally in Italy.
Source: Adapted from Zincone 2000; Caritas 2001, 2002, 2003, 2004, 2005, 2006.

Table 14.2   Italian and foreign residents in Italy (non-EU, including minors)

Population – official data	1991	2001	2004
Total population of Italy	56,778,031	56,995,744	58,462,375
Of which foreigners	692,630	1,448,000	2,786,340
In %	1.2	2.5	4.5

Source: Istat (http://www.istat.it/); Dossier Caritas 2002, 2005.

The migrant population in Italy is quite heterogeneous in terms of ethnic origin. There are no dominant nationalities, although the 10 largest groups at the end of 2003 were Romanians (10.9 per cent of the total foreign population), Albanians (10.6 per cent), Moroccans (10.4 per cent), Ukrainians (5.1 per cent), Chinese (4.6 per cent), Filipinos (3.4 per cent), Poles (3.0 per cent), Tunisians (2.8 per cent), Americans (2.2 per cent), and Senegalese (2.2 per cent). In sum, these 10 groups represent just over half of the total immigrant population (see Table 14.3).

Table 14.3   Stocks of immigrant population by country of origin (December 2003)

Country of origin	Number	% of total number
Romania	239,426	10.9
Albania	233,616	10.6
Morocco	227,940	10.4
Ukraine	112,802	5.1
China	100,109	4.6
Philippines	73,847	3.4
Poland	65,847	3.0
Tunisia	60,572	2.8
USA	48,286	2.2
Senegal	47,762	2.2

Source: Caritas 2004.

Owing to an increasing demand for care-providers, the number of female immigrants registered in Italy has increased significantly in more recent years. From a total number of approximately 2.2 million foreign residents in Italy at the end of 2004, 1,344,000 were women (Caritas, 2005, p. 132). The largest groups originate from Romania, Ukraine, Albania and Morocco. There are significant differences in gender distribution among different nationality groups. For instance, the Ukrainian community is characterized by a strong female presence (84.6 per cent). The same gender distribution applies to the Polish and other East-European Communities (Russian, Moldavian), as well as the Latin American ones (Caritas, 2005, p. 140). On the other hand, Moroccans, Tunisians, Senegalese and Egyptians are, by a large majority, men.

The impact of family reunification on Italian immigration flows is still relatively low. In 2003, 24.3 per cent of residence permits were issued for reasons of family reunification (Caritas, 2004). Foreigners who have held a permit for dependent work or self-employment, study or religious reasons for at least one year, or a residence card (Art. 29) can apply for reunification with: a) their spouse; b) dependent children; c) dependent parents. Parents over the age of 65 are allowed to enter under family reunion only if they can prove that no other child can provide for them in their native country, while siblings and other relatives are not entitled to legal entry.

There is no dominant religion among immigrants in Italy. According to Caritas (2005), in December 2005 22.6 per cent of immigrants were Catholic, 20.3 per cent professed other Christian religions and 33.0 per cent were Muslims, while the remainder claimed they belonged to either another or to no religion.

Most immigrants are young people, aged between 20 and 40 years, who are in Italy for economic reasons. As regards integration into the labour market, immigrants are employed in specific sectors usually characterized by tough working conditions, namely strenuous physical effort, endurance, overtime and night shifts (that is, working in small manufacturing firms, the construction industry, agriculture, catering and domestic services). Immigrant workers usually take jobs that the native population is unwilling to take. These occupations have been described by Ambrosini and Berti (2003) as the 'five-p jobs': *pesanti, precari, pericolosi, poco pagati, penalizzati socialmente* (heavy, precarious, dangerous, poorly paid, socially penalized), also known as the 'three-d jobs': dirty, dangerous, and demanding. Immigrant women are typically employed in the informal economy as housekeepers or private carers for the elderly. Research on the Italian labour market suggests that self-employment is a desirable objective for immigrants and, in fact, in more recent years the number of 'ethnic' enterprises has increased. In June 2004, 71,843 ethnic enterprises were registered at the Chamber of Commerce (Caritas 2004: 296).

Earlier studies (Reyneri, 1998; Zanfrini, 2002) found that high percentages of immigrants have a relatively high level of education and professional skills, yet take up unskilled jobs in Italy, as these are the only ones available. According to Caritas (2005, p. 99), among adult immigrants resident in Italy, 12.1 per cent possess a university degree, 27.8 per cent have a high school diploma, and only a mere 2.5 per cent have not had any schooling. Very few immigrants obtained the recognition of their previous educational attainments by Italian authorities (Zanfrini, 2002).

Asylum seekers have traditionally been only a small component of total migration flows in Italy (around 10,000 applications annually), and delays in the asylum procedure, coupled with a lack of housing and social support, have meant that many asylum seekers fail to appear at their hearing and are presumed to have moved elsewhere. Under the Dublin Convention,[6] many are sent back to await a new hearing. The average wait for an asylum hearing is 12–15 months, during which applicants have no right to work. Public support is available only for the first 45 days, after which applicants are left without any support, although medical care is guaranteed. In recent years, requests for asylum have come primarily from Turkish and Iraqi Kurds, Pakistanis, citizens of former-Yugoslavia (Kosovo in particular) and some African countries. In 2003, Italy received 13,455 asylum applications (Caritas, 2004, p. 502), of which less than 10 per cent were accepted. Nevertheless, acceptance rates have varied significantly during the last decade. When recognized, refugees receive a two-year renewable residence permit allowing them to work and have access to public assistance. After five years, they can apply for citizenship.

Naturalization

Italian citizenship and the possibilities for the naturalization of foreigners are defined by Law 91/1992 implemented by Presidential Decree No. 572/1993. The law is based on a combination of the *ius sanguinis* and *ius soli* principles. A child can become a citizen through descent (parental citizenship) or by birth within the Italian territory, if certain conditions are satisfied. Citizenship is automatically granted to children of at least one Italian parent, regardless of place of birth; to children born in Italy to unknown or stateless parents, to minors whose parents become Italian citizens, and to foreign children adopted by Italian citizens. The law also provides that foreign citizens who are able to demonstrate that at least one parent or grandparent was born with Italian citizenship have the right to citizenship.[7] The 1992 citizenship law also allowed those who had 'lost' their citizenship under the previous law to regain it. When the re-acquisition period ended in 1997, 163,756 former Italian citizens had regained their citizenship. Of these, 75 per cent were emigrants to the Americas, and almost all the rest were emigrants in Europe. There is an accelerated procedure for those born in Italy from non-Italian parents and continuously resident in Italy until 18 years of age. Upon turning 18, these second-generation individuals have one year to request citizenship. Moreover, citizenship may be acquired following marriage with an Italian citizen. Among the 13,420 applications accepted in 2003, 11,300 were through marriage (Caritas, 2004, p. 148).

---

6   The 1990 Dublin Convention (ratified by Italy in 1992, but effective since 1997) introduced a second norm by which a request for asylum can be refused if such a request has already been made in a country which guarantees political and civil rights.

7   In this case, certain conditions have to be satisfied: male applicants must undergo their military service in Italy; the applicant must work for the Italian state, either in Italy or abroad, and request citizenship; or the applicant is an 18-year-old, resident for at least two years in Italy.

An individual can request citizenship based on length of residence in Italy. Residence requirements vary depending on the country of origin. For EU citizens, four years are required; for adopted foreigners who are no longer minors, or for refugees and stateless persons, five years; and for non-EU citizens, ten years of residence are necessary. Double citizenship is also permitted. However, the bureaucratic procedure when applying for naturalization is complex, time-consuming and hard work. As a result, it effectively acts as a deterrent to potential applicants. Italy has one of the lowest naturalization rates, a high rejection rate of applications (45 per cent) and a very long time for receiving a decision (Caritas, 2003, p. 159).

Immigrant rights and participation in public life – issues of immigrant integration

Italy's integration policy adopts a rather 'paternalistic' approach: immigrants are seen as socially weak subjects and, as such, are marginalized as civic actors (Kosic and Triandafyllidou, 2006). An overview of the literature on civic participation of immigrants revealed that the integration of immigrants in Italy has not been given its due attention in the literature.

As early as 1986, immigration laws set up structures and channels that have encouraged civic participation of immigrants in consultative bodies at the municipal, provincial, regional and national levels. Particularly relevant for the promotion of immigrant civic participation was Law 40/1998 (Caponio, 2000; Caponio and Dota, 2001; Zincone, 2001). This law includes provisions for the support of immigrant associations, through governmental bodies, NGOs and non-profit associations, which assist both the social integration of immigrants and the promotion of 'knowledge and [the] valorization of cultural, social, economic and religious expressions of legally resident immigrants ...' (Art. 40.) Furthermore, of great relevance was the implementation of Art. 3 (paragraph 6), which stated that representatives of immigrant associations should take part in the Territorial Immigration Councils. According to Article 57 of Law 40/1998, immigrant associations must be represented in these Councils by at least two members, and another two members must be Italian citizens representing volunteer associations.

Nonetheless, the wide range of consultative bodies instituted at the local, regional and, to a certain extent, national level have not significantly contributed to increasing the political involvement and/ or influence of immigrants even though they have institutionalized their involvement in local issues (Martiniello, 1999). Such integration and immigrant civic participation is given scope to function bottom-up through non-state agencies such as the Church, non-governmental organizations and trade unions (CNEL, 1999, 2003; Carpo et al., 2002; Meli and Enereuzor, 2003; Attanasio and Facchini, 2004; Bentivogli and Geria, 2005). Their networks are active in various fields ranging from primary assistance (food, accommodation, help to find a job) to new immigrants, including those who arrive undocumented, to a wider range of social services (such as assistance in dealing with the national bureaucracy, organization of cultural festivities, or courses in the Italian language). Immigrants actively engage in these organizations either as appointed or as elected members.

Immigrants are also active in ethnic (both mono- and multi/interethnic) associations. The number of associations varies among immigrant groups. We know little about the type and level of involvement of members of these associations. Nonetheless, these associations are an important referent, both for the communities to which they belong, and for the local institutions, since they may represent immigrant populations in the consultative bodies mentioned above as well as in instances of formal social dialogue. The immigrants' associations' field of action is focused on the reproduction and protection of the culture of origin, or to offering assistance to immigrants.

Many difficulties that affect civic participation have to do with structural problems which may prevent civic activism both at the individual and at the group level. The most important hurdles include lack of funds, logistic support, information, space, and suitable resources. The limited political rights that are offered to third country nationals residing in Italy necessarily restrict the scope and frequency of independent migrant activism.

European legislation has become increasingly open to the granting of political rights to non-EU citizens. The granting of the local vote to resident immigrants is provided for by Article 8b of the Treaty of Maastricht, and subsequently by Article 19 of the Treaty of Amsterdam. Italy, however, has never ratified the latter. Moreover, in 1992, the Council of Europe issued the 'Convention on the Participation of Foreigners in Public Life at the Local Level', which Italy only partially ratified in 1994. The Convention aims to improve the integration of foreign residents into the life of the community. This is thought to be achieved through guaranteeing them the basic rights which are also important for the maintenance and expression of their cultural identity. Such rights include freedom of expression, freedom of assembly and the right to free association. Furthermore, the European Convention stipulates that every foreign resident should be granted the right to vote and to stand for election in local authority elections, provided that s/he has been a lawful and habitual resident in the State concerned for the five years preceding the elections. The chapter which provides for the granting of the right to vote in local elections, however, had not been accepted in Italy at the time of writing (June 2007).

Law 40/1998 originally contained the proposal of extending the vote in local elections to non-EU citizens who are holders of the residence card (Carta di soggiorno). That proposal was later presented in the Parliament by Gianfranco Fini, secretary of Alleanza Nazionale and Minister of Foreign Affairs between 2001 and 2006. A proposal to revise Article 48[8] of the Constitution (Chamber Act 4,167) was also put forward, but did not get onto the parliamentary agenda for discussion before the end of that legislature (April 2006). One of the most common concerns regarding immigrant participation in local elections was that granting the right to vote would lead to the formation of ethnic parties (Zincone, 2000). Some municipalities (such as Genoa, Venice, Turin, Pisa, Ragusa, Brescia and others) have proposed to modify their Statute to allow immigrants the right to vote at the local level.

Political parties are principal players in matters concerning migrant civic participation in Italy. This becomes particularly problematic when one considers that there is a strong (at least implicit) reluctance in the effective integration of immigrants in Italian political party rank and file. This is partly because, unless they have been naturalized, immigrants do not yet enjoy voting rights, and partly because non-EU citizens are still widely perceived as outsiders to national politics.

Public and media discourses on migration

Italians with their long emigration history have often considered their country to be 'different' and 'immune' to the racism experienced in other countries. However, Italian public attitudes, initially characterized by 'social tolerance' towards immigrants, have given way to hostile and xenophobic behaviour in recent years (Bonifazi and Cerbara, 1999; Triandafyllidou, 1999). It is since the 1990s that creeping xenophobia in new forms (Balbo and Manconi, 1990) or virulent and explicit racist reactions, such as those seen in the propaganda of the northern Lombard League, have emerged.

These hostile attitudes have surfaced against a backdrop of various factors. First, the number of immigrants to Italy has steadily risen over the past few years (that is, an average influx increase of 11.4 per cent between 1990 and 2000[9]). Second, the country has suffered from unclear and

---

8   Article 48 confers the right to vote to 'all the citizens': the problem is if the reference to citizens should be understood in its strict sense or simple as a synonym of 'person' (Zincone, 2000).

9   See EUROSTAT at http://europa.eu.int/comm/eurostat/.

underdeveloped immigration and settlement policies, combined with an inefficient public administration responsible for the management of the phenomenon (Zincone, 1999). Immigrants in Italy, as in many countries, were suitable 'scapegoats' for all kinds of problems that society was facing. The idea of immigration as a 'problem' develops with reference to three main points: a) a security threat (the invasion threat, undocumented immigration, and criminality); b) a threat to jobs (the destabilisation of the labour market); and c) a threat to cultural and religious identity (Diamanti and Bordignon, 2002).

During the last two decades, the Italian mass media have promoted a negative and highly stereotyped image of immigrants (e.g., CENSIS, 2002; for a review, see Sciortino and Colombo, 2004). The main criticism against the media is the tendency to transmit alarmist information on immigration. News reports have been linking immigration and undocumented (clandestine) entry to Italy, transforming all immigrants into 'illegals', 'criminals' or 'threats' for a large part of public opinion.

Several studies carried out during recent years have shown how mass media have focused on immigrants mainly when they were involved in criminal episodes (CENSIS, 2002; ter Wal, 2001). On the contrary, the everyday aspect of integration processes does not appear in communications. Research carried out by Cotesta (1999) revealed that, between 1991 and 1997, nearly half the articles dealing with the presence of immigrants in Italy concerned incidents of conflict and only about one-third was devoted to some in-depth analysis of their living conditions. A study of the language used in the newspaper titles and articles reveals that 'Albanians', 'immigrant', 'arrested', 'public force', 'clandestine', '*extracomunitari*', 'drugs', 'Moroccan' and 'refugee' were the words used most frequently to describe migration-related events (Stoppiello, 1999). The ethnic, racial and national identity of the groups or individuals involved were consistently referred to by the media when immigrants' arrests or accusations were mentioned (Dal Lago, 1999).

The other common theme in Italian political discourse and mass media is their perceived threat to Italian 'national identity' (Marletti, 1995; Tambini, 2001). Italy is a country that lacks a strong sense of nationhood (Diamanti, 1999; Doumanis, 2001; Triandafyllidou, 2005); but the perceived threat posed by Muslim immigration produces a re-interpretation of religion as an identity marker for the definition of national identity. When reporting on cultural and religious difference at the collective level, namely as regards the cultural and religious rights of the immigrant population, the coverage becomes ambivalent at best. Media discourse emphasizes that diversity can pose a threat to social cohesion and national culture. While living together with people from different cultures may be feasible at the individual level, it is presented as an almost insurmountable challenge at the societal level (Triandafyllidou, 2002).

In recent years, some media have developed a more sensitive approach when addressing immigrants. Moreover, they have paid some attention to immigrant integration and to the issue of multiculturalism. In July 1999, the AGCOM (Italian Regulatory Authority in the Communications Sector) approved a project for the monitoring of the content of television programmes. This monitoring project focuses on four main areas: 1) user protection (especially of minors); 2) programming obligations of licensees (for example, European quotas); 3) advertising (for example, transmission time); and 4) pluralism (political, cultural, social). The Service Contract (2000–02),[10] signed by the Ministry of Communications, the Government and RAI (*Radiotelevisione Italiana*), defines the functions, contents and mission of the Italian public broadcasting service. One of the assumptions underlying the contract is that it is 'an explicit duty of the public broadcasting service to guarantee the display of the multi-coloured realities of the world of employment and emerging social and cultural realities in a weak condition on the level of information tools, paying particular

---

10   http://www.medialaw.it/Rai/contratto.htm.

attention to those relating to voluntary services, feminism, environmentalism, problems of elderly, immigration, and so on'. Moreover, Art. 6 *bis* stipulates that special attention shall be paid to programming for foreign citizens: '...the licensee shall undertake to dedicate special attention, possibly with special programmes in foreign languages, to the social, religious, employment problems of foreign European Union and non-European Union citizens in Italy, also for the purpose of promoting integration processes and for guaranteeing adequate information about the rights and duties of immigration citizens'.

Despite these generous provisions defining the role of the public media as a lever for promoting multiculturalism, equality and social inclusion of foreign residents in Italy, the reality on the ground is disappointing. Several studies (for example COSPE, 2003) have shown that ethnic media are largely non-existent while cultural diversity/minority broadcasting is scheduled outside peak times or is outsourced to special channels and thus plays a marginal role in promoting multiculturalism.

Concluding remarks

This chapter has provided an overview of recent immigration trends in Italy. It has focused on employment characteristics, labour market dynamics and the characteristics of the immigrant population itself. It has also covered the main elements of current Italian immigration policy; namely the quota system for workers, permit types and conditions of stay. Moreover, it has offered a description of Italy's national integration policy, looking at the main features of policy for settlement of migrant workers and their civic participation.

It is important to specify the meaning accorded to the word 'integration' in Italian immigration policy. Italy, as a whole, is not formally a 'migration' country, like Canada or Australia, nor is it declaredly 'multicultural', as are the Netherlands and Britain. Its migration policy is based on limiting migration into the country to specific labour market sectors. At the same time, immigrant workers have certain rights such as family reunification, gradual reassurance regarding the possibility of staying in the country, and parity of access to public services. The Italian citizenship law is separate from the 1998 immigration framework law and, with 90 per cent of applications for naturalization being rejected, it is highly restrictive in both rhetoric and practice. Nonetheless, Law 40/1998 rests on three pillars, of which one is 'integration'. The broad assumption underlying the legislation is that labour market integration – employment – is a necessary and sufficient condition to guarantee social integration, when coupled with parity of right of access to public services.

Several NGOs, trade unions and charitable organizations have been active since the 1980s in providing assistance to immigrants in the process of integration. To facilitate contacts, these organizations have encouraged the civic participation of immigrants and their involvement in representative bodies. Furthermore, these organizations have provided support to immigrant associations. Immigrant participation in trade unions, voluntary organizations and immigrants' associations ensures their access to what is called 'intermediate political rights'. From an institutional perspective, civic and political participation remains mostly the realm of Italian citizens and naturalized immigrants.

References

Ambrosini, M. and Berti, F. (2003), *Immigrazione e lavoro* (Immigration and Labour). Milan: FrancoAngeli.

Attanasio, P. and Facchini, A. (2004), 'Rappresentanza politica e diritto di voto' (Political Representation and Right to Vote), in Caritas and Migrantes (eds) *Immigrazione: Dossier Statistico*, 186–95. Rome: Antarem.

Balbo, L. and Manconi, L. (1990), *I razzismi possibili* (Possible Racisms). Milan: Feltrinelli.

Bentivogli, F. and Geria, A. (2005), 'Immigrati, tutela contrattuale, associazionismo' (Immigrants, Protection of Work Contract, and Associationism), in Caritas and Migrantes (eds) *Immigrazione: Dossier Statistico*. 308–317. Rome: Antarem.

Bonifazi, C. and Cerbara, L. (1999), 'Gli immigrati stranieri: valutazioni, conoscenze e giudizi degli italiani' (Foreign immigrants: evaluations, knowledge and opinions of Italians). *Studi Emigrazione*, **133**(133), 3–38.

Butt, P. A. (1994), 'European Union Immigration Policy: Phantom, Fantasy or Fact?' *West European Politics*, **17**(2), 168–91.

Caponio, T. (2000), 'Partecipazione politica' (Political Participation), in Zincone, G. (ed.) *Primo rapporto sull'integrazione degli immigrati in Italia* (First report on imimigrant integration in Italy), 355–400. Bologna: Il Mulino.

Caponio, T. and Dota, S. (2001), 'Partecipazione politica e rappresentanza' (Political Participation and Representation), in Zincone, G. (ed.) *Secondo rapporto sull'integrazione degli immigrati in Italia* (Second Report on Immigrant Integration in Italy), 309–327. Bologna: Il Mulino.

Caritas (2001), *Immigrazione: Dossier Statistico*. Roma: Antarem.

—— (2002), *Immigrazione: Dossier Statistico*. Roma: Antarem.

—— (2003), *Immigrazione: Dossier Statistico*. Roma: Antarem.

—— (2004), *Immigrazione: Dossier Statistico*. Roma: Antarem.

—— (2005), *Immigrazione: Dossier Statistico*. Roma: Antarem.

—— (2006), *Immigrazione: Dossier Statistico*. Roma: Antarem.

Cotesta, V. (1999), 'Mass Media, Ethnic Conflicts and Migration. Research on Italian Newspapers in the Nineties', *Studi Emigrazione*, **XXXVI**(135), 387–499.

D'Alimonte, R. and Bartolini, S. (eds) (1997), *Maggioritario per caso. Le elezioni politiche del 1996* (A majoritarian system by accident. The 1996 election). Bologna: Il Mulino.

Dal Lago, A. (1999), *Non persone. L'esclusione dei migranti in una società globale* (Non persons. The exclusion of immigrants in a global society). Milano: Feltrinelli.

Diamanti, I. (1999), 'Ha senso ancora discutere di nazione?' *Rassegna Italiana di Sociologia*, **XL**(2), 293–321.

Doumanis, N. (2001), *Italy: Inventing the Nation*. London: Arnold.

Kosic, A. and Triandafyllidou, A. (2006), 'Urban cultural policy and immigrants in Rome: multiculturalism or simply "paternalism"?', in Meinhof, U. H. and Triandafyllidou, A. (eds) *Transcultural Europe: Cultural Policy in the Changing European Space*, 157–78. Basingstoke: Palgrave Macmillan.

Marletti, C. (1995), *Televisione e islam: immagini e stereotipi dell'islam nella comunicazione italiana* (Television and Islam: images and stereotypes of Islam in the Italian communication media). Torino, RAI - Nuova ERI.

Martiniello, M. (1999), 'The Limits of Consultative Politics for Immigrants and Ethnic Immigrant Minorities', in Council of Europe, Directorate of Social and Economic Affairs (ed.) *Political and Social Participation of Immigrants through Consultative Bodies*. Strasbourg: Council of Europe Publishing.

Meli, A. and Enereuzor, U.C. (2003), *Participation of Foreigners in Public Life at the Local Level.* COSPE: National Focal Point of the European Monitoring Centre on Racism and Xenophobia.

Reyneri, E. (1998), 'The Mass Legalization of Migrants in Italy: Permanent or Temporary Emergence from the Underground Economy?' *South European Society and Politics*, 3(3), 82–102.

Sciortino, G. and Colombo, A. (2004), 'The Flows and the Flood: The Public Discourse on Immigration in Italy, 1969-2001', *Journal of Modern Italian Studies*, 9(1), 94–113.

Stetter, S. (2000), 'Regulating migration: authority delegation in justice and home affairs', *Journal of European Public Policy*, 7(1), 81–103.

Stoppiello, S. (1999), 'Nomi e Immagini dell'Altro. Un'Analisi Multidimensionale della Stampa' (Names and Images of the Other. A Multidimensional Analysis of the Press). *Studi Emigrazione*, 36(135), 417–42.

Tambini, D. (2001), *Nationalism in Italian Politics: the Stories of the Northern League, 1980-2000.* London: Routledge.

ter Wal, J. (2001), 'Minacce territoriali, socio-economiche e di sicurezza: immagine degli immigrati nella stampa quotidiana' (Territorial, socio-economic and security threats: the image of immigrants in the daily press). *Incontri*, 16(1–2), 67–78.

Triandafyllidou, A. (1999), 'Nation and Immigration: a Study of the Italian Press Discourse', *Social Identities*, 5(1), 65–88. [DOI: 10.1080/13504639951626]

—— (2005), 'Italy and Europe: Internal Others and External Challenges to National Identity' in Ichijo, A. and Spohn, W. (eds) *Entangled Identities: Nations and Europe*, 88–105. Aldershot: Ashgate.

Triandafyllidou, A. and Veikou, M. (2001), 'Immigration Policy and its Implementation in Italy' in Triandafyllidou, A. (ed.) *The State of the Art in Migration Pathways: A Historic, Demographic and Policy Review of four Countries of the European Union*, 63–85. Brussels: European Commission Research Directorate.

Zanfrini, L., *Sostenere il lavoro. Le attività dei Centri per l'Impiego a favore dei lavoratori extra-communitari* (Employment support. The Activities of Employment Centres for Non-EU Workers), unpublished report.

—— (2003), 'Employment Needs of Firms and Planning of Flows', in unpublished IRES Report.

Zincone, G. (1999), 'Rappresentanza e diritto di voto' (Representation and the Right to Vote), in Atti del Convegno 'Partecipazione e rappresentanza politica degli immigrati' (Conference proceedings 'Participation and political representation of immigrants'), Commissione per le Politiche di Integrazione degli Immigrati, Dipartimento degli Affari Sociali, Presidenza del Consiglio dei Ministri, Roma, 21 giugno, 1999.

—— (2000), *Primo rapporto sull'integrazione degli immigrati in Italia* (First Report on Immigrant Integration in Italy). Bologna: Il Mulino.

—— (2001), *Secondo rapporto sull'integrazione degli immigrati in Italia* (Second Report on Immigrant Integration in Italy). Bologna: Il Mulino.

Zincone, G. and Ponzo, I. (2006), 'Out of Paradigms: the Italian Reasonable Way to Integration', *Canadian Diversité*, 5(1), 51–56.

Internet-based references

Campani, G. and De Bonis, A. (2003), *Migration Policies in Italy* (available at http://www. emzberlin.de/projekte_e/pj32_1pdf/MigPol/MigPol_Italy.pdf).

Carpo, F. et al. (2002), *Immigrants and Political Participation: the Case of Italy*, SATCHEL Research/action on citizenship education for old, new and future EU citizens (available at http:// www.retericerca.it/Satchel/documents/Rapporto%20finale%20Italia-EN.pdf).

CENSIS (2002), *L'immagine degli immigrati e minoranze etniche nei Media* (The Image of Immigrants and Ethnic Minorities in the Media), Final Report (available at http://www.edscuola. it/archivio/stranieri/immagine_immigrati.pdf).

Chaloff, J. (2003), 'Italy', in Niessen, J. and Y. et al. (eds) *EU and US Approaches to the Management of Immigration*, Brussels: Migration Policy Group (available at http://www.migpolgroup.com/ publications/default.asp).

CNEL (1999), *Primo rapporto sulla rappresentanza degli immigrati* (First Report on Immigrant Representation), Roma: Documents CNEL (available at http://www.portalecnel.it/portale/ pubblicazioni.nsf/).

—— (2003), *Secondo rapporto sulla rappresentanza degli immigrati* (Second Report on Immigrant Representation), Roma: Documenti CNEL (available at http://www.portalecnel.it/portale/ pubblicazioni.nsf/).

COSPE (2003), *Media e Immigrazione Rapporto sulla Settimana Europea di Monitoraggio dei Media in Italia* [Media and Immigration. Report on European Week of Monitoring Media in Italy]. Documents COSPE (available at http://www.cospe.it/news/media.pdf).

Diamanti, I. and Bordignon, F. (2002), 'Migration and Citizenship Rights in Europe: European Citizens' attitudes', Quaderni FNE. Collana Osservatori, No. 21 – November 2005 (available at http://www.fondazionenordest.net/uploads/media/english_version.pdf).

Excelsior Unioncamere (2004), *Ministry of Labour*, Documento programmatico 2004–2006 [Programme Document 2004–2006] (available at http://excelsior.unioncamere.net).

Triandafyllidou, A. (2002), 'Religious Diversity and Multiculturalism in Southern Europe: The Italian Mosque Debate', *Sociological Research Online*, 7(1) (available at www.socresonline. org.uk/7/1/ triandafyllidou.html).

Chapter 15

Latvia

Inese Šūpule

Since the collapse of the Soviet Union Latvia has changed its status from a destination country to an immigrant-exporting country. The main migratory inflows between 1951 and 1990 were from the nearest Soviet Republics, and particularly Russia, Belarus and Ukraine. As a result, the percentage of ethnic Latvians decreased from 77 per cent in 1935 to 52 per cent in 1989, while the percentage of Russians, Belarusians and Ukrainians increased. The significant changes in the ethnic composition of Latvia's population are the core reasons for the rather negative attitudes towards immigrants and immigration in Latvia. Nonetheless, since 1991 net migration in Latvia has been negative as, on average, more people leave Latvia than arrive. Indeed, every year about 1,500 people immigrate, and about 4,000 people emigrate.

The statistics regarding the resident population by citizenship at the beginning of 2006 show that 80 per cent of all residents in Latvia are citizens of Latvia, whereas 18 per cent are non-citizens. The group of non-citizens comprises those who immigrated into Latvia during the Soviet time, as well as their descendants. Under Latvian legislation, former USSR citizens who had neither Latvian nor other citizenship received the status of Latvian non-citizens in 1995. People who have citizenship of other countries and live in Latvia are termed as foreigners. Altogether, the number of foreigners is very small (about 1.6 per cent), including 1 per cent of residents who are citizens of the Russian Federation, and about 0.6 per cent who are citizens of other countries.

Three phases of migration can be observed in Latvia after regaining independence. The years 1991–1993, which were characterized by the collapse of the Soviet Union and the fall of the iron curtain, were marked by radical changes in Latvia's political and economic systems. These changes provided the fertile ground facilitating emigration from Latvia. After a second phase of normalization when migration decreased (the years 1994–2000), a new wave of short-term emigration for work in different EU countries, and in particular Ireland, marked the third phase (beginning with 2000, increasing in 2004). According to official estimates, approximately 50,000 people moved for work purposes to other EU countries. Recently, going abroad for work has gained a lot of public attention, and experts note both the positive and negative consequences of this trend. The question that is posed is whether emigration for work purposes can be expected to be a rather short-term migration experience, and whether people currently working in different EU countries will eventually return or decide to stay in other EU countries.

Major developments in Latvia's immigration policy

In order to understand the attitudes towards immigration and Latvia's immigration policy, it is necessary to retrace the history of migration in Latvia. The most important immigration flows to Latvia occurred during the Soviet time. After the Second World War many people from other USSR republics were brought in and the newcomers received different kinds of benefits, including new flats in newly built houses, while a number of local people lived in modest flats without modern conveniences. The discontent with Soviet policy, the sharp decrease in the percentage of ethnic Latvians and the increase in the number of Russians, Belarusians and Ukrainians, have influenced both the public debate and Latvia's post-independence immigration and citizenship policies.

The possibility of regulating immigration policy in Latvia appeared only after 1991. The 1992 Law on Migration (Vēbers, 1997, p. 152) stopped the practice adopted during the years of Soviet occupation of not regulating immigration from other parts of the USSR and recommended the regulation of immigration and residence in Latvia.

After independence, the early 1990s were characterized by net emigration (see Table 15.1). This has been explained by the radical changes in political and economic systems in Latvia and the USSR in general, the fact that the USSR army left Latvia, and the possibility of moving to Western countries.

Table 15.1   International long-term migration

Year	Immigration		Emigration		Net migration	
	total	average per year	total	average per year	total	average per year
1951-1960	639,880	63,988	459,832	45,983	180,048	18,005
1961-1970	476,934	47,693	335,872	33,587	141,062	14,106
1971-1980	548,643	54,864	428,235	42,823	120,408	12,041
1981-1990	506,576	50,658	423,953	42,395	82,623	8,263
1991-1995	30,842	6,168	168,230	33,646	-137,388	-27,478
1996-2000	12,223	2,445	47,064	9,413	-34,841	-6,968

Source: Central Statistical Bureau of Latvia (2006), Demographic Yearbook of Latvia. 2005 (Riga: Central Statistical Bureau of Latvia).

The data on long-term migration show that, after 1995, departures from Latvia decreased from the high number observed in the early 1990s. Between 1996 and 2000, the net outflow from Latvia averaged 6,968 persons/year. Between 2001 and 2004, however, the corresponding number fell to an average of 2,229 persons/year.

During the last few years, long term international immigration to Latvia has not changed significantly. During 2000, 627 immigrants were recorded, while during 2004, 1,665 immigrants were recorded. The migration statistics indicate that out of all immigrants in 2004, 16 per cent came from the Russian Federation, 15 per cent from Lithuania, 10 per cent from Germany, 7 per cent from the USA and 7 per cent from the UK. The data on emigration show that 38 per cent have moved to Russia, 8 per cent to Germany, 6 per cent to Ukraine, 6 per cent to the USA, 5 per cent to Lithuania, 4 per cent to the UK and 4 per cent to Belarus. Altogether, data analysis of the long-term migratory flows reveals that migration to and from Russia, Belarus and Ukraine has decreased. On the contrary, immigration from and emigration to other countries, particularly westwards, has slightly increased. Indeed, in 1995, more than 80 per cent of all immigrants were from Russia, Belarus and Ukraine and less than 20 per cent from other countries.

Immigration policy in Latvia has also been influenced by the process of Latvia's accession to the European Union. From 1998, Latvia began adapting its national legislation to the standards of the European Union. Moreover, both the Immigration (2003) and Asylum Laws (2002) were developed. The 2003 Immigration Law has not triggered much public attention, as economic conditions do not encourage immigration into Latvia.

The latest migration trends show an increase in short-term emigration for work purposes and this process has caused particular social problems and concerns in Latvia. Since the EU enlargement in 2004, only three countries, namely Ireland, Great Britain and Sweden, have been open for the free movement of workers. Many inhabitants of Latvia have moved for work abroad (mostly to Ireland), but this process has not been accurately recorded, as this has been considered as short-term migration. According to estimates by the Ministry of Economics, about 50,000 people have moved to EU countries for work purposes. The main reasons for labour emigration are sharp differences in salaries and discriminating and unprofessional attitudes of employers in Latvia. Employers in Latvia have to compete with employers in other countries, and, as the workforce has diminished in Latvia, for demographic and labour emigration reasons, experts have already begun to warn of the need to stop the process of labour emigration and to think about changes in regulations for workers from third countries, particularly from Russia, Belarus and Ukraine. Moreover, immigration policy has set up a rather long procedure to immigrate from Russia, Belarus and Ukraine to Latvia. However, there are thus far no policy initiatives to stop short-term emigration for work or to facilitate the immigration of guest workers.

The Latvian immigrant population: main demographic and social features

The statistics about the resident population of Latvia show that 80 per cent of all residents in Latvia are citizens of Latvia, 18 per cent have the status of Latvian non-citizen, 1 per cent of residents are citizens of the Russian Federation, and less than 0.6 per cent are citizens of other countries (see Table 15.2).

In fact, two groups of immigrants exist in Latvia – non-citizens and foreigners. Non-citizens are people who immigrated during the Soviet time and their descendants. Officially, former USSR citizens who did not have Latvian or any other citizenship, in 1995 received the status of Latvian non-citizens. Most foreigners – people who have citizenship of other countries and live in Latvia – are citizens of the Russian Federation. The peculiarity of this group is that after the USSR split, they chose to receive Russian citizenship, despite having lived in Latvia for years. So, almost all immigrants in Latvia have lived in Latvia for at least 15 or 20 years, and this is true of non-citizens and of most foreigners.

Table 15.2   Resident population of Latvia by citizenship status (1 January 2006)

	Number	%
Citizens of Latvia	1,834,282	80.07
Latvian non-citizens	418,436	18.27
Refugees	0	0.00
Alternative protection	3	0.00
Not specified	198	0.01
Others (foreigners with permanent or temporary residence permits):	37,846	1.65
Russian Federation	*25,338*	*1.11*
Lithuania	*2,674*	*0.12*
Ukraine	*2,618*	*0.11*
Belarus	*1,672*	*0.07*
Estonia	*749*	*0.03*
United States	*482*	*0.02*
Germany	*474*	*0.02*
Israel	*282*	*0.01*
Poland	*275*	*0.01*
Other countries	*3,282*	*0.14*

Source: Office of Citizenship and Migration Affairs (2006b), Resident population of Latvia by citizenship status, 01.01.2006. Statistics page (published online 14 January 2006) <http://www.pmlp.gov.lv/images/documents/8.pdf>.

Non-citizens

The problem of Latvia is the big number of non-citizens (18 per cent). The fundamental principles of the Citizenship Law (1994) were based on the fact that Latvia's independence was renewed and that all laws and the Constitution adopted during the period before Soviet and Nazi occupations remained in force. Consequently, holders of Latvian citizenship before 1940 and their descendants were automatically granted citizenship after 1991.

According to the Citizenship Law, a naturalization procedure must be followed in order for non-citizens or foreigners with permanent residence permits to become citizens of Latvia. The requirements of the naturalization procedure include five years of residency in Latvia, a legal source of income and knowledge of the state language, of the Constitution, of the Latvian anthem and of Latvian history. In general, the success rate of naturalization tests has been high, as more than 90 per cent of applicants pass at their first attempt.

The admission to citizenship through naturalization in Latvia started in February 1995. According to a number of international experts, the naturalization requirements laid down by the Citizenship Law comply with generally accepted international standards and basic principles for the formation of an integrated society (Brands Kehre and Stalidzane, 2003, p. 5). From the beginning of the naturalization process in 1995 up to the beginning of 2006, the number of non-citizens decreased from more than 29 per cent to 18 per cent.

At the beginning of 2006, there were 418,436 (18.27 per cent) non-citizens in Latvia, compared to 735,000 in 1995. Citizenship of Latvia through naturalization has been granted to 106,324 persons (data on 28 February 2006), namely, one-third of the total decrease of the number of non-citizens. Obviously, the tendency of the number of non-citizens to decrease is largely attributable to the demographic situation and to emigration rather than naturalization.

During the first three years of the process the naturalization was very slow because of the 'naturalization windows' designed to manage the anticipated large number of people wishing to naturalize by staggering the eligibility for naturalization according to the year of birth. (Priority was given to younger age groups – 20 year-olds were eligible to naturalize in 1996, 25 year-olds in 1997 and 30 year-olds in 1998).

The pace of naturalization increased rapidly after the 1998 referendum, when naturalization windows were abolished. The increase in the naturalization rate and the number of applications for naturalization which have been observed during recent years have been largely attributed to Latvia's accession to the EU.

As regards the ethnic categorization of non-citizens in Latvia, two-thirds (66 per cent) of them are Russians, 13 per cent Belarusians, 9 per cent Ukrainians, 3 per cent Poles, and 9 per cent others (see Table 15.3). Half of the non-citizens of Latvia (210,164) live in Riga, the capital of Latvia, where they represent almost one-third of the residents (29 per cent).

Table 15.3   Permanent residents of Latvia by ethnicity (1 January 2006)

	Citizens of Latvia	Non-citizens	Foreigners	Total	Total %
Latvians	1,348,354	2,053	1,082	1,351,489	59.00
Lithuanians	17,828	11,799	1,680	31,307	1.37
Estonians	1,532	630	374	2,536	0.11
Belarussians	29,238	55,254	2,102	86,594	3.78
Russians	351,876	278,213	22,115	652,204	28.47
Ukrainians	14,637	39,633	3,905	58,175	2.54
Poles	40,685	14,385	612	55,682	2.43
Jews	6,452	2,704	369	9,525	0.42
Others	23,680	13,769	5,804	43,253	1.89
In total	**1,834,282**	**418,440**	**38,043**	**2,290,765**	**100.00**
%	**80.07**	**18.27**	**1.66**	**100.00**	

Source: Naturalization Board of the Republic of Latvia, The, Facts and Statistics on Residents. A Breakdown of the Residents of Latvia Based on Nationality. Statistics page (published online 25 January 2006): <http://www.np.gov.lv/index.php?en=fakti_en&saite=residents.htm>.

Children born to non-citizens in Latvia after 1991 are entitled to register as Latvian citizens. At the beginning of 2006, 4,748 children of non-citizens have been registered as citizens of Latvia, and approximately 15,000 have remained non-citizens.

Foreigners with temporary and permanent residence permits

According to the Office of Citizenship and Migration Affairs, 37,846 foreigners resided in Latvia on 1 January 2006. Approximately one-fifth of them held temporary residence permits, while the remaining held permanent residence permits. Most foreigners enter Latvia either for family reunification purposes or for employment.

The right to apply for a permanent residence permit is extended to ten different groups. Among these are spouses and parents of a Latvian citizen or Latvian non-citizen, foreigners who have continuously stayed in the Republic of Latvia with a temporary residence permit for at least ten years, their spouses if they have continuously stayed in Latvia with a temporary residence permit for at least five years, under-age children of a foreigner who has received a permanent residence permit, and foreigners (and their spouses) who have received refugee status.

In general, to obtain a temporary residence permit a foreigner is required to present a valid health insurance policy. The temporary permits are issued for different lengths of time and according to the reason for stay in Latvia. With regard to employment permits, these are issued for the period of the employment contract if it does not exceed one year; or for a period of five years, if the employment contract is for a period longer than one year. In connection with family reunification, a temporary residence permit for one year is issued upon the first submission of documents. At the second submission of documents, a temporary residence permit for four years is issued and, at the third, a permanent residence permit is issued.

To obtain a permanent residence permit a foreigner shall present a certificate on state language skills evidencing the knowledge of the state language at level 1B. The last condition has not been applied to under-age children, to those who have received a secondary education in Latvia, to those who have made an investment of not less than LVL 600,000 (EUR 420,000) and who hold a temporary residence permit for at least last five years, to refugees and to repatriates. The right to vote in national or local elections is reserved for Latvian citizens only. Immigrants have thus to naturalize to obtain political rights in Latvia.

Asylum seekers, refugees and illegal immigrants

The number of asylum seekers and refugees is very small in Latvia. Since 1998 only 161 persons have asked for asylum in Latvia (40 from Russia, 13 from Azerbaijan, 13 from Iraq, 10 from Afghanistan, 10 from Georgia and 75 from other countries). Of these, only eight persons have received the status of refugee according to the Geneva Convention. In 2005, only 20 persons asked for the asylum in Latvia, yet no one was accorded the status of refugee (Office of Citizenship and Migration Affairs, 2006a).

The Asylum Law which came into force on 1 September 2002 provides a subsidiary protection to asylum seekers who cannot claim refugee status, yet are in need of protection. Persons under subsidiary protection (for nine or 12 months) are paid benefits in the form of a minimum monthly salary and receive the status of asylum seeker in Latvia. Persons with the status of refugee or asylum seeker may freely leave and enter Latvia, as well as invite their family members residing in foreign countries (family reunification). They also have the right to apply for a permanent residence permit, as well as all other economic, social, personal and other rights, freedoms and responsibilities provided by the Article 8 'Basic Human Rights' of Satversme ['The Constitution of Latvia']. On 1 January 2006, Latvia counted three persons with asylum seeker status.

According to the evaluation of experts, the number of asylum seekers in the near future will increase in Latvia but not as rapidly as in other European countries. This is because asylum seekers usually choose an economically stable, developed country with a high standard of living, a country where good social benefits are provided to those who have obtained asylum seeker status (Indans 2004, p. 9). In Latvia, however, social benefits are minimal.

As reported by representatives of the State Border Guards and experts from the International Migration Organization in Latvia (Indans 2004), the number of illegal immigrants in Latvia is small – some dozens – and they try to enter Latvia mainly from Ukraine and Lithuania. Ivars Zālītis, Head of the Main Office of the State Border Guards, considers that more often than not, these immigrants try to enter Latvia with the aim of continuing toward the 'old' countries of the European Union.

Immigrant rights and participation in public life – issues of immigrant integration

The legislation on immigrant (non-citizen and foreigner) rights can be divided into two parts: those regulating issues concerning citizenship and rights inherent to citizens, and those regulating issues concerning national minority rights.

The most important legislative acts regulating non-citizen rights are the legislative acts on Latvian Citizenship.

The 1991 Decree on the Renewal of Latvian Citizenship gave the legal basis for the identification of the Latvian citizenship population. According to the decree, citizenship was granted to those people who were citizens of Latvia before 1940 and their descendents. The Citizenship Law (1994) prescribes who are citizens of Latvia and who are not, and the process of naturalization. The Citizenship Law (1994) was liberalized after the referendum held on 3 October 1998, and the most important amendments made regarded the naturalization procedure – abolition of the 'window' system and simplification of the language test. The Law on the Status of Former USSR Citizens Who Do Not Have Latvian or Any Other Citizenship (1995) states that among the rights and obligations of the subjects of this law is the right of non-citizens to preserve their mother tongue and culture.

Non-citizen and foreigner participation in political life is affected by the following laws regulating participation in elections and referenda:

- the Constitution of the Republic of Latvia (Articles 8, 37, 80, 101)
- the Law on Referenda and Legislative initiatives of 31 March 1994
- the Law on the Register of Electorate of 29 January 2004.

According to these legislative acts, the right to participate in parliamentary elections, referenda and elections of local government is only granted to citizens of Latvia. Although in other countries non-citizens have the right to vote in local elections, in Latvia non-citizens are not granted this right and despite recommendations by several international institutions to change this legislation, the prevalent mood among the majority of politicians – including the President – does not provide any indication that this will even be considered.

For non-citizens, freedom of association has been limited to the right to found a political party. The 1992 Law on Public Organizations and their Associations requires a minimum of 200 founding members who are citizens in order to register a party. Although Latvian non-citizens may also participate as founders, their number must be no more than half of the founding members (Latvian Centre for Human Rights and Ethnic Studies, 2005, p. 21).

The Restoration of Independence rights of national minorities have been granted by the Law on the Unrestricted Development and Right to Cultural Autonomy of Latvia's National and Ethnic Groups passed in 1991. While the law does not define what is meant by 'national and ethnic groups', they have been granted rights to cultural autonomy and cultural self-rule.

The Council of Europe Framework Convention for the Protection of National Minorities was signed by Latvia in 1995, but was not ratified until 2005. The Convention was ratified on 26 May 2005 on the pretext that the Convention applies only to the citizens of Latvia, and that Articles 10 and 11 are in force only when they do not contradict the legislative acts of Latvia. The last pretext is stipulated so as to maintain the current situation where local names, street names and other topographical indications intended for the public are in Latvian. The pretext to Article 10 is provided to maintain the current situation in which minority languages are not used in administrative authorities and national minorities.

Both these pretexts are intended not so much to discriminate the language of national minorities but, rather, to protect the official language. Indeed, in certain areas, including the capital, Latvian is not the dominant language and Latvian legislation after regaining independence was intended to strengthen its position lost during the Soviet time.

Besides the legislative acts mentioned so far, documents concerning integration policy in Latvia are also important. In 1998, the government created a working group to draft a new policy document, notably a Framework Document for the Integration of Society in Latvia. In 2001, the Government of Latvia adopted the National Programme for the Integration of Society in Latvia, a policy framework which lays out the goals and means for minority policy and promotes social cohesion in realms such as civic participation, education and culture. Also in 2001, parliament adopted a law creating a Society Integration Foundation to administer government and donor money in support of integration-related projects. In November 2002 a new ministerial portfolio responsible for integration – that for Special Assignments for Society Integration Affairs – was created.

Under the Regulations made by the Cabinet of Ministers Nr. 612, the Secretariat of the Minister for Special Assignments for Society Integration Affairs took up its role on 1 January 2003. The main tasks of the Secretariat are to implement and coordinate the State programme 'Society Integration in Latvia' and 'The Lives in Latvia' and to implement and coordinate state support for cultural associations of ethnic minorities.

On the 25 August 2004, the Cabinet of Ministers adopted the five-year National Programme for Tolerance developed by the Secretariat of the Minister for Special Assignments for Society Integration Affairs. Ethnic and religious minorities are singled out as especially relevant groups to include in the plan to promote tolerance. The action plan includes various activities such as events to raise public awareness, seminars, brochures, travelling exhibitions, work with media and others (Latvian Centre for Human Rights and Ethnic Studies, 2005, p. 23).

The Society Integration Foundation was established on 5 July 2001. The purpose of the Foundation is to financially support projects in relation to society integration, including NGO projects in the field of ethnic integration and assistance programmes to minority cultural societies and associations, Latvian language training to naturalization applicants, research into society integration process, and others. The Foundation works closely with the Secretariat of the Minister for Special Assignments for Society Integration Affairs. The latter is producing the guidelines for the Foundation.

The participation of immigrants, namely non-citizens and foreigners, in public life is rather hard to evaluate as there are no, or very few, organizations targeting only non-citizens and foreigners. Studies of the civic participation of citizens and non-citizens reveal that citizens had participated more often in different political activities and NGOs than non-citizens. Sixty-two per cent of citizens and 88 per cent of non-citizens had taken no part in any of the political activities proposed in the optional answers. Seventy-three per cent of citizens and 85 per cent of non-citizens were not involved in any social or non-governmental organization (Baltic Institute of Social Sciences, 2001). These data indicate that both citizens and non-citizens generally have low participation rates in various organizations. Their range of communications is usually limited to that of their family, friends and colleagues at work and this is a typical feature of a weakly organized society.

The reason why the participation rate among non-citizens is lower than among citizens can be sought in the alienation between the state power elite and the inhabitants. The inhabitants of Latvia are dissatisfied with the authorities' attitude towards them. They are dissatisfied with the fact that they cannot influence the work of the government, and that they do not feel that the government treats every individual equally and fairly. People most often perceive themselves as subject to power, with no possibility of influencing power. Moreover, people lack belief in their political efficacy. Indeed, approximately two-thirds of Latvia's inhabitants (67 per cent of citizens, 70 per cent of non-citizens) do not believe that they can do anything to change any decision taken by the government. Similarly, 60 per cent of citizens and 67 per cent of non-citizens do not believe that they can influence decisions at the municipality level.

On the other hand, the most active and visible NGOs are the minority NGOs which comprise both citizens and non-citizens of the same ethnic group. As the minorities issue is one of the core issues shaping public discussions, minority NGOs are rather important actors in public policy. In addition, they have more access to grants opportunities than other organizations.

Currently, there are more than 200 ethnic minority NGOs operating in Latvia, a great deal of which work with third-country immigrants or their descendants. Such third-country immigrants include Russians, Belarusians, Ukrainians, Armenians, Azerbaijanis and others. It has to be noted that with respect to minority organizations in Latvia, it is impossible to separate first- and second-generation migrants from those who have lived in Latvia for centuries. Only a few organizations can be recognized as organizations targeting first-generation immigrants from third countries. Such organizations target ethnic groups who have settled in Latvia during the last decade, such as the Afro-Latvian association, the Latvia-Lebanon Club of Education and Culture, and the Latvian Foreigners' and Refugees' Association (which is no longer active).

The activities of these organizations have two main aims: to contribute to the development of ethnic culture and, second, to influence ethnic minority policy in Latvia. Russian organizations actively try to affect ethno-political circumstances in Latvia, as they maintain a critical attitude towards Education Law (1998) and State Language Law (1999). Other minority NGOs, such as those representing Jews, Poles, Lithuanians, and Estonians are aimed particularly at preserving their ethnic identity, and at promoting the process of social integration and ethnic tolerance in Latvia.

Altogether, one can conclude that there are various possibilities for different ethnic groups in Latvia to develop their language, culture and different interests. At the same time it should be added that there are differences between citizens and others concerning political rights and the right to hold certain professional positions.

Public and media discourses on migration

There was a high level of media attention on migration towards the end of the 1980s, when the debate on the consequences of the Soviet policy in Latvia and the restoration of Latvian independence was opened. At the centre of the debate was the fact that Soviet policy promoted 'Russification', and that immigrants from other USSR Republics rarely learned the Latvian language and remained ignorant of local history and culture. This discussion persisted until 1995 when the Citizenship Law (1994) came into force.

During recent years, the question of immigration has rarely been touched upon in public discussions. The problem of immigration arose as one of the most important objections and concerns regarding accession to the EU. A content analysis of the newspapers with the largest circulation reveals that between May and October 2003, foreigners and immigrants were mentioned mainly within the context of the EU accession (Tilts, 2004, p. 9).

An extreme example of the public discourses on migration is the discussion on the racist television advertisement clip that was produced in the election campaign material of *Brīvības partija* ['Freedom party'] (Indans 2004, p. 45). This television advertisement clip was broadcast once before parliamentary elections and before the referendum on accession to the EU. The clip showed an African man dressed in Latvian military uniform in front of the Freedom monument, followed by an image of a black man kissing a blonde girl in Latvian national costume. The background text read 'Today – a guard of Latvia, tomorrow – perhaps your son-in-law'. Finally, there was a text that some 20 million economic migrants from Africa and Asia will come to the European Union within the next few years, and the clip ended with the question: how many of them will choose Latvia as a place of residence?

The musicians Christopher Edjugbo from Nigeria and Peter Mensah from Sierra Leone, who were featured in the clip without knowing the purpose to which it would be put, prosecuted the Freedom party and won a civil case against it in 2002. It should be added that this party was not successful in elections and did not get any seats in parliament. However, according to the report on human rights in Latvia, the racist television advertisement clip continued to be available on the party's home page in 2003 and early 2004 (Latvian Centre for Human Rights and Ethnic Studies, 2004, p. 30).

Recent studies of ethnic tolerance (Zepa et al., 2004) show that public opinion in Latvia is against immigration. This is primarily based on people's fear of the unknown and the alien, of competition and loss of status. Immigrants in Latvia are usually seen as potential competitors. This is true with respect both to wealthy Europeans ('they have money and experience') and to people from less wealthy countries ('they'll be willing to work for a lower salary'). Eighty-four per cent of ethnic Latvians and 78 per cent of non-Latvians agreed with the statement 'It would be terrible if a lot of people from economically less-developed countries were to come to Latvia'.

From the interviews, researchers concluded that people from visually different nationalities encounter very different attitudes in Latvia, ranging from interest to suspicion and scorn. Because they look different and because they are few, these people always attract particular attention – intense gazes, various remarks and, occasionally, physical violence. These are situations which usually occur late at night, when one encounters intoxicated young people on the street (Zepa et al., 2004, p. 47).

Although Muslims are very few (about 1,500 people), people in Latvia hold negative attitudes toward them. Fifty-two per cent of ethnic Latvians and 59 per cent of non-Latvians agreed with the statement: 'The views and traditions of Muslims may be dangerous to Latvia's residents' (Zepa et al. 2004, p. 54). In focus group discussions some respondents even said that Islam should be banned: 'I favour religious discrimination specifically against Islam. This religion might even be banned in Latvia' (Zepa et al., 2004, p. 28). Many people in Latvia still believe that a culturally homogenous society is both the norm and the ideal and should be pursued.

After Latvia's accession to the European Union and especially at the end of 2005, the issue of Latvian workers abroad, particularly in Ireland, surfaced in public discourse. The study of public opinion about the migration of the workforce (SKDS, 2005) shows that people in general are positive towards Latvian workers working abroad, although they consider that the government should make efforts to stop the workforce emigration.

At the same time, people hold very negative attitudes towards the invitation of guest workers to Latvia. Only 16 per cent of all Latvian inhabitants support the idea that Latvia should invite guest workers in order to solve the problem of a lack of labour. On the contrary, 70 per cent hold a negative attitude towards the invitation of guest workers. People asked about the possible countries of guest workers' origin admit that the most convenient would be guest workers from Belarus (43 per cent), Ukraine (40 per cent) and Russia (20 per cent), but most unwelcome would be guest workers from China (41 per cent), Africa (32 per cent) and Vietnam (30 per cent).

In sum, it should be noted that immigration is not a core issue in Latvia, because during the last 10 years many more people have left Latvia than have come into the country. Nevertheless, people hold negative attitudes towards immigrants. By contrast, emigration for work reasons is positively evaluated, although this trend might cause negative consequences for employers in Latvia.

Concluding remarks

Given that, historically, Latvia was a destination country, politicians and officials have only recently acknowledged that emigration is more problematic than immigration. Accordingly, Latvia's immigration policy has up to now been developed with the aim of stopping immigration from other parts of the former USSR, and almost nobody cared about workforce emigration. Indeed, there will soon be a substantial lack of workers due both to demographic decline and emigration.

The same lack of foresight can be found on the issue of naturalization of Latvian non-citizens. In 1994, many more people (including politicians) were concerned about the possible high number of naturalized citizens, although in reality the naturalization rate in the early 1990s was very low.

The adaptation of Latvian legislation to the standards of the European Union in this area can be seen as a balancing process. Because of this process, the norms of naturalization were gradually liberalized and the 2003 Immigration Law was introduced in accordance with international obligations and human rights instruments.

Surprisingly for Latvian society, the expected immigration after EU accession has not occurred yet. On the contrary, it has turned to emigration, as at least three EU countries are already open for the free movement of labour. If the main concern of Latvian society was previously migration to Latvia, now the central issue on the agenda is the lack of labour and the problem of workforce emigration. Nevertheless, fear of immigrants is strong enough, as people hold xenophobic attitudes towards Muslims, for instance, and hold very negative attitudes towards the invitation of guest workers to Latvia.

Recently, politicians in Latvia have recognized the need to develop instruments which will promote the return of Latvians working abroad, increase birth rates, and so on. However, what kind of mechanisms will be developed, and how they will be made effective, are questions for future research.

References

Apine, I., Dribins, L., Jansons, A., Vebers, E., Volkovs, V. and Zankovska, S. (2001), *Etnopolitika Latvijā*. Riga: Elpa.

Brands Kehre, I. and Stalidzane, I. (2003), *The Role of Regional Aspects in Dealing with Citizenship Issues*. Riga: The Naturalization Board of the Republic of Latvia.

Indans, I. (2004), *The Impact of Immigration on Ethnic Relations in Latvia in the Context of Enlargement of EU*. Riga: Latvian Institute of International Affairs.

Latvian Centre for Human Rights and Ethnic Studies (2004), *Human Rights in Latvia in 2003*. Riga: Latvian Centre for Human Rights and Ethnic Studies.

Latvian Centre for Human Rights and Ethnic Studies (2005), *Human Rights in Latvia in 2004*. Riga: Latvian Centre for Human Rights and Ethnic Studies.

Vēbers, E. (1997), *Latvia and its Ethnic Minorities*. Riga: Latvia Academy of Sciences, Institute of Philosophy and Sociology.

Zepa, B., Supule, I., Krastina, L., Penke, I. and Krisane, J. (2004), *Ethnic Tolerance and Integration of the Latvian Society*. Riga: Baltic Institute of Social Sciences.

Internet-based references

Baltic Institute of Social Sciences (2001), 'Towards a Civic Society − 2000: Survey Report' (available at http://www.bszi.lv/downloads/resources/civicSociety/civicSociety2000.pdf, accessed 10 December 2004).

Īpašu uzdevumu ministra sabiedrības integrācijas lietās sekretariāts (2004), 'ĪUMSILS darbība − fakti' (updated 10 December 2004) (available at http://www.integracija.gov.lv/doc_upl/prese_ (1).doc).

Office of Citizenship and Migration Affairs (2006a), *Statistics on Asylum Seekers*. Statistics page (published online 14 January 2006, available at http://www.ocma.gov.lv/?_p=422&menu__ id=111).

Office of Citizenship and Migration Affairs (2006b), *Resident Population of Latvia by Citizenship Status, 01.01.2006*. Statistics page (published online 14 January 2006 available at http://www. pmlp.gov.lv/images/documents/8.pdf).

SKDS (2005) (The Research Centre), 'Study on Public Opinion about the Migration of Labour Force'. The Public Policy Site, PolitikaLV (published online 23 January 2006 available at http:// www.politika.lv/index.php?id=112482&lang=lv).

Tilts, M., 'Mediju kontentanalīze: neiecietības veicināšanas/mazināšanas aspekti. 2004', *Īpašu uzdevumu ministra sabiedrības integrācijas lietās sekretariāts* (available at http://www. integracija.gov.lv/doc_upl/prezentacijas_materials.doc, updated 10 December 2004).

The Naturalization Board of the Republic of Latvia, *Facts and Statistics on Residents. A Breakdown of the Residents of Latvia based on Nationality*. Statistics page (published online 25 January 2006, available at http://www.np.gov.lv/index.php?en=fakti_en&saite=residents.htm).

Chapter 16

Lithuania

Rita Zukauskiene

From the end of the Second World War, Lithuania was annexed to the Soviet Union and underwent rapid, large-scale industrialization, urbanization and colonization. Until the late 1980s, international migration in Lithuania was both intensive and stable. At that time, there were almost no migration relations with other foreign countries except the Soviet Union. However, after 1989, as a result of political, social and economic changes in Lithuania, the migration situation started to change, with some migration flows even reversing their direction. Over the last decade, Lithuania has a negative migration balance[1] (Table 16.1).

The current flow of immigrants to Lithuania mainly consists of the following three categories of persons: returning citizens (that is, Lithuanians whose entry is unlimited; they receive Lithuanian citizenship and can, therefore, stay indefinitely), reunion of family members (limited) and a smaller percentage of migration for business. The majority of immigrants come from Russia and the CIS (Commonwealth of Independent States) countries.

The number of illegal transit migrants and refugees is relatively low. Although initially none of the transit migrants intended to stay in Lithuania or to find work in the country, eventually some of them seek refugee status with the intention of staying. The law provides for the granting of asylum and refugee status in accordance with the provisions of the UN Convention Relating to the Status of Refugees and its 1967 Protocol.

There is a legal and institutional framework at the national level for putting into effect the principle of equal treatment and combating discrimination on the basis of racial and ethnic origin in Lithuania. Equal social benefits, health and social insurance, pensions, loans, subsidies for the education of children, maternity leave and employment opportunities are equally available to citizens and permanent residents. The social, political, and economic changes that took place ten years ago have influenced the situation of all ethnic groups (including both majority and minority groups) when acting in the social sphere, adapting themselves to new requirements (citizenship, civic loyalty, knowledge of the state language, value changes, and participation in the newly formed bodies such as the private or non-governmental sector) in a more active or passive way.

Major developments in Lithuania's immigration policy

Lithuania's location at the crossroads between Eastern and Western Europe has resulted in its complicated and turbulent history. Over the centuries its geopolitical situation has frequently changed. Lithuania was an independent grand duchy in the Middle Ages. The state of Lithuania, founded in the thirteenth century, lost its independence several times and for long periods. In the sixteenth century, it united with Poland to form a commonwealth. During the partition of this commonwealth by Russia, Prussia and Austria in the eighteenth century, Lithuania was absorbed

---

1   Net migration is negative when the number of emigrants exceeds the number of immigrants.

Table 16.1   Migration flows (2003–2005)

	2003			2004			2005		
	Immigration	Emigration	Net migration*	Immigration	Emigration	Net migration	Immigration	Emigration	Net migration
Total	4,728	11,032	-6,304	5,553	15,165	-9,612	6,789	15,571	-8,782
Males	2,594	5,173	-2,579	2,968	7,146	-4,178	3,816	7,558	-3,742
Females	2,134	5,859	-3,725	2,585	8,019	-5,434	2,973	8,013	-5,040

*The difference between the total number of persons arriving and the total number of persons departing.
Source: Department of Statistics to the Government of the Republic of Lithuania (Statistics Lithuania), 2005.

into the Russian empire. After the First World War, on 16 February 1918, the Lithuanian Council proclaimed the restoration of the Lithuanian state. The secret protocol of the Soviet-German frontier treaty in 1939 assigned the greater part of Lithuania to the Soviet sphere of influence and, on 3 August 1940, Lithuania became a Soviet Socialist Republic of the USSR. On 11 March 1990, the Lithuanian Supreme Soviet proclaimed independence and, since 2004, Lithuania has been a member of the European Union.

Fifteen years of independence marked not only by a strengthening statehood but also by a transition from a totalitarian to a democratic society and from a centrally planned to a market economy, have brought about great changes in the political, socioeconomic and cultural life of the country. They have also had a considerable impact on the country's demography. The last few years have been characterized by the continued decrease in inflation, by GDP growth, increased foreign investment and privatization, and a stabilization of unemployment at approximately 9.8 per cent (end of 2003). Indeed, since 2003 Lithuania has been one of the fastest growing economies in Europe (Statistics Lithuania, 2005; *CIA World Factbook*, 2003).

The current ethnic composition of Lithuania has suffered great changes due to its historical course. The main role in the process of formation of ethnic groups and communities in Lithuania is ascribed to migration. Considerable changes in the population began in 1940 and were related to the loss caused by the Second World War. This period also included the Holocaust, emigration of the Polish intelligentsia and Soviet deportations. Overall, between 1940 and 1958 Lithuania lost about one million people. The relative population losses in the Baltics in the 1940s were among the highest in the world.

Between 1940 and 1989, Lithuanian borders were open to an influx of Soviet immigrants. At the end of the Second World War, Lithuania underwent – from a very low base – rapid and large-scale industrialization, urbanization and colonization. Inward labour migration created an ethnic group of first-generation immigrants. Large numbers of workers moved from the neighbouring Soviet Republics to Lithuania. After the territorial annexation of Lithuania by the USSR, industrialization caused the migration of workers from Ukraine, Byelorussia (now Belarus), Russia and Transcaucasia. Only incomplete migration statistics exist for the post-war period and, moreover, migration amongst the rural population was not registered at all until 1956. However, as the results of immigration research show, immigration intensity was highest in Estonia and Latvia and noticeably lower in Lithuania (Zvidrins, 1997).

This period was characterized by weak contacts with Western countries and a constant increase in the population due to immigration from the republics of the former USSR (http://web.inter.nl.net/users/Paul.Treanor/europlan.html#gigantism). Soviet industrialization policy accelerated Lithuanian urbanization after 1950 and, in fact, today Lithuania remains highly urbanized, with 68 per cent of the population living in urban areas. Forced urbanization and deliberate decisions influenced the distribution and migration trends of the population.

The implementation of giant Soviet projects resulted in a significant extension of the network of settlement, with the accompanying mass migration to certain regions. This resulted in Lithuania's ethnic variety being supplemented by various nationalities of the USSR. The first decades of the Soviet period (1945–1979) covered the industrialization and centralization of the Soviet economy. Up until 1988, due to the forced military and economic migration, groups of labour migrants (mainly the Russian-speaking population) came to Lithuania. Ethnic groups were formed as a result of the flows of labour migrants, who were mainly specialists and qualified workers. The fact that persons with advanced qualifications had immigrated to Lithuania became salient in the first years of the independent state. Because of certain industrial developments, certain towns served as destinations for immigrants, for example Visaginas, Mažeikiai and Vilnius. Lithuanians comprise a minority in the regions of Šalčininkai, Vilnius, Švenčionys and the town of Visaginas (where

52.4 per cent of the population is Russian, 15.0 per cent Lithuanian and 8.6 per cent Polish). In Lithuania there are two Soviet mega-projects in rural areas: the Mažeikiai oil refinery, and the Ignalina nuclear plant, resulting in a Russian majority in the new town of Visaginas.

The clear intention of the Soviet Government was to dilute the Baltic populations and bolster pro-Soviet loyalties (Lieven, 1993, p. 184). In all the Baltic States, the numerically second largest nationality is Russian. Their total in the Baltics at the end of the 1980s reached almost two million. The third largest ethnic group were the Poles (321,000 in 1989), who lived mainly in Lithuania (258,000). The number of Poles was slowly growing (Lieven, 1993). But Lithuania's rates of immigration were considerably lower than those of Latvia and Estonia. After the war, Lithuania was less modernized and had a labour surplus (Zvidrins, 1997).

Moreover, local Russians, in comparison with the other former Soviet Baltic Republics, were more adapted and more involved in the local cultural and linguistic environment. This could be supported by the data form the 1989 census regarding the bi-lingual level of the Russian population in the former the Soviet Republics. In Lithuania, 37.8 per cent of Russians were fluent in the language of the titular nation or treated it as their mother tongue, while in Latvia and Estonia these indicators were 22.4 per cent and 15.15 per cent respectively (Kasatkina and Beresnevičiūtė, 2004).

Naturalization

The legal and institutional framework for putting into effect the principle of equal treatment and combating discrimination on the basis of racial and ethnic origin consists of the Constitution, the laws, Lithuania's obligations under international treaties, and explanations of the Constitutional Court of the Republic of Lithuania.

On 29 November 1989, the Lithuanian Socialist Soviet Republic adopted a Citizenship Law which introduced the so-called 'zero-option' for acquiring Lithuanian citizenship. This law allowed all members of national minorities living permanently in Lithuania to apply for Lithuanian citizenship, regardless of nationality and without any language requirements. The law remained in effect until 4 November 1991. During this period, 87 per cent of those who had not already been granted citizenship were granted it (Sipaviciene and Kanopiene, 1999).

Between 1999 and 2004, approximately 300 persons were naturalized per year. In the following years, however, there has been a decreasing trend.

According to the 2001 Population and Housing Census, citizens of other countries amount to a mere 0.7 per cent, while those without citizenship constitute 0.3 per cent. (See Table 16.2.) Overall, 659 persons had double citizenship (Kasatkina and Beresnevičiūtė, 2004). Remarkably, the 2001 Population and Housing Census recorded the highest number of Lithuanians throughout the history of Lithuania. Poles, having been the second minority, became the first, while Russians moved to second place.

In its report on minority rights in ten European Union candidate states, the Open Society Institute stated that Lithuania does not have a comprehensive anti-discrimination law that expressly prohibits discrimination in specific areas of public activity. Many non-ethnic Lithuanian public sector employees were required to attain a functional knowledge of Lithuanian within several years, although the authorities have been granting liberal extensions of the time frame in which this is to be achieved. There is no documented evidence of job dismissals based on the language law.

Table 16.2   Lithuanian population by citizenship

	Percentages
Citizens of Republic of Lithuania	99
Citizens of Russian Federation	0.4
Citizens of other countries	0.2
People without citizenship	0.3
Not indicated their citizenship	0.1

Data for 2001 from: Population by Sex, Age, Ethnicity and Religion. Statistics Lithuania, Vilnius 2002.

The Law on Citizenship of the Republic of Lithuania, adopted on 17 September 2002, came into effect on 1 January 2003. The law expanded the category of persons who have an inherent right to citizenship up to the fourth generation, and introduced a new citizenship status – namely, reservation of citizenship and the conditions for the simplified restoration of citizenship for the persons who lost their citizenship of the Republic of Lithuania and who have an inherent right to that citizenship.

In 2003, the Migration Department received the documents of 4,808 persons concerning the attainment, retention of right, implementation thereof, or loss of citizenship (up from 4,345 in 2002). In 2003, the department passed 2,081 resolutions over citizenship (up from 1,398 in 2002), 129 resolutions on the retention of the right to citizenship, 93 resolutions over citizenship upon determination that the issue of that person's citizenship was resolved in violation of requirements of the Law on Citizenship. The documents of 152 individuals were transferred to the Citizenship Group of the office of the President of the Republic of Lithuania for the reservation of citizenship. Moreover, 161 certificates evidencing the retained right to citizenship were issued (replaced). Furthermore, in 2003 the Department submitted documents on 715 persons to the commission that had to produce recommendations despite the shortage of documents evidencing Lithuanian citizenship before 15 June 1940 or Lithuanian origin, citizenship of children and other disputable citizenship issues.

The principle of equal treatment of ethnic minorities is addressed by a number of Lithuanian laws. For example, Article 3 of the Law on Presidential Elections states that 'any direct or indirect abridgement of a citizen of the Republic of Lithuania's right to vote on the grounds of their sex, race, nationality, language, descent, social status, religion, convictions, or views shall be prohibited'. Article 2 of the Law on the Employment Contract stipulates as one of the principles of legal regulation of labour relations, 'equality for all employees, regardless of their sex, race, nationality, citizenship, political convictions, religious beliefs, or any other factors which do not affect their professional qualifications'. The Penal Code provides for a sentence of from two to ten years' imprisonment for the incitement of racial or national hatred or incitement of violence against foreigners.

The Lithuanian immigrant population: main demographic and social features

Lithuania is a multiethnic state in which one ethnic group, Lithuanians, accounts for an overwhelming majority of the population. However, statistical data show a change in the last decade in the ethnic composition of the population. The percentage of Lithuanians increased from 79.6 per cent in 1989 to 83.5 per cent in 2001; the percentage of Poles has decreased from 7.0 per cent to 6.7 per cent, and of Russians from 9.4 per cent to 6.3 per cent (Table 16.3). Although legislation does not provide a definition of a 'national minority', it is generally accepted that a national minority is a group of residents who identify themselves as belonging to a nationality other than Lithuanian. The 2001 Population and Housing Census recorded nationality (ethnic origin) as indicated by the respondent. Parents indicated the nationality of their children. In 2001, representatives of 115 nationalities lived in Lithuania, of which only 29 accounted for 100 or more people. According to the Census data, Lithuanians accounted for 83.5 per cent of the population, Poles comprised 6.7 per cent, Russians 6.3 per cent, Belarusians 1.2 per cent and Ukrainians 0.7 per cent. Jews, Germans, Tatars, Latvians and the Roma people accounted for 0.2 per cent, while 0.9 per cent of the population did not indicate their nationality at all. The official language is Lithuanian, but ethnic minorities have the right to use their language in private and in public, to carry on their own educational activities, including the maintenance of newspapers, schools and the use or the teaching of their own language where they form a substantial part of the population.

The migration situation in Lithuania differs from that of most other Central and Eastern European countries. Until the late 1980s, international migration in Lithuania was both intensive and stable. It was characterized by a constant increase in the population, due to immigration from the republics of the former USSR, amounting to net immigration of some 6,000–8,000 persons a year. At that time, there were almost no migration relations with other foreign countries. The foreign-born proportion population in 1989 was 10 per cent in Lithuania and 26 per cent in Latvia and Estonia.

Table 16.3   Lithuanian population by nationality (1923–2005) (per cent)

Nationalities	1923	1959	1969	1979	1989	2001
Lithuanians	84.1	79.3	80.1	80.0	79.6	83.45
Poles	3.2	8.5	7.7	7.3	7.0	6.74
Russians	2.5	8.5	8.6	8.9	9.4	6.31
Belarussians	0.2	1.1	1.5	1.7	1.7	1.23
Ukrainians	0.0	0.7	0.8	0.9	1.2	0.65
Tatars	0.04	0.1	0.1	0.1	0.1	0.09
Jews	7.6	0.9	0.8	0.4	0.3	0.12
Latvians	0.6	0.2	0.1	0.1	0.1	0.08
Roma	-	0.1	0.1	0.1	0.1	0.07
Germans	1.4	0.4	0.1	0.1	0.1	0.09
Armenians	-	-	-	-	-	0.04
Other	0.2	0.2	0.1	0.4	0.4	0.18
Not indicated	-	-	-	-	-	0.94

Data for 2001 from: Population by Sex, Age, Ethnicity and Religion. Statistics Lithuania, Vilnius 2002.

However, since 1989, as a result of the far-reaching political, social and economic changes in Lithuania, the migration situation started to change, with some migration flows even reversing their direction (Sipaviciene and Kanopiene, 1999). The process of restoration of independent states has stimulated emigration (and re-emigration) of the population of non-titular nationalities from the Baltic States. Up to now, Lithuania has a negative migration balance. Moreover, the Lithuanian population growth rate in Lithuania is −0.29 per cent (2000 est.). Substantial demographic changes started to become visible in 1990 when the population's growth rate fell to 0.76 per cent and, since 1992, the population has been decreasing. The level of emigration reached a peak in 1992, when emigration to the CIS countries was 27,000 people. Most emigrants left for Russia, Ukraine or Belarus, that is the Republics that represented the major part of the net immigration in the past. Emigration was decreasing and the net migration balance with the CIS countries was positive between 1997 and 1999. However, in 2000, 1,400 persons left permanently for the CIS. This was twice as many as in 1999, and net migration became negative again. In 2000, 1,200 persons emigrated and 400 immigrated.

With Lithuania's EU accession many Lithuanian citizens have emigrated to other EU Member States for employment purposes. At the same time, since 1991, there has been no active and massive immigration into the country. The flows of immigrants to Lithuania mainly consist of returning citizens (that is Lithuanians whose entry is unlimited), reunion of family members (limited) and migration on business (the number is not high). The majority of immigrants come from Russia and the CIS countries (Table 16.4).

Among the immigrants, Lithuanians and relatives of the former already naturalized migrants, namely Russians, Belarusians and Ukrainians, prevail. In 1993, Lithuanians were the largest group of immigrants, accounting for 41.5 per cent, and in 2000 they accounted for 44.1 per cent (Kasatkina and Beresnevičiūtė, 2004). The analysis of applications submitted has revealed that the majority of arrivals in the Republic of Lithuania are related to family reunification (2,387) or the pursuit of commercial or other legal activities in Lithuania (1,066).

Grants of Lithuanian citizenship to persons who have previously been citizens of another country or who have been stateless was 825 in 1997, 562 in 1998, 567 in 1999, 490 in 2000, 507 in 2001 (Eurostat yearbook, 2004).

Table 16.4 Main nationalities in the flows of immigration (1990–2000) (per cent)

	Lithuanians	Russians	Ukrainians	Belarussians	Poles	Jews	Other
1990	23.1	42.7	13.8	7.5	10.2	0.9	1.8
1991	25.3	43.3	10.1	6.4	7.2	0.9	6.8
1992	34.1	40.2	7.9	6.6	5.4	0.6	5.3
1993	41.5	34.8	5.1	5.3	6.5	0.6	6.1
1994	33.1	35.6	6.1	7.7	5.9	1.0	10.6
1995	26.9	41.0	6.3	7.4	4.5	1.6	12.3
1996	33.4	35.7	7.9	5.1	4.8	0.6	12.7
1997	34.9	34.5	6.5	5.6	4.9	1.1	12.4
1998	31.9	33.6	6.9	6.9	4.9	0.8	15.1
1999	30.1	33.1	6.9	5.1	4.2	0.4	20.2
2000	44.1	21.6	4.9	2.0	4.6	0.5	22.4

Source: Population of Lithuania 1990-2000. LFSI. Demografiniu tyrimu centras. Vilnius, 2002. p. 79.

In late 2003, citizens of European Union Member States residing in the Republic of Lithuania on a permanent basis comprised a meagre 0.53 per cent. Citizens of European Union Member States residing in the Republic of Lithuania on a temporary basis amounted to 19.2 per cent of all foreigners residing in the Republic of Lithuania on a temporary basis (up from 15.4 per cent in 2002) (www.migracija.lt) (Table 16.5).

Table 16.5   Number of foreigners residing in the Republic of Lithuania on a permanent or temporary basis (2002–2003)

	On a permanent basis		On a temporary basis	
	2003	2002	2003	2002
Foreigners in total	27,905	25,109	4,833	5,361
Citizens of Russian Federation	12,425	1,136	1,051	1,300
Citizens of Republic of Belarus	2,007	1,758	578	589
Citizens of Ukraine	1,413	1,241	444	699
Stateless persons	7,917	9,033	n.a	n.a
Citizens of USA	n.a	n.a	289	321

Foreigners may reside permanently in Lithuania if they have a residence permit issued by the Ministry of Internal Affairs and an identity document. A permit for permanent residence in the Republic of Lithuania can be issued if a foreigner is an immediate relative of a citizen of the Republic of Lithuania; is a dependant of a citizen of the Republic of Lithuania; financially maintains a citizen of the Republic of Lithuania; is married to a citizen of the Republic of Lithuania, and in some other cases. These provisions of law on the legal status of foreigners in the Republic of Lithuania are not applicable to persons who, up to the date of entry into force of this law, have been permanent residents in the Republic of Lithuania and have not acquired citizenship under the 1989 Law on Citizenship. Such persons are qualified as foreigners permanently residing in the Republic of Lithuania. Foreigners who are in the Republic of Lithuania on a basis other that that specified in this law are qualified as foreigners temporarily residing in the Republic of Lithuania. They must register their passport or another equivalent document, and must leave the Republic of Lithuania after their visa and residence permit have expired.

Illegal migration

The emergence and gradual increase in illegal migration for work in Lithuania can only be understood in the broader context of its development throughout the region, and particularly in the countries of the former USSR.

During the Soviet period, illegal migration of any kind (immigration, emigration or transit migration) in either Lithuania or any of the other countries of the former USSR was practically impossible. Surrounded by the *iron curtain*, on which the army acted as border guards and implemented a closed door migration policy, none of these countries was either easily accessible or attractive to migrants. Migration was regulated by special secret decrees, including Secret Decree No. 200 of the Ministry of the Interior of the USSR, supplemented by secret KGB instructions. In general, only immediate relatives were allowed to emigrate. Immigration, or even repatriation, was not welcome. A similar policy was applied to short-term foreign migration, with the aim of minimizing temporary foreign visits in and out of the country (Stankuniene, 1995a, 1995b).

However, the collapse of the former USSR, the liberalization of migration policy, and the considerable weakening of frontier controls led to the revival of traditional migration patterns. The first illegal transit migrants were apprehended in Lithuania only in 1992, when the operational service of the Border Police Department was first established. It is not, therefore, possible to state with any certainty that illegal transit migration did not occur previously. Since then, transit migration (trafficking), particularly of Asians and Africans, has gradually increased and has come to account for a significant proportion of all illegal crossings of the Lithuanian border. Investigations have shown that very few Asian or African migrants who arrive in Lithuania intend to stay in the country and that their objective is mainly to reach Western Europe or the United States. The greatest recorded increase occurred in 1994 and 1995 before it slowed down in 1996. However, the official figures refer only to the illegal migrants who have been detected (Sipaviciene and Kanopiene, 1999).

In 1999, the new Law on the Legal Status of Aliens of the Republic of Lithuania laid the foundation for a uniform asylum system. In 2002, the only ground for prohibiting the entry of an asylum seeker to Lithuania was if a person sought to enter Lithuania from a 'safe third country'.

Over the last few years, irregular immigration decreased dramatically due to improved border control, stricter laws against human smuggling and more effective detention and return of migrants to their countries of origin. In 2003, officials of the State Border Guard Service detained a total of 581 illegal immigrants at the Lithuanian frontier. Two hundred and eighty-one detainees arrived from neighbouring countries (111 were Russian nationals, 92 Belarusian, 73 Latvian and 5 Polish), whereas 300 came from other states (48 citizens of Ukraine, 28 stateless persons, 27 Turkish nationals, 24 Pakistani nationals, 24 Indian citizens, 14 Chinese nationals). Two hundred and fifty-nine of those individuals were detained while attempting to cross the state border illegally. One hundred and forty-six individuals attempted to enter the country with forged or somebody else's travel documents, whereas 176 resided in the country illegally. Following the new assessment criteria, Lithuanian border guards also detained 12 citizens of Israel, and an identical number of citizens of Moldova and the Netherlands, who were treated as illegal immigrants (www.migracija.lt).

Immigrant rights and participation in public life

Under the laws of the Republic of Lithuania, foreigners staying in Lithuania can enjoy freedom of thought, conscience, religion and convictions. They cannot elect or be elected to the representative bodies of state power and other elective state bodies, or participate in referenda. Foreigners who permanently reside in the Republic of Lithuania may hold any post in state service, with the exception of those posts that under the laws of the Republic of Lithuania can only be held by citizens. Foreigners cannot be subjected to military service in the army. Under the laws of the Republic of Lithuania, foreigners are guaranteed inviolability of person and of abode, as well as other personal freedoms. A foreigner staying in Lithuania cannot be detained or arrested except when he or she: 1) has attempted to illegally enter the Republic of Lithuania and been detained; 2) has been illegally staying in the Republic of Lithuania and been detained; 3) has committed a crime or any other violation of law for which he or she has had to be detained or arrested under the laws of the Republic of Lithuania. Each detained foreigner must be informed, without delay, of the reasons of his/her detention or of the accusations brought against him/her if there are such, in the language understandable to him/her. Each foreigner possessing citizenship of a foreign state and staying in the Republic of Lithuania is allowed to get in touch with a diplomatic or consular mission, or with any other body representing the interests of that foreign state in the Republic of Lithuania. If there are no such bodies, contact may be made with the diplomatic or consular mission of another foreign state which is authorized to defend the rights and lawful interests of citizens of that state of which the detained foreigner is a citizen. The Procurator must notify a diplomatic or consular mission of the state whose citizen has been detained, of his/her detention or arrest not later than within 48 hours.

A foreigner staying in the Republic of Lithuania has the right to appeal to court or other state bodies personally or through a person authorized by him, in the same manner as citizens of the

Republic of Lithuania. Foreigners permanently residing in Lithuania may engage in any labour or economic activity if it is not prohibited by law or if it is not exclusively reserved for citizens of the Republic of Lithuania. Foreigners permanently residing in the Republic of Lithuania and having lawful employment enjoy the same economic and social rights as citizens, and the same rights to social security. Foreigners enjoy the same rights to cultural properties of the Republic of Lithuania, they are guaranteed the right to use their native language, to protect and foster their culture and traditions. Foreigners staying in Lithuania may contract or dissolve a marriage with a citizen of the Republic of Lithuania, according to the procedure established by the laws of the Republic of Lithuania. In their marital and family relations, foreigners are entitled to the same rights and duties as citizens of the Republic of Lithuania.

Both citizens and permanent residents are equally supported by the state. Equal social benefits, health and social insurance, pensions, loans, subsidies for the education of children, maternity leave and employment opportunities are equally available to all. Education is offered in native languages: in 69 schools in Russian, 73 in Polish, 1 in Belarusian, 1 in Hebrew, 1 in German and 29 mixed-language schools.[2] All schools except one private Russian school are owned by the State. Twenty-seven Sunday schools in nine languages are also available. Radio and television programmes are broadcast in nine languages and newspapers in seven minority languages (43 in total) are run with government support. National minorities publish 41 periodicals in their language (35 newspapers and 6 magazines). Thirty-one of them are published in Russian, seven in Polish, one in Belarusian and two in German. *The State* radio broadcasts one hour daily in Russian and Polish. There are weekly editions in Ukrainian and Belarusian. There is a daily news broadcast in Russian on state television. Private regional television companies broadcast news and other programmes in Russian, Polish and Belarusian. However, as Nina Mackevič emphasized in her paper 'Russian Press in the View of Marginalization', newspapers in Russian, for instance, are written in bad Russian; they depend on the information from the Russian press, and largely the reviews of this press. The same may be said about other minority press.

However, being the largest ethnic minority, the Russians never thought of themselves as a minority during the Soviet period. Even now, there is a dominance of the Russian environment and language in many settlements. This language is often also used by non-Russians, and many children of Belarusian, Ukrainian or Jewish ethnicity attend schools where lessons are taught in Russian. The Russian communities maintain close contacts with Russia. Not surprisingly, ethnic Russians make up a large part of those with relatives in Russia, resulting in the fact that many political events in this country have a direct resonance in the Baltics. However, the extensive emigration of Russians from the Baltic States has aggravated their own national identity issue and has tended to stimulate their ethnic consolidation. At the same time, their large size and the recent history of the Russian-speaking communities' dominance have created a certain inertia and reluctance on behalf of Russians to adapt to the local cultural communities. The former so-called 'Russian towns' and 'Russian zones' are the most problematic from the point of view of integration (Blaschke, 1994, p. 88).

However, despite some temporary problems, Lithuania is able to successfully integrate most of the ethnic communities into society, while maintaining their own national and cultural identity. In 2002, 213 schools operated in a language other than Lithuanian (Moskvina, 2004). Forty-nine minority language periodicals were published and 225 national minority organizations were operating. Special programmes are prepared by the Ministry of Education and Science for bilingual pupils in the schools in which the language of instruction is Lithuanian (Moskvina, 2004).

---

2   Russian-Lithuanian, Polish-Lithuanian, Russian-Polish, Belarusian-Russian and Lithuanian-Russian-Polish.

Public and media discourses on migration

Lithuania is a fairly homogeneous country and not an overtly xenophobic one. Lithuanians do not suffer from ethnic and cultural tension, or discrimination against migrants. However, the danger can be found among public attitudes towards refugees and asylum seekers who trickle across our borders. The mainstream media often look for negative stories only. They focus on so-called illegal migration, on those people entering the country clandestinely and on criminality among migrants. Lithuanians usually hear negative things, and a common concept of a refugee is often of someone who has come to cause trouble.

One of the major concerns of the media between 1997 and 1999 was illegal immigration. Publications described growing public anxiety about illegal immigration, mainly the flow across the Belarusian border with Poland. The Public opinion and market research company *Sprinter tyrimai* carried out a public opinion survey asking the question 'What is most frightening about entering the EU?' Responses indicated that the main disadvantages identified were: the increase in prices (55 per cent), increased competition (19 per cent) and the flow of immigrants (9 per cent). Both younger and older generations were worried about the influx of immigrants. Some people expressed concern that they would lose their jobs to foreigners who would work for next to nothing.

As regards Lithuanian media portrayals of ethnic minorities, there have been very few studies on this topic over the last ten years in Lithuania. In the case of ethnic minorities, Tereskinas (2003) examined the representations of four ethnic groups – Russians, Poles, Roma and Jews – living in Lithuania, in the largest Lithuanian daily *Lietuvos rytas* (LR) from 27 November 2000 to 9 May 2001. *Lietuvos rytas* published a total of 88 news stories and articles mentioning Lithuanian Russians, Poles, Jews and Roma. Most stories touched upon the subject of Jews and the Holocaust in Lithuania (37), Lithuanian Russians attracted 22 reports, and Poles 10. There were a total of 22 stories about those of Russian ethnicity living in Lithuania published in LR during the studied period. Of those, seven dealt with active Lithuanian-Russian politicians, nine with crimes, four with culture and education and two with historical justice (Tereskinas, 2003).

In the Representative Population Survey on Human Rights in Lithuania in 2002, the respondents mentioned three rights which, in the respondents' opinion, receive sufficient attention: 1) the rights of ethnic minorities: 46.8 per cent said sufficient attention and 9.9 per cent insufficient, 2) the rights of migrants and refugees: 28.8 per cent said sufficient and 16.2 per cent insufficient attention. People favourably evaluated the work of two institutions protecting and ensuring human rights in Lithuania: the mass media (58.4 per cent evaluated favourably and 9.4 per cent unfavourably) and NGOs (24.4 per cent evaluated favourably and 14.2 per cent unfavourably) (www3.lrs.lt/owa-bin/owarepl/inter/owa/U0075489.doc).

Concluding remarks

The absence of large numbers of new immigrants and specifics of settlement of those few who do go to Lithuania provides the background for there being no migration-issue-based opposition in the local communities. Massive immigration is not typical in Lithuania and, if immigration does take place, then the flow of persons entering the country is normally directed to the capital city Vilnius or to a few other big cities, which offer better economic and social opportunities.

Immigrants who arrived in Lithuania during the Soviet period have been naturalized and consider themselves Lithuanian citizens. Their civic participation takes place in religious associations, in NGOs on an ethnic basis, and also in political parties. The lack of a new inflow of immigrants to

Lithuania results in invisible civic participation. From the review of the little existing material, studies, and non-academic sources, it appears that the main fields of civic participation are ethnic associations and participation in legal and illegal labour markets. Unfortunately, there are no studies of immigrants' relations with mainstream society organizations on which one could base a comparison. Immigration is a rather new phenomenon in Lithuania and, as a result, no research has so far been conducted in analysing the civic participation of new immigrants and their involvement in social and political life. Future studies on this topic are therefore needed.

References

Blaschke, J. (1994), 'East-West Migration in Europe and the Role of International Aid in Reducing the Need for Emigration', in Böhning, W.R. and Schloeter-Paredes, M.-L. (eds) *Aid in Place of Migration?* 73–100. Geneva: ILO.

Kasatkina, N. and Beresnevičiūtė, V. (2004), 'Ethnic Structure, Inequality and Governance of the Public Sector in Lithuania', paper for UNRISD project presented at the international conference 'Ethnic Inequality and Public Sector Governance', Riga, 25–27 March 2004.

Lieven, A. (1993), *The Baltic Revolution: Estonia, Latvia and Lithuania and the Path to Independence*. New Haven and London: Yale University Press.

Moskvina, J. (2004), *Possibilities for Developing Social Integration of Ethnic Minorities in Lithuania: EU Integration Process from EAST to EAST: Civil Society and Ethnic Minorities in a Changing World*. A round table for young social scientists, University Lucian Blaga, Sibiu, Romania, 17–19 December 2004.

Sipavičienė A. (1997), *The Baltic Route: The Trafficking of Migrants through Lithuania*. Budapest: IOM MIP.

Stankuniene, V. (1995a), 'Demographic Development of Vilnius in Historical Context', in *Demographic Changes and Population Policy in Lithuania*, 21–41, Vilnius: Lithuanian Institute of Philosophy and Sociology.

Stankuniene, V. (1995b), *The New Migration Features in Lithuania: Directions and Ethnic Composition. Demographic Changes and Population Policy in Lithuania*. Vilnius: Lithuanian · Institute of Philosophy and Sociology.

Statistics Lithuania (2005), *Statistical Yearbook of Lithuania 2005*. Vilnius.

Zvidrins, P. (1997), 'Changes in the Ethnic Composition of the Baltic States since the End of World War II', in *50 Years after World War II*, 81–94. Gdansk: Wydawnictwo Uniwersytetu.

Internet-based references

CIA World Factbook 2003, Washington, DC: Central Intelligence Agency.

Eurostat yearbook (2004), (available at http://epp.eurostat.cec.eu.int/pls/portal/url/PAGE/PGP_ DS_YEARBOOK/PGE_DS_YEARBOOK_03, accessed on 12 December 2004).

Sipaviciene, A. and Kanopiene, V. (1999), 'Foreign Labour in Lithuania: Immigration, Employment and Illegal Work', *International Migration Papers No. 31*, p. 37. Geneva: International Labour Organization (available at http://www.ilo.org/public/english/protection/migrant/download/imp/ imp31.pdf).

Tereskinas, A. (2003), 'Towards a New Politics of Citizenship: Representations of Ethnic and Sexual Minorities in the Lithuanian Mass Media' (available at http://www.policy.hu/tereskinas/research.html, accessed on 15 November 2004).

Chapter 17

Luxembourg

Serge Kollwelter

During the last century, migration has significantly contributed to the economic and social development of the Grand Duchy of Luxembourg. In 2006, Luxembourg's total population of 450,000 included 38 per cent foreigners. The overwhelming majority of foreign nationals residing in Luxembourg are citizens of other EU Member States, while only five per cent come from non-EU countries. To a large extent, this is the result of a very effective policy carried out by the authorities and centred on accepting almost only white, Catholic, European immigrants. In effect, given Luxembourg's ageing population,[1] immigration is considered necessary for the country's economy. In addition, the active working population includes only 36 per cent of Luxembourgers; 26 per cent of the working population is third-country nationals and the remaining 38 per cent comprises people crossing the border each day from France, Belgium and Germany. Immigration is thus a triple challenge. While immigration is necessary for economic growth and demographic survival, it creates an important democratic deficit and, hence, a political challenge for the country.

This chapter reviews the immigration policy developments of the past 15 years, paying particular attention to three related issues that have marked the policy debate on immigration. First, the question of the pension system in Luxembourg is addressed, as is the issue of asylum seekers and the special regularization campaign of 2001. Moreover, an overview of the demographic and social features of the immigrant population, as well as the participation of immigrants in public life with particular attention to immigrant activism and participation in political parties, trade unions and NGOs are also provided. Lastly, the chapter concentrates on the public debates on immigration mainly in the media during recent years.

Major developments in Luxembourg's immigration policy

The last quarter of the twentieth century was a period of almost full employment and saw the creation of many new jobs in Luxembourg, as well as an increase in the active population. The unemployment rate over the last 20 years has remained stable between two and three per cent, and had only risen up to five per cent by the beginning of 2006. During this period, there was no real debate on immigration: immigrants arrived and settled in the country and due to the economic growth it was perceived as a 'win/win' situation. The only discourse regarded the successful and smooth integration that was expected by all, though there was no explicit policy regarding immigration and integration. The Law on the entry and residence of foreigners was passed in 1972 and was conceived for non-EEC workers and only a few minor changes have taken place since. This legislation was mainly drawn up in reference to Portuguese, which were Luxembourg's main foreign labour force for a long period. However, given that Portugal has become a member of the

---

1   Average age of the total population: 38.13 years; average age of Luxembourgers: 41.27 years; average age of foreigners: 33.99 years (1 January 2006, Source: Statec).

EU since the mid-1980s, this legislation is now only applicable to a small section of Luxembourg's foreign population, namely migrants from third countries.

There are three types of work permits for immigrants in Luxembourg. The first is for one year and one employer. The second is for four years in the same economic sector, and the third has neither time nor sector limitation. Residence permits are valid for five years. The employer has to prove that s/he could not find an EU employee who is suitable for the job and, therefore, must look for a non-EU national.

With regard to family reunification, while there is no legal text clearly specifying requirements and conditions for family reunification, the Ministry of Justice has issued an information sheet (with neither official header nor reference), wherein it stipulates that:

- Authorizations are provided for minor children and elderly parents who are incapable of providing for their own needs.
- Employees have to prove that they have sufficient means of subsistence and that they are able to assume the financial responsibility for the person they wish to bring to Luxembourg. Moreover, they have to have adequate accommodation.
- Independent professionals can claim the right to family reunification after three years of stay in Luxembourg. They are issued with authorizations that are renewed annually on the basis of proof of sufficient income resources and they must provide a unique bank guarantee of 12,350 euros per family member.

Restrictive asylum policy and the regularization campaign

In the early 1990s, Luxembourg received a few thousand refugees, mainly from Bosnia. There was no specific legislation relating to living and working conditions for asylum seekers. Thus, conditions similar to those applicable to economic migrants were applied in their case as well. In short, asylum seekers were instructed to find a job and accommodation. With the Kosovo War at the end of the 1990s, a few more thousand refugees arrived in Luxembourg. Meanwhile, a law on asylum was passed on April 3rd, 1996. While the legislation regarding asylum seekers became more restricted, the economic situation in Luxembourg remained unchanged. Five to six thousand new jobs were being created annually and these had to be filled either by cross-border workers or by immigrants.

In the spring of 2001, a regularization campaign took place, as a 'one-shot action'. The conditions to be fulfilled were the following: applicants had to prove their presence in Luxembourg before 1 July 1998, or to prove that they had worked without the necessary documents since 1 January 2000. People from Kosovo were entitled to regularization if they had arrived before 1 January 2000. Persons fulfilling one of these conditions were given a six-month period during which they had to find a job.

One of the main side-effects of the regularization was to provide a few hundred people who had applied for asylum with immigrant worker status and, thus, also alleviate the pressure on the asylum procedure. However, many asylum seekers were excluded from this regularization procedure, particularly those from Sandjak, an area covering the south of Serbia and the north of Montenegro, which is populated mainly by Muslims. At the end of the campaign, of the 2,894 people who had applied for regularization, 2,244 had been regularized. Of these, 2,041 came from the former Yugoslavia, and practically all were asylum seekers.

The asylum procedure in Luxembourg is very strict and, as a result, most asylum seekers see their application rejected. In effect, the recognition rate of refugee status in Luxembourg ranges between two and five per cent per year. The government started a large scale operation to repatriate rejected asylum seekers on 5 November 2002. However, when the government started the repatriation process, it became clear that a large number of rejected asylum seekers had been living in Luxembourg for three, four or even five years, and that their children were, in general, well integrated in Luxembourgian schools. In order to exert pressure on the government, on the 17 May 2003, asylum seekers whose cases had been dismissed organized, jointly with ASTI (Association in Support of Foreign Workers), a human chain of 2,000 persons, that ran from the Ministry of Employment to the Ministry of Justice, and demanded that the status of those individuals who had been in Luxembourg for a period of 30 months be regularized.

Three weeks later, the Prime Minister received a delegation of the protesters and reconfirmed that the government would carry out the 'assisted' repatriations in the summer of 2003. In order to apply additional pressure and to encourage them to leave of their own free will, the government cut off their food supplies. Protests were organized on six consecutive Fridays in front of the offices of the Prime Minister during the scheduled time for his weekly press conference. Media coverage was thus guaranteed and, after six weeks, the government restored the provision of food supplies.

The '700,000 state' and the debate on the pension level

Migration policy and measures influencing the admission and integration of the immigrant population are intimately connected with the debate on pensions that has been ongoing for the last 15 years in Luxembourg. In effect, the pensions issue has led to the creation of a political party (ADR[2]) that has based its political platform on asking for a fair deal regarding pension levels in the public and private sectors.

Some background information on this matter is pertinent in this context. In the present pension system, which is based on repartition, the constantly growing working population produces more than needed to pay for pensions. As a result, there is growing political pressure to raise pension levels. However, the present level of pensions can only be maintained for future generations if the active population continues to grow. In his address to Parliament in May 2001, the Prime Minister launched the discussion about a potential future of a state with '700,000 inhabitants'. Using a demographic projection based on a four per cent growth of the economy and of the active population in the next 50 years, he argued that higher pension levels in the future would require a larger number of contributors. However, this raised much debate given that population growth implies more immigration and that rapid population growth may have negative consequences for the Grand Duchy's environment, infrastructure and quality of life.

In 2001, a Special Parliamentary Commission on Immigration was created and a round table discussion was also organized, bringing together the country's main social and economic actors. This meeting led to an increase in the pension levels though it was not coupled with higher contributions. Employers disagreed with the adoption of this reform, arguing that the system would no longer be functional in a few years. The debate was so focused on the figure of 700,000, which was supposed to be reached in 2050, that closer projections, such as the one according to which the Luxembourg/foreign residents rate could reach a 50:50 ratio within a decade, were neglected. Moreover, the possible increase in border-crossing workers, who could reach 300,000 in the year 2050, was also neglected.

As the economic growth predictions dropped from 3–4 per cent to 0.5–1 per cent, the debate on the future '700,000 inhabitants state' seemed far away, but the question of funding the pension system remained. The demographic challenge persisted and in fact according to 2003 data, the foreign population that totals approximately 37 per cent of the country's population had 2,782 children, while the remaining 63 per cent (that is the native population) had only 2,521. See Table 17.1.

---

2   The ADR secured seven parliamentary seats out of 60 in the 1999 elections.

Table 17.1   Births of Luxembourgers and foreigners

Births	1990	1995	1996	1997	1998	1999	2000	2001	2002	2003
Luxembourgers	3284	3151	3288	3084	2947	2875	2917	2723	2692	2521
Foreigners	1652	2270	2401	2419	2439	2707	2806	2736	2653	2782

Source: IGSS (Social Security General Inspection) 1.1.2003.

Thus, given the ageing population and the low birth rates, Luxembourg's younger population can only come from abroad. As a result, in spite of slower economic growth, the need for further immigration remains pressing.

The immigrant population in Luxembourg: main demographic and social features

Luxembourg has relied on a foreign labour force since the end of the nineteenth century when individual workers for the steel industry were called upon for temporary engagements between one and three years on a rotation basis. From 1960 onwards, in reaction to an economic boom and a declining birth rate, the government endorsed a policy that was implicitly relatively open to immigration. For example, in the 1970s, there were significant numbers of economic migrants, particularly from Portugal, who entered Luxembourg without work permits or invitations. Given the country's economic prosperity and the labour market's needs, it was very easy for these 'illegal' immigrants to become legalized almost immediately. Thus, the 'sans-papiers' (paperless) is a semantic creation in Luxembourg and appeared only on the political agenda at the end of the 1990s. See Table 17.2.

Most foreigners are white, European, Catholics. Of these, the Portuguese constitute the majority. Non-EU foreigners make up about five per cent of the local population and include numerous nationalities such as former Yugoslavia, USA, Cape Verde and others. Luxembourg has the highest percentage of foreigners among all OECD countries but, at the same time, it has the lowest rate of naturalization (SOPEMI, OECD 2003: 860).

The proportion of naturalizations by country of origin as indicated in statistics provided by the Ministry of Justice shows some clear trends. It is mainly citizens from non-EU countries who choose to become Luxembourgers. Citizens from other European countries who live in Luxembourg generally choose to adopt a new nationality only if requirements to do so appear reasonable and uncomplicated, and if they are allowed the 'dual nationality' option.

Table 17.2   Foreign nationals by country of citizenship (on 1ˢᵗ January 2003)

Portuguese	66,876
French	24,603
Italians	20,658
Belgians	15,967
Germans	11,556
Serbians & Montenegrins	8,397
British	5,690
Dutch	4,258
Spanish	3,448
Bosnians	2,718
Danish	2,352
Cape Verdeans	1,938
US citizens	1,703
Greeks	1,416
Swedish	1,472
Irish	1,313
Russians	1,086
Finns	941
Poles	885
Austrians	661
Swiss	542
Others	14,740
Total foreign nationals	**193,220**

Source: IGSS (Social Security General Inspection), 1.1.2003.

Luxembourgers work mainly in the civil service, making the production and innovation sectors the principal sectors within which foreign workers are employed. One-third of the workforce in Luxembourg is comprised of Luxembourgers, while the rest is made up of foreigners residing in Luxembourg and by commuters mainly from neighbouring countries (Belgium, France and Germany). Indeed, the workforce represented by commuters from neighbouring countries has come to represent approximately 38 per cent of employees, as Table 17.3 shows.

Table 17.3   Evolution of the active workforce

	Luxembourgers	Foreigners	Commuters
1970	79,500	25,700	7,400
1980	85,100	40,000	11,900
1985	84,500	38,100	16,900
1990	85,700	49,400	33,700
1995	85,300	56,300	55,500
2000	89,000	69,300	87,400
2003	91,200	76,100	106,900

Source: Statec.

As in most other EU Member States, and at the other end of the spectrum, the immigration of highly qualified people is not mentioned in official discourse as it tends to take place without difficulty. That is the case, for instance, for the management of the numerous foreign banks and financial institutions as well as US companies.

Immigrant rights and participation in public life – issues of immigrant integration

In Luxembourg, the debate about the civic participation of foreigners focuses on the right to vote in municipal elections. It has centred on this demand and on the open discourse led by the NGO ASTI (Association in Support of Foreign Workers), which was founded in 1979. It started to popularize this idea through debates and through a big annual celebration, the Festival of Immigration, under the slogan 'to live, to work and to decide together'.

History of democracy equals economic history[3]

If the right to vote was historically linked to real estate, fiscal duties and masculinity, in many countries the ultimate barrier is formed by nationality. If this last requirement is softened, economic grounds speak in favour of a policy of granting political rights on the basis of residence. Given the important role of foreigners to economic development, political integration of this workforce is inevitable. Without immigrants' contributions, the social and insurance systems could not persist in their current form. However, the ageing of the electorate has not facilitated this development or any rearrangement of social contributions. Thus, the political parties that advocate a conservative stance towards pension policies have had the wind behind them. It seems that only through the involvement of younger (foreign) voters will there be a chance for these new policies, which promise modes of financing and are geared towards the future, to find an electorate. This latter may explain why Luxembourg's conservative Prime Minister Jean-Claude Juncker put forth a rather new proposal allowing dual nationality.[4] The aim is to mobilize a younger electorate whose main preoccupation does not lie with the conservation of their pension rights but, rather, with making a living.

---

3   Pauly, 'History of democracy equals economic history', *Forum* 241, October 2004, pp. 44–51.
4   In his speech about the state of the nation on 7 May 2002.

Voting rights: from a claim to a timid application

Political participation was granted to EU nationals on the basis of an EU directive (EC Directive 94/80 1994) on the right to vote in local elections and in European Parliament elections. This directive stipulates that a member state with more than 20 per cent of its population comprised of other EU citizens may obtain three derogations: 1) to ask for a longer duration of stay; 2) to not provide the right to stand for election; and 3) the restriction in the composition of its electoral lists. These derogations have been obtained by Luxembourgian authorities (the only member state with more than 20 per cent of foreign EU citizens) in the field of local and European elections and the admission of EU nationals to these elections.

In the public discourse that was associated with this EU directive, the political forces celebrated more the derogations granted to Luxembourg than the enlargement of the electorate. At that time, the main argument brought forward in support of these derogations was the particularly high percentage of foreigners in Luxembourg, which necessitates a restrictive policy. Critics pointed out the democratic incoherence engendered by this restrictive attitude because in no other country was a similarly high percentage of the population deprived of the right to vote. Furthermore, there existed a necessity to bridge the gap between the realm of the 'real' and the 'legal' society.

Of the 3,226 candidates standing for election at the 1999 municipal elections, 138 (or 4.3 per cent) were foreigners. This, however, is in contrast to the figures for EU citizens resident in Luxembourg which, at that time, comprised 32.1 per cent of the population. Moreover, few immigrants (13.1 per cent) registered in the electoral lists.

EU citizens are under-represented, while non-EU citizens are not represented at all in local decision making processes. Generally, local political activists from other EU Member States tend to be younger and better qualified than the average Luxembourgian and foreign non-EU population.

In terms of European elections, non-Luxembourgian citizens may, since 1994, both elect and be elected through the Grand-Duchy's lists for the European Parliament. As Table 17.4 shows, eight foreign candidates stood for office in 1994, six in 1999 and eight in 2004. In 2004, none of the main parties was represented by a non-Luxembourgian national.

Table 17.4   Foreign candidates for European elections

	1994	1999	2004
ADR	0	0	0
DP	0	0	0
CSV	1	0	0
LSAP	1	1	0
Greng	3	2	1
KPL	1	Common list KPL Left	3
Lenk	2	3	4

Note: Each list has a total of 12 candidates.[5]
Source: electoral lists for the European elections.
Key: ADR = right, DP = liberals, CSV = Christian party, LSAP = social democrats, Greng = greens, KPL = communist, Lenk = left

---

5   In order to obtain an idea of the respective importance of the political parties, here is the number of seats they won in the 2004 national elections (which took place on the smae day as the election for the European Parliament): CSV: 24, LSAP: 14, DP: 10, Greens: 7, ADR: 5.

Registration on the electoral lists for the elections of October 2005[6]

Voting is compulsory for Luxembourgers so there is no need for registration. Once foreigners have registered, voting is compulsory for them as well.

For the October 2005 municipal elections, 23,937 foreigners had registered on the electoral lists. Of these, 22,706 were EU citizens and 1,251 were from third countries who, meanwhile, had been granted the right to vote but not the right to be elected. This represents an increase of 73 per cent as compared to 1999. The highest increase was among Portuguese nationals (+ 117 per cent), followed by Italians (+ 82 per cent), British (+ 60 per cent) and French (+ 52 per cent). Overall, the rate of registration for the municipal elections amounted to 15 per cent. Among EU citizens the rate was 17 per cent and for non-EU citizens it amounted to 6 per cent. Among the nationalities most strongly represented were Italian (21 per cent), Portuguese (20 per cent) and Dutch (19 per cent). Citizens from the 10 new Member States who joined the EU in 2004 had only a 3 per cent representation.

It is worth noting that the growing number of registrations on the municipal electoral lists has direct consequences on the proportion of foreign voters in relation to the overall electorate. In 1999, out of 100 voters, 6 were foreign and 94 Luxembourgian. In 2005, the ratio was 10 foreigners to 90 Luxembourgers. Indeed, in certain municipalities, the electoral weight of foreigners was above average. Larochette, for instance, has the highest ratio with 33 per cent of non-Luxembourgian nationals, followed by Medernach (18 per cent) and Sandweiler (18 per cent).

Immigrant participation in mainstream organizations

In principle, all political parties present in Parliament accept non-Luxembourgian nationals as members. It is, however, impossible to know how many or in what percentage as the parties do not grant access to their register. Some parties such as the CSV (Social-Christian), LSAP (Social-Democrats) and the Green Party have specific internal structures for foreigners wherein Luxembourgers and foreigners discuss their party's issues. This is notably the case for the LSAP's 'Group for Political Integration' which, however, does little to publicly promote its proceedings.

As an indication, below are some relevant figures obtained through a postal survey carried out in November 2004 by the author and aimed at the political parties and trade unions. The CSV (Social Christian) has 250 foreigners within its 9,800 members, the LSAP (Social Democrats) has 5.69 per cent of non-nationals among its members, namely Portuguese (24.31 per cent), Italians (22.15 per cent), French (13.54 per cent), Belgians (10.46 per cent), Germans (15.38 per cent) and others (14.16 per cent). No reply was received from the DP (liberals). The Green Party does not classify its members in terms of their nationality, but estimates them at approximately ten per cent. The ADR also does not distinguish nationalities, but estimates approximately 5.18 per cent of foreign nationals on their municipal electoral lists of 1999. No reply was obtained from the left-wing parties.

As regards trade unions, the OGBL (Social Democrat orientation) has some 45 per cent of foreigners among its 57,000 members. The LCGB (Christian orientation) has approximately 37.41 per cent of non-nationals among its 40,000 members.

---

6   SeSoPi 2004, Sesopi is a catholic research center.

Immigrant participation in NGOs

The situation is more complex in the field of NGOs and other associations. In July 2004, 140 associations fulfilled the requirements needed to take part in the election of the members of the national consultative body CNE which, by law, advises the government. Of these, only 40 exercised their right to vote. It would appear that there is limited interest in participating in this body, which is the only one that has a legal basis, but almost no public visibility. The political voice for these associations is the CLAE, the 'Comité de Liaison et d'Action des Etrangers' (Coordination and Action Platform of Foreigners) which changed its name in 2006 into 'Comité de Liaison des Associations d'Etrangers' (Coordination of Foreigners' NGOs).

The CLAE has signed an agreement with the Ministry for the Family which finances a dozen permanent staff members for its political, cultural and social activities. Until 2003, the CLAE organized training and information seminars for members of municipal consultative bodies (CCEs). It can be estimated that some 100 associations are members of the CLAE.

The CLAE was created in 1985 and generally holds a moderate public profile in terms of its political engagement. The public perception of the CLAE is primarily shaped by the Festival of Immigration, inaugurated by the ASTI in 1981, with the aim of gaining support amongst public opinion in favour of the right to vote for foreigners. The political aims are no longer the main aspect of this event and have been put on the back burner, as priority has been given to promoting the cultural dimensions, considered as less controversial.

Internal differences have hindered the participation of the associations in CLAE. Again, the organization failed to take a common stand with the unions OGB-L and LCGB on the debate on migration held by the parliamentary committee in spring 2004. CLAE refused to contribute to a common paper about a new migration policy launched by the Unions and the NGO community in June 2005 without giving any reason.

Most Portuguese associations are grouped in the CCPL, the Confederation of the Portuguese community in Luxembourg, which holds a biannual conference. Overall, 84 associations of all kinds belong to the membership of the CCPL. The Confederation regularly speaks out in public, notably during its congresses and in the Portuguese press in Luxembourg. Other interventions mainly take place within the communities or are aimed directly at Portuguese authorities. The CLAE has often reproached the CCPL for promoting a restrictive communitarian approach instead of a more transnational one. The relationship between the two seems to have normalized, the current president of the CCPL drawing his paycheck from the CLAE, but at its 2006 spring congress, CCPL took a very critical public position vis-à-vis CLAE. And, in fact, CCPL along with ASTI did not participate in the 2006 General Assembly of CLAE, claiming disrespect of internal rules.

Integration of immigrants

While the governmental programme requires that language and civic education courses be followed by foreigners wishing to acquire Luxembourgian nationality, it remains silent on integration courses for new arrivals. Nevertheless, the relevant department of the Ministry of Family, Social Solidarity and Youth has set up an informal group consisting of officials and NGOs to discuss integration courses. Although this group has been set up, unfortunately it did not meet for 12 months. Meetings resumed in the summer of 2006.

A seminar was held at the end of May 2005 in Luxembourg which brought together government representatives and experts from France, Belgium, Germany and the Netherlands, for an exchange of views on current practices with regard to integration courses. For the moment the only conclusion is a modest pilot project on integration courses.

In addition, in November 2004, Lionel Fontagné, a French expert, proposed a series of reforms relating to immigration and integration in his report (Fontagné, 2004, p. 40) on competitiveness. Fontagné proposed to open the public service to foreigners. He argued that 'nothing decisive can probably be done without changing the balance of the political economy. (...) [the fact that] the dynamic of employment is based essentially on employees who migrate or commute, while voting is concentrated among the working population of the public sphere and non-working population, is a source of blockage, which could be solved by re-examining the questions of dual nationality/ citizenship and political participation of foreigners in elections'. Though these recommendations have not been considered by the authorities, they have contributed to the general debate towards further integration of the immigrant population in Luxembourg.

The major challenge: school and qualification

More than elsewhere, the children of immigrants run into unavoidable obstacles in the officially trilingual Luxembourgian educational system. Luxembourgian, German and French languages co-exist, and half the students leave school without a certificate or a diploma. In general, it has been observed that Luxembourgian children encounter many difficulties in the French language, whereas the children of immigrants fail because of German, which is taught on the basis of an extensive knowledge of the Luxembourgian dialect, a dialect foreign children generally do not have. While the overall failure rate is 4.9 per cent for children in primary education, it is 3.6 per cent for Luxembourgers and 11.9 per cent for Cape Verdean children. There have been some parliamentary documents and debates on the educational situation of foreign children over the past 25 years, but they have not led to any far-reaching legislative actions. Efforts have been made in the area of language teaching, and some pilot projects have been set up by the present government.

Nevertheless, the education of foreign children remains a major challenge. Characteristic of this challenge is the fact that there are 41.4 per cent foreigners in the elementary schools, 13 per cent in high schools, and 60.4 per cent in the modular classes of technical education. The last two editions of the PISA (Programme for International Student Assessment) programme of the OCDE have ranked Luxembourg among the last in the field, and they have emphasized the selective character of Luxembourgian education and its socially unjust character which exacerbates social inequalities instead of reducing them. The result is an excess number of failures. Indeed, at the age of 15, half of the children will have repeated a class at least once.

Public and media discourses on migration

As stated above, Luxembourg is characterized by little unemployment and an increasing workforce due to immigration. The continuously growing foreign population and the traditionally good level of integration seem to be accompanied by a changing discourse. The arrival of a significant number of asylum seekers, especially since the end of the 1990s, may have contributed to this change. The population was accustomed to the many foreigners who were usually employed in the growing labour market needs. However, suddenly, the reference to foreigners' 'laziness' became easy, as the government did not explain why it did not and does not allow asylum seekers to work.

The rather receptive attitude towards immigration of the political parties was challenged by the right-wing party, the National Movement (NB), which adopted an openly anti-immigration position. This party, however, never obtained more than three per cent of the votes (in the 1994 general elections). The Liberals also benefited from a growing concern among the electorate at the increase in the immigrant population and secured significant support from civil servants and from their influential Union (CGFP), which tries to keep public jobs for nationals.

The events of 9/11 had far-reaching effects in Luxembourg as well. The Muslim community was close to obtaining both formal recognition and public financing (just as the Catholic, Protestant, Orthodox and Jewish communities do), when accusations and speculations where launched by the media about Islamist activism. There were no openly anti-Islamic reactions, but suspicions developed. The fact that a large part of asylum seekers from the Sandjak region were also Muslims contributed to the situation and prejudice was often reflected in random police checks in accommodation occupied by Muslim families, and so on.

Automatic association between immigrant and asylum seekers on the one hand and references to criminality and drug trafficking has been frequent, and socially insensitive remarks, particularly in pre-election periods, have often stigmatized large segments of the foreign population. In effect, the discourse regarding foreigners has tended to become more rigid, even accusative at times, while the number of foreign workers and asylum seekers has continued to grow.

Concluding remarks

In the near future, Luxembourg will face a multiple challenge in the field of immigration and integration. The revision of the 1972 law is scheduled for 2006/07. It will be a challenge for politicians to demonstrate the political will for a comprehensive immigration and integration policy. Unfortunately, those two aspects are run by two Ministers of two different parties (Jean Asselborn and Marie-Josée Jacobs), thereby, complicating matters further both in terms of consistency and ideological compatibility. Luxembourg has to create a new legislation and languishes between the known necessity of immigration and the growing reluctance among the population.

Fortunately, all attempts by a right-wing, openly xenophobic political group or party have, thus far, failed. The risk of a kind of soft political apartheid exists, however, despite the Prime Minister's statement in Parliament that 'The participation of the greatest possible number of people in the process of decision-making is for us a national interest' (6 May 2002). Nothing, however, has since happened in this field.

According to Statec, the population of Luxembourg will grow only with the addition of foreign workers. Social cohesion may be greatly tested, given that the autochthonous population fears becoming a minority. The 2003 annual report of the OCDE identifies four immigration-related challenges for the Grand Duchy. The first is integration through education and training. The second is the overloading of the infrastructure, namely the means of transport. The third is an overheated housing market and the fourth is the survival of the welfare state, which entails expenditures for health and ageing.

The legislation regarding citizenship will be changed. The question is open, however, as to the extent to which there will be a real opening to dual citizenship or simply a 'facelift' of the current legislation.

In the field of transposition of EU directives, the Grand Duchy shows little enthusiasm. The directives against discrimination have been waiting five years, and no action has been taken regarding the family reunification or long term residents directives.

In terms of registration for elections, for instance, the overall increase of registrations across all social strata and geographical regions shows the positive impact of a well-targeted information campaign. A mobilization campaign bears fruit only if there is sufficient political engagement, targeted efforts and adequate sensitization campaigns. The efforts targeted at the Portuguese community must be continued and widened to include, for example, the Cape Verdean community, whose registration rate is very low for a community that has been present in Luxembourg for three decades. The work that has been carried out so far must be continued and the activities and meeting points should be used to their best extent, as these have been proved efficient means.

The next few years will be decisive. Indeed, the *laissez-faire* attitude of recent decades can no longer be pursued, given present conditions and the evolution predicted.

References

Fontagné, L. (2004), *Compétitivité du Luxembourg: une paille dans l'acier*. Luxembourg: Ministry of Economy.
OECD (2003), *Report about Luxembourg*. Paris.

Internet-based references

Kollwelter, S. (2005), *Active Civic Participation of Immigrants in Luxembourg*: A contribution to a project on 'Immigrant Civic Participation in the 25 EU countries' (available at http://www. uni-oldenburg.de/politis-europe/download/Luxembourg.pdf).

Chapter 18

Malta

Katia Amore

Immigration to Malta is a relatively recent phenomenon. The country has a long history of emigration which was often used as a 'safety valve' to ease population pressures. With an area of just over 300 square kilometres and a total estimated population of 402,668 at the end of 2004, the Maltese Islands have for several decades been one of the most densely populated countries in the world. As a result, Malta has been facing the problem of how to strike a balance between population growth and the limited economic resources of the country.

An increasing inflow of immigrants began to arrive on the Maltese Islands in 2002, progressively transforming Malta into a country of immigration. The political approach to immigration is generally quite protectionist and mostly based on the very same observation that led so many Maltese to emigrate in the past, namely, that Malta is a small, densely populated country with limited resources and, therefore no space for newcomers. So far, within the country, the issue of immigration has been seen as a question of border control, especially in the context of the EU accession as well as in the face of irregular immigration pressures. Indeed, the debate focuses mostly on irregular migration and the issue of asylum, given the increasing number of asylum claims submitted.

Major developments in Malta's immigration policy

The combination of overpopulation and unemployment in Malta has, during particular historical phases, resulted in the emigration of thousands of Maltese. Indeed, this was also reflected in policies, which consequently focused on emigration. Early efforts to encourage and assist the Maltese to migrate began under British colonial rule and the outflow started to develop on a more permanent basis during the two World Wars when the government established the Department of Emigration to manage the emigration flow (NSO, 2003). After the Second World War, Maltese emigration reached its peak. Government efforts to facilitate it were intensified and turned migration into one of the main political solutions for the country's post-war economic hardship.

Since the 1980s, however, such emigration has slowed down and when, in 2002, the flows reversed, with immigration being on the rise and the specific issues of irregular immigration and asylum increasingly dominating public debate, the government was unprepared for dealing with the influx, and the existing infrastructure was put under considerable strain. These developments brought the need for changes in the legislative frame regarding migration at a time when the country was also going through a general revision of its overall legislative framework in preparation for European Union (EU) membership.

Malta became a Member State of the EU in May 2004 and the years before accession were marked by a wave of rapid and unprecedented changes in various sectors in order to bring laws and policies in line with the *acquis communautaire*. Within this general framework, the area of migration and asylum posed, without a doubt, one of the greatest challenges, since it required significant changes to national laws and policies at a time when the country was also challenged by the sudden surge in the number of irregular migrants arriving in Malta (Camilleri, 2004).

The main legislative instruments that regulate the life of immigrants in Malta are the Immigration Act and the Asylum Act. The Immigration Act (Chapter 217 of the Laws of Malta) was first enacted in 1970 and has since undergone several amendments in order to respond to changing national and international circumstances. As already mentioned, many of the most recent amendments (that is, those brought in by Acts IV and IX of 2000 and Act XXIII of 2002) were introduced to align Malta's immigration law with the EU *acquis*, in view of accession. The Immigration Act regulates matters related to entry, visa regime and border control, as well as the granting of temporary and permanent residence permits and the granting of permission for foreigners to work in Malta. However, in general, the country has a rigid protectionist approach to labour immigration aimed at regulating the employment of foreigners and thereby protecting the national labour force from external competition. Malta has a Work Permit Scheme, giving permission to reside and work in the country for a definite period of time to migrants whose skills requested by the employer are locally absent or in short supply. The Department for Citizenship and Expatriate Affairs is the department responsible for issuing the licences. A board, which includes representatives from different government departments and agencies, examines each application for an employment licence and gives its recommendations. This process takes approximately three to four months. The licences issued are usually valid for one year and may be renewed further, provided such requests are justified. For renewal of the permit, it is recommended that a renewal form be submitted at least five months before the expiration of the current permit. If the foreigner applying is an investor in the manufacturing or financial sectors and holds substantial shareholding in the enterprise, the relative licence may be issued on an indefinite basis.

According to the National Statistics Office, during the past ten years the number of work permit holders has fluctuated, but over the last few years it has almost remained constant. At the end of 2003 the number amounted to 2,928, of whom 813 were females (NSO, 2004). Table 18.1 below indicates the number of work permit holders at the end of June 2002 and the distribution by nationality and sex.

Until recently, the country lacked a refugee law and asylum system, and the Emigrant Commission, set up more than 50 years ago by the local church to deal with emigration issues, was the body in charge of asylum procedures as an operational partner of the UNHCR.

It was only in 2001, with the Refugee Act, that Malta finally established national provisions and procedures with regard to refugees and asylum seekers. The Refugee Act (2001) incorporates the obligations that Malta assumed when signing the 1951 Geneva Convention on asylum and the 1967 Protocol, and provides the framework for procedures and policies for refugees and asylum seekers. The following year, in 2002, a record of 21 boats landed in Malta bringing a total of 1,680 irregular immigrants, who had neither personal documents nor any other means of identification. For the country this was a record number, as it represented almost half its birth rate. Many of the migrants were asylum seekers and had to be dealt with by the Refugee Commission (REFCOM) that had become operational just a few months earlier. When the commission was set up, no one had envisaged such a relatively huge caseload on the basis of previous years' experience. The Act provides that individuals who have been recognized as refugees and those who are given humanitarian protection are granted a residence permit and a work permit when requested (Eurydice, 2003/04).

Table 18.1   Work permit holders by nationality and sex (end of June 2002)

Country	Males	Females	Country (cont.)	Males	Females	Country (cont.)	Males	Females
Afghanistan	1	-	Ghana	5	-	Peru	7	-
Albania	5	11	Greece	6	3	Philippine	25	20
Algeria	9	3	Hungary	3	4	Poland	8	10
Angola	1	-	Iceland	3	-	Portugal	3	-
Armenia	3	1	India	152	14	Rumania	19	10
Australia	25	15	Iran	1	1	Russia	75	76
Austria	25	5	Iraq	17	3	Seychelles	1	-
Bangladesh	4	-	Ireland	9	6	Sierra Leone	10	-
Byelorussia	1	-	Israel	1	-	Slovakia	4	10
Belgium	17	11	Italy	131	12	Slovenia	1	-
Bosnia-Herzegovina	67	8	Japan	-	4	Somalia	4	-
Brazil	2	1	Jordan	4	1	South Africa	3	1
Britain	254	133	Kazakhstan	-	1	Spain	5	6
Bulgaria	101	45	Kenya	1	-	Sri Lanka	7	-
Cameroon	2	-	Korea	1	1	Sudan	5	-
Canada	8	5	Latvia	42	2	Sweden	77	13
China	127	105	Lebanon	9	2	Switzerland	10	2
Columbia	1	-	Libya	133	8	Syria	18	-
Congo	1	-	Lithuania	1	2	Taiwan	-	1
Croatia	8	5	Luxemburg	-	1	Thailand	9	6
Cuba	1	-	Macedonia	3	1	Tunisia	17	5
Cyprus	-	1	Malaysia	4	-	Turkey	38	15
Czech Republic	8	7	Moldavia	-	1	Ukraine	15	16
Denmark	12	10	Morocco	6	8	United States	17	10
Egypt	27	4	Netherlands	32	19	Uzbekistan	-	1
Estonia	-	2	New Zealand	5	1	Venezuela	1	-
Finland	2	7	Nigeria	17	7	Yugoslavia	263	43
France	34	23	Norway	11	2	Stateless	1	-
Georgia	5	2	Pakistan	19	4			
Germany	72	69	Palestine	7	-	**Total**	**2,083**	**830**

Source: NSO 2002.

In general, the issues of irregular immigration and asylum are often intertwined in public debate, as many immigrants who arrive irregularly in the country apply for asylum. According to the National Statistics Office (2005) 'records show that of 3,576 irregular immigrants who arrived in Malta between 2002 and 2004, an average of 85 per cent were coming from Africa' and that 'between 2002 and 2004, Malta granted refugee or humanitarian protection status to 53 per cent of all asylum applicants, thus emerging as the country with the highest acceptance rate in Europe'. In March 2005, UNHCR (2005a) noted that after Cyprus and Luxembourg, Malta had the third highest number of asylum applications per capita in 2004.

These data, together with the consideration that Malta is a small country which has only recently turned into a transit country for immigrants, has maintained the focus of the political debate on matters of border control, irregular immigration and asylum as well as on the need for more cooperation with North African transit countries, and more support from EU Member States.

In terms of border control, the government has assumed the role of the mediator between Europe and North Africa, especially Libya, relying on Malta's strategic geographic position and its historical relations with both sides of the Mediterranean.

In July 2005, speaking at the Libya-European Union seminar on 'Saving Life at Sea and in the Desert', Deputy Prime Minister and Minister for Justice and Home Affairs, Tonio Borg, stated that Malta's adhesion to the new European family should in no way diminish Malta's relationship with North African countries but, on the contrary, it should bring with it a special responsibility of always maintaining a Mediterranean dimension to decisions taken at the core of Europe (Borg, 2005). In few words, the government's approach to immigration has focused mostly on the efforts to stop the flows and obtain support from other EU countries. In line with this, once the immigrants actually land in Malta, the predominant policy is detention in closed centres followed by repatriation, unless they are accorded refugee or humanitarian status.

Detention policies and practices in Malta were harshly criticized for the duration of detention which lasted between one and two years and for the low standards of treatment of the migrants (AI, 2004b). According to government officials, these conditions were due to the difficulties of coping with the unprecedented inflow of migrants and asylum seekers between 2001 and 2003. Lately, some of the problems have been tackled by the government by opening more reception centres, improving general standards and reducing waiting times for processing asylum applications. The most relevant change is the introduction of a temporary limit to detention for asylum seekers, whereby they can only be detained for a maximum of 18 months while they wait for an answer on their application. If this period is exceeded they are moved to an open centre which provides for their accommodation and other basic needs, and which they are free to leave.

However, many organizations working with migrants in Malta, such as the Jesuit Refugee Service, still consider the limit of 18 months to be far too long and consider conditions in the detention centres to be far too harsh. In January 2005, UNHCR criticized Malta's policies and practices in the centres, the strictest in the EU, and condemned certain episodes that were considered deliberate attacks by Maltese soldiers on asylum seekers who were demonstrating peacefully in a detention centre (UN News Centre, 2005). At the end of March 2006, a six-member delegation from the European Parliament inspected the four centres and described the conditions as 'awful, degrading and in breach of the immigrants' human rights' (Kelleher (2006). The delegation also criticized the government's policy of keeping irregular immigrants in detention for 18 months and insisted that this was inhumane and in breach of their human rights. It was also affirmed that, although the government was partly to blame for the situation, it was also true that a lack of a common European Union policy on immigration was creating problems for certain Member States, Malta included, thereby partly supporting Minister Borg's call for help.

As far as integration policies are concerned, minor efforts have been made towards the integration of immigrants and refugees. Malta is still taking its first steps towards realizing and accepting its new role as an immigration country and, at the moment, the accent is still on its role as a transit country towards the rest of Europe. Therefore, there is a predominant view that migrants are not there to stay. Some important developments on this front are taking place in relation to refugees, given the predominance of such a category among the new arrivals, and new policies are developing around the issue of refugee integration. In December 2003, the Ministry for the Family and Social Solidarity took responsibility for refugees and asylum seekers in Malta and for developing an integration programme. In the first year of activities the Ministry has set the priority areas of intervention as accommodation, health and education. New open centres for refugees and asylum seekers were set up using a community model rather than a shelter model, encouraging them to elect their own leaders and play an active role in the centres. Other activities were also organized such as English classes and training courses to improve employability. It is believed by policy-makers that the limited response to some of these initiatives on behalf of refugees and asylum seekers suggest that they are not interested in staying in Malta but rather aim to continue their journey to mainland Europe.

The Maltese immigrant population: main demographic and social features

The fact that immigration is a relatively recent phenomenon in the Maltese context is reflected by the lack of detailed statistics on the issue. In the latest demographic review of the year 2004, the Malta National Statistics Office (NSO, 2006a) explains that the estimated net inflow, based on the last three years' figures on migration, stood at 1,913 persons. This showed a natural net increase of 888 persons in the local and foreign population in Malta. Over the past ten years, the incidence of foreigners within the Maltese population has increased gradually from 7,231 to 11,999 persons.

The 2004 Demographic Review (NSO, 2006a) does not contain a detailed list of the country of origin of non-EU settlers or naturalized citizens. The largest group of aliens living in Malta is constituted of Maltese emigrants, or descendants of Maltese emigrants, returning to Malta and of citizens of other EU Member States, with British expatriates being the main group. Other groups of interest are the historical Indian community, the Arab-Muslim community, predominantly constituted by Libyans, and the smaller Nigerian and Albanian communities.

Many people belonging to these groups have acquired Maltese citizenship, which can be acquired through two different procedures: registration or naturalization. Registration is a process open to specific categories of people who were previously Maltese citizens or are related to a Maltese citizen, while naturalization is a process open to foreigners who meet specific requirements which are defined by the Citizenship Act.

Among the eligible people are those who can prove that have resided in Malta for at least five years, a person born abroad whose father was also born abroad, but whose grandfather and great-grandparent were both born in Malta, a minor child of a Maltese citizen. In short, the granting is discretionary.

The number of people who acquired Maltese citizenship between 1997 and 2002 is listed in Table 18.2 below. Unfortunately, no details in relation to the countries of origin were available.

Table 18.2   Number of people who acquired Maltese citizenship via registration or naturalization between 1997 and 2002

Year	Registrations	Naturalizations	Total
1997	111	128	239
1998	111	110	221
9/98-8/99	76	66	142
9/99-8/2000	299	31	330
9/2000-8/2001	1072	129	1201
9/2001-7/2002	651	105	756

Source: Borg 2001–2002.

Returnees often hold Maltese citizenship or have a background that allows them to obtain it. Moreover, the vast majority of British citizens in Malta holds a resident permit or has acquired Maltese citizenship.

Currently, there are some 45 families, around 300 people, of Indian origin, all from the town of Hyderabad in Sindh, who have adopted Maltese nationality. Their relationship with Maltese society is mostly related to business. The majority of 'l-Indjani' (the Indians), as the Maltese call them, belong to a well-established and respected business community which has been part of Malta's commercial life for the last 115 years and has integrated fully into Maltese society while retaining its cultural roots.

The Arab-Muslim community in Malta is made up of approximately 3,000 individuals, many of whom are now Maltese citizens and the majority of whom come from Libya. The existence of this Libyan population in Malta can be explained by the fact that under Mintoff's government in the late 1970s and 1980s, Malta and Libya developed a special political partnership. Even at the time when Libya was in the international limelight for its alleged involvement in terrorist attacks, Malta maintained friendly relations despite UN sanctions, and opened the door to cooperation. Overall, the number of Libyan tourists increased drastically in 1992, when the United Nations imposed a number of sanctions on Libya as a response to its refusal to surrender suspects wanted in the US and Britain in connection with the 1988 Pan Am plane bombing over Lockerbie. For many Libyans, Malta came to be considered as a stepping stone to the world and thousands of them travelled to Malta as a stopover to other destinations, or to buy essential foodstuffs, American cigarettes and other products that had been rendered scarce by the imposition of sanctions.

Albanians began to arrive in Malta as refugees in the early 1990s. Over the years, some of them have settled, some have married Maltese citizens, others have moved to a third country or returned to Albania. Kosovo Albanian refugees arrived in Malta during the Kosovo crisis in 1999, when the country accepted 110 refugees through the UNHCR evacuation programme (ECRE, 1999).

Nigerians in Malta seem to be the most well known group of foreigners, as they are mostly engaged in football, a sport loved by the whole country, which has over 50 football clubs. Despite the lack of statistical data on their presence in the islands, we can safely claim that while they may not be one of the largest groups, they are one of the most visible ones.

There are no official data available on irregular immigrants, but it is estimated that a significant number are illegally employed, especially in the construction and catering sectors. Finally, according to UNHCR (2005b) data available on the refugee population in 2003, there were 176 Somalis, 70 Iraqi and 52 Congolese in Malta.

Immigrant rights and participation in public life – issues of immigrant integration

Considering the relatively small scale of immigration in Malta, it is not surprising that immigrants' participation in public life in Malta is mostly limited to ethnic associations and self-help groups, followed by religious associations.

With regard to political participation, in general, aliens have the right to vote at local elections if they meet the following requirements: they have an identification card; they are over 18 years of age; they are resident in Malta and have been residing in the country for at least 6 months before registering; they are not declared incapable on account of any mental illness by a Maltese court; they have registered as voters in the Special Register. If the migrant is registered as a voter in the general Electoral Register or the Special Register, he/she automatically qualifies to be elected as a member of the local council (IOM, 2003).

With regard to civic participation, below we give a brief account of the public activities of the main immigrant groups in Malta.

Maltese returnees have various associations, housed by the Emigrants' Commission, which organize activities and meetings. Each of these associations deals with a specific group of migrants and their needs:

- the Association of Families of Migrants (AFE)
- the Maltese–American Association (MAA)
- the Friends of Australia Association (FOAA)
- the Maltese–Canadian Association (MCA)
- the International Wives' Association (IWA).

They might have a far more active level of participation in Maltese society than any other group, but there is a lack of information on their specific involvement in the current political life of Malta or in any other national associations.

The Indian community, once very isolated, seems to have turned into a national local minority and is mostly engaged within Maltese society through business partnerships and relations. The other activities of the community are focused on maintaining the Indian traditions in Malta, dealing mostly with the organization of activities such as Diwali parties and running both the temple and the community centre.

The Arab-Muslim community is more active in pursuing its goals in the attempt to achieve a better degree of integration and participation in Malta and challenge the negative stereotypes and discriminatory behaviour targeted at Arabs and other Muslims. The main public figure is the Imam of the Maltese Muslim community, Sheikh Mohammed El Sadi, who has often been interviewed by the media on matters related to the Muslim community in Malta or to international affairs. The opening of a Muslim primary school represents a great achievement for the community. The school is recognized by the state and has obtained the support and cooperation of the Education Ministry. This is officially a Maltese school that follows the national curriculum but also includes the teaching of Islam and of Arabic. It has the aim of maintaining the identity of children of the Muslim community in Malta and enhancing tolerance and mutual respect between Muslims and other faiths. In fact, the majority of the school's teachers are not Muslims and the headmistress herself is a Christian.

There are other organizations in Malta that involve immigrants, especially asylum seekers and refugees, in their activities and operate mainly to combat racism and xenophobia and promote human rights and integration.

The Integra Foundation, a Maltese not-for-profit organization working to facilitate the integration of minority groups into mainstream society in Malta, focuses especially on refugees and asylum seekers. The aim of the organization is to bridge the gap between minorities and other segments of Maltese society, in order to facilitate their long-term integration. The Foundation organizes activities to oppose racism and xenophobia in Malta, provides support to refugees and asylum seekers through community development projects, promotes the active participation of refugees and other minority groups to maximize their potential as full members of Maltese society and lobbies for the integration of minority groups into Maltese society.

The Jesuit Refugee Service (JRS) Malta focuses on the issue of asylum seekers in detention, offering legal assistance and social work services within detention centres, and lobbies to change the government's detention policy. Moreover, JRS Malta also works actively to raise awareness of the plight of refugees through campaigns and projects such as the EU funded Sahha fid-Diversita campaign (Diversity Strengthens) which includes, among its main activities, the visits of JRS

Malta members of staff and volunteers to secondary schools in Malta and Gozo in order to raise awareness through hands-on activities.

The European Anti-Poverty Network, which was set up by a number of non-governmental organizations and groups involved in the fight against poverty and social exclusion, operates with a special focus on refugees and asylum seekers. The goal of the network is to strengthen the voice of people experiencing or living at the risk of poverty and/or experiencing social exclusion in Malta.

Finally, The National Commission for the Promotion of Equality, which is an autonomous body set up in January 2004, has the task of monitoring the implementation of the Act to Promote Equality for Men and Women that came into force in December 2003, and to promote equality in spheres where it may be lacking. So far the work of the Commission has focused mostly on gender issues. In the future, their work should also include activities aimed at ensuring that Maltese society is free from any form of discrimination.

Public and media discourses on migration

Two main issues have dominated the public debate in relation to migration in Malta in the early 2000s. First, accession to the EU and, second, irregular immigration. In both cases, the starting point for the debate was the aforementioned consideration that Malta is a small and highly densely populated country with 'limited space' to accept newcomers.

Malta's concerns for the potential influx of other EU citizens coming to work in the country after accession and competing with nationals in the job market was a central issue of interest to the general public, the media, politicians and trade unions. These concerns have been particularly expressed by the General Workers Union Policy Paper on Social Security and Migrant Workers, who are concerned about the potential influx of workers coming from EU countries in parallel to the possible outflow of the best trained and the best qualified Maltese citizens wanting to work in other EU countries (General Workers Union, 2000). These points were incorporated in the negotiations with the EU on free movement of persons that were concluded in June 2001.

In general, the issue of irregular immigration remains the most relevant migration issue discussed in the country. The highest circulation newspapers, *The Times of Malta* (TOM), *The Sunday Times of Malta* (STOM), *The Malta Independent* (daily) (TMI), The Malta Independent on Sunday (TMIS) and *Malta Today* (a Sunday newspaper) and the rest of the national media regularly report news of immigrants landing illegally in the country. The main stories usually cover: vessels overcrowded with immigrants stuck off the Maltese coast (between Malta and Sicily, or between Malta and Tunisia), and accidents with immigrants dying at sea. In 2004, special attention was given to relations between Malta and Italy on the issue of irregular immigration and border control, and to the efforts to find a solution to human trafficking in collaboration with the Libyan Government. In May 2004, an Amnesty International Report (AI, 2004a) claimed that the majority of around 220 Eritrean illegal immigrants, who had been forcibly repatriated by Malta in 2002, had been imprisoned and tortured upon arrival in Eritrea, with many still being held captive. The story was taken up by the Maltese press and was in the media from around mid-May right up to European Parliament (EP) election week (Pace, 2004). It was presented as mismanagement by the Maltese Government.

In the 'pre-accession to the EU' phase, both the issue of migration in relation to EU membership and irregular immigration were brought together by the widespread worry that joining the EU might also lead to an increase in the number of irregular immigrants arriving in Malta. MIC, the Malta-EU Information Centre, addressed these concerns in a pamphlet titled 'Question & Answer on Malta and the EU' which dealt with various issues of public concern related to accession.

The pamphlet answered the question 'If we join the EU, will the number of illegal immigrants increase?' It stated that immigrants would not increase because most immigrants would not see Malta as their final destination. However, it continued, if, in the future, Malta were to be perceived as an economically advanced EU country, it may start attracting illegal immigrants in its own right. Moreover, membership of the EU would certainly place on Malta a greater sense of responsibility to police its coastal borders; a point which is included in the membership obligations (MIC 2002, 13).

In conclusion, the main focus of the debate on immigration in Malta is the phenomenon of irregular immigration and asylum. The worry about more immigrants on the Maltese shores and the questions related to the best solution to this problem dominate both the public and the political debates. However, as Camilleri (2004) explains, the worries over irregular immigration and the general protectionist approach to immigration in Malta are confronted every day by a different reality. Indeed, a number of migrants, including those who are staying illegally on the islands, are actually employed in various sectors, and in particular in the construction and the catering industries. Despite the fact that there are no reliable statistics available on the true extent of this phenomenon, reports carried in the local media highlight the continued relevance of this issue.

Another aspect which has been widely discussed publicly is that regarding Malta's detention policy. This became especially poignant after Amnesty International's Report against Malta's policy and practices was published in 2004. A special case is that of 100 journalists who signed a petition against the government's refusal to allow them access to immigrants' detention centres in February 2005.[1] The majority of Maltese media journalists and editors disapproved of this refusal and insisted that the government should, in the interest of the public, alter its stance. It was strongly maintained that refusing all media requests for access limits local media coverage of immigrants' detention, and denies the possibility of ascertaining the veracity of the news and gathering first-hand information.

It is also interesting to note that, in recent years, the question of Maltese national identity has also acquired a central role in the political and intellectual debate in Malta. This was mostly prompted by the possibility of joining the EU rather than by the increasing number of immigrants reaching the Islands, and became an integral part of the political debate on Malta's positioning in relation to Europe. Nevertheless, the general debate on Maltese identity and the relationship between Malta and Europe, on the one hand, and Malta and the south of the Mediterranean on the other, has relevant implications for the life of ethnic minorities and immigrants in the Islands. The political debate on the possible role of Malta within the EU focused on the assumption that Malta could assume the role of a bridge between Europe and North Africa and, as explained earlier, this remains the case. The geopolitical position of the Islands and their historical role as a crossroads between the North and the South, the West and the East has been presented both as an asset in terms of bridging the two sides of the Mediterranean and as a source of challenges in terms of identity, border permeability and border security. In this strategic geographical position between Europe and North Africa, the Maltese tend to stress their sense of belonging to Europe as a way of distinguishing themselves from North Africans (Schembri, 2004). As a matter of fact, much of the public debate on immigration reflects general stereotypes and xenophobic reactions to North Africans in Malta, especially Libyans, with serious consequences for the local immigrant North African population, which faces the highest level of prejudice and discrimination. While, at the

---

1   The petition was signed by editors, journalists, photographers, cameramen, columnists working for *PBS, MediaLink, One News, Where's Everybody, The Times, The Sunday Times, MaltaToday, the Malta Independent, the Malta Independent on Sunday, l-Orizzont, It-Torca, the Malta Business Weekly, the Malta Financial and Business Times, di-ve.com*, as well as by correspondents and independent journalists (MaltaMedia News, 2005).

governmental level, Malta and Libya enjoy good relations, the general attitudes of the Maltese vis-à-vis Libyans have degenerated over the years (Vella Gauci, 1996). The problem touches everyday relations between the Maltese and the Libyans, from the customs at the airport to banks and hotels, to shops and rental agencies, to the streets. Arabs, especially young males, are generally perceived as criminals or potential criminals. Indeed, this has reached such levels of racism that some night-clubs in Bugibba (an area famous for its nightlife) have started to refuse entrance to so-called 'Arab looking' people and one specific place has displayed a sign, in Arabic, stating that 'Arabs are not welcome here' (Schembri, 2004).

Equally worrying is the overall growing level of racism against refugees and asylum seekers. Between 2005 and 2006, an increasing number of arson attacks against houses or vehicles belonging to human rights activist journalists and JRS volunteers, as well as members of staff who are actively working against discrimination, have raised the levels of tension and have prompted several anti-racist initiatives by various local organizations.

Concluding remarks

The new millennium brought with it two major changes in Malta which have undoubtedly affected present and future developments in Maltese society. These have been accession to the EU in 2004, and the gradual switch from a country of emigration into one of immigration from 2002. Both issues have been tightly connected in the Maltese political and public debates by underlining Malta's potential role of mediator between North Africa and Europe in relation to the problem of managing migration flows.

The political rhetoric on immigration is largely based on the consideration that Malta is a small, densely populated country that cannot cope with the influx of immigrants. This is a key point that influences both the public debate and the development of policies which consequently focus mostly on border control. This is also strengthened by the assumption that immigrants do not want to stay in Malta, but rather use it as a transit country to the rest of Europe. As a consequence, efforts have been directed at finding solutions to reduce the flows and ensure that those migrants who reach Malta irregularly are sent back to their country of origin or their last country of transit. The government's strict detention policies are directly linked to these efforts and are intended to deter and control. Despite repeated criticism from international organizations, refugee agencies and MEPs, detention policies seems to be 'here to stay' and they have also been used to show the rest of the EU that Malta cannot cope alone with the pressures present at the EU's external borders.

On the contrary, little effort has been directed towards facilitating the integration of immigrants and refugees, and promoting their participation in Maltese public life. Exceptions are mostly in respect of Maltese returnees, other EU nationals and communities of immigrants which have a longer historical presence on the Islands, such as the Indian community. Policies designed to receive and integrate newcomers have only recently made their first steps. On the one hand, this can be justified by the relatively recent development of the phenomenon which has clearly caught the country unprepared; on the other, if governmental policies and the public debate continue to focus predominantly on border control, Malta runs the risk of ignoring the urgent need for better reception and integration policies for its 'new' immigrant population.

Now mostly used as a transit country, Malta could soon realize that a number of immigrants are coming to stay and, especially, that the country actually needs them. According to the 2005 Preliminary Report of the Population Census (NSO, 2006b), if the current socio-demographic trends continue in the future, with a declining fertility rate and a low immigration intake of younger persons, a steady increase in the old age-dependency ratio is expected in the coming years. This will bring with it many of the economic and social problems that other EU countries are already experiencing.

Finally, the need for more research on various aspects of the migration phenomenon is pressing. There are both quantitative and qualitative gaps which range from the political to the economic and sociological perspectives. A deeper analysis of the relationship between Maltese society and immigrants could play an important role in the general debate on immigration. It could contribute to a better understanding of the impact of immigration in Malta, to the development of more efficient integration policies and antidiscrimination strategies and, ultimately, to furthering Malta's acclaimed role of mediator between the north and the south of the Mediterranean.

References

Borg, T. (2005), Opening Address by the Deputy Prime Minister and Minister for Justice and Home Affairs, Tonio Borg, on 'Saving Life at Sea and in the Desert', Libya-European Union seminar, 20 July 2005.

IOM (International Organization for Migration) (2003), *Informed Migration – Malta*. IOM: Malta.

Kelleher, D. (2006), 'European Parliament delegation visits detention centres: "Conditions are awful and degrading"', *The Independent*, 25 March 2006.

MIC (Malta-EU Information Centre) (2002), *Question and Answer on Malta and the EU*. Malta: MIC.

NSO (National Statistics Office Malta) (2002), *Demography – The Migration Factor*, News Release E-stats Service No. 107/2002.

NSO (National Statistics Office Malta) (2003), *Migration Results from the 1995 Malta Population and Housing Census: Comparison with other Data Sources Regarding Coverage and Reliability*, Working Paper No. 8, 23 April 2003.

NSO (National Statistics Office Malta) (2004), *Official Statistics of Malta*, Demographic Review 2003.

NSO (National Statistics Office) Malta (2005), *World Refugees' Day 2005*, News Release, No. 133/2005, 20 June 2005.

NSO (National Statistics Office Malta) (2006b), *Census 2005 Preliminary Report*.

NSO (National Statistics Office) Malta (2006a), *Official Statistics of Malta*, Demographic Review, 2004.

Schembri, K. (2004), 'Will Malta be a bridge to the south?' *Europe Mag*, 9 May 2004.

UNHCR (2005a), *Asylum levels and trends in industrialised countries – 2004*. Geneva: UNHCR.

UNHCR (2005b), *Statistical Yearbook 2003: Trends in displacement, protection and Solutions*. Geneva: UNHCR.

Vella Gauci, J. (1996), *Christian-Muslim Relations as a Topos in Maltese Historiography, Literature, and Culture*. PhD thesis. Birmingham University.

Internet-based references

AI (Amnesty International) (2004a), Open Letter to the Maltese Minister for Justice and Home Affairs. AI Index: EUR 33/002/2004, 7 June 2004 (available at http://web.amnesty.org/library/Index/ENGEUR330022004?open&of=ENG-MLT, accessed 18 December 2004).

AI (Amnesty International) (2004b), Malta (available at http://web.amnesty.org/report2004/mlt-summary-eng, accessed 18 December 2004).

Borg, T. (2001–02), Rapport mill-Onor. Tonio Borg Ministru ta' l-Intern u l-Ambjent, Ministeru ta' l-Intern u l-Ambjent 2001–2002 (available at http://www.doi.gov.mt/EN/archive/gverninsahhupajz/minreports/intern.pdf, accessed 31 January 2006).

Camilleri, K. (2004), *European Union and Member State Migration and Asylum Law and Policy – Malta* (Dublin: International Federation for European Law (FIDE) XXI Congress), 2–5 June 2004.

ECRE (1999), Country Report 1999 (available at http://www.ecre.org/publications/2specificgroups.shtml accessed 20 March 2005).

Eurydice (2003/04), *Integrating Immigrant Children into Schools in Europe: Malta* (available at http://www.mszs.si/eurydice/pub/eurydice/migranti/Malta.pdf, accessed 12 April 2006).

General Workers Union (2000), 'Policy Paper – Social Security and Migrant Workers' (available at http://www.gwu.org.mt/mea.html, accessed 1 January 2006).

Malta Media News (2005), 'Journalists insist in accessing immigrants' detention centres', 16 February 2005 (available at http://www.maltamedia.com/news/2005/gp/article_5150.shtml, accessed 20 March 2005).

Pace, R. (2004), The European Parliament Election in Malta, 12 June 2004, European Parliament Election Briefing No. 5 Sussex European Institute, European Parties Elections & Referendums Network (available at http://www.sussex.ac.uk/sei/1-4-2-2.html, accessed 20 October 2005).

UN News Centre (2005), UN refugee agency condemns Malta's treatment of asylum seekers, January 2005 (available at http://www.un.org/apps/news/story.asp?NewsID=13071&Cr=Malta&Cr1=, accessed 1 April 2005).

Chapter 19

The Netherlands

Jessika ter Wal

Until 1961, the Netherlands had a negative migratory balance as many Dutch left to settle in Canada and Australia after the Second World War. During the 1950s, the main incoming flows were citizens from the former colony of Indonesia. Starting a bit later than other Northern European countries, in the 1960s and 1970s, the Dutch Government recruited unskilled workers from Southern Europe, Turkey and Morocco. The labour migrants recruited from Southern Europe and Yugoslavia in part returned home during the economic crisis in the 1970s and the ending of the recruitment policies. By contrast, the Turkish and Moroccan migrants, despite initial government plans to stimulate re-emigration, often ended up staying and are now among the largest migrant populations in the Netherlands. Starting in the mid-1970s, they benefited from possibilities of family reunification; and family formation began in the 1980s. Since the 1970s, there has also been a consistent and continuing migration from the Dutch overseas territories, mainly from Suriname and from the Dutch Caribbean islands (Antilles and Aruba), which continue to be part of the Dutch crown and, as a result, have no restrictions on immigration.

The Dutch multicultural model which followed during the 1980s, and partly continued during the 1990s, was put under strain in the 1990s and 2000s. The persisting socioeconomic disadvantage of the migrant population and their descendants has been a key issue in media coverage and political debate. In particular the socioeconomic position of migrants with a Muslim background and the affirmation of Muslim communities' identity in public life have been presented as a problem by media and politicians alike. The general policy framework regulating immigration to the Netherlands is discussed below. Secondly, some basic figures for the main groups and motives of migration are presented, and some information is provided about the active participation of migrants in public life. Finally, the main issues in recent public debates about migration and integration of migrants in Dutch society are summarized.

Major developments in the Netherlands' immigration policy

Until the late 1970s the Netherlands was a reluctant country of immigration in which the idea of temporary migration was maintained. However, by the mid-1970s, a number of factors convinced the political elite that the benign neglect of immigrant communities justified by the official stance that the Netherlands was not an immigration country was counterproductive. It became clear that immigrants were here to stay, and that as the economy worsened and industrial restructuring was under way, they were not faring well.

During the 1980s an 'ethnic minorities' policy was developed, aimed at those immigrant groups 'for whose presence the government feels a special responsibility (because of the colonial past or because they have been recruited by the authorities), and who find themselves in a minority situation' (Minderhedennota, 1983, p. 12). The ethnic minority policy aimed to promote the participation of immigrants in social and economic life, and to stimulate good inter-ethnic relations, with a focus on equal opportunity and the fight against discrimination. Rath (1991) characterized the effects of this policy of 'integration with maintenance of own identity' as 'minorization' (see also Koopmans and Statham, 2000). The policy included initiatives that protected religious and cultural diversity, following the segmented pluralism of Dutch pillarized society until the 1960s.[1] For example, education in the languages of the country of origin was stimulated, Hindus and Muslims were allowed to set up their own primary schools and airtime on radio and television was reserved for the different religious and migrant groups.

In the 1990s, the perceived failure of the ethnic minority policy expressed, among other things, in the persisting disadvantaged position of the groups concerned, led to a more individualist 'assimilationist' stance that replaced the separateness nourished in the previous multicultural policy. The emphasis in this new policy is on integration and increasing the civic participation of migrants. In 1996, the government introduced compulsory courses of civic integration on a national scale that offered orientation on the Dutch language and society for newcomers. Later, these courses were also directed at 'old-comers' but the institutions have difficulty reaching this group. A new law for compulsory civic integration was due to be introduced on 1 January 2007.

In the field of asylum, a strict regime has been adopted with the 2000 Aliens Act. This law introduced shorter procedures for establishing the right to asylum, one single form of residence permit for those granted asylum, with a duration of three years, and with the possibility of obtaining a fixed residence permit. Those with a temporary residence permit were allowed to work and to apply for study allowances and public housing. In 2004, the government decided to send 26,000 asylum seekers back to their countries of origin. These were asylum seekers whose application had not been accepted.

Several other policy changes introduced after 2003 have produced an increasingly strict entry regime. As of November 2004, in a bid to reduce 'marriage immigration', the minimum salary required for Dutch residents who want to bring their foreign partner into the Netherlands was raised by 230 euros, and the age limit was raised from 18 to 21 years.[2] In 2005, the figure of granted residence permits for family formation dropped by 25 per cent, as compared to the previous year. After mid-2005, non-EU nationals who want to immigrate to the Netherlands must pass an integration test in their home country before arrival, that is, in the Dutch embassy in the country of origin.[3] In 2005, the Senate approved a draft bill, excluding citizens from Western-orientated third countries such as Australia, Canada, Japan, New Zealand, United States and Switzerland from this

---

1   Historically, there have been several 'pillars' in Dutch society reflecting religious pluralism: a Protestant pillar, a Catholic pillar and a non-denominational or lay pillar (Lijphart, 1975). Peaceful coexistence among various groups in society rested upon their equal access to societal and political institutions (equal opportunities) and the emancipation of all segments of society so that there would not be groups with a lower social position (equality in outcomes). Although the pillar system influenced the organization of society and politics, Dutch society in the second part of the twentieth century became largely secularized.

2   'After' (1 November 2004), Dutch residents must earn at least a net EUR 1,319 a month if they want to bring their foreign partner into the Netherlands; this figure equals 120 per cent of the minimum wage (used to be 100 per cent). This requirement is only applicable for family formation, that is, the non-national who wishes to obtain a residence permit in order to live in the Netherlands with a married or registered partner, where the relationship has started while the Dutch partner was already living in the Netherlands. Single parents who take care of children under the age of five, and people above the age of 57½, who were hitherto exempted from the income requirement, now need to have sufficient means of living as well.

3   The Netherlands government announced plans to require those applying for immigrant status to pass a test of Dutch language and culture in their countries of origin before receiving immigration visas.

obligation. This bill has been criticized by the National Bureau against Racial Discrimination[4] for making distinction on the basis of nationality.

The latest regularization programme for illegal aliens in the Netherlands was in 1999. Between October and December of that year, illegal aliens could apply for legalization of their status. Five thousand applicants saw their application refused, while 2,000 were accepted.[5]

Naturalization

The policy regime for naturalization has also seen fundamental changes that reflect more assimilationist positions. As of 1 October 1997, maintenance of dual nationality is no longer allowed and, with exceptions, naturalization requires the renouncing of one's original nationality.[6] Currently, the condition to apply for naturalization is that one must have resided for at least five consecutive and preceding years (three years if one is married to a Dutch citizen) on Dutch territory and must be considered a 'participating citizen' of Dutch society (this is, proved to have achieved a reasonable knowledge of the Dutch language, and socioeconomic and sociocultural integration into Dutch society). As of 1 April 2003 this knowledge is tested using a naturalization exam. Exempted from the test are those who have attended the Dutch educational system or have already completed the compulsory newcomers' course.

In addition, as of 1985, children born and residing on Dutch territory since birth can acquire Dutch state citizenship between the ages of 18 and 25 (Jacobs, 1998, p. 351). This option is also available for stateless persons born in the Netherlands and who have lived in the country for at least three consecutive years. People married to a Dutch national for at least three years and who have lived at least 15 consecutive years in the country are also eligible to apply. Finally, children under 18 born from such a marriage can also obtain Dutch nationality in the same procedure.

The immigrant population in the Netherlands: main demographic and social features

The current Dutch migrant population is characterized by a growing number of descendants of immigrants from former recruitment countries and post-colonial minorities. Moreover, it is characterized by a new migration based on family reunification, asylum and, in particular, family formation. In 2004, 'foreign-born' immigrants categorized as first-generation immigrants were ten

---

Visa applicants would have to pay an exam fee of €350, and eventually the 755,000 non-EU foreigners living in the Netherlands may also have to pass the language and culture test.

4   The *Landelijk Bureau ter Bestrijding van Rassendiscriminatie* acts as the coordinating body of several official discrimination monitors, both for national and international organizations (http://www.lbr.nl).

5   The conditions to apply under the 'Temporary Measure for Illegal Aliens' were: i) a proven permanent residence in the Netherlands since 1992; ii) possession of a Dutch social fiscal number since 1992; iii) possession of a valid passport; iv) no expulsion from the Netherlands after 1991; v) no use or possession of false documents or false data, and vi) no criminal record.

6   Exceptions are when the applicant has the nationality of a state whose legislation does not allow the renouncing of nationality; the applicant is born on Dutch territory and remains there during the application; the applicant's spouse is of Dutch nationality, or the applicant has obtained refugee status from the Dutch state. Because of official policy in the country of origin, Moroccan citizens automatically keep their Moroccan nationality; immigration minister Rita Verdonk announced in 2004 that she wanted to ask the Moroccan authorities to reconsider this policy. The Dutch policy of avoiding dual nationality is allegedly part of the assimilationist philosophy and of the practical aim of effective terrorism prevention.

per cent of the population. Another nine per cent was formed by descendants of immigrants, who are referred to in the Dutch statistics as 'second generation' (see Table 19.1).[7]

Table 19.1   Population total and major migrant groups (1 January 2004)

	1st generation (foreign born)	2nd generation	Total
Total population			16,258,032
Foreign-born and foreign-background total	1,602,730	1,485,422	3,088,152
Non-western total	1,021,074	647,223	1,668,297
Turkey	194,319	157,329	351,648
Morocco	166,464	139,755	306,219
Surinam	187,990	137,291	325,281
Netherlands Antilles and Aruba	84,024	46,698	130,722
Indonesia	133,503	264,999	398,502
Former Yugoslavia	55,381	20,965	76,346
Former Soviet Union	32,734	9,299	42,033
Poland	20,773	14,769	35,542
Afghanistan	32,123	3,920	36,043
China	29,422	12,272	41,694

Source: Central Bureau for Statistics, The Netherlands.

By 2003, only 25 per cent of incoming migrants were from those countries of origin comprising the four largest ethnic minority groups (Turkey, Morocco, Suriname, the Antilles/Aruba). They migrated mainly under the label of family reunification and family formation.[8] As can be seen in Figure 19.1 below, family formation increased considerably between 1995 and 2003. In 2003, it was the most important motive, especially amongst non-Western migrants (CBS, 2004).

---

7   The operational definition is that people have a foreign background if at least one of their parents is born abroad. Persons with a foreign background (or origin) are distinguished in two different ways. Firstly, persons who were born abroad constitute the first generation and are distinguished from persons where were born in the Netherlands and are referred to as second generation. Secondly, persons with a foreign background are classified as Western or non-Western, according to their country of birth. If they are born in the Netherlands (the second generation), the classification is based on the mother's country of birth. If she was also born in the Netherlands, the background is determined by the father's country of birth. The category 'non-Western' includes persons with a Turkish, African, Asian and Latin American background. Persons with a Japanese and Indonesian background are classified as Western on the basis of their social and economic position in Dutch society. The category 'Western' consists of persons from Europe (excluding the Netherlands and Turkey), North America, Oceania, Japan and Indonesia (including the former Dutch East Indies).

8   Family formation means when a non-national obtains a residence permit in order to come and live with a partner in marriage, registered partnership, or living together, where the relationship was formed while the partner lived in the Netherlands. Family reunification occurs when a non-national wishes to have a residence permit in order to come and live in the Netherlands with another member of the family (for example children wishing to live with their parents).

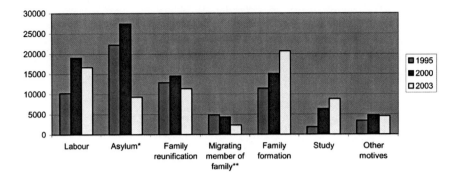

*Asylum seekers registered in the municipalities after obtaining residence permit, or after 6 months'
residence in a reception centre.
**Members of family who immigrate (family reunification) in the same year as, for example, the labor
migrant.
Source: Central Bureau of Statistics.

Figure 19.1   Development of migration motives (1995–2003)

In 2003, one-third of the group of migrants who came for family formation was made up of Turks
and Moroccans. According to official figures from 2003, three-quarters of Turkish and Moroccan
migrants, both of the first and second generation, living in the Netherlands were married to partners
from their country of origin (Hooghiemstra, 2003).

Table 19.2   Immigration of non-nationals by migration motive (2003)

	Labour	Asylum	Family reunification*	Family formation	Other**	Total
Western	13,200	1,700	6,600	5,500	6,400	33,400
Non-Western	3,400	7,600	7,000	15,100	6,800	39,900
Turkey	900	200	1,200	3,900	200	6,400
Morocco	100	100	1,200	2,900	200	4,500
Suriname	-	-	700	1,400	300	2,400
Other non-Western	2,300	7,300	3,900	6,900	6,100	26,500
Total	16,600	9,300	13,600	20,600	13,200	73,300

*Including members of the nuclear family who migrate.
**Group composed of students, interns, au pairs, economically inactive and people entering for medical visits.
Source: Central Bureau for Statistics/Central Registration Foreigners.

By the end of the 1980s and throughout the 1990s, requests for asylum rose to a peak of over fifty
thousand in 1994, and over forty-five thousand in 1998. With the introduction of more restrictive
measures, in 2001 the number of asylum requests started to substantially decrease. In 2003, asylum
requests had dropped to 13,000, of which only 9,000 were granted (CBS, 2004; see Figure 19.2
below). On 1 January 2004, approximately 200,000 people of refugee origin were registered in the
municipal administrations with a residence permit. This figure not only included refugees, but also

asylum applicants, persons who joined the asylum applicant under a family reunification scheme, as well as children of applicants who were born in the Netherlands. The largest refugee groups were Iraqis (mainly Kurdish), Afghans, Iranians and Somalis. Almost one-third of the Somali refugees who were first accepted in the Netherlands have migrated to the UK.

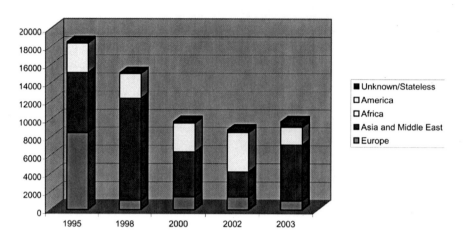

Source: Central Bureau of Statistics.

Figure 19.2   Accepted asylum applications by region of origin (1995–2003)

In 2002, a research group at the Universities of Rotterdam and Utrecht estimated the number of illegal aliens in the Netherlands between 112,000 and 163,000. This was based on police reports from 25 police regions and interviews with 156 undocumented aliens (Engbersen et al., 2002). The population of undocumented aliens at the time was made up mostly of men of between 20 and 40 years of age. This figure included asylum seekers whose requests had been refused, but who had not left the country, as well as people illegally employed or self-employed in various sectors of the underground economy.

Naturalization

Although naturalization has been common practice for many years, the conditions set by the government have become more stringent, and rates have dropped in recent years. This is partly due to changing regulations and partly due to a harshening of the attitudes towards foreigners. In anticipation of a change in the law in 1997 which ended the possibility of maintaining dual nationality, almost 80 thousand non-Dutch were naturalized in 1996. This remains the highest annual figure for naturalization. In 2000, over 90 per cent of those born in Suriname and residing in the Netherlands had Dutch nationality. The second largest naturalized group were the Hong-Kong Chinese, followed by Vietnamese migrants, of whom over 80 per cent hold Dutch nationality. Also over 50 per cent of the Ethiopian, Somali, Egyptian, Polish, Iranian, Chinese, Turkish and former Yugoslavia-born people held Dutch nationality in the year 2000 (de Valk et al., 2001).

Recently, however, the number of naturalizations has dropped consistently, from 42,000 in 2002 to 21,000 in 2003 (CBS, 2005). In particular, the number of Turkish residents who obtained naturalization has declined. In 2003, less than 4,000 Turkish obtained Dutch nationality. The same applies to Moroccans, who, while they form the largest group of those naturalized (25 per cent in 2003), have seen their numbers decrease at almost twice the rate of the three preceding years. The difference in naturalization rates between Turkish and Moroccan citizens is mostly the result of different legislation in the country of origin. Moroccan law does not accept the renouncing of Moroccan nationality. By contrast, Turkish immigrants lose their Turkish nationality if they opt for naturalization.

Segregation

Residential segregation is a serious problem in the Netherlands and has been on the rise since the mid-1990s (van Praag, 2003). Most people with a 'non-Western' foreign background live in the most urbanized part of the country and in particular in the four major cities, namely Utrecht, Amsterdam, Rotterdam and The Hague. Indeed, as much as 40 per cent of the largest minority groups (Turks, Moroccans, Surinamese, Antilleans) are concentrated in these four major cities (SCP, 2003). In addition, minority groups are also concentrated within specific neighbourhoods (van Praag, 2003). Segregation indices are highest for Turks and Moroccans and lowest for Surinamese and Antilleans. Moreover, ethnic segregation overlaps greatly with socioeconomic segregation (Veld, 2003). In 2004, unemployment among young people with a Moroccan background was twice as high as among young native Dutch people. Furthermore, among the Moroccan population as a whole (aged between 15 and 64) unemployment was four times as high as among native Dutch people in the same age category.

Immigrant rights and participation in public life – issues of immigrant integration

Article 1 of the 1983 Constitution forbids discrimination 'on the grounds of religion, belief, political opinion, race, or sex, or on any other grounds'. The Constitutional principle of anti-discrimination implies that migrants and (ethnic, cultural and religious) minorities have the same rights as Dutch citizens to assembly and to access or to set up civic organizations. Moreover, foreign-born people can be elected representatives of political parties and clubs.

The Dutch reliance on a system of consultation has implied a favourable position towards ethnic minority organizations. These organizations are eligible for public funding although they are non-governmental. However, the fragmentation and internal division of religious organizations in general has made it difficult to provide effective consultation mechanisms. According to scholar Jean Tillie, the turn to a more republican approach adopted by local authorities in Amsterdam, and the abolition of the advisory boards, has had the effect of further isolating ethnic and/or religious self-organizations.[9] Furthermore, the de facto segregation in the labour market and housing has also had its impact on the persistence of segregation in other areas of life, such as education and sports.

Traditionally, the Dutch system has supported the functioning of associations on the basis of religious denominations through the pillar system and the constitutionally defended freedom of

---

9   'There are still ethnic organizations, but with the abolition of the advisory boards, these have become islands. Individuals and groups have become isolated and isolation favors radicalization. An example is the Grey Wolves, an ultranationalist Turkish organization. They had their own mosque and soccer club in Amsterdam. The president of the soccer club was also represented in the Turkish advisory board on minorities policies. There were also many other connections with 'normal' Turkish organizations. That seems dangerous, but because of this social network the radicalization of the Grey Wolves was in fact limited. Democracy is contagious' (Jean Tillie 'Democratie is besmettelijk' interview met Jean Tillie, *Folia* **58**(26), 11 March 2005, pp. 14–15).

religion (Rath et al., 1996; Fennema and Tillie, 1999; Sunier, 2000). Due to the separation of Church and State, the latter does not subsidize religious organizations as such, but rather those organizations maintaining educational facilities. Hence, the Dutch system hosts and financially supports not only state schools, but also those of Catholic, Protestant and Jewish orientations, as well as schools based on other philosophies and religions, such as Muslim and Hindu primary schools. Schools receive public funding as long as they respect the rules laid down by law regarding the curriculum and educational methods. The constitutional freedom of education means that parents can choose to send their children to any of the available schools.

In the religious domain, the active civic participation of ethnic minorities is found to be much stronger than that of the native Dutch. While 60 per cent of the Dutch population are members of a religious association, for Turks and Moroccans this reaches 93 per cent and for the Surinamese and Antilleans 82 per cent. In all other domains (politics, trade unions, sports and recreation, hobbies, the environment) native Dutch have a (much) higher participation (de Hart, 2005). The most active religious groups are the Muslims. An analysis of claims made in press coverage during 1998–2002 revealed that Turkish migrants were more visible in the public debate as representatives of ethnic and/or religious self-organizations. Instead, Moroccans were more often represented individually among mainstream Dutch organizations, both at the political level and in the public institutions and debate (ter Wal, 2004).

In the 2000s, subsidies are primarily aimed at national umbrella organizations, and 'expertise-' and 'knowledge centres' that mediate between migrant organizations on the one hand and decision-making bodies on the other. There is a greater emphasis on broader cross-category initiatives which do not focus solely on ethnicity, religion and cultural diversity but also on gender and other forms of diversity in these organizations. Their existence indicates the increasing possibility (and stimulation) of synergies with mainstream organizations.

Besides the institutionalized forms of participation, more spontaneous initiatives exist. These are not always visible, however. For instance, voluntary work is not registered because it is neither labelled nor perceived as such within the ethnic community structures (Penninx, 2004). A more visible example is that of migrant youth organizations that have sprung up in recent years to counter prejudice and negative media portrayal, and that set up debate meetings and Internet forums (van Heelsum, 2004).

Political participation

Representation in local politics is the one field where participation of migrants/ethnic minorities has been more effective. However, it has not reached levels of proportional representation and participation, as naturalization is still a condition for full participation in the democratic political process (Jacobs, 1998). A change in the 1983 Constitution, together with a modification of the electoral law in 1985, made it possible for non-nationals to vote and be voted for in municipal elections, on the condition that they had held a legal residence permit in the municipality for the five preceding years. In national and provincial elections (where the provincial states elect the members of the Dutch Senate or First Chamber), only Dutch nationals are entitled to both vote and stand for office.

Whereas political participation among migrants is considerable, it is also characterized by high amounts of ethnic candidate preference votes. Migrants far more often than Dutch natives cast a candidate preference, but not at the expense of party preference. Left-wing parties are successful among migrants, more with Moroccans than Turks, and ideological party choices appear to be consistent over time (Tillie, 2000; Michon and Tillie, 2003).

In the municipal elections of March 2006, the Dutch Labour Party (PvdA) regained many of the votes lost in 2002, thanks to the migrant electorate. In Rotterdam, for instance, over 80 per cent of the migrant electorate voted for the PvdA, largely due to candidacies of their own ethnicity. In Amsterdam and Rotterdam, candidates of migrant origin on the lists were voted on to the city council thanks to votes of preference from their constituent migrant community members. In Rotterdam, 8 of the 18 new council members from the party are of migrant origin (van Rhee et al., 2006). Instead of welcoming this change, the PvdA leadership came into the public arena with a discussion about the way in which the qualities of their candidates as council members should be assessed. The introduction of more ethnically diverse political representative bodies, therefore, came to be presented as a problem. At the same time, party members reinstated a colour-blind attitude, by emphasizing the sameness of all Rotterdam citizens, and the need to avoid polarization. Allegedly, this discussion had the aim of avoiding non-migrant voters being alienated from the party.[10]

Public and media discourses on migration

During the 1990s, issues linked to immigration and asylum, Islam and ethnic minorities came to the forefront of the Dutch political and media debate. The politicization of migrant issues had also been used in election campaign rhetoric by populist movements and established political parties. Public discourse witnessed an increasing problematization of the existence of segregated, disadvantaged and culturally different groups. The religious diversity of migrant groups was thereby either explicitly or implicitly mentioned as being an important factor.

Debates about the 'failure' of Dutch integration and multicultural policy

Since the late 1990s, various intellectuals and politicians have picked up the discussion about the failure of Dutch integration policy. One of the recurring arguments is that large parts of the first-generation migrants are not integrated because they do not speak the Dutch language, they have not adapted to the Dutch culture, and that efforts to introduce compulsory language and civic integration courses appear to remain largely unsuccessful. Over-representation of first- and even second-generation migrants of, in particular, Turkish and Moroccan (but also other migrant) origin among the unemployed and dependent on social welfare, and higher drop-out rates of migrant youth in secondary education, as well as the increasing level of ethnic segregation in urban schools, constitute a major object of debate.

Migrant youth deviance

In an increasingly overt way, the media have described incidents of deviance, confrontations with the police, and involvement in petty crime among Moroccan youth in particular. Besides stigmatization of the group of Moroccan youth as a whole, this also aggravates the problems of discrimination and prejudice they face when seeking employment, or, for example, when entering bars or discotheques (Harchaoui and Huinder, 2003; ter Wal, 2004).

Moroccan youth are not the only 'problem group' in the public discussion. Antillean youth are also often associated with crime (in particular drugs smuggling), deviance, violence and disturbance of public order. In addition, the media frequently report on the adherence to cultural norms of

---

10   Article in daily newspaper *NRC Handelsblad*, 18/19 March 2006: 2, 'Rotterdamse allochtonen stem den vooral op de vele "eigen" kandidaten'.

vengeance and honour-related violent crimes against women within various Muslim communities. Adherence to and manifestations of religious-political movements within, for example, the Turkish extremist 'Grey Wolves', as well as manifestations of Kurdish movements, have raised media attention. Finally, young third-generation Moluccans have protested against the Dutch authorities for not taking a clear enough stand and taking diplomatic action in the present political situation in Indonesia.

Religious difference

In recent years, public discourse has featured a strong connection between ethnicity and religion. In the 1990s, the former right-wing leader Frits Bolkestein had already made harsh statements about Islam. Between 1998 and 2002, the three main issues which were discussed by both majority and minority actors in the leading Dutch quality newspaper *de Volkskrant* regarding migrants were religion (Islam), discrimination and crime (ter Wal, 2004). Although these discussions were not explicitly referring to Muslim migrants, in reality the focus was often on these groups. Indeed, one of the characteristics of the public debate was the ambivalent and generalizing use of 'Muslim' and the juxtaposition of 'migrant' and 'Muslim' categories.

The most important media debates about Islam during 1998–2002 concerned the presence of reactionary – and for Dutch public opinion unacceptable – positions about homosexuality, the curriculum and orientations of Islamic schools and mosques/imams, the wearing of headscarves in public office and in schools, and political mobilization and radicalism among Muslim youth. These issues were connected to a wider debate about the presumed demise of Dutch integration policy. The debate revealed that in dealing with concrete claims for religious difference, the application of principles of freedom of expression and religion, and of the separation of Church and State, were put under strain.

These debates have been particularly intensified by domestic reactions to 11 September 2001. In the period following these events, arson attacks and other violent incidents aimed at 'Muslim' targets (mosques and Islamic schools) reached a peak (EUMC, 2002). In the run up to the 2002 elections, politician Pim Fortuyn became popular by restating old populist slogans, and by proposing a stop on Muslim immigration. The discussion about Islam became more polarized. Fortuyn was killed (by a Dutch environmentalist activist), but others picked up his rhetoric, both within and outside the Fortuyn movement.

Film director and editorialist Theo van Gogh was murdered by a Muslim radical in November 2004. His murder was related to a film he made together with MP Ayaan Hirsi Ali, entitled *Submission*, which was first shown on Dutch television in the summer of 2004. The film depicts the women-unfriendly practices legitimated by the Koran and Muslim belief, in an attempt to stir up the debate about the degrading position and treatment of women in Islam. The murder of Theo van Gogh has further polarized the debate about Islam.[11] This has revitalized the debate about the limits of tolerance of Dutch society and about the way to handle constitutional principles of freedom of speech and religion. Media and politics called for an end to the culture of political correctness, and opinion makers refused to defend the positions of Muslim minorities more vividly than the views

---

11   The biography of the murder convict, Mohamed B, as reconstructed in the media, is interesting. He successfully completed an educational career, was involved in local youth work and attempts to work within the existing support structures to improve employment opportunities for migrant youth. This was, however, followed by a disaffection with the existing 'opportunity structure', apparently followed by a shift to the outside and identification with radical Islamic ideals offered by homeland-orientated and transnational media, and religious institutions and networks operating in the Netherlands (*de Volkskrant*, 'De Zachte Krachten', 20 November 2004, pp. 13–14).

of their critics. After the murder, a wave of anti-Islamic incidents was registered throughout the country, particularly in smaller cities in the south of the Netherlands. The government started a series of highly mediatized actions to clamp down on groups of Muslim radicals.

In this debate, the Dutch policy approach is often questioned. Some say that the generous Dutch social welfare system and initial emphasis on supporting cultural pluralism has allowed immigrants to isolate themselves (Koopmans, 2002). A consequence some politicians and researchers draw from this interpretation is that this form of state support to ethnic groups has indirectly and unintentionally helped to create forms of Islamic extremism. Other academics emphasize that the radicalization of Muslim youth is limited (cf. Phalet and ter Wal, 2004) and in particular migrants themselves argue it is a result of the marginalization and exclusion of (part of) their groups from mainstream society.

Islamophobia

The hostility towards Muslims in general, and young people of Moroccan descent in particular, has been manifested on several occasions, both in the general public sphere and in statements by political leaders. An example of the latter was during the Amsterdam municipal election campaign in the first months of 2002, when future local Labour Party councillor Rob Oudkerk spoke in very offensive terms about 'Moroccan youth'. The fact that this was not punished, and that Oudkerk could become a councillor was perceived by the Moroccan youth as a sign that society remains indifferent toward them (van Heelsum 2003, p. 104). Subsequent media attention to disturbances during a mass demonstration in Amsterdam against the Israeli-Palestinian conflict, and during the annual national memorial for Second World War victims, further stigmatized the position of Moroccan youth (ter Wal, 2004).

The hostility and sharpened societal climate has also led to stronger claims in the public sphere on behalf of some organizations. In 2002, Moroccan youth were attracted to the positions of the leader of the Arab European League in Belgium, Abu Jahjah. Televised interviews with Abu Jahjah, following the publication of his book, caused a boom in discussions on Dutch-Moroccan websites.

Although with the developments mentioned, most youth organizations have a growing tendency to accord value to their own identity, they also stress positive examples to challenge existing prejudice (van Heelsum, 2003). Indeed, the majority of initiatives among the youth try to deal with the current polarization in the societal climate, by engaging in activities that promote dialogue; Moroccan youth play a primary role here. The number of debate meetings has risen since 11 September, 2001 (van Heelsum, 2004), and increased again after other cases in the public discourse, such as the murder of Theo van Gogh, and the tightening and strict interpretation of immigration policies.

Concluding remarks

Shifts and contradictions in Dutch policy or 'philosophies' of integration, from policies that propagated 'integration with maintenance of the own identity' towards more assimilationist models, leave their imprint on the position of migrants and the modes of participation of migrant groups in the Netherlands. On the one hand, inclusion and integration in mainstream society is sought and also imposed by policies for entry and stay, with increasingly stringent criteria. On the other hand, the Dutch societal configuration, its history of pillarization which supports the manifestation of different religious and political groupings in their own niches, and the legal constitutional framework with freedom of religion as one of its core values, have created favourable conditions for the cultivation of migrants' separateness in their own ethnic and religious organizations.

The balance between separateness and inclusion, from a policy perspective, tends to shift towards more inclusive or assimilationist forms. The assertion of diversity in religious terms, including both moderate and extreme forms of Muslim radicalism in recent years, and the public and media debate surrounding the 'problems' extremism poses to Dutch society, have revealed that more effort is needed for such integration expectations to become effective in practice. A major downside of the public and media debate is the generalizing discourse about 'Muslims' and 'migrants' where, in fact, as the literature reveals, many diverse realities exist and great differences among and within different ethnic groups prevail.

References

de Hart, J. (2005), *Landelijk verenigd*. The Hague: Social Cultural Planning Bureau.

de Valk, H.A.G. et al. (eds) (2001), *Oude en nieuwe allochtonen in Nederland. Een demografisch profiel*. The Hague: Wetenschappelijke Raad voor het Regeringsbeleid.

Engbersen, G. et al. (eds) (2002), *Illegale vreemdelingen in Nederland. Omvang, verblijf en uitzetting*. Rotterdam: Erasmus Universiteit Rotterdam/RISBO.

EUMC (European Monitoring Centre on Racism and Xenophobia) (2002), *Anti-Islamic reactions within the European Union after the acts of terror against the USA*. Vienna: EUMC.

Fennema, M. and Tillie, J. (1999), 'Political participation and political trust in Amsterdam: Civic communities and ethnic networks', *Journal of Ethnic and Migration Studies*, **25**(4), 703–726.

Harchaoui, S. and Huinder, C. (2003), *Stigma: Marokkaan! Over het afstoten en uitsluiten van een ingebeelde bevolkingsgroep*. Utrecht: FORUM.

Hooghiemstra, E. (2003), *Trouwen over de grens. Achtergronden van partnerkeuze van Turken en Marokkanen in Nederland*. The Hague: Social Cultural Planning Bureau.

Jacobs, D. (1998), 'Discourse, politics and policy: the Dutch parliamentary debate about voting rights for foreign residents', *The International Migration Review*, **32**(122), 350–373. [DOI: 10.2307/2547187]

Koopmans, R. (2002), 'Zachte heelmeesters… Een vergelijking van de resultaten van het Nederlandse en Duitse integratiebeleid en wat de WRR daaruit niet concludeert', *Migrantenstudies*, **18**(2), 87–92.

Koopmans, R. and Statham, P. (eds) (2000), *Challenging Immigration and Ethnic Relations Politics*. Oxford: OUP.

Lijphart, A. (1975), *The Politics of Accommodation: Pluralism and Democracy in the Netherlands*, 2nd edn. Berkeley, Calif.: UC Press.

Michon, L. and Tillie, J. (2003), 'Politieke participatie van migranten in Nederland sinds 1986', in Pellikaan and Trappenburg (eds) *Politiek in de multiculturele samenleving*, 126–59. Amsterdam: Boom.

Minderhedennota (1983), *Regeringsnota over het minderhedenbeleid*. The Hague: SDU Uitgevers.

Penninx, R. and van Heelsum, A. (2004), *Bondgenoot of spelbreker? Organisaties van immigranten en hun mogelijke rol in integratieprocessen*. Utrecht: FORUM Instituut voor Multiculturele Ontwikkeling.

Phalet, K. and ter Wal, J. (2004), *Moslim in Nederland*. The Hague: Social and Cultural Planning Bureau.

Rath, J. (1991), *Minorisering: de sociale constructie van 'etnische minderheden'*. Amsterdam: SUA.

—— et al. (eds) (1996), *Nederland en zijn islam; een ontzuilde samenleving reageert op het ontstaan van een geloofsgemeenschap*. Amsterdam: Het Spinhuis.

SCP (Social Cultural Planning Bureau) (2003), *Rapportage Minderheden 2003*. The Hague: SCP.

Sunier, T. (2000), 'Verzuilen of niet? dat is de vraag', *Migrantenstudies*, **16**(1), 54–58.

ter Wal, J. (2004*), Islam in de publieke discussie. Een analyse van artikelen in de Volkskrant*. The Hague: SCP.

Tillie, J. (2000), *De etnische stem, opkomst en stemgedrag van migranten tijdens de gemeenteraadsverkiezingen 1968-1998*. Utrecht: FORUM.

van Heelsum. A. (2003), 'Reacties van zelforganisaties op stigmatisering', in Harchaoui, S. and Huinder, C. (eds) *Stigma: Marokkaan! Over het afstoten en uitsluiten van een ingebeelde bevolkingsgroep*. Utrecht: FORUM.

—— (2004), *Migrantenorganisaties in Nederland. Deel, 2: Functioneren van de organisaties*. Utrecht: FORUM.

van Rhee, M. et al. (2006), *Analyse Gemeenteraadsverkiezingen 2006*. Rotterdam: Centrum voor Onderzoek en Statistiek.

Veld, T. (2003), *Etnische minderheden in Rotterdam*. Rotterdam: ISEO-COS.

Internet-based references

CBS (Central Bureau for Statistics) (2004), *Allochtonen in Nederland 2004*. Voorburg: CBS (Central Bureau for Statistics) (2005), 'Aantal naturalisaties bijna gehalveerd', *Webmagazine* (updated 11 January 2005, available at http://ww.cbs.nl/publicaties/artikelen/algemeen/webmagazine).

Chapter 20

Poland

Krystyna Iglicka

For Poland, 1989 marked a turning point in the migration process. Profound political, legal and institutional changes in the country brought about, *inter alia*, an opening of borders and the abolition of limits on movement. Along with the political, social and economic transitions which occurred across Central and Eastern European, the mechanisms and patterns of migration also changed. Although Poland is still a country of emigration, it has recently experienced: massive short-term mobility of citizens from the former Soviet Union; labour migration from both Eastern and Western Europe; permanent migration into Poland, mainly from other Eastern European countries; the formation of new and, for this part of Europe, rather exotic immigrant communities of Chinese, Vietnamese and Armenian origin; inflows of asylum seekers; lower levels of emigration; and the return of Polish citizens living abroad. Indeed, a new ethnic diversity and creation of a new ethnic consciousness can gradually be observed (Iglicka, 2001).

The arrival of various categories of foreigners and their numbers created a qualitatively new migratory situation. However, Polish immigration policy was shaped mainly by political circumstances such as system transformation and European integration and the country had neither the time nor the possibility to shape its immigration policy according to its own needs.

The existing immigrant groups are too new to engage in civic activities and their efforts are concentrated primarily on their economic situation rather than their social integration. Certain associations and organizations focus on religious and cultural activities but, as far as the active civic participation of immigrants – that is, activities by political parties or socio-cultural associations or other organizations of immigrants and non-EU citizens – in Poland is concerned, the situation is rather under-developed. Currently, there are no structures enabling immigrants to influence political decisions at any level. There are no consultative bodies or immigrants' parties. The question of voting rights at the local level for (non-EU) immigrants is not on the political agenda of any party and the public debate on the subject is extremely limited.

Major developments in Poland's immigration policy

Polish immigration policy developed under the influence of quite different factors from those commonly recognized in the literature. Neither the economic need for immigrants' labour nor socially destabilizing large inflows of asylum seekers, nor political and public debates on immigration creating certain opinions had real impact on this policy.

At the heart of Polish immigration policy lay processes related to the historical and political circumstances, namely, the system's transformation and European integration. Poland had neither the time nor the possibility to shape its immigration policy in accordance with its own needs (Weinar, 2006).

At that time of political, social and economic transformation, the Polish Government realized it did not have any experience with immigration, and did not possess the legal foundations or policies to deal with people coming in. Up until 1989, the only law dealing with migration was the Aliens Act of 1963, implemented at a time when few foreigners entered Poland. The Act defined cursorily the conditions of entry into the country, internal movement and departure (Iglicka, 2005).

The country also lacked the money to fund the government structures necessary for handling asylum and immigration-related procedures and paperwork. Nevertheless, Poland's immigration policy had to be formulated in reaction to rapid and unexpected changes in the political situation and, as a consequence, migration patterns.

In the first half of the 1990s, policies concentrated on the issues of entry, covering four basic areas:

- establishing border control on all frontiers
- entry into the pan-European system of controlling transit migration (entering into readmission agreements with the Schengen and neighbouring states)
- constructing a legal and institutional asylum framework
- facilitating cross-border traffic with the neighbours (maintaining non-visa regimes with all European states, including CIS) (SOPEMI, 2004).

In the second half of the 1990s, Poland had also been gradually able to develop an increasingly complex set of laws to regulate immigration matters. Work on a new Aliens Act began in 1992, yet it took five years to complete an updated version. Although The Aliens Act of 1997 focused mostly on the conditions for entry, it also described conditions for stay, and transit through Poland. As soon as it was passed, the Act was already outdated due to Poland's obligations stemming from the forthcoming EU enlargement and further changes in migratory patterns (Weinar, 2006).

The issue of the resettlement of co-ethnics, raised in public debates at the beginning of the 1990s, obtained its legislative framework as well. The first official decisions to facilitate and channel the resettlement of people of Polish ethnicity from the former Soviet Union to Poland were taken by the government in May 1996. The inflow of this particular group was categorized as repatriation, and those involved were granted Polish citizenship upon their arrival in Poland. The Aliens Act of 1997 launched repatriation visas and (due to the lack of financial resources) more rigid rules for recognizing if a person is truly of Polish origin.

The EU accession process provided, perhaps, the most direct incentive for legislative change in Polish immigration policy. In April 2001, the Polish Parliament passed comprehensive amendments to the 1997 Aliens Act which would help clear the path toward EU membership. The amendments defined a new, accelerated procedure to avert the initiation of the asylum procedure for migrants from 'safe countries' and 'manifestly unfounded' claims, the obligation of *non-refoulement* to an unsafe country as well as the concept of temporary protection status (SOPEMI, 2003).

As far as institutional changes are concerned, one of the significant changes introduced was establishing the first separate government agency dealing with immigration issues, the Office for Repatriation and Foreigners. The first complex legislative document relating to repatriation issues came into force in January 2001. However, in recognition of the lack of financial resources to facilitate the resettlement of all co-ethnics living in the former Soviet Union, the 2000 Repatriation Act limited repatriation only to Asiatic republics of the former Soviet Union.

In 2003, Poland implemented two laws, the Act of Protection of Aliens and the 2003 Aliens Act which further refined the 2001 changes. The Act of Protection of Aliens clearly divides asylum from economic migration issues. It includes principles and conditions for extending various forms of protection for foreigners, including refugee status, asylum status, temporary protection status and tolerated status. The 2003 Aliens Act marks Poland's first regularization programme for unauthorized immigrants (Iglicka, 2005).

Within the negotiations in the area of Justice and Home Affairs (JHA), Poland resolved to implement the JHA in full, including the Schengen *acquis*, by the time of accession without asking for any transition periods or derogations. The Schengen *acquis* was formally incorporated into Polish law before accession, but full implementation was not finalized, and is now not expected to be complete until 2007. This is largely because Poland is awaiting a positive assessment of the state of border infrastructure and operational capacity of all the institutions involved.

The most important area of disagreement in the negotiations is related to the visa policy for CIS neighbours, where Poland opted for the introduction of a visa requirement at the very last moment before the date of accession. Many worried that such visa requirements could weaken cross-border trade, cause the collapse of exports to CIS neighbours, and decrease the income of people depending on trade-related services. This last point was important because residents of Poland's eastern territories have almost completely depended economically on cross-border trade-related services. Poland waited for the introduction of visas for CIS neighbours until the last moment, October 2003 (Iglicka, Kazmierkiewicz and Weinar, 2005).

2004 was marked by Poland's accession to the European Union and resulting changes in relevant legislation concerning asylum law and the conditions of entry and stay of EU citizens and their family members in Poland. It was also marked by changes in labour market regulations concerning foreigners. Since 1 May 2004, Poland has been bound by the asylum law in force in the EU Member States, which provides the rules for determining the country responsible for asylum procedure (the so called Dublin II Convention). The Act on Conditions of Entry and Stay of EU Citizens and Their Family Members, adopted in July 2002, also entered into force. The new Act introduced two new documents: the EU residence permit and the EU temporary residence permit, both of which allow EU citizens and their families to stay on Polish territory longer than three months. On 1 June 2004, the Act on the Promotion of Employment and Institutions of the Labour Market entered into force. This Act enumerates categories of foreigners who are not obliged to obtain a work permit. These are: recognized refugees and settlement permit holders (already included in the old Act of 1994), family members of Polish citizens who are EU citizens, foreigners (spouses and children below 21 years and dependent children irrespective of age) who are not EU citizens and who are temporary residence permit holders, foreigners granted a temporary residence permit in Poland because of marriage to a recognized refugee, tolerated status or temporary protection status holders (SOPEMI, 2004).

Polish immigration policy has many faces, but its integration component is among the least significant. Although, in theory, the Polish state pursues a policy of integration based on European standards, the implementation of this policy lags far behind. The standards that exist have been adopted by a narrow political elite and are incorporated into the legal system without any grass roots action that would legitimize them and sensitize society. In consequence, integration programmes generally tend to fail for lack of social support (such as support from the non-governmental sector). The financial difficulties of the Polish state only serve to make the limited integration efforts less effective. Foreigners who manage to integrate do so mainly due to their own determination (Iglicka, 2003; Iglicka and Okolski, 2005, Weinar, 2006).

The immigrant population in Poland: main demographic and social features

During the last 16 years Poland has become host to thousands of immigrants – both legal and illegal – and refugees.

Detailed data on migratory flows into Poland were collected for the first time in Poland's post-war history at the time of the 2002 population census (PC). According to some experts, due to the lack of experience with the methods of immigration data collection and a misleading official definition of who should be defined as an immigrant, there are serious underestimates observed in this source. Even analysts from the Central Statistical Office (the body responsible for the Census structure and data collection) say that the 'migration part' failed to some extend (RAPORT, 2003).

In spite of the lack of accurate and complete data, a number of observations may be drawn on the basis of the PC 2002 results and an analysis of the 2004 immigration trends. First, temporary residence and settlement permits reflect two stages of the regularization of stay for a foreigner in Poland. Temporary residence permits are granted to foreigners who prove that they have a well-founded reason for staying in Poland for longer than six months, for example migrant workers, family members, students, refugees, foreign spouses of Polish citizens or permanent residents who stay in Poland on a basis of settlement permits (SOPEMI, 2004).

Settlement permits are granted to foreigners who wish to settle in Poland for a longer period, up to ten years. Currently, applications for a settlement permit can be lodged only after having resided in Poland on the basis of a temporary residence permit for five years. The settlement permit is also the only category that allows for registering a foreigner as an immigrant. They appear in the official statistics only if they have a settlement permit (SOPEMI, 2004).

In May 2002, at the time of the PC, 34,100 people who were permanent residents of other countries had been residing in Poland on a temporary basis for at least two months. They originated mainly from Ukraine (22 per cent), Germany (13 per cent), Russia (6 per cent), Belarus (6 per cent), the USA (5 per cent), Armenia (4 per cent), the United Kingdom (3 per cent), France (3 per cent) and Vietnam (3 per cent). Two out of three temporary immigrants had already been residing in Poland for over 12 months, that is, they could be considered as long-term immigrants (though not having permanent resident status).

One out of four temporary immigrants, or 7,700 people, held Polish citizenship. Of these, 3,400 were multiple citizenship holders. The remaining 24,100 (70 per cent) were 'actual foreigners' – without Polish citizenship.

According to the Office for Repatriation and Foreigners data, the number of applications for temporary residence permits was 28,324 in the year 2004. This number was lower by almost ten per cent than in 2003. As in previous years, the biggest number of applications was lodged by citizens of the former USSR (55 per cent in 2004; 46 per cent in 2003; 44 per cent in 2001). Positive decisions were issued for 90 per cent of the applications, meaning 25,649 temporary permits were issued. As far as the nationality of foreigners granted a temporary residence permit is concerned, Ukrainians constituted 33 per cent, Belarusians 7.5 per cent, Vietnamese 7 per cent, Armenians 7 per cent and Russians 6 per cent.

At the time of the PC (2002) there were 40,500 foreigners working legally on Polish territory. The number is given on the basis of all work permits issued for this year and comprises all types of employees, from low-skilled construction workers, to highly qualified managers of international companies. Only some of them were intent on permanent immigration involving settlement. Their motives for coming to Poland vary substantially, the labour factor not being the main driver. The economic purpose might be connected with self-development; so, temporary immigration to Poland can signify future profits (SOPEMI, 2004).

In 2004, 5,169 foreigners applied for a settlement permit. This number was 70 per cent higher than 2003. The same nationalities as in the case of temporary residence holders prevailed: Ukrainians 37.5 per cent; Russians 15 per cent; Belarusians 10 per cent; Vietnamese 8.7 per cent; and Armenians 6 per cent. The numbers of permits issued are shown in Table 20.1.

Table 20.1   Settlement permits, top ten nationalities (2004)

Country of origin	Number of permits
Ukraine	1,670
Russia	447
Belarus	394
Vietnam	385
Armenia	250
Kazakhstan	80
Germany	63
USA	61
China	58
Mongolia	57

Source: Office for Repatriation and Foreigners Data, 2005.

According to PC 2002, in the period between 1989 and 2002, a total of 85,500 people moved (or returned) to Poland from abroad. Women constituted 51 per cent of all movers. 'Actual foreigners' (people without Polish citizenship), who became permanent residents of Poland during the transition period comprised 17 per cent (14,500) of the total. The remaining population included either Polish citizens who moved back to Poland (return migration) or the second generation of Polish emigrants, who decided to settle in their parents' homeland. In most cases, these so-called 're-emigrants' hold multiple citizenships. The former countries of residence were: Germany (27 per cent), the USA (14 per cent), Ukraine (6 per cent), Italy, Canada, United Kingdom and France (SOPEMI, 2004).

In 2004, Poland's migration balance was still negative, though it was the lowest recorded since 2000 and one of its lowest levels since the mid-1950s. A total of 18,877 persons emigrated from Poland, whereas the largest growth in the immigrant population was recorded among Ukrainians (up by 21 per cent), Russians (up by 108 per cent), Armenians (up by 38 per cent) and Kazaks (up by 30 per cent). See Table 20.2.

Table 20.2   Emigration and immigration data, Poland (2000–2004)

Year	Emigrants	Immigrants
2000	26,999	7,331
2001	23,368	6,625
2002	24,532	6,587
2003	20,813	7,048
2004	18,877	9,495

Source: Central Statistical Office, CSO, Warsaw 2005.

According to PC (2002) 37.3 million persons (96.4 per cent of the total population) were born within Poland's post-war territory, whereas 775,300 (2 per cent) were born abroad (including territories that belonged to Poland before the Second World War). In the case of 385,000 persons, due to interviewer inaccuracy, the country of birth remained unknown.

Moreover, more than 98 per cent of the country's permanent residents held Polish citizenship. Of these, 1.2 per cent (444,900) held multiple citizenship and the category of dual citizenship holders included 279,600 (62.9 per cent) German citizens, 30,100 (6.8 per cent) US citizens, 14,500 (3.3 per cent) Canadian citizens, 7,300 French citizens and almost 1,000 citizens of Ukraine (SOPEMI, 2004).

A further 40,200 persons held only foreign citizenship, with Germans (7,900), Ukrainians (5,400) and Russians (3,200) topping the ranks.

According to Art. 8.1 of the 1962 Act on Citizenship, citizenship may be acquired after at least five years of legal residence on the basis of the settlement permit. However, Art. 8.2 of the Act stipulates an exception from the five-year-residence requirement by stating that in exceptionally justified cases, not included in the Act, Polish citizenship may be granted even if the above requirements are not met (that is, for third-country nationals residing in Poland for less than five years on a settlement permit, or for a foreigner who does not stay in Poland, but who is resident abroad). This exception pertains particularly to Poles who, during the communist era, had to give up their Polish citizenship in order to emigrate. It also applies to ethnic Poles whose ancestors were deported by Soviet authorities to various former USSR republics (Iglicka, 1998). In these cases, all applications are considered individually by the President of the Republic of Poland. A supplementary opinion on these cases is provided by the Chairman of the Office for Repatriation and Foreigners. If Polish citizenship is granted, it is also extended to the children of the applicants; if the child is over 16, s/he must decide whether s/he wants to become a Polish citizen.

Over the past 11 years, the number of citizenships granted under Article 8 of the Act has undergone quite a few fluctuations. See Table 20.3.

Table 20.3   Number of approved applications for Polish citizenship (1992–2003)

Year	Number	Year	Number
1992	1,522	1998	871
1993	834	1999	1,000
1994	751	2000	975
1995	1,038	2001	766
1996	679	2002	988
1997	555	2003	1,471

Source: Office for Repatriation and Foreigners, 2005.

The importance of the above is that it seems that the number of approved applications is growing again to the 1992 level. This might be because a growing number of foreigners can finally meet the five-year-residence requirement. See Table 20.4.

Table 20.4   Polish citizenship applications approved, top nationalities (2004)

Country of Origin	Percentage
Ukraine	25
Russia	12
Israel	10
Belarus	8
Germany	5
Vietnam	3
Sweden	3
Armenia	2
Kazakhstan	2
USA	2
Other	28

Source: Office for Repatriation and Foreigners, 2005.

According to estimates of the Polish Ministry of Labour and Social Policy, there are between 100,000 and 500,000 foreigners working illegally in Poland each year. The majority of these come from Poland's eastern neighbours, particularly Ukraine. Men work mainly in construction, forestry and fruit farming. Women also work in fruit farming and as seamstresses, housekeepers, nurses for the elderly and babysitters.

According to some estimates there are about 30,000 Vietnamese in Poland, at least half of whom are illegal migrants.

It is impossible to estimate the number of illegal migrants created by failed asylum seekers. The vast majority of them definitely left Poland, but some of them quietly joined a fairly large group of undocumented migrants.

Refugee status is granted on the basis of the Act on Providing Protection to Foreigners on the Territory of the Republic of Poland of 13 June 2003. The Act does not contain a definition of the refugee, yet it complies with the 1951 Geneva Convention and New York Protocol. Refugee status can be granted in Poland if the applicant has not yet been granted refugee status in any other safe country. The asylum seeker has to apply for refugee status in person at the Polish border.

The inflow of asylum seekers continues to play an important role in the inflow of foreigners to Poland, if only for its high proportion relative to other migratory movements to Poland and its largely irregular character.

Table 20.5   Number of refugee applications (1994–2003)

Year	Numbers
1994	641
1995	843
1996	3,212
1997	3,544
1998	3,423
1999	3,061
2000	4,662
2001	4,528
2002	5,170
2003	6,906
2004	8,079

Source: Office for Repatriation and Foreigners data, 2005.

The number of applications has been growing steadily over the last 10 years (see Table 20.5), with the exception of the drop in 1999 which, however, was immediately replaced by a significant increase in 2000 (right after the beginning of the war in Chechnya). The number of applications increased almost by half in 2003, which could have been caused by the expected Polish accession to the EU or entry into force of the Dublin II regulations.)

The growth trend in refugee applications was confirmed in the year 2004 as well. The number of applications lodged was 16 per cent greater than in 2003. In 2004, one significant peak in a growing trend was observed. In April 2004, namely a month before the enlargement, the number of applications reached almost 1,000 and then in May dropped suddenly to 355. However, in the second half of 2004, especially from September, the numbers started to systematically increase and, in December 2004, the number of applications lodged exceeded 1,000.

The growth of applications in autumn 2004 can be explained by the Beslan tragedy. At that time thousands of civilians left Chechnya terrified by the threat of being persecuted. Actually, the Beslan tragedy lies at the core of the first Polish refugee crisis. Since the Chechens apply for refugee status mainly in Poland, and the law requires the asylum seekers to stay in refugee centres during the procedure, the Polish administration reached its logistic capacity in a few weeks.

As far as the nationality of asylum seekers is concerned, 2004 was no different from 2003. Again, asylum seekers from Russia of Chechen origin dominated the flow, amounting to over 7,100 applications, which was almost 89 per cent of all applications. The second and third position was occupied by asylum seekers from Pakistan (only 2.6 per cent), and India (1.85 per cent) – a tendency observed in 2003 and 2002, but now more established. Armenians and Afghans had been at the top of the list at the end of the 1990s. In 2004, asylum seekers from Ukraine (52) and Afghanistan (40) were in fifth and sixth position respectively.

As in previous years, positive decisions on refugee status constituted around 3 per cent of the total number of applications in 2004. Positive decisions in 2004 amounted to 315 whereas in 2003 positive decisions were granted to 243 persons.

In compliance with the Act of 15 June 2003, concerning granting protection to aliens on Polish territory, an asylum seeker can be granted tolerated status, that is s/he is not considered a refugee as stipulated in the Geneva Convention, but cannot be expelled to his/her country of origin (*non-refoulement* principle). The tolerated status grants the right to work (without a work permit), to social welfare, medical care and education in Poland. Tolerated status has been granted since September 2003 and is granted more readily than refugee status. Between September and December 2003, 72 positive decisions on tolerated status were issued, whereas in 2004 tolerated status was granted to 1,097 persons (of whom 870 had previously been refused refugee status).

Immigrant rights and participation in public life

There are no structures enabling immigrants to influence political decisions at the local or national levels. There are no immigrants' parties. The question of voting rights at the local level for non-EU citizens is not on the political agenda of any party. Conditions enabling immigrants' incorporation into labour markets are of a restrictive nature.

The question of possible forms of civic participation of immigrants in Poland has not been discussed either by policy-makers at any level, or NGOs or immigrants themselves. The existing immigrants' groups are still too weak and too new on Polish soil to create organizations, parties or associations focused on civic participation. They mainly concentrate on the social and economic situation of their existence in Poland. A few others focus on religious or cultural activities of their fellow-countrymen and women. New immigrant groups, now in the process of formation in Poland (such as Ukrainians and Armenians), tend to bond with their ethnic group that has been living in Poland for centuries. So far, almost any new immigrant structures have been created only within or by the organizations set up by the old ethnic minorities or within the structures of Ukrainian church operations in Poland.

So far, the most visible and successful immigrant associations are those set up by the Vietnamese. The role of the Vietnamese associations in organizing Vietnamese migrants and creating their positive image in Poland is similar to that played by the strong and resilient ethnic associations in Hungary that integrate and organize Chinese migrants. Membership of the 'Socio-Cultural Association of Vietnamese in Poland' includes the socio-cultural (and often financial) elite of the Vietnamese, consisting of 200–300 former students and their families. These people have been living in Poland for the longest time. Usually they have Polish citizenship or at least permission for settlement. They know the Polish language and culture and are well integrated within Polish society. Members of that association act as leaders for the whole 'community'. Some of them occupy key positions in a second organization, 'Solidarity and Friendship', which seeks to gather, organize and control all the Vietnamese migrants in Poland (Halik, 2000).

As far as third-sector actors and international organizations dealing with immigrants issues are concerned, the most active are: UNHCR, the Helsinki Foundation for Human Rights, Polish Humanitarian Action and the Polish Red Cross:

- A liaison Office of the UNHCR was established in 1992 in connection with the admittance of the first refugees' group where no legal instruments and technical possibilities to secure their protection were present. The role of UNHCR in Poland concentrated at first on co-operation with government agents to develop effective procedures as well as refugees' centres. With time there has been an evolution towards the representation of refugees' and asylum seekers' interests, especially towards government institutions as well as organizations which provide integration programmes.
- The Helsinki Foundation for Human Rights provides permanent assistance and advice on legal issues: several lawyers are at the disposal of asylum seekers and refugees.
- The Polish Humanitarian Action has the task of providing help to victims of war and disaster in Poland and abroad as well as to refugees. The assistance programme for refugees supports

medical aid. Particular attention is paid to the integration process of foreigners who are recognized as refugees. Since 1996 PHA has been running the Refugee's House, where homeless asylum seekers can find shelter. The promotion actions (for example Refugee Day in co-operation with another NGOs) and educational activities are of great importance.

• The Polish Red Cross takes care of refugees. The role of the PRC was enormous, especially in 1990 and 1991, when no mechanism which would ensure protection from the state authorities was present.

Recently, there is a new EU funded initiative under the EQUAL programme in Poland. The Equal Community Initiative Programme Education for Integration – Partnership for Refugees (EDI) Project is coordinated by the Jagiellonian University Human Rights Centre within the theme 'Socioeconomic integration of asylum seekers'. The main objective of the project is based on a pre-integration model and it aims to promote asylum seekers with the necessary information and skills to start an independent existence and facilitate their integration into Polish society.

State run public programmes aim to integrate two groups of foreigners: asylum seekers and repatriates. In fact, the only programme that fulfils its aims is an integration programme for repatriates. However, one should remember that according to Polish law, repatriates are not considered to be foreigners. In fact, foreigners who manage to integrate do so mainly because of their own determination and a helping hand offered by friends and family.

Asylum seekers' integration

The only governmental programme for refugees lasts one year, and is run by the provincial authorities. Refugees receive a monthly payment of 1600 PLN (ca 400 euros) and are helped with finding a flat. They are also registered at the Labour Office. Participation is not automatic – it is conditional upon attending Polish language courses offered as part of the programme. After a year, the integration aid stops and refugees can use the support offered by social assistance centres. It is obvious that a mere 12 months cannot guarantee any successful integration (Iglicka, 2003).

The most important problem is housing. Refugees cannot easily find accommodation. There are fewer flats than refugees participating in the programme. Some of them have to find their own a place to live and they face many obstacles.

Refugees consider housing as a starting point for further insertion into society. The rent, especially in Warsaw, is very high, and finally they are caught in a situation where they earn money only to pay for it. They are very often forced to change houses and thus they have the feeling of constantly lacking stability.

The other important factor in the integration process is employment. Refugees can be employed on the same terms as Polish citizens. The difficult economic situation in Poland drives refugees to look for some other solutions, for example employment in the grey economy. The majority of them understand perfectly that Poland cannot afford integration programmes of the kind offered in Western European countries. Especially in the last two years, the economic slowdown has hit Polish society. Refugees see the growing problem of unemployment and they clearly assume their right to demand jobs is somehow questionable. They feel like guests who have overstayed, and these feelings are deepened by the Polish authorities, who openly admit that Poles are too poor to afford asylum seekers (Iglicka, 2003; Weinar, 2006).

Repatriates' integration

According to Polish law, repatriates are not foreigners. Their status has been defined in the Repatriation Act of 9 November 2000. Although the Repatriation Act has been in force since January 2001[1], real repatriation started many years earlier, initiated by the national campaign of the Church and right-wing parties.

A person coming into Poland within the framework of repatriation is reimbursed for their one-way trip by train from Kazakhstan to Poland (the ticket for moving their possessions is also refunded). Repatriates are granted Polish citizenship almost automatically. Two months after they receive citizenship, the following measures are foreseen: money transfer amounting to double the average monthly salary for each family member to cover the expenses of establishing a new household; allowance for the education of minors; reimbursement of any required renovation or adaptation of the offered accommodation (this money is transferred over a two-year period).

The employment arrangements for repatriates are obviously preferential. The local administration can refund part of the following expenses related to the repatriate: salary, social security tax, bonuses, workplace equipment, training. The right to this funding is valid for five years after arrival, and it can be effective in two years, provided that the employment is guaranteed for four years. If the repatriate cannot find employment in her/his profession, the local authority can address a potential employee and offer reimbursement of the cost of training, provided that employment is guaranteed for two years. Another important provision is a national register of accommodation and employment possibilities for repatriates (Iglicka, 2003; Iglicka and Okolski, 2005).

In practice, the question of employment and, thus, of gaining independence is solved for some newcomers. It all depends on the local community they come to live in. Repatriates often are misinformed and they therefore cannot reduce the obstacles to employment.

Persons with repatriation status get Polish citizenship. As a result, they have the right to social security on the same terms as Poles do. They get welfare if unemployed, and some get a pension. They are also victims of Polish survival strategies – they can find employment, but only illegally, as many Poles do in the poorer regions of the country. The most successful were settlements where the local administration ran a complex repatriation service and engaged the local community. Decent housing and employment may therefore not only protect repatriates from entering the welfare chain, but may also provide the basis for further integration (Iglicka and Okolski, 2005).

Public and media discourses on migration

The arrival of various categories of foreigners and their numbers created a qualitatively new migratory situation at the very beginning of the 1990s. At the same time, all the countries of Central and Eastern Europe were undergoing changes. A possibility of East-West mass migratory movements was seriously considered in light of the break-up of Soviet Union. There were fears of the eruption of ethnic conflicts and acts of violence which might facilitate the exodus as well as large-scale returns of Poles to the homeland (Iglicka and Sword, 1999).

The Polish state was neither prepared for that new migratory situation nor could it render assistance and care for the asylum-seekers arriving in ever greater numbers. Migratory movements and their consequences raised concerns about state security, in view of Poland's precarious

---

1   Because of the state's financial difficulties, the Repatriation Act has been applied to ethnic Poles from Asiatic Republics of the former Soviet Union only and, more specifically, to those arriving from Kazakhstan.

geopolitical location, and the absence of legal foundations for the policy on aliens, as well as of effective state structures and procedures, aggravated by the shortage of funds and relative lack of experience in dealing with problems of the kind. It was not the rapid rise in the number of border entries by the citizens of the USSR and later of the former USSR alone which fuelled the anxiety (Iglicka, 2003). Of greater concern was the onset of organized criminal activities, smuggling of illicit drugs and dangerous substances, car thefts, prostitution, illegal trade and related financial operations, document forgeries and arms trade on unprecedented scale. The bazaar trade and the presence of foreigners on the Polish labour market also raised some controversy, reflected in public opinion on migrations. The imposition of restrictions on the entry of citizens of the former USSR was current in the debate. Several experts concurrently pointed to various public security threats and called for a state response.

The appearance on Polish streets of a lot of foreigners – mostly from beyond the eastern border – had undoubtedly enlivened the urban landscape. However, foreigners soon became the source of unknown troubles and danger. Although they generally declared tourism as the purpose of their trips, the vast majority came to Poland to work, generally informally. With increasing frequency, foreigners became the subject of negative reports in the mass media and this, in turn, reinforced adverse attitudes towards them. Articles concerning foreigners in the Polish press at the beginning of the 1990s tended to concentrate, according to Mrozowski (2003, p. 232), on the following themes:

- the influx of immigrants into Poland. In these articles immigrants were often viewed as a threat to the nation, since many of them crossed the border illegally or remained in Poland beyond the time permitted by their visas;
- reporting on criminal behaviour by immigrants in Poland, immigrants who disturbed public order and broke the law;
- focus on the economic activities of immigrants. Such material presented immigrants as people looking for work and whose activities bring benefits not only for them but also for Poles;
- reporting on the daily lives of immigrants in Poland, their striving to settle and to lead a normal life.

The concerns of journalists were raised in equal degree by the presence of immigrant groups with such characteristics as a need to integrate, self-organization and loyalty – as with, for example, Armenians and Vietnamese – and by groups characterized by a lack of need for integration or by loose self-organization, such as Ukrainians, Belarusians, Russians, Bulgarians and Romanians. In the case of the former, fears were caused by the possibility of the creation of transnational organized crime structures as well as economic activities which might threaten the existence of Polish firms. In the case of the latter, anxiety was fuelled by such features as impulsiveness, recklessness and a lack of moral scruples which led, in some cases, to brutal criminal behaviours (Mrozowski, 2003).

Immigrants' portrayal in the mass-media has changed since the second half of the 1990s. When it became clear that the mass inflow of foreigners which had been feared did not actually occur, and that the majority of third-country nationals seek formal employment and a normal livelihood, the media changed their stance. Since the second half of the 1990s one can observe an idealistic element when describing foreigners' presence in Poland. Articles about the revival of multiculturalism have been appearing quite often and the cultural differentiation has started to be perceived not as a threat but, rather, as an element enriching Polish culture (Weinar, 2006).

Concluding remarks

Two issues of deep concern have a great importance in analysing the future of migration trends into Poland. The first is connected with the difficulty of being an EU border country, and a country absorbing flows of transit, temporary and permanent migrants, mainly from its eastern neighbours.

Poland's neighbours include many countries going through a difficult phase of their economic development and with significant migration potential. These countries will not become EU members for the next 20–25 years. Of special concern here is Ukraine which, with its 50 million inhabitants, deep economic crisis, and language and historical ties with Poland, is the largest 'exporter' of immigrants to Poland.

A serious threat to the internal security of Poland in the context of human migration is the non-existence of a readmission agreement with Russia. Destabilization caused by war, terrorism, ecological disasters and so on could increase the volume of migration from third countries through Russia. As a result, Poland, as the border EU country, could face a very difficult internal security problem.

A second issue is connected with the growing presence of legal and irregular immigrants in Poland and a lack of integration policy in the country. As we know even traditionally immigrant countries' approaches to immigration may cause ethnic and racial tensions. From this perspective, the challenges facing the totally inexperienced Polish immigration policy are enormous; especially given that under this policy certain types of migrants, especially refugees, have already been allowed to fall into the socioeconomic margins, and that a significant shadow zone of immigration has already been formed. What model of integration will be developed by the Polish state? What model will be affordable? Will the growing number of migrants cause a growth in xenophobic attitudes in Polish society, which is not used to living side by side with foreign cultures, and which can feel demographically, economically and culturally threatened?

It is difficult to provide immediate answers to all the questions posed here, but it is certainly worth posing them now. Ethnic questions have been a vital and sensitive issue for Western democracies for a long time. With ten new EU Member States, with their own historical burden and a lack of experience in dealing with immigration issues, these questions are becoming more salient than ever.

References

Central Statistical Office and Data (2005), Warsaw: Central Statistical Office.

Halik, T. (2000), 'Vietnamese in Poland: Images from the Past, Present and Future', in Hamilton, F.E.I. and Iglicka, K. (eds) *From Homogeneity to Multiculturalism. Minorities Old and New in Poland*. London: SSEES, UCL Press.

Iglicka, K. (1998), 'The Migration of Ethnic Poles from Kazakhstan to Poland', *International Migration Review*, **32**(4), 995–1015. [PubMed 12294305] [DOI: 10.2307/2547669]

Iglicka, K. (2001), *Poland's Post-War Dynamic of Migration*. Aldershot: Ashgate.

Iglicka, K. (2003), *Integracja czy dyskryminacja? Polskie wyzwania i dylematy u progu wielokulturowosci* (Integration or discrimination? Polish Challenges and Dilemmas at the Threshold of Multiculturalism). Warszawa: ISP.

Iglicka, K. and Okolski, M. (2005), 'A Central European Perspective', in Süssmuth R. and Weidenfeld, W. (eds) *Managing Integration: The European Union's Responsibilities Towards Immigrants*. Washington: Migration Policy Institute.

Iglicka, K. and Sword, K. (eds) (1999), *The Challenge of East-West Migration for Poland*. London: Macmillan.

Iglicka, K., Kazmierkiewicz, P. and Weinar, A. (2005), 'Poland', in Niessen, J., Schibel, Y. and Thompson C. (eds) *Current Immigration Debates in Europe*. Brussels: Migration Policy Group.

Iglicka, K., Mazur-Rafal, M. and Kazmierkiewicz, P. (2003), 'Poland', in Niessen, J. and Schibel, Y. (eds) *Current Immigration Debates in Europe*. Brussels: Migration Policy Group.

Mrozowski, M. (2003), 'Obrazy cudzoziemcow i imigrantow w prasie polskiej' (Portrayal of Foreigners and Immigrants in Polish Newspapers), in Iglicka, K. (ed.) *Integracja czy dyskryminacja? Polskie wyzwania i dylematy u progu wielokulturtowosci* (Integration or discrimination? Polish Challenges and Dilemmas at the Threshold of Multiculturalism). Warsaw: ISP (Office for Repatriation and Immigration data, 2005).

RAPORT z wynikow Narodowego Spisu Powszechnego Ludnosci i Mieszkan (2003), (Report from Census Data) Warsaw: CSO.

SOPEMI (2003), *Recent Trends in International Migration in Poland: The 2003 SOPEMI Report*. Paris: OECD.

SOPEMI (2004), *Recent Trends in International Migration in Poland: The 2004 SOPEMI Report*. Paris: OECD.

Weinar, A. (2006), *Polityka wobec cudzoziemcow w swietle debat parlamentarnych w Polsce, 1990–2003* (Policy towards foreigners in the light of parliamentary debates in Poland, 1990–2003). Warszawa: Scholar.

Internet-based references

Iglicka, K. (2005), *EU Membership Highlights Poland's Migration Challenges*. Washington: Migration Information Source, Migration Policy Institute (available at www.migrationinformation.org, accessed April 2005).

Chapter 21

Portugal

Ana Teixeira and Rosana Albuquerque

Portugal's long experience as a country of emigration can be traced back to the fifteenth century, when the main migratory flows were directed toward Portuguese colonial territories. From the nineteenth century onwards, Portugal began to export labour into non-colonial regions, and the Americas were the main destination of outflows. In the 1950s, however, Central and Northern Europe, especially France and Germany, became the main destinations of Portuguese emigrants.

Significant immigration flows into Portugal began roughly in the 1970s. The main third-country foreign nationals in Portugal originate from Brazil and Portuguese-speaking African countries, namely Cape Verde, Angola, Guinea Bissau and São Tomé e Príncipe.

In 2001, a newly created immigrant status aiming at regularizing the situation of undocumented foreign workers uncovered both a quantitative and a qualitative change in the structure of the immigrant population in Portugal. First, there was a quantitative jump from 223,602 foreigners in 2001 to 364,203 regularized foreigners in 2003. Secondly, there was a substantial qualitative shift in the composition of immigrants.

The majority of the new immigrants are now coming from Eastern European countries, such as Ukraine, Moldavia, Romania, and the Russian Federation. Thus, European countries outside the EU zone now rank second (after African countries) amongst sources of Portugal's immigrant population.

The differences between the new and traditional immigration flows are visible in the geographical distribution of immigrants and in their insertion into the labour market. While, previously, immigrant communities would mostly concentrate around Lisbon's metropolitan area and in the Algarve, the new migratory flows tend to be more geographically dispersed and present in less urbanized areas of Portugal. In terms of employment, although most immigrants tend to be absorbed into the construction sector, Eastern European workers may also be employed in the agricultural and manufacturing sectors.

The present chapter outlines the Portuguese immigration policies regarding the control and integration of immigrants, the most important types of immigration status and permits, and the recent developments in the existing naturalization law. Next, we present a demographic and social characterization of the immigrant population in Portugal, including the country's most important ethnic groups. This is followed by an overview of the civic integration of immigrants in Portugal, with a special focus on immigrants' civic rights and their participation in Portuguese public life. Finally, the chapter offers an overview of the media coverage and media discourses on immigration in Portugal.

Major developments in Portugal's immigration policy

Immigration policies in Portugal were fragmented and almost non-existent until 1992, when Portugal's adherence to the Schengen Agreements in 1991 forced the Portuguese Government to reinforce a more structured immigration policy. Until then, the country's historical ties with Portuguese-speaking African countries (PALOP) and Brazil made Portugal a privileged port of entry and stay for people originating from these countries. As a result of the Schengen Agreements, and later the Amsterdam Treaty, the Portuguese Government has had to tighten control over the entry, stay and exit of third-country nationals on Portuguese territory.

One of the consequences of this new direction taken by Portugal's immigration policy was the creation of social strains between Portugal, PALOPs and Brazil's immigrant communities and governments. Hence, Portugal found itself in the double bind of complying with European Union regulations while, at the same time, trying to preserve the strong ties that attach it to other Portuguese-speaking countries. As a result, the Portuguese Government tried to give preferential treatment to third-country nationals originating from Portuguese-speaking countries in relation to other third-country nationals. This special treatment is most apparent in two areas. First, in the different time periods required to acquire either permanent residence or naturalization for PALOPs nationals and Brazilians. Second, in the signature of special bilateral agreements with these countries with regard to visas, entry and stay in Portugal (Leitão, 1997).

The first regulatory immigration measures can be divided between those measures addressing the presence of undocumented immigrants in Portugal (see discussion of this topic below), and policy measures addressing the integration of immigrants in Portuguese society.

The first measures catering to the integration of immigrants included a fragmented set of initiatives in the area of professional training and intercultural education. These measures paved the way to a more consistent policy in the integration of immigrants through the creation of structures such as the Coordinating Secretariat for Multicultural Education Programmes in 1991 and the High Commissioner for Immigration and Ethnic Minorities in 1996. However, many association leaders and politicians have negatively assessed these policies and structures.

Concurrently, the legal framework regulating the entry, stay and exit of immigrants in Portugal has gone through rapid and constant change, with the creation of new regimes and laws (Santos, 2004) which try to adjust Portuguese law and the special circumstances of Portuguese society to its European Union role.

Portuguese law currently distinguishes between several immigrant statuses: residence permit, stay permit and different types of visa.

The residence permit (*autorização de residência*) can be temporary (valid for a period of two years and renewable for successive periods of three years) or permanent (without limit of validity and renewable every five years). Permanent-residence permits may only be acquired by foreigners who have legally resided in Portugal for a minimum period of five consecutive years (for Portuguese-speaking countries' nationals) or eight consecutive years (for nationals of other countries). This regime does not apply to European Union nationals who have a special type of residency card.

Stay permits (*autorização de permanência*) represent a special status created in 2001 (Decree-Law 4/2001) to address the existence of undocumented foreigners who either had a work contract or a work contract proposal with a favourable assessment from the Ministry of Employment. This specific legal status was revoked by the 2003 Law regulating the entry, stay and exit of immigrants on Portuguese territory. Although this permit is no longer available, stay permit holders can still renew and exercise all their rights granted by this status. Portuguese law recognizes the right to family reunification for residence permit (RP) and stay permit (SP) holders.

Additional immigrant visas include short-duration visas, residence visas, student visas, work visas, temporary stay-visas (Decree-Law 34/2003) and asylum (Law 15/98) (Silva, 2004). However, the number of immigrants who hold these types of visas is very low when compared to those with RPs and SPs. The current work visa acknowledges four different levels of qualification and lines of work, namely sports and entertainment activities, highly qualified work or scientific professions, independent professionals and low-qualification workers.

Portuguese law defines the term 'illegal immigrant' as a person who has entered and who remains in national territory without legal documents or with false documents. Moreover, the term includes those individuals who have entered national territory with legal documents but have remained after the document's validity has expired or have stayed on after having been expelled from Portuguese territory (Malheiros and Baganha, 2000). An important contributing factor to the existence of undocumented immigrants in Portugal is the strict requirements that immigrants have to comply with in order to obtain a residence authorization or to extend their visa. Indeed, a significant number of applicants are denied residence, thereby acquiring illegal status (Rosa et al., 2003).

In order to address the human and social problem of irregular immigration, the Portuguese state has organized special periods during which undocumented immigrants can apply for regularization. The first regularization process took place during 1992 (from October 1992 until March 1993) and was extended to immigrants' spouses and offspring under 14 years of age. From the roughly 80,000 immigrants who applied for legal status, only 38,400 were granted residence permits (Fonseca, Malheiros and Silva, 2005). Some of the reasons cited for the discrepancy between the number of applications made and permits granted are immigrants' lack of information regarding the regularization process and the difficulty of complying with the legal requirements (Rocha-Trindade et al., 1995). As a result of the number of regularization requests which were denied, a second special period of regularization took place in 1996. This time, of the roughly 35,000 requests, approximately 31,000 permits were granted (Fonseca, Malheiros and Silva, 2005).

In 2001, the above-mentioned stay permit status absorbed many of the individuals who were in an irregular situation but had a work contract and paid their contributions to social security. Approximately 185,000 individuals, mostly Eastern Europeans, received stay permits (idem). In 2004, two other special regularization processes took place, one aimed at the general immigrant population holding work contracts and contributing to social security, and another specifically targeting Brazilian nationals. There are still no definitive data available for these numbers.

The Portuguese nationality law has been extensively and frequently adjusted in the past 20 years in order to reflect the new migratory realities experienced by Portugal.[1] During this period, regulatory changes show increasingly more restrictive conditions to obtain Portuguese nationality (Rocha-Trindade et al., 1995). It should be noted, however, that the current laws slightly reinforce the *jus soli* principle as a criterion for the acquisition of Portuguese nationality.

Foreign citizens may acquire Portuguese nationality by way of marriage, by adoption (a child adopted by a Portuguese citizen is entitled to Portuguese nationality) and through naturalization. In the case of naturalization, there is a set of requirements which need to be fulfilled. These include: 1) to be of age, 2) to legally reside on Portuguese territory for at least six years, 3) to possess some knowledge of the Portuguese language and 4) to not have a criminal record (Lei Orgânica 2/2006).

The recently approved law concedes the following:

- 'native nationality' can be obtained by individuals who fulfil the following conditions: 1) 'third-generation immigrants', that is, individuals born in Portugal of foreign parents who were themselves born in the country but who had never acquired the nationality; and 2) 'second-generation immigrants', that is, individuals born in Portugal of foreign parents, if

---

1   The Nationality Law 37/81 was recently revised by Lei Orgânica 2/2006.

either the mother or the father has resided in the territory for at least five years, regardless of their immigrant status;
- the right to nationality through naturalization for 'second-generation immigrant minors', that is, children born in the territory whose parents have become legalized or have a legal status in the past five years, or if a child finishes the first cycle of compulsory education in Portugal;
- the right for 'second-generation immigrants' (individuals born in the country) to obtain Portuguese nationality when they are 18 years old if they have lived in Portugal for the last 10 years, albeit in an irregular situation.

In spite of these changes, however, one can still argue that this law – based in the *jus soli* principle – offers a very restrictive interpretation of this principle. In fact, in both the previous law and the current one, the right to acquire citizenship for children born on Portuguese territory to foreign parents is restricted in three important ways. First, bar some exceptions, the parents need to have a legalized immigrant status. Second, the parents must have resided in Portugal for a relatively long period of time. Third, the acquisition of citizenship is not automatic, but rather, requires a declaration from the child or the legal representatives that the child desires to obtain Portuguese nationality (see Silva, 2004, for an analysis of Law 25/94).

The immigrant population in Portugal – main demographic and social features

During the 1970s, two major events modified the patterns of Portuguese migratory flows. First, the oil crisis of the mid-seventies put a cap on the number of immigrants Central and Northern European countries were willing to accept. Mechanisms restricting the entry of new immigrants were put in place, along with policies that encouraged the return of immigrants and their families to their countries of origin. As a result, Portuguese migratory outflows toward European countries – which had been the most significant trend since the 1950s – slowed down and assumed a different shape; that of short-term temporary emigration and family reunification (Rocha-Trindade et al., 1995; Baganha and Góis, 1999). At the same time, Portuguese emigrants began to look for alternative host countries, and emigration flows were re-directed to the USA and Canada (Rocha-Trindade et al., 1995). Furthermore, overall, Portuguese emigrants were gradually returning to Portugal at an increasing rate. For instance, during the period between 1980 and 1985, it was estimated that there were 210,000 returns (Baganha and Góis, 1999).

At present, the main Portuguese emigrant communities abroad may be found in Brazil (one million), France (798,837), South Africa (600,000), Canada (523,000), USA (500,000), and Venezuela (400,000) (data for 1994 in Rocha-Trindade et al., 1995, p. 167).

The second major event that changed the patterns of Portuguese migratory flows was the 1974 'Revolution of Carnations'. This was a major political change that put an end to the existing authoritarian regime and paved the way for the establishment of a democratic political system in Portugal. This political event led to the de-colonization of the Portuguese colonies in Africa and in East-Timor. Because of the de-colonization process initiated in 1975, there was a major influx of individuals from the former colonies into Portugal, with estimates varying between 500,000 and 800,000 individuals. The 'retornados'[2] were mostly from Angola (61 per cent) and Mozambique (34 per cent), and only 5 per cent came from the remaining former colonies (Cape Verde, Guinea Bissau, and S. Tomé e Príncipe). Roughly 60 per cent of this population was born in Portugal; the

---

2   Individuals who returned to Portugal from the former African colonies.

remaining population groups included Portuguese descendents born in either Portugal or Africa, and individuals of African ancestry born in Africa (Pires et al., 1987; Rocha-Trindade et al., 1995). Thus, a significant portion of African foreign immigrants in Portugal are Portuguese nationals of African descent who either resided in Portugal or who came to Portugal between 1975 and 1981 and lost their Portuguese nationality as a result of decolonization. Although this is a 'problematic' population in that it does not fully fit under the terms 'immigrant' or 'foreign' (Baganha and Góis, 1999), they are usually included by Portuguese scholars in the bulk of the foreigners residing in Portugal. One of the main reasons for lumping together such a diversity of social groups is the absence of statistics that would allow researchers to differentiate this particular social group from the remaining foreigners.

In 1975, there were roughly 32,000 foreigners legally residing in Portugal and, by 1980, that figure had increased to 58,091. Since the 1980s, the number of foreigners has increased steadily. In 1990, there were 107,767 foreigners and, as of 2001, that number rose to 223,602. At present, the main places of origin for immigrants with a residence permit in Portugal are African countries (especially Portuguese-speaking African countries), European Union member countries, and Central and South American countries (especially Brazil). As of 2001, the largest third-country immigrant groups (for example non-European Union countries) with residence authorization were Cape Verde (49,930 individuals), Brazil (23,439), Angola (22,630), Guinea Bissau (17,783), USA (8,027), São Tomé e Príncipe (6,304) and Mozambique (4,749) (SEF, 2001). The composition of these immigrant groups is, as expected, strongly influenced by the Portuguese historical links to the former African colonies and to Brazil.

Table 21.1 presents data on the foreign-born population in Portugal based on residence permits (RPs) and stay permits (SPs). As can be observed from the table, the 2001 stay permits introduced both a quantitative and a qualitative change in the documented immigrant population in Portugal. First, there is a quantitative jump from 223,602 foreigners in 2001 to 364,203 foreigners in 2003. Second, there is an important qualitative shift in the immigrant population with a greater proportion of immigrants coming from Eastern European countries. Thus, European countries outside the EU zone are now the second in rank after the African countries.

Table 21.1 also presents data on the foreign-born Portuguese population residing in Portugal in 2001. In contrast to other countries, data on the foreign-born Portuguese population residing in Portugal is not a reliable indicator of the rates of naturalized foreign population. In fact, the data reflect the specificities of Portugal, in that they include the Portuguese who were born in the former colonies, chose to return to Portugal after de-colonization and retained their Portuguese nationality. In addition, it includes the descendants of Portuguese emigrants born abroad and who returned to Portugal. In fact, the Portuguese population born in PALOP, and especially in Angola (124,756) and Mozambique (68,826), represents the most important group of Portuguese foreign-born individuals. Within the group of EU countries, France and Germany — the main destinations of Portuguese emigration in Europe — are also the main places of birth for the Portuguese foreign-born, with 59,151 and 13,453 individuals, respectively. In the case of the American continent, Brazil (with 7,441) and Venezuela (with 8,889) are the most frequent countries of birth for the Portuguese foreign-born (INE, 2001).

Table 21.1   Stocks of foreign national population residing in Portugal (2003) and foreign-born Portuguese population residing in Portugal (2001), by region of nationality*

Country of origin/birth	Foreign-national population residing in Portugal			Foreign-born Portuguese population residing in Portugal (2001)
	Residence permits (RP) (2003)	Stay permits (SP) (2001-2003)	Total (RP + SP) (2003)	
EU countries	69,805	–	69,805	82,608
Non-EU countries	180,607	183,596	364,203	265,028
Africa	118,632	29,751	148,383	226,106
America	42,598	38,961	81,559	18,872
Asia	11,571	13,719	25,290	10,123
Europe (non-EU countries)	7,248	101,021	108,269	9,672
Oceania	558	20	578	255
Other (stateless and unknown)	285	124	409	n.a
Total	250,697	183,596	434,293	347,636

The total population residing in Portugal in 2001 was slightly over 10 million (10,356,117).
Source: SEF (2003) and INE (2001).

Table 21.2 reflects the new trends in Portugal's immigrant population. It illustrates that the traditional African immigrant groups are no longer the largest in Portugal. Ukraine is the main nationality, with 65,214 individuals. Brazil has also benefited from the introduction of the SP status, maintaining its rank as the second largest immigrant community in Portugal.[3] Finally, the former Portuguese colonies of Cape Verde, Angola and Guinea Bissau are now followed by Moldavia and Romania as important immigrant communities in Portugal.

As regards irregular immigration, the number of undocumented immigrants in Portugal is currently estimated to be between 80,000 and 100,000 (Fonseca, Malheiros and Silva, 2005). However, it is very difficult to make an accurate estimate. As the special regularization processes seem to demonstrate, illegal immigration in Portugal exhibits a shift from the traditional individual movements of people coming from the PALOP with established social networks in Portugal (from the 1970s through to the 1990s), to the structured illegal trafficking networks controlled in the sending countries and composed mainly of Eastern European immigrants (from 2000 onwards) (Malheiros and Baganha, 2000).

---

3   Brazil is also the nationality that is expected to become the most numerous nationality of origin after the 2004 special period of regularization.

Table 21.2   Twelve major nationalities in Portugal by immigrant status in 2003 (residence permit, stay permit, asylum seeker, and acquisition of nationality)

Immigrant groups	RPs (stocks 2003)	SPs (2001–2003)	Total	Asylum seekers* (1999–2003)	Acquisition nationality (1995–2000)**
Ukraine	519	64,695	65,214	15	n.a
Brazil	26,561	37,920	64,481	3	1,179
Cape Verde	53,858	8,558	62,416	–	687
Angola	25,681	8,533	34,214	114	349
Guinea Bissau	20,209	4,318	24,527	17	217
Moldávia	266	12,632	12,898	12	n.a
Romania	766	10,926	11,692	25	n.a
São Tomé e Príncipe	7,313	2,553	9,866	1	90
P. R. China	4,814	3,909	8,723	–	62
USA	8,004	62	8,066	–	649
Russian Federation	852	7047	7,899	48	n.a
Mozambique	4,946	461	5,407	–	178

Data refer to asylum applications and not to granted asylum status. Data cover the years from 1999 to 2003. Data are incomplete for the year 2003, since only major nationalities were presented. Source is SEF (2003).
**Data on acquisition of nationality cover the years from 1995 to 2000, and are based on SOPEMI (2001). Source: Serviço de Estrangeiros e Fronteiras (SEF 2003, 2002, 2001, 2000, 1999) (see notes below).*

Immigrant rights and participation in public life – issues of immigrant integration

Portugal's existing regulatory context does not restrict immigrants' rights of access to social housing, public health services, social security or education. In fact, the law is explicit on this matter, clearly stipulating that even illegal immigrants are entitled to health care, and that the children of illegal immigrants are entitled to education (Marques and Rosa, 2003).

With regard to political rights, in 1996 third-country immigrants acquired the right to vote and be candidates in local elections (Law 50/96). However, the law imposes some restrictions. On the one hand, reciprocity between states must be observed and, thus, only certain nationalities are entitled to political participation (namely, Argentina, Brazil,[4] Cape Verde, Israel, Norway, Peru, Uruguay, Venezuela and Iceland).[5] On the other hand, only legal residents who have resided in the country for a minimum of two years (if they are nationals of Portuguese-speaking countries) or a period of three years (for other nationals) may exercise their right to vote. Regarding the capacity to run for local elections, the conditions are the same, except for the minimum periods of residence which are raised to four and five years respectively (Mendes and Miguéis, 1997; Costa, 2000; *ACIME/STAPE* n.d).

---

4   Exception is made for those nationals from Brazil who have the special status of equality of political rights. Holders of this status may vote in other elections besides local elections. Not all Brazilians are entitled to this status.

5   Chile was included by Declaration 10/2001 but was excluded by Declaration 9/2005, the same legal document that extended this right to Iceland.

Moreover, the number of foreigners who are actually registered to vote is extremely low. According to data from the National Census Commission (Comissão Nacional de Recenseamento), as of December 2003, the number of third-country foreigners registered to vote amounted to 17,922. This number was distributed among the following nationalities: Cape Verde (15,635), Brazil (1,974), Venezuela (168), Argentina (61), Peru (28), Norway (25), Uruguay (16), Chile (12) and Israel (3).[6] According to these numbers, the most important immigrant community in terms of their political participation is the Cape Verdean community, the oldest and one of the largest groups in Portugal.

Another area where immigrants' civic rights are restricted is employment. Here, immigrants are prevented from accessing state employment or joining public administration careers (Marques and Rosa, 2003). The exclusion is applicable when the job involves political functions and not only technical ones (Torres, 2001).

The Portuguese local and central state and Portuguese civil society have created some institutional structures and opportunities to encourage immigrants' participation in Portuguese public life.

At the state level, the main organizational state structure is the High Commissioner for Immigration and Intercultural Dialogue (Alto Comissário para a Imigração e Diálogo Intercultural/ ACIDI) and a set of interrelated initiatives, which act as mediators between state officials and civil society, with a particular focus on immigrant communities. This structure was formerly designed as High Comissioner for Immigration and Ethnic Minorities (Alto Comissário para a Imigração e Minorias Étnicas/ACIME). It was created in 1996 and restructured in 2003 and 2007 in order to extend its initial roles. ACIDI is an interdepartmental structure which offers the Portuguese Government a supportive and consultative role on matters of immigration and ethnic minorities (Decree-Law 167/2007). While ACIDI became the political mediator between the government and immigrant associations, immigrant associations became the mediators between public administration offices and the diverse immigrant groups (Albuquerque, Ferreira and Viegas, 2000).

The organization's mission is threefold. First, to promote the integration of immigrants and ethnic minorities in Portuguese society. Second, to assure the participation and collaboration of the different representatives of immigrants' interests (such as immigrant associations, social partners, and social solidarity institutions) in the policies promoting social integration and eradicating social exclusion. Third, to oversee the application of legal tools aimed at preventing discrimination based on race, nationality, or ethnic origin. Additional tasks held by ACIDI include, among others, the development of research on the integration of immigrant and ethnic minorities, as well as collaboration with the different public offices involved in the control and surveillance of flows of foreigners in Portugal (ACIME;[7] Santos, 2004). In order to achieve these aims, ACIDI is equipped with specific competences such as the right to apply penalties to any violation of the specific law banning discrimination based on race, nationality or ethnic origin. It also has the competency to grant legal recognition to immigrant associations.

ACIDI is Portugal's overarching institution in matters of immigration policy. A plethora of programmes, working groups and other semi-autonomous organizations stem from and depend on ACIDI. Until now, the role played by ACIDI has been praised by both government officials and immigrant representatives alike. However, it is worth noting that the dependence of the majority of state initiatives and programmes on a single institution may, eventually, pose a risk to the entire system if the centralizing institution suffers from blockages or inefficiencies. The progressive

---

6   STAPE, www.stape.pt/recensel/quadro14.htm, date of visit: 2004/12/11.
7   www.acime.gov.pt, date of visit: 2004/12/10.

organizational autonomy of these commissions and working groups may drive the decentralization of state initiatives.

There are some initiatives which have been created at the local level, aiming at the integration and higher involvement of immigrants in local structures and at the municipal level. The Municipal Council of Immigrant Communities and Ethnic Minorities (Conselho Municipal das Comunidades Imigrantes e Minorias Étnicas) created by the City Council of Lisbon in 1993, and the Municipal Council for Ethnic and Immigrant Communities (Conselho Municipal das Comunidades Étnicas e Imigrantes), created by the City Council of Amadora in 1995, are consultative bodies which are composed by community and immigrant associations leaders. Their aim is to involve the most representative immigrant groups in local policies. This is related to the social integration of immigrants, to the safeguarding of immigrants' rights, and to racism and xenophobia prevention (Rocha-Trindade et al., 1995; CML 1993). However, today both councils are inactive.

Two other local structures are municipal departments which specifically address matters concerning ethnic and immigrant groups. Such departments are the Cabinet for Religious and Social Issues (Gabinete para Assuntos Religiosos e Sociais Específicos – GARSE), created in the City Council of Loures in 1993, and the Cabinet for the Support of Immigrants and Ethnic Minorities, in the City Council of Santarém, formed in 2002. This type of structure offers technical and logistic support to immigrant initiatives, especially associations, and facilitates communication between immigrant communities and local offices, among others (Rocha-Trindade et al., 1995; Albuquerque, Ferreira and Viegas, 2000; Albuquerque, 2002).

Civil society structures: immigrant associations, non-immigrant associations and unions

A crucial piece of legislation for immigrant associations was Law 115/99, which approved the legal regime regulating immigrant associations. Until then, immigrant associations were not regulated by a special status, and were formed as non-profit cultural associations or private institutions of a social solidarity character. The approval of the legal regime of immigrant associations in 1999 paved the way for a higher visibility of these associations as political partners and legitimate representatives of the interests of immigrant groups in the public domain. Immigrant associations are, thus, important partners in the shaping of public policies concerning immigration (Rocha-Trindade et al., 1995; Albuquerque, Ferreira and Viegas, 2000).

Since the 1950s, when the first immigrant association was established, the movement has witnessed a slow and stable increase in the number of associations, with the 1990s and 2000s registering the highest number of new establishments. Indeed, the number of immigrant associations amounted to 184 in 2002 (Albuquerque, 2002). Also, several inter-organizational platforms have been created, thereby facilitating the associations' role as political interlocutors and representatives of the immigrant groups vis-à-vis the political powers.

A 2002 survey organized by SOS Racismo identified 52 third-sector associations catering to immigration issues formed by non-immigrant members. An important part of this sector is comprised of organizations linked to the Catholic Church (ibid.). However, because of the rising diversification of ethnic groups in Portugal, religious third-sector organizations are also becoming diversified with the presence of Orthodox, Hindu and Muslim religions. Other important components of the non-immigrant organizational sector are the anti-racist organizations, human rights activists, and educational and cultural associations (ibidem).

In Portugal, unions have traditionally been involved with immigration issues. The main unions, CGTP-IN and UGT, have developed special departments dealing with immigration issues, having launched several initiatives catering for immigrant populations. The activities developed by these unions include information sessions during the special regularization periods, development of professional training programmes for immigrant populations and their descendents, and also legal counselling offered to migrant workers, given that most immigrants are not unionized and are, therefore, less knowledgeable of their employment rights (Albuquerque, Ferreira and Viegas, 2000).

Public and media discourses on migration

Immigration is not a constant topic of debate among the political forces in Portugal. Its discussion and debate in the political and public arena is intermittent and dependent upon certain events, such as political campaigns or specific incidents that attract media coverage and where immigrants play a central role. These latter are usually connected with crimes suffered or committed by immigrants.

Media coverage of immigrants can be divided into two categories: one type covers particular stories where immigrants have a central or secondary role but where the main theme is not immigration (that is a crime, an accident); and another category in which the main theme is immigration issues, such as education, adjustment to a new society, cultural differences, employment and so on. However, whenever immigration is a topic in the newspapers or on television, it is rarely presented as an informative piece on immigrants' living and working conditions. Rather, the image depicted is that of single stories or trajectories of specific individuals.

A recent and significant example is the media coverage of an incident which took place in June 2005. On 10 June, a Portuguese national holiday, television news reported a robbery involving 500 young black individuals on a crowded beach near Lisbon. Several television channels portrayed this assault as having been organized by a criminal gang of young people living in degraded suburban quarters of the Lisbon metropolitan area. All of them based their reports on the statement of a bar owner who called the police because, as he explained, he felt frightened when he saw several black youngsters arriving at the beach. The day after, the police reports announced that 30–40 individuals were involved in that incident and that it was a spontaneous and unplanned action. It was explained that it was usual to have robbery incidents on that beach and, as there were around 15,000 people that day, things got out of control and people got frightened when they saw the police officers arriving. These statements were not widely and clearly communicated by the media and in the following days the criminality of young blacks in Lisbon's suburbs took centre stage.

A year later, the High Commissioner for Immigration and Ethnic Minorities published a report about the 'pseudo-robbery of Carcavelos' which presents the report of the High Authority for the Media (*Alta Autoridade para a Comunicação Social*). The report underlines that the media did not follow the necessary rules of journalistic research and were disseminating false news. Today, it is clear that the media capitalized on this event for sensationalist reasons (ACIME, 2006).

This case is important for two reasons. First, it reveals the power of the media in building and reinforcing stereotypes. Second, it introduced the discussion of social integration and exclusion of second- and third-generation immigrants in relation to the issue of Portuguese nationality. When Parliament approved the new nationality law, the debate underlined that access to Portuguese nationality was crucial for a sense of belonging and will to participate and nationality was considered a crucial instrument in the integration of second- and third-generation immigrants.

Two recent studies have analysed the media coverage of immigrants and ethnic minorities in Portugal. One of the studies covered the national and regional print media (newspapers and magazines) from January 2001 to March 2002 (Cádima and Figueiredo, 2003). According to this study, the topics most covered by the print media were associated with 'crime and offences'. These were followed by themes related to the 'reception of immigrants', 'sociabilities', and 'exploitation and Mafia'. Interestingly, among the themes least covered by both the national and regional press are topics related to the discussion of 'living conditions and housing', 'illegal networks, exploitation, and slavery', 'measures supporting integration', and 'access to health services' (ibid., p. 46). The immigrant and ethnic groups most frequently cited by the newspapers are the 'Eastern Europeans', followed by the generic category 'immigrants', immigrants from the 'Portuguese speaking countries – PALOP', and 'gypsies' (ibid., p. 40).

The study examining print media and the main television broadcasters conducted in 2003 by Cunha et al. (2004) also found that the topic most frequently associated with immigrants and ethnic groups was 'crime'. Nevertheless, the data suggest that there is an emergent interest in other themes related to the identity and culture of foreigners (ibid., p. 93). In this regard, different media highlight different subjects: if tabloid newspapers cover 'crime', non-tabloid newspapers choose 'work-related' news. Comparing newspapers to television, both give prominence to 'crime' segments, but television channels allocate a higher percentage of their time to 'crime-related' news (28.6 per cent against 17.9 per cent). In this study, the nationality most frequently mentioned in the news is Brazilian.

Another finding of interest is that immigrants and ethnic minorities have acquired more centrality and agency, since they are more often quoted or used as information sources by the media. However, according to the authors, this fact does not reflect an accurate depiction of the realities experienced by immigrants in Portugal by the media, since the news is constructed as *fait-divers*, or as personalized singular narratives (ibid., p. 103).

Concluding remarks

Portugal's migratory experiences are strongly influenced by the country's historical past. The same countries which first received population inflows from Portugal (PALOP and Brazil) became major senders of labour in a post-colonial phase. However, the last five years have seen dramatic changes in the national origins of the immigrant population arriving in Portugal. Eastern European immigrants are now becoming important immigrant communities and important providers of labour. Portugal's accession to the European Union has contributed to determining the country's position within a wider global migratory and labour market system, not only as a 'sending' country, but also as a 'receiving' country. On the other hand, Portugal suffers the impact of the European Union's policies toward migratory flows at the level of its own policies and regulatory frameworks.

Present migratory trends are mainly characterized by the stabilization of Eastern European inflows along with family reunification, and significant inflows from Brazil and other South American countries. The latter see Portugal as a port of entry into the European Union, taking advantage of their geographical proximity to Brazil and the numerous daily flights between the two countries. PALOP inflows are almost non-existent. A major concern of Portuguese political authorities is to fight illegal immigration, which is strongly connected to criminal networks of women-trafficking for prostitution, especially from Brazil.

Immigration policies in Portugal were initially fragmented and almost non-existent, and only from the mid-1990 s onwards was there an effort to offer more structured and encompassing policies on the integration of immigrants in Portuguese society. However, policy packages are not nearly enough to rectify the unequal access of immigrants to education, jobs, housing, health services and civic life, and to lessen the acute social exclusion suffered by some immigrants in Portugal.

Some of the positive developments towards the integration of immigrants include the role of ACIDI – the main state initiative – which has been investing in maintaining communication channels with immigrant associations and populations, and in involving associations in participatory policy-making structures. However, the dependence of the majority of state initiatives and programmes on a single institution may eventually pose a risk to the entire system. The progressive organizational autonomy of the several commissions and working groups may be a necessary step in order to maintain efficient communication channels between the central power and immigrant associations. Another positive development has been the strengthening of the *jus soli* principle in Portugal's nationality law, although access to nationality is still a restrictive process, even for the children of immigrants. There is, however, some sensitivity on the part of the political elites in understanding that access to nationality is a fundamental condition for the social inclusion of immigrants in Portugal.

References

ACIME (2006), *O 'pseudo-arrastão' de Carcavelos: Documentos*. Lisboa: ACIME.

ACIME/STAPE (n.d), (Alto Comissário para a Imigração e as Minorias Étnicas/Secretariado Técnico de Apoio Processo Eleitoral) in Recenseamento Eleitoral. *Direito de Voto dos Estrangeiros*. Leaflet.

Albuquerque, R. (2002), 'Dinâmicas associativas e comunidades imigrantes', in SOS Racismo (ed.) *A imigração em Portugal. Os movimentos humanos e culturais em Portugal*. Lisboa: SOS Racismo.

Albuquerque, R., Ferreira, L. and Viegas, T. (2000), *O fenómeno associativo em contexto migratório. Duas décadas de associativismo de imigrantes em Portugal*. Oeiras: Celta.

Baganha, M.I. and Góis, P. (1999), 'Migrações internacionais de e para Portugal: o que sabemos e para onde vamos?' *Revista Crítica de Ciências Sociais*, **52/53**, Novembro (1998), Fevereiro (1999), 229–80.

Cádima, R. and Figueiredo, A. (2003), *Representações (imagens) dos imigrantes e das minorias étnicas nos media*. Lisboa: ACIME.

CML (Câmara Municipal de Lisboa) (1993), 'Regulamento do Conselho Municipal das Comunidades Imigrantes e Minorias Étnicas, Câmara Municipal de Lisboa', *Diário Municipal*, **16596**, 1993.04.01.

Costa, P.M. (2000), 'A participação dos portugueses não residentes e dos estrangeiros residentes nas eleições portuguesas', *Documentação e Direito Comparado*, **81/82**, 179–216.

Cunha, I.F. et al. (2004), *Media, imigração e minorias*. Lisboa: ACIME/Observatório da Imigração.

Fonseca, L., Malheiros, J. and Silva, S. (2005), 'Portugal', in Niessen, J., Schibel, Y. and Thompson, C. (eds) *Current Immigration Debates in Europe: A Publication of the European Migration Dialogue*. Brussels: European Migration Dialogue, MPG.

INE (2001), *Recenseamento Geral da População e Habitação*. Lisboa: INE.

Leitão, J. (1997), 'The Portuguese Immigration Policy and the New European Order', in Baganha, M.I. (ed.) *Immigration in Southern Europe*. Oeiras: Celta.

Malheiros, J. and Baganha, M.I. (2000), 'Imigração ilegal em Portugal: padrões emergentes em inícios do séc. XXI', *Janus 2001 – Anuário de Relações Exteriores*, Novembro, 190–91.

Marques, M.M. and Rosa, M.J.V. (2003), 'L'intégration des immigrés au Portugal: Singularité ou Retard?' *Sociologia, Problemas e Práticas*, **41**, 9–36.

Mendes, F.A. and Miguéis, J. (1997), *Orgãos das Autarquias Locais: Lei Eleitoral*. Vila Franca de Xira: Comissão Nacional das Eleições.

Pires, R. et al. (1987), *Os retornados. Um estudo sociográfico*. Lisboa: IED.

Rocha-Trindade, M.B. et al. (1995), *Sociologia das Migrações*. Lisboa: Universidade Aberta.

Rosa, M.J.V., Seabra, H. and Santos, T. (2003), *Contributos dos 'imigrantes' na demografia Portuguesa, O papel das populações de nacionalidade estrangeira*. Lisboa: ACIME.

Santos, V. (2004), *O discurso oficial do Estado sobre a imigração dos anos 60 a 80 e imigração dos anos 90 à actualidade*. Lisboa: ACIME/Observatório da Imigração.

SEF (1999), *Relatório estatístico*. Lisboa: SEF.

—— (2000), *Relatório estatístico*. Lisboa: SEF.

—— (2001), *Relatório estatístico*. Lisboa: SEF.

—— (2002), *Relatório estatístico*. Lisboa: SEF.

—— (2003), *Relatório estatístico*. Lisboa: SEF.

Silva, J.P. (2004), *Direitos de cidadania e direito à cidadania: princípio da equiparação, novas cidadanias e direito à cidadania portuguesa como instrumentos de uma comunidade constitucional inclusiva*. Lisboa: ACIME/Observatório da imigração.

SOPEMI (2001), *Trends in International Migration. Annual Report*. Paris: OECD.

Torres, M. (2001), 'O estatuto constitucional dos estrangeiros', *Scientia Iuridica*, **290**, 7–27.

Internet-based references

ACIME (available at http://www.acime.gov.pt, home page).

STAPE (available at http://www.stape.pt, home page).

Chapter 22

Slovakia

Boris Divinský

In its modern history, Slovakia has been an emigration rather than an immigration country. Intensive emigration movements from the territory of the current Slovak Republic were particularly evident from the second half of the nineteenth century until the First World War, when more than 500,000 persons left for the United States of America and another 350,000 for other regions of the world (Divinský, 2004a). Emigration continued both during the interwar period and under communism. While mainly economic factors contributed to emigration until the Second World War, emigrants after 1948 were largely motivated by political reasons (persecution, political pressure, disagreement with communist ideology, impossibility of self-fulfilment and so on).

The fall of communism and the establishment of a new social and economic order in Slovakia after 1989 resulted in fundamental shifts. Following a long period of negative net migration, migration trends in the Slovak Republic began to alter. During the last 15 years, the country has experienced previously unknown and dynamic phenomena, such as large-scale irregular immigration, human smuggling, a rise in asylum seekers, problems with foreigners' integration, naturalization issues and so forth.

At first, public authorities, State institutions, NGOs, the academic community and other actors dealing with migration underestimated the developmental trajectory and did not react in a prompt, effective and adequate manner. Matters of international migration remained on the periphery of public interest despite their growing relevance and influence on Slovak society (namely in the economic, social, cultural, political, security, legal and institutional areas). Much of this changed during the process of Slovakia's accession to the European Union. New migration policy has gradually been articulated while some of the challenges are being addressed. Yet there are still many essential tasks in the field of immigration and integration to be done in the country (Divinský, 2005a; Divinský, 2006a).

Major developments in Slovakia's immigration policy

One cannot define migration policy in Slovakia up to 1990, as it basically did not exist. But, as elsewhere in the former Soviet bloc, the country provided opportunities for immigrants from ideologically close countries in the world to study and work in its territory. In this way, hundreds of Palestinians, Afghans, Syrians, Cubans, Ethiopians, Angolans, Vietnamese, Mongolians and so on resided in Slovakia. However, it should be noted that their total number was not very significant.

After the collapse of the Iron Curtain, migration patterns were considerably transformed and the Central and Eastern European countries, including Slovakia, were fully incorporated into the system of European migration movements. As a consequence, the stock of foreign nationals in the country began to increase slowly. Simultaneously, Slovakia for the first time encountered the phenomenon of refugees to the country. Still in 1992, the number of asylum seekers reached just 87 individuals and undocumented immigration was little known. The general opinion prevailed that there was no need to develop or formulate a specific immigration policy (Divinský, 2004a).

Indeed, the Slovak Republic did not feel the necessity for substantial legal, institutional or other changes or a special approach to migration. Nevertheless, the Slovak Government founded the *Migration Office of the Ministry of the Interior of the Slovak Republic* with the 1993 Resolution No. 501. In order to meet international obligations, the Government also passed the *Principles of the Migration Policy of the Slovak Republic*. However, the document consisted of merely 10 paragraphs. Likewise, the then laws pertaining to asylum issues (Act No. 283/1995) and the entry, stay or expulsion of foreigners (Act No. 73/1995) were rather sketchy and formal.

The above mentioned Principles became the important guideline for migration management in Slovakia until early 2005. They perhaps reflected objective reality in the 1990s. However, at the beginning of the new millennium it was still more evident that the provisions of the Principles were largely obsolete and coincided little with the contemporary situation in the country, the region of Central Europe, or Europe as a whole. In addition, according to many experts and NGOs, State migration policy based on these Principles was not carried out in a pro-immigration way (Divinský, 2005c; Divinský, 2005e). Unlike its neighbours, the country was more inclined to restrict than to support legal migration.

In the meantime, particularly since the mid-1990s, the situation in the field of migration in the Slovak Republic has radically changed. Slovakia became a country with (officially registered) positive migration balance figures (Table 22.1). The country was also affected by rapidly and unexpectedly growing numbers of undocumented migrants and asylum seekers with such a concomitant phenomenon as the operation of a wide network of organizations smuggling (trafficking) migrants; delay in the building of the asylum system with polarized views on its (restrictive) character; the inadequate analysis of labour immigration and imprecise registration of labour immigrants; the complete absence of naturalization and integration policies; the increasing occurrence of manifestations of intolerance, xenophobia towards or discrimination of migrants; insufficient evaluation of impacts resulting from the presence of immigrants in the territory of Slovakia on the autochthonous society, and so on.

Below, one can find some selected characteristics and trends in the main categories of migrants in Slovakia. (For a more detailed analysis see Divinský, 2004b; Divinský, 2005a; Divinský, 2005b; Divinský, 2005d; Divinský, 2006b.)

During the past 15 years, Slovakia has undergone several stages in the quantitative development of *undocumented migrants*. Dramatic growth in numbers began in 1998, peaking with over 15,000/year in 2001 and 2002 (Table 22.1). The inflow of undocumented migrants in Slovakia then increased to approximately seven times the 1993 rate. As a result, the ratio of apprehended undocumented migrants to the total population of the country was almost the highest in the region of Central and Eastern Europe. The given dynamics mirrored the recent expansion of migration to Slovakia due to migration pressure, especially from some Asian countries, a well-functioning network of smugglers across the country and the relatively difficult protection of the eastern Slovak border.

Table 22.1   Developments in the major categories of migrants in the Slovak Republic (2000–2006)

Year / Category of persons	2000	2001	2002	2003	2004	2005	2006
People changing their permanent residence (inflows)							
Emigration from Slovakia	811	1,011	1,411	1,194	1,586	1,873	1,735
Immigration to Slovakia	2,274	2,023	2,312	2,603	4,460	5,276	5,589
Net migration	1,463	1,012	901	1,409	2,874	3,403	3,854
Foreigners with stay permits (stocks)							
Holding a permanent stay permit	17,410	17,287	17,108	17,008	17,003	20,927	26,028
Holding a temporary stay permit	11,391	12,131	11,333	10,505	4,517	4,286	5,894
Holding a registered stay permit	0	0	1,050	1,683	477	188	0
Holding a tolerated stay permit	0	0	14	23	111	237	231
Persons, total	28,801	29,418	29,505	29,219	22,108	25,638	32,153
Foreigners with stay permits (inflows)							
Persons, total	4,622	4,723	4,799	4,574	8,081	11,299	12,631
Persons in the asylum procedure (inflows)							
Number of asylum seekers	1,556	8,151	9,743	10,358	11,395	3,549	2,871
Procedure suspended	1,366	6,154	8,053	10,656	11,782	2,930	1,940
Asylums rejected	123	130	309	531	1,592	827	861
Asylums granted	11	18	20	11	15	25	8
Naturalized citizens (inflows)							
Persons, total	4,241	2,122	3,484	4,047	4,016	1,537	1,050
Apprehended undocumented migrants (inflows)							
Those transiting illegally	6,062	15,548	15,235	12,493	8,335	5,178	4,129
Those staying illegally					2,612	2,871	3,491
Total number of inhabitants in Slovakia (stocks)							
Persons, total	5,402,547	5,378,951	5,379,161	5,380,053	5,384,822	5,389,180	5,393,637

Source: Office of Border and Alien Police; Migration Office; Ministry of Interior of the Slovak Republic; Statistical Office of the Slovak Republic.

Quantitative development in the group of *asylum seekers* in Slovakia has been even more remarkable. In 2004, their annual inflow for the first time exceeded 11,000 individuals and reached 131 times the 1992 figure. This extreme upsurge began in 2001, shocking authorities and the public. In 2003 and 2004 the ratio of asylum seekers to the number of inhabitants in Slovakia was among the highest in Europe.[1] But only a minimal number of asylum applicants have been granted asylum. This circumstance has often been subject to criticism by non-governmental organizations, international institutions and migrants themselves. On the other hand, after time to take stock and 'catch their breath', asylum seekers usually leave the Slovak refugee camps for Western European countries, thereby breaching the conditions of the asylum procedure, which has then to be suspended (Table 22.1).

Developmental trends in *foreigners holding a residence* (stay) *permit*[2] in the country are of a different character. After modest growth in their stock since the establishment of an independent Slovakia, the country saw their stagnation from 1998. There are three reasons for this. First, a natural one – both external and internal conditions to stay in the country were not particularly favourable for foreigners. Second, a legal one – the category of expatriate Slovaks was exempt from the register of foreigners. Finally, a 'technical' one – this register was revised in 2004 and numerous doubly-registered permits were eliminated. At the end of 2006, the stock of foreign nationals with a residence permit reached over 32,000 (Table 22.1) thus representing the most numerous and significant group of migrants in the territory of Slovakia. It is worth noting that their annual inflow is currently on the rise again as a result of the country's accession to the EU.

As regards *naturalized immigrants* in Slovakia, their numbers were quite large in the first half of the 1990s – over twelve thousand persons a year. This group was then formed primarily by ex-citizens of Czechoslovakia, and later by citizens of the Czech Republic, wishing to be holders of both citizenships for mainly economic reasons. At present, naturalized citizens in the country are predominantly represented by persons with the former status of expatriate Slovaks (that is those with Slovak roots). The annual inflow of those naturalized was stabilized at the level of 4,000 individuals in 2000–2004 (Table 22.1).[3]

---

1   The situation in 2005–2006, however, suggests a surprising decrease in the number of asylum applicants in the country.

2   Act No. 48/2002 on the Stay of Foreigners distinguishes between three essential kinds of residence permit for foreign nationals in Slovakia: a temporary stay permit, a permanent stay permit and a tolerated stay permit. A *permit for temporary stay* is granted to a foreigner who intends to perform a particular activity in the country for a short period (usually up to five years); this permit can be renewed. A temporary stay permit may be granted only for a single purpose of these six: doing business, employment, study, special activity, tasks of civilian employees of foreign armed forces, and family reunification. (Within this kind of stay, before Slovakia's accession to the Union, its citizens were entitled to a special *registered stay permit* regulating their stay in the country in an above-standard, administratively much simpler, way.) A *permanent stay permit* entitles the foreigner to stay in the country's territory for a longer (five-year) period or for an indefinite period – because of family reunification, employment or doing business – under the respective conditions. Permanent stay permits are also granted to refugees. Finally, a *tolerated stay permit* is granted to any foreigner who cannot be expelled from the Slovak Republic for various administrative/ technical reasons, has been incarcerated or has been granted temporary shelter. It is valid for a maximum period of 180 days, but may be repeatedly renewed.

3   Since 2005, conditions for granting Slovak citizenship have been considerably tightened. It may be granted to those foreign nationals who have a permanent stay permit and live in the country for five years uninterruptedly, can speak the basics of Slovak and have not been convicted for an intentional crime. Within the naturalization procedure, there is no special policy in favour or disfavour of any nationality/ group of foreigners.

Despite the given facts and obvious enormous quantitative growth in some categories of migrants in the Slovak Republic, as well as subsequent grave qualitative consequences, most of the major State institutions still claimed that the above mentioned Principles provided a satisfactory framework for the management of migration. Some other institutions, NGOs and independent experts in the country expressed the opinion that coordination among actors involved in the areas of immigration, asylum and integration of foreign nationals – and the existing legal instruments – were not sufficient (Divinský, 2004a).

On the eve of the third millennium, one external factor appeared that substantially changed the whole situation. Within the EU accession process, the Slovak Republic was obliged to pass, amend or harmonize a multitude of legal standards, including those referring to various migration issues. For instance, entirely new and qualitatively much better legal norms altering the conditions for the entry and stay of immigrants in the country (Act No. 48/2002 on the Stay of Foreigners from 2001) or improving the asylum procedure (Act No. 480/2002 on Asylum from 2002) were adopted. A set of other laws on border protection, social and health care, employment, entrepreneurship, ownership, antidiscrimination and so on, also dealing with the position of immigrants in Slovak society were approved too. Analogically, the formation of comprehensive and modern migration policy was discussed for a longer period but responsible institutions did not manage to prepare it until the country's accession to the European Union.

At the very end of 2004, the Migration Office of the Slovak Ministry of Interior presented a draft of the *Conception of the Migration Policy of the Slovak Republic* and submitted it to expert debate. After it was examined and completed by the competent State authorities, self-government bodies, NGOs, IGOs and other relevant subjects, the Conception was passed by the Government in January 2005. It outlines policies in the fields of international cooperation; legal migration; the integration of immigrants; asylum; combating undocumented migration; collaboration among the respective migration actors; human rights protection; preventing xenophobia, intolerance and discrimination (see more in Divinský, 2005a).

The document has been drawn up as a general framework. Its objectives are further specified for the years to come (basically until 2010) and already being fulfilled by the individual institutions concerned, mostly State organizations – Ministries of Interior, Labour and Social Affairs, Foreign Affairs, Justice, Health and Education. There is an apparent significant qualitative shift in the philosophy of the Conception in comparison with the old Principles. As a fundamental strategic document, it reflects the ongoing process of integrating immigration and asylum policies in the European Union.

Naturally, the Conception cannot be perfect. For example, numerous aspects of the process of foreigners' integration into society; the development of missing national integration, naturalization or regularization policies; a series of issues pertaining to labour immigration; the foundation of a parliamentary or governmental Committee for the Matters of Foreigners (Migrants); the workings of the media; the activation of immigrant associations; the improvement of statistical databases on migrants; greater support for the academic community in studying migration phenomena and some other challenges should have been given more emphasis in the document. However, all this also requires a common political and societal consensus and adequate financial means. Therefore, in principle, comprehensive immigration policy in the Slovak Republic is still at the beginning of a long journey (Divinský, 2005a; Divinský, 2005d).

The immigrant population in Slovakia: main demographic and social features

Both in its legal norms and in practice, the Slovak Republic only applies the concept of *foreigner* (not that of foreign-born person). The citizenship of a person is thus the crucial criterion to assess his/her status and to recognize the corresponding rights. According to the Constitution and other laws, a foreigner is any person who is not a (State) citizen of the Slovak Republic.[4]

As of 31 December 2006, the stock of registered foreigners in the country with any of the stay permits reached 32,153 persons, thus representing almost 0.6 per cent of the total population. In comparison with other countries, this is quite a low figure and the lowest proportion in the entire European Union. The gradual growth of their absolute number and share in the total population is evident: at the beginning of the 1990s, the proportion of foreign nationals in the country fluctuated around 0.2 per cent.

Since the category of foreigners with a stay permit already existed in Slovakia, albeit to a smaller extent, during the communist regime before 1990, both their quantitative development and the structure of their source countries are markedly dissimilar to those of asylum seekers or undocumented migrants (Divinský, 2004b).

Among the 30 most represented countries of origin in 2006 it is possible to identify several groups with different histories, characteristics or motives to immigrate to and stay in the Slovak Republic. The largest group is formed by persons from the neighbouring countries who have strong kin/labour bonds in Slovakia. The immigrants from the Czech Republic naturally dominate in number, accounting for 16 per cent of all immigrants. They are primarily employed or do business in various economic sectors, but for a good part of them, family reunification too provides an important reason to stay in Slovakia. Almost the same can be said of the immigrants from Poland and Hungary. On the other side, the Ukrainians – predominantly men – are employed as low-skilled workers in construction, manufacturing, forestry, auxiliary works and so on. The Ukrainians, Poles and Hungarians usually come from regions adjacent to Slovakia.

The next group of foreign populations in the Slovak Republic is constituted by persons from the countries with historically developed communities of immigrants in the territory of Slovakia (Russia, Bulgaria, Croatia). They work, study or create families and gradually join their national minorities in the country. Likewise, immigrants from Serbia and Romania may partly be included in this category. However, as a great number of them are expatriate Slovaks (Divinský, 2006b), they were lately excluded by law from the register of foreigners.

The increasing inflow of immigrants from Asian countries is a new trend in the country. The Vietnamese have been in Slovakia for some decades already and newcomers just join them. But the Chinese community is recent and very dynamic. Economically, both these nationalities are mostly active as small entrepreneurs, retailers, vendors, wholesale importers of cheap goods and in gastronomy. The immigrants from South Korea represent an absolutely contrasting subgroup of Asians. A few years ago they were almost unknown in the country, yet they increased from fewer than 50 individuals in 2003 to over 800 persons in 2006. This extraordinary growth has been brought about by the construction of a huge new car factory in northern Slovakia (Kia/Hyundai). Koreans work there as top executives and high-skilled employees.

One of the most dynamic developments in Slovakia over recent years has been among immigrants from 'old' countries of the European Union. They have substantially increased in number; currently they make up more than one-fifth of the foreign population (in 2002 merely 9.5 per cent). Particularly remarkable have been their inflows since the accession of the country to

---

4   The Constitution of the Slovak Republic (Act No. 460/1992) and Act No. 48/2002 on the Stay of Foreigners (both with later amendments).

the EU.[5] The fastest-expanding EU population in Slovakia is the French one. In 2004–2006 its size almost tripled because of the construction of another large car factory in the country (PSA Peugeot Citroën near Bratislava), which launched production in mid-2006.

In general, immigrants from the EU, U.S.A., Canada and other 'western' countries in Slovakia carry out economic activities in the tertiary and quaternary sectors as high-skilled employees or businessmen in such professions as manager or company representative, expert, consultant, teacher, university lecturer, researcher and so on (Divinský, 2006a). The reunification of family is rarer in this group.

A detailed overview of the top 30 countries whose nationals resided in the Slovak Republic at the end of December 2006 is given in Table 22.2 below.

Table 22.2   Thirty major immigrant populations in Slovakia (end of 2006)

Czech Republic	5,113
Ukraine	3,927
Poland	3,646
Germany	2,289
Hungary	2,106
Russia	1,311
Austria	1,202
Serbia	1,073
Vietnam	1,063
China	896
France	865
South Korea	837
United Kingdom	744
USA	701
Romania	700
Italy	695
Bulgaria	547
Croatia	333
Macedonia	251
Netherlands	245
Spain	182
Belgium	169
Norway	165
Israel*	153
Denmark	149
Turkey	148
Japan	127
Greece	115
Switzerland	114
Belarus	112
Others	2,175
Immigrants in total	32,153

Mostly Israeli Palestinians.
Source: Office of Border and Alien Police.

---

5   The share of immigrants from all countries of the European Union in the total stock of foreigners in the Slovak Republic is 56 per cent (2006).

During the recent period, changes having a serious impact on the structure of residence permits in the country occurred (Divinský, 2005a). By the end of 2006, several new legal norms on the stay of foreign nationals were passed by the Slovak Parliament and other measures were taken by the police, thus adopting the respective EU directives and improving the legal and registration systems in the relevant field.

As a consequence, the stock of foreigners with a temporary stay permit has dramatically dropped (Table 22.1). As previously mentioned, this is because the category of expatriate Slovaks (by then usually granted this kind of permit) was exempt from the register of foreigners. Moreover, most of the eliminated doubly-registered permits were also temporary stay ones and the citizens of the European Union are still granted these permits, albeit to a diminishing extent. At the same time, the registered stay permits were systematically replaced by the permanent ones, which also led to a contemporary increase in the stock of foreigners holding the latter permits in the country. Lastly, the number of persons with a tolerated stay permit in Slovakia obviously grows as the number of individuals with reasons for its granting increases.

As to the geographical distribution of immigrants in the Slovak Republic, the majority of them are concentrated in the regions of Bratislava and Košice. In 2006, over one-quarter of foreign nationals lived in the former, one-seventh of them in the latter (out of the eight administrative Slovak regions). The spatial concentration of immigrants in the country apparently reflects the distribution of labour and business opportunities, advanced infrastructure, existing educational facilities and the provision of housing.

As far as the demographic and social characteristics of immigrant populations in Slovakia are concerned, the official data are quite limited (Divinský, 2005a). As of 31 December 2006, children (age 0–14) formed less than 6 per cent of the foreign population, persons between 15 and 64 made up 88 per cent, and the elderly (over 65) constituted more than 6 per cent of the total. The most represented age category was that of 30–39, comprising almost a quarter of the total non-native population in the country.

Unfortunately, the other relevant statistics on immigrants are not recorded. As a result, data on the gender, education, professional background, religion, family status, mother tongue and so on of foreigners with a stay permit in Slovakia are lacking.

As regards the economic activity of immigrants, available data on the basis of both the permits issued by the Ministry of the Interior and the work registration statistics from the Ministry of Labour and Social Affairs are of a rather incoherent nature. For instance, each category of the stay permits legally relates to a certain purpose for which they have been granted. One may thus clearly quantify the numbers of foreigners who came to Slovakia because of employment, business, research, lecturing, and other activities on the one side, to study or for family reunification on the other. But in the given classification there are also other confusing and intermingled purposes of stay such as 'citizen of the European Economic Area', 'first permit', 'second permit' or 'refugee' – that is referring to persons a majority of whom are probably economically active. Moreover, the statistics also fail to specify the economic activity of a good number of persons..

It has to be emphasized that the figures presented above do not cover the group of immigrants who have been naturalized in the country over the past period. They are considered citizens of the Slovak Republic now and for this reason no separate statistics on their demographic and social characteristics are collected (with the exception of their gender, age and country of origin at the moment of naturalization).

All data provided here pertain purely to the immigrants residing legally in Slovakia. No expert studies on, or correct estimates of, those residing in the country unlawfully have been carried out so far. A few rough estimates (with a high potential risk of error) speak about at least several thousand foreign nationals staying and working in Slovakia illegally (Divinský, 2004a). It is commonly known that they are, above all, engaged in the building industry, retailing, and gastronomy.

Immigrant rights and participation in public life – issues of immigrant integration

The Constitution of the Slovak Republic (Act No. 460/1992 with later amendments) states that foreign nationals in the country enjoy the same fundamental human rights and freedoms as Slovak citizens, unless such rights are explicitly granted exclusively to native citizens.

Foreigners holding a permanent stay permit (including refugees) have the right to vote and to stand for election. However, this applies merely to the *authorities of local and regional self-government*; immigrants in Slovakia are not allowed to vote in, or to stand as a candidate for, the *national parliament*. Hence, they cannot be engaged in the activities or be members of the political parties and this fact is increasingly criticized by some NGOs as well as immigrants themselves (Divinský, 2005a).

The right to establish immigrant organizations, to assemble and associate is guaranteed by law and these activities represent the cardinal aspect of civic life for foreign nationals in Slovakia.

The undocumented migrants who do not ask for asylum are the most restricted group of migrants in the country. Their freedom of movement is usually limited by their being placed in detention centres until the date of their expulsion. But they have the right to apply for asylum at any time during their detention. Some NGOs, however, have warned that these migrants have not been allowed to do so in some cases.

In 2004, the Slovak Parliament – after a long and stormy political discussion and under a certain pressure from the European Union – passed an entirely new law: Antidiscrimination Act No. 365/2004. Its provisions also apply to the immigrants in the country. Any discrimination because of their racial, national or ethnic origin, denomination or belief, skin colour, language, political or other persuasion and so on is explicitly forbidden by this law.

The employment of migrants and their business activities in the country are rather complicated, since individual categories have different rights and restrictions. The fundamental legal norms dealing with the issue are Act No. 5/2004 on Employment Services, Act No. 455/1991 on Trade Law, Act No. 513/1991 – Commercial Code, Act No. 311/2001 – Labour Code, Act No. 82/2005 on Illegal Work and Illegal Employment (all with later amendments) and several others. These, as well as the already mentioned Act No. 48/2002 on the Stay of Foreigners, define exactly under what conditions foreigners may or may not work in Slovakia.

As regards the legal background of immigrant rights in the Slovak Republic as a whole, this may generally be considered medium-developed (Divinský, 2005c). Immigrant rights are ensured by a complex of various laws mostly harmonized with those in the EU over recent times. Notwithstanding, there is considerable scope to improve the situation in this area.

Table 22.3 gives an overview of the extent of rights for the main categories of foreign nationals in the country.

Table 22.3   Overview of some elementary rights and opportunities for civic participation in the major groups of migrants in Slovakia (2006)

Group of migrants	Right to free stay & movement of persons	Right to self-organize and associate	Electoral right	Membership of political parties	Right to work
Naturalized immigrants	yes	yes	yes	yes	yes
Those with a permanent stay permit	a few administrative limits	yes	yes local and regional self-government, no Parliament	no	yes (information card)
Those with a temporary stay permit	a few administrative limits	yes	no	no	depends on situation (yes with permit / yes with information card / no)*
Those with a tolerated stay permit	depends on situation (limited / no)**	yes / no**	no	no	depends on situation (yes with permit / yes with information card / no)**
Refugees	a few administrative limits	yes	yes local and regional self-government, no Parliament	no	yes (information card)
Asylum seekers	limited	hardly accomplishable	no	no	no / yes after 1 year of stay
Undocumented migrants	limited / no	no	no	no	no

Under the respective conditions stipulated by law, some groups of foreigners in this category need a work permit, some may work with an information card only, and some are prohibited from working.
**This category of foreign nationals covers various groups of persons – those in temporary shelter, those who cannot be expelled but are at liberty, as well as those in prison.*
Source: author.

In practice, the participation of immigrants in public life and their integration into society is not manifested much in the Slovak Republic. There are several factors in this (Divinský, 2005c):

- no long history of immigration to the country;
- low numbers of foreign nationals in Slovakia, particularly in comparison with the neighbouring countries or the autochthonous population;

- no specific territorial concentration of migrants in the country (with the partial exception of Bratislava and its region);
- extremely low or even practically zero chances to succeed as a candidate in the elections to the organs of local and regional self-government; impossibility to vote for/be elected to the Slovak Parliament;
- no lobbies, economic groups or parties act in favour of immigrants. As a consequence, there are no significant political subjects and structures in the Slovak Republic directly defending immigrant rights;
- the amount of financial means attributed to the associations of immigrants in Slovakia is insufficient. According to a personal survey, there are just a few subsidies to ethnic-cultural-religious associations of foreigners in the country. A more generous approach would be necessary in this context;
- the recency of adoption of laws on immigration, asylum and integration or their harmonization with respective European Union legal norms or Council of Europe conventions;
- the considerable level of xenophobia and the prevailing negative public opinion of the native population about foreign nationals in the country;
- the lack of interest of principal Slovak actors, the media and common people in many of the issues of immigration, asylum and integration of foreigners;
- the geopolitical position of the country – Slovakia is still primarily a transit country for migrants, therefore a good part of them see it merely as a temporary stop and have no intention of being further integrated into society.

Those factors discourage and/or restrict (some) immigrants in the country from more active engagement in civic participation or, more generally, in the integration process as such. At the same time, however, these shortcomings also make the quicker articulation of the national integration policy of the Slovak Republic an essential objective for today.

Public and media discourses on migration

Public opinion in the country is mostly negatively inclined towards immigrants (though this is very recently slowly changing in a positive way). There are obvious forms of xenophobia against foreigners, sometimes multiplied by their social exclusion or manifestations of intolerance. The level of *xenophobia* especially is high in Slovakia but to varying degrees: some people are open to immigrants and regard them positively or in a neutral manner, whilst others express a general distrust. Other persons look at foreign nationals explicitly negatively (Divinský, 2004a; Divinský, 2006b).

For instance, 68 per cent of respondents in a representative public opinion survey conducted recently in the country (UNHCR et FOCUS 2005) identify themselves with the statement that refugees[6] are costly to the Slovak Republic, 51 per cent believe that these migrants contribute to the growth of criminality, and 66 per cent are convinced that they bring various diseases into the country. On the other side, 73 per cent agree with the statement that refugees should be accepted, given assistance and shelter in Slovakia if they were forced to flee their own country. Besides, 53 per cent of Slovaks say they would not mind if their neighbours were refugees (immigrants). Thus, the results reflect mixed attitudes of the autochthonous population towards foreigners.

---

6   Since most of the native inhabitants do practically not distinguish among the various groups of foreign nationals in Slovakia, results of the survey are of a general character.

Several factors synergistically operate in generating and maintaining xenophobia in Slovakia with the *relative isolation of the country* during 1939–1989 probably playing a dominant role. Slovak society was then not widely confronted with immigrants, and not at all with refugees or undocumented migrants. This resulted in a lower level of acceptance of immigrant cultures in the country. Particularly older generations or those less educated, unemployed, living in the countryside, with no prior personal contact with foreign nationals and so on did not manage to break their stereotypes (Divinský, 2005a; Divinský, 2005b).

Unfortunately, one cannot say much positive about the operation of the Slovak media in modifying outlined stereotypes and attitudes of the public. Negative perception, xenophobia, intolerance or discrimination of immigrants in the country are then to a great extent a natural reflection of approaches presented by the local mass media as well as of the lack of balanced information.

In general, the main weaknesses in terms of the media's reporting on issues related to immigration can be summarized as follows (see more in detail Divinský, 2005c):

First, information on immigration is given *only occasionally* in the Slovak media. Questions on the life, activities and problems of foreign nationals in the country, their integration and interrelations with the majority population are not considered important and attractive for either journalists or readers/viewers; the subject is seen as peripheral. Therefore, few Slovak journalists occupy themselves with it, and if they do so, it is only in a part-time, marginal and sporadic manner.

Second, when relevant migration issues are covered, they are seldom handled with the necessary experience and competence. Rather, they are presented *superficially and inadequately*. Since journalists and reporters are not well-educated or knowledgeable on the topic, their outputs are of inferior quality, with various methodological and other mistakes. Deeper analyses of causes and consequences, studies of significant background documents, more extensive comments and so on are commonly absent. On the contrary, the media not infrequently cite authorities out of context, provide imprecise data and adopt other unprofessional work methods.. In this way, readers/viewers get a distorted picture of reality.

Finally, *negative dimensions and impacts* of (or even misleading information on) immigration in the country are all too often offered by the media, since they are believed to be more attractive for people. True images of immigrants and positive messages are seldom shown or are even completely missing.

More specifically, the following migration issues are the most presented in the Slovak media, usually in a negative light:

- apprehensions of undocumented migrants on the borders or in the interior of the country;
- smuggling of migrants, activities of traffickers, the difficult protection of the eastern Slovak border as a Schengen border;
- excessive numbers of asylum applicants flooding the country, problems connected with the Slovak asylum system and asylum procedure;
- campaigns and petitions by natives against building new refugee camps in their cities and communes;
- recent developments in European immigration and asylum policies;
- crisis of the multicultural model, further co-existence of immigrants and native populations;
- employment and enterprises of foreigners in Slovakia, their alleged negative contribution to the unemployment rate and fiscal burden on the State budget;
- supposed considerable impact of foreign nationals on the crime level in the country;

- potential danger of spreading infectious diseases through immigrants;
- some legal aspects, particularly amendments to laws on immigration and asylum;
- some migrants' dirty appearance, street begging, petty thefts and harassment.

On the other hand, the themes below are either neglected, very rare, or totally absent in the Slovak media:

- pictures from the everyday life of migrants (including asylum seekers in refugee camps) in the country;
- examples of the successful integration of immigrants into Slovak society;
- contribution of foreigners to the national economy, culture, education, building civil society, political life, and so on;
- personal statements of immigrants living in the country and their life stories;
- the majority population's perception of foreign nationals, the necessity to combat xenophobia, intolerance, discrimination and racism;
- making personal contacts and friendships between natives and immigrants, stories of mixed couples and families;
- relevance and nature of Slovak migration policy, its vital role for the successful integration process and other aspects of migration management;
- activities of non-governmental, international and other organizations dealing with migration matters;
- operation and problems of immigrant associations;
- promotion of the active civic participation of immigrants;
- the position and development of migration in the contemporary world, the categories of migrants, general causes and implications of migration.

Concluding remarks

Until only a decade ago, the *immigration issue* practically did not exist or was not recognized in the country. Slovakia was, for a long period, associated with emigration as an immanent demographic and social feature of its population; an opposite movement was hardly imaginable.

The collapse of communism and new political, social and economic changes after 1989 brought about a radical reversal in migration patterns and the country began to face a set of entirely new immigration phenomena. These included larger-scale irregular migration, soaring numbers of asylum seekers, labour immigration, rebuilding the legal and institutional systems, the need for migration policy and so on. In connection with dramatically rising numbers of undocumented migrants and asylum applicants since the end of the 1990s, the country's tasks within the pre-accession period and also various qualitative changes in society from 1998, the Slovak Republic has been undergoing an evident transformation in perceiving migration challenges and things have been – though belatedly – set in motion.

In this context, the greatest progress has been achieved in passing new, and updating old, laws. This has been especially prominent in areas concerning conditions for the entry, stay or expulsion of immigrants, the asylum procedure, the Dublin convention and implementing EURODAC, the Schengen *acquis* and border protection, the smuggling of and trafficking in migrants, the naturalization of foreign nationals, the antidiscrimination, employment, social and health care of immigrants and other domains. This process still continues as further EU legal acts are being transposed into the Slovak legal system.

However, the institutional sphere lags behind developments in legislation. The system of institutions dealing with migrants in Slovakia is incomplete, fragmented and unconsolidated. Some of them are unstable (for example certain NGOs) or subject to frequent organizational modifications (for example State organizations) thus making collaboration between them awkward and less effective. In order to improve the smooth operation of hitherto independent institutions at the State level, it is planned to merge them all and establish one central authority in the country – with clear competencies – by 2010. A new *Immigration and Naturalization Office* should then cover the areas of immigration, integration, asylum, naturalization and repatriation of migrants. Again institutionally, the absence of an official parliamentary or governmental *Committee for the Matters of Foreigners (Migrants)* to support the issue legally and politically is currently being discussed in the country, too (Divinský, 2006a).

In early 2005 a (new) migration policy in the form of a Conception was finally articulated in the Slovak Republic. It is the first coherent and comprehensive document on migration management in the country; however, it merely outlines policies in particular areas. National integration and naturalization policies are still considerably lacking, which is felt to be a serious shortcoming. Also for this reason, immigrants face *integration problems* such as the lack of cheaper housing, few employment opportunities, difficulties with commanding the Slovak language, minimal support for cultural and other activities, social exclusion, shortage of essential information; and their civic and political participation is negligible. The first steps have quite recently been taken in the field of education of foreign nationals, defending human rights and preventing manifestations of intolerance, discrimination and racism (Divinský, 2005a).

As has also been presented in this chapter, the media's role in informing people about the immigration situation in the country is crucial, but not a very positive contribution. As a result, the level of xenophobia and prevailing negative attitudes of the autochthonous population towards immigrants are only slowly declining, the lack of interest of politicians in the phenomenon persists and the extent of public debate remains limited.

Thus, at the dawn of the twenty-first century, the Slovak Republic is just at the beginning of its metamorphosis into a pro-immigration society. The country's modern migration and integration policies are only just created, so their concrete shapes will be better known in the years to come. Despite this fact, it is believed that with the assistance of more migration-experienced members of the European Union, on the basis of running strategic initiatives (for example the Hague Programme) and within commonly shared visions, Slovakia will be able to fulfil its commitments in the field of international migration for the benefit of the country, the Community, Europe and immigrants themselves.

References

Divinský, B. (2004a), *Migration Trends in Selected EU Applicant Countries, Volume V-Slovakia – An Acceleration of Challenges for Society*. Vienna: International Organization for Migration.

—— (2004b), 'Zahraničná migrácia v Slovenskej republike: súčasný stav a predpokladaný vývoj po vstupe krajiny do Európskej únie' [International Migration in the Slovak Republic: Its Contemporary State and Expected Development after the Accession of the Country to the European Union] *Medzinárodné otázky*, **13**(2), 16–38.

—— (2005a), *Zahraničná migrácia v Slovenskej republike – Stav, trendy, spoločenské súvislosti* [International Migration in the Slovak Republic – Situation, Trends, Social Context]. Bratislava: Friedrich Ebert Stiftung.

—— (2005d), 'Zahraničná migrácia' [International Migration], in Kollár and Mesežnikov (eds) *Slovensko 2004: Súhrnná správa o stave spoločnosti* [Slovakia 2004: A Global Report on the State of Society]. Bratislava: Institute for Public Affairs.

—— (2005e), 'Selected Problems of Foreigners in Slovakia in the Context of Current Migration Policy in the Country', in *Social and Cultural Diversity in Central and Eastern Europe: Old Factors and New*. Prague: Multicultural Center.

—— (2006a), 'Zahraničná migrácia v SR: potreba nových prístupov' [International Migration in Slovakia: a need for new approaches]. *Zahraničná politika*, **10**(3), 3–5.

—— (2006b), 'Medzinárodná migrácia' [International Migration], in Mládek et al. (eds) *Demogeografická analýza Slovenska* (Demographic analysis of Slovakia). Bratislava: Comenius University.

UNHCR et FOCUS (2005), *Prieskum verejnej mienky pre UNHCR – Postoje verejnosti k utečencom v SR* [A public opinion poll for UNHCR – Attitudes of the public towards refugees in Slovakia]. Bratislava: Úrad Vysokého komisára OSN pre utečencov et FOCUS.

Internet-based references

Divinský, B. (2005b), 'Mezinárodní migrace a Slovensko v roce 2004' [International Migration and Slovakia in 2004] (available at http://www.migraceonline.cz/e-knihovna/?x=1955233).

—— (2005c), *Active Civic Participation of Immigrants in Slovakia*, Country Report prepared for the European research project POLITIS (Oldenburg: Carl von Ossietzky Universität) (available at http://www.uni-oldenburg.de/politis-europe/9812.html).

Chapter 23

Slovenia

Svetlozar A. Andreev

After the collapse of both communism and the Federal Republic of Yugoslavia in the early 1990s, Slovenia emerged as an independent state which was soon to embark upon regional integration in the EU. Currently, Slovenia presents one of the most interesting cases of migration control and management, not only in post-communist Eastern Europe, but also among the current EU Member States. Regarding immigrant integration, the situation is still far from clear. Nevertheless, the first signs of active civic involvement are present, especially in the large Slovenian cities and among the 'old migrants' from the former Yugoslav republics. These latter include Serbs, Bosnians and Croats. Parts of the media and the NGO community have also taken a proactive stance not only to defend immigrants' rights, but also to give them a voice in public life. Last, but not least, with the entry of Slovenia into the EU, some groups of foreign nationals have been granted new political and social rights, namely, participating in local elections, purchasing property, residence, work and social benefits.

Major developments in Slovenia's immigration policy

Migration policy in Slovenia is a relatively recent development. Before the 1950s Slovenia used to be predominantly a country of emigration. During the 1960s and 70s, the picture gradually changed: new migrants from the east and south (mainly from the other Yugoslav republics) were attracted to Slovenia by the availability of work there, while Slovenians still continued to (e)migrate as 'guest workers' to the wealthier West.

Before the 'watershed' year of 1991, when Slovenia gained its independence, migration flows between Slovenia and the other Yugoslav republics were predominately the consequence of economic factors. Another important reason for immigration to Slovenia was the absence of a common immigration policy in former Yugoslavia which could regulate the movement of workers. Temporary migration was not uncommon between Slovenia and the other SFRY republics as well. It was mostly seasonal, as, for example, employment in the construction sector, tourism and agriculture (see Mežnarič, 1986; Malačič, 1991; and Genorio, 1989). In a study of Slovenia's immigration situation during the early 1990s, Kodelja (1992) defines three territories of inflow of migrants from former Yugoslavia. First, the Slovenia-Croatia border municipalities, second, the northern and western parts of Bosnia, eastern Slavonia (Croatia), Bačka, Srem in Vojvodina and Mačva in western Serbia, and, third, 'the southern Yugoslav' emigration territory, comprising the central part of Kosovo, Metohija, the north-eastern region of Macedonia, and the area of Sandžak.

During the late 1980s, and especially during the 1990s, with the intensification of ethnic conflicts across Yugoslavia, a large number of refugees from the other federal republics came to Slovenia. Situated on important 'migration routes' from East to West and North to South, Slovenia also started to attract immigrants from countries in the Developing World. Initially, the influx of sizeable migrant groups, representing as much as 10 per cent of the entire Slovenian population, was perceived as a clear threat to national identity. The young democratic institutions, civil society and the media were either not always adequately prepared, or lacked previous experience of dealing with migration problems.

Slovene immigration policy has largely been a policy 'imposed by events' rather than a carefully crafted and deliberated strategy regarding the organization and monitoring of migration flows from and through the country's territory. The dissolution of Yugoslavia and the proclaimed independence in the early 1990s led to a great uncertainty regarding both national identity and the international position of Slovenia in a post-Cold War world. Citizenship problems persisted well into the early 2000s, when the last few thousand legal residents from the Yugoslav times, who had been stripped of political and social rights at the time of Slovenia's independence (25 June 1991),[1] were regularized and given passports (Andreev, 2003a, 2003b; see also the section regarding the problem about the 'erased' foreign persons).[2] The EU expansion to the east and Slovenia's proximity to Central Europe predetermined its elites' and peoples' predominantly pro-enlargement stance. With this choice, however, came the difficulty of working out comprehensive asylum and immigration policies in a relatively short time which would suit a small country situated at the Schengen Zone periphery.

Today, there are four main groups of immigrants, the outcome of consecutive migration flows over the last 20 years.

First, there are ethnic Slovenians returning to their country of origin (or at least what had been Slovenia before 1991 during the Austro-Hungarian Empire, the Kingdom of Serbs, Croats and Slovenes and the Socialist Federal Republic of Yugoslavia) and claiming citizenship on the basis of *jus sanguinis*. They have been returning to Slovenia from predominantly two regions:

---

1   The actual deletion of the names of the Yugoslav nationals from the Republic of Slovenia registries took place at the end of February 1992 (some people even posit that the exact date is 26/02/92), when the 'grace period' given by the Slovenian authorities to foreign nationals who had been long-term residents in the country, to acquire Slovenian citizenship expired (see Andreev, 2003a). Nevertheless, those people who did not choose to do so were effectively deprived of both citizenship and social rights at the moment of Slovenia's secession from SFRY. Thus, for instance, the years that some of the 'erased' foreign nationals had spent working, studying or residing unemployed in the Federal Republic of Slovenia before June 1991 did not count for pension, maternity and other social benefits after Spring 1992. This was because the public registries in Slovenia were updated by the Ministry of Interior in February 1992 or shortly after that, and the modified information was forwarded to other Ministries and the local authorities, who could not basically tell those foreign nationals who had previously had residence and worked in Slovenia, from the new arrivals after, for example, the civil war in Bosnia and Herzegovina and the conflict in Kosovo.

2   According to some Slovenian civil society activists – the members of the Slovenian Helsinki Committee in particular – there are still a few hundred persons who are claiming to be stateless and without proper documents due to the problem with the 'erased' in Slovenia from the early 1990s. Allegedly, many of these migrants reside in other EU Member States (Germany, Italy, Austria and Belgium), but not in Slovenia. A significant number of them are war refugees and Roma from previously conflict-torn zones. Despite the sweeping claims of a relatively small group of civic activists and academics in Slovenia, that those persons are a product of 'administrative genocide' by the Slovenian authorities, it is very difficult to say whether those migrants really belong to the 'erased' contingent, or simply took the opportunity to claim Slovenian and, thence, European citizenship on the basis of their refugee status in the country during the 1990s and occasionally the 2000s. Overall, and compared with other EU Member States having faced a similar problem (that is the Baltic States during the 1990s and Western European countries such as Italy, Spain and Malta during the 2000s), Slovenia has always had quite a liberal policy of granting citizenship and of accommodating different kinds of refugees.

Western Europe (Germany, Austria and the Scandinavian countries) and Latin America (Argentina, Uruguay and Brazil).

Second, there are migrants and long-term residents having established themselves in Slovenia since the times of ex-Yugoslavia. Many of them were left stateless by the dissolution of SFRY and decided to become citizens of the Slovene Republic following its independence on the basis of *jus soli*. These are usually Serbs, Bosnians, Kosovars, Macedonians and the Roma.

The third group is immigrants and refugees driven by the wars in former Yugoslavia arriving from conflict zones, such as Croatia, Bosnia and Herzegovina and Kosovo.

Fourth are economic immigrants, asylum seekers and occasional migrants who had settled in the country either temporarily or permanently, as well as those who were intercepted by the police authorities 'en route' to Western Europe and were forced to remain in Slovenia for a given period of time. All these people are customarily defined as 'new immigrants' and they represent quite a heterogeneous group. For example, among them one could find asylum seekers from the Developing World, seasonal workers from the ex-Yugoslav republics, economic migrants from Eastern Europe and persons being smuggled through Slovenian territory.

The second and third groups of immigrants are the largest ones, while the fourth has experienced great fluctuations, yet is steadily growing. People from ex-Yugoslavia present by far the largest segment of the country's migrant population due to a) overlapping migration flows dating back from half-a-century ago, and b) a relatively liberal migration policy in the Slovenian republic practised during the first couple of years of its independence. This policy led to the granting of citizenship and refugee status to many foreign nationals who had decided to establish themselves permanently in Slovenia (see Andreev, 2003a).

The integration of immigrants in the public life of new societies involves a wide range of policy fields and practical issues ranging from economic to social, political and cultural. Slovenia's immigration policy is specifically stipulated in both the 2002 Resolution on the Immigration Policy of the Republic of Slovenia, and the 1999 Resolution on the Immigration Policy of the Republic of Slovenia. However, the general legal framework for treating immigrants and asylum seekers is provided by the Slovenian Constitution (Official Gazette of the Republic of Slovenia, No. 33/91) and the latest versions of two fundamental laws: the Aliens Act (Official Gazette of the RS, No. 87/2002) and the Asylum Act (Official Gazette of the RS, No. 61/1999).

The institutions dealing with migration issues are primarily the Ministry of the Interior and its Migration Directorate. The Office for Immigration and Refugees that was part of the Ministry was abolished in March 2004 and replaced with a Directorate. The police are also part of this Ministry. Other ministries regulating migration at different levels of social life include the Ministry of Labour, the Ministry for Family and Social Affairs and the Ministry of Culture. There are also parliamentary committees occasionally debating migration issues. However, their activity is more politically motivated and less policy orientated.

The role of the EU in the second half of the 1990s was paramount in promoting the rights of various minority groups (Zagar, 1997; Lozar, 2002). Far from being a hegemonic power, the EU exerted considerable pressure on the Slovenian authorities in a number of areas, the most important of which were the border regime, competition policy, the free movement of persons, and minority rights. One of the critical issues in EU-Slovene relations was the possibility given to foreign nationals to buy land in Slovenia. Being a very sensitive issue for the young Slovenian state, this problem was counteracted by the issue of the free movement of workers from Slovenia into the current Member States after enlargement. Transitional periods were being asked for from both sides regarding these issues (Bucar and Brinar, 2001; Šabič, 2002).

The problem of the 'erased' foreign residents and asylum seekers in Slovenia

This section analyses the issue – quite fascinating from both an empirical and a theoretical point of view – of people deleted from the Slovenian public registries. They are foreign nationals and asylum seekers who were left stranded in the country after the dissolution of Yugoslavia, practically without political and social rights. Even though the problem of the so-called 'erased' foreigners does not exclusively hinge upon migration issues, it provides the opportunity to raise a set of quite pertinent questions about the treatment of potential migrants in Slovenia, that is a) how Slovenian citizenship was defined and implemented in practice after the country's independence, b) what was the reaction of the public authorities, civil society and the media, and c) who benefited from the 'erased' people saga, and d) how this crisis and future crises with foreign nationals asking for Slovenian residence or citizenship had to be resolved?

Slovenia is one of the youngest and smallest states in terms of both its territory and population. Approximately two million persons live on a territory of a little more than 20,000 square kilometres. According to the most recent census results, the country's population is 1,995,718 people, of whom 1,949,419 are citizens of the Republic of Slovenia (excluding citizens temporarily residing abroad), 15,285 have permanent residence in Slovenia, 28,682 have temporary residence, and 2,332 persons are under temporary protection. Slovenians often joke that they are always 'short of' or 'missing' about 50,000 persons in order to reach 2,000,000 citizens. This 'missing group' may, in fact, be the last three categories of inhabitants, the majority of whom are demanding Slovenian citizenship.

From the point of view of its ethnic composition, Slovenia virtually represents a nation-state: around 90 per cent of its population is of Slovenian ethnic origin.[3] Tiny communities of Slovenian origin have also been living in the neighbouring countries (Austria, Croatia and Italy), in the republics of former SFRY, and further abroad (for example in Argentina, Canada and the United States). All of these factors were taken into account while drafting the constitution and state-forming laws with respect to citizenship. In the provisions of these laws, Slovenian citizenship was mainly defined in terms of blood relationship (*jus sanguinis*). Notable exceptions were also made in order to recognize the existence of certain 'historical nationalities' living on Slovenian territory like the Italians and Hungarians, as well as the Romany community (*jus soli*).[4] However, no special provisions were made to recognize a sizeable community of citizens coming from the other SFRY republics, or the war refugees who had been permanently residing in Slovenia.

One of the principal hypotheses advanced by a recent study of this problem (Andreev, 2003a) regards the structural weakness of the Slovenian state. Historically, Slovenia was always vulnerable in its relations with an external dominant power – be it the Austro-Hungarian Empire in the distant past, or the former SFRY at the end of the twentieth century. In both cases the Slovenian leadership needed the support of the international community and its domestic population to assert its legitimate authority over the national territory. Since both the Austro-Hungarian Empire and the SFRY possessed the exclusive means and international legitimacy to represent Slovenia in its external relations, it was very difficult for an unrecognized state entity to seek support unilaterally in the international arena. However, in the early 1990s the desire of the Slovenian leadership to move the country away from the rump Yugoslav federation was quite strong and, hence, it had to

---

3   At the time of national independence, 87.84 per cent of the country's inhabitants were of Slovenian ethnic origin, while small Croatian, Muslim, Italian and Hungarian communities (each below 1.5 per cent) also existed (Population census of the Socialist Republic of Slovenia: 1991).

4   Article 64 of the Slovenian Constitution grants extensive rights and privileges to the 'autochthonous Italian and Hungarian ethnic communities in Slovenia', while Article 65 vaguely mentions the need for protecting the 'Romany ethnic community'.

look for additional support from its entire domestic constituency.[5] By promising to grant citizenship to all permanent residents shortly before the Plebiscite on the Sovereignty and Independence of the Republic of Slovenia (23 December 1990), the ruling elite aimed to achieve two things:

- Obtaining greater support for the country's independence domestically;
- Convincing both the international community and the federal authorities in Belgrade that even nationals of other Yugoslav republics residing in Slovenia supported a democratic and free Slovenia.

The proposal to grant citizenship to all permanent residents was made for the first time in the *Statement of Good Intents* and enshrined in the new Citizenship Act of the Republic of Slovenia after independence. It was one of the most far-reaching and comprehensive in post-communist Eastern Europe. In such a way, the then Slovenian leadership concluded a more or less explicit deal with all segments of society to treat them equally before the law.

During the early 1990s, this deal was almost completely fulfilled by the Slovenian public authorities. However, because of the unexpectedly high number of applicants from within Slovenia, the influx of refugees following the initiation of military and civil conflicts on the territory of the other SFRY republics, and the rising nationalism and xenophobia among parts of the Slovenian population instigated by extremist politicians, the state has proved incapable of following the previously liberal policies of granting citizenship and residence to foreign nationals at the same pace and intensity as at the beginning of the independence period. On the contrary, some of the public institutions (for example, the Ministry of Interior) began to work against the provisions of Article 40 of the Constitution and of related laws. This led to a certain reaction by the members of civil society and the more moderate politicians in the Slovenian parliament, who opposed changes to the existing Citizenship Act. However, these groups fell short of proposing a more liberal policy towards minorities and immigrants alike. Left on their own, former nationals of the other republics of the former SFRY either converted into 'good Slovenes' by speaking the language and following the local customs, or sank into anonymity by continuing to practice their largely marginalized ethnic cultures (Komac, 2001).[6]

Despite a set of critical points, however, Slovenia's democratic credentials have never been seriously questioned at the European level. This has been mainly because a) Slovenia's performance regarding the protection of ethnic minorities has been better-than-average compared to that of the other candidate states from post-communist Europe, and b) some of the current EU Member States have experienced similar problems with their own minorities and would not welcome international monitoring and advice regarding issues that have been perceived as a predominantly domestic affair (European Commission, 2002).

---

5   In April 1990 Slovenia held its first democratic elections and on 2 July, 1990 a Declaration on the Sovereignty of the Republic of Slovenia was passed by the republican parliament.

6   Finally, on 29 September 1999, after having previously been heavily pressured by the Constitutional Court and the Ombudsman, the Parliament adopted the Act Regulating the Status of the Citizens of Other Successor States to the Former SFRY in the Republic of Slovenia. This special law gave the opportunity to more than 10,000 people to apply for citizenship, while those actually residing in Slovenia were granted temporary or permanent residence permits much more easily.

Immigrant population in Slovenia: main demographic and social features

According to official statistics, there have been approximately 40,000 foreigners living in Slovenia from the end of the 1990s and early 2000s. This number represents 2 per cent of the total population (much less than the EU average, however, which ranges between 3.6 and 9 per cent). Among them, three-quarters have been people with a temporary residence in Slovenia, 15 per cent have been foreigners with a permanent residence and 10 per cent have been refugees. On average, foreign nationals with permanent residence in Slovenia have been the oldest, while the refugees have been the youngest. Among the latter, the majority has been women, and men have prevailed in the group of foreigners with permanent or temporary residence permits in Slovenia (Bevc et al., 2000).

Taking as an example the data provided by the Ministry of the Interior for 2002, one sees that a total of 5,855 foreign nationals have been permanently living in Slovenia while 37,091 have been residing temporarily. Virtually all of these persons' permits were issued in the previous 11 years – that is, following the independence of Slovenia from SFRY. Most of the permanent permits have had a duration of more than one year, since they concerned war refugees and political dissidents. Moreover, one could easily observe that, first, permanent residence permits have amounted to a significantly lower number compared to the temporary residence permits issued. Second, the highest share of residence permits has, in both cases, been issued to persons originating from Bosnia and Herzegovina, followed by individuals from the other former Yugoslav republics (see Table 23.1 and Table 23.2).

Table 23.1   Permanent residence permits issued (1997–2002)

Country of origin	1997	1998	1999	2000	2001	2002
Bosnia and Herzegovina	336	211	1,192	3,673	913	3,638
Croatia	172	188	401	1,319	327	766
Serbia and Montenegro	196	100	275	713	332	739
Former Yugoslav Republic of Macedonia	30	34	72	135	94	295
Germany	14	28	10	4	2	24
Ukraine	3	6	11	11	3	34
Other	585	475	668	904	362	359
Total	**1,336**	**1,042**	**2,629**	**6,759**	**2,033**	**5,855**

Table 23.2   Temporary residence permits issued (1997–2002)

Country of origin	1997	1998	1999	2000	2001	2002
Bosnia and Herzegovina	3,385	3,472	8,892	15,946	16,167	15,404
Croatia	2,072	1,491	4,154	8,263	7,699	5,814
Serbia and Montenegro	1,988	2,102	4,161	6,358	5,846	5,784
Former Yugoslav Republic of Macedonia	550	935	2,442	6,547	5,972	4,642
Ukraine	171	359	661	1,420	1,242	1,050
China	86	88	173	372	490	361
Russia	101	164	209	354	359	347
Italy	176	199	190	276	277	277
Germany	119	106	137	284	212	208
Romania	22	71	125	260	236	260
Slovakia	6	9	97	214	224	361
Moldova	5	10	61	251	285	272
Other	4,391	3,877	4,630	4,860	3,204	2,311
Total	13,072	12,883	25,932	45,405	42,213	37,091

Source: Ministry of the Interior, 2003.

Permanent and temporary employment ranked first for over 47 per cent of the migrants as an indicative reason for establishing themselves in Slovenia. This was followed by family reunification (24 per cent), seasonal work (15 per cent), daily migrants (5 per cent), contract workers (4 per cent), study (2 per cent), a child born in Slovenia (2 per cent), and other reasons (2 per cent).

Because of the deepening socioeconomic crisis and the eruption of military conflicts in the other parts of former Yugoslavia during the 1980s and 1990s, as well as due to the increased prospect of Slovenia joining the EU in the early 2000s, a large number of foreign nationals attempted to cross the Slovenian border illegally. In the first nine months of 2000, 27,000 illegal immigrants entered Slovenia, most of them from Croatia and Hungary. According to the Minister of Internal Affairs, this was a 70 per cent increase over the same period in 1999. Moreover, according to data published on the website of the Slovenian police, the Slovenian authorities registered a total of 6,926 illegal crossings in 2002, down 67 per cent over the previous year, when there had been 20,883 cases. Most of the illegal migrants were from Yugoslavia (Serbia and Montenegro) (2,015), FYROM (1,221), Turkey (820), Iraq (596) and Bosnia and Herzegovina (405). The vast majority of persons attempting to enter Slovenia illegally were apprehended at the border with Croatia. Based on bilateral agreements regarding the return of persons, 2,372 persons were returned to foreign security services, most of them to Croatia. Meanwhile, neighbouring countries returned 1,369 persons to Slovenia. Austria, for instance, returned 1,013 persons.

The size of irregular migration in Slovenia and illegal border crossings could also be explained by the fact that many third-country nationals have attempted to enter the EU, and the Schengen Zone (specifically Austria or Italy), through Slovenia. The Roma minority, actively travelling between the former SFRY republics and the West, has been a sizeable portion of these migrants. The war in Kosovo was an additional reason for the increase in illegal border crossing by refugees fleeing the war and trying to reunite with their families already residing in some of the EU and Western European countries (for example, the Kosovar community in Switzerland).

It is, however, worth mentioning that relatively few foreign nationals have attempted to stay in Slovenia as refugees. There are two possible main reasons for this. First, that Slovenia has primarily been seen as a 'transit country' and, second, the Ministry of Interior and the other state authorities have been reluctant to grant refugee status to a large number of persons. Indeed, for an entire decade, namely between 1995 and 2004, there were a total of only 111 officially recognized refugees in Slovenia. The lowest numbers were during the period 1995–99, while the relative peak of refugee intake for the country was during the years 2001, 2003 and 2004 with 27, 40 and 30 persons, respectively.

The overall situation regarding the Slovenian policy towards refugees could partly be clarified by taking into account the *temporary protection status* granted to persons fleeing from the military and civil conflicts of the former Yugoslavia, and Bosnia and Herzegovina in particular. Table 23.3 shows the official figures with respect to granting such status for the period 1997–2003. Unfortunately, the Ministry of the Interior's statistics reflect only the number of temporary refugees accommodated in public centres. It does not include people in private accommodation, residing with relatives and acquaintances. According to Slovenian specialists' estimates, if both types of accommodation were included, the overall numbers of refugees would be much higher, especially for the early stages of migration from the wars in former Yugoslavia (1992–1995) (Zavratnik Zimic, 2003).

Table 23.3   Refugees from Bosnia and Herzegovina with temporary protection status (TPS) (1997–2003)

Date	Number of TPS	Accommodation in refugee centres	Number of centres
31.12.1997	4,609	2,263	12
31.12.1998	3,453	1,702	10
31.12.1999	3,113	1,621	10
31.12.2000	2,800	1,420	9
31.12.2001	2,406	1,226	9
31.12.2002	537	809	7
03.03.2003	98	768	7

Source: Ministry of the Interior, 2004.

Immigrant rights and participation in public life

The employment and stay of immigrants are regulated on the basis of different legal instruments, the two most relevant being the Employment and Work of Aliens Act (Official Gazette of the RS, No. 66/2000) and the Aliens Act. National statistics indicate that in 2004, 17,100 work permits were granted to migrants. This amounts to 1.96 per cent of the total population. In 2003, this number was 17,579, representing 2.02 per cent of the entire working population. It is also worth mentioning that the yearly seasonal foreign workers' quotas have often not been filled to their maximum capacity (that is, 5 per cent of the entire working population). EU and other EU-associated states' nationals have not been included in this quota.

Immigrants are also entitled to different social welfare benefits, such as pension and health care. These conditions are set out in the Social Welfare Act, the Pensions and Disability Act and the Health Insurance Act.[7] Immigrants have free access to the educational system at the level of primary school.

The Act Amending the Local Election Act (Official Gazette of the RS, No. 51/2002) brings new elements into the field of political participation and representation. The novelty in this Act is that all those foreign nationals with permanent residence in the country have the right to vote and stand as members of the municipal councils. The voter has the right to vote in the municipality of his/her permanent residence (Article 1). There have been no reported cases of immigrants or other foreign nationals (for example, EU citizens) running for local elections. However, this legal act provides an important means for foreign nationals to press for their political and social concerns, albeit locally, in the near future.

The Act on Promoting the Public Interest in Culture (Official Gazette of the RS, No. 96/2002) in its Article 65 determines that the state financially supports projects that are especially intended for the cultural integration of minority communities and immigrants. This act directly relates to the possibility of immigrants' social participation, although there is a condition that the intended cultural programmes and projects meet local interest. Article 66, defining the competence of the municipalities in this respect, determines that the municipalities should support amateur cultural activities, including those intended to culturally integrate minority communities and immigrants. Both acts, however, are intended primarily to support the indigenous ethnic communities in Slovenia, such as the Germans, Hungarians and Italians. The Roma community has also been targeted as a potential recipient of state aid.

Despite all of the above provisions for increased foreigners' social inclusion and political activism, immigrants, as in many parts of post-communist Europe and even in most EU Member States, rarely take the opportunity to voice their social and political concerns. Whenever foreigners decide to take an active part in the public life of the receiving country, these are usually individual acts, rather than a collective response to particular decisions of the state authorities and the challenges of the social environment. Slovenia's immigrants have not been an exception to this trend. Below are several examples of the types of social and political activities that a number of individuals from the 'new' and 'old' minorities in Slovenia have been engaged in.

First, in 2001, Bi Fine, a singer fleeing Sierra Leone for political reasons, came to Slovenia and applied for asylum. In the period 2001–2002 he was very active in the field of culture by organising concerts. The songs he sang had a large political impact, reflecting the nature of contemporary migration and its consequences.[8]

Second, during the late 1990s and at the beginning of the 2000s, Inacio Bintchende became a widely known figure. He was an immigrant from Africa and used to perform as an actor in a popular television show (*TV Poper*) aired on a public television station. In 2001, Bintchende was physically attacked in the centre of Ljubljana in front of his apartment. This xenophobic act gained a lot of media attention, while Bintchende became publicly active. He tried to defend his and other migrants' right to live a normal life in Slovenia.

Third, the Slovene mufti Osman Đogić has often spoken on Slovenian media, in order to explain why the Muslim community needs a cultural centre and a new mosque (for many years Slovenia's Muslims have been practising their faith in a gym hall). As already mentioned, the great majority of the so-called 'Muslim community' in Slovenia came from other Yugo-republics, so, it has been naturally difficult for the rest of the Slovenians to imagine these migrants or naturalized citizens

---

7   Foreign nationals are generally provided with immediate medical treatment, but the conditions for payment/repayment could differ from case to case.

8   The lyrics are published in Pajnik et al. (2001).

as radically different from them culturally, and to anticipate their needs in terms of religious and other social institutions.

Fourth, the case of 18,000 'erased' Slovenian residents was publicly presented by Aleksandar Todorović, a Serbian born archaeologist, and President of the Association of the Erased People. During 2002–2004 he was among the few who kept on reminding the public about the illegal erasure of thousands of persons and this act's consequences. His position was given publicity by a number of international human rights institutions and civic organizations (for example, the Helsinki Committee and the Human Rights Watch).

Public and media discourses on migration

During the 1990s, Slovenia was, for the first time, faced with the pressing issues of dealing with mass migration. Related to this, it had to devise a refugee policy and to protect asylum-seekers. The social impact of this inflow of immigrants was tremendous. The main question that many people tried to answer regarding that period was 'How did the Slovenian state and society – that is the governmental institutions, civil society and NGOs – react to mass migration?' The opinion of public officials and politicians, on the one hand, and civic activists and immigrant group leaders, on the other, regarding how this issue was dealt with were often in contrast to each other (see Zavratnik, 1996; Vrečer, 1999).

At the beginning of the twenty-first century, Slovenia faced quite a different set of challenges related to migration. This time, immigrants came from more distant non-European countries and they were more diverse than ever before (Zavratnik Zimic, 2003). In public discourse, especially in the media, immigrants were frequently described as 'the others', 'foreigners', and those with a 'different identity'. Immigrants were presented as having 'a different cultural, ethnic, and religious background', and as potentially being a 'threat to the emerging national identity', not least because of their 'high numbers'. The populist use of identity differences by politicians and the media was rather common too.

Slovenian migration specialists usually refer to two 'crises' or 'hypes' in the national media discourses related to the arrival of immigrants in the early and mid-1990s and at the beginning of the 2000s (Zavratnik Zimic, 2003). The first set of public debates occurred as a reaction to a perceived 'refugee influx' during the period 1992–1995, when the wars in the former Yugoslavia displaced hundreds of thousands of people from Croatia and Bosnia and Herzegovina and compelled those people to look for safety in nearby countries, Slovenia included. The second negative media portrayal of immigrants came as a result of a campaign orchestrated by the Ministry of Interior against some illegal residents (mainly Roma) and asylum seekers (usually from countries in the Developing World and Kosovo). These people were traditionally described as 'unruly', 'dirty' and 'a threat to the local people' (Pajnik, Petra and Gregorčič, 2001).

Regarding the first crisis, Doupona Horvat and her colleagues (1998) conducted thorough research on Slovenia's elites' rhetoric from April 1992 to March 1993. The authors carried out textual analyses which monitored different media discussions in newspapers, as well as on radio and television. Special attention was paid to the implicit aspects of attaching values to and explaining the meaning of the country's refugee policy and decisions taken by the state authorities on this subject. According to this research, politicians, state administrators and media representatives tended to classify the Republic of Slovenia as a country which tried to respect human rights and this fact made it different from the 'autocratic darkness' and instability of the conflict-ridden Balkans. A closer look at the media debates, however, revealed some divergent (that is non-democratic and intolerant) principles in addressing the so-called 'refugee crisis' in Slovenia, which was allegedly the outcome of international conflicts such as those in the former Yugoslavia. For instance, eminent public figures used the metaphor of a 'refugee wave' which was reportedly flooding Slovenia. Moreover, refugees were often portrayed as 'endangering the young Slovenia democracy', whist the international (and especially some neighbouring EU countries') experience of refusing entry and documents for stay of foreign nationals was frequently invoked in order to legitimate certain 'protectionist policies'. These latter included denying immigrants the right to work and to have access to social services in Slovenia.

The second media-sponsored 'drama' in Slovenia's public space occurred at the end of 2000 and the first months of 2001, when the main topic of discussion was the future of immigrants who had entered Slovenia without valid documents (Pajnik, Petra and Gregorčič, 2001). An extensive analysis of the biased and occasionally xenophobic attitude of Slovenia's printed media in the first three-and-a-half months of 2001 is provided by Jalušič (2002). She reports a deliberate strategy of 'emotionalization' of the media discourse – a deliberate policy of 'exaggerating the situation' and provoking a crisis by laying the blame on both the immigrants and the state institutions for a difficult conundrum of dealing with an allegedly large number of 'unwanted' foreigners. Overall, the media reports focused exclusively on the victimization of the local Slovenian residents by immigrants, thereby emphasizing the excessive rights given to foreigners. According to Jalušič, this led to 'the normalization of xenophobia as a response', but the media reporting triggered other 'social defence mechanisms' (for example, 'we (Slovenians) are normal' not xenophobic, and 'xenophobia is a marginal phenomenon' and is not representative of our society).

Nevertheless, the attitude towards immigrants in Slovenia has not been uniform, either in the early 1990s or during the 2000s. Throughout those years, influential counter-trends to the dominantly negative media discourse emerged both in civil society and in the political class as well (see Milohnić, 2001; Pajnik, Petra and Gregorčič, 2001; and Kramberger et al., 2004). For instance, at the beginning of 2001, groups of prominent politicians and leaders of NGOs launched a number of joint public appeals to put an end the hostility towards immigrants. A bottom-up organization, the Bureau for Interventions, announced a series of solidarity actions. Such actions included a rally against xenophobia ('Solidarity with Immigrants'), the collection of toys for the children of immigrants, the organization of a number of public forums in Ljubljana which attracted many people, as well as the attention of the media (Kogovšek, 2001). As result of this strong collective response to xenophobia, the media began to publish articles referring to immigrants as individuals rather than a homogeneous mass of people presenting a threat. It might be said that, already in late 2001, there was some kind of positive shift of opinion towards immigrants in the Slovenian public. In parallel, there was also a gradual media 'change-of-heart' that was taking place (Drolc, 2003; Zavratnik Zimic, 2003).

Concluding remarks

The evolution of Slovenia's immigration policy has been the result of complex historical and political processes. First, emerging both as a post-communist regime and a young nation-state during the early 1990s, Slovenia's political and administrative elites, as well as the majority of the population, had major problems accepting immigrants and minorities in general. Hence, foreign-born residents and some non-Slovenian ethnic groups were usually treated with great suspicion and sometimes open animosity by the majority of society. Foreigners have usually been perceived by the media and the various elites as 'subjects' bound by the Slovenian administrative and legal immigration system to abide by local customs and regulations. They have not been perceived as active citizens (or denizens), endowed with full rights and capabilities to participate in public life in their own way. Second, because of the very dynamic circumstances characterizing recent Slovenian state history (the disintegration of SFRY, national independence, EU accession and full membership of the EU – all this during slightly more than a decade), there has generally been an ambivalence about what should be done in several policy areas, such as migration, border control, citizenship, social and employment policy and national security, to name just a few which affect the destiny of immigrants and some of the already legal foreign residents. Finally, the heterogeneous and quite mobile nature of the migrant population in Slovenia has not permitted all immigrants to accumulate sufficient knowledge about Slovenian culture or the necessary resources to organize themselves and to claim a greater role in political and social life. This has, in turn, led to the relatively slow integration in Slovenian society of some of these groups, especially the so-called 'new immigrants' from the Developing World and the Roma.

Yet, despite these obvious problems, one should not forget the tangible results achieved by the Slovenian authorities and civil society in particular in trying to make Slovenia more welcoming to immigrants and a better living place for its minorities. The embryonic, but seemingly sustainable, participation of migrants in Slovenia's social and political life is one such source of optimism. The unique, albeit sometimes painful, experience of the country's public administration, the media and civil society is helping to define a set of priorities in dealing with its immigrant and ethnic minority populations. This is potentially a useful lesson for some of the other CEE and CIS post-communist regimes facing the same kinds of problems.

References

Andreev, S. (2003a), 'Making Slovenian Citizens: The Problem of the Former Yugoslav Citizens and Asylum Seekers Living in Slovenia', *Southeast European Politics*, **IV**(1) (May 2003), 1–24.

Andreev, S. (2003b), 'Measuring the Quality of European Citizenship in View of Slovenia's Joining the European Union', *European Paper Series*, April 2003. Ljubljana: Mirovni Institut.

Bevc, M., Prevodnik-Rupel, V. and Verlič-Christensen, B. (2000), *Migracije v Sloveniji v luči vključitve v EU* [Migration in Slovenia in Light of its Accession to the EU]. Ljubljana: Inštitut za ekonomska raziskovanja.

Bucar, B. and Brinar, I. (2001), 'Lessons from Transition and Accession Periods of Slovenia', *Central European Political Science Review*, **2**(6) (Winter 2001).

Drolc, A. (2003), 'Immigrants between a Common Europe Migration Policy and Local Peculiarities', in Pajnik, M. and Zavratnik Zimic, S. (eds) *Migration – Globalization – European Union*, 328–46. Ljubljana: Mirovni inštitut. (Published in both Slovenian and English).

European Commission (2002), *Regular Report on Slovenia's Progress towards Accession, COM*, 2002, 700.

Genorio, R. (1989), 'Slovenci v Kanadi' [Slovenians in Canada] *Geographica Slovenica*. Inštitut za geografio Univerze v Ljubljani.

Horvat, D., Verscheueren, J. and Žagar, I.Ž. (1998), *The Rhetoric of Refugee Policies in Slovenia: The Pragmatics of Legitimation*. Ljubljana: Open Society Institute. (Published in both Slovenian and English).

Jalušič, V. (2002), 'Xenophobia or Self-protection? On the Establishing of the New Slovene Civic/Citizenship Identity', in Pajnik, M. (ed.) *Xenophobia and Post-Socialism*, 45–72. Ljubljana: Mirovni inštitut. (Published in both Slovenian and English).

Kodelja, J. (1992), 'Iz katerih območij v Jugoslaviji so prihajali, kje so se naselili' [Which part of Yugoslavia did they come from, and where did they settle?] *IB revija*, **26**(6–7), 34–38.

Kogovšek, N. (2001), *Spreminjanje slovenske azilne zakonodaje v letu 2001* [Changing Slovenian Asylum Legislation in the year 2001]. Ljubljana: Mirovni inštitut.

Komac, M. (2001), 'Forming a New Nation-State and the Repression or Protection of Ethnic Minorities: The Case of Slovenia', in Nagel, S.S. and Robb, A. (eds) *Handbook of Global Social Policy*, 267–92. NY: Marcel Dekker.

Kramberger, T., Mihelj, S. and Rotar, D.B. (2004), 'Representations of the Nation and of the Other in the Slovenian Periodical Press before and After 1991', in Spassov, O. (ed.) *Quality Press in Southeast Europe*. Sofia: Southeast European Media Centre.

Lozar, M. (2002), 'Scenarios for Institutional Reform in the EU: Before and After the Nice Summit', *EU Monitor*, 3. Ljubljana: Peace Institute.

Malačič, J. (1991), 'Zunanje migracije Slovenije po drugi svetovni vojni' [International migration in Slovenia after World War II] *Zgodovinski časopis*, **45**(2).

Mežnarič, S. (1986), *Bosanci. A kuda idu Slovenci nedeljom?* [Bosnians. Where do Slovenians go on Sunday?]. Ljubljana: Krt.

Milohnić, A. (ed.) (2001), *Evropski vratarji: Migracijske in azilne politike v Vzhodni Evropi* [European Door-keepers: Migration and Asylum Politics in Eastern Europe]. Ljubljana: Mirovni inštitut.

Pajnik, M., Petra, L.T. and Gregorčič, M. (2001), *Immigrants, who are you? Research on Immigrants in Slovenia*. Ljubljana: Mirovni inštitut. (Published in both Slovenian and English).

Šabič, Z. (2002), 'Slovenia and the European Union: A Different Kind of Two-Level Game', presented at the 3rd Joint Convention of CEEISA/NISA/RISA in Moscow, Russia, 20–22 June 2002.

Vrečer, N. (ed.) (1999), *Vsakdanje življenje beguncev in begunk v Sloveniji* [Everyday Life of Asylum Seekers in Slovenia]. Ljubljana: Slovensko Etnološko Društvo.

Zagar, M. (1997), 'Rights of Ethnic Minorities: Individual and/or Collective Rights? Some New(er) Trends in Development and the (Universal) Nature of Human Rights – the European Perspective', *Journal of International Relations*, 4(1/4), 29–48.

Zavratnik, S. (1996), *Social Integration vs. Social Exclusion: the Case of Bosnian Refugees in Slovenia, Austria and Ireland*. MSc Thesis, Ljubljana University.

Zavratnik Zimic, S. (2003), 'Migration Trends in Selected EU Applicant Countries, Volume VI – Slovenia: The perspective of a Country on the "Schengen Periphery"', *IOM Report*. Vienna: International Organization of Migration.

Chapter 24

Spain

Carmen González Enríquez

A country of emigration since the nineteenth century, Spain began to receive immigration in substantial numbers after its entry into the European Union and the economic growth which followed it. Spain has become the main destination point for new immigrants in Europe. In 2005, immigrants represented 10 per cent of the population, three-quarters of which originated from non-EU countries. A good portion of recent economic development, indeed one of the highest in Western Europe, is produced in sectors which employ mainly foreign manpower, namely construction and tourism. This dependence on immigrant labour constitutes an important political and social base for permissive policies toward immigration. Public opinion in this realm is one of the least negative in Europe, but an increase in feelings of rejection, particularly in areas where immigrants concentrate, poses a dilemma for politicians, who have used regularizations as the main policy instrument to control immigration flows.

Major developments in Spains's immigration policy

The first measure designed to regulate immigration in Spain was approved in 1985 in order to adapt Spanish legislation to European policies before entering the European Community. At that time, the foreign population in the country barely amounted to 200,000 people, most of whom were European citizens. The 1985 Law was passed without public debate, approved in the Parliament almost unanimously and only provoked significant reactions in Ceuta y Melilla, the two Spanish towns in North Africa with a high percentage of immigrants of Moroccan origin. The Law was restrictive, mainly directed to facilitate the expulsion of irregular immigrants (Pajares, 1998), while social integration and attention to immigrants' needs were implicitly left in the hands of Autonomous Communities and local councils. This meant that immigrants' circumstances and treatment varied greatly, since they depended on their place of residence.

In 2000, the second and third laws on immigration were passed, both known as 'Ley de Extranjería' (Law on Foreigners).[1] The first one was proposed by the Catalonian nationalist party CiU (Convergencia I Unió), the leftist IU (Izquierda Unida) and the Mixed parliamentary group (mainly nationalists from different areas of Spain). Their proposal tried to create a legal framework to pursue the integration of immigrants, and was thus in opposition to the 1985 Law, which mainly focused on controlling their arrival and stay. The Socialist Party later presented its own, more detailed proposal. All these were rather generous – in comparison with other European countries' standards – with regard to the social rights of immigrants, be they legal or illegal, or the legal guarantees offered to irregular immigrants.

When the first Law was discussed in the Spanish Parliament, the Popular Party did not hold a sufficient majority and the Law was approved against its will. However, the 2000 general elections

---

1   Ley Orgánica 4/00 and Ley Orgánica 8/00.

granted the Popular Party the necessary majority and a new version of the Law was presented. This version was more restrictive, claiming that the change was necessary in order to adapt Spanish standards to those of the EU. The debate around the proposed reform of this Law was the first occasion that immigration became an important public matter, attracting wide coverage in the media. The Popular Party was alone in its defence of a more restrictive Law, when all other political parties, NGOs, the Catholic Church and trade unions were against the reform. The visibility and media coverage of the debate was increased because of the confrontation between members of government, in particular the Minister of Labour who was openly against the reform, and the Minister of Interior who was openly in favour. The reform of the Law was approved with the votes of the Popular Party only, and it included many small changes (BOE [State Gazette] 23 December 2000) (Pérez Díaz, Álvarez Miranda and González Enriquez, 2002). Public attention focused on two issues: first, the restrictions directed to facilitate the expulsion of illegal immigrants, and second the limitations to the right of association, strike and demonstration. Compared with the first Law on Foreigners (4/2000), this was a restrictive Law, but not when compared with the 1985 Law or with most European provisions.

The Law was modified again in November 2003. This modification was agreed by all the main parties, and was concerned with the intense and unexpected increase of immigrants in the first years of the decade. The reform's main declared objective was to improve the instruments so as to address illegal migration and the traffic and smuggling of human beings. For instance, the regulations allow the Police to access the data collected in the Municipal Registers, oblige international transport enterprises to give notification of passengers who do not use their return ticket, include new penalties for smugglers and enterprises who hire irregular workers, and oblige foreigners without a permanent residence permit to renew their inscription in the Municipal Register every two years (BOE [State Gazette] 21 December 2003).

Since the mid-80s the economic development experienced after joining the European Community, the growing access of women to the labour market, and the general increase in the level of education, created new spaces for migrant workers, who arrived in spite of the difficulty in obtaining legal status. The response of successive governments – be they socialist or liberal-conservative – to this increase of unauthorized residents was regularizations. In 1991, 1995, 2000, 2001 and 2005 there were processes of 'normalization' or regularizations which, on the whole, allowed for the legalization of one million migrants (1,041,000), more than half of whom were 'regularized' in the 2005 process. Each of these measures was presented as 'extraordinary' and 'the last one', and all of them have had a 'call effect' or 'pull effect' which has attracted more immigrants who, in turn, have found themselves in a situation of irregularity. 'Extraordinary' regularizations have, de facto, become the main instrument used in controlling immigration flows, and have turned into a 'cheap way' to adapt labour market demands to foreign workforce supply, relying on the efficiency of the 'invisible hand of the market' (Martín Urriza, 2006).

After the 2001 regularization, the Popular Party Government (1996–2004) announced that, in order to avoid the 'pull effect', it would not offer any more special regularization processes and maintained this policy until it was defeated in the March 2004 elections. However, the struggle against illegal immigration which, in official rhetoric, was the main feature of the immigration policies of Popular Party governments, was never a systematic policy involving the expulsion of irregular immigrants from the country. The Spanish state lacks the financial and administrative resources to effectively expel illegal immigrants. Thus, between 1 January 2002 and 14 June 2004, a period of two-and-a-half years, the Administration made 117,768 expulsion orders for aliens, but only 32,749 (28 per cent) were executed.[2] The financial cost and the lack of repatriation agreements with the countries of origin are the main reasons hindering these expulsions.

Finally, the political leaders understand that a large part of the Spanish population would be opposed to a policy involving raids and massive expulsion of irregular immigrants. Thus, irregular immigration is tacitly accepted in the social and political environment, as is the underground economy in which a substantial part of immigrants work. Unlike other developed countries which are hosts to immigrants, in Spain a private citizen would hardly ever report the presence of illegal immigrants. When such reports do occur, they refer exclusively to cases involving forced prostitution or exceptionally harsh exploitation at work. In this regard, immigrants benefit from a traditional political culture of tolerance towards illegality. On the other hand, the frequent changes in the legal framework and the strong occurrence of 'befallen illegality' resulting from slow bureaucracy and the understaffing of public services dealing with renewal of residence and labour permits, make illegality a common feature. In fact approximately 90 per cent of present legal immigrants coming from non-EU countries have passed through a phase of illegality (Pajares, 2004; Díez Nicolás and Ramírez Lafita, 2001). Most Spaniards who have any contact with immigrants are aware of this and, hence, do not necessarily attribute any negative connotations to irregular stayers (González Enríquez, 2006).

The assistance to, and the destiny of, irregular immigrants arriving by sea in Andalusia or the Canary Islands has become a source of confrontation between Autonomous Governments and the Central Government over recent years. The Canary Government in particular, asks from time to time for more financial help to assist immigrants and has obtained the periodical transfer of irregular migrants to the Peninsula, organized by the Ministry of Interior. Once there, after 40 days of stay in special centres (the maximum allowed by Law for illegal immigrants), they are freed, as most of them cannot be expelled. This, in turn, provokes protests from the Autonomous Governments of Madrid, Valencia, Andalusia or Catalonia, the main points of destiny, who feel pressured by the presence on their streets of highly visible irregular immigrants in need of social help.

In August 2004, soon after their electoral victory that year, the Socialist Party announced the launching of a 'normalization process' which, after negotiations and doubts, offered the chance to regularize their status to foreigners who were offered a labour contract and who could prove they were living in the country before 8 August 2004. To access to this normalization, immigrants should have been registered with their local council before that date, have been offered a work contract of at least six months (three months in the agricultural sector) and have no criminal record in their home country or in Spain. The application had to be filled in by the employer, except in the case of domestic employees, and a channel to denounce employers who refused to apply for their workers was thus opened. In this process, held during the first months of 2005, 691,655 people asked for regularization and 573,270 were granted residence and labour permits. This translated into 550,000 new contributors to the Social Security fund. The process was presented as an attempt to combat the hidden or 'second' economy and it was supposed to be accompanied by a strengthening of labour inspection services to avoid the employment of illegal immigrants.

The launching of this process was contested both domestically and internationally, as some European leaders saw it as a measure directed in the wrong direction and against the tendency of most European countries toward more restrictive policies regarding immigration. In the domestic arena, the Popular Party headed the protest against what they labelled a 'call effect' measure. The Popular Party, however, remained isolated in their confrontation, as trade unions, business associations and NGOs supported this measure. The Socialist Party also modified the regulations governing access to residence permits, which can now be obtained after two years of effective

---

2   Data provided by the Secretary of State for Immigration and Emigration, July 2004.

stay and 12 months of labour, or three years of effective stay and an offer of a work contract,[3] thus providing a way for continuous regularization of irregular stayers.

At the beginning of 2007, after the entry of Romania and Bulgaria into the European Union which legalized the stay in Spain of persons coming from these two countries, the data pointed to 730,000 irregular immigrants.

According to Eurostat, since the beginning of the twentieth century Spain has become the main point of entry of immigrants into Europe. In fact it is almost impossible to produce an accurate comparison as Spain is the only country which promotes local council registration of unauthorized migrants. The 2000 Aliens Law granted regular or irregular immigrants the right to free health care with the single condition that they were included in the municipal registers. But the use of local council registers as a source of information regarding the number of foreigners living in Spain entails many difficulties. Immigrants do not cancel their registration when they leave the country permanently and there are many who register themselves only to get medical treatment, without really living in Spain. A legal change introduced in 2003 obliges foreigners without a permanent residence permit to renew their registration with the local council every two years, but many immigrants ignore it and do not renew their registration in time. On the other hand, local councils have their own reasons for preferring to keep the number high, as financial and material resources are assigned to them according to the number of inhabitants.

There are some factors than can help explain why Spain is at present so attractive to immigrants. First, there is the existence of a strong and rather vibrant informal economy where irregular migrants can find employment. Second, the relatively positive social attitudes towards immigrants, in comparison with other European countries (Triandafyllidou, 2001),[4] the traditional tolerance towards illegality embedded in South European political culture, and, third, the treatment of social rights for irregular immigrants in Spanish regulations (González Enríquez, 2005).

At present, the integration of immigrants and attention to their special needs are in the hands of Autonomous Governments, local councils and NGOs mainly financed by public funds. They provide services such as language classes, information to find a job or accommodation. But this kind of support to immigrants is very unevenly distributed across the country, and a good portion of immigrants do not have access to it. On the other hand, this role of regional and local administrations creates an extra financial burden for many local councils and Autonomous Governments, which frequently demand more resources from the State in order to attend to the immigrant population. In 2001, the government of the Popular Party approved the GRECO Plan (Programa Global de Regulación y Coordinación de la Extranjería y la Inmigración) which was during the period 2001–2004 the only nationwide instrument directed toward the integration of immigrants. But its lack of financial resources and the failure of the government to develop the general regulations included on the Programme, made it nothing more than a catalogue of good intentions (Laparra and Martínez, 2003). As an answer to the demands from regional and local administrations, in 2005 the Socialist Party Government approved the first Fund for the Integration of Immigrants, with 120 million euros directed to both administrations and, in 2006, increased it to 182 million euros.

The immigrant population in Spain: main demographic and social features

In 1980, only 180,000 aliens were resident in Spain, and the majority of these were Europeans from Germany, the United Kingdom and other countries of Central and Northern Europe, who had settled

---

3   Under the previous norm it was five years of effective stay, or three years in the case of immigrants who could show integration in the work market or family ties with Spaniards or regular immigrants.
4   See the European Social Survey (2005).

permanently on the coasts and islands of Spain and were mainly retired. Besides the Europeans, there was a small group of Latin Americans, most of whom had fled from the dictatorships of South America. This feature changed after 1985 as the immigrants who have arrived since then come from a broad range of countries: Moroccans, Chinese, Sub-Saharan Africans, Ecuadorians, Colombians, Dominicans, Western and Eastern Europeans. At the end of the eighties, immigrants born in other EU countries accounted for half the total number, yet now, they do not even constitute a quarter (22 per cent in 2005). The remaining come mainly from developing countries or countries in crisis, namely from Latin America and Africa. Moroccans formed the biggest group of non-EU immigrants in the nineties but they have been overtaken in number by the rapid growth in immigrants from Latin America (INE [Instituto Nacional de Estadística], 2005 Municipal Registers).

In January 2007, the number of foreign-born people registered with the local councils (including EU citizens) represented 11.7 per cent of the total population, but the percentage could be lower, as experts agree that the data in these registers magnify the alien population (Arango, 2004; Garrido and Toharia, 2004). Table 24.1 shows the growth in the totals since 1980, and Table 24.2 gives a breakdown by country of origin for 2006.

Table 24.1   Number of foreign-born residents in Spain (1980–2007)

	Foreign-born residents in Spain
1980	182,045
1990	276,796
1992	402,350
1994	461,364
1996	538,984
1998	719,647
2000	1,034,210
2001	1,370,657
2002	1,977,944
2003	2,664,168
2004	3,050,847
2005	4,391,484
2006	4,837,622
2007	5,214,390

Note: Data up to 1998 refer to legal residents. As from the year 2000, the data refer to persons registered in the census of the municipalities, and include irregular immigrants. The 2000 Aliens Law granted irregular immigrants the right to free healthcare with the single condition that they were registered in the municipal register, which led to the statistical 'blossoming' of a large portion of this population.
Source: Instituto Nacional de Estadística y Ministerio del Interior [National Institute of Statistics and Interior Ministry].

Table 24.2   Major non-EU nationalities in Spain (1 January 2006)

Main origin of residents born outside the EU (1 January 2006)			
	Total	Percentage	Cumulative percentage
Morocco	606,000	16	16
Ecuador	456,600	12	28
Romania	397,300	11	39
Colombia	287,000	8	47
Argentina	271,400	7	54
Peru	123,500	3	57
China	104,800	3	60
Bulgaria	100,800	3	63
Other	1,412,600	37	100
Total non-EU	3,769,000	100	-

Source: Instituto Nacional de Estadística, Padrón Municipal de Habitantes, [National Institute of Statistics. Municipal Registers of Inhabitants] 2006.

Although there are no official figures on the total number, there are only a few aliens with the status of political refugee in Spain. Successive governments have maintained a very restrictive policy as regards the granting of this status and have accepted an average of less than five per cent of applications. Moreover, the aid offered to refugees is very sparse in comparison with that offered by other countries. Finally, the opportunities provided for obtaining work in the irregular economy make illegal immigration a preferable option for possible asylum seekers in Spain. During the previous decade, applications amounted to more than 10,000 annually during the years coinciding with the successive crises in Yugoslavia, and at no time did the figure reach 15,000. Subsequently, and up to now, the figure has oscillated between 4,000 and 8,000 a year. Thus, in 2003, 7,500 applications for political asylum were submitted but only 370 were successful (CEAR. Comisión Española de Ayuda al Refugiado [Spanish Commission for Aid to Refugees]).

Geographically, the immigrants are distributed very unevenly on Spanish territory, with high concentrations on the Mediterranean coast, the Balearic and Canary Islands, and Madrid, while their presence is scant in the rest of the country. Forty-five per cent of non-EU immigrants were living in Barcelona or Madrid in January 2005, and all around the Mediterranean coast the number of extra-community immigrants is twice the Spanish average. Even in the 'regions of immigration', the distribution is very unequal and the aliens are concentrated in certain villages and towns. Moreover, within the cities they concentrate in particular districts. Thus, in 2005 in the city of Madrid, some districts had over 30 per cent of alien population, while others did not reach 5 per cent.

Immigrants concentrate in two types of areas: districts of the historic centres where the housing is of poor quality (as in El Raval in Barcelona or Lavapiés in Madrid) and peripheral districts which are well connected to public transport and have relatively cheap housing built in the 1960s and 1970s. Prices of housing and accessibility are clearly the two factors which condition the choice, together with the previous presence of acquaintances or family members who help in the first stages of arrival, thereby also explaining the tendency of immigrants to concentrate in a certain area according to their country of origin. The high cost of housing in Spain and the scarcity of rental flats form the main difficulty that immigrants face. Many of them (19 per cent) live in crowded flats, with less than ten square metres per person and half of them share flats with non-family persons (Pereda, Actis and de Prada, 2005).

Immigrants are found in the areas where there is a strong tourist industry, intensive agriculture or, generally speaking, where there are dynamic economies such as in Madrid or Barcelona. However, there are also political reasons, such as the presence of a violent nationalism, which would explain why areas which are economically rich, such as the Basque Country, are hosts to only a small percentage of immigrants (4.4 per cent of the total population.) (Municipal Registers of 2005).

The arrival of immigrants in Spain has coincided with a period of economic growth which has enabled an increase in the active domestic population and, in the meantime, the absorption of this foreign labour force. Between 1996 and 2005 six million new jobs were created, and now 80.5 per cent of men between 16 and 64 years old are active, while only 6.5 per cent of them are unemployed (Martín Urriza, 2006). Although unemployment continues to affect eight per cent of the total active population, a large number of unemployed persons are reluctant to work in the sectors where immigrants find employment. Hence, the latter fill an 'occupational gap' which has been left by the Spaniards. These jobs are often unskilled and involve some of the following features: low wages, long working hours, hard physical conditions and low social prestige. By sector, male immigrants are concentrated in agriculture (18 per cent of the total), construction (23 per cent) and services (47 per cent), while females are concentrated in services (86 per cent), especially domestic service, small businesses and catering, and hotels (CES, 2004). There is a certain sector specialization depending on national origin, thus 28 per cent of East Europeans and Africans (basically Moroccans) are employed in construction, while only 16 per cent of Latin Americans are found in this sector. On the other hand, 26 per cent of Latin Americans work in domestic services (almost all women), while only 4 per cent of Africans, 18 per cent of East Europeans and 2 per cent of Spaniards work in this sector. The Africans are also concentrated in agriculture (13 per cent) and the Latin Americans in catering and hotels (16 per cent). Due to the concentration in these sectors and the short period of time in the employment market, their turnover rate is much higher than the average for the Spanish working population. 70 per cent of the contracts for African males are temporary, a percentage which is twice the Spanish figure (Garrido and Toharia, 2004). The sectors the immigrants concentrate in are also those which feed the underground economy, whose weight in the Gross Domestic Product is estimated to be around 23 per cent, the fourth biggest in Western Europe after Greece, Italy and Belgium, and on the same level as Portugal (Schneider, 2004).

Immigrant rights and participation in public life

Only about 1 per cent of non-EU immigrants who live in Spain have managed to obtain Spanish nationality (18,000 persons from 1992 until the end of 2004). This percentage will be substantially increased in the next few years as Spanish regulations allow those persons coming from countries with special cultural and historical bonds with Spain to obtain nationality after two years of legal stay in the country. This applies to Latin American countries, Andorra, the Philippines, Equatorial Guinea, Portugal, as well as Sephardim Jews. At present, as was mentioned above, most immigration is from Latin America, but most Latin Americans have not yet fulfilled the two years of legal residence requirement. As regards immigrants with other countries of origin, Spanish Law requires ten years of legal residence (reduced to five years in the case of refugees), in order to obtain nationality (Aparicio and Tornos, 2003). Table 24.3 gives the figures for naturalizations for the six years from 1999.

Table 24.3   Number of applications for naturalization (1999–2004)

	No. of aliens who applied for and obtained Spanish nationality					
	1999	**2000**	**2001**	**2002**	**2003**	**2004**
Applications	16,838	18,035	23,260	32,778	46,354	60,346
Granted	16,374	11,994	16,735	21,799	26,540	38,335

Source: Ministry of Justice and Yearbook of the OPI [Observatorio Permanente de la Inmigración].

Spanish nationalization rules are governed by a mixture between *jus sanguinis* and *jus soli*. The principle that the descendents of Spaniards are Spaniards is complemented by the concession of nationality to those born in Spain when the father or the mother was also born in Spain, and the concession of nationality based on residence. The reform of the Civil Code approved in 2002 favours the nationalization of children born in Spain of immigrant parents (they obtain their nationality after one year of continuous legal stay in the country before the application). This reform was also directed to favour the re-naturalization of grandchildren of Spaniards who emigrated to Latin America or to other areas during the nineteenth and twentieth centuries, have failed to maintain Spanish nationality and now, confronted with the grave economic crisis of some Latin American economies, desire to live in Spain.

The granting of nationality based on residence is subject to some restrictions such as 'good civic conduct' and 'sufficient integration in Spanish society'. The interpretation of this last condition is left to the discretion of judges and the lack of knowledge of the Spanish language is the most common cause of rejection which has, till now, mainly affected Moroccan and Chinese immigrants (*El País*, 9 November 2004).

Social and political rights of foreigners are regulated by the above-mentioned Law 4/2000 on the Rights of Aliens and their Social Integration (known as Ley de Extranjería). In accordance with this law, immigrants with a residence permit enjoy the same social rights as Spaniards. As for irregular immigrants, they must register themselves with the local councils in order to get access to free health care (on the same basis as regular migrants and Spaniards) and to education for children and teenagers from 3 to 16 years old. Registration with the local council is easy and simple, and almost all irregular migrants are registered.

Regarding political rights, aliens who have a residence permit in Spain have the right to meet, demonstrate, associate, and join a trade union and professional organizations. As for electoral political participation through active and passive suffrage at the municipal and Autonomous Community elections, this right is granted to all EU citizens (who can also vote in the European Parliamentary elections) and to the nationals of countries with whom Spain has reciprocal agreements (Argentina, Chile, Uruguay and Norway). The right to vote in national elections is only granted to naturalized aliens. Recently, the two main political parties, Socialist and Popular, have announced their will to extend the number of immigrants entitled to vote in local elections, by signing reciprocal agreements with some countries of origin of immigrants, such as Ecuador.

The irregular immigrants in Spain lack political rights. However, these legal restraints have not prevented illegal immigrants from participating in immigrants' associations or trade unions, nor from attending demonstrations or sit-ins requesting 'papers'. Although the political sectors with more pro-immigrant attitudes protested at the time (in 2000) because of the governmental refusal to include in the Aliens Act the right of irregular immigrants to strike, it is difficult to imagine how this can affect persons who, supposedly, cannot work.

The presence of immigrants in public social life is, up to now, very scarce and limited to some famous foreigners in the world of professional sports, mainly football, in television and in the entertainment industry. Immigrants are frequently 'objects' of reports, debates and news in the media but only on exceptional occasions do they produce this information themselves and become active participants in the diffusion of news or opinions. As regards their political and civic participation, it is by now channelled through immigrants' associations, whose activities are frequently encouraged by State subsidies and by the existence of the Forum for the Social Integration of Immigrants, which assesses the government on issues related to immigration. Many Autonomous Communities and town halls have also created bodies for consultation and co-operation with immigrant organizations, but there is a lack of studies at the local level to compare this variety of structures of political opportunity. There are, up to now, no prominent immigrants in the main political parties, trade unions or civic associations of any kind, nor are they occupying visible posts in public institutions.

Most immigrants do not take part in any kind of association, as they have been in the country for a short period (half of them less than two years) and they are still in precarious situations which hinder any kind of civic participation. The main field of activity of immigrant associations is assistance. In practice, this translates into legal aid for obtaining 'papers' and all types of social support such as help in finding accommodation, finding a job, connecting with the social and charity services, and so on. Secondary areas of activity are political pressure on the Central Administration –demands for new regularizations or changes in the legislation on aliens – and cultural activities such as leisure and the maintenance of the culture of origin. Immigrant associations are highly dependent on state funds, as they lack their own financial resources, and this state funding (be it from the national, the regional or the local government) has diminished their cultural or political features and has deepened their role as service providers (Veredas, 2003).

In 1995, the Forum for the Social Integration of Immigrants was set up as a consultative body. The Forum is composed of representatives of the Public Administrations, immigrants' associations and NGOs, trade unions and business associations. The criteria used for the selection of immigrant associations which take part reinforce the dominance of a small group which receive more financial help and, in turn, are in a better position to take part in the Forum. Those who received more financing in the past are those who subsequently receive more financing thanks to the structural and organizational dimension achieved in the first stages of the aid programmes. Thus, there is an unequal distribution between the consolidated associations and those aspiring to receive funds (Veredas, 2003).

Public and media discourses on migration

Attention devoted by the media to immigration in recent years has been consistently focused on irregular immigration, especially that from Africa. The most common reports refer to police success in dismantling networks, small boats arriving at the coast, cases involving the exploitation of immigrants, cases of extortion and kidnapping among immigrants, and so on (MUGAK, 2002; Lorite García, 2004, Nash, 2005). Of all the news coverage of immigration, 20 per cent related to illegal immigration in 2001, 27 per cent in 2002 and 31 per cent in 2003, with a clear progression showing that everything related to the irregular aspects of immigration has been gaining ground (CIPIE, several years). During the summer months, when the arrival of small boats in Andalusia and the Canary Islands increases, the arrest of their occupants or the sinking of one of these boats is reported on an almost daily basis. In spite of the fact that only a small minority of foreigners arrive in the country in 'pateras' or 'cayucos' (small boats coming from Morocco or lately from

Mauritania and Senegal), or jump the fence in Ceuta or Melilla, they occupy the majority of the space that the media devote to immigration.

During the months following the terrorist attack of 11 March 2004, which caused 191 deaths, public attention focused on the results of police searches which discovered the participation of Muslim immigrants in the attack or in the preparation of new ones. Since then, reports on the integration of Muslim migrants all over Europe have become a common occurrence in the media. Due to this attack, a debate arose in 2004 on the relationships between the State and the Mosques and Muslim oratories, similar to those developed in other European countries, which has confronted freedom of expression and religion with demands for security. The Socialist Government attempted to imitate the French model with the creation of a body representing the Muslim population, but it came up against the internal division of this community and the reluctance of the main Moroccan immigrants' association, ATIME (Association of Moroccan Workers in Spain), which was opposed to granting more political weight to the Imams. Before 11 March 2004, the Moroccan immigrants, who make up more than 90 per cent of Muslim immigrants in Spain, were those least accepted by the population, and this rejection increased notably after the attack (Real Instituto Elcano, Barómetro, 2004 www.realinstitutoelcano.org).

The political debate on immigration over recent years has focused on irregular immigration and the issues related to it, such as extraordinary regularizations and the humanitarian assistance to immigrants arriving in boats. During the second legislative period of the Popular Party Government (2000–2004), after the closing of legal ways to immigrate and the subsequent growing number of illegal immigrants, leftist parties, NGOs and immigrant associations accused the government of benefiting the employers in the underground economy, by putting undocumented and, therefore, cheaper labour at their disposal. At the same time, they asked for the opening of new legal ways to immigrate and for a new regularization process. The period with the greatest growth in immigration (1998–2004) coincided with the government of the centre-right Popular Party (1996–2004), which was immobilized between two contradictory pressures. On the one hand, the vast social sectors benefiting from having an immigrant workforce at their disposal, and on the other, the increasing social unease due to the growth of immigration. Trapped in this blocked situation, the Government made 'the fight against the immigration mafias' a rhetorical motto planned to cover up the absence of a real policy of control of immigration flows.

After the electoral victory of the Socialist Party in 2004 and its announcement of a process of 'normalization', the Popular Party and the right-wing media accused the Government of favouring the increasing of irregular immigration by rewarding it with 'papers'. They predicted a strong increase in the arrival of immigrants and the inability of the welfare system to bear the weight of this added population. The Popular Party, freed after March 2004 from the responsibilities of government, began to issue warning messages which are well received by a good part of public opinion, since half of Spaniards favour more restrictive immigration policies. After the arrival of some thousands of African irregular immigrants in the Canary Islands during the summer of 2006, even the Socialist Party and the Government modified their public discourse on this topic, insisting on their will to send back irregular immigrants.

However, leaving aside the discussions on the regularization of immigrants, the political debate on immigration has, so far, been weak in Spain. Immigration only became one of the main 'issues' in the domestic political debate after the Popular Party went into opposition in March 2004. Until that time, immigration had taken a back seat in the political debate at domestic level. Unlike other European countries with a longer experience of immigration, there have been no deep debates on the advantages or inconveniencies of immigration, nor on the policies needed for their integration, nor on the costs or economic benefits involved, nor the consequences for the welfare system. The political elite are aware that numerous social sectors in Spain benefit from immigration, including the large number of middle-class families which hire immigrant workers for domestic service or the care of children or the elderly. This constitutes a social support base for permissive policies towards immigration. In addition, the idea that immigrants are needed in order to save the pension system, which is threatened by an ageing Spanish population, has become generalized despite the fact that specialists have not reached a consensus in this regard (Herce and Jimeno, 2003).

On the other hand, public opinion surveys show that the very fast increase in immigration over the last few years is beginning to cause unease among the autochthonous population which still is the least racist and xenophobic in Europe. At present, immigration is perceived as the second most important problem in Spain, after unemployment. Sixty per cent of interviewees believe that there are already too many immigrants in Spain, 56 per cent maintain that provisions regulating immigration are more tolerant than they should be, and the fear of the labour competition of foreigners and its effect on salaries is high and increasing. Spaniards tend to associate immigration with the rise in criminality,[5] and the role played by immigrant Moroccans in the terrorist attack of 11 March 2004 has led to greater pessimism regarding immigrants' integration (Real Instituto Elcano, Barómetro, January 2006, www.realinstitutoelcano.org).

Distrust and ill-feelings are especially strong among the population of the zones where immigration is concentrated, that is to say, in Madrid and the Mediterranean coast, where feelings of rejection towards immigrants appear the strongest.[6] Some outbursts of collective violence against immigrants have occurred in the Mediterranean area, such as the attack on Moroccans in El Ejido (Almería) in 2000, or the sacking of a Chinese footwear warehouses in Elche (Alicante) in September 2004 (Cachón, 2005).

Concluding remarks

Ten years ago, Spain was an almost monoethnic society and, in a very short period, it has become a country of immigration, with ten per cent of foreign-born population. A good part of its economic growth, one of the strongest in the European Union during this decade, is due to the presence of immigrants, although most of them have been, or still are, staying irregularly in the country. Their arrival has not been planned, and there have been no systematic or coordinated measures devoted to their social integration. Access to adequate housing is the main difficulty that immigrants face and it provokes or reinforces the tendency to their concentration in towns, while the right granted to regular or irregular immigrants to enjoy free access to health services diminishes the negative consequences of difficult living conditions in general.

The absorption by the labour market of more than four million immigrants in the last 15 years looks like a success history, but there are some clouds appearing in the near distance. The first one concerns Spain's ability to maintain its high rate of economic growth. The construction industry has been the main engine of this growth in recent years and it is beginning to show signs of exhaustion. It is not yet clear that in the next few years the economy will support the present high rate of employment of Spaniards and immigrants, many of whom will begin now to regroup their families. Moreover, despite having been in recent decades a scarcely xenophobic society, public opinion is beginning to turn against immigration, not only due to the role of Moroccan immigrants in the terrorist attack of 11 March 2004, but also to other criminal activities of some foreigners, and as a result of the tensions appearing in districts where immigrants concentrate. The increasing presence of immigrants as users in all kinds of public and social services, whose size and offer has

---

5   For the statistical relationship between criminality and foreign population in Spain, see Avilés, 2004.

6   See the barometer surveys on immigration carried out by the CIS (www.cis.es) and González Enríquez and Alvarez-Miranda (2005).

not grown at the same pace as population, sometimes provokes their saturation and the discontent of autochthonous citizens. In this situation, a brake on economic growth could have very negative effects on public opinion towards immigration and probably on public policies too.

References

Aparicio, R. and Tornos, A. (2003), 'Towards an Analysis of Spanish Integration Policy', in Heckmann and Schnapper (eds) *The Integration of Immigrants in European Societies*, 213–52. Stuttgart: Lucius and Lucius.

Arango, J. (2004), 'La población inmigrada en España', *Economistas*, **99**, 6–14.

Avilés, J. (2004), 'Inmigración y seguridad ciudadana', Working Paper of the Instituto Universitario de Investigación sobre Seguridad Interior. Madrid: IUISI.

Cachón, L. (2005), *Bases sociales de los sucesos de Elche de septiembre de 2004*. Madrid: Observatorio Permanente de la Inmigración.

CIPIE (2001, 2002 and 2003), *Inmigración y racismo* (Press Journal). Madrid: IMSERSO. (Publication ceased in 2003).

Consejo Económico y Social (2004), *Informe sobre la inmigración y el mercado de trabajo en España*. Madrid: CES.

Díez Nicolás J. and Ramírez Lafita M.J. (2001), *La voz de los inmigrantes*. Madrid: IMSERSO.

Garrido L. (2004), 'Para cuantificar a los extranjeros', *Economistas*, **99**, 28–37.

Garrido, L. and Toharia, L. (2004), 'La situación laboral de los españoles y los extranjeros según la Encuesta de Población Activa', *Economistas*, **99**, 74–86.

González Enríquez, C. (2005), '¿Qué Ofrece España a Los Inmigrantes? Factores de Atracción de la Inmigración', *Panorama Social*, **2**. FUNCAS, Madrid, 2005, pp. 102–111.

—— (2006), 'The Fight against Illegal Immigration, Smuggling and Trafficking in Human Beings in Spain: Ambiguities and Rhetoric', in Guild and Minderhoud (eds) *Immigration and Criminal Law in the European Union: The Legal Measures and Social Consequences of Criminal Law in Member States on Trafficking and Smuggling in Human Beings*, 325–45. Leiden: Martinus-Nijhoff.

González Enríquez, C. and Álvarez-Miranda, B. (2005), *Inmigrantes en el barrio. Un estudio cualitativo de opinión pública*. Madrid: OPI-MTAS.

Herce, J.A. and Jimeno, J.F. (eds) (2003), *Mercado de trabajo, inmigración y estado de bienestar*. Madrid: FEDEA-CEA.

Laparra, M. and Martínez, A. (2003), *Extranjeros en el purgatorio*. Navarra: Bellaterra.

Lorite García, N. (2004), *Tratamiento informativo de la inmigración en España, 2002*. Madrid: IMSERSO.

Martín Urriza, C. (2006), 'El modelo español de reclutamiento de trabajadores extranjeros. Un modelo barato', *Revista del Colegio de Economistas de Madrid*, **107**, 93–98.

MUGAK (2002), *Análisis de prensa 2002. Inmigración, Racismo y Xenofobia*. San Sebastián: MUGAK-Gobierno Vasco.

Nash N. (2005), *Inmigrantes en nuestro espejo: Inmigración y discurso periodístico en la prensa española*. Barcelona: Icaria.

Pajares, M. (1998), *La Inmigración En España*. Barcelona: Icaria.

—— (2004), *Inmigración irregular en Cataluña, análisis y propuestas*. Barcelona: CCOO.

Pereda, C., Actis, W. and de Prada, J. (2005), *Inmigración y vivienda en España,* Madrid: Observatorio Permanente de la Inmigración.

Triandafyllidou A. (2001), *Immigrants and National Identity in Europe*. London and New York: Routledge.

Veredas, S. (2003), 'Las asociaciones de inmigrantes en España: práctica clientelar y cooptación política', *Revista Internacional de Sociología*, **36**, 207–225.

Internet-based references

Pérez Díaz, V., Álvarez Miranda, B. and González Enríquez, C. (2002), *Spain and Immigration*, Barcelona: Fundación LaCaixa (available at www.estudioslacaixa.es).

Schneider, F. (2004), 'The Size of the Shadow Economies of 145 Countries all over the World: First Results over the Period 1999 to 2003', IZA (Institut für Zukunft de Arbeit) DP No. 1431 (available at www.iza.org).

Chapter 25

Sweden

Miguel Benito

The immigrant population in Sweden was 790,445 in 1990, or 9.2 per cent of the total population. At the end of 2004 the number of immigrants increased to 1,100,262 persons, or 12.2 per cent of the total population. Moreover, about 800,000 persons born in Sweden are children of parents from another country of origin. Together with their children they represent 21 per cent of the population today. Nearly 40 per cent of the immigrants who came to Sweden during the last 60 years have returned to their home country or have emigrated to a third country. The immigrant population includes nationalities from all over the world.

Immigration to Sweden is very restricted and is free only for citizens from the European Union and European Economic Area countries (EEA). There are very few asylum seekers who can obtain refugee status today. Still, it is possible to get a residence permit for humanitarian reasons.

The main reforms for immigrants took place in the 1970s. From 1990–2005 a new law on integration was passed. Moreover, a new immigration law was also passed on 31 March 2006 with the establishment of new Migration Courts for appeals against the decisions of the Swedish Migration Board.

The first immigration law was passed in 1913. Immigration from the Nordic countries has, since 1954, been ongoing and without restrictions, and the Finnish population remains the largest immigrant group to date. Labour immigration began at the end of the 1940s, the 1950s and part of the 1960s. It stopped at the end of 1969 after pressure from the trade unions and the creation of the Swedish Immigration Board. Since then the majority of immigrants who come to Sweden are either asylum seekers, or come for family reunification reasons.

Immigration from the EEA countries has been without restriction since 1992. Citizens from the new EU countries can also move freely into Sweden provided they find a job. Citizens from third countries can come to Sweden as refugees, for family reunion purposes, or for studies and research. Immigrants with a residence permit enjoy almost the same rights as Swedish citizens.

The immigrant population in Sweden: main demographic and social features

In the last 150 years, Sweden has been characterized by emigration. From 1851 until 1930, 1.2 million persons emigrated from Sweden. This period is referred to as the period of the great Swedish emigration. 1930 marks the start of Sweden as a country of immigration, as the number of immigrants grew in relation to that of emigrants. Indeed, from 1941 to 2005, nearly 2.5 million persons came to Sweden and nearly 950,000 foreign citizens left Sweden. This means that approximately 40 per cent of the immigrants returned to their home country or emigrated again to a third country. The issue of the return of the immigrants has, until now, been given very little attention by governments or by public opinion.

The agreement on freedom of movement between the Nordic countries in 1954 resulted in a very large emigration wave from Finland to Sweden. In the mid-seventies, there were almost half a million persons from Finland living in Sweden. Nowadays, the Finnish population in Sweden amounts to approximately 200,000 persons. A new immigration policy was approved in the Swedish parliament in 1968, which meant that immigrants coming from outside the Nordic countries would need work permits before arriving in Sweden. The Swedish Immigration Board was created in 1969 and, since 1970, the majority of immigrants to Sweden have been refugees. In the 1990s and 2000s the biggest refugee groups have come from Bosnia, Somalia, Iraq and Iran.

During the 1970s a reform programme took place, starting with a political reform allowing immigrants who are not Swedish citizens to vote in the municipal and regional elections. Other reforms included the teaching of the mother tongue at school, the teaching of Swedish for immigrants free of charge during working time, and equal social rights for all residents. Swedish public libraries were financially supported in buying books in various immigrant languages. Other religious organizations are also supported in the same way as other churches outside the official Swedish church. Equality, freedom of choice and co-operation (*jämlikhet, valfrihet* och *samverkan*) were the three honour words for this new policy, which lasted until 1997, when the Parliament approved a new integration policy for equal rights, responsibilities and opportunities.

In 1984, the responsibility for refugees was transferred from the Employment Office to the Swedish Immigration Board. Parliament decided that rather than being concentrated in few places, refugees should move to different cities around Sweden. This was called the 'whole-country strategy'.

In 1986, a new ethnic discrimination ombudsman was appointed. The ombudsman's work is to help immigrants in cases of discrimination due to their ethnic background. The entry of Sweden to the European Union in 1996 and the enlargement of the Union in 2004 have, so far, not led to a massive influx of people similar to that experienced with the Nordic agreement. In 2001, a new law on Swedish citizenship was implemented, allowing dual citizenship. It also allowed children of stateless parents to become Swedish from birth. In 2003, a new law on discrimination, which comprises all kinds of discrimination on the grounds of ethnicity, religion, sexual preference or handicap, was approved. Finally, a new law on immigration was approved in 2005 and was implemented on 31 March 2006. The main addition of this law is that the Appellation Board is replaced by three Migration Courts. At the same time, a provisional law made it possible for many asylum seekers who had received a negative answer to their refugee appeal to have a fresh chance to prove their case until 30 March 2006. This was possible thanks to a very large campaign by many NGOs, and especially the Swedish Church, to give amnesty to asylum seekers who had been in Sweden for a long time and whose application had been rejected.

Today, Sweden is faced with a more restricted refugee policy than before 1990. As a result of the appearance in 1991 of a new political party against immigration, New Democracy, and the war in the Balkans driving many refugees to come to Sweden, it became more and more difficult to cross the frontiers to Sweden. The Schengen Agreement was very soon implemented by the Swedish Government and the migration authorities. Later on, in 2004, a proposal was put forward in parliament by the government to restrict the free movement of citizens from the new EU-countries, but this proposal was rejected by the parliament and Sweden is one of the countries in Europe with free movement of persons between the old and the new EU Member States.

Table 25.1 shows the changes of the immigrant population during the last 35 years. The biggest percentage increase of immigrants in the last 15 years has been by persons from Asia and Africa, while in the 70s and 80s the increase was higher by immigrants from South America after the Pinochet military coup.

Table 25.1   Foreign-born population by region of origin (1970–2004)

Region	Population 1970	Population 1990	Population 2004
Nordic countries	320,913	319,082	277,103
Europe – other countries	176,463	220,806	392,637
Africa	4,149	27,343	65,249
North and Central America	15,629	19,087	26,515
South America	2,300	44,230	55,488
Asia	9,841	150,487	272,279
Oceania	558	1,866	3,517
Former Soviet Union	7,244	7,471	6,954
Unspecified	488	73	520
Total immigrants	537,585	790,445	1,100,262
Foreign-born as per cent of total population	6.7	9.2	12.2
Total population of Sweden	8,081,229	8,590,630	9,011,392

Source: Statistical Central Office. Work by the Immigrant Institute.

There are different ways of immigrating to Sweden:

Residence permits

Residence permits in Sweden are generally issued for three years, and are automatically renewed every three years. People who marry someone living in Sweden cannot obtain a residence permit before two years of residence in Sweden have passed. During that time they can obtain a permit for one year and, later, for one more year. If they divorce during this time frame, they lose the right to renew the residence permit and are asked to leave the country. The application for residence permits has to be filed before entry into the country, through Swedish embassies or consulates. If an individual attempts to arrive in Sweden and then apply for a residence permit, he/she automatically forfeits the right to the permit. Relatives may also obtain residence permits but, again, this procedure must be completed before their arrival in Sweden. In general, only wives/husbands and children under 18 years of age are considered relatives. Parents of adult immigrants can also obtain residence permits under special circumstances.

Work permit

Work permits are automatically granted to those with residence permits. In addition, work permits are also granted to experts and to asylum seekers after four months of being in Sweden and while they wait for a final decision of their asylum application. With regard to the latter, however, a work permit does not mean so much, as employers usually do not employ persons who do not speak the Swedish language.

Asylum

Traditionally, Sweden was characterized by a rather generous refugee policy. However, over the past 16 years this has gradually changed and has taken a more restrictive turn. From a country that had always welcomed refugees, Sweden has turned into a country where the majority of asylum seekers are not granted refugee status. With a restrictive policy there is no place for an anti-immigration party. But even if not so many can get asylum according to the UN Geneva Convention of 1951, they can get a residence permit for humanitarian reasons which, in practice, amounts to almost the same thing.

Asylum seekers could, until March 2006, send an appeal against a negative decision by the Migration Board to an administrative board called '*Utlänningsnämnden*' (Aliens Appeals Board). If the decision there remained negative, they could then be expelled from the country. For years, the opposition parties in the Swedish Parliament had criticized the Aliens Appeals Board for not taking decisions according to the law. In 2001, the parliament requested that the government pass a new law by which the appeals against the decisions taken by the Swedish Migration Board could be handled by a special migration court. First, in 2005, the government sent a bill to be approved by parliament for the creation of this court. This was possible thanks to the parties supporting the government, the Greens and the Left, who made this issue a precondition for supporting the Social Democratic Party in power. The appeals cases were transferred from the Aliens Appeals Board to the Administrative Migrations Courts from April 2006. The most significant difference is that the asylum seeker can present his/her case to the court and that the Migration Board has to present its reasons for refusing a permit to the court.

As a result of the war in the Balkans, the number of refugees granted residence permits in 1994 was 44,875. This decreased to 3,399 in 2004. The acceptance rate of asylum seekers has dropped to under ten per cent.

Since 2002 a new phenomenon has appeared in Sweden: that of the so-called 'apathetic children', or in official terms 'children with severe withdrawal behaviour'. During the last five years around 10,000 children have being waiting to be granted refugee status and many of them have got a negative decision not only once but often two or three times. They have been in Sweden for up to three or four years. Most of them come from former Yugoslavia or the former Soviet Republics and have seen persecution against their parents or relatives or witnessed torture. A government report (Asylum-seeking children with severe withdrawal behaviour, 2005) states that around 150 of these children have developed a sickness which makes them apathetic. A last report was published at the end of 2006.[1]

At the end of 2004, the Swedish Church started a campaign in favour of immigrant families with children who have been in Sweden for a long time. The 'apathetic children' was the first group the church and other humanitarian organizations asked the government to give residence permits to on humanitarian grounds.

Sweden perceives an administrative problem with asylum seekers who arrive without any personal documents confirming their identity. This situation has been the result of a perceived doubt on behalf of the authorities that those asylum seekers who carry documents were really persecuted in their country of origin. At the same time, however, it remains ironic that those without documents are also viewed with distrust as the Swedish authorities have no way of confirming their identity.

Today, Swedish authorities claim that almost 85 per cent of asylum seekers lack documents. Many asylum seekers are told by their helpers to throw their documents away before they cross the Swedish border so that they cannot be sent back to other European transit countries. This is partly a result of the Dublin Convention, which stipulates that an asylum seeker has to ask for asylum in the first country they come to, even if it was only a transit country. Sweden sends asylum seekers immediately to the first country when this is known.

---

1   SOU 2006:114.

The last years immigration and emigration flow is shown in Table 25.2. As emigration from Sweden is very seldom discussed it is considered important to have some figures about the relation between immigration and emigration.

Table 25.2   Immigrants and emigrants (1990–2005)

	Immigrants	Swedish citizens included*	Emigrants	Swedish citizens included**	Net immigrants
Total	905,020	186,601	537,804	272,241	367,216
Average per year	56,564	11,663	32,998	18,183	22,51

Swedish citizens resident in other countries are registered as immigrants when they come back and register in Sweden.
**They can be Swedish citizens by birth or naturalised Swedish citizens who want to return to their original country or to migrate to a third country.*
Source: Statistical Central Office. Work by the Immigrant Institute.

Undocumented immigration

There is a group of immigrants who do not seek work permits, but work and stay illegally in Sweden. Despite possessing documentation regarding their identity, this group is also counted by the Swedish authorities as non-documented. This is because they lack a residence permit. Some of them work with fake documents. People, especially from South and Central America, are told to come to Sweden by travel companies under false promises of work. Groups supporting immigrants are working to legalize their situation, but the government has, so far, refrained from getting involved in an official discussion, as it is not possible to know if these immigrants are living illegally in the country given that they are not registered. Humanitarian organizations working for refugees believe that there are approximately 10,000 persons in this situation. Experience indicates that those persons also spend a short period of time in Sweden, during which they work without permission. However, the degree of social control is so extensive that they usually feel that they must leave the country. There are no official reports on this issue.

Finally, Sweden also faces the problem of human trafficking. A lot of work is being done by the police to stop it, but without much success so far. There are an estimated 200 women who are exploited in this way, but there is a current lack of research on this issue.

Citizenship

Sweden applies the rule of *jus sanguinis* in the case of citizenship. In 2003, a new law made it possible for children born in Sweden to get Swedish citizenship more quickly than the adults if the parents desired it, independently of the nationality of the parents. Children who, as a result of their parents being stateless, were found stateless themselves, can now register as Swedish citizens from birth.

Table 25.3   Naturalizations by former nationality (1997, 2000 and 2003)

Previous citizenship	1997	2000	2003
Europe	13,22	22,042	14,909
Denmark	296	310	310
Finland	1,882	1,389	2,816
Norway	186	289	395
Bosnia-Herzegovina	2,550	12,591	3,090
Yugoslavia/Serbia and Montenegro	6,052	5,134	2,061
Croatia	233	231	1,531
Poland	523	264	1,325
Romania	747	266	268
Russia	174	410	642
Federal Republic of Germany	118	154	209
Other Europe	1,061	1,004	2,262
Africa	2,525	4,634	2,520
Ethiopia	995	343	222
Somalia	491	2,843	1,121
Other Africa	1,039	1,448	1,177
North America	422	436	781
South America	1,230	1,457	1,159
Chile	545	687	548
Peru	244	332	205
Other South America	441	438	406
Asia	9,187	12,669	11,812
India	207	173	120
Iraq	2,328	4,181	4,678
Iran	2,423	2,798	1,350
China	302	434	675
Lebanon	33	366	388
Syria	567	693	1,218
Thailand	343	525	443
Turkey	1,402	1,398	1,375
Vietnam	601	580	330
Other Asia	981	1,521	1,235
Occania	19	5	116
Former USSR (excluding Russia)	151	–	–
Other countries incl. stateless persons	1,528	2,230	1,925
Total	28,884	43,473	33,222

Source: SCB Befolkningsstatistik (www.scb.se). Part 4.

There are different ways of becoming a Swedish citizen through naturalization. Immigrants from the Nordic countries, including Norway, can become Swedish citizens after two years of residence. They only need to register in the national demographic register run by the tax authorities. Persons with refugee status can become Swedish citizens after four years. They have to apply to the Swedish Migration Board. On average, the application procedure can take from several months to one year to be approved. Other immigrants can apply for Swedish citizenship after five years of residence in Sweden. The price for the application is 1,500 Swedish crowns, which is equivalent to more than 155 euros.

In some cities there is a municipal ceremony on 6 June (or on the eve), which is Swedish National Day, where those who have become citizens during the last 12 months are welcomed as Swedes by the local authorities. Until the mid-1970s, knowledge of the Swedish language was a precondition for Swedish citizenship, but this condition disappeared with the new reforms taken after 1976, and especially with the introduction of the right to vote in local elections for foreign nationals (which was voted in Parliament in 1975 and implemented for the first time in the 1976 elections). The Popular Party, which for many years personified unconditional support for refugees, had, nevertheless, proposed in its 2002 programme to make knowledge of Swedish compulsory for those willing to become Swedish citizens. The party almost doubled the votes received in 2002 thanks to this and other similar proposals in relation to immigration policy, but their influence in parliament remains marginal.

Statistically, 50 per cent of all foreign-born persons resident in Sweden for five years or more become Swedish citizens. There exists, of course, a big variation between naturalization from one to another country of origin depending on the socio-political situation.

Table 25.3 shows some of the countries from which larger numbers of immigrants apply for Swedish citizenship. Interest in becoming a Swedish citizen is very low for citizens from the Nordic countries or from the European Union. For nationals of other countries it is more important.

Immigrant rights and participation in public life

The Swedish constitution guarantees freedom of assembly, freedom of association and freedom of speech. Registration is not required in order to start an association for whatever purpose. This applies even to immigrants, as the constitution does not mention them specifically. Financial support for migrant organizations is under the same conditions as those for Swedish organizations.

Some Swedish municipalities also engage in a dialogue with immigrant organizations in so-called 'immigrant councils'. As the municipalities are autonomous in deciding, there is a large range of variation between municipalities. In some municipalities the 'immigrant councils' have a consultative status, while in others the immigrant council is an umbrella organization for representatives from organizations to engage in a dialogue with the municipality as well as other parts of society.

Sweden was a pioneer in the rights of immigrants and especially in their participation in municipal elections. Indeed, as mentioned above, immigrants residing in Sweden for more than three years can both vote and be elected. Unfortunately, the vote of immigrants who are not Swedish citizens dropped from 60 per cent in 1976 to 38 per cent in 2002. There are some studies carried out by the Universities of Stockholm and Gothenburg as well as by the Integration Board and the former Immigration Board, but they cannot explain why immigrants vote in local elections less than Swedish citizens. The only reason appearing in all the reports is that immigrants, as long as they do not become Swedish citizens, do not feel concerned with Swedish society to the extent that they want to participate politically. Swedish citizenship is still required for voting in parliamentary elections. Almost 7 per cent of parliamentary seats were occupied by naturalized immigrants after the 2002 elections. Indeed, from the very beginning, Swedish legislators have aimed to give immigrants the same rights and responsibilities as those given to Swedes.

Moreover, as soon as asylum seekers obtain their residency permit, they have the same treatment as other immigrants. The only difference is that the authorities have a programme for integration of refugees during their first three years, which does not apply to other immigrants. When a refugee and his/her family obtain a residence permit they are placed in a municipality through an agreement with the Integration Board and the municipality. The idea is that the family learns Swedish at the beginning before they get a job, while the children go to school.

Persons with temporary permission as married persons or students cannot be granted social security or other rights before they get a permanent permit. In the case of married couples, this means that one spouse is dependent on the other, given that he/she does not qualify for social rights by themselves through employment. The right of residence is not renewed if they divorce before 2 years have passed. Otherwise, immigrants are not excluded from non-contributory social rights, including family benefits, child allowances and housing benefits.

Many of the reforms of the 1970s were directed towards the improvement of the cultural rights of immigrants. The creation of the National Cultural Board in 1974 followed the idea of giving economic support to immigrants' activities in their own language, as well as in Swedish.

Public municipal libraries provide literature and magazines in the languages of immigrants living in the municipality. There is also a national distribution centre for the less used languages, so that everybody may have access to literature in their own language through their local library. Today, after a new law on ethnic minority status was adopted by Parliament in 2000, the cultural support is different from immigrants belonging to an ethnic minority group accepted as such. The minority status applies to language, not the country of origin. The languages accepted as minority languages are Sámi, Finnish, Tornedalen Finnish, Yiddish and Roma languages.[2]

During the seventies and eighties there was widespread support of cultural immigrant organizations by the Swedish municipalities. This is still the case, but many municipalities have either reduced the total amount provided or they have more or less decided not to continue with the economic support.

Immigrant children have had the possibility of studying their mother language officially since 1977. This was partly possible thanks to the work of two Finnish researchers, Tove Skutnabb-Kangas and Pentti Toukomaa,[3] who emphasized the importance of learning the mother tongue to improve the efficiency of learning Swedish and participate in school. Before 1977 it depended upon each municipality and, in consequence, on whether the community was interested in the issue. Nevertheless, since 1990, there has been a move to not fully support the idea of learning the mother language at school. This has partly been the case following a debate of some leading immigrants who were against the teaching of the mother tongue at school, claiming that it posed an obstacle to integration. By law, however, immigrant children are guaranteed the right to study their own mother tongue in school. Almost 50 per cent of immigrant children attend these classes.

Freedom of religion is safeguarded in the Swedish constitution. This means that religious organizations have the right to exist and work in Sweden. However, often, when immigrants want to build a mosque or even a church for a lesser-known Christian congregation, there are very often protests from the local population. These protests are mostly centred on the issue of location, environment and practical problems such as parking or heavy traffic, even if these reasons are sometimes used as excuses to disguise different reasons such as prejudice and a negative attitude

2   Regeringens proposition (1998).
3   Skutnabb-Kangas and Toukomaa (1976).

towards specific groups. There is not much research on this issue, but a large number of newspaper articles show that this happens very often.[4]

The Swedish Church has, until recently, been the official state church. In 2000, it was first decided to separate the Swedish Church and the state. The Swedish Church still maintains some privileges with regard to the right to collect taxes and also the responsibility for the cemeteries, for which all employed persons pay taxes regardless of their religious beliefs.

There are co-operation committees between different religious denominations at the national level as well as at the regional level. The government provides economic support through these committees. No distinction is made between churches where the majority is Swedish and other religious groups run by immigrants. The existing discrimination applies more or less to the local people's refusal to allow the building of mosques or other religious facilities.

The Swedish Immigration Board became two different organizations in 1997: on the one hand, the Swedish Integration Board, with the task of working for integration in society, and, on the other, the Swedish Migration Board, with responsibility for immigration permits, assignment of refugee status and citizenship.[5] A division of power in the government was also introduced: there are now two Ministers, one for integration, since January 2007 in a new department of Integration (earlier as part of the Ministry of Culture and until the end of 2006 in the Ministry of Justice), and the other as Minister of Migration, placed in the Foreign Office.

There is no restriction of membership of political parties for immigrants. Although immigrants are not affiliated to the same degree as 'natives', there is still a considerable level of participation at all organizational levels of political parties. Some parties even have special sections just for immigrants, in order to help them to participate in their own way. The Social Democratic Party has many sections, each of them for a specific language or country group, mostly in Stockholm.

Another form of political activity is home-country related. Immigrants establish Swedish sections of political parties that are active in their home countries. Many immigrants come as refugees from countries which have been or still are under authoritarian regimes and, therefore, their work is often aimed towards changing the political situation in their home country. This is allowed by the Swedish law and even supported to different extents by the Swedish political parties.

The challenges of the immigration policy of today are threefold. First is the integration of immigrants living in the suburbs. There are many reports about the so-called 'one million programme'. This refers to the one million apartments built during the 1960s and 1970s to address the shortage of dwellings in Sweden. Many suburbs of the big cities were created very quickly and are not so attractive today. The more recently arrived refugees are placed together in these downgraded urban areas.[6]

Second is the discrimination young people, children of immigrants, face when searching for a job. Despite the fact that they can be born in Sweden, can be Swedish citizens, and they have gone to Swedish schools, often they will not be called to employment interviews because their names are foreign. There is an increasing number of immigrants and children of immigrants who leave Sweden for other countries such as England or Canada after they have finished university in Sweden, thereby resulting in the brain-drain phenomenon.

Third, the high rate of unemployment among newly arrived refugees means that it may take a very long time for refugees to be accepted in society.[7]

---

4   Karlsson and Svanberg (1995).
5   Encyklopedi om invandring (online).
6   På rätt väg? (2002).
7   Ekberg (2004).

Currently, there is a debate to open the country to third-country citizens. The trade unions are still opposing the idea, as they fear a slump in wages if immigration is opened up again. The right-wing parties discuss the possibility of accepting immigrants for both very qualified work and for household purposes as well.

While there was agreement about immigration policy in the 1960s and 1970s between the political parties and the trade unions, this changed during the 1990s as a result of the influence of the xenophobe party called New Democracy.

A government proposal, *Sverige, framtiden* och *mångfalden* (Sweden, the future and diversity)[8] was sent to the Parliament and was approved in 1997. This marked the end of the immigration policy and the beginning of a new integration policy which focuses on the whole population. Also, the municipalities began adjusting their practices to the new integration policy, and created integration bodies with a less concrete task than the immigrant service used to have.

The disagreement between the political parties began to increase with the governmental proposition *Sverige, framtiden och mångfalden* in which 'integration policy' was introduced, and the immigration policy was not dropped but changed in words.

The Popular Party was the party that fought New Democracy from the beginning, supporting immigrants and refugees, and was supposed to support the new integration policy. Nevertheless, they too soon changed their strategy in the 2002 elections, with a list of demands for immigrants and with an idea that the Social Democratic integration policy had failed. They doubled their seats in parliament.

Since 2001 the number of asylum seekers who have obtained a residence permit has been dropping drastically each year. On the other hand, the restrictions posed in the neighbouring country Denmark do not apply to Sweden. There has been some immigration from Denmark to the south of Sweden by Danes and other residents. Persons under 24 years old who marry a person from a third country without a residence permit may not live together with that person in Denmark. Some of these couples move to Sweden. Family reunion is a well established right in Sweden.

Public and media discourses on migration

Swedish Radio airs programmes in 15 immigrant languages, while Swedish television has programmes in Sámi and Finnish. Immigrants themselves are involved in community radio, and publish around 200 magazines in 40 languages. The content varies depending on the country of origin. Some magazines are orientated towards the integration of immigrants into Swedish society, while others are engaged in the political struggle in their home country. They nevertheless play an important role in immigrants' life, despite the fact that they are not so well known to the public.

The Swedish media play an important role in the shaping of immigration policy. Integration and discrimination have dominated the Swedish mass media regarding immigrants, and they have been addressed through three different issues.

The first issue has been the restricted refugee policy, where the media have criticized the authorities' decisions. Many cases of families and persons who have been rejected as refugees have been followed by the media over long stretches of time, even after they have been expelled to their home country.

The second issue has been the increasing opposition to immigration, especially from some political parties. New Democracy won a place in Parliament thanks to media campaigns. The party

---

8   Regeringens proposition (1997).

was dissolved before the following elections of 1994. Overall, it is not widely accepted in the media to argue against immigration and almost any criticism is labelled as racism.

The third issue has been the increasing discrimination in some areas of public life, especially in restaurants and nightclubs, as well as the discrimination that immigrants face when they are searching for work or an apartment to settle in.

During recent years, a new discussion has surfaced about Muslims' right to, for instance, wear a veil in school, or start private religious schools. There is a fear of isolation, which doesn't improve integration in society.

There have also been some vendetta and honour killings by members of families originating from the Middle East. The media have reported extensively on this phenomenon, but a distinction has been made between religion and the cultural and social background in which these murders have been possible. The same applies to the circumcision of girls, mainly from East Africa, a practice which is forbidden in Sweden.

While the media, in general, side with asylum seekers as long as they have not got a residence permit, and also support more open immigration, immigrants themselves are commonly presented as a problem by the media.

There is a big difference in the media in how they approach the areas where mostly Swedes live and the areas with a bigger concentration of immigrants. A big difference is that while criminality committed by Swedish persons is seen as an individual case, when criminality is committed by immigrants it is still seen collectively, especially if it is committed by people from the big housing estates. Statistically there is no substantial difference between immigrants and Swedes.[9] There is some awareness of the prejudices of the media in this area and the new trend is to try to employ journalists coming from the immigrant groups themselves.

Concluding remarks

The integration of immigrants continues to be the main issue in Swedish public life. A discussion on whether to allow immigration for work purposes as well as a new awareness of the difficulties refugees face to get permission to stay in Sweden is currently under way.

For a while now, Swedish immigration policy is going to be very restrictive as authorities do not want to give refugee status to asylum seekers. The fear of some politicians about an increasing number of persons coming to Sweden from the new EU-countries and making use of Swedish social security did not prove to be a real threat.

At the same time the authorities are worried about the easiness with which persons can move freely between countries. Overall, criminality today no longer seems to be associated with immigrants to the extent it was before. There is still difficulty for the labour market in integrating immigrants and refugees, despite the amount of work done by authorities and organizations. As in many other countries there are also racist groups. The confrontation between groups is well portrayed in the media. As mentioned at the beginning of this chapter, there is no political consensus today in Sweden as to what integration means. With the change of government that took place in the autumn 2006 a new integration policy is announced. The government decided as a first step the close of the Integration Board after the 30th of June 2007. The issue of integration is probably the major challenge that Sweden, along with other European countries, will have to face in the twenty-first century.

---

9   Ahlberg (1996).

References

Ahlberg, J. (1996), *Invandrares och invandrares barns brottslighet: en statistisk analys.* Summary in English: Criminality amongst Immigrants and Children of Immigrants.

Asylsökande barn med uppgivenhetssymtom – trauma, kultur, asylprocess (2006), Stockholm: Fritze. (SOU 2006:49).

Asylsökande barn med uppgivenhetssymtom - ett svenskt fenomen år 2001-2006 (2006), Stockholm: Fritze. (SOU 2006:114).

Asylum-seeking children with severe withdrawal behaviour – status of knowledge and survey (2005), Report 2005:2 from the national coordinator, Sweden, for children in the asylum process with severe withdrawal behaviour. Stockholm: Fritze.

Ekberg, J. (ed.) (2004), *Egenförsörjning eller bidragsförsörjning? Invandrarna, arbetsmarknaden och välfärdsstaten,* Rapport från Integrationspolitiska maktutredningen.

Karlsson, P. and Svanberg, I. (1995), *Moskéer i Sverige. En religionsetnologisk studie i intolerans och administrativ vanmakt* (Mosques in Sweden. An ethnological and religious study in intolerance and administrative powerlessness). Uppsala: Svenska kyrkans forskningsråd.

På rätt väg? (2002), *Slutrapport från den nationella utvärderingen av storstadssatsningen* (Norrköping: Integrationsverket). (In the right way? Final report from the National Evaluation on Resources invested in the Big Cities).

Regeringens Proposition (1998), *Nationella minoriteter i Sverige.* (Proposition 1998/99:143) (National Minorities in Sweden).

Regeringens proposition (1997), *Sverige, framtiden och mångfalden. Från invandrarpolitik till integrationspolitik* (Proposition 1997/98:16) (Sweden, the future and pluralism. From immigrant policy to integration policy).

Skutnabb-Kangas T. and Toukomaa, P. (1976), *Teaching migrant children's mother tongue and learning the language of the host country in the context of the sociocultural situation of the migrant family.* Tampere: University of Tampere.

Internet-based references

Encyklopedi om invandring [online] (Borås: Immigrant-institutet) (available at http://www.immi.se/alfa/, accessed 20 May 2006) (Encyclopedia on immigration).

Chapter 26

United Kingdom

Franck Düvell

The UK qualifies both as a country of immigration and of emigration. Given that the majority of its current immigration is of a temporary nature, the UK can, perhaps more precisely, be described as a country of temporary migration flows. Moreover, conventional categories of emigration and immigration no longer provide an adequate conceptual framework. Rather, migration to the UK is better thought of in terms of global integration and global geographic mobility.

In the early 1970s, after less than three decades of barely regulated post-war flows from the Commonwealth, the UK closed its doors to further immigration, as did other European countries. As a consequence, labour migration came to a halt, but family reunification increased. The late 1980s were characterized by an inflow of refugees, whilst irregular migrants became a prominent feature in the 1990s. Meanwhile, low levels of unemployment, high demand for workers, and relatively successful equal opportunities legislation facilitated increasing migration. Successively, legal migration channels have been introduced and previous restrictions have been liberalized, culminating in a policy of open borders toward Eastern Europe.[1] The interplay between economic growth and migration is further intensified by the UK's successful bid for the 2012 Olympic Games. Consequently, migration will almost certainly continue.

Major developments in Britain's immigration policy

The British Isles have always been a region of migration movements: first Saxons, Danes, Vikings and Normans; then Huguenots; later Jews and refugees from continental Europe and, throughout history, large numbers of Irish immigrants. From the eighteenth century onwards, Britain's ports accommodated small communities of seafarers and other migrants from its overseas colonies who, after the abolition of slavery in 1833, were free to settle in the UK. The two World Wars led to the settlement of non-white service personnel and of displaced persons and refugees from Germany and Poland. But, it was only the specific historical conditions following the Second World War – the economic boom, the demand for cheap labour and a liberal migration policy within the British Commonwealth – which set the conditions for mass immigration from outside of Europe. Labour migration from Southern Europe (Italy, Spain and Portugal) or the Mediterranean (Cyprus) was comparably small in numbers.

The key events and main periods of non-European immigration that ought to be highlighted are the following. First, the arrival of the steamship 'Empire Windrush' in 1948 signalled the starting point of post-war Caribbean mass immigration which peaked in the 1950s. Up to 1976, the Black Caribbean immigrant population grew to 500,000 people. Immigration from the Indian sub-continent dates back to the settlement of servicemen and seafarers after the First and Second

---

1   With the exception of Romania and Bulgaria, which joined the EU in 2007, and the European non-EU countries.

World Wars. Asian mass immigration, however, began ten years after West Indian immigration, namely around the late 1950s. Nonetheless, it soon outnumbered West Indian immigration. Indian, Pakistani and Bengali immigration reached its first height in the 1960s and continued at such high levels well into the 1970s, reaching over one million people in the late 1970s. A third source of mass immigration is related to the expulsion of Asians from the newly independent African states, namely Uganda, Kenya, Malawi and Tanzania. By 1981, 155,000 African Asians had immigrated to the UK. Further immigrant populations were Chinese (often, but not only, from Hong Kong), West Africans (from Nigeria, Gambia, Sierra Leone and so on), Cypriots (Cyprus was under British control until 1960) and Somalis. In fact, many of the UK's post-war immigrants were actually refugees, victims of early ethnic or religious 'cleansing' (Muslims in India and Hindus in Pakistan), displaced by post-war policies or Africanization policies (for instance Indians in Uganda). On the other hand, the UK accepted, actively encouraged and, to a lesser extent, recruited migrant labour for its post-war economic development. The years following immigration restrictions (1968 and 1971) were characterized by family reunion, asylum immigration, the temporary migration of students and, to a lesser extent, labour migrants.

The first immigration restrictions were introduced in 1905 when the Aliens Restrictions Act, aiming to restrict East European Jewish immigration, came into force. Subsequent acts were the 1948 British Nationality Act, which granted freedom of movement to all Commonwealth citizens, and the 1962 Commonwealth Immigrants Act which introduced work voucher quotas. The 1968 Commonwealth Immigration Act then restricted African Asian migration. Finally, the 1971 Immigration Act ended primary Commonwealth immigration altogether. The 1981 Nationality Act withdrew the right to settlement for most Commonwealth citizens. Numerous follow-ups introduced visa requirements (1986), regulated asylum applications and appeals (1993) or dealt with illegal employment (1996). These restrictive measures have, recently, been further reinforced by the 2002 Nationality, Immigration and Asylum Act (NIA). As a result, the legal framework is complex and fragmented.

Meanwhile, there exist around 85 different immigration categories, each with specific rights, conditions and limitations. The three major immigration categories are the European Economic Area (EEA) and Swiss nationals, EU-8 and EU-2 nationals,[2] and non-EU/non-EEA nationals. Separate treatment of EU-8 and EU-2 nationals with regard to employment is only a temporary measure. Non-EU nationals are then further categorized on the basis of the purpose of their entry into the UK. The purpose may range from tourism to reunification with family members, students, au pairs, businessmen, asylum seekers and labour migrants. The latter are further distinguished between work permit and permit-free categories. There exist numerous labour migration categories, according to profession or skills level. Here, mainly in the areas of overseas domestic workers and agricultural workers, they are regulated via quotas but, overall, most are not. The immigration system is constantly changing and further major reforms lie ahead.

Regulations for asylum seekers, as laid down in the 1999 Immigration and Asylum Act, are rather stringent. Until 1996, when changes to the immigration rules came into force, asylum seekers were basically free to choose where to live, had access to benefits and were entitled to work. With rising numbers of applications, numerous restrictions have been imposed. One very important one is, for example, that employment is prohibited. The 1999 Immigration and Asylum Act introduced the dispersal of asylum seekers throughout the country, their collective accommodation, and minimum provisions under the National Asylum Support Scheme (NASS). As a consequence, asylum seekers are cut off from communities of co-nationals and from refugee and exile organizations.

---

2   EU-8: Poland, Hungary, Lithuania, Estonia, Latvia, Slovakia, Slovenia, Czech Republic. EU-2: Romania, Bulgaria.

Even though the UK is not included on the list of countries known for having adopted major regularizations, two policies deserve to be mentioned. In 2003, a discretionary 'family amnesty' was granted to all asylum seekers who had a dependent minor, regardless of whether their case was pending or had even been refused. Until January 2006, 16,870 families had benefited from this measure. Furthermore, regulation is possible on humanitarian and compassionate grounds on a case-by-case basis, which was at the discretion of the Home Secretary.[3] In 2004 alone, 4,080 grants of settlement were issued on this basis, thus reaching a total of 48,360 persons since 1994 (IND, 2005). Finally, in summer 2006, the new immigration minister Liam Byrne did not rule out a possible amnesty for irregular migrants (*Daily Telegraph*, 14 June 2006).

Overall, it appears that UK immigration policy is structured along four dimensions. First, the government encourages economic migration and offers 'legal [migration] routes', aiming at a) providing for the needs of UK-based businesses, and b) reducing illegal movement (Home Office, 2002). Second, it intensifies, at least in its rhetoric, its efforts to combat illegal immigration and employment, but without adequately gearing-up immigration enforcement agencies. Third, it concentrates on reducing asylum migration and on removing failed applicants. Finally, more recently, the external aspects of migration control have been highlighted, including the nexus of migration and development.

The immigrant population in the UK: main demographic and social features

Identifying the size and composition of the UK's immigrant, refugee and ethnic minority population is not an easy task. There are ten different data sets to be considered, all of which show considerable discrepancies. The five main sources are the 2001 Population Census, the International Passenger Survey, the Home Office's annual immigration control figures, the annual Labour Force Survey, and the statistics from the Department of Social Security. None of these is comparable with any other, nor can their interpretation be consistent. Whilst the population census does not cover immigration status but only asks for country of birth, immigration control figures and passenger surveys only reflect annual inward movements – no departure records are held – and do not show the status or size of the foreign population in the country. For example, in 2002 the number of immigrants admitted as students was 369,000, but this figure does not show the total number of overseas students residing in the UK in that year. Furthermore, the census question for 'country of birth' only distinguishes migrants by their nationality, while they may be overseas-born whites, blacks or Asians. Moreover, the question for ethnicity only offers the Indian, Pakistani, Bangladeshi, Chinese or 'other' nationalities, thereby not allowing any room for other ethnic groups such as Kashmiri, Bengalis (who can be Indian), Tamils and so on. In addition, the 'Black' category only distinguishes between Caribbean, African and 'others' and does not differentiate between, for example, Twee-speaking Ghanaian, Mandingo-speaking Gambians, or even French-speaking nationals from Ivory Coast. The question for 'ethnicity' can even produce unexpected outcomes. For instance, Turks may chose to tick 'white', 'black', 'Asian' or 'other'. Finally, the four most commonly used categories – ethnic minorities, foreign-born nationals (migrants), foreign-born workers, asylum seekers/refugees – show considerable overlap.

For decades, the UK's rising numbers of passenger arrivals illustrate increasing global mobility and increasing interconnectedness. Since 1994, figures have increased by 50 per cent and, in 2004, amounted to 97.2 million. The figure of non-EEA passengers, however, has increased by only 30 per cent. The majority were returning UK nationals, whilst 17 million were from the EU and

---

3   Under the provisions of the Nationality, Immigration and Asylum Act (NIA) 2002, the long-residence concession was meanwhile brought within the scope of the Immigration Rules.

another 12 million from non-EEA countries. Amongst these arrivals were tourists and businessmen, students and workers, family members and irregular immigrants.

Since 1983, the migration balance has been positive, though until 1993 the annual gain was small (Home Office, 2001, p. 39). During the period 1994–2004 however, the UK registered a positive net migration flow of 1,339,700 persons (ONS, 2005a). Of these, 877,400 were from the Commonwealth (trend increasing), 859,400 from other third countries, and 194,800 (trend increasing) were from the European Union. The statistics also show that the positive net migration of foreign nationals corresponds to a negative net migration of 624,900 British citizens. The number of work permit holders has nearly tripled, family reunification has doubled, and the number of students has increased by about 18 per cent.

A specific dynamic is related to the 2004 EU enlargement. Passenger arrivals from the eight accession countries of Eastern and Central Europe nearly doubled from 677,000 in 2003 to 1.29 million arrivals in 2004. The main increase occurred between the second (262,000) and third quarter (602,000) (ONS, 2005b). Within 12 months, 232,000 EU-8 nationals registered with the Workers Registration Scheme (WRS) and by the end of 2005 this figure had increased to 345,000 (Home Office, 2006). The overwhelming majority of WRS applicants were Poles (131,290) followed by Lithuanians (33,775), Slovakians (24,470), Latvians (16,625), Czechs (14,610), Hungarians (6,900), Estonians (3,480) and Slovenians (250). These figures do not indicate, however, that 345,000 EU-8 workers had been in the country at that time, the overwhelming majority of whom only stayed for short periods of time.[4] The same source suggests that an additional 30 per cent did not register, and therefore worked irregularly (ALP, 2005).

Between 1996 and 2004, 498,149 applications for asylum (excluding dependants) were received (trend decreasing). The total number of refugees, asylum seekers and persons under temporary protection in Britain is not known (see Stewart, 2004), because no data on departure are kept (only enforcement actions are recorded), and Home Office data on persons and addresses are not disclosed. Between 1996 and 2004, 131,340 asylum seekers and their dependants have been granted settlement as refugees or because of leave to remain (IND, 2005). In 1998, and according to various calculations, the total number of refugees and asylum seekers was between 220,000 and 300,000 (Kelly and Joly, 1999). The numbers shows a sharp decrease in 2004. Applications went down to 33,960, mostly because there were fewer applications from Somalis, Zimbabweans, Sri Lankans and Iraqis and from former Yugoslavia, Angola and Algeria (Home Office, 2005a). Table 26.1 brings together the numbers of immigrants in the various categories.

The overwhelming majority of migrants are temporary migrants. These include work permit holders, those under the Workers Registration Scheme, students and au pairs. Those who finally get settled seem to be migrants whose circumstances change due to marriage, because of employment extension, and employment which follows the end of university studies. Otherwise, migrants coming under provisions of family reunification (89,095 in 2004), refugees (19,490 in 2004), work permit holders, and permit-free employees (17,530 in 2004) seem to be a major source of settlement cases. Altogether, these amounted to 139,260 in 2004. By and large, acceptance for settlement has tripled since 1992.

---

4   According to some sources the average staying time was only one month (ALP, 2005).

Table 26.1   Immigrants in the UK by immigration status

All immigrants/foreign nationals 2004		2,854,000
Work Permit holders incl. dependants (2002)		120,115
Workers Registration Scheme (2004-2005)		232,000
Seasonal Agricultural Workers Scheme (SAWS) (Quota)		25,000
Sector-based Schemes (SBS) (Quota)		20,000
Highly Skilled Migrant Programme (1 2001-9 2002)		3,721
Domestic workers (Quota)		9,000
Working holidaymakers		42,000
Au pairs		12,800
Students		369,000
Husbands, wives and children (probationary year, 2002)		31,750
Refugees	Total (refugees, asylum seekers, temporary protection in 2002)	350,000–420,000
	Refugees, exceptional leave to remain incl. dependants (1993-2002)	135,500
Asylum applicants awaiting decision in 2002		*106,630

Sum of first applications (84,130) and cases awaiting outcome (41,300), minus an overlap of at least 18,800 cases which have been received within the previous six-month.
Source: Author's compilation.

For a long time, no estimates of the illegally resident population existed (National Audit Office, 2004). However, recent figures published by the Home Office suggest that there might be between 310,000 and 570,000 irregular immigrants in the UK, with a median of 430,000 (Home Office, 2005a). Many were thought to be of Eastern European origin. While 70,000 of these regularized their stay due to EU accession (Home Office, 2006), another 120,000 are assumed to have ignored registration procedures and to have continued working irregularly (ALP, 2005). Meanwhile, in 2004, only 36,550 illegal entry actions were initiated (IND, 2005). There are reasons to assume that the number of illegal immigrants is below the estimated average of other European states for two reasons. First, the extent of the shadow economy in the UK was 12.6 per cent of the GDP in 1999/2000, well below the OECD average of 18.0[5] (Schneider, 2002, p. 17). This comparably lower UK level appears plausible because of the lower level of regulation. Low taxes and more entrepreneurial freedom create an economic environment which results in fewer incentives for strategies to deal with irregulars. Equally, trends toward a liberalization of immigration regulations by way of, for example, increasing legal migration channels, further close the gap between individual aspirations and institutional goals. Thus, migrants find more opportunities for legal migration whilst there are fewer incentives for irregulars strategies. It is usually assumed that illegal immigrants do not only come from the 'typical' emigration countries (India, Pakistan, Poland and so on), but also from the USA, Canada and Australia. Indeed, it is estimated that up to 40,000 illegal immigrants from Australia alone live in the UK (JCWI, 1999). These are assumed to be mostly overstaying their working holidaymaker visa.

In 2001, according to a Home Office report, 8.3 per cent (4.9 million) of the total population of the UK (58.7 million) was born outside the UK (Kempton, 2002). This is almost twice as many as in 1951 (4.2 per cent). Almost a third of the total migrant population currently living in the UK arrived during the last decade, thereby reflecting the increases in migration through all channels over this period (ibid.). Around ten per cent of the population (5.75 million people), including Irish people, have community roots outside of Britain (Parekh, 2000, p. 372). According to the Office

---

5   It was 16.3 per cent in Germany, 27 per cent in Italy and 28.6 per cent in Greece.

for National Statistics (ONS, 2001), 4.9 million people are defined as belonging to ethnic groups 'other than white'. In 1995, nearly half of Britain's ethnic minority population was estimated to be born in the UK (CRE, 1995, p. 1), thereby not counting as foreign-born. It must be assumed that, whilst the size of the foreign-born population is known (excluding the illegally residing population), the ethnic minority picture is blurred.

Among the overseas-born population, country of birth does not always correspond closely with ethnic origin. Overseas-born people from the White ethnic group are the most diverse with regard to their countries and continents of birth. One in five (21 per cent) were born in Ireland and a further two in five (41 per cent) were born elsewhere in Europe. Substantial proportions of overseas-born White people were also born in Asia (11 per cent), North or South America (11 per cent), Africa (10 per cent) and Oceania (6 per cent). These are often white residents from Hong Kong or South Africa returning to where their parents or grandparents once emigrated from.

Table 26.2   Population by ethnicity

Ethnicity	Number	Born overseas	% of total population	% of all ethnic minorities
Total population	58,789,194	4,900,000	100	
White	54,153,898		92.4	
- Irish	691,000		1.0	
All ethnic minorities	4,635,296		7.9	
Mixed	*677,117*		1.15	11.0
All black	*1,148,738*		1.95	
- Black Caribbean	565,876	238,000	1.0	13.6
- Black African	485,277	322,000	0.9	12.9
- Black Other	97,585		0.1	1.5
All Asian	*2,331,423*		3.97	
- Indian	1,053,411	570,000	1.7	21.7
- Pakistani	747,285	336,000	1.3	16.7
- Bangladeshi	283,063	152,000	0.5	6.1
- Chinese	247,403	176,000	0.42	4.2
Other Asian	*247,664*		0.4	4.7
Other ethnic	*230,615*		0.39	7.4

Source: Census 2001, author's compilation.

The table on ethnicity (Table 26.2 above) does not further identify groups with a distinct background, and in particular groups categorized as 'white.' For example, East, South-East and Central Europeans, such as Poles, Russians, citizens from the Baltic republics, citizens from former Yugoslavia, Hungarians, Turks and Cypriots are not separately recorded.

In 1995, 'it is estimated that some three-quarters of them [ethnic minorities] are British citizens' (CRE, 1995, p. 1). Meanwhile, and because of positive net immigration, this has decreased to an estimated 47 per cent who have acquired British citizenship (Kempton, 2002). Fifty-four ethnic or national groups have been identified that are larger than 10,000 individuals. Nineteen have more than 50,000 members (see Table 26.3). The 2001 Census reveals that the UK today is more culturally diverse than ever before.

Table 26.3   Country of birth and size of community in the UK

Irish Republic	691,000	Cyprus, Greek and Turkish	78,000
India	409,000	Poland	74,000
Northern Ireland	245,000	Australia	73,000
Pakistan	234,000	Hong Kong	73,000
Germany	216,000	South Africa, Black and White	68,000
USA	143,000	Canada	63,000
Jamaica	142,000	Middle East	57,000
Kenya	112,000	France	53,000
Bangladesh	105,000	Uganda	51,000
Italy	91,000	Ghana	30,000

Source: Census 2001.

In all, some 200 languages are spoken. Regarding major religious faiths, 37 million are Christian: 26.2 million Anglican or Episcopalians, 5.7 million Roman Catholics, 2.6 million Presbyterians, 1.3 million Methodists, and 500,000 belong to Pentecostal and Holiness Churches communities (Parekh, 2000, p. 236). Other religious groups are Muslims (1.55 million), Hindus (550,000), Sikhs (330,000), Jews (260,000) and Buddhists (144,000) (ONS, 2003b).

Immigrant and refugee communities are not equally distributed throughout the UK, but are concentrated in England. Of their total, 95.5 per cent (or 9 per cent of the population as a whole) are concentrated here, whereas only 5 per cent live in Scotland and Wales. In 2001, 45 per cent of the black and minority ethnic (BME) population resided in Greater London (19 per cent of all residents) and another 8 per cent in the South-East of England. Thirteen per cent live in the West Midlands (Birmingham conurbation), 8 per cent in the North West (Liverpool, Blackburn), 7 per cent in Yorkshire & Humberside (Bradford) and 6.3 per cent in the East Midlands, mainly Leicester, where they represent one-third of the population. There are 23 constituencies with a BME population between 40.5 and 66.3 per cent in Vauxhall and East Harrow respectively (ONS, 2003b). Eighty-five per cent of all refugees and asylum seekers reside in London or the South-East.

Ethnic minorities display socioeconomic features that distinguish them from the average population which indicate that they still suffer from disadvantages and discrimination.

Compared with a national average of 79.6 per cent of economic activity, the rate for ethnic minorities is 65.3 per cent. This is mainly because women are less likely to be economically active. However, economic inactivity is also due to a higher level of students (over 30 per cent) compared with the average (21 per cent). White men and ethnic minority women are more likely to be in full-time employment than black men or white women. The level of self-employment between white and BME groups is similar, but Pakistanis are most likely, and Black Africans are least likely, to be self-employed. Whites are over-represented in production, whilst ethnic minorities are over-represented in services, hotel and catering, and transport, indicating a racially segmented labour market. Unemployment is more than twice as high for BME men and women alike, as for white people (9.6 per cent compared with 4.6 per cent), whilst ethnic differentiation shows that Indians are least likely to be unemployed (4.8 per cent), whereas the contrary is true for Pakistani women (20.2 per cent) and Bangladeshi men (15.7 per cent). In terms of income, average pay is £8.00 per hour for whites and £7.50 for ethnic minorities, on average. In sum, white men earned more than black men in 2005, but black women earned more than white women (CRE, 2006a).

Performance and opportunities vary greatly between ethnic groups and sexes. Whilst deficiencies in English seem to be the main obstacle to successful participation in school, pre-school education has been identified as crucial for future educational performance. Bangladeshi and Afro-Caribbean pupils 'fare worse at school', whilst those who have English as an additional language achieve less than the others. On the other hand, Indian and Chinese out-perform all other groups, and girls often out-perform boys. Ethnic minorities are much more likely to be at university than white youths (26.9 per cent white, 35.5 per cent Asian, 31.3 per cent Black, 63.4 per cent Chinese) (see CRE, 2006b).

With respect to housing, only 56 per cent of ethnic minorities compared with 71 per cent of the white population are owner-occupiers, 28 per cent (whites 19 per cent) are in social housing. They are more likely to live in overcrowded conditions (2 per cent white, 7 per cent Indian, 9 per cent black, 23 per cent Pakistani/Bangladeshi), in poor housing (13.7 per cent white, 22.9 per cent black, 18.6 per cent Indian, 34.8 per cent Pakistani/Bangladeshi) and in poor neighbourhoods (27 per cent of the ethnic minorities, 10 per cent whites). These figures illustrate disparities in housing conditions and some level of residential segregation (CRE, 2006c).

Naturalization

It is pertinent to note that the UK also has three categories of citizenship, British Citizenship, Citizens of the United Kingdom and Colonies, and Commonwealth Citizenship. Whilst the first two categories have 'right of abode' and are therefore not subject to immigration control, the right of abode only applies to certain categories with Commonwealth Citizenship. Most Commonwealth citizens are subject to standard immigration controls and restrictions, such as limits on stay, as well as to particular regulations on marriage and employment. In order to qualify for UK citizenship, a minimum of a legal five-year stay in the UK is required, one year of which must be with an 'indefinite leave to remain' status. The 2002 Nationality, Immigration and Asylum Act introduces new naturalization requirements such as good character, sound mind, ceremony, oath, and language proficiency and will be coming into effect in 2007.

Between 1993 and 2002, citizenship was granted to 736,205 people. This indicates a rising trend since 1999. Of the 139,350 people granted citizenship in 2003, 32 per cent were from Africa, 24 per cent from the Indian sub-continent, 14 per cent from European countries outside the EEC area, 8 per cent from the Americas and 5 per cent from the Middle East (Dudley and Woollacott, 2004). Looking at the decade from 1992 to 2002, 34 per cent of grants of settlement in 2001 were from Africa. Indeed, the Indian sub-continent accounted for 21 per cent. The Middle East and the remainder of Asia accounted for 19 per cent, Europe 10 per cent, the Americas 10 per cent and Oceania 5 per cent. Usually, between about two-thirds and three-quarters are dependents of people already settled in the UK, and between one-quarter and one-third are accepted in their own right. Of the latter category, in 2000 about two-thirds were refugees, but in earlier years these provided for only a tenth of the total number (1990). Given that the number of asylum seekers has been decreasing since 2003, refugees will account for less and less. It must be assumed that many of those having been granted settlement will also apply and most of the time will also be granted citizenship. See Table 26.4 for numbers naturalized and settled.

Table 26.4   Naturalizations and settlement

Naturalized citizens (1993–2002)	736,205
Grant of settlement (1992–2002)	847,150

Source: Immigration and Nationality Directorate (IND) 2005.

Immigrant rights and participation in political life

After a period of exclusion, discrimination, and racism which, during the 1970s and 1980s resulted in a strong 'black social movement' and a series of inner city uprisings, the tide has changed. Since the mid-1980s, and even more so since the mid-1990s, serious efforts have been made to address exclusion, discrimination and racism. This, however, has not met with complete success, as the figures above have indicated. The legal framework and the conditions of ethnic civic participation are rich and complex. What is clear, though, is that there are no legal restrictions on the civic participation of foreigners, immigrants or refugees of any kind.

Whilst the initial 1965 Race Relations Act was only of a declaratory nature (Layton-Henry, 1984), its successors, the 1968 and the 1976 Race Relations Acts, went much further. The 1968 Act made discrimination unlawful and set up an enforcement agency – the Commission for Racial Equality (CRE) – which has been successively provided with statutory powers. Moreover, the 1976 Act finally defined racial discrimination as discrimination based on colour, race, nationality (including citizenship), and ethnic or national origins. Racial discrimination did not, however, include discrimination based on religion or beliefs (for criticism see Parekh, 2000). It covers all areas of employment, education, housing and, more recently, urban planning. The major innovations were i) the distinction between direct and indirect discrimination, ii) granting individuals access to courts and iii) the introduction of legal remedies (for example compensation). Shortcomings of this act were finally revealed in the course of the McPherson Inquiry (1999) into the murder of Stephen Lawrence which, for the first time, acknowledged the existence of institutional racism. The 2000 Race Relations Amendment Act introduced and strengthened the 1976 Race Relations Act in its application to public authorities, which now have a general duty of promoting race equality. This requires public authorities to: eliminate racial discrimination; promote equal opportunities; and promote good relations between people of different racial groups. (For an overview of the history of the racial equality legislation and its regulations see House of Commons, 2000.)

While the UK does not have a written constitution, the 1998 Human Rights Act serves this purpose to some extent. Whilst reinforcing anti-discrimination it allows the restriction of the 'political activity of aliens' (Article 16). In particular, under the 2000 Prevention of Terrorism Act and the 2001 Anti-Terrorism, Crime and Security Act, a limited number of associations of immigrants have been banned. Civil rights organizations often criticize, and increasingly so since 9/11, the fact that entire immigrant communities have been put under surveillance and, thereby, intimidated, discriminated against and limited in the exercise of their civil rights (see, for example, Statewatch bulletin or European Race Audit, several issues).

On the other hand, concepts of social cohesion and social inclusion have gained relevance. Since the beginning of the millennium, the government has been deliberately enhancing the participation of all parts of society in public affairs, policy and decision-making, at the local, regional and national levels. For example, the Treasury's Public Service Agreement (PSA 8) with the Home Office aims to build strong and active communities to increase civic participation (HM Treasury, 2004). As a result, a space is created in which civil society organizations can manoeuvre.

In particular, ethnic minority, immigrant and refugee communities are encouraged by the Home Office to have a stake in society (Home Office, 1999; for a detailed analysis see Düvell, 2005).

The right to vote depends on being registered in the Electoral Register. This is regulated by the 1983 Representation of the People Act and a 2000 substitution. The right to vote is based upon nationality and residence. Basically, British, Irish, EU and Commonwealth citizens of over 53 countries who reside in the UK and who are in the electoral register are entitled to vote as well as run for election, whilst migrants from non-Commonwealth countries are not. Even illegal immigrants considered to be from a Commonwealth country may find that they can both register and vote due to the lack of immigration checks. In addition, Operation Black Vote was launched in August 1996, thereby encouraging African, Asian, Caribbean and other ethnic minority communities to participate in policy life. Electoral registration and turnout is normally high, and often above average. However, in 2004, only 12 out of the 652 Members of Parliament were of an ethnic minority background, there were 18 members of the House of Lords, and 662 local councillors (3 per cent of 21,498 councillors in England and Wales). Of course, these figures are not at all commensurate with the proportion of the ethnic minority populations.[6]

The Labour Party, the Liberal Democrats, to some extent also the Conservative Party, and also the Trade Union Congress and member trade unions actively encourage the participation of BME members in their organizations. Even more encouraged, and increasingly well funded, is civic participation on all levels. The National Council for Voluntary Organisations, the National Association for Voluntary and Community Action (a network of 360 local voluntary and community sector organizations), London Voluntary Service Council and, more specifically, the Council of Ethnic Minority Voluntary Sector Organisations represent over 9,000 BME community organizations. Research (McLeod, 2001) on 5,500 Black and Minority Ethnic Organizations (BMEO) found that 90 per cent had a formal legal status and 50 per cent had a regular annual income between £50,000 and £250,000. Furthermore, over half reported a rising income.

BMEOs mostly serve people with significant social and economic needs, and commonly work on a town or borough basis. Many originate from specific ethnic, cultural or religious backgrounds. Services include education and training, health support, welfare and legal advice and advocacy, day care facilities, housing and accommodation, cultural, sports and other leisure activities. Some research (Craig et al., 2002) is nevertheless sceptical about the impact such agencies have on local policy. In addition, while women's organizations play a key role in community development, they are often understaffed and underfunded (Davis, 2002).

Finally, bodies such as:

- the 1990 Trust and its Black Information Link
- Ubuntu
- the Union of Muslim Organisations
- the Muslim Council of Britain
- the Council of Mosques
- the National Association of British Muslims
- the League of British Muslims
- the Indian Muslim Federation and
- the British Refugee Council

illustrate the well-organized nature of black, Asian, Muslim and refugee communities. Although competition may occur over funding and other issues no major tension is recorded.

---

6   A proportionate representation would be, for example, 36 MPs.

Public and media discourses on migration

During the 1970s, UK immigration discourse was dominated by racial considerations and race relations. A policy trade-off was developed whereby 'good race relations require firm immigration controls'. The 1990s, on the other hand, were dominated by an 'asylum panic', much of which is still noticeable today. Meanwhile, the discourse has become dominated by economic considerations. Improving national economic performance and labour productivity, and increasing labour market participation on the one hand, whilst on the other reducing benefits dependency, are at the heart of contemporary British politics. New Labour was anxious to rebut the Old Labour image of being hostile to financial and commercial interests. Instead, it promoted British business, emphasizing that the flexibility of UK labour markets gave Britain a competitive edge when compared to its European partners. Rooting out fraud of all kinds (avoidance of taxes, black markets, shadow labour markets, social security fraud) is another topic, albeit secondary when compared to the dominating economic goals. Furthermore, any discourse regarding the 'modernization' of public services is balanced between references to three major principles – individual freedom, entrepreneurial freedom and racial equality – and two major policies – promoting social inclusion and civic participation. Any regulations, in whatever policy field, have to be carefully balanced against these guiding principles. Finally, the UK Government is driven by the aim to win the public's confidence with regard to controlling immigration. Hence, pro-immigration measures are often combined with other, tough, measures. For example, asylum seekers seem to be sacrificed at the expense of labour migration, and liberal labour migration channels are complemented by tough enforcement measures.

The change of tide was marked by a speech of the then Immigration Minister, Barbara Roche, made on 8 September 2000 at a conference on 'UK Migration in the global economy' (at the Institute for Public Policy Research) in which major changes were announced. This speech reflected the dualism of UK immigration politics on migration issues in its attempt to balance the requirements of an open economy under conditions of global competition, and a society that embraces multiculturalism and racial equality but fears overcrowding, competition for collective goods and pressures on its public services. Migration was welcomed as a 'central feature' of a globalized environment, and one in which 'there are potentially huge economic benefits for Britain if it is able to adapt to this new environment' (Roche (2000, p. 1). Since then, 'properly managed legal migration' has become a prominent key phrase (Hughes, 2003). The UK perceives itself to be in competition with other EU countries with regard to skilled migrants and success in the economy and immigrant integration (Hodge, 2000). The positive economic effect of migration has since been frequently repeated (for example Home Office, 2005b) in an almost mantra-like manner. In line with this approach, public policy and media display a positive approach to immigration from the new EU-8 member states; despite concerns over the accession of Romania and Bulgaria. Meanwhile, this positive approach has been supplemented by, first, some emphasis on enforcement measures, specifically deportations of refused asylum applicants, and second, by security concerns triggered by 9/11. Moreover, as a result of the July 2005 terrorist attacks in London, concerns over cases of failing integration and occasional radicalization of immigrants have been expressed (Home Office, 2005b, p. 22).

In the mass media, a continuous battle is fought between 'restrictionists' and liberals. Whilst the liberal media (*Independent*, *Guardian*, *Observer* and *Times*) tend to emphasize the benefits of migration, the conservative *Daily Telegraph* is more likely to be critical and to emphasize the negative aspects. Two tabloids in particular, the *Daily Mail* and *News of the World*, are known for their anti-immigration stance (NCADC, 2004). The issue of immigration in the UK remains highly politicized and public opinion is volatile on this particular issue. Indeed, the government's strategy of restricting asylum but encouraging certain categories of economic migration remains fragile, and media discourse can often take a highly critical point of view on the matter.

Concluding remarks

The UK was for long a country of immigration and, after a period of rather closed doors, it has once again become a country of immigration. Both temporary and, to a lesser extent, permanent immigration are encouraged and facilitated, as is subsequent naturalization. Increasing immigration, continuous economic and job growth plus positive fiscal effects illustrate that the present arrangements seem to benefit migrants and host society alike. Because this liberal approach is motivated by overwhelming economic considerations, any change in economic conditions will affect immigration policy. Integration is considered comparably successful. However, whilst recent labour migrants seem to provoke no xenophobic backlash, asylum seekers and some ethnic communities bear the brunt of lurking racism. Moreover, recent terrorist incidents provide cause for concern over issues of alienation of some sections of the ethnic minority, immigrant and refugee population. Immigration ranks near the top of the list of public concerns and race relations are fragile. Hence, continuous proactive integration policies ensuring peaceful cohabitation must accompany liberal immigration policies.

References

ALP (Association of Labour Providers) (2005), *Workers Registration Scheme, the Case for Abolition*. London: ALP.

CRE (Commission for Racial Equality) (1995), *Ethnic Minorities in Britain*. London: CRE.

—— (2006a), *Employment and Ethnicity, Factfile 1*. London: CRE.

Craig, G. et al. (2002), *Contract or Trust? The Role of Compacts in Local Governance*. Bristol: The Policy Press.

Davis, S. (2002), *The Role of Black Women's Voluntary Organisations*. London: Joseph Rowntree Foundation.

Dudley, J. and Woollacott, S. (2004), *Persons Granted British Citizenship. United Kingdom 2003*. London: Home Office.

HM Treasury (2004), *2004 Spending Review: Supporting Britain's Communities*. London: HM Treasury.

Hodge, M. (2000), *Work Permit System Will Make it Easier for Firms*, Press Release 416/00. London: Department for Education and Employment.

—— *Strengthening the Black and Minority Ethnic Voluntary Sector Infrastructure*. London: Home Office.

—— *International Migration and the United Kingdom: Recent Patterns and Trends*. London: Home Office.

—— *Secure Borders, Safe Haven: Integration with Diversity in Modern Britain* (White paper). London: Stationery Office.

—— *Sizing the Unauthorised (Illegal) Migrant Population in the United Kingdom in 2001*. London: Home Office.

—— *Controlling our Borders: Making Migration Work for Britain. Five Year Strategy for Asylum and Immigration*. London: Stationery Office.

——*Accession Monitoring Report, May 2004–December 2005.* London: Home Office.

House of Commons (2000), *The Race Relations Amendment Bill*, Research Paper 00/27. London: House of Commons.

Hughes, B. (2003), '*Working in the UK' Website Goes Live.* Press Release. London: Immigration and Nationality Directorate.

IND (Immigration and Nationality Directorate) (2005), *Control of Immigration 2004.* London: Home Office.

JCWI (Joint Council for the Welfare of Immigrants) (1999), 'Time for an Amnesty?' *JCWI Bulletin* (Summer), 1–2.

Kelly, L. and Joly, D. (1999), 'Refugees' Reception and Settlement in Britain'. Unpublished report for the Joseph Rowntree Foundation.

Kempton, J. (2002), Migrants in the UK: their Characteristics, Labour Market Outcome and Impacts, *RDS Occasional Papers No 82.* London: Home Office.

Layton-Henry, Z. (1984), *The Politics of Race in Britain.* London: Allen and Unwin.

McLeod, M. (2001), *Black and Minority Ethnic Voluntary and Community Organisations: Their Role and Future Development in England and Wales.* London: Policy Studies Institute.

McPherson, W. (1999), *The Stephen Lawrence Inquiry Report.* London: Stationery Office.

National Audit Office (2004), *Asylum and Migration: a Review of Home Office Statistics.* London: National Audit Office.

NCADC (National Coalition of Anti-Deportation Campaigns) (2004), 'A Brilliant Success – European Wide Days of Action', *NCADC News Service,* 3 February 2004.

—— (2003a), 'Total International Migration: Time Series 1992 to 2001', *Country of Last or Next Residence.* London: ONS.

—— (2003b), *Census 2001: Report for Parliamentary Constituencies.* London: ONS.

—— (2005a), *Migration to the UK Rises*, News Release, 20 October 2005. London: ONS.

—— (2005b), *International Passenger Survey. Visits to the EU from the Enlarged Europe.* London: ONS.

Parekh, B. (ed.) (2000), *The Future of Multi-Ethnic Britain:* Report of the Commission on the future of multi-ethnic Britain. London:, Profile Books (for Runnymede Trust).

Roche, B. (2000), *UK Migration in a Global Economy*, Speech given at Institute of Public Policy Research (IPPR) seminar, 11 September 2000.

Stewart, E. (2004), 'Deficiencies in UK Asylum Data: Practical and Theoretical Challenges', *Journal of Refugee Studies,* **17**(1), 29–49. [DOI: 10.1093/jrs%2F17.1.29]

Internet-based references

Commission for Racial Equality (CRE) (2006b), *Statistics: Education.* London: CRE (available at http://www.cre.gov.uk/research/statistics_education.html, accessed February 2006).

—— (2006c), *Statistics: Housing.* London: CRE (available at http://www.cre.gov.uk/research/statistics_housing.htm, accessed February 2006).

Düvell, Franck (2005), *Civic Participation of Third Country Nationals in the United Kingdom.* Oldenburg: Universität Oldenburg (available at http://www.uni-oldenburg.de/politis-europe/download/UK.pdf, accessed June 2007).

ONS (Office for National Statistics) (2001), *People and Migration: Ethnicity* (available at http://www.statistics.gov.uk/cci/nugget.asp?id=455, accessed 4 August 2004).

Schneider, F. (2002), *The Value Added of Underground Activities: Size and Measurement of the Shadow Economies of 110 Countries all over the World.* Paper presented to Centre for Tax System Integrity, Canberra, 17 July 2002 (available at http://ctsi.anu.edu.au/workshop.schneider.doc, accessed 5 May 2004).

Chapter 27

Concluding Remarks[1]

Ruby Gropas and Anna Triandafyllidou

According to the latest data presented by the EU Commission (European Commission, 2006, p. 3), on 1 January 2003, 15.2 million persons residing in the 25 Member States were third-country nationals. This amounts to 3.35 per cent of the total EU-25 population. Moreover, the two million population increase that was registered in the EU-25 in 2005 was mainly due to registered net immigration of 1.7 million. Positive net migration has been recorded in almost all Member States with the exception of Estonia, Latvia, Lithuania, the Netherlands and Poland, while Cyprus, Spain and Ireland registered the highest rates.

Although such generalized information is useful in providing us with the global picture of migration trends, what the preceding chapters of this book have highlighted is that it is nearly impossible to provide accurate information on the size and nature of the third-country nationals' population in the EU. Available statistics do not offer a consistent and reliable numerical picture of immigrants within the EU. Each Member State uses different sets of statistical categories, different definitions, different ways of recording residents and citizens. Stocks and flows of immigrant populations (presented in the preceding chapters) are rarely, if at all, directly comparable.

Despite these difficulties in developing a meaningful comparison between the countries studied in this volume, we have to note that a basic trend is common across the EU: the past few decades have been characterized by significant population movements across and within the European continent. Europeans have increasingly migrated from east to west and people from around the world have increasingly migrated to EU Member States. All Member States, regardless of their geographical and population size, and irrespective of previous migration history, have experienced population movements that have altered the EU demographically, socially and – all the more so – politically. Migration is the main determinant of demographic growth in the EU and will unquestionably have far-reaching consequences and implications for the socio-cultural landscape of Europe, as well as for its labour markets and economies.

The 25 country chapters of this book provide a brief presentation of the immigration situation in each of the European Union Member States, the size of their immigrant population and recent trends of inflows and outflows. Each chapter has commented upon the different definitions of migration categories in the national policies as well as the different types of migration statistics kept by each country. Each chapter has also offered a brief overview of migration policy developments during the last 15 years or so and has outlined the main provisions and conditions for the participation of immigrants in public life. Last but not least, each chapter has discussed the main media and political debates in relation to migration.

Against this background, this chapter highlights and discusses critically some aspects of the national studies with special reference to a typology of countries (in relation to their migration experience), a typology of migration pathways, and a typology of migration regimes. These typologies constitute a first attempt to provide an overview and to compare different EU countries

---

1   This chapter draws from Cyrus et al. (2006).

without over-generalizing and with a view to recognizing and taking into account their different migration experiences. In other words, our aim in this chapter is to draw some comparative readings of the trends and issues currently characterizing EU migration patterns, while also pointing out some of the most marked differences.

Comparing experiences of migration

In this section, we propose a provisional typology (see Table 27.1) of migration experiences among EU countries which takes into account the following factors: relations between sending and receiving countries (for example, colonialism), past migration experience (earlier or recent conversion from senders to hosts, experience in migration management and integration policies), the size of the immigrant population (in absolute and relative terms, that is as percentage of the overall population), and the factors that have triggered migration flows (geopolitical changes, political or economic factors).[2]

Old host countries

During the first decades of reconstruction following the end of the Second World War, northern and western EU Member States shifted from being senders (for instance to the USA, Australia or Canada) to becoming hosts. France, Germany, Belgium, the Netherlands and the UK in particular have a relatively long immigration history related to their colonial past but also due to labour shortages after the end of the Second World War. These countries ran state or company-led recruitment schemes from Southern Europe as well as northern Africa, Asia and the British Commonwealth. Austria and Denmark joined this group more recently (since the 1970s) even though they have no special colonial ties to any countries. The migration pattern they have experienced is similar: economically motivated migration with migrants and their families gradually settling in large numbers.

At present, these countries are generally faced with ageing first-generation immigrants and the challenge of combating the social exclusion and marginalization of second- or third-generation immigrants. In parallel, the economic difficulties, or even crises, that characterize most of these economies and the accompanying social frustration are manipulated by extreme right-wing parties to gain voters. This has been steadily leading to the exacerbation of xenophobic reactions on the part of the majority populations. Religion, in particular Islam, is also becoming increasingly visible as a dividing factor between 'native'[3] populations and those of immigrant origin. These countries certainly have a long experience in migration and admission policies and have arguably developed elaborate (more or less successful) integration policies.

---

2   This typology pays less attention to the new forms of migration (King, 2002) (for example, shuttle migration, gendered migration, youth and study migrations, co-ethnic movements, asylum seekers under humanitarian protection) and to special aspects of a country's legislation related to co-ethnic returnees for instance. These aspects are discussed in the section on migration pathways.

3   The term 'native' is used in inverted commas to note that populations of immigrant origin are also often natives of the country of settlement.

Table 27.1 Typology of countries in relation to their migration experience

Category	Type of migration pattern	EU Country
Old hosts	• Long migration history • Sizeable migrant population • Initially economic migration later followed by family reunification • Currently: only high skill migrants welcome, limited low skill programmes for specific sectors • Advanced integration policies and relatively liberal citizenship policies • Public debates on migration are politicized and mainly concern the dilemma between multiculturalism and assimilation	Austria, Belgium, Denmark, France, Germany, the Netherlands, Luxembourg, Sweden, United Kingdom
Recent hosts	• Countries on the geographical periphery of Europe • Transition from emigration to immigration in the late 1980s or early 1990s • Large immigrant populations developed quickly • Ad hoc immigration policy planning (marked by repeated regularization programmes in the Southern European countries) • Limited and still hesitant integration policies • Public debates on migration focus on control, criminality, fears of losing national cultural authenticity	Greece, Italy, Portugal, Spain, Ireland and Finland
Countries in transition	• Former communist countries in Central Europe • Caught in between sending, receiving and being a place of transit for migrants • Performing well in terms of their economic and political transition to capitalism and democracy • Small legal immigrant populations but potentially growing undocumented immigration from Eastern European states outside the EU • Non-existent integration policies, debates on immigration are very limited	Czech Republic, Hungary and Poland
Small islands	• Very small island countries facing increasing migration and asylum-seeking pressures • Ad hoc immigration policy planning and very limited integration policies • Still experiencing emigration of their own citizens • Public debates on immigration concentrate on fears of being 'inundated' by foreigners	Cyprus and Malta
Non-immigration countries	• Very low levels of new immigration whether legal or irregular • Important population changes and minority formation in the course of the 1990s, resulting from recent nation state building and ethnic unmixing (Brubakers 1996)	Estonia, Latvia, Lithuania, Slovenia and Slovakia

During the 1990s, a gradual shift took place towards increasingly restrictive admission policies,[4] and towards a revisiting of their own integration policies. In an environment of heightened security concerns, the value and success of multicultural citizenship policies adopted by most of these European countries has increasingly been questioned (Gropas, 2007). Recent trends in their integration policies are marked by new (and in many cases stricter) integration obligations towards new immigrants, for instance through obligatory language and civic orientation courses. A telling example is the case of the Netherlands where, as of 2005, immigrants coming for family creation must pass an integration test in the Dutch embassy in their country of origin. Also, the Dutch Government has recently announced plans to require tests of Dutch language proficiency and knowledge of Dutch culture for labour migrants applying for an entry visa.

Recent host countries

Over the course of the last two decades, countries on the geographic periphery of the EU have seen their traditional emigration patterns being reversed and have become destination countries. This is the case for Southern European states (Greece, Italy, Portugal and Spain) and for smaller countries in the western and northern periphery of the European Union (Ireland and Finland).

In part, this reflects a gradual improvement in the economic situation and the living conditions in these countries. It has also, however, been an unintended side effect of the restrictive immigration measures taken by the UK, France, Germany and Switzerland since the mid-1970s. Moreover, immigration patterns in these countries have been significantly affected by the implosion of the communist regimes in Central and Eastern Europe and the liberalization of population movements from east to west.

The immigration experience in this group has been characterized by the absence of consistent migration policies – that is, policies with a long-term approach to the issues of admission and integration. This has led to a high number of migrants remaining in these countries unofficially or without proper documentation and to high numbers of illegal immigrants. This is particularly the case in Southern European countries, which have land and sea borders that are difficult to patrol and control. The irregular or illegal status that is common to large segments of the migrant population has implications not only for their employment conditions but also for their effective integration in the host society.

The large inflow of undocumented immigrants that has been common to the southern Member States has led to repeated regularization programmes as governments gradually admitted that the immigration situation was getting out of their control and that large populations were present in the country illegally. Since 1986, there have been five such programmes in Italy involving more than two million immigrants, and Greece has implemented three similar programmes of which the most recent was in 2005. Since 1992, Portugal has adopted four regularization initiatives and Spain began its third and most far-reaching regularization scheme in 2005.

Finland and Ireland have also recently been transformed from countries of emigration to host destinations and the largest influx came with the end of the Cold War. Traditionally, Finland has been a country with very restrictive migration policies, mainly due to its geographical position (bordering with the Soviet Union during the Cold War), while Ireland's economic situation did not render it a destination choice for migrants. Political and economic changes in the 1990s altered this, leading to a significant change in the socio-demographic and economic landscape of both countries. Unlike the southern EU countries in this general category, Ireland and Finland have not

---

4   Immigration policies in these countries had put a halt to recruitment of foreign labour since the mid-1970s as a result of the oil crisis and the slowing down of their economies.

been faced with noteworthy illegal immigration and they have been more proactive in formulating integration policies for the influx of newcomers and in particular for the integration of asylum seekers and refugees.

Countries in transition

The third group of countries experienced major changes in migration patterns since the 1990s fundamentally as a consequence of the 1989 'Autumn of Nations.' While these new EU Member States experienced large emigration towards the other EU states in the early to mid-1990s, they have also become transit migration countries and appear to be in the preliminary stages of becoming hosts of third-country immigrants. The inflow of immigrants is primarily from former Soviet Union countries (and in particular from Ukraine) or other neighbouring nations with which there was a formal relationship (for example between former Czechoslovakia and Yugoslavia).

In addition, small, albeit well organized, immigrant populations in these countries come mainly from Asia and in many cases are the continuation of migratory movements during the Communist times. Thus, we find small groups of Vietnamese or Chinese emerging in Poland or the Czech Republic. In addition, Central and Eastern European Member States have also become an attractive destination for entrepreneurs from Western Europe and the USA. These immigrants are predominantly involved in economic activities in the tertiary sector as highly-skilled managers, experts, consultants or scientists.

In all cases, the new Member States have encountered a series of challenges in the field of integration and administrative hurdles (lack of qualified personnel and financial means) in implementing integration initiatives and the national action plans for employment (European Commission, 2006, p. 7).

Small island countries

The islands of Malta and Cyprus have experienced increased immigration, both as transit and host countries, since the 1990s. Cyprus has received both legal and irregular migration in a pattern similar to that of Greece or other Southern European countries. Malta, by contrast, has been concerned with increasing amounts of illegal migration and growing numbers of asylum seekers and refugees who reach its coasts on wrecked dinghies from North Africa. What these two countries share is their small size, which makes even a few thousands or tens of thousands of foreigners a large population; their lack of previous experience with migration management and integration policies; and the developing xenophobic and racist attitudes among their populations. Debates in these countries frame migration in terms of fear and threat. At the same time, both island countries continue to experience emigration of their youth, who go to study abroad in other European countries and often remain there.

Non-immigration countries

For some of the former communist states, migration is still of minor importance. This is the case for the Baltic States, and also for Slovenia and Slovakia. With regard to the Baltic States, the previously steady migration flows from the former Soviet Union have generally ceased since the 1990s. Moreover, all three countries experienced a population decrease in the early to mid-1990s mainly due to the repatriation of Russian-speaking residents to Russia or other former Soviet states. These outflows have eventually levelled out after the first few years. The Russian speakers who chose to remain in these three countries have been turned into ethnic minorities through the process of nation building. In the case of Lithuania, minorities were given citizenship status and are therefore recognized as ethnic minorities. In the case of Latvia and Estonia, many among the Russian speakers were unable to acquire citizenship status and have therefore been labelled as immigrants who are permanent residents in those countries. Theoretically, these populations may be considered immigrants but they are in most cases second generation (as it was their parents who moved within the Soviet Union) and have known no other country as their own. The linguistic issue, and in particular the question of education in minority languages, has been the main policy issue in recent years and the main topic of public debates on 'immigration'.

The situation of Slovenia resembles that of the Baltic States to a certain extent, as part of its population stems from internal migration from other states of former Yugoslavia. There again, nation state building has led to problematic citizenship policies which were further complicated by the war in neighbouring Croatia and Bosnia. Slovenian immigration has mainly to do with former Yugoslav citizens from Bosnia or Serbia who now reside in Slovenia with or without appropriate legal status.

Slovakia has also been grouped within this set of countries because it has also experienced virtually no immigration other than transit migration towards the west and because it has similarly been affected by nation building. Slovakia has accepted a number of Czech citizens but has also 'lost' part of its population which chose to stay in the Czech Republic and naturalize. Currently, debates about migration have mainly to do with the movement of Roma populations between Slovakia and the Czech Republic and are tainted by prejudice and racism against this ethnic minority, regardless of their citizenship.

All five countries in this group may be characterized as non-immigration countries, as they have experienced very little immigration or emigration in recent years, except for population movements related to nation building. The special nature of these cases is that populations did not actually move; it was the borders that moved over them after the end of the Cold War, thereby changing their status or requiring them to change their citizenship.

Immigration pathways

The existing diversity in immigrant populations within the 25 EU Member States is the result of the history of migration flows in Europe, specific political and economic configurations between sending and receiving countries, geopolitical circumstances, and national differences in immigration policies. Below, we provide for a typology of the main 'old' and 'new' forms of migration in Europe today. Our classification includes the old typical labour migrations that were triggered by economic inequalities between the sending and the receiving countries and were managed through recruitment schemes and bilateral agreements. It also attempts to encompass new forms of migration that are more fluid, often irregular, involve circular or pendular movements between several countries, and are related to specific economic sectors of seasonal or heavy jobs.

To provide a structured scheme for comparison and categorization, we use here the term 'migration pathways' borrowed from the work of Psimmenos and Kassimati (2003). The term 'pathways' suggests sets of relationships, policies and opportunities that come together to form a specific pathway, a channel through which information and people flow between the sending and receiving country.

Based on this understanding and following from a comparative reading of the 25 country overviews, we have identified eight such main migration pathways that are analysed in turn below: the pathway of co-ethnics and returnees, the colonial and post-colonial pathway, the pre-1989 internal migration pathway, the labour migration pathway, the asylum-seeking pathway, the pathway of temporary and seasonal migration, the 'gold-collar' pathway and the pathway of irregular migration.

The pathway of co-ethnics and returnees

Favourable admission patterns for co-ethnics, returnees and their descendants are widespread across many Member States. In each case, preferential reception schemes are justified on the basis of unique historical circumstances and are excluded from general, restrictive immigration policies.

Two types of migrants can be distinguished within this pathway of migration: returnees and co-ethnics. Returnees are individuals born in the EU country, who have emigrated and have subsequently returned after a long absence abroad. Co-ethnics are descendants of emigrants or members of co-ethnic communities abroad who result from past migration movements. Co-ethnics may also be populations which are ethnically and culturally akin to the receiving country but which have never, in this or previous generations, lived in that country. In practice, the two categories are often merged, while the logic that regulates policies towards them is the same: they are of the same ethnic origin as the citizens of the receiving country.

While some EU Member States have a larger presence of returnees, other Member States have a higher proportion of co-ethnics. Poland is one country that clarifies this distinction; persons who emigrated from Poland as adults and returned to the country after the system transition (mainly from the USA) are considered returnees (also referred to as expatriates) whereas co-ethnics are the descendants of settlers and deportees, mainly from Kazakhstan. In the case of Germany, immigrating co-ethnics (*Aussiedler*) come mainly from Kazakhstan, whereas in Finland co-ethnics come from Estonia. Greece has received co-ethnics (Pontic Greeks) from the former Soviet Republics of Georgia, Kazakhstan, Russia and Armenia, and a large number of ethnic Greeks from Albania. Portugal's *retornados* are the descendants of former Portuguese settlers and come mainly from Angola and Mozambique. Swedish Finns and mainly Ingrian Finns are currently regarded as return migrants with special status in Finland. Hungary is also a country with a high number of immigrants of Hungarian ethnic origin. Indeed, since 1989, immigrants and temporary workers are mostly from ethnic Hungarian communities beyond the borders of contemporary Hungary (for example Romania, Ukraine and former Yugoslavia). Another country that has experienced co-ethnic migration, albeit in small numbers, is Italy. Here, immigrants (mostly from Argentina) who can identify Italian parenthood up to three generations prior, are still considered co-ethnics and have a preferential channel to naturalization. Finally, there has been an inflow of returnees towards the Baltic countries in recent years. This migration predominantly consists of a high percentage of repatriated citizens (returnees) who returned to Latvia, Lithuania and Estonia when independence was restored.

In all cases, the reception of co-ethnics and returnees is better than that of 'other' immigrants. They usually enjoy the right to naturalize through preferential channels and, even if they do not have the right to naturalization upon arrival, they enjoy privileged conditions compared to other migrants as regards the financial and institutional support provided to them by the state with a view to helping them settle down and integrate into society as smoothly as possible.

The colonial and post-colonial pathway

This pattern mainly pertains to Member States with a colonial past, and seems to have worked as a de facto substitute for the recruitment of workers. This is particularly the case for the UK, France, the Netherlands and, to a certain extent, Belgium, Spain and Portugal. In these countries, immigrants were granted access to the territory as citizens of the former colonies, with certain sets of rights associated with their status. The United Kingdom has received several immigrant groups from Commonwealth states of the West Indies, Asia and Africa, while France has received immigrants mainly from former African colonies (for example West Africa and the Maghreb). The Netherlands has welcomed former colonial subjects from Indonesia and Suriname, and Belgium has received migrants from its former African colonies such as the Congo (former Zaire), Rwanda and Burundi. Spain has large immigrant communities from Ecuador, Argentina and Peru, and the main countries of origin of immigrants in Portugal are Portuguese-speaking African countries (for example Angola, Cape Verde, Guinea Bissau, Mozambique), and Brazil. Initially, immigration from Africa and Asia mainly took place within the framework of post-colonial migration, but the receiving countries gradually put legal obstacles in place so as to curb post-colonial immigration.

In terms of immigrant integration, the colonial relationship has offered some advantages to the migrants in that they were usually familiar with the language, the culture, and even the institutions and political system of the colonial 'mother' country. It also brought with it important disadvantages such as prejudice, discrimination and racism that were built into the social and political system of the country of settlement and that were widespread among its population. Moreover, some colonial populations had had particularly traumatic and divisive experiences in their relationship with the mother country (for example Algerians in France) that could not be easily forgotten or settled (emotionally and politically) even if they lived in the mother country for decades.

Pre-1989 internal migration pathway

This pathway has mainly affected countries located in Central and Eastern Europe and the Baltic region. During Soviet rule, large population movements took place and, as a consequence, large numbers of Soviet citizens (mainly but not always of Russian nationality) settled in areas that became independent states after 1989. In these countries, internal migration movements were typical of the Communist era.

Communist countries in Europe had no migration relations with countries outside the Warsaw Pact. The governing regime tightly controlled emigration, and political reasons for emigration were often intertwined with economic motives. The Czech Republic (then part of Czechoslovakia) experienced immigration within the framework of 'international aid cooperation' schemes and the consequent intergovernmental agreements drafted between Czechoslovakia and other socialist countries including Poland, Yugoslavia, Hungary, Cuba, Mongolia, Angola and North Korea. In contrast, it is worth noting that there was hardly any immigration to Hungary between 1949 and 1989, with the exception of two politically motivated movements when Greek and Chilean communists were granted asylum protection in the early 1950s and 1970s.

Throughout the large-scale industrialization of the 1960s and 1970s, significant numbers of people from different parts of the Soviet Union (mostly from Ukraine, the then Byelorussia and Russia) settled in the three Baltic States. Because of nation state (re-)building, most of the settlers are now identified as foreign nationals. However, these populations are not the outcome of international migration but, rather, of formerly internal migration and the reshuffling of states and their borders.

What is common among these movements is that they all happened within the context of a centrally governed economy and an authoritarian society. They all resembled internal movements within some sort of 'empire' which was the communist part of the world. In some cases, populations that used this pathway to migrate were offered the opportunity to naturalize and to become fully integrated into their societies of settlement while, in other cases, naturalization has been very difficult and these groups remain labelled as foreign immigrants despite their long-term settlement in the receiving countries.

The labour migration pathway

This pathway includes two main patterns of movement that have historically been inter-related: initial labour migration that came as a response to labour recruitment by the receiving countries and, later, family reunification or family formation migration. This latter had to do with the settlement of the workers in their host country and their wish to bring their family over or to form a family with a person from the same country of origin.

The labour migration pathway is probably the numerically most important one in Europe today. It has been the dominant form of migration in Western and Southern Europe from the 1950s up to the present day. Recruitment programmes were implemented in the older host countries of Northern and Western Europe from the late 1950s until the early 1970s. These programmes, also known as guest-worker recruitment programmes, were established through bilateral governmental agreements mainly with Southern European and Mediterranean countries (such as Morocco and Turkey).[5] The recruitment was initially intended to be strictly temporary and recruited workers were expected to return to their country of origin. However, the return aspect of the agreements was not implemented in a strict and consistent manner. Instead, policies allowing for the repeated renewal of residence rights were commonplace. In the end, this led to settlement and subsequent family reunification migration. This has been the case for immigrants from Italy, Greece, Spain, Portugal, Yugoslavia, Turkey, Morocco and Tunisia who have settled predominantly in Germany, Sweden, France, Belgium, the Netherlands, Austria and Luxembourg. Although Italy, Greece, Spain and Portugal are EU Member States today and immigrants in these countries enjoy free mobility within the Union, immigration from the former Yugoslav states, Turkey and North Africa is still of third-country status. Today, family formation (marrying a partner from the parents' country of origin) is an important source of new immigration linked to this historical recruitment pattern.

The asylum seeking pathway

Since the mid-1970s, Western European countries have received three major migration flows from other parts of Europe that were initiated by political persecution and war. The first wave was from the socialist countries of Central and Eastern Europe. These migrants were perceived as legitimate refugees escaping communist suppression and received preferential reception until the end of the 1980s. Due to restrictive passport regulations in most socialist countries, the largest refugee migration came from the least restrictive Polish People's Republic. These migrants went primarily to Germany and secondarily to Italy, France and Greece when martial law was imposed in Poland in 1981.

The second most important refugee migration wave came from Turkey in the 1980s when members of the Kurdish minority and the religious minority of Alevits sought refuge predominantly in Germany, but also in Greece.

The third wave of asylum-seeking migration was a result of the civil war in former Yugoslavia. Between 1991 and 1995, hundreds of thousands of refugees arrived in Germany, the UK, France, Austria, Italy, Ireland, Sweden and Slovenia. These refugees only received temporary protection as civil war refugees and the majority have returned to their home country. However, a considerable proportion has remained in the receiving countries, among them Roma people who in particular have experienced problems of discrimination and intolerance in the countries of settlement.

---

5   There were also some bilateral schemes with more geographically distant countries, such as the scheme linking Germany and South Korea.

From the mid-1970s until the early 1990s, the number of non-European persons applying for asylum increased drastically throughout all EU12 and EU15 (at the time) Member States. The majority of asylum seekers came from countries affected by political intolerance, ethnic conflicts and civil or international wars. Accordingly, the main regions of origin were Latin America (Chile, Columbia, Ecuador), Africa (Ghana, the Republic of the Congo, Nigeria, Somalia), the wider Middle East (Palestine, Iraq, Iran, Algeria, Morocco) and Asia (Socialist Republic of Vietnam, Sri Lanka, Afghanistan).

As a response to the constant rise in the number of asylum applications, by the mid-1990s some European countries had made the relevant regulatory frameworks and assessment criteria more restrictive. Germany, for example, has changed the respective article in its Constitution with a view to reducing the numbers of asylum seekers that selected Germany as their destination-country. This change has made provisions for asylum seekers who are legally identified as being from 'safe countries' to be returned to their country of origin. Changes in asylum-seeker reception policies in some countries have also resulted in the partial shift of asylum applications to other destinations. Thus, there is currently an increasing trend for asylum applications in Poland and other Central and Eastern European countries from Chechen refugees, for instance.

The pathway of temporary and seasonal migration

Temporary migration programmes have also been a permanent feature of migration regimes. The recruitment programmes of the 1960s were planned and propagated as temporary programmes, although not administered accordingly, and resulted in the settlement of recruited workers. After the recruitment stopped in the early 1970s, temporary programmes were used with greater reluctance in many countries. However, with the implosion of the communist regimes in 1989 in Central and Eastern Europe and the liberalization of population flows that resulted, older programmes increased in scope or new temporary programmes were introduced in order to find a legal way to respond to the pressure of migration.

Temporary immigrants from non-EU countries have responded to the structural imbalance of developed economies in Europe. They have occupied specific niches in the secondary labour market, becoming cleaners, home carers, construction workers and generally filling jobs in the lower-skilled, more labour-intensive and volatile sectors of the economy. Seasonal migrants have been a similar case, accepted mainly for jobs in agriculture and tourism or catering services. Temporary and seasonal recruitment programmes have been adopted by several EU countries (including for instance Austria, France, Cyprus, Greece, Italy, Germany and the UK). The aim was to provide a legal path for migrants to enter these countries and fill positions that were not taken by natives because they were low-pay, low-prestige jobs with difficult working conditions. Whether these temporary and seasonal labourers have remained temporary sojourners or have legally or illegally converted into long-term migrants is a question only half explored.

The 'gold collar' pathway

During the last 15 years there has also been increasing temporary and permanent immigration of highly qualified professionals such as managers, investors and business persons, researchers in academia and industry, engineers in multinational companies, sport professionals and people in the arts in the western and southern EU countries. This migration occurs to a lesser extent in the new Member States in the east. Immigration law often provides for preferential treatment for highly qualified people and even when there are no such provisions in the law, implementation practices tend to be different when it comes to multinational company employees or highly qualified professionals. This group is also referred to as 'knowledge migrants' in the Netherlands.

Although some highly qualified migrants have received particular media attention and have used their position to defend the cause of other immigrants, the majority of these migrants seem to be largely invisible and are not considered part of the immigration issue. In recent years, the discourse in many countries has had a tendency to actively address the issue of attracting this 'gold-collar' immigrant labour force. It is perceived to be a major challenge for developed economies (especially of the larger EU Member States such as Germany, France and the UK) to attract and keep a part of this highly qualified, multilingual, internationally mobile cosmopolitan elite, in order to enhance the knowledge-based competitiveness of their economy. The UK for example has created the Innovators immigration category since 2000 to encourage the immigration of innovative entrepreneurs, and the Highly Skilled Migrant Programme since 2002 to supplement its labour market needs (European Commission, 2006, pp. 17–18). Numerically speaking, this pathway involves a rather limited number of immigrants in Europe today.

The pathway of irregular migration

A large percentage of new immigrants in EU countries are undocumented. Owing to either the gradual establishment of restrictions on migration or the absence of an appropriate migration policy, a proportion of the immigrant population currently has or has had an irregular or illegal status. Some have entered host countries illegally; others have entered with a valid visa or residence permit and have overstayed or abused their visa. Depending on the control regime of the receiving country, some undocumented migrants may only work in unregistered jobs in the shadow economy, whilst others may work in registered jobs. While old host countries generally reject regularization campaigns as an option and react with further internal controls to curb irregular migration, recent host countries have made regularization or the so-called 'amnesty' programmes their main axis of immigration policy. Gaps in the regularization laws, inefficient public bureaucracies, and the lack of incentives for employers to ensure or facilitate the legal status of many migrants have complicated the situation. This has led to the perpetual revitalization of this pathway, which is constantly re-fuelled by new irregular immigration or where migrants live in limbo, shifting frequently between legal and illegal status. In effect, a common story of many third -country nationals falling into this category involves illegal entry, later regularization of their status but, often, the inability to retain official status when their permit is due for renewal, for a variety of reasons ranging from lack of a proper work contract (that is full, formal employment with social security benefits, and so on) to not satisfying other requirements (for example, they risk bringing their family to the host country even if their family reunification application is rejected because their taxed income is not sufficient). This contributes to the marginalization and exploitation of a significant part of the immigrant labour force.

Comparing integration policies and practices

A comparative examination of immigrant integration practices regarding naturalization regimes, the granting of local voting rights and the extent of immigrant participation in the civic and political life of the host countries presents a rather disjointed picture. Immigrants encounter very different integration prospects and opportunities depending on the country in which they live, on the rights that may be linked to their specific country of origin and to their individual status, as well as to the implementation of rights at the local level.

A full comparative overview of the conditions and regimes for immigrant integration in the EU countries would go beyond the scope of our chapter. Therefore, we have chosen to address two topics that, we believe, are of crucial importance for immigrant integration and that may also be considered as emblematic of the 'integration philosophies' (Favell, 1998) currently present within the Union. Thus, we discuss the naturalization options and the different types of migrant status available to third-country nationals in the EU-25 and the question of local voting rights.

Naturalization and migration status regimes

All 25 EU Member States have participation regimes that distinguish between their own nationals, EU citizens and third-country nationals. As a rule, only own-country citizens enjoy full political and civic rights, while third-country nationals (non-citizens) are subject to different kinds of restrictions. Within the immigrant population, however, there are also numerous distinctions, depending on the status of the individual and the specific national group to which s/he belongs.

Most states have designed a variety of migration status levels for specific groups – temporary workers, asylum seekers, family members of settled immigrants, immigrants with renewable residence permits and permanent residents. Each type of permit may encompass a specific set of rights which more or less deviates from citizens' rights, and which changes from country to country, in spite of EU efforts (that is, the European Commission mainly) to define minimum conditions. While legal permanent residents sometimes enjoy full equality except for enfranchisement at the national level, undocumented workers may be de facto excluded from all rights or may only be allowed to access specific services such as emergency health care. Asylum seekers may be restricted in their mobility in various ways ranging from detention and an obligation to live in specified places, to being forbidden to leave a municipality or region.

Full political and civic rights and obligations may be acquired by immigrants from third countries through the naturalization process. Most EU states primarily base citizenship on ancestry (*jus sanguinis*) rather than on place of birth (*jus soli*), although most citizenship laws contain elements of both. Member States also differ in their acceptance of dual citizenship and, hence, their requirement for the migrant to abandon her/his citizenship of origin if s/he is to naturalize.

The naturalization process is long and complicated in almost all countries, requiring a very long list of documents that should accompany the application. Naturalization rules often also include vague conditions that are open to different interpretations during their day-to-day implementation by administrative personnel.

Eligibility for naturalization is basically defined on the basis of the length of stay. Other core determining factors include language proficiency, good character, sound mind and no criminal record. Acquisition of citizenship via marriage with a national of an EU Member State is subject to specific conditions, as are the procedures for refugees and asylum holders.

In practical terms this means that first-generation immigrants can request citizenship on the basis of length of residence in a country of the EU. Residence requirements vary between countries, but also in relation to country of origin and residence status (for example, EU citizens, adopted foreigners, refugees, stateless persons, non-EU citizens, and so on). Children born to immigrants in the EU are usually considered to be 'foreigners', even though many EU Member States have decreased residency and other naturalization requirements for 'second-generation' immigrants and have extended automatic citizenship for the 'third generation'. In most EU countries, refugees and foreigners with regular residence permits may request citizenship if they have permanently resided in the territory of the country for periods of between five and ten years.

Ireland is exceptional, as it granted unconditional citizenship to all children born in Ireland until 2004. Since 2005, automatic rights to children of immigrants have been abolished unless one of the parents or grandparents has Irish citizenship or if the parent had been living in Ireland for three of the four years preceding the birth of the child. On the contrary, Greece holds one of the longest residence requirements in Europe. According to a policy which is currently under revision, immigrants are required to reside in the country for ten out of the past twelve years in order to be eligible for Greek citizenship.

In the CEE countries, the number of naturalizations was relatively high in the first half of the 1990s, reflecting mainly returning emigrants who had lost their citizenship while abroad. Since 2000, this number has been much lower. A specific situation was created in the newly formed Baltic States and Slovenia, where immigrants from other regions of the former larger unit were not granted citizenship. While there is some preferential treatment for gaining citizenship in the Baltic States, in the case of Slovenia, no special provisions have been made to recognize the sizeable community of citizens from other former Yugoslavian republics and war refugees who have resided in the country for many years. Between 18,000 and 40,000 people were 'erased' from the citizenship registers in the period immediately following national independence.

In Latvia and Estonia (but not in Lithuania) after the Restoration of Independence, all those who were not citizens of the country in the pre-1938 period were declared aliens and had to apply for naturalization. Requirements for the naturalization procedure included five years of residence, a legal source of income, and a thorough knowledge of both the constitution and the state language. Indeed, language became the main obstacle (and contested issue) for naturalization as these 'internal migrants' from other parts of the Soviet Union were Russian speakers and had not needed, nor had they been required during Soviet times, to learn the language of the country in which they settled. While alienating some of their residents, the Baltic countries welcomed emigrants who wished to return and who could prove their link to the country through their own or their parents' citizenship of the pre-1938 states.

Most of the immigrants who arrived in Latvia and Lithuania during the Soviet period have now been naturalized, but the situation is more difficult in Estonia. The annual number of naturalizations has grown smaller, and the majority of the people who have received citizenship in recent years have been children.

In fact, for many countries of Central and Eastern Europe, naturalization policies appear to be more strongly shaped by concerns about expatriates, diasporas and ethnic kin minorities in neighbouring countries than by immigration. It should be noted, however, that a number of older EU Member States, have also long pursued policies of preferential access to citizenship for persons who are considered ethnic or linguistic relatives. This is the case for Germany, Portugal, Spain, Italy and Greece. Germany awards German citizenship immediately to ethnic Germans from the former Soviet Union who have been accepted as co-ethnics in the application procedure, as does Greece with Pontic Greeks from the former Soviet Republics. Spain reduces the ten-year legal residence requirement for naturalization to two years for persons from countries that hold special cultural and historic bonds with Spain such as Andorra, the Philippines, Equatorial Guinea and most Latin American countries. Portugal also has a preferential regime for Portuguese-speaking countries, since PALOP nationals require a minimum of a six-year residence permit to be eligible, whereas a minimum of ten years is required for other third-country nationals.

The different migrant status and naturalization regimes of each country result in different distributions between nationals and non-nationals in each country. In other words, in some countries a large part of the migrant population has naturalized and disappeared from the migration registers. Sweden is illustrative of this, where approximately half of all foreign-born persons residing in the country for five years or more become Swedish citizens. In other countries, even second- or third-generation migrants remain aliens. Some countries continue to keep a record of their naturalized foreigners and/or generally of their population that has some foreign ancestry (for example France and the Netherlands) while other countries do not (for example Germany and the UK).

Local voting rights

We have chosen to discuss local voting rights here as these are the most advanced political right conceded to non-nationals in some countries. While voting in national elections remains the privilege of citizens,[6] some countries have offered to third-country nationals the possibility to vote and also stand for office in local elections. More specifically, there are three variations of this policy: the denial of voting rights at the local level; the granting of the right to vote but not to stand as a candidate in local elections; and the granting of full political rights, active and passive (see table below).

Table 27.2   Voting rights for third-country nationals in EU Member States

Political rights	EU Member States
No local voting rights	Austria, Cyprus, Czech Republic, France, Germany, Greece, Hungary, Italy, Latvia, Lithuania, Luxemburg, Poland
Granting of voting rights but not of the right to stand as candidate	Belgium, Estonia
Full voting rights at the local level conditional to the fulfilment of special requirements	Denmark, Finland, Ireland, Netherlands, Malta, Portugal, Slovakia, Slovenia, Spain, Sweden, UK

Source: Table 2 in Cyrus et al. (2006: 80); see also POLITIS project country reports (http://www.uni-oldenburg.de/politis-europe/index.html).

Nearly half of the EU Member States belong to the first group of countries, those that do not grant voting rights at the local level to their resident foreign population. Altogether 12 countries strictly deny local enfranchisement. But the fact that these countries deny immigrant voting rights at the local level does not mean that the issue is not part of the political debate. In those western countries with a higher percentage of immigrant population, such as Luxembourg, Italy, Germany or Austria, the introduction of voting rights for immigrants was at one moment or another a significant issue on the political agenda. While the Government of Luxembourg did not even consider the matter, legislators in some of the other countries took the proposal to enfranchise foreign residents more seriously, though ultimately did not adopt relevant legislation. The case of Germany, with its federal constitution, is illuminating. Here, some of the federal states had passed a law that foresaw the voting right for resident non-EU nationals. However, the project was cancelled after a court ruling by the Federal Constitutional Court in 1994, which underlined the fact that the right to vote at every level of political decision-making is perceived to be the exclusive privilege of citizens. The only way to acquire political voting rights is through the acquisition of citizenship.

Two countries, Belgium and Estonia, have introduced a reduced voting right at the local level that gives resident non-EU citizens the right to vote but not to stand for elections. In the case of

6   With some small but notable exceptions related to each country's history (for example citizens of Commonwealth countries in Britain).

Belgium, where voting is compulsory for citizens, the enfranchisement of foreign nationals at the local level was due to come into force for the first time in 2006. The main requirement is to maintain a legal residence for at least five years. The regulation is a response to the claims of immigrant associations and their supporters for local voting rights. In the case of Estonia, foreign citizens and stateless persons – here the relatively large group of former Soviet citizens who lost their citizenship with the formation of the Estonian nation-state – are entitled to vote in local council elections if they hold a permanent residence permit and have resided legally on the territory of the corresponding municipality for at least five years by January 1st of the election year. However, the right to stand as a candidate is reserved to Estonian citizens.

At the time of writing (2006) at least 11 EU Member States have enfranchised the resident foreign population at the local level. Local voting rights were introduced in some countries several decades ago (for example, Sweden, 1976; Denmark, 1981), while in other countries, foreign nationals will enjoy local voting rights for the first time in forthcoming elections. All countries require the observance of particular conditions that define the eligibility of non-EU citizens to participate in local elections as voters or candidates. The most general requirements are legal status of a minimum duration (usually five years) and that individuals have to register in order to vote. In some countries enfranchisement is restricted to immigrants who hold the citizenship of specific countries. A notable exception to these obligations is Ireland where, since 2004, third-country nationals who are 'ordinary residents' have enjoyed full local voting rights from the first day of their registration in the local register.

Three EU Member States have only enfranchised individuals from particular countries. In the UK, citizens of Commonwealth countries qualify to vote for local elections. In Spain and Portugal only those citizens of countries which have signed a mutual agreement to grant local voting rights can participate in local elections. In 1996, for example, Portugal introduced the immigrants' right to vote and stand for election at the local level. However, only citizens from some countries are entitled to this political participation (namely Argentina, Brazil, Cape Verde, Chile, Israel, Norway, Venezuela, Uruguay and Peru) because enfranchisement is based on the principle of reciprocity between states.

The granting of voting rights does not appear to be influenced by the size of the immigrant population, nor by its composition. It is not subject to how mature the migration history of the Member State is, although long experience with migration seems to encourage local enfranchisement. Local voting rights are partly related to post-colonial ties. Also, states with a strong ethnic or national element tend to be in the group that denies local voting rights, even though there is a certain trend towards local enfranchisement of immigrants in the European Union.

Final remarks

This chapter has provided a comparative overview of immigration in the EU-25. More specifically, we have proposed a typology of countries based on their migration experience during the last decades. We have thus distinguished between old hosts, recent hosts, countries in transition, small island countries and non-immigration countries. We have also constructed a typology of migration pathways, that is, sets of opportunities, policies, motivations and constraints that open a specific channel where people and information flow more easily and more intensely than when these conditions are not in place. The notion of migration pathways is tentatively introduced here. Its scope or usefulness needs to be developed further in empirical research (see also Psimmenos and Kassimati, 2003). Our two typologies aim at providing a broad description of migration phenomena and a first attempt at creating up-to-date theoretical classifications that respond to contemporary

European realities. The last section of this chapter has given some brief insights into two main issues of immigrant integration, notably the question of naturalization and the issue of local voting rights. These are only two among several important contested issues that European Union countries need to address if they are to respond to the challenge of migration for the twenty-first century. We believe that this book is an important first step in the systematic exploration and comparison of contemporary European migration. Further comparative research is needed to develop the field of comparative migration studies, highlighting the similarities and differences between the EU-25 as regards migration and migrant integration.

References

Brubaker, R. (1996), *Nationalism Reframed.* Cambridge: Cambridge University Press.

Cyrus, N., Gropas, R., Kosic, A. and Vogel, D. (2006), 'Comparative Perspectives: Opportunity Structures for Immigrants' Active Civic Participation in the European Union: Sharing Comparative Observations', in Vogel, D. (ed.) *Building Europe with New Citizens? Civic Participation of Immigrants in Europe: POLITIS project state of the art report*, 67–87. Brussels: European Commission Office for Publications,

European Commission (2006), *Second Annual Report on Migration and Integration*, SEC(2006) 892, Brussels, 30 June 2006.

Favell, A. (1998), *Philosophies of Integration: Immigration and the Idea of Citizenship in France and Britain.* Basingstoke: Macmillan.

Gropas, R. (2007), 'The State of the Issue: Social and Cultural Integration in Europe', in *Multiculturalism in Europe (Visions of Europe, College of Europe project).* London: Orion-Weidenfeld; Paris: Odile-Jacob. (Forthcoming.)

King, R. (2002), 'Towards a New Map of European Migration', *International Journal of Population Geography*, **8**, 89–106.

Psimmenos, I. and Kassimati, K. (2003), 'Immigration Control Pathways: Organisational Culture and Work Values of Greek Welfare Officers', *Journal of Ethnic and Migration Studies*, **29**(2), 337–71. [DOI: 10.1080/1369183032000079639].

Index

Second 7, 27, 40, 64, 69, 80, 91, 116, 119, 129,
    158, 191, 252, 253, 257, 267, 279, 280, 366,
    372
Third 14, 40, 258, 279, 286, 362, 372

Immigrant
    Associations 27, 39, 79, 108, 110, 122,
        135–136, 143, 192, 195, 271, 284–288, 295,
        303, 329, 330, 375
    Civic participation 39, 45, 53–54, 57, 65–69,
        80–81, 94, 123, 134–136, 147, 155, 163,
        178–178, 192–193, 195, 206, 222, 230, 243,
        250, 256, 263, 271, 300–301, 303, 329,
        355–357
    Integration 13, 15, 26, 53–54, 61, 65–66, 77, 92,
        106, 113, 118, 124, 134, 146–147, 149, 151,
        163, 178, 185–186, 192, 194, 205, 230, 242,
        255, 283, 299, 307, 357, 368, 371–372, 376
    Test 143, 250, 364
    Organizations 27, 285, 299, 329, 341, 342

Jus sanguinis 8, 23, 40, 62, 308, 310, 328, 339, 372
Jus soli 8, 36, 40, 129, 279, 280, 288, 309, 310, 328,
    372

Media discourse 28, 40, 47, 55, 68, 71, 82, 95, 108,
    116, 123–124, 136, 148, 151, 165, 179,
    193–194, 207, 221, 234, 244, 257, 273, 277,
    286, 301, 316–317, 329, 344, 357–358
Migrant
    Gold collar 15, 367, 370–371
    'guest worker' 10, 19, 25, 33, 34, 64, 128, 201,
        208, 209, 307, 369
    highly skilled 4–6, 14, 21, 35, 42, 53, 95, 136–8,
        187, 230, 266, 279, 296–297, 351, 363, 365,
        370–371
    return 1, 9, 10, 15, 53, 59, 63–64, 72, 91, 99,
        106, 127, 130–132, 141–142, 144–145,
        155–158, 160, 163, 175, 178, 211–217, 219,
        241–243, 246, 249, 263, 267, 273, 280–281,
        308, 335, 339, 349, 352, 366–367, 369, 373
Migration
    Circular 19, 63, 69, 366
    Colonial 1, 14, 15, 33, 169, 180, 237, 249, 277,
        362, 366, 367–368
    Commuting 60, 156, 162–163, 229–230, 234
    gender 1, 2, 5, 25, 29, 82, 92, 160, 180, 190,
        244, 256, 298, 362
    illegal 3, 5, 10, 12, 14–15, 28, 49, 56, 60, 61,
        63–65, 68–69, 77, 90–91, 93, 104, 109, 115,
        128, 138, 141–143, 150, 163, 165, 170, 173,
        185, 188, 194, 204, 211, 218–219, 221, 228,

244–245, 251, 254, 265, 268–269, 274, 279,
    282–293, 299, 313, 321–323, 326, 328–330,
    339, 349, 351, 356, 364–365, 371
irregular 3, 14–15, 22, 35, 37, 42, 65, 119, 141,
    156–157, 163, 188, 219, 237–240, 242,
    244–245, 275, 279, 280, 282, 291, 303, 313,
    321–325, 328–331, 347, 349–351, 363–366,
    371
marriage 15, 21, 22, 34, 53, 55, 76, 77, 79–80,
    82–83, 100, 103, 106, 109, 130, 136, 148,
    164, 191, 250, 252, 265, 279, 350, 354, 372
pathways 3, 15, 26, 76, 361, 366–375
post–colonial 15, 60, 96, 113, 124, 251, 287,
    366, 367–368, 375
post Cold War 1, 364, 366
return 1, 100, 101, 103, 109, 128, 144, 209, 267,
    280, 313
    illusion of 135
seasonal 10, 15, 21, 29, 60, 128, 131, 132, 137,
    158, 163, 186–188, 307, 309, 313, 314, 351,
    366–367, 370
security concerns 3–4, 20, 28, 95, 99, 114, 119,
    130, 135, 151–152, 165–166, 194, 273–275,
    330, 357, 364
shuttle 1, 6, 362
suitcase 6
temporary 1, 2, 3, 5, 6, 8, 10, 14–15, 19, 21, 41,
    45, 46, 53, 57, 59, 64, 69, 127, 129, 131,
    136, 138, 163, 164, 228, 249, 266, 275, 307,
    327, 347, 348, 350, 358, 367, 369, 370, 372
    residence 9, 34, 47, 49, 53, 63, 76, 90–91,
        96, 101, 114–115, 133, 137, 142, 167, 187,
        202–204, 218, 238, 250, 265–266, 278, 293,
        294, 298, 300, 310–313, 342
transit 14, 60, 62, 163, 186, 211, 218–219, 246,
    264, 275, 293, 366
    transit country 19, 34, 63, 65, 240, 246, 301,
        314, 338, 363, 365
undocumented 1–3, 10, 14, 34–35, 37, 45, 49,
    51, 53–56, 131, 134, 141–143, 145–146,
    151, 163, 173, 185–186, 188, 192, 194, 254,
    269, 277–279, 282, 292–293, 295–296,
    299–300, 302–303, 330, 339, 363, 364, 371
Multicultural
    Advisory boards 107–108,
    policy 38, 42, 67, 249–250, 257, 302, 364
    society 41–43, 45, 57, 119, 195
Multiculturalism 40–43, 56, 68, 95, 124, 194–195,
    274, 357, 363
    Anti- 41
    Ethnic 68
Muslim
    European Islam 41